Also by Will Friedwald

A Biographical Guide to the Great Jazz and Pop Singers

Stardust Melodies: The Biography of Twelve of America's Most Popular Songs

Tony Bennett: The Good Life (with Tony Bennett)

Warner Bros. Animation Art (with Jerry Beck)

Sinatra! The Song Is You

Jazz Singing: America's Great Voices from Bessie Smith to Bebop and Beyond

Looney Tunes and Merrie Melodies: A Complete Illustrated Guide to the Warner Bros. Cartoons (with Jerry Beck)

The Great Jazz and Pop
Vocal Albums

The Great Jazz and Pop Vocal Albums

Will Friedwald

PANTHEON BOOKS, NEW YORK

Library of Congress Cataloging-in-Publication Data

Name: Friedwald, Will, [date] author.
Title: The great jazz and pop vocal albums / Will Friedwald.
Description: First edition. New York : Pantheon, 2017.
Identifiers: LCCN 2016027178. ISBN 9780307379078 (hardcover). ISBN 9781101871751 (ebook).
Subjects: LCSH: Jazz vocals—Discography. Popular music—Discography. Singers—
Discography. Sound recordings—Reviews.
Classification: LCC ML156.4.J3 F76 2017. DDC 016.78242164026/6—dc23
LC record available at lccn.loc.gov/2016027178

www.pantheonbooks.com

Front-of-jacket image: The Great American Songbook Foundation
Jacket design by Janet Hansen
Book design by Iris Weinstein

Printed in the United States of America
First Edition
2 4 6 8 9 7 5 3 1

For Bob—
four books in and I hope this isn't the end

And for Billye—
because it's about time

Contents

Preface and Acknowledgments

Over the decades I've been listening to jazz and the American Songbook, it's become increasingly apparent that there are certain albums that are more important than others. You can tell the standout albums—sometimes even without actually listening to them—because it seems as if all roads lead back to them. I'll frequently hear a vocalist at Birdland singing "They Say It's Wonderful" in such a way that there can be no doubt that he or she learned that Irving Berlin song from hearing it on *John Coltrane and Johnny Hartman* rather than from the *Annie Get Your Gun* original cast album. When pianists at Dizzy's or the Jazz Standard play "But Beautiful," it's almost inevitable that they'll employ the same substitute chord changes used by Bill Evans on his sessions with Tony Bennett. Singers at 54 Below or the Metropolitan Room frequently do "Black Coffee," and while it's possible that they might have discovered the song from the recordings of either Ella Fitzgerald or Sarah Vaughan, it's much more likely that they'll have learned it from Peggy Lee. (In fact, Miss Lee's idiosyncratic mannerisms have become so much a part of the music that one fully expects all contemporary singers to bend the note on the phrase "black *cof*-fee" the way she does.)

In jazz and pop, more than in classical music or opera, certain recordings have become a kind of textbook. Generations of musicians, singers, and listeners have grown up with these albums; music teachers have made them required listening in schools with jazz education departments. They are the gold standard, the yardstick against which all subsequent efforts have been measured. Every time there's a new edition of one of these records, fans and collectors line up to buy it. They have become a kind of canon unto themselves.

Between 2001 and 2010, when I was writing *A Biographical Guide to the Great Jazz and Pop Singers*, I would repeatedly come across these albums—in a very real way they were at once landmarks and land mines. When talking about Rosemary Clooney, for instance, it would occur to me that her 1956 meeting with Duke Ellington and Billy Strayhorn stood out as a milestone apart from the other work she was doing in that period. I would suddenly realize that I had just spent six thousand words on a single album. Gradually it occurred to my editor, Robert Gottlieb, and myself that there was a need for a whole other book, one that would focus on these essential albums.

Compiling the "playlist," as it were, for this current volume was for the most part remarkably straightforward: most of these albums just jumped out at us without our having to give the question a lot of soul-searching thought. We began by listing those albums that absolutely had to be in here, most of which immediately leapt to mind. What we didn't need to do was study lists of artists and proceed from there; in other words, we thought at once of *Lullabies of Birdland* and *Mack the Knife* rather than ask ourselves, "What are the essential albums by Ella Fitzgerald?"

When we considered our basic list, we were hardly surprised that there were two albums on it by Nat King Cole, Ella Fitzgerald, and Peggy Lee, although it was somewhat startling to realize that we had decided to go with a mere two by Frank Sinatra. (And, oddly, there are actually three by Doris Day, Jo Stafford, and Louis Armstrong.)

In a certain sense, the current work completes a trilogy that began fifteen years ago with the publication of *Stardust Melodies*. That book was about songs, and the subsequent book, the *Biographical Guide*, was about singers. This new work connects the two: how the great singers have shaped and organized collections of songs into albums. The great albums are almost invariably more than a superior singer rendering a superior set of songs: usually there's an overarching idea of some kind that links the songs together and connects the tracks on the album from the first to the last.

In some cases, these are first albums, as in Marilyn Maye's well-named *Meet Marvelous Marilyn*

Maye, and Lambert, Hendricks & Ross's *Sing a Song of Basie*. In some instances, they're the last albums, or the final works of a major artist before entering a long dry spell, as in Maxine Sullivan's *Memories of You: A Tribute to Andy Razaf* and Jimmy Scott's *The Source*. In other cases, they're the late-career summations of a so-called legacy artist moving into the long-playing era, such as Fred Astaire's *The Astaire Story*, Bing Crosby's *Bing with a Beat*, Billie Holiday's *Lady in Satin*, and all three Louis Armstrong albums.

Others represent a veteran singer turning a corner into a new phase (like Peggy Lee's *Black Coffee*, *Mel Tormé with the Marty Paich Dek-Tette*), or at least trying to, as in Dick Haymes's *Rain or Shine*. Some albums are about an artist tackling a body of music that few others would attempt to address: Jo Stafford collecting American folk songs and Scottish ballads, Nat King Cole swinging and crooning the blues of W. C. Handy, Steve Lawrence and Eydie Gormé putting their stamp on hits of the big band era, Ray Charles rocking country and western, Jack Teagarden testifying and purging his sin-sick soul through the uncategorizable compositions of Willard Robison. Some are traditional songbooks built around a composer (Margaret Whiting's Jerome Kern songbook, *Bobby Troup Sings Johnny Mercer*) or a performer (*Dinah Washington Sings Fats Waller*).

In a few cases, these albums are milestones in the history of American musical culture, especially the Frank Sinatra and Billie Holiday sets, and likewise Barb Jungr's *Every Grain of Sand*—an album that opened a thousand doors for contemporary singers. Others are just plain silly and fun (*Della Della Cha Cha Cha*) and are not expected to be anything more than that. Some represent artists working in unusual, one-of-a-kind settings (*Nina Simone and Piano!*, Carmen McRae's *As Time Goes By: Live at the Dug*); others are notable for their lack of uniqueness, e.g., the Ella Fitzgerald *Lullabies of Birdland* and *Mack the Knife: Ella in Berlin*, which capture the greatest-ever lady of jazz or song at her most typical, singing the same way she did every night of her life. In Fitzgerald's case, the most typical is also the absolute greatest. Then there are the live albums, each special in its own way: the

Judy at Carnegie Hall concert from 1961, *Ella in Berlin* in 1960, a year before the Wall, and remarkable shows by the equally amazing Sarah Vaughan and Carmen McRae, both recorded in Japan.

In some instances, these albums represent unique collaborations: *John Coltrane and Johnny Hartman*, Rosemary Clooney's meeting with Duke Ellington *(Blue Rose)*, and Sarah Vaughan's with Clifford Brown *(Sarah Vaughan)*, *The Tony Bennett / Bill Evans Album*, Doris Day and Robert Goulet's *Annie Get Your Gun*. (Louis Armstrong is easily the champion collaborator of all time, having made no fewer than three classic team-ups, with Ella Fitzgerald, Bing Crosby, and Oscar Peterson.) Every album captures an artist doing what he or she does best—especially Kay Starr's *I Cry by Night*, Blossom Dearie's *My Gentleman Friend*, Billy Eckstine's *Billy's Best!*, and Bobby Short's *Songs by Bobby Short*—although not always what's expected of them. At least one album that I consider worthy of inclusion is by an artist that few people would consider one of the all-time great American singers but who's a talented, thoughtful artist, who found the right combination of collaborators (producer and orchestrator) in order to produce a work that probably sounds even better today than when it was first released: *God Bless Tiny Tim*.

I find it particularly gratifying that I've been able to use this book as an opportunity to talk about several artists I have never before written about at length, even in the leviathanic *Biographical Guide* (all 831 double-column pages of it). I've written about Marilyn Maye briefly in *The Wall Street Journal* and, before that, *The New York Sun*, but this is the first chance I've had to analyze some of her greatest work in depth. As for *God Bless Tiny Tim*, this is an album I loved as a kid in the early 1970s, and upon hearing it more recently as a CD reissue, I concluded (and Bob agreed) that it was a work of superior quality that had to be in the book.

A basic rule of storytelling is that you can't tell a story until it's finished. The saga of the jazz and pop vocal album can now be told in the light of current, overwhelming evidence that the album format itself is becoming a thing of the past, rapidly receding into the recesses of history. Since the beginning of the current century, sales of physical media have plummeted to somewhere in between *nada* and *bupkis*. (Surprisingly, sales of vintage vinyl LPs have been on the increase; as a recent *New Yorker* cartoon observed, this is a format for those who are drawn to both the expense and the inconvenience.)

The rapid fade-out of the CD occasioned this new book in other ways too. With the end of the disc comes the end of the album's accompanying annotation. Once upon a time it was possible to glean backstory, context, and commentary in what was called a CD booklet. As my grandfather, Aristotle Sophocles Confucius Friedwald, wisely put it, "There are no liner notes on an MP3." (I myself have written roughly seven hundred sets of liner notes for albums going back to the late LP period, though lately that stream of work has dwindled to a trickle.) The current book seems like more of a necessity if you want to be reminded of what makes Doris Day different from Jo Stafford, who is different from Margaret Whiting and Kay Starr.

We began this book just as the *Biographical Guide* was being put to bed in 2010. It was just around that time, in May of that year, that I began writing a weekly column titled "The Jazz Scene" for *The Wall Street Journal*. Coincidentally, five years and 260 columns later, the final entry for "The Jazz Scene" was filed the very same week that I submitted the final essay for this current book to Bob.

This time around, I would like to thank Mike and Leah Biel, Bill Boggs, Jim Burns, Ken Burrows and Erica Jong, Eric Comstock, Roger Crane, Jim Davison, Alan Eichler, Anthony DiFlorio, Dan Fortune, James Gavin, Vince Giordano, Charles "Chuck" Granata, Tom Hallett (of "Buster's Blogs"), Cary Hoffman, Michael Katsobashvili, Steve Kramer, Michael Kraus, Jeff Leibowitz, Mark Mairowitz, James Fox Miller, Dan Levinson, Gio Molla, Dan Morgenstern, David Ostwald, Jim Pierson, Ricky Riccardi, David Rosen, Michael B. Schnurr, Roger Schore, Dan Singer, and David J. Weiner and other collectors and friends who helped me organize the book, find material to listen to, albums to consider.

At Pantheon, I would like to thank Altie Karper and Ryan Smernoff.

I also want to thank William Clark, a literary agent of Job-like patience (not to mention unerring taste). And most of all Bob himself, for putting up with me for not less than four books now (over a period of roughly twenty years) and fitting me in between such infinitely more illustrious authors as President Clinton and Miss Piggy—and also for many, many Greek omelettes and gyros. And perhaps even more so to Patty, who has more than earned her place, not only in this book but in the long-playing album of my heart.

May the music never end.

Will Friedwald
New York, 2017

Introduction:
The Origins and Development of the Pop Music Album from
To Mother to *The Voice*

(1926–1945)

"Ha ha ha. Who's got the last laugh now?" In 1937, George and Ira Gershwin immortalized, in an irreverently syncopated style, a sequence of celebrated accomplishments of innovation and invention. Chief among them was the widely accepted fact that Thomas Edison was the first man to record sound. For well over a hundred years, it was taken for granted that sound recording was perhaps Edison's first great achievement, even before the electric light or the motion picture camera.

Yet in recent years, it has become known that sound recordings were actually made (and still exist) at least twenty years before Edison's tinfoil experiments. As early as 1857, a Frenchman named Édouard-Léon Scott de Martinville had invented a device called the phonautograph, which successfully captured soundwaves and represented them visually. At that time, it was not actually possible to play back the sound in any way, although in 2008, the recorded noises of 150 years earlier were extracted and made available on the Internet. (Where else?) The fidelity is far from wonderful—in fact, it's hard to tell exactly what you're listening to—yet they constitute a genuine precedent to Edison.

Which goes to show that you can never say that something is the "first" of anything. Inevitably there's something else out there, waiting to be discovered.

I offer the above "cautionary tale" as a preamble before attempting to track the history of the popular music album. No one can say what the first pop album actually was, but one point that needs to be made at the outset is that the album—as both a concept and a commercial reality—predates the long-playing record (or LP) by many years. Albums were, in fact, a viable and familiar concept to record producers and buyers deep into the 78 era, well before World War II. It's often reported that the technology of the long-playing album inspired creative musicians like Frank Sinatra, Miles Davis, and Duke Ellington to craft more ambitious, extended projects for a bigger canvas, but in fact it was the other way around: it was artists who drove the technology. Likewise, albums too were very much a part of the pop music market for at least a decade before the long-playing disc was perfected, thereby enabling record labels to release eight (later twelve) songs on a single disc.

The concept of the album had a long and respectable run. We know of pop albums going back to at least 1926, when the dominant format—virtually the only format—was individual 78 rpm discs. The 10-inch LP medium, introduced in 1948, was the next step forward, succeeded by the 12-inch LP, which became the standard, in America at least, about 1955, and then the compact disc (from 1985 on). The CD would be, so far, the last physical format for which artists would put together programs of creative and interesting music. In the post-physical age of listening to music, the album is more or less passé: kids primarily download individual tracks, and pay attention to entire albums only secondarily. Thus the age of the pop music album is finite, stretching for roughly eighty years, picking up speed slowly from the mid-1920s onward and then losing momentum quickly in the mid-"aughts."

The purpose of this book is to talk about the great jazz and pop vocal albums, and in this introductory chapter we trace the development of the concept—the events that led up to the development of the pop music "album." We'll go from the first pop albums, well before the start of the Depression, up to the successful introduction of the long-playing record after the war. By the time that the LP was good to go, creative artists like Frank Sinatra and Duke Ellington (not to mention forward-looking producers like Jack Kapp, George

Avakian, and Norman Granz) were truly ready for it.

Throughout this whole period, for our purposes, there were essentially three types of albums:

* Existing Songs / Existing Recordings: The most basic kind of album (then as now) was a collection of tracks that had already been recorded, and, in most cases, already released. Usually these were collections of songs that had been hits in the singles format; more often than not, they sport titles like *The Best of So-and-So* or *So-and-So's Greatest Hits.*
* New Songs / New Recordings: On the other end, there was the all-original album, which actually began in 1946 with the release of *Manhattan Tower,* a groundbreaking and genre-defying work which all but singlehandedly invented what later became known as the concept album. In the 1960s, this idea came to dominate in rock-oriented pop music (although there already was a precedent in the jazz world). In most classic rock albums from the Beatles onward, the tracks were all newly recorded and all the songs were completely original as well, written in almost all cases by the performing artist.
* Existing Songs / New Recordings: There was a halfway point between the two above extremes (completely unoriginal and completely original), which was perfected by Frank Sinatra in 1945 with the first pop music "concept" album, *The Voice.* Nearly all of the great pop and jazz vocal albums would follow this format: the songs themselves were already of a certain vintage, well known and well loved enough to be considered classics. But the recording itself was new, and so was everything else: the interpretations, the arrangements, the sequencing. It became a challenge for the singers, orchestrators, and producers of the era, which reached a peak in the 1950s and '60s, to be able to take standard songs and use the album concept—i.e., the act of taking individual songs, written for different purposes by different composers, and making them relate to each other, thus forging a new collective statement out of songs that already existed.

It's the contention of this book that the most creative, interesting, and memorable albums (starting with those of Sinatra and Ella Fitzgerald) belong to this third category. There was, quite possibly, more creativity and more great results from this particular combination of the old and the new (a new spin on songs the listeners already knew) than in any other use of the album format. The central idea behind this book is to show how this format (old songs in a new context) evolved, and to identify and discuss the classics of the genre. (For the most part, I'm leaving original cast albums out of this categorical discussion, although I will mention a few—they are a distinct genre unto themselves.)

If Edison (the phonautograph aside) is the father of the recording industry, the mother of the pop album is, it turns out, "mother" herself. In 1926, RCA Victor issued three pop albums, each with a slightly different strategy, and this is as good a place to start as any. Again, there are precedents: there already were combination record and storybooks for children, such as the famous Bubble Books, and these do count as albums. There also already existed a tradition of issuing classical music in the album format, though there were only a few such releases by the mid-1920s.

The first album, for the purpose of this discussion, was *To Mother.* As the title suggests, this was a Mother's Day collection, from 1926. In a sense, it's perfectly natural that the idea of the record album should originate with mother: mother, traditionally, was the keeper of family lore, and the most prominent use of the word "album" prior to the twentieth century was the venerable old photo album, usually maintained by mother. Mother's photo album had a lot in common with at least one of the 1926 Victor phono albums, and, it turns out, even more with the MP3 downloads of the twenty-first century. Photo albums consisted of images that the user personally placed therein; no one ever sold an "album" of predetermined pictures. A picture book was and is a very different thing from a photo album.

To Mother would seem to be the first pop music album that we know of. As recording historian Mike Biel has documented, this clearly was a "modern" pop album in every definition. It consisted of six songs on three 10-inch double-faced 78s, all of which concerned themselves with mother, home, family, and childhood. Like later albums, *To Mother* was clearly programmed with regard to both consistency and variety; the set alternates between three different solo vocalists (two tenors, Lewis James and Henry Burr; one soprano, Della Baker), one boy-girl duet, and two instrumentals by the Victor Salon Orchestra.

The six tracks were all recorded within ten days of each other in March 1926, which could indicate that whatever pioneering A&R man "produced" the album (Victor's Eddie King or Nathaniel Shilkret both would be good guesses) recorded these tracks explicitly for this album. It also bears an illustrated album cover: the words "To Mother" shown to the right of a few simple flowers. It looks more like a greeting card than anything else, but it is, in fact, a genuine album cover. (Much later, a myth emerged that the album cover was "invented" by designer Alex Steinweiss at Columbia Records in 1940. The story is widely propagated, especially on the Internet and Wikipedia, but there were, in fact, album covers dating back at least to 1917, the year Steinweiss was born.)

Another precedent was instantly established: even at this point, new songs and hit songs would continue to be released as singles, while the album format would become the province of the formal, even conservative side of pop music. In the *To Mother* album, two older, traditional songs were played instrumentally by the Victor Salon Orchestra, which was a considerably more formal ensemble than, say, the label's other "house" band, the snappy, peppy Victor Dance Orchestra. Even the relatively recently written songs on the Mother's Day album were composed in a more old-fashioned style.

Victor followed *To Mother* a few months later with an album promoting recent advancements in audio technology, *New Victor Records Orthophonic Recordings*, in October. The process which we now call "electrical" recording was then only in use for about a year, and many record labels had not yet made the transition. Victor was using the album medium to show off the cutting edge of tech in exactly the same way that they would thirty years later with all those stereo and hi-fi demonstra-

tion albums of the late 1950s and early 1960s—the recording process itself was as much the selling point as the music. Victor recommended six specific discs to go in the set (at twelve songs, it was twice as long as *To Mother*), but, the catalogue explains, "you may substitute other records of your own choice—either a complete set of six or single records." Biel notes, "No price is given [in the catalogue] because it would vary with the choice of records."

Lastly, in time for the holidays, the label released *The Victrola Christmas Album*. Importantly, this was a completely empty storage album, with three pockets. Buyers were encouraged to pick out records of their own choosing, and, the catalogue states, "your selection of records need not be confined to Christmas numbers." In other words, the "album" itself was essentially an elaborate form of gift-wrapping, a very lovely package in which to present three records of any kind. In a way that makes for a technological wormhole, RCA was in a sense inventing the CDR and the download in 1926: a concept of an album whose specific contents were determined by the listener. *The Victrola Christmas Album* was the first "playlist."

It's possible someone will unearth something from earlier that amounts to a true pop music concept album, but, for now at least, the three Victor albums of 1926 represent a good point with which to begin talking about the development of the album. There was certainly nothing else like them, released by Victor or anyone else, for a few years to come. As mentioned, even classical albums were hardly common currency at this point. As far back as 1917, HMV in England had launched an ambitious series of complete albums of Gilbert and Sullivan, beginning with *The Mikado*. (And these were full albums in the most modern sense, with elaborately illustrated covers.) There were roughly only ten full albums of classical music released by Columbia as "Masterworks" (a term still in use today) by the end of the acoustic era in 1925.

Other albums from the late 1920s and early 1930s could be said to reflect both classical and pop interests. Bandleader Paul Whiteman, who was the acknowledged leader in inspiring extended works of concert music that combined jazz and pop with the classical tradition, released several of his more ambitious pieces in album packages, notably George Gershwin's Concerto in F in 1929 and Ferde Grofé's *Grand Canyon Suite* recorded in 1932. It wouldn't be until some time later that there would be albums of Whiteman's popular song and dance hits. One of the more surprising releases of the era is Victor's *Jimmie Rodgers: America's Blue Yodeler,* a collection, the liner notes tell us, selected by the pioneering country singer himself (obviously before his death in 1933).

Thus, at the turn of the 1930s, the industry was heading slowly but steadily toward accepting the idea of the classical music album, with pop and jazz albums trailing not far behind. The concept, along with a great many other things, was slowed down considerably by the start of the Great Depression, which put an end to the unprecedented boom market that the music business was enjoying (along with most of the rest of the economy) during the Jazz Age. Apart from Victor, Brunswick Records was also releasing albums of classical music (much of it recorded in Europe) in the late 1920s. Brunswick A&R guru Jack Kapp then produced the next two most important pop albums, both of which were driven by Broadway, *Show Boat* (1932) and *Blackbirds of 1928* (1933). Both were inspired by musical shows that were roughly half a decade old at the time, but neither was a true "original cast album" in the way that we define that term today. Both were deluxe packages—luxury items—that directly foreshadow the ultra-elaborate packaging found on limited-edition, collector's-item releases over the next eighty years.

Show Boat was a recording of the score of the already iconic 1927 show, done roughly around the same time as the 1932 Broadway revival, but only two singers involved in the project had ever performed in a company of the show, Helen Morgan and Paul Robeson, both equally irreplaceable. The other "cast members" were semiclassical vocalists then popular on radio, soprano "Countess" Olga Albani and tenors Frank Munn and James Melton. The set consisted of three 12-inch discs, with six tracks (including "*Show Boat* Overture" and "*Show Boat* Finale") totaling twenty-four minutes. The orchestral accompaniment, conducted by Vic-

tor Young, then one of Brunswick's star maestros, likewise didn't attempt to re-create the Broadway orchestration. Rather, it was arranged like an elaborate show medley, of the kind that had been widely popular almost from the inception of commercial recording. (Original cast recording was much more prevalent in Europe; in fact, there already was an extensive series of *Show Boat* original cast discs from the 1928 London production, although they were not collected in an album at the time.)

Similarly, *Blackbirds* paid its respects both to the popular, long-running series of all-black revues produced by impresario Lew Leslie, and also to African American musical achievement in general. Kapp assembled an ambitious collective of black talent, looking more toward artists who had worked with him on Brunswick (which was nearly everyone) than had appeared in any of the *Blackbirds* editions on Broadway. The most prominent actual cast members were headliners Ethel Waters and Bill "Bojangles" Robinson. (Duke Ellington had never worked with Leslie, but he did collaborate at the Cotton Club with songwriters Dorothy Fields and Jimmy McHugh, who wrote most of the songs for the *Blackbirds* revues as well. In general, there was considerable spillover between the *Blackbirds* revues and the Cotton Club productions.) Kapp drew most of the album's songs from the spectacularly successful 1928 edition of *Blackbirds*—the high point of the series—but didn't hesitate to use songs from other years as well. Still, there was a Great Depression on, and few jazz or Broadway lovers could afford the elaborate *Blackbirds* album. (The set was also released in England, but the pressings from either country are exceedingly scarce. At the time, Brunswick also issued an Ellington album, but only in England.)

The early 1930s were the bleakest for the country in general and, correspondingly, for the music industry—it was the wrong time to be experimenting with new technology and formats. (Along with the idea of the album, there also were early forays into both long-playing pressings and stereophonic sound.) But when the nation began to breathe somewhat more easily, starting from the mid-1930s, then the 78 rpm album gradually began establishing itself as a viable format. In 1936, Victor had notable success with an album of music from Walt Disney's *Snow White and the Seven Dwarfs;* this was both a children's album and a movie soundtrack/original cast project. (And though we're not getting into them here, children's albums were also gathering momentum in the mid to late 1930s, especially as tie-ins to Disney films.)

Some of the earliest jazz albums were memorials released to honor fallen heroes, which served the collectors of the period while further underscoring the notion that the album format was already a repository for music that was part of the past. The famous *Bix Beiderbecke Memorial Album* (as it was later known) on Victor was issued in 1936 as *All Star Album Presenting the Original Pioneers of Swing.* In November 1937, Columbia honored another pioneer with *The Bessie Smith Album.*

The first all-original jazz album—or at least the earliest to make a major impression—was RCA Victor's *A Symposium of Swing* (also released in November 1937). It consisted of all 12-inch sides, specially recorded for the project by the bands of Benny Goodman, Tommy Dorsey, Bunny Berigan, and Fats Waller. In 1940, Decca offered a response with their own 12-inch anthology, a fact that they referenced in the title, *Five Feet of Swing.* But in between, there had already been an extensive series of jazz albums, including sets by Artie Shaw (Bluebird) and Benny Goodman (Victor), both of which featured previously unissued material. (It might be an academic distinction to differentiate between material expressly recorded for an album and tracks that were simply not yet issued for one reason or another.)

Dedicated jazz collectors—no less than the classical market—were a major factor in helping to push the record business toward the album format. By 1940, it was indirectly established that standard singles were more for basic pop music, records by big bands that everyone danced to (especially teenagers), whereas the albums were for the more serious collectors. By this point, vintage tracks—both issued and unissued—that were only, say, ten to fifteen years old by the start of the war, were more likely to be found in the album format. In addition to jazz packages old and new on Victor, Decca, and Columbia (or rather ARC, which became Colum-

bia again in 1939), even independent outfits like Blue Note and Commodore got into the act.

Though all the major labels showed some interest in the new format, the biggest booster continued to be Jack Kapp of Decca Records, whose series of nonclassical albums was by far the most extensive of any label. In 1939, Decca could advertise "More than 100 Albums to Choose From." Further catalogues inform us that by March 1941 the number had reached 210 albums; by the start of America's entry into the war at the end of that year, the total was up to 290. Around the same time, Columbia had released about sixty popular albums, and for RCA Victor the number was somewhere around one hundred.

Interestingly, a look at the "1939 Decca Album Series" catalogue (which contains ninety-five titles) reveals that pure pop, as we understand it today, is only one of many varieties of music being offered—it's hardly the majority shareholder. It's a marvelously eclectic mix: there's small-group jazz and there's calypso, there's folk music and there's Viennese waltzes, there's American Civil War songs and songs of Old New York, there's "Spanish and Mexican Folk Dances," the "Cloister Bells Album," "Traditional Hebrew Prayers," and "Gypsy Memories." Surprisingly, there's no separate series for more classically oriented packages: Decca Album No. 59 is *Blues Sung by Teddy Grace* and No. 60 is *Classical Spanish Guitar Selections, Vol. II.*

Throughout this whole period and for many years to come, the industry leader was Bing Crosby, who was by far Decca's signature artist. You would think it would be a no-brainer that the first Crosby album would be a hits collection, but no, it's Decca Album No. 69, *Cowboy Songs Sung by Bing Crosby,* which tells us that even in the realm of mainstream pop, the album format is, at this point, thought of as a medium for slightly more marginal kinds of music—you can buy Bing singing "Home on the Range" in an album but not "Pennies from Heaven." It's significant that Bob Crosby, Bing's younger brother, had released an album somewhat earlier, Decca 32, *Bob Crosby Showcase.* Decca's most popular female singer—in terms of albums at least—was neither a traditional pop star nor a jazz singer, not Judy Garland (who had one package, *Judy Garland Souvenir Album,* No. 75) or Ella Fitzgerald (who had none), but Deanna Durbin; the precocious movie soprano had four albums of her own by 1942.

What must have seemed surprising in 1939 was that two of the first jazz album producers for Decca were both ensconced at Yale: Marshall Stearns, then working toward his PhD, and George Avakian, at the time a twenty-year-old undergrad. In May, Stearns supervised what must certainly be the first album by a major jazz-blues-big-band singer, *Blues Sung by Teddy Grace* (No. 59).

"I felt that jazz should be treated the way the classical music was treated, in albums with annotations," Avakian told me at the time of his ninetieth birthday in 2009. "And the way to start the excitement would be to record one of the pioneers of the three cities that were responsible for spreading jazz: New Orleans, Kansas City, and Chicago. Decca had started a series of six-pocket 78 albums; that was a standard thing, three discs for $2 to $2.25 or six discs for $2.50 to $2.75. When I made the proposal to Jack [Kapp], he sent me a penny postcard saying 'Drop in during your vacation.' So the first album I made was *Chicago,* with the Eddie Condon guys, because they were working at Nick's, and I got to know them real well. That was my first project as a producer."

By the time of *Blues Sung by Teddy Grace* and *Chicago* (and even on Kapp's earlier *Show Boat* and *Blackbirds* albums), it was increasingly common for producers to record new material expressly for release in the album format. The medium was no longer strictly a secondhand shop, a holding place for previously released tracks or even historical material that was being released for the first time. No less importantly, by 1939, the songbook concept was well established. Decca's first two songbooks were skewed toward classically oriented pop and the recent past: *George Gershwin Music* (No. 31) was recorded in 1938, the year following the composer's death, and consisted of Gershwin concert works (rather than his songs), as played by Paul Whiteman, while No. 38 was *Victor Herbert Melodies.* (The popularity of the American operetta king should not be underestimated: Decca released no fewer than four full albums of Victor Herbert by 1939.)

Hoagy Carmichael Songs (No. 43), however, honored a songwriter who was still very much active—and unlike later songbook albums, this one featured the participation of the subject himself. This was by far the most ambitious songbook project of the period: the bulk of the selections featured the Casa Loma Orchestra backing Louis Armstrong (who dueted with Pee Wee Hunt, the Casa Loma's trombonist and "rhythm" singer), the vocal group the Merry Macs, Kenny Sargent (the band's regulation crooner), and Carmichael himself, as well as two instrumentals by the band. Clearly, *Hoagy Carmichael Songs* was planned, produced, and recorded (in February 1939) as an all-original "concept" album from the ground up. (It can't be a coincidence that in 1939, Paramount Pictures, which had Carmichael under contract as a singer, featured him on-screen in a short subject that amounted to a one-reel Carmichael songbook movie.)

By 1939, there were two kinds of songbook album: anthologies like *Victor Herbert Melodies* and *Hoagy Carmichael Songs,* involving multiple artists, and albums where the works of a single composer were done by a single artist. Decca had two albums of Paul Whiteman playing *Irving Berlin Songs* (Nos. 70 and 71) and no less ambitious was *Noël Coward Songs* (No. 77), which featured six numbers by the future Sir Noël all by Hildegarde, the singer, pianist, and transcontinental superstar, accompanied by Ray Sinatra's Orchestra.

In 1940, Columbia released *Smash Song Hits by Rodgers & Hart,* which had the distinction of featuring Richard Rodgers himself at the piano and conducting. That album, which is the first to feature a cover by Alex Steinweiss, is for no logical reason frequently described as the first pop album, or the first to have an illustrated cover—both claims, as Biel points out, are completely spurious. Not only that, according to pianist and later composer Joel Herron, "Rodgers was a basket case and Johnny Green wound up playing for him. One of the songs was 'The Girl Friend,' and Rodgers couldn't make it. But he wrote good enough melodies, it didn't matter that he couldn't play." (Herron, who later wrote "I'm a Fool to Want You," was working with Green at the time on various radio projects.)

On a smaller scale, the highly jazz-oriented singer Lee Wiley recorded three early songbook albums in quick succession: George and Ira Gershwin (November 1939), Rodgers and Hart (February 1940), and Cole Porter (April 1940). (Then, two years later, Wiley recorded a follow-up package of Harold Arlen songs in February 1942.) The four Wiley packages have been incorrectly described (by me, among others) as the first songbooks. These were released on very small boutique labels—literally. Before the war, there was a short-lived precedent for music stores to morph into independent labels, most successfully the jazz label Commodore. Where Commodore catered to jazz fans, Gala-Rabson and Liberty Music Shop appealed to theater buffs; Broadway buffs would attend a matinee of some snappy new revue, then stop by the Liberty Music Shop on their way home to pick up a new recording of a song they'd just heard.

It's safe to say the Wiley albums were hardly heard by anyone at the time, yet they have been kept steadily available over the decades on both LP and CD. Paradoxically, most of the other songbook albums of the era, like the Decca projects mentioned above and even Columbia's *Rodgers & Hart,* have scarcely been heard from since.

Thus there's plenty of evidence that the pop music album was a viable and ever-expanding format well before World War II and, subsequently, the successful introduction of the long-playing disc in 1948. The concept album was not invented in the wake of the long-playing format; rather, the LP was developed as an easier means of distributing the concept albums that were already being produced. That's especially true when some of those albums, like the original cast recording of *Oklahoma!* and Frank Sinatra's *The Voice,* turned out to be blockbusters. There were, in fact, three milestones in the album format produced during World War II that would all have a widespread, game-changing effect on the way popular music was produced, recorded, and disseminated.

In retrospect, the original cast album of *Oklahoma!* may seem like a foregone conclusion, but it's actually precisely the opposite: at the time it took quite a lot of brains to get the idea off the ground. Out of all ninety-five albums listed in the 1939 Decca catalogue, there's only one devoted to music from a Broadway show, *Song Hits from "The Boys from Syracuse"* (No. 33), and only one further release devoted to a film, *The Wizard of Oz* (No. 74). Up to 1943, recordings of cast members from Broadway shows—even major hits—were scatter-shot; some productions were covered extensively, while many hit shows were completely ignored; in general the concept of the original cast recording was only considered a viable commercial proposition in Europe. Decca's 1938 *Boys from Syracuse* wasn't anything like an original cast album; it featured the Rodgers and Hart score as sung by two contractee entertainers, Rudy Vallee and Frances Langford, who were both well known from their work on radio.

Kapp's decision, working with the same Richard Rodgers, in 1943, to document the score of *Oklahoma!* with the actual cast then appearing at the St. James Theatre, was a giant leap forward. Clearly he knew what he was doing when he picked *Oklahoma!* for this experiment; the show, which had opened in March 1943, was already a blockbuster by the time Kapp recorded it in October. (He would have brought the cast into the studio earlier, but there was a musicians' strike on throughout most of 1943.) Kapp included as much of the show, with the original songs sung by the original actors and singers, as he could in this six-side package.

The *Oklahoma!* album was a landmark comparable to the show itself. Following that success, composers, lyricists, and playwrights became inspired to write similarly constructed "integrated" shows. Likewise, producers and audiences now wanted authentic cast recordings, capturing on record the way the score sounded onstage. With *Oklahoma!* Kapp made the original cast recording a staple of the album format, which it remains to this day. There had been considerable precedent, but the original *Oklahoma!* album can be said to be the release that fully put the concept of the cast album on the map, even as Rodgers and Hammerstein's show itself celebrates the Oklahoma territory achieving statehood and becoming part of the map of the United States.

Contrastingly, Duke Ellington's *Black, Brown*

and Beige was regarded (by some, at least) as a misfire in its day, but has generally been considered a triumph ever since. Written at the tail end of 1942, *Black, Brown and Beige* was described by its composer as "a tone parallel to the history of the Negro in America"; others have referred to it as a "jazz symphony." *BBB* doesn't adhere to any specific classical model, though it comes closer to the sonata form than most of Ellington's other extended works. Ellington had planned the work as the centerpiece of what would be his first of a series of Carnegie Hall concerts in January 1943.

Previewing the event in *Down Beat* (reprinted in *The Duke Ellington Reader*), Helen Oakley announced, "Ellington's performance will be a serious program hailing the attention of Carnegie's customary patrons." However, in the same article, she also quoted Ellington as saying, "We are not attempting to produce a magnificent affair. We desire to remain true to self." That was, in fact, the conflict represented by *Black, Brown and Beige*—or indeed of the very idea of Ellington performing in a formal concert hall like Carnegie. It was widely believed by jazz advocates at the time that for a jazz artist to work in any kind of extended form, whether informed by European classical music or not, was the opposite of being "true to self."

Yet from very early in his career, Ellington was ambitious enough to aspire to compose jazz works beyond the length of the three-minute tracks that were customary for radio broadcasts and for standard 10-inch 78 rpm singles. His early extended works include the 1931 "Creole Rhapsody" and the 1935 "Reminiscing in Tempo." One of his most remarkable early works is his soundtrack to the 1935 short film *Symphony in Black,* which also deserves to be described as an extended concert work, even though Ellington incorporated some existing pieces into the nine-minute work.

Ellington and his orchestra premiered *Black, Brown and Beige* at Carnegie on January 28, 1943, but after only two additional performances Ellington would never play the complete original work in that same format again. Clearly, the musical world wasn't ready for a jazz composition, undeniably brilliant but also undeniably flawed, of that length and ambition. At that point, the major newspapers reviewed classical music but jazz was, for the most part, only covered in specialist publications like *Down Beat* and *Metronome.* Still, nobody knew what to make of *BBB,* and critics on both sides of the press divide accused Ellington of having gone "longhair" and highbrow. John Hammond, who had long been critical of Ellington, accused him in print of "deserting jazz," a claim that seems even more ridiculous today than it did in 1943. More recently Alex Ross proclaimed, "All music becomes classical sooner or later": many jazz fans of the period were determined not to let Duke get away with it, and likewise classical reviewers (particularly Paul Bowles) were hardly any more supportive.

At the time, Ellington was under contract to RCA Victor, which, like the other recording concerns, was embroiled in the ban on commercial recordings imposed for roughly two years by the American Federation of Musicians. When RCA settled with the union, one of the very first orders of business was making some kind of commercial recording of *Black, Brown and Beige.* Yet, rather than the complete work, Ellington recorded eighteen minutes of excerpts in an album of four 12-inch tracks. (Another section of *BBB,* "Carnegie Blues," was released by Victor on a regular 10-inch single, and not included in the original *BBB* 78 album.) Undoubtedly, the reaction of the press discouraged RCA from considering a full recording of the forty-five-minute work, but Ellington was famous for tinkering with his works even after they were introduced, and even without the critical reaction, he probably would have played *BBB* somewhat differently in December 1944 than he had almost two years earlier.

Considering the hit that Ellington took at Carnegie, RCA's trimmed-down version of *BBB* was surprisingly well received. One prominent classical critic, Kurt List (a student of Alban Berg), writing in *Classical Records* in 1946, praised it effusively: "The work is remarkable, not because it transcends actual jazz clichés, which it doesn't, but because it endows them with a great deal of imagination and with a wealth of invention clearly borrowed from the vocabulary of modern serious music."

List laments that the complete work wasn't recorded, but it's my theory that he wouldn't have liked it as much had he been there at Carnegie in 1943. The main problem with the full-length *BBB* was not content but form: Ellington had composed a series of marvelous "movements," but getting from one to the next was his downfall: in the Carnegie performance of *BBB*, Ellington continually gets bogged down in tiresome transitional passages. In that respect, the work was an ideal candidate for the 78 rpm album, a format in which it was physically impossible to make a seamless transition from one disc to the next. The technology demanded that there had to be a clear break, and thus essentially solved Ellington's problem, or at least freed him from having to deal with it. RCA transformed *BBB* from an amorphous, undefined classical form into a clear-cut suite. In a suite, one can go from one piece to the next with a break and without any musical transition, and that form suited Ellington much better—it may not be a coincidence that he introduced his next extended work, *The Perfume Suite,* at his December 19, 1944, Carnegie Hall concert, just a week after recording the RCA version of *BBB*.

Indeed, nearly all of Ellington's subsequent long-form works would use the suite format, including *The Liberian Suite, The Queen's Suite, Such Sweet Thunder (Shakespearean Suite), The Far East Suite,* not to mention his rightfully acclaimed adaptation of the most famous of all classical suites, Tchaikovsky's *Nutcracker.* The medium just happened to ideally suit the record album format, whether in the 78 album-style package of 1943 or the long-playing format of 1948 onward. Upon first hearing these, it becomes immediately apparent that Ellington is not being in the least bit "arty" or pseudo-classical, even when addressing Shakespeare or Tchaikovsky. He is merely writing a series of Ellington-style pieces that flow into and out of each other, which can be enjoyed individually or in sequence. He is, as he said in 1942, being "true to self."

With these works, Ellington consolidated the idea that a jazz or pop band, as opposed to a classical ensemble or a theatrical cast (of solo singers and a chorus), could present an entire, album-length work of original compositions, all designed to follow each other sequentially, but which can also stand as single-like tracks on their own. There

would be many jazz musicians and composers who would follow the format, often (but not always) working orchestrally, like the marvelous *Cuban Fire!,* written for the Stan Kenton Orchestra by Johnny Richards, who wrote a similar work titled *The Rites of Diablo* for his own band, or Benny Carter's excellent *Kansas City Suite* for Count Basie. Album-length orchestral jazz suites continue to be composed up to the present day, by such prominent musicians as Wynton Marsalis and Ted Nash (who both write for the Jazz at Lincoln Center Orchestra), Bobby Watson, and the storied veteran (now late) Gerald Wilson.

Yet, while jazz suites are hardly rare, the prevailing mode of the jazz album for the last sixty years is not the suite, the idea of a single work connecting an entire album, but a combination of original compositions and fresh interpretations of standards and other pre-existing songs. The idea of the newly composed suite became much more prevalent in pop music in the 1960s, especially with the Beatles' albums of 1965 to 1969. *Sgt. Pepper's Lonely Hearts Club Band* is the most celebrated, and most of the second side of the 1969 *Abbey Road* is a sixteen-minute, uninterrupted piece, comprised of eight shorter themes: it's generally described as a medley, but it could also be called a suite or a song cycle—and the parallels to *Black, Brown and Beige* are obvious.

Sgt. Pepper, the Beach Boys' *Pet Sounds,* Marvin Gaye's *What's Going On,* as well as *Blonde on Blonde, Nashville Skyline,* and other albums by Bob Dylan, became the gold standard of rock-era "concept albums"—in fact, the "concept" became the concept that connects all rock-era pop of the last fifty years, from psychedelia to soul to heavy metal to punk to new wave to disco to grunge, from the Clash to Michael Jackson to Bruce Springsteen to Madonna to Jay Z and whatever comes after that. It became the Olympian goal for a pop band to create a classic album, an effort that was applauded much more loudly by other musicians and the press than simply having a chart hit single. By the twenty-first century, there was an implicit intellectual prejudice connected to the two formats: any moron, like "Hannah Montana" or Britney Spears, could land a hit single, but it takes a bunch of so-called geniuses, like Radiohead, to create a classic album. In a way, perhaps all of this is an extension of Duke Ellington's legacy.

A year after the recording of *Black, Brown and Beige* in 1944, Frank Sinatra made *The Voice* (more fully titled *The Voice of Frank Sinatra*), which, when released in 1945, would set the standard for thousands upon thousands of pop and jazz vocal albums, many still being made today. On one level, *The Voice* seems entirely unprecedented; after all, none of Sinatra's forebears, not Al Jolson, not Crosby, not Billie Holiday, had done anything like it. Yet at the same time, in retrospect *The Voice* seems like the next logical step after the profusion of albums released in the immediate prewar years.

Somewhere along the way, the term "concept album" got attached to Frank Sinatra and later to the mature works of the Beatles and the Beach Boys, etc., although I'm not sure that the phrase itself is entirely accurate. It's only when there's a completely extramusical programming conceit, such as songs of travel (Bing Crosby and Rosemary Clooney's *Fancy Meeting You Here*) or songs bemoaning the state of the world (Marvin Gaye's *What's Going On*), that any of these is truly described as a concept album. (A few more examples: Steve Lawrence's *Swinging West*, Mel Tormé's *Swinging on the Moon*, Jack Jones's *Shall We Dance*, all albums built around songs that share a common idea.)

By that standard, which I think is an entirely reasonable one, relatively few of Sinatra's (or the Beatles') albums qualify, save *Moonlight Sinatra, Come Fly with Me,* and not many others. Alas, there isn't a convenient term for what Sinatra created with *The Voice,* and then elaborated upon with *Sing and Dance with Frank Sinatra, In the Wee Small Hours, Songs for Swingin' Lovers, Only the Lonely, Where Are You?, Come Swing with Me,* and dozens of others.

What made *The Voice* especially remarkable is Sinatra and musical director Axel Stordahl's use of a classical-style "chamber music" group, consisting of a string quartet and a four-piece rhythm section (piano, guitar, bass, drums), plus occasional classical woodwinds (flutes, oboes). This particular instrumental format was something brand-new, an attempt to combine the sounds of a jazz group at its most intimate with that of a classical ensemble at its most personal. Sinatra and Stordahl planned the tracks in sequence to a remarkable degree: the album opener, "You Go to My Head," begins with a string passage that approximates the one used in the Sinatra-Stordahl arrangement of "Night and Day." Since this was during a period when that Cole Porter song was Sinatra's radio theme, listeners in 1945 would have instantly recognized that flourish, and in hearing it would be receiving a mental cue that something was about to start, and indeed it was. It's a remarkable contrast, on the radio show and on the Columbia recording of "Night and Day," the flourish is played by several dozen strings, and here it's just a quartet: it sounds the same, yet different.

The Voice consists of eight songs that were already standards in 1945; "These Foolish Things," from 1936, and "You Go to My Head," from 1938, are the most recent. All eight numbers can be described as love songs or romantic ballads. Where some of Sinatra's own later albums would be even more specific, the messages here contain a lot of variety: "Someone to Watch over Me" and "Why Shouldn't I?" are about looking forward to finding love, whereas "You Go to My Head," "I Don't Stand a Ghost of a Chance with You," and "I Don't Know Why" all lightly bemoan the unhappy fact that the one whom the speaker loves will never love him back. "These Foolish Things" is the only one that's specifically about a lost love and a finished affair, and "Paradise" is the only one about being in the middle of a happy relationship, with no dark clouds on the horizon. "You Go to My Head" quotes the title of "A Ghost of a Chance" in its last line, which further connects the two.

Fully titled, "These Foolish Things (Remind Me of You)" is a perfect song for the first-ever real pop song album, since it not only was a song that most people would have known in 1945, but the song itself is a kind of album of memory, a catalogue of the inconsequential bric-a-brac and folderol that accumulate during a relationship, beginning with "a cigarette that bears a lipstick's traces, an airline ticket to romantic places." It's not like the person is deliberately or joyfully remembering all these foolish things, rather, they're being haunted by them ("oh how the ghost of you clings") whether they like it or not. Fittingly, some of the "things" are musical, like "the waiter whistling as the last bar closes" and "a tinkling piano in the next apartment" and, most tellingly, "the song that Crosby sings." The lyrics are a prescient illustration of what the pop song album would become; not one of the foolish things is significant in itself, but they add up to a vivid story, much the way that the eight individual songs on *The Voice* add up to a narrative.

Yet unlike in Sinatra's classic later concept albums, such as *A Swingin' Affair* or *No One Cares,* none of the songs here are ecstatically happy or morosely sad, some are vaguely more optimistic, others are slightly more melancholy—they all hang around the middle mood-wise, and are all rapturously romantic. They are all in what was then considered a slow tempo; in this era when practically every record was a dance record in danceable foxtrot tempo, they're not nearly as slow as Sinatra would get later on. In this premiere album, his first shot out of the gate, he's already found the perfect balance of consistency and variety. All the songs sound like they belong together, yet neither he nor musical director Axel Stordahl ever seems to be repeating himself.

The first LP issue, the 10-inch LP released in June 1948, upheld the sanctity of the original 78 rpm album, but the later 12-inch edition (released after Sinatra had left Columbia, and presumably without his input) added some tracks, took others away, and completely botched everything that Sinatra and Stordahl had achieved. (Needlessly too, as there were other, far more compatible tracks that could have been added to expand the set to twelve cuts.) Unfortunately, this is the version that was around for roughly thirty years, until the beginning of the CD era, and the one that most people know.

Sinatra would complete five more albums during his Columbia period, the later ones being originally released as 10-inch LPs: *Songs by Sinatra, Volume 1* (1947), *Christmas Songs by Sinatra* (1948), *Frankly Sentimental* (1949), *Dedicated to You* (1950), and *Sing and Dance with Frank Sinatra* (1950). *The Voice* was the "purest" of his original

six Columbia albums in that it was the only one that was totally planned as a goal unto itself from the ground up, and that every track was explicitly newly recorded for the project. For the others, he generally combined previously unissued tracks with newly recorded ones. But in virtually all cases the arrangements were by Axel Stordahl, and Sinatra made sure that they flowed in and out of each other seamlessly. *Frankly Sentimental* opens with two tracks featuring the full-sized, near-symphonic Stordahl orchestra, "Body and Soul" and "Laura," but when it then transitions to the *Voice*-style chamber group for most of the remaining six songs, the segue bothers no one. (Interestingly, not one of the original six Sinatra Columbia albums, released during the period when Sinatra was still under contract to the corporation, was either a "greatest hits" collection or a songbook.)

What Sinatra and Stordahl have achieved is no less remarkable, in its own way, than what Ellington created with *Black, Brown and Beige* (and the subsequent suites) or what Rodgers, Hammerstein, and Kapp wrought with the *Oklahoma!* cast album. He took eight songs from eight different sources or composers, and made them relate to each other; in its own way, as I once described it elsewhere, it was comparable to what the early Soviet filmmakers called "montage" theory or what the ancient Egyptians did with hieroglyphics: the idea that image, or song, is meaningful unto itself, but acquires an even greater meaning cumulatively. You're listening to eight songs with a similar mood (wistful, slightly melancholy songs about love) set in arrangements similar enough to obviously be from the same source. In the hands of a lesser vocalist-orchestrator team, you might feel like you're hearing the same song eight times in a row, or a stack of eight singles. Yet Sinatra uses the accumulated meaning of sequential songs to convey a deep sense of overarching destination; you feel like you're going from point A to point B in a meaningful way. (Others would take the idea even more literally to create a direct musical theater–style narrative, following an "I met a girl"–type song with a "now I'm happy"–type song and then a "boy loses girl" song, like Jimmy Rushing's *Cat Meets Chick,* but Sinatra realized that to take it that far would be overkill.)

The singer Steve Lawrence once compared Sinatra doing a love song to a three-act play, with a beginning, a middle, and a distinct ending, but a Sinatra program of songs, like *The Voice,* is even more so.

Listening to eight songs in a row felt like a complete experience. Sinatra was giving the songs of Cole Porter ("Why Shouldn't I?") and the Gershwin brothers ("Someone to Watch over Me") the same kind of sustained attention that Ellington was aiming for in his extended compositions, or that Rodgers and Hammerstein had brought to Broadway, and that had long existed in the individual movements of a symphony. Of the three models, Sinatra's is the one that had the most relevance for jazz and popular singing—not only on recordings but in live performance as well. Vocalists were heading from ballroom bandstands and movie theater stages (where they generally did cameos in big band stage shows) and into nightclubs, and, eventually, concert halls, and amphitheaters. Most of them would be following Sinatra's example of using what was being established (though not yet named) as the "Great American Songbook" as their basic bread and butter. The overwhelming majority of the great jazz and pop vocal albums— virtually all of those covered in this book—follow this basic format.

And just as Sinatra perfected the basic outline of the pop and jazz vocal album (one utilized by a great many instrumentalists in addition to singers) well before the commercial introduction of the long-playing disc, it remains to be seen if and how the idea survives the demise of physical media (the LP and the CD). Indeed, we have reached a turn of the wheel that takes us back to the original *Victrola Christmas Album:* now when you buy an album of Christmas music from iTunes or Amazon, you can select the tracks you want and construct your own album out of them. It's taken us ninety years to get back to where we were in 1926.

The concept of the pop album was a key element that helped the great songs endure for generation after generation. Yet even in an age of intangible media—of pure downloads and album-less sound files—there's every reason to believe that the songs of Porter and the Gershwins and their contempo- raries will continue to thrive. Ha, ha, ha. Who's got the last laugh now?

A special footnote about "You Don't Know What Love Is." Because this song is heard on four albums included in this book (by Chet Baker, Tony Bennett, Billy Eckstine, and Billie Holiday), it was decided to discuss its etymology here, up front, rather than in any (or, worse, all) of the individual essays. The song was the work of Don Raye (1909–1985) and Gene de Paul (1919–1988); the former mostly wrote lyrics and the latter mainly music, but they each wrote both at different times. As a songwriting team, Raye and de Paul worked for Universal Pictures during the World War II era, a period in which they enjoyed a huge popular success with two very different strains of songs. Famously, they were among the first to capture the boogie-woogie trend of the era in mainstream popular songs, and had substantial hits with "Down the Road a Piece" (Raye solo), "Beat Me, Daddy, Eight to the Bar," "Scrub Me, Mama, with a Boogie Beat," "Bounce Me Brother, with a Solid Four," and "The Boogie-Woogie Bugle Boy of Company B." They also wrote very lovely, lyrically and harmonically sophisticated ballads, like "I'll Remember April," "Star Eyes," and "You Don't Know What Love Is." In both strains, their songs were enthusiastically played by jazz groups and singers, and many became jazz and Great American Songbook standards.

At this time, they were constantly working on war-related Universal musical comedy pictures, the casts and scores for which were highly interchangeable. "You Don't Know What Love Is" was apparently originally written for the (Bud) Abbott and (Lou) Costello movie *Keep 'Em Flying* (1941), in which it was supposed to have been sung by leading lady Carol Bruce. However, the song was dropped from that movie, but Universal apparently considered using it in another wartime comedy-variety production starring a famous comedy team, the Ritz Brothers vehicle *Behind the Eight Ball.* According to many sources, the song was sung by Carol Bruce in that 1942 film, but if that is the case then it has been cut from all known prints—I've screened multiple copies of that movie and the song isn't heard in any of them. My conclusion is that it was also dropped from *Behind the Eight Ball* as well, and not heard in any movie.

Despite not being introduced in a picture, the song became an instant jazz standard—it was almost immediately recorded by Ella Fitzgerald, Harry James, and the Earl Hines Orchestra (featuring Billy Eckstine) in the fall of 1941. (A check of the labels on the original 78s reveals that the first one, the Fitzgerald, states "from the Universal Picture *Keep 'Em Flying*," but none of the other labels mention any movie at all, and none mention *Behind the Eight Ball*.) The jazz community responded to both its musical and its emotional richness— it's not only one of the most profound love songs (in the literal sense of "profound," meaning deep) but one of the darkest. It's heavily romantic and extremely nihilistic at the same time, conveying a sense of sexual hopelessness that many jazz artists are drawn to—both Eckstine and Baker recorded it more than once. It has, in fact, become one of the most recorded of all standards—1,077 different versions are listed in the basic jazz discography. It's not surprising that "You Don't Know What Love Is" would turn up on four of the fifty all-time greatest jazz and pop vocal albums.

The Great Jazz and Pop
Vocal Albums

Louis Armstrong

Louis Armstrong Meets Oscar Peterson

(1957)

Louis Armstrong once described the singing of his friend and peer Bing Crosby as "having a mellow quality that only Bing's got. It's like gold being poured out of a cup." It was a quality that Armstrong himself aspired to. The great trumpeter famously described himself as having a "sawmill voice," and, indeed, in his younger years particularly it was a deep, gruff, bearlike growl. In fact, he was the prototype for many successive generations of growlers, any list of which would start with the many jazz-singing horn men who tried to follow in his footsteps (most successfully Jack Teagarden) as well as many distinct individuals in disparate fields such as Howling Wolf, Tom Waits, and even the Cookie Monster. But Armstrong himself always wanted to be a crooner, just as he always tried to get his big band to play as sweet as Guy Lombardo's; it's clear as early as on recordings like "Sweethearts on Parade" (1930), a song by Carmen Lombardo that he sings as romantically as possible. One reason Armstrong was so successful as a pop singer in his fifties and sixties is that his voice had mellowed so much—by this point it was sweet as well as rough—and also because he had kept growing as an artist. Specifically, he was astute enough to learn from the singers who had learned from him—not only Crosby, but the giants of the next generation, like Billie Holiday, Frank Sinatra, and Ella Fitzgerald.

Unlike such contemporaries as Duke Ellington and Sinatra, who both went through a fallow period in the early 1950s and then experienced what was regarded as a "renaissance," Louis Armstrong never required a "comeback"; his popularity never flagged, and neither did his touring schedule or his recorded output. Whereas most recording stars of the period were under contract to only one label at a time, Armstrong was a freelancer throughout the LP era, and (particularly when reissues of 78-era material are factored in) seemed to have a zillion albums coming out all the time from every existing record company. Some were more purely jazz-oriented, some had a definite pop appeal, some were about re-creating the past and others were about living in the present, some emphasized his trumpet and some his band, and others his singing. But of all these releases, the one that showcases Armstrong best as a vocalist (call him jazz or pop or whatever) is *Louis Armstrong Meets Oscar Peterson* (1957). This is the one project in which all the elements most fully coalesced: the best accompanist and the most Olympian rhythm section, as well as a sympathetic producer who wanted him to record songs of substance rather than take a quick and often cheap shot at the Hit Parade. This is the record that offers the most irrefutable evidence as to why Louis Armstrong is one of the great singers of all time.

• • •

For Louis Armstrong, the album format was the opportunity to go middlebrow.

By the 1950s, jazz purists—meaning critics, historians, and collectors—were regarding Armstrong's classic recordings of the 1920s as high art. These same scholars were at the same time openly dismissive of the pop singles that he was then turning out. Even as Columbia Records was gathering his Okeh 78s of thirty years earlier onto 12-inch LPs, Armstrong was recording 45s of quasi-novelty tunes with titles like "The Dummy Song." In between the high art of the Hot Five years and the low-slung singles of the 45 rpm era, Armstrong's albums were what some would consider middlebrow—that's how the Great American Songbook was regarded in the years the concept was coming into existence. The extreme purists (including most of his biographers) would rather that he had just played blues, traditional New Orleans songs, and his own originals—but if he had to play pop songs, then the Gershwins were surely a step up from "It Takes Two to Tango."

For all his success, Armstrong found himself in a rather awkward place, culturally, during the Eisenhower era: one segment of his audience castigating him for changing his music too much since the Hot Five era, with another group taking him to task for not having changed his politics and general deportment since the 1920s. It seems, in retrospect, that rather too much of this was made by the music press of the moment (who, like virtually all journalists before and since, were always looking for a conflict), and then by historians and biographers in the last fifty to sixty years. When we look back at the era, we have little choice but to see through the eyes of writers with all kinds of biases. But the unprejudiced reality is that the overwhelming majority of listeners and fellow performers (excepting a few modern jazz militants) adored Armstrong and couldn't get enough of him, on singles, albums, TV shows, concerts, club appearances, movies, whatever. They loved his songs, his delivery, his energy, his eagerness to please, his stage antics, and most of all, his playing and singing.

Producer Norman Granz was among the first to discover the often intertwined markets for both the older (premodern) styles of jazz and the emerging notion of a standard songbook. The market for both forms was substantial and in 1956, Granz, who had been recording mostly jazz (and certain select singers) for various labels including several of his own, launched Verve Records. Verve was notable in that it was exclusively directed at jazz fans and song buffs; albums containing classic jazz and standard songs were the primary focus, and what singles it released were strictly an afterthought. Granz was a canny businessman who knew exactly when to get into a market and when to get out. Far from appealing only to highbrows, Verve was so successful that less than four years after the company was founded, he sold his interests outright to MGM for a huge profit. As Granz and, later, George Wein would learn, this was a period when it was possible to get rich presenting jazz. In a famous phrase attributed to Jerome Kern, "Go on being uncommercial—there's a lot of money in it."

Granz's operation could hardly have been possible without Oscar Peterson; as a name artist, he turned out dozens of albums on a songbook theme (and every other theme) with his various trios, and as a sideman he enabled Granz to produce session after session. No matter whom he backed up, Peterson had the sheer chops, taste, skill, and attitude to keep every date going smoothly. If the discographies are accurate, Peterson recorded the greater part of four albums in four long sessions over two days, July 31 and August 1, 1957: *Soft Sands,* in which the pianist's trio was backed by a string orchestra and mixed choir in a format that would later be dubbed "easy listening," "mood music," or "make-out music"; a session with the tenor saxophone icon Lester Young released as *Going for Myself . . . ;* an all-star jam session with trumpeter Sweets Edison and saxophone stars Stan Getz and Gerry Mulligan that was released as *Jazz Giants '58;* and in addition, he and his trio taped four tunes for the album that became *Louis Armstrong Meets Oscar Peterson.*

Armstrong's career as an album artist was a particularly vital one: although he had been making records steadily for well over thirty years before the invention of the 12-inch LP, thanks to creative producers like George Avakian and Granz, most of his albums were special projects—quite distinct from his singles. Armstrong in particular utilized the format as a vehicle for team-ups—both actual and virtual. He worked not only with Peterson, but with musicians as modern as Dave Brubeck, as traditional as the Dukes of Dixieland, and as iconic as Duke Ellington, as well as two of the only singers who flew in his general orbit, Ella Fitzgerald and Bing Crosby. These team-ups were, in a sense, an extension of the variety show sensibility that was uppermost in pop music at the time—when stars like Dean Martin, Perry Como, and Dinah Shore hosted weekly TV shows in which the singing host was expected to sing duets with the guests. Armstrong not only sang with nearly all of them but with many others, including Frank Sinatra, Eddie Fisher, and Jimmy Durante. Then, too, his successful songbook albums *Louis Armstrong Plays W. C. Handy* (1954) and *Satch Plays Fats* (1955) were presented like team-ups; you looked at the cover of the latter album, with pictures of Armstrong and Waller side by side, and many customers who had more taste (and money) than knowledge probably assumed that Fats was actually playing with Pops.

The title of *Louis Armstrong Meets Oscar Peterson* is a bit of a stretch, but a forgivable one. So too is the cover, which shows Armstrong and Peterson sitting side by side, very casually, on adjacent stools. However, this isn't *The Tony Bennett / Bill Evans Album*(s), where two collaborators are on equal footing. Peterson and his working group of the period (customarily guitarist Herb Ellis and Ray Brown, here joined by drummer Louis Bellson) are strictly accompanying Armstrong. The pianist and several of the others solo occasionally, but there's no attempt to have them share the spotlight. It's Pops's show, and they're just along for the ride; the four men function as wheels on a car—he couldn't get anywhere without them, but make no mistake, Pops is the one steering.

Armstrong's relationship with Granz and Verve Records was centered around his initial two team-up albums with Ella Fitzgerald, *Ella & Louis* (1956) and *Ella and Louis Again* (1957), followed by the duo's epic recording of *Porgy and Bess*. The collaboration with Peterson was recorded in between all these, not exactly as an afterthought but rather

as a collateral benefit. Following the previously mentioned August 1 date, there would be a subsequent Armstrong-Peterson session on October 14, and the two dates became the album. Between the two sessions, a total of fourteen different songs were recorded, all of which are on the current CD edition of the album. (In recent years, a generous amount of "bonus" session material has also surfaced, particularly from August.)

"That Old Feeling" is a prophetic opener: This is the same Satchmo many listeners had been loving for thirty years prior to 1957, and the song itself was twenty years old at that point. (It's one of many standards by lyricist Lew Brown from the years after the highly successful trio of DeSylva, Brown, and Henderson went their separate ways.) But there's definitely a new feeling to this old feeling; never before has that old Satchmo sung with a new piano player like this. The most important feeling—what musicians sometimes call "the time feel" (the overall groove generated by the rhythm section)—is quite new and different from any ensemble that Armstrong had worked with in the past. Obviously, it was beneficial that Armstrong had already worked with Peterson on the album with Fitzgerald; to my ears at least, he seemed a little tense on those earlier dates, whereas in August and October he seems blissfully relaxed, and much more comfortable with the material. Peterson's riffy intro on the first track reveals the influence of the King Cole Trio, and it's apparent from Armstrong's entrance that the mighty man is in rare form. There's no trumpet on this track, but he's never been greater at using his voice like a horn, punctuating Brown's lyric with a wide range of nonverbal, hornlike phrases, especially on the second chorus and the coda.

"Let's Fall in Love" testifies to Granz's knowledge of the American Songbook. Harold Arlen and Ted Koehler wrote the song in 1933 as the title number for a Columbia Pictures comedy, marking their first Hollywood venture and virtually their first assignment of any kind outside the Cotton Club. It was hardly overlooked in 1933–34 but had seldom been heard in the two decades since. Armstrong backs into the second eight bars like an Olympic athlete getting ready for a jump, positioning himself by getting a running start with a momentary scat interlude. The trumpet solo here is especially fine; he holds the climactic note much longer than you'd think, and then enters singing with "Yessss, let's fall in love," holding that "yes" again much longer than he has to. Both vocals and trumpet are immersed in super-high energy here.

Two of the next few songs had started life as jazz instrumentals before lyrics were added. "I'll Never Be the Same" was first heard in 1931 as a melody written by two New York dance band musicians, violinist Matty Malneck and pianist Frank Signorelli, whom Armstrong probably knew in the early days. It was originally titled "Little Buttercup" before Gus Kahn gave it the lyric and the title that it's been known by for the last eighty years, after which point it would, in fact, never be the same. The tempo takes us closer to ballad territory; there's just a slight tinge of melancholy in Satchmo's vocal: "Once love was king," he sings, emphasizing the high note, "but kings can be wrong . . . yes!" This is a letter-perfect interpretation: you can see why Sinatra, Holiday, and Fitzgerald all cited Pops as their major inspiration, and, in turn, what he was learning from them. In his younger years, Armstrong might have ended with his signature "oh yeah," but here he channels that same feeling into the lyric's final word, "again," stretching the "a" as if it were the extended "ohhhhhh" of the "oh yeah."

"What's New?" was also a natural for Armstrong, having been originally conceived as a trumpet feature for Billy Butterfield (himself a Satchmo scholar), as composed by bassist-arranger Bob Haggart, who titled it "I'm Free" before Johnny Burke made it into the song we all know and love. Yet Armstrong's treatment doesn't include any trumpet—or bass and drums, either; it's a remarkably moving duet for voice and piano, one of the very few times Armstrong ever recorded in such a format. This is one of his all-time-best ballads, particularly among the few he sang in something close to rubato. When he emphasizes "Probably I'm boring you" in the second chorus, he makes the written words seem like an ad lib, and prepares us for a genuine spontaneous interjection when he sings

"Mama, I understand." This is another superlative lyric reading; Johnny Burke meant the last line to be something of a twist ending: after thirty-two bars of chitchat, the hero surprisingly comes out and admits he still loves the person he's singing to—he's been trying to focus on what's new, but the truth is that he can't get beyond that old feeling. Armstrong has, of course, been communicating love in every word, every note, every syllable along the way, making the last line seem even more natural when he reaches it.

Harold Arlen and Johnny Mercer intended "Blues in the Night" as a movie theme song that encapsulated the true feeling of the blues, both musically and lyrically, in pop song form; when they finished, the unusual structure and extended length of the piece also gave it something in common with classical lieder. There's no denying it's a brilliant and beautiful song, particularly as performed in the 1941 film of the same name. Still, as a song—especially compared with the trim economy of other Arlen-Mercer masterpieces like "One for My Baby" and "Come Rain or Come Shine," "Blues in the Night" has always seemed too much of a muchness. The point of the blues is to be direct and to the point, but "Blues in the Night" is rather overbaked, there's just too much of it, especially the long, rambling middle section that seems completely unnecessary. Any kind of a bridge is usually out of place in the blues, and this one (beginning with "The evening breeze will start the trees . . ." and continuing through "The mockingbird will sing the saddest kind of song . . .") is especially so. Bing Crosby didn't sing that section in his 1941 version, relegating it to a female vocal group, and it still doesn't need to be there.

It won't surprise anyone that Armstrong—the greatest jazz singer of all time and a mean blues musician—brilliantly brings out the jazz and blues elements of this movie song, but by making that middle section work so well, he's also, in a way, making the classical side of the number work better than it has with any other performer. At 5:17, the length and tempo are perfect, as is the relaxed and bluesy tempo provided by Peterson's quartet—and the great man's trumpet solo adds even more to the overall impact. There's no doubt that Arlen and Mercer heard Armstrong's recording; one can only imagine what they felt upon discovering how Armstrong realized their aspirations better than any other interpreter, even Sinatra or Ray Charles. The coda is perfect, with Armstrong altering the final words to "My mama was right—oh, blues every night!"

The first words of "How Long Has This Been Going On?" are priceless in and of themselves: "As a tot when I trotted in little velvet panties / I was kissed by my sisters, my cousins, and my aunties." Everybody—Granz, Peterson, and especially the mighty man himself—is clearly having a joke on the sheer incongruity of this singer with that voice doing those lines. The laughter is productive, it warms us up for what is one of Armstrong's greatest vocals on record; he sings with absolute conviction and a sense of humor that brilliantly suits one of the wittiest of all songs by the Gershwin brothers. It's also one of the very best of the thousands of recordings of this classic from the 1927 *Funny Face;* the song was a cornerstone of the 1950s Gershwin revival, an era when there were new Gershwin movies (*An American in Paris, Funny Face*), many performances on television, and tons of 12-inch LPs. Gershwin was by far the most popular subject for songbooks—Ella Fitzgerald alone did no fewer than three. Ira Gershwin wrote two different verses for "How Long," one for a man and the other for a woman—although it may seem surprising ninety years later that the "little velvet panties" line was actually the start of the male lyric. (Of all the many heavyweights to tackle the song in this period, man or woman, Armstrong was the only one to sing those particular lines; both Fitzgerald and Carmen McRae begin with the female verse, which starts "'Neath the stars, at bazaars . . .")

"I Was Doing All Right" is a comparatively lesser-known Gershwin classic, from the brothers' final project, the 1937 film *The Goldwyn Follies,* in which it was introduced by the recently emigrated Scottish entertainer Ella Logan. Armstrong feels comfortable enough with the tune to open with a trumpet solo—just eight tasty bars at the start—and both the horn solo and the vocal are of an extremely high quality. He's never been more excited by the prospect of interpreting a lyric on

a line-by-line, word-by-word basis, like Sinatra; more than ever, Satch's famous asides are offered in the service of the text, especially when he takes the word "suffer" out of time and just says it (in both choruses): he doesn't need to overemphasize it—in fact he makes "suffer" sound more insufferable merely by speaking it. At the closer, he throws in "I was doing all right, but I'm doing a little better than ever now." And indeed he is.

"Moon Song" had been popular when it was new (introduced by Kate Smith in the 1933 film *Hello, Everybody!*) but then, like many other songs, was sorely neglected for almost twenty-five years, before experiencing a major resurgence in the album era. It was usually sung as a slow, melancholy ballad (as Doris Day did it), but Armstrong turns it into a medium-tempo romper (the kind he would describe as "half-fast"). Louis and Oscar are enjoying themselves so much that they go for a full four and a half minutes—it's not a second too long, and there's no shortage of trumpet.

In the natural order of things, Armstrong had recorded the music of George Gershwin under several circumstances: there was a wonderful "Love Walked In" from 1938, and numerous versions of "I Got Rhythm." But for most of his career, Pops had the misfortune to almost completely miss out on the Cole Porter songbook. Finally, in the mid-1950s, that began to change: First, in 1954, Armstrong and the All-Stars played "Don't Fence Me In" as a duet feature for himself and Velma Middleton; then, in 1956, the All-Stars were part of the all-star cast of MGM's *High Society.* Finally, no fewer than three Porter classics were selected by Granz and crew for this album: "Let's Do It (Let's Fall in Love),""I Get a Kick Out of You," and "Just One of Those Things."

"Just One of Those Things" is also full-out Porter at his Porter-iest, a song laden with fantastic imagery ("a trip to the moon on gossamer wings") and complex, multiple layers of irony—a very different kind of irony than that which had been part of Armstrong's musical makeup since his boyhood in New Orleans. In "Just One of Those Things," the speaker is a typical Porter protagonist—a nonchalant, blasé, presumably upper-class character who pretends not to care when his love affair is finito: "It was great fun / But it was just one of those things," but the interpreter's job is to show more pain and passion than the lyric lets on at first, to go behind Porter's sophisticated veneer—and this Armstrong does brilliantly, both with his voice and his trumpet, in a full-chorus solo. "I Get a Kick Out of You" and "Let's Do It" were both done at the August session (although not included on the original album release); obviously, Armstrong was getting his feet wet with Porter in a serious way. "Let's Do It" became the archetype for what Porter called his "laundry list" songs (later examples include "They All Fall in Love" and "Can-Can"). In a less overt way, "I Get a Kick Out of You" also has elements of a "list" song; it could be called a "reverse list" song, since it catalogues those items that do not thrill the speaker. Armstrong opens with the minor-mood verse: "My story is much too sad to be told . . ." Yes, this character is another one of Porter's blasé sophisticates; however, Armstrong doesn't try to make us believe that he could be such a character—clearly, he has never fought vainly that old ennui in his whole life (or been bored "terriff-ically too")—instead, he reverses the mood, accentuating the positive, and thus making us feel the joy of those things that he actually does get a kick out of.

"Let's Do It" is also full-fledged Norman Granz; it can be viewed as a follow-up to what the producer achieved a year earlier with Fitzgerald and the song "Bewitched, Bothered and Bewildered" on her Rodgers and Hart songbook. As in 1956, the idea was to start with a classic show tune, one that had already gone on to become a jazz standard, one with a slightly risqué attitude, and a long, long list of choruses. At the time these songs were written, deep in the 78 era, it was assumed that only a small portion of the words would ever fit on a single of the day, but just as he recorded marathon jam sessions, Granz was also one of the first to record ultra-length versions of these now iconic standards, including chorus after chorus. Armstrong and Peterson take the whole thing very slowly, in order for the singer to extract the maximum value out of every one of Porter's witty turns of phrase, the first chorus (which describes courtship rituals among various nations of the world), skipping then to the third written chorus from the show

(which delineates the mating habits of the denizens of the deep), and then on to chorus four (now it's the turn of the bugs, starting with "dragonflies, in the reeds"), and finally the last chorus (officially number five, but only Armstrong's fourth), which talks about jungle animals ("chimpanzees in the zoos"). The insectoid chorus contains Armstrong's funniest ad lib yet; where Porter's line is "Moths in your rug do it, what's the use of mothballs," Armstrong comes up with "Moths in your rug do it—well, looky here, what's the use of balls—hmmm?" There's no verse and no trumpet, but we don't need either. Armstrong builds and builds, finding a different way to be funny and funky with every line. This is a mature Armstrong masterpiece.

"There's No You" and "You Go to My Head" are the two strongest ballads on the album, and are also, respectively, the shortest and the longest tracks. Like every other musician of his generation, trombonist-bandleader Tommy Dorsey was a major Louis Armstrong fan, and he instilled that love of Pops—as if it needed any instillation—in everyone who ever worked for him. "There's No You" was published by one of Dorsey's companies and first recorded by his orchestra in 1945, and it was forever associated with four Dorseyites: writers Tom Adair and Hal Hopper (whose day job was singing as one of the Pied Pipers), and singers Frank Sinatra and Jo Stafford. Armstrong's "There's No You" could also be called "There's No Band"—the whole 2:19 track is just Armstrong's voice and guitarist Herb Ellis. The mighty man is most celebrated for his extroverted exuberance, but, particularly in his maturity he knew well how to sing and play in an intimate manner, thus forming a remarkably direct connection with his audiences.

On "There's No You," that intimacy is expressed entirely vocally, and "You Go to My Head" starts out with one of his best trumpet solos of the period; there's no flash or dazzle here, none of the trumpet "theatrics" that first made him a superstar, none of the operatic-style high drama. Rather, every note he plays is at the service of the melody, the lyrics, and the inner meaning behind them both. I've never heard him so relaxed and yet so passionate; and after a full, glorious chorus on trumpet, he sings in a way that's equally potent and communicative. One can't imagine any of Armstrong's trumpet progeny, even those who sang, delivering "You Go to My Head" so meaningfully—not Roy Eldridge, Red Allen, Bunny Berigan—well, maybe Chet Baker. For such an interpretation, no matter what the means of delivery (vocal or instrumental—well, maybe Lester Young), you'd have to go to Armstrong's vocal descendants—Fitzgerald, Holiday, Sinatra. At six and a half minutes, it is, again, a powerful argument for the LP's ability to break down the time barrier of the standard single-length format that dominated recorded music up until 1950; some performances are actually worth listening to for longer than three minutes. Not many, I'll grant you, but this is one of the few.

"Sweet Lorraine" is a unique ballad that spent its whole history firmly within the world of jazz musicians and singers; not, for once, originating in a show, it was composed by Clifford (sometimes credited as "Cliff") Burwell, a journeyman pianist of the 1920s who, among other things, played in Rudy Vallee's Connecticut Yankees. (Lyrically, it's the earliest song of note by famed wordsmith Mitchell Parish.) "Sweet Lorraine" was immediately picked up by clarinetist Jimmie Noone, who in 1928 was, like Armstrong, a New Orleans musician who had settled in Chicago. Early on, it was associated with Noone's Apex Club Orchestra, and in particular with Noone's pianist and co-leader, the young Earl "Fatha" Hines. And then it was thanks to Hines that another, even younger transplanted Southerner in Chicago, Nat (not yet "King") Cole, learned the song. Cole was playing "Sweet Lorraine" with his trio as far back as the late 1930s, but it was after he recorded it for Capitol Records in 1943 that it became a hit and a jazz standard. Armstrong's treatment defers to the Fatha and the King (and Peterson is especially mindful of his two piano predecessors), but Armstrong adds his personal stamp, especially with the trumpet; it's a bit more emphatic than "You Go to My Head"—something about him seems the tiniest bit competitive with Noone, Hines, and Cole—but still amazingly mellow.

Armstrong sings "Makin' Whoopee" (not on the original album) rather like a veteran campaigner back from the wars, imparting his wisdom to his younger charges—and, in this case, that includes all of us. He's playing the old stud here, telling us what he's learned in a lifetime of loving, losing, and loving again. The tempo is slow, perfect for romantic dancing, but even better for storytelling. Satchmo sings as though he's seen many a season come and go, and many a reason as well, and, in his many years, much whoopee has been made.

Billie Holiday had been doing "Willow Weep for Me" a lot in the mid-1950s, before both Armstrong and Sinatra, neither of whom had any previous connection to the song, recorded it. It's safe to say that both Armstrong and Sinatra were inspired by her. Sinatra's version, on *Only the Lonely,* is by far the slowest and the most doleful; Armstrong's (also left out of the original recording) is much faster and looser, a few beats away from an R&B-style shuffle, and definitely in a solid dance tempo, which he reinforces with a powerful trumpet solo. (Since it derives from the August date, there is, as with the other three tunes, an abundance of alternate takes and session material, and it's possible to listen to Armstrong and Peterson working out the arrangement, point by point.)

Norman Granz is definitely to be commended for his efforts to record Armstrong as a "serious" popular singer. It may have been the Columbia studio albums *Louis Armstrong Plays W. C. Handy* and *Satch Plays Fats* (both produced by George Avakian) that showed that the All-Stars could play more than "Sleepy Time" and "Indiana," but it was Armstrong's Verve albums that showed how much he had grown as a singer in the thirty years since he'd first started to vocalize regularly on recordings. All the well-meaning efforts of these producers were, to an extent, stymied by Armstrong's manager Joe Glaser; where Granz, Avakian, and Milt Gabler, who produced Armstrong's singles and albums for Decca, tried to take the long view, Glaser sold Armstrong short in trying to maximize his time by booking recording sessions on the same nights that he was also doing concerts and clubs. As a result, Armstrong was often exhausted by the time he arrived at the studio. It wasn't in his nature to hold anything back—he always gave his audiences everything he had, often over two or three sets a night; not surprisingly, sometimes when the tape started rolling at two a.m., the exhausted Armstrong had nothing left to give. With the best of intentions, Granz produced what should have been two classic albums with Armstrong backed by an orchestra led by arranger Russ Garcia, *Louis Under the Stars* and *I've Got the World on a String* (both mostly also recorded in August 1957). I always enjoyed those two albums on LP, but hearing them under the closer scrutiny of digital remastering reveals how tired Armstrong was. His trumpet work particularly suffers here, but the vocals too are just not as rich and ripe as his work on the Peterson sessions.

Which underscores why *Louis Armstrong Meets Oscar Peterson* ranks as Armstrong's single best vocal album. All the stars were in alignment, and it was simply the luck of the draw; his vocal and trumpet chops were in particularly amazing shape. Alas, where there were two full albums with Fitzgerald and two with Garcia (followed by the *Porgy and Bess* double-album magnum opus with both Fitzgerald and Garcia), there was only one album costarring Armstrong and Peterson— and he would never make anything else like it, an album of classics from the Great American Songbook with a "modern" rhythm section. It wasn't like Satchmo the Great to repeat himself, but, just this once, we wish that he had. More than on any other Armstrong album, this is the one where his voice most sounds like gold being poured out of a cup.

2

Fred Astaire
The Astaire Story
(1953)

Another left-field and entirely personal note, one that has little or nothing to do with Fred Astaire: In the 1980s and early 1990s, I worked for an independent record label called Stash Records, which was run by a music buff, former industrialist, and World War II veteran named Bernard Brightman. Before the war, Bernie had been an avid swing dancer in the glory days of the Savoy Ballroom, and, back when it was still legal, a marijuana enthusiast (as his choice of a company name indicates). We both loved the music of the swing era and traditional jazz from New Orleans, but we had differing ideas on how to preserve and disseminate it. My idea was that we should gather historical recordings (meaning 78s) and get a sound engineer to perform what later would be called "audio restoration" on them, and then issue vintage recordings. Bernie's idea was that we find a contemporary band that could play the music—Vince Giordano's Nighthawks were already playing around Manhattan—and produce new recordings of vintage songs and orchestrations.

THE ASTAIRE STORY

A NEEDLE IN A HAYSTACK
OH, LADY BE GOOD!
A FOGGY DAY
NOT MY GIRL
JAM SESSION
SO NEAR AND YET SO FAR
YOU'RE EASY TO DANCE WITH
THEY CAN'T TAKE THAT AWAY FROM ME
I'M BUILDING UP TO AN AWFUL LETDOWN

The difference between us was that I was thinking like a record collector, and Bernie was thinking like a record producer. And that was the way that most producers of the early LP era tended to think. There were LP reissues of classic jazz and pop, but the general inclination was to record new albums—especially after hi-fidelity and then stereophonic recording came in. It was much more profitable to do new sessions, and legacy artists like Benny Goodman or Duke Ellington stood to make more profits from new albums (between being paid for the new sessions and royalties afterward, which were rarely included in 78-era contracts). There was a thin line between re-creation and tribute albums; if you felt like listening to Russ Columbo, who had died in 1934, you were more likely to find the tribute album by Jerry Vale; if you wanted the historic King Oliver–Louis Armstrong sessions, there was always *Satchmo Plays King Oliver* from 1959.

For veteran recording stars, the LP medium was a format of the past as well as for the future. In the mid-1950s, Bing Crosby, Louis Armstrong, and Ethel Merman would all release album packages titled *A Musical Autobiography*. But the first "musical autobiography," although it wasn't titled that, was Fred Astaire's *The Astaire Story*, recorded in 1952 and released in 1953 as a deluxe four-LP package.

The year is significant in terms of the technology, but not with regards to anything else; there's no occurrence in Astaire's professional life that would have motivated him to want to take stock and recap everything he had done up until this point. By that yardstick, he should have made the album in 1957–58, after finishing *Funny Face* and *Silk Stockings*, which would turn out to be his last major "traditional" movie musicals (although he couldn't have known that at the time). In 1952, he starred in *The Belle of New York,* which is regarded by no one as classic Astaire (it actually lost money at the box office, although it hardly seems like a dog or a turkey today), but in 1953 he would make *The Band Wagon,* which is on nearly everyone's list of all-time-great movie musicals.

By 1952–53, however, there was an encroaching element of autobiography in Astaire's work: *Royal Wedding* (1951) vaguely incorporated some real-life experiences from the dancer's early career with his sister, Adele, and *The Band Wagon* (1953) borrowed the title and many of the songs from Astaire's 1931 Broadway hit. (Later, *Funny Face,* 1957, would be a new movie musical constructed around the bones of a thirty-year-old Astaire Broadway vehicle.) It's also true all this merely seems like reflection from the present point of view, and one doubts that Astaire was consciously thinking about any of this at the time. At this point as well, the producer Norman Granz was keenly aware that even while Astaire himself was still active and vital, the songs that he had introduced were increasingly regarded as classics, in spite of how Astaire himself, unlike his character Tony Hunter at the start of *The Band Wagon,* was anything but a museum piece.

In the cinematic productions of both *The Band Wagon* and *Funny Face,* he was reprising many classic Astaire songs he had introduced decades earlier, but by that time, so was everyone else: virtually every classic Sinatra "concept" album included at least one song associated with Astaire; virtually every songwriter in the Ella Fitzgerald songbook series had written a film or show for Astaire; virtually every TV variety show—and there were dozens on the air in the 1950s, from Perry Como to Dinah Shore to Ed Sullivan to Steve Allen to *The Colgate Comedy Hour*—did the same. In short, considering that everybody was singing Astaire songs, whether they acknowledged it or not, it certainly made sense that Astaire himself should do something with the classic songs he'd introduced.

It also makes sense that Norman Granz would be the one to get him to do it. *The Astaire Story,* as related in Tad Hershorn's 2011 biography, *Norman Granz: The Man Who Used Jazz for Justice,* started out as a labor of love. (All historical details here

come from that source, unless otherwise noted.) Born and raised in Los Angeles, Granz grew up a devotee of both jazz and the American Songbook from a very early age. During the time of Granz's youth, neither of these closely interconnected areas of music needed either moral or financial support; but by the late 1940s, both were on the path to becoming increasingly marginalized. At war's end, novelty songs were more popular than Jerome Kern, and improvised small-group jazz was less popular than the big dance bands, which themselves were now less popular than star singers. As an independent recording producer and concert promoter, Granz would make himself a considerable pile in presenting both.

"The whole thing started when Norman Granz called me up one day and said he wanted to do a record album with me," Astaire wrote in the album booklet, "not just an ordinary album, but a special one." The great entertainer didn't exactly jump for joy at the idea. Rather than approaching Astaire through an agent, Granz had gotten hold of the dancer's personal phone number and, on February 9, 1951, called him directly. "He'd never heard of me [and] said he wasn't interested," Granz reported. "He was curious as to why I wanted to do it. I knew I was dead and nothing would come of it. For starters, Astaire was no fan of his own singing, and could not understand why anyone wanted to record him."

Astaire was savvy enough about his own talent to realize that he was one of the greatest dancers on either the stage or the screen, and he had considerable pride in his ability not just to flawlessly execute those moves but to stage and direct them; as a "dance-maker," Astaire was also the best. But despite the increasing testimony of admirers who knew what they were talking about, including both Mel Tormé and Tony Bennett, Astaire had little faith in his ability as a singer, especially in the purely aural medium of the phonograph recording. When Granz pitched the idea, Astaire recalled, "I was most reluctant about accepting."

The idea seemed, as Granz said, dead in the water. It was only revived by a rather remarkable coincidence. A few hours after the phone call, Granz wound up literally bumping into Astaire at a

Duke Ellington concert at the Shrine Auditorium. If Astaire didn't know who Granz was, his fifteen-year-old son (Fred Astaire Jr.), who was apparently even more of a jazz fan than his father, recognized the producer's name instantly. It turned out that Astaire Sr. was very familiar with Granz's work, though not his name; the Astaires owned a set of the Jazz at the Philharmonic recordings at home. With his son's encouragement, Astaire started to take Granz's idea seriously. He was particularly impressed, not only with the JATP concert recordings, but with an early concept album Granz had produced titled *The Jazz Scene*. "As he explained his purpose and how it would be done, I began to see it, the idea was attractive to me because of his attitude and approach to the concept," the dancer wrote. "Well, anyway, we decided to do it."

Then they selected the songs. In the thirty years since Fred and Adele first made it to Broadway (the year was 1921, when he was twenty-two years old), he'd sung close to a hundred songs in shows and films, and an amazingly high percentage of them had become standards, worthy of reprise and inclusion in this project. Narrowing those down necessitated a period in which Granz "practically lived with Astaire for weeks," he said. The final package—all four LPs of it—would include thirty-eight tracks, among which were thirty-four songs and four instrumental "dances," about which more later.

Apparently Granz at one point considered backing his star with a full-sized orchestra. That too would have been welcome. Had Astaire also done that—an album with a contemporary-sounding arranger—it would likely have been glorious as well. But in 1952, Astaire and Granz both fell in love with the idea of putting him in the context of a small jazz group, and Granz picked a number of musicians from the pool of players he employed on his studio dates and on the JATP concerts—the versatile trumpeter Charlie Shavers, the exciting tenor saxophonist Flip Phillips, prolific guitarist Barney Kessel, stalwart bassist and drummer Ray Brown and Alvin Stoller. On piano, there was only one choice: Oscar Peterson was not only rapidly becoming one of the most celebrated jazz pianists of his generation, but he was a brilliant accompa-

nist as well. In his own solos, it sounded like he was playing everything at once, not just every note and every chord, but every string on the piano, even the legs and wheels of the instrument, the paintings on the wall, the carpet on the floor, and the drapes in the window. Yet Peterson could also lie back when accompanying a singer or soloist; he knew exactly where the dividing line was between being supportive and being intrusive.

We don't know how many sessions there were, or exactly what dates in December 1952 they fell on. Granz was a record producer, not an inch-worm of a record collector, who might have kept track of such details. But the results were extraordinary. This was indeed a musical autobiography, and a later-in-life career summation (although Astaire was only fifty-three at the time of the sessions, that was later then than it is now, and later still for a dancer). As we shall see, Astaire had not previously recorded quite a few of the thirty-four songs in the package, but even on the songs that he previously recorded, the new tracks are remarkable. Up to 1952, Astaire's career as a recording artist was magnificent but sporadic; he regarded his commercial 78s as a side dish and never the main course, and there are huge milestone songs that he never got around to recording. (Even in 1952, it's hard to believe that Astaire and Granz could have somehow passed over both "Pick Yourself Up" and "One for My Baby," among others.)

So, there were many tunes that Astaire never recorded the first time around, and there are others that he didn't include on *The Astaire Story*. But in the many cases where he recorded the song twice, I would hate to have to choose. The vintage recordings have period charm and an exuberant youthful Astaire, and a great many of his classic Brunswick sides have audio shtick—the choir of singing telegram boys who chant "Paging Mr. Fred Astaire" on "I Can't Be Bothered Now," his comically blundered false steps at the start of "Pick Yourself Up," his banter with Ray Noble on "The Yam." These were the audio equivalents of his movie song-and-dance routines, and proof that he took the art of recording seriously—and the absence of such bits of business is a notable liability on the 1952 album.

The downside, however, of this boost in cultural credibility was what might be considered a loss of street cred. In other words, when Astaire was recording twenty years earlier, he was considered pop, and by the time he made the mega-album, he was art—whether he liked it or not. Even the fact that this was to be a jazz album increased the risk that it could be self-conscious, in contrast to the earlier recordings, which were so, as the title one of his films proclaimed, carefree. In *The Band Wagon*, Astaire (as Tony Hunter) is shocked to learn that his old movies are being shown in museums, and within a year after the release of that film, jazz began to be presented in festivals—in no less *recherché* a destination than Newport, Rhode Island—a locale where the plutocratic natives would have traditionally not welcomed jazz musicians into their neighborhood.

Still, even a cursory listen reveals that none of this was a real issue for Astaire: he took his dancing very seriously, but not himself. He loved the idea that this was going to be a jazz album, and to him jazz still meant fun, not a festival in an upper-crust postal code. He loved Ella Fitzgerald and Joe Williams, but he didn't try to be Ella Fitzgerald or Joe Williams. His singing is loose, swinging, and relaxed, but he's never deliberately trying to prove that he's a jazz singer; there's one passage that might be described as something like scat singing, but it could also be called an extended hum. Likewise, he doesn't try to wail the blues; he never feels the need to be what he's not. In fact, he doesn't feel the need to prove anything.

Astaire is still himself; he still sings with that high baritone voice. Twenty years earlier it was up near the tenor range, but now it has comfortably lowered. In fact, the voice itself is more sonically pleasing. The other aspect one can't help but notice is that most of Astaire's vintage Brunswick records were made with dance bands (Ray Noble, Leo Reisman, Johnny Green) and were, in fact, not merely recordings of a dancer but also records made for people to dance to. Nearly all the 1930s sides are in strict dance tempo. Although the 1952 sides are also in tempo—and are all swinging—they're much more relaxed; Astaire has more room, rhythmically, to stretch out as an interpreter, to show what

he can do with a lyric. I would argue that he gains considerably with this turn of events, but what he loses is minimal; he never sounds forced or self-conscious in any way.

The songs selected cover what would be, when the album was released in 1953, a thirty-year-profile of the great dancer's career. By 1953, most listeners who purchased *The Astaire Story* knew of him only as a movie star; he hadn't been seen onstage for twenty years at that point. But the earliest songs on the four-LP package come from four Broadway shows of 1924 to 1932: *Lady, Be Good!* (1924), *Funny Face* (1927), *The Band Wagon* (1931), and *Gay Divorce* (1932). All but the last costarred his sister, Adele, and the first two were collaborations with another pair of siblings, George and Ira Gershwin. Between *Lady, Be Good!* and *Funny Face,* both of which had long runs in New York and in London, the Astaires spent five key years starring in two key Gershwin shows and singing little else besides Gershwin songs.

"Oh, Lady Be Good!" is one of a handful of songs on the album that Astaire felt so strongly about that he wanted to introduce them in his own words and his own voice. He does so in roughly the same manner that Crosby and Armstrong would introduce their own key songs on their later musical autobiographies: "Before I started doing pictures, my sister Adele and I were a very active part of the New York and London stage—and all points east and west, I might add. Oh, we covered a lot of territory! One of the most important of our shows was *Lady, Be Good!* George Gershwin did that score, of course. I don't think George Gershwin ever dreamed that the title song was destined to become a jazz classic, but of course it has become just that. In the show it was performed as a plot song, slow and straight. How it ever developed into a standard jam session number, I'll never know! But of course it has. I always love to hear it."

What Astaire apparently didn't feel worth mentioning in 1952 was that neither "Oh, Lady Be Good!" nor "Fascinating Rhythm," the two songs from *Lady, Be Good!* reprised here, was sung onstage in that show by either Fred or Adele; the second was sung by Cliff Edwards, who was followed by the two Astaires doing what George

Gershwin himself, writing ten years later, described as a "miraculous dance," and the first, the title song, was sung by comedy lead Walter Catlett to a line of chorus girls. The Astaires did make a commercial recording of "Fascinating" in London, but "Oh, Lady Be Good!" is one of many songs on *The Astaire Story* that was indelibly associated with him although he had never actually sung it (or, in this case, even danced to it).

"Oh, Lady Be Good!" actually sounds more like a Granz-style jam session than a show tune, which is the way both the star and the producer wanted it. After the spoken intro, it begins with the rhythm section, first drums, then an arco bass break, finally Astaire and Peterson come in together. Astaire's singing in the bridge is especially notable: most singers who came of age musically in the teens and twenties would have held the second note on "Oh, please have some pity," but Astaire cuts it off immediately, in keeping with the late-swing/early-bebop-style phrasing that one might hear on a JATP concert—and, for another thing, he skips the verse. Then there's also a very longish rest, before he speaks the phrase "I'm all alone in this big city," very conversationally. Like the great dancer he is, Astaire plays with the time throughout, dancing in and out and around where the syllables would fall if the song were being sung completely straight. There follows what amounts to a jam session—everybody solos for a chorus: Phillips, Peterson (soloing on celeste rather than piano, and making it sound rather like Lionel Hampton playing the vibraphone), Shavers, Kessel, and then Astaire for a second chorus. In what we have come to think of as the classic Ethel Waters model, the second vocal chorus is even jazzier and more playful than the first; here he's not just dancing around the melody notes, he's rewriting it wholesale in a manner more closely akin to Armstrong or Fitzgerald.

"Fascinating Rhythm" opens with Oscar very much in a King Cole Trio bag; there's a bright, declamatory intro, then he dances around the notes for a whole chorus with a keyboard touch that's obviously reminiscent of Nat King Cole. More to the point, what Peterson plays here also sounds like what Astaire would play if he had Peterson's piano chops. Astaire's vocals even have

a light quality somewhat reminiscent of the early King Cole. Shavers gets a half-chorus solo, before Astaire returns after the bridge ("I know that once it didn't matter . . ."). Here Astaire's biggest line is the ending; he fairly shouts "Stop picking on me!"

"'S Wonderful," from *Funny Face,* follows a similar format, opening with a full chorus of Peterson, with a muted Shavers taking the bridge. Again, on a blindfold test, I might have guessed that the pianist was Cole; generally there's no drummer on most of Cole's piano recordings, but here Stoller plays in a highly unobtrusive fashion, and there's also a 's wonderfully Cole-ish piano introduction, in which Peterson seems to dance backward into the melody. One suspects that Astaire was grateful to sing it after having waited some twenty-five years after Adele introduced it with her leading man, Allen Kearns. By substituting "'S" for "It's," the Gershwins were instilling both a musical syncopation and what amounts to a verbal one as well; in clipping the word they align themselves perfectly with the argot of the Jazz Age. In 1952, Astaire takes that 1920s-style syncopation and does something different with it: instead of making the melody more syncopated, he makes it more casual; he sounds so relaxed and low-key that it's like he can barely muster the energy to sing the full word "it's," so he just sings the "'S" instead and renders the whole first chorus like that. Love's got him in a lazy mood. Flip Phillips captures that lazy mood perfectly, and plays his chorus in a laconically Lester Young–like style. When Astaire returns at the bridge for a half chorus ("You've made my life so glamorous"), he reverses the Ethel Waters pattern, singing the second chorus more solidly on the beat and less lazy-like.

The next production that Astaire references is *The Band Wagon,* with three songs, "Dancing in the Dark," "New Sun in the Sky," and "I Love Luisa." He talks about the show in a spoken intro to "Luisa"; whereas the later musical autobiographies were scripted, here Astaire really seems to be speaking extemporaneously. He says of the show, "This one my little sister Adele and I did in *The Band Wagon* at the New Amsterdam Theatre in New York . . . back in, let me see, 1929, I think, yeah. Well anyway it was one of our biggest shows, a terrific cast—

Frank Morgan, Helen Broderick, Tilly Losch, lots of wonderful people, it was a colorful revue produced by Max Gordon, a wonderful score by Arthur Schwartz and Howard Dietz." Astaire is to be forgiven for getting the year wrong for his own show (two years early is close enough), although it's curious that he would describe Adele as his "little sister," unless he meant in terms of size, rather than the customary meaning in terms of age, since she was two and a half years older than he was.

"Dancing in the Dark" again opens with Peterson, playing a harmonically astute and highly romantic chorus on piano; Astaire croons it in an exceedingly mellow manner, much more so than anybody would have sung it in 1931; even Bing Crosby's very successful recording seems loud and intense by comparison. After the chorus, Astaire sings the verse ("What though love is old . . ."), before Phillips plays a whole chorus—just as Peterson continues to sound like Cole, Phillips continues to wear his Lester Young porkpie hat. Astaire sings a second chorus. While in the first he seemed as if he was crooning to his leading lady, in this second full chorus he now seems to be dancing with her. At four and a half minutes, it's a highly satisfying performance.

Still, the difference between 1929 and 1931 is a crucial one in that both "Dancing in the Dark" and "New Sun in the Sky" are key songs of the Great Depression. "Dancing in the Dark" can be taken as a highly romanticized view of the direction in which the whole world was going, an era in which the dark was all that we had to dance in. "New Sun in the Sky," more optimistically, points to the possibility of finding the light. The title even sounds like something Franklin D. Roosevelt might have said in one of his speeches. (FDR was governor of New York in 1931–32, when The Band Wagon was running on Broadway.) The track is a comparatively short one, much faster and less heavy than "Dancing in the Dark." At 2:30, it's less of a production, featuring Astaire with just piano, bass, and drums (brushes?). Astaire himself sounds blissfully casual.

Astaire must have been thinking about singing the next song in his upcoming film The Band Wagon, which he would shoot a few months later, in 1953. In the spoken intro he says, "In this number, 'I Love Luisa,' we were all on a merry-go-round, gay German atmosphere, military uniforms, and all the trappings. Here the boys give it a sort of picnic treatment." This is virtually the only song on The Astaire Story that doesn't work; the exaggerated dialect, Dutch Uncle–German-accent komedy-und-gesang is ill-suited for the JATP jam session format, and someone decided not to let Astaire do the whole routine, with all the additional choruses. When it fades at 2:41 (fades themselves being very unusual at this time and place), it seems like it's being cut off arbitrarily. One wishes that Astaire had picked another song from The Band Wagon, such as "Sweet Music," but "Luisa" was obviously a personal, sentimental favorite of his.

After The Band Wagon finished its run on Broadway, Adele Astaire, then thirty-five, retired from the stage to become Lady Cavendish, and Fred Astaire's first show without his sister (which would also turn out to be his only show without her) was Gay Divorce (1932). He introduces the song "Night and Day" as follows: "The only stage show of mine which subsequently became a motion picture was Gay Divorce. For the screen, the title was changed to The Gay Divorcee. Cole Porter wrote the original score, and from the many fine songs in that score, 'Night and Day,' as you may know, has become one of the biggest hits of all time. Although I've done the song a lot through the years, I'm particularly intrigued by the background that the boys have given me on this record."

Intriguing, yes. It starts with Kessel playing a countermelody that's thoroughly beboppish and somewhat tropical at the same time—referring to those jungle tom-toms—and something that captures the very essence of Cole Porter's music, exotic and sophisticated at the same time. Astaire sings the verse with a kind of resignation, as though he realizes it's kind of weird to be obsessed with someone to this extreme, but there's nothing he can do about it. This is more than infatuation, this is the kind of obsession that, as Stephen Sondheim would say, "is not a choice / and not much reason to rejoice." There's a kind of a Mickey Mouse/Spike Jones moment when Astaire sings "the roaring traffic's boom" and Al Stoller gives his bass drum the tiniest kick, more of a thud than a boom. We hear the four-piece rhythm section here; Peterson and Kessel exchange whole sections of the song following Astaire's first vocal. We think Astaire will return for a second chorus, but instead he comes back just to chant the opening line of the verse ("Like the beat, beat, beat of the tom-toms when the jungle shadows fall") three times. The repetition reinforces the idea that this particular obsession isn't ending with the song, but going on and on.

The rhythms of Broadway and Hollywood are very different: remember that from 1924 to 1930, the Astaires were in only two shows, *Lady, Be Good!* and *Funny Face*, and that this was very much the desired goal, to have two huge hits in a row, both with long runs on Broadway and then the West End. *Gay Divorce* too had a long run on Broadway—November 1932 to June 1933, which constituted a hit at the time. However, by the time the London production opened (a year after Broadway), Astaire had already made his first two movies—*Dancing Lady* and *Flying Down to Rio;* apparently he shot his scenes in both of them between July 1933, when *Gay Divorce* closed at the Shubert Theatre, and November, when it opened at the London Palace. In 1952, Astaire chose to forget *Dancing Lady*, MGM's oddly enjoyable but thoroughly demented take on a gritty Warner Bros.–style backstager, in which the dancer made his film debut in a cameo as Joan Crawford's dancing partner (his was a mock-Bavarian number obviously inspired by "I Love Luisa," which he must have enjoyed). For the album, he chose to remember *Rio* as his first picture; he may have only been a supporting player, but it was in *Rio* that Astaire and his new partner, Ginger Rogers, totally walked off—or rather, danced off—with the picture.

As Astaire remembers in his spoken intro, "I think that I ought to say something about this next one, 'The Carioca.' It was the big tune from *Flying Down to Rio,* my first important picture with that wonderful gal Ginger Rogers, and it really started that series of Ginger Rogers–Fred Astaire pictures." In 1933, North American musicians didn't know—and weren't interested in—playing authentic South American rhythms, and many of the early recordings of this song, written for the movie by Vincent Youmans, sound more like a Cuban rhumba or an

Argentine tango than anything Brazilian. The original word, *carioca,* in Portuguese, refers to the citizens of Rio de Janeiro. Later, Artie Shaw, who had made a hit out of Cole Porter's approximation of a Martinique beguine, did the same for Youmans's "Carioca." Neither of these swing-era classics, great as they are, have the slightest hint of Pan-American rhythm in them.

Astaire and Rogers were such a hit dancing "The Carioca" in *Flying Down to Rio* that RKO decided to make a movie out of *Gay Divorce*, into which they shoehorned a follow-up song to "The Carioca." This was "The Continental," by Con Conrad and Herb Magidson, and it turned out to be an even bigger success. Astaire likely included both "The Carioca" and "The Continental" as a means of settling old scores. As with "Oh, Lady Be Good!" and "'S Wonderful," which Astaire didn't actually sing on stage, he also didn't sing either of these two songs that did so much to make him into a movie star. "The Carioca" was sung in *Rio* by Etta Moten, and "The Continental" was rendered in *The Gay Divorcee* by Rogers, comic Erik Rhodes, actress Lillian Miles, and seemingly everybody but Astaire. Both songs are the basis of spectacular Busby Berkeley–style production numbers, each with a huge dancing chorus and more bodies undulating on screen than in a Cecil B. DeMille Bible epic. Still, it was the sight of Astaire and Rogers dancing together that had audiences walking on air as they left the theater.

Finally, with *The Astaire Story*, Astaire at last gets to sing both "The Carioca" and "The Continental." After the spoken intro, the five-minute "Carioca" opens with a sequence of instrumental intros, many of which suggest Old World Spain rather than New World Brazil. There's a flamenco-style guitar, a trumpet blast such as one would hear at a bullfight, a distinctly Iberian piano passage in which Peterson seems to be dusting the glitter off the keyboard with his fingertips, and Stoller hitting the rim of his drums in a Latin pattern. The 1933 movie production number is highly erotic; North American tourists watch dark-skinned Brazilians intertwine in a way that wouldn't have been possible two years later under the Production Code. (Their comment: "No wonder it never gets cold here!") But the 1952 Astaire version is warm and romantic. He starts with the central refrain ("Say, have you seen the Carioca?") and then, after a transitional piano passage, he moves to the patter chorus ("Two heads together, they say, are better than one"). Astaire astutely and abruptly signals a shift of the rhythm with the final words "And you are mine!" Then, Peterson plays a full-fisted piano solo in North American swing-to-bop style, further differentiated from the rest of the track by having the drums lay out and the guitar and the bass work with the piano. (The instrumentation is that of the King Cole Trio, but the piano solo itself is more like Art Tatum or Bud Powell, especially in the audible humming.) After the fast 4/4 piano solo, it reverts back to Astaire singing the last half of the lyrics, with the rat-tat-tat-ing drums and the mock-Brazilian pattern, and Shavers supplying obbligatos.

"The Continental" doesn't get a spoken introduction. You'd have thought that in 1952, Astaire would deem it noteworthy to inform us that he introduced the song that won the first Academy Award, but no, he doesn't mention it. Where all the various vocalists who sing the song in *The Gay Divorcee* are loud and declamatory, Astaire takes the lyric line "It's very subtle, the Continental," to heart—his vocal is soft and subdued; although the story is set in Europe, the production number of "The Continental" recalls nothing so much as Rio at Carnival time (making it very much a sequel to "Carioca"). But where the movie number is way over the top, the 1952 Astaire is consistently understated throughout, and again, romantic. He sings mostly over a rhythm pattern from Kessel and Brown; the piano and the drums are barely audible for the sung intro ("Beautiful music, dangerous rhythm . . .") as well as the first chorus ("It's something daring, the Continental . . ."). Peterson enters after the vocal, and now it's his turn to dance. Astaire returns singing the patter section ("You kiss while you're dancing . . .") and concludes with a reprise of the phrase "beautiful music, dangerous rhythm."

Another song by Conrad and Magidson, "A Needle in a Haystack," was an unexpected choice in 1952, in that it was added after the fact to the movie version of *Gay Divorce/Gay Divorcee,* and it never became anything like a standard. But it's an excellent song, and Astaire and company make the most of it. The three principals—Astaire, Phillips, and Shavers (who exchange fours during the instrumental break)—sound so relaxed they seem to be lounging about on top of the haystack rather than eagerly searching through it. Astaire's out-chorus, from which he returns at the bridge, is a bit more anxious, but never strained or forced.

There was yet one more "transitional" movie before the Astaire-Rogers series began proper, RKO's 1935 film of the 1933 show *Roberta.* Again, Astaire doesn't get enough of a chance to sing "Lovely to Look At." In the movie the number is dominated by Irene Dunne, with a full-on soprano, and Ginger Rogers, with a comic faux-French accent. (Both, it cannot be denied, are lovely to look at.) In 1952, Astaire sings "Lovely" following a slightly rubato intro by Peterson. Once more, the movie performance is rather outsized for such an intimate lyric ("It's thrilling to hold you terribly tight"); Astaire's 1952 reading, mostly with guitar and piano (Kessel gets one of his most impressive solos in here), is much more personal—and lovely to listen to. When, following the guitar solo, he hums eight bars of the chorus, it seems like the aural equivalent of romantic partner dancing.

The two horns introduce "I Won't Dance" and Shavers plays continual muted obbligatos behind the singer, getting one of his own best solos in the break. The lyrics, originally by Oscar Hammerstein and then brilliantly rewritten by Dorothy Fields, are a glorious rat's nest of ironic implications; the idea of dancing is clearly a metaphor for something else, something even more personal, and when Astaire sings it he seems to be dancing verbally even while he's ostensibly refusing to. When Fields rewrote Hammerstein's original text (which originated not in the Broadway production of *Roberta* but in *Three Sisters,* a 1934 British show by Kern and Hammerstein), she included one of Astaire's first self-references, "When you dance, you're charming and you're gentle / Especially when you do the Continental." And that's the line that Astaire comes back to for his out-chorus, picking it up at the bridge and taking us out.

Top Hat (1935), at long last, marks the formal beginning of the Astaire-Rogers series. For the first time, he and she were top-billed, and everyone else was in support of them. To make the occasion even more special, RKO commissioned the score from Irving Berlin, who hadn't written for a film since 1931, and, unbelievably, had yet to work with Astaire. (Berlin would be Astaire's most frequent songwriter from 1935 on, just as Gershwin was earlier.) You can tell it was extra special to Astaire in 1952: *Top Hat* is the only production to rate a full four songs in *The Astaire Story*. Of the four, two— "No Strings (I'm Fancy Free)" and "Top Hat, White Tie and Tails"—were Astaire solos in the original picture, and "Cheek to Cheek" and "Isn't This a Lovely Day?" were partner dances with Rogers.

"No Strings" starts with an imposing intro—it's hard to imagine that Peterson could have just come up with this off the top of his head. Buffered by a muted Shavers, Astaire is right on top of the beat, filled with testosterone and what P. G. Wodehouse would call "beans." Peterson solos on celeste for a whole chorus, while Shavers and Phillips riff in the background behind him, and the two-and-a-half-minute track also has room for a full solo by Kessel. Astaire's final chorus is even more energetic; he seems to be working extra hard to express all that dynamic energy with his voice, since he knows he doesn't have the usual visual element.

"Isn't This a Lovely Day?" is the opener of the four-LP set, and it's also the first of Berlin's "lovely day" trilogy (that also includes "It's a Lovely Day Tomorrow" from *Louisiana Purchase* and "It's a Lovely Day Today" from *Call Me Madam*). Peterson prefaces Astaire with a few gentle notes, and Astaire's vocal, starting with the verse, captures perfectly the meaning of Berlin's text: he may be describing "thunder and lightning," but since he's "caught" with the one he loves, his mood is all rainbows and lollipops, and he sings of tumultuous weather with the same rapturous tone one might use to describe fluffy pink clouds. Phillips's tenor solo is languidly Lesterian. This is another case where the 1952 recording is much slower and more romantic than in the movie; if Fred and Ginger were to have tried to dance at this tempo, said dance would have been strictly horizontal. "Cheek

to Cheek" is even more low-key. Astaire seems to be milking what comes after the first word "Heaven . . . [rest] . . . I'm in Heaven." More than in 1935, he sounds as if he's been listening to Armstrong and Crosby here; rather than being in a hurry to get into the dance number, he seems to have all the time in the world. Fittingly, this is the longest vocal in the package, one of the few in which everybody gets a solo: Phillips, Kessel, Shavers (muted), Peterson, then a round of two-bar breaks by the four of them again, followed by a break from Ray Brown. (We expect Astaire to return, but, surprisingly, it ends there.) More than on most of his recordings, here he sounds more like a singer than a dancer.

"Of all the songs I've done, I think perhaps this next one has been the nearest thing to a trademark. I am particularly fond of this old 'fella' and when Irving Berlin wrote it for me, I, of course, found it a real inspiration, 'Top Hat, White Tie and Tails.'" As in the movie, Astaire sings the verse, the key part of which is the singer-dancer quoting from an invitation that he's received "through the mails," which reads, "Your presence requested this evening, it's formal: top hat, a white tie and tails." (Famously, in real life Astaire was never especially pleased about being associated with that particular fashion statement.) Onscreen, he punctuates the beats by literally tapping on the paper invitation with a cane; on the recording here, he achieves the same effect using just his voice, singing those words in a clipped, staccato fashion as if reading a telegram (the pauses indicate the "stops" of telegraph operators).

Astaire had the most remarkable gift: he would slave away on a routine for months, work his dance-maker's brain to the bone, and rehearse until his feet bled. But when you see him onscreen, the only thing you see is the fun and the illusion of spontaneity; the sense of sheer enjoyment that he projects is even more palpable than his obvious virtuosity, his ability to perform the impossible. "Top Hat" is his most perfect balance of fun and formality: he's willing to go to all the trouble of getting himself decked out in the fanciest topper and tailcoat imaginable, just for the delight of being able to toss caution to the winds and muss it up when he starts dancing. Berlin and Astaire perfectly mirror each other, the songwriter's lyrics parallel the careful preparation that he put into a number, and then Astaire perfectly captures the exuberance of the dance itself. The instrumental break is first a back-and-forth dance, an exchange of phrase between Shavers and Kessel, and then Peterson takes a lengthy solo on his own. Astaire's second chorus has him underscoring the text by spontaneously throwing in the exclamation "yeah," then he puts in a special twist on "when I step on the gas" to make it sound even gassier. He ends by demonstrating what his dance (at the forthcoming formal event) will be like with an exuberant tap break.

The first two major Fred and Ginger vehicles, *Top Hat* and *Follow the Fleet,* were simultaneously planned by producer Pandro S. Berman and composed by Berlin at roughly the same time. Still, *Follow the Fleet* (released in 1936) doesn't get nearly as much love as *Top Hat;* somehow Astaire as a humble gob resonated less with Depression audiences than Astaire as a top-hatted hoofer—although he doubtlessly preferred being out of tails for most of the picture. Just as the sailor suit is quite the opposite of the tailcoat, so "I'm Putting All My Eggs in One Basket" is the philosophical opposite of "No Strings." Rather than singing of the glories of having no connections, no ties to his affection, here the singer is happy to be giving all his love to one baby, even though, he confides, "Lord help me if my baby don't come through." (He emphasizes that thought by delivering the line in singspiel.) It starts with Shavers playing a whole chorus in a mood so ebullient that it's all Astaire, who enters with the verse ("I've been a roaming Romeo . . ."), can do to keep up with it, but keep up with it he does. Flip Phillips reminds us of why he's one of the all-time favorite tenors of swing-era saxophone connoisseurs like Granz, and Astaire underscores the emotion further by scatting, which is to say, dancing with his voice, before he caps the piece by delivering the last line all by itself.

By now the Fred and Ginger series was in full swing, and the team of Fred, Ginger, and producer Berman were engaging one Olympian songwriter after another. Astaire had sung a score by Jerome Kern in the 1922 Broadway show *The Bunch and Judy* as well as the 1935 *Roberta* movie, but the 1936

Swing Time represents an all-time pinnacle for composer, lyricist (Dorothy Fields), and the two costars. For *The Astaire Story,* he reprises one of the most thrillingly romantic love songs of all time, "The Way You Look Tonight," and one of the funniest, the sarcastically titled "A Fine Romance."

Peterson introduces "The Way You Look Tonight" unaccompanied and rubato, then Astaire enters, crooning at his mellowest, especially in the first eight bars; he gets slightly more aggressive in the second eight, as the piece kicks into something more like a dance tempo (and Kessel, Brown, and Stoller enter behind Astaire and Peterson). The way Peterson and Kessel phrase Kern's famous two-note counter-riff is especially memorable, although it might have been even more so had Astaire hummed those phrases the way Bing and Dixie Lee Crosby did, for instance (at the end of their 1936 recording of the song). Astaire is filled with humor in "A Fine Romance," especially when he shifts into talking mode at various spots: "At least they flap their fins to express emotion." Kessel is the main soloist in the break, but there's also room for some low-key Peterson. This is the opposite of most tracks in the set in that Astaire is more relaxed and less intense in his final chorus (or half chorus in this case).

The two 1937 Astaire RKO films mark the climax and conclusion of the dancer's remarkable relationship with the Gershwins. There are five songs on *The Astaire Story* from the scores of *Shall We Dance* and *A Damsel in Distress,* and these are all among the cornerstones of what later became known as the Great American Songbook: "Let's Call the Whole Thing Off," "They All Laughed," "They Can't Take That Away from Me," "A Foggy Day," and "Nice Work if You Can Get It." These are all among the most recorded, most sung, most played, most heard, and most loved songs of all time.

"A Foggy Day" and "Nice Work if You Can Get It" are from *A Damsel in Distress,* a picture remembered by history as a Fred and Ginger movie minus Ginger; it feels exactly like every other film in the series, except that the leading lady, Joan Fontaine, was charming but nonmusical, and Astaire's dancing cohorts were the deliciously nimble-footed team of George Burns and Gracie Allen. "A Foggy

Day" is one of the great ballads of *The Astaire Story*. He doesn't enter until more than two minutes in, giving Peterson a chance to essay a whole chorus. In his vocal, which is just one chorus and no verse (Phillips helps with an ace obbligato), he more than makes it clear that though the words begin with the phrase "A foggy day in London town," the song is really about a person more than a place. No one knows better than Astaire how to articulate the difference between what the lyrics are saying, at least on the surface, and what a song actually means. "Nice Work if You Can Get It" is the shortest vocal on the package. Astaire romps through it with Shavers in pursuit, and there's time for a brief but memorable rhythm section break; for the second, even more swinging, chorus, he alternates with the ensemble, just singing the title lines at the end of each eight-bar section. He ends by commenting "Nice work," and we can't help but agree.

Of the *Shall We Dance* songs, "Let's Call the Whole Thing Off" is a built-in duet, but here Astaire sings it solo, and very relaxed indeed at over four and a half minutes. Astaire and Granz both clearly loved Ira's lyrics so much that they wanted to include the verse and both refrains, separated by a chorus by Peterson with Kessel taking the bridge; the second refrain has Astaire very carefully delineating the pronunciations, i.e., "laff-ter" vs. "loff-ter" as well as "vanilla, van-ella, choc'late, strawberry!" "They All Laughed" is another perfect Astaire number, a romantic song with a comic twist, a list song in which the points add up to a highly coherent story—this is what the American song does best. Astaire in particular loves this format: if he can deliver a lyric that's essentially a set of one-liners ("They all laughed at Fulton and his steamboat, Hershey and his chocolate bar"), and still sneak in a love message in the middle of it, that's the way he likes it. For Astaire, the idea of a stealth erotic communication, as in "They All Laughed," is even more appealing than an overt one, as in "Night and Day." The 1952 "Laughed" is agreeably relaxed and features a few well-placed chuckles from the singer. There's no verse or instrumental break here, and Peterson and Brown are the only musicians audible, but Astaire sings both choruses of Gershwin lyrics.

"They Can't Take That Away from Me" is another long one, but far too intimate to be an epic; Kessel plays an introduction, and then the guitarist winds around Peterson through the first eight bars of this iconic melody. Astaire enters quietly with the verse to a song that begins with an ending, "Our romance won't end on a sorrowful note," then he only gets through one full chorus before the four and a half minutes are up. This is the very essence of what Granz was hoping to achieve with *The Astaire Story*: to have Astaire sing his best songs in the most direct, personal way, enhanced by the jazz accompaniment but without all the trappings of a Hollywood production number.

The 1938 *Carefree* is an underappreciated entry in the Fred-Ginger oeuvre, marking the return of Irving Berlin to the series. The verse of "I Used to Be Color Blind" tells us, "What a difference when your vision is clear / And you see things as they really are," and Astaire intones those words, and the whole song, with absolute crystal clarity. The track, which features just the rhythm quartet (no horns), also has a few bonus bars of Astaire humming. "Change Partners" is another song that became bigger in later years than it was at the time; Astaire's vocal is especially direct and plaintive, and he's gloriously accompanied by Shavers, who knows how to say a lot in a few choice notes.

Carefree is the last Astaire-Rogers film to be referenced in *The Astaire Story* (neither the 1939 *Story of Vernon and Irene Castle* nor the team's 1949 reunion, *The Barkleys of Broadway*, was deemed worthy). The RKO-Fred-Ginger series was, in 1952, viewed as the centerpiece of Astaire's overall career: there's stuff before and stuff after, but those ten 1934–39 RKO pictures are the main event. Five post-Ginger movies are addressed in *The Astaire Story*: *Broadway Melody of 1940*, *You'll Never Get Rich* (1941), *Holiday Inn* (1942), *Blue Skies* (1946), and *Easter Parade* (1948), all of which are reunions with Porter and Berlin.

On the minus side, the nondancing parts of *Broadway Melody of 1940* (MGM) aren't nearly as much fun as the RKO series, but on the plus side, Eleanor Powell was one of the most talented partners of Astaire's entire career, and the Porter score is absolutely tremendous. "I Concentrate on You" was sung in the picture by the underappreciated baritone Douglas McPhail while Powell and Astaire pirouetted about, all three in harlequin masks and Pierrot drag. Today it's all but forgotten that Astaire didn't sing it until this album, and it's become one of the most frequently revived of all Porter songs. Astaire's vocal here is short and to the point, and highly concentrated. Shavers is right behind him; at 2:45, neither one of them wastes a second. "I've Got My Eyes on You" is Astaire's major solo turn in *Broadway Melody*, he not only demonstrates his piano-playing prowess (for virtually the only time on-screen), but he makes the piano a virtual partner in his dance routine. "Eyes" is a highlight here, even though he restricts himself to only singing, and the band is restricted to just the rhythm section. "So Near and Yet So Far" (*You'll Never Get Rich*) is given a lightly Latin treatment, with Astaire and Peterson addressing the verse in the middle, rather than the opening.

Throughout the set, Astaire makes one think of Irving Berlin's well-known one-liner about Ethel Merman: "Never write a bad song for Ethel," he famously said, "because if you do, everyone will hear it." The same thing goes for Astaire; he didn't bellow or blast or project to the rafters like Merman, but you don't miss a word of what he sings—not a single nuance is lost or wasted. That resonates especially in Porter's "So Near and Yet So Far," as well as in the Berlin songs that Astaire sings from *Holiday Inn* and *Blue Skies*. (In those latter two, his costar was Bing Crosby, whereas the leading ladies in each have since become questions for Trivial Pursuit.) In the movie itself, the blockbuster "White Christmas" overshadowed everything, and Astaire's long-awaited duets with Crosby were also memorable; as excellent as "You're Easy to Dance With" was, it was hard for the song to be noticed in a movie with so much going on. Kessel opens "You're Easy to Dance With" with a bluesy, jivey lick, and Astaire ends the mood by phrasing the melody in short, staccato bursts, at least in the lead-in lines ("I—could—dance—nightly / Just—hold—ing—you—tightly"), but then relaxing when he gets to the title phrase at the end of each eight bars. Phillips takes solo honors.

The last two numbers in the chronology of Astaire's career as represented here are two classic Berlin songs that are even riff-ier, and jive-ier, with Astaire in a very funky, very minor, highly syncopated mode. "Steppin' Out with My Baby" (from *Easter Parade*, with Judy Garland) became one of Astaire's best-remembered numbers from the period, a status that was reinforced fifty years later when Tony Bennett made a whole new generation conscious of the song and of Astaire and Berlin. The mood is more undisguisedly erotic than most; as in Berlin's clever wordplay, "the big day may be tonight," we know exactly what he means. There's some ace minor-key riffing by Peterson and Kessel in tight unison, sometimes joined by the horns. Astaire gets two full choruses in, in a mere 2:24; rather than wish it were longer, I just keep playing it again and again.

"Puttin' on the Ritz" is a unique song in Astaire annals: it was originally written by Berlin for a 1930 film of the same title, starring Harry Richman, an early talkie rival to Al Jolson. Clearly, Astaire was enamored of it, and the song was one of the few that the great star recorded (in 1930) not from one of his own productions, and he clearly welcomed the chance to create a dance to it a decade and a half later. It's even more riffy and staccato than "Steppin' Out."

Which brings the Astaire story up to 1948, or roughly three years before Granz approached him with the idea of *The Astaire Story*. The inclusion of two songs composed by the dancer himself was undoubtedly his own idea; it's doubtful that Granz even realized that Astaire was a persistent, if not always successful, songwriter, writing both music and lyrics on several occasions. The two Astaire songs included in the album are "Not My Girl" (1929) and "I'm Building Up to an Awful Letdown" (1935).

Of the first, Astaire tells us, "Here's another one. This one always amused me. I wrote it over twenty years ago, I guess, with a very clever English lyricist named Desmond Carter. This one gained a little recognition over there." It's an excellent snappy-peppy song of the Jazz Age; the reference to "Annabelle Lee" has nothing to do with Edgar Allan Poe but to another song of the era, "Miss Annabelle Lee." Astaire continues, "As I said before, piano playing was a very serious hobby of mine, so, you know, I was bound to sneak some of it in here someplace. I'll start off by playing the first chorus in the same style as I used to do it then. Oscar rescues me, and takes it from there. Here I go with 'Not My Girl.'" After the spoken intro, we get a chorus of Astaire playing highly syncopated piano; he then sings the verse, apparently Peterson is now playing for him in a very Jazz Age style, using several famous piano figures associated with Fats Waller, but not quite breaking out into a full stride solo.

Regarding "I'm Building Up to an Awful Letdown," Astaire tells us, "I suppose that almost everyone has a secret yen to be a songwriter. Well, I was a sort of frustrated one in my early youth, and still am." The song was anything but a letdown in 1935, it was recorded by several prominent American and British bands, as well as by Astaire himself; Benny Goodman also played it on the air, which must have pleased Astaire very much. The 1952 track uses the full lineup and finds time for the verse as well as solos by Phillips and Shavers (muted). Astaire's return, wherein he takes it from the bridge onward, is especially warm and appealing.

Granz and Astaire also recorded three tracks of Astaire dancing with the rhythm section, plus one, "Jam Session for a Dancer," featuring the whole band, with no Astaire presence. "You know, I've always felt that dancing for records wasn't too effective as far as my stuff was concerned, because I get off the floor a great deal and there may be a lot of empty spots for me. But I'd like to take a stab at it! I'll tell you what, I'll step in and ad-lib with the boys. If you hear some strange noises out there, remember that's me. All right, let's go!" The three dances are all fast riff numbers, and are differentiated by tempo, fast, slow, and medium. The track titled "Fast Dances (Ad Lib)" (which is the one with the above spoken intro) has a recognizable bridge, while the others are based on blues changes. For the most part, they're meetings between Astaire and Peterson, with the others mostly in supporting roles (although Kessel gets a chorus in the

"Medium Dances [Ad Lib]" and there's a trade of fours at the end).

"Slow Dances (Ad Lib)" is the one most clearly a blues, as Astaire reports: "You know, this album is a kind of jazz album too, and jazz means the blues. Oscar, Barney, Alvin, and Ray are going to ad-lib some of those blues now and I'm going to walk in and throw a little hoofing in there. We like these slow blues so much that we decided to do a couple of them." The comment suggests that they must have recorded at least one additional slow blues, since there's only one on the album—this is the only track where you can hear a few seconds of Astaire grunting as he dances, and there's a stop-break, a familiar blues device, that allows him to get a few taps in a cappella.

The final side of the original package (LP4, Side B) begins with the earliest tune in the set, "Oh, Lady Be Good!," followed by the two Astaire compositions, "I'm Building Up to an Awful Letdown" and "Not My Girl" (in that order), followed by "Jam Session for a Dancer." He introduces the last as follows, "Now we get back to normal again! Here comes some music that I didn't write. But seriously, the fellows are going to step out on their own and do some jamming. I'll sit this one out. Go ahead, Oscar!" It's a six-and-a-half-minute instrumental, the longest track in this package but hardly the longest as far as Norman Granz's epic jam sessions, both live at Jazz at the Philharmonic and in his studio session series, were concerned. It's a fast, major blues (with no discernible bridge) that starts with Peterson and Kessel riffing together, before the phrase is repeated by the whole group with the two horns. Peterson solos first (whizzing by "Autumn Nocturne") followed by Phillips, very up and in a Coleman Hawkins–esque bag, then Kessel, then Shavers in his most aggressive open-bell statement on the package, after which the group riffs together, with Peterson manning the charge, toward a climax—there's no trade of fours, or drum or bass solo: it was obviously felt that nothing could satisfactorily follow Shavers.

(Some editions of the album follow the "Jam Session for a Dancer" with "The Astaire Blues." This was a quartet piece recorded by the lineup ten months earlier in February 1952. The original LP edition apparently included two takes of this number, a twelve-minute "original" and a seven-minute "sequel." Neither of these takes appears on the CD edition, issued as a double-disc set for the first time in 1988, a year after the dancer's death.)

The Astaire Story was released around the summer of 1953, likely just as *The Band Wagon* was hitting movie theaters. It was probably the most deluxe album package of any kind issued up until that point, and probably for many years to come (or until Granz's five-LP *Ella Fitzgerald Sings the George and Ira Gershwin Song Book* in 1959). The big box contained four LPs, each pressed on "virgin vinyl from India" and sub-packaged in an individual jacket, as well as a deluxe booklet with photos by Gjon Mili (the *Life* magazine regular, and one of the great music photographers of all time), plus a set of lithographs of drawings by David Stone Martin. By including Mili and Martin in the package, Granz was extending the all-star team beyond Astaire, Peterson, and the musicians. He pressed 1,834 copies of the package, all of which were signed by Fred Astaire.

In 1953, the box sold for $50, which was an all-time high. In the era of eBay, the few copies that have turned up regularly go for at least $2,000. The full set doesn't appear to have been easily available until the mid-1970s, when DRG Records reissued it as a three-LP box with booklet; thankfully, it's been on compact disc (a two-CD set) since the beginning of the CD era.

Astaire presented each member of the sextet with a gold bracelet inscribed, "With thanks, Fred A." In his spoken introductions, Astaire talks about being an amateur songwriter as well as an avocational pianist, but he doesn't talk about playing the drums, something he did in several of his films (e.g., *Damsel in Distress*), admittedly more for visual and terpsichorean purposes than for strictly musical ones. But yes, he was an amateur drummer as well, and kept a trap set next to his piano in his music room. During one of the rehearsals for the album, Astaire asked Stoller if he might sit in on the drums for one number, unfortunately not recorded. As Peterson later described what transpired, "What a riot! To hear his time with Ray's vast sound was quite an event, and the look of rapt intent on Fred's face was a joy to behold." As well, he should have been pleased: it was on this album that he proved his singing was every bit as good as anything else he did.

3
Chet Baker
Let's Get Lost: The Best of Chet Baker Sings
(1954–1956)

Where does a sound like the voice of Chet Baker come from? There's no obvious precedent. The most likely place to look is in the work of the major singing musicians who came before him, which quickly becomes a fruitless quest: he has little of the overwhelming emotion of his fellow trumpeter Louis Armstrong, the soulful, aged-in-the-wood blues of Jack Teagarden, the rambunctious party energy of Fats Waller (and his many followers), or the suave, immaculate romanticism of Nat King Cole. In a certain sense, Baker may have been the polar opposite of Armstrong: Armstrong gave everything, and held nothing back; Baker seemed, on one level, to be holding everything back. Armstrong gave it all to you, Baker made you work for it. There was never any doubt about

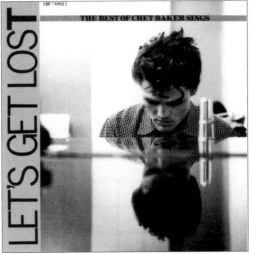

what Armstrong was thinking at any given point, it was all there, right in front you; with Baker, it was, for the most part, a mystery. And yet, though the emotion and the mental process are not constantly in your face—they're always there. Baker's singing is passive, rather than aggressive, and not passive-aggressive either. He is completely defenseless, open, and vulnerable. In his own way, no less than Louis Armstrong, Chet Baker is totally fearless.

As a singing musician, Baker might also be considered unprecedented for technological reasons. He's part of a continuum of "soft"-spoken singers who all emerged in the mid-1950s, among them Blossom Dearie, Bobby Troup, Julie London, and Matt Dennis. Theirs was a sound, collectively, that cried out for such relatively recent innovations as tape recording, long-playing discs, and microgroove. None of these voices would have been nearly as effective on a coarse-groove, 78 rpm single.

Indeed, Baker's entire oeuvre as a vocalist was so entirely without precedent that it seems to have taken most of the trumpeter's career before it was fully appreciated. No one, least of all Baker, seems to have fully fathomed the widespread, long-term appeal of his singing. He made relatively few vocal albums, and when performing live, rarely sang more than a single song on any given set. Even Richard Bock, the rabbi of Baker's recording career, who encouraged him to step out in front both as a bandleader and as a vocalist, doesn't seem to have completely understood the force that he had unleashed: at one point, Bock took a few of Baker's vocal recordings, and then removed the vocal tracks, replacing them with instrumental solos by other musicians, apparently assuming they were more valuable as instrumentals than as vocal sides. When Baker's popularity had reached such a level that Columbia Records wanted to do an album, the resulting project was entirely instrumental: an album of Baker soloing against a string background. Obviously, someone thought that Baker's trumpet plus strings would sell more records than his singing.

His singing only began to attract more attention after his death in May 1988. Roughly a year or so after his shattered body was found in front of the hotel where he was staying in Amsterdam, Baker's first and best recordings as a vocalist, the twenty tracks that he made with pianist Russ Freeman, were gathered for the first time on a single release. (Then too such a release was only possible with the recent invention of the compact disc.) This CD was first issued under the title *Let's Get Lost: The Best of Chet Baker Sings,* but then RCA Records, which was releasing the soundtrack album to the Bruce Weber documentary *Let's Get Lost,* objected, and future pressings of the Pacific Jazz compilation were released with the cover changed to simply *The Best of Chet Baker Sings.*

There would be many future pressings. As it turned out, the album didn't need whatever help a tie-in to the film might have provided. The documentary helped generate a stir over Baker's life and art in the year or so after his departure, but then the soundtrack album more or less vanished, and has been hard to find over the last twenty-five years. The 1989 CD, no matter what the title, was quite a different story. Up to that point, the Baker Pacific tracks had been known mainly to jazz buffs and collectors, and apart from Brazilian devotees like João Gilberto, who absorbed his vocal style, few vocalists even knew about Baker's singing. The CD edition marked the first time those recordings had the benefit of being widely distributed on a major label, since the Pacific catalogue had by then been acquired by Blue Note Records, which itself was part of the vast EMI empire. For the first time, the best tracks of Baker singing were commonly available, and as a collected unit they quickly attained a reputation comparable to *John Coltrane and Johnny Hartman* or *The Tony Bennett / Bill Evans Album.* *The Best of Chet Baker Sings* became a "given," an album that everybody in the jazz world immediately loved. For the first time, young jazz singers began learning "Let's Get Lost."

Technically speaking, *The Best of Chet Baker Sings* is the only entry in this book that could be considered a compilation rather than a "pure" album, a work planned as an album unto itself from start to finish. This compact disc consists of twenty tracks collated from a series of sessions done over four years, originally released, for the most part, on two albums, *Chet Baker Sings* and *Chet Baker Sings and Plays with Bud Shank, Russ Freeman and Strings.* Given the circumstances of its production and the quality of the music—and its long-term impact on the art of jazz singing—this exceptional album is well worth making an exception for.

These twenty songs constitute all the vocals that Baker recorded with his original quartet, which costarred the remarkable pianist Russ Freeman, and which flourished in the years 1953–55, followed by a brief but vital reunion in 1956. These are the first vocals that Baker ever recorded, and they're not only the best of his career, but they amount to some of the most distinguished singing of the body of work known as the Great American Songbook that's ever been documented. The playing too is on an equally high level. Perhaps there's some technological irony at work here: it was only after his death that Baker became a major influence on young singers. It was the LP medium that made Baker a star to begin with, but it was the compact disc that made him immortal.

Within a few years of the introduction of what has since been called modern jazz, several instrumental formats were quickly put into place. The basic combination for the bebop era was a two-horn front line, usually trumpet and saxophone (tenor or alto), plus a rhythm section of piano, bass, and drums. If the group was a sextet rather than a quintet, the additional instrument was usually either a trombone or a second saxophone in the front line. There also were piano trios, and when a group was a quartet almost always it was a saxophone in front of a three-piece rhythm section. These formats were fairly rigidly set, and probably accounted for 90 percent of all the activity in the modern jazz era: such innovators as Miles Davis and Dave Brubeck helped set these parameters, and for the most part stayed within them. As the music digressed through such spinoffs as cool jazz and hard bop, these instrumental combinations stayed more or less the same.

At the point when he first became a star of the jazz world, Chet Baker was known for being part of two of the rarer groups that made a point of not following this particular road map. The first and most famous was the Gerry Mulligan Quartet; the idea of a band consisting of saxophone, particularly the baritone, and trumpet plus bass and drums seemed so unusual—even radical—that it helped make the Mulligan Quartet a national sensation in 1952–53. The level of contrapuntal interplay between the two front-liners was amazing, even by the jazz standards of the day, largely, in fact, because both principals had such an innate understanding of harmony and amazing empathy for each other that they could communicate by sheer thoughts and notes. (Baker was never one much for words, except when he was singing.) They were instantly one of the most visible and popular combinations of the era, and the tiny clubs they played in the Los Angeles area were quickly overflowing with customers.

The group didn't last long. This wasn't because of any internal tensions—the two stars got along very well—but because of external issues. In 1953, Mulligan was a heroin addict, and, remarkably, Baker was still clean at this early stage of the game. The situation would quickly be reversed. The Mulligan-Baker quartet made almost all of its classic recordings between January and May 1953. Mulligan was even then planning to deal with his problem, and, obviously, he and producer Richard Bock wanted to record as much music as possible before the big interruption of his career that they both knew was coming. For most of the middle of the year, Mulligan would be residing at a police-run rehab institution known as "the Sheriff's Honor Farm" and receiving the treatment that would save his life.

Mulligan was off the scene by June 1953. The first thought of Bock and Baker was to keep the two-horns, two-rhythm quartet going, but with another saxophone. Thus, they recorded an amazing live session with Stan Getz on tenor, which wouldn't be issued for about fifty years. That album more recently has become an after-the-fact classic, but the Baker-Getz quartet was not regarded as an ongoing proposition in 1953.

Instead, Baker started a wholly different quartet in a format all his own. In 1953, the idea of a trumpet in front of a rhythm section all by itself was almost as radical as Mulligan's two-horns, two-rhythm format. There had been occasional recordings by swing players like Charlie Shavers and Roy Eldridge with just a rhythm section and no other horns, but there hadn't yet been a headlining touring jazz quartet with trumpet, piano, bass, and drums. (Jonah Jones would use this format later on, to major mass-market success.) Whenever a trumpeter started his own band—from Miles Davis on down—they went out and hired not just a three-piece rhythm section but also a saxophonist.

But Baker had a warmer sound than any other trumpeter, even more than Eldridge, whose goal, as he frequently said, was to play with the greater fluidity of a saxophone. Although known for the soft, vulnerable quality of much of his playing, Baker could also play with a sharp, hard-driving sound when he needed to; Baker's horn was, in fact, almost two instruments at once. At the very least, his singing would have been a helpful addition to the lineup, particularly on recordings where the recently invented process of multitrack recording allowed him to play and sing at the same time. All by himself, Baker could be all the front line that anyone needed.

Baker was actually experimenting with his "saxophone-less" quartet in the studio even while the Mulligan-Baker group was still active, doing two sessions with the new format in December 1952 and April 1953. Following his key collaborations with Charlie Parker and then Mulligan, the key partner in Baker's vocal sessions would be pianist Russ Freeman (1926–2002). Like Baker, he grew up (in Chicago) with the big bands and World War II, and though he was too young to participate in either one of those experiences, the effervescent, swinging sound of the early 1940s was a permanent part of his musical makeup, even though after settling in Los Angeles he became one of the major exponents of bebop piano on the West Coast. As with Mulligan, Baker and Freeman shared a level of empathy that was almost literally telepathic. There was a healthy degree of contrast between Mulligan and Baker, especially in that the baritone sax is, at heart, a big, heavy instrument, even if Mulligan played it with a deft, light touch in a manner inspired by the great ballet dancer of the saxophone, Lester Young. Freeman, however, almost sounded like Baker himself would have sounded on the piano—or like an attempt to replicate Baker's whole approach on another instrument, the keyboard: light and swinging, but with great harmonic profundity, upbeat and driving. No less than Baker and Mulligan, Baker and Freeman were a perfect team.

The Baker-Freeman Quartet, like the Mulligan-Baker group, flourished briefly, lasting two very valuable years from 1953 to 1955, during which time they too were recorded prolifically by Pacific Jazz. The first session (December 1952) had Baker and Freeman, with bass (the famous Red Mitchell) and drums (Bobby White) testing the format on "Isn't It Romantic?" and though the track was entirely instrumental—Baker wasn't singing just yet— the understated wit of both the trumpet and the piano solos owed just as much to the verbal style of Lorenz Hart as to the melodic and harmonic acumen of Richard Rodgers. The next date (April 1953) had Mitchell replaced by Bobby Whitlock, and this time they tried three numbers: two standards, "The Lamp Is Low" and "This Time the Dream's on Me," and a Latinate original by Freeman titled "Maid in Mexico," which anticipated the kind of contributions that the pianist would be making to the quartet's band book. On the next two sessions, Carson Smith and Larry Bunker arrive on bass and drums, as the quartet continues to build up a repertoire of standards and originals by Freeman.

October 24, 1953: the quartet is now Baker, Freeman, Joe Mondragon, bass, and the iconic drummer Shelly Manne. This time there are three tunes: two slow ballads, and one peppy Christmas song ("Winter Wonderland"). One can't imagine what thoughts crossed Bock's mind when he heard Baker sing for the first time, as he obviously did on live dates prior to this session. In 1953, every week seemed to bring some major new innovation into the modern jazz field, but here was something completely new—and totally disarming. "I Fall in Love Too Easily," which Sammy Cahn and Jule Styne wrote for *Anchors Aweigh* (1945), is a perfect

premiere vocal, a song about a guy who's not in control of his own emotions. On his first singing on record, Baker is already a cipher—he may feel good, he may feel bad, whatever happens, it's out of his control, and he assumes no responsibility for his emotional state. (This version of "I Fall in Love Too Easily," however, is not the one that most of us know from *The Best of Chet Baker Sings;* that more familiar version was recorded at the February 1954 date.)

Baker obviously associated "I Fall in Love Too Easily" with the young Sinatra (who introduced it). Although "The Thrill Is Gone" was written by Lew Brown and Ray Henderson for Rudy Vallee in *George White's Scandals* (1931 edition), Baker more likely knew the 1931 recording by Bing Crosby. But where the Crosby version is hot and lusty, Baker's is regretful but cool—he laments the loss of the thrill but is resigned to it. This 1953 track is also an early—and highly effective—example of multi-track recording; even though it's in mono, the trumpet obbligato that Baker plays behind his own vocal is no less moving than the singing itself.

Singing was only the beginning: there were several other different ideas that Baker and Bock were messing around with at the end of 1953. On December 14 and 22, Baker cut eight tunes with a septet, which essentially was the quartet (including Freeman) plus a three-man saxophone section. Even more ambitiously, this was the point when Columbia Records came a-calling: Bock, who had Baker under exclusive contract, worked out a deal whereby he would produce what would be one of Baker's few albums for a major label and his first in a large format aimed at a more popular audience. *Chet Baker & Strings* was taped in Los Angeles (on December 30 and 31), utilizing the same musicians and arrangers familiar from Pacific Jazz sessions. The only difference was that at the end of the project, the engineer shipped the tapes to Columbia Records.

Having tested the waters with those two vocals in October, when Baker returned to the studio in February, it was time for more singing. On February 15, the quartet (with Carson Smith and Bob Neel plus Baker and Freeman) reconvened and struck pay dirt. In one day, they laid down seven tracks, all vocals, and all instant classics. The first tune of the day turned out to be one of the great jazz performances of all time, on a par with anything anybody was doing in 1954, even exceeding anything by the Mulligan-Baker quartet. "But Not for Me," the Gershwin brothers' classic from *Girl Crazy*, had transitioned into a torch song by the mid-1950s, but Baker restores it to its origins as a serio-comic aria of humorously exaggerated self-deprecation. He plays the verse on the trumpet not in the least bit ad-lib or rubato (it's totally danceable), after which he sings the chorus, entering precisely on the beat; both singing and playing, he captures perfectly Ira Gershwin's air of comic resignation.

"Time After Time"—more Cahn/Styne/Sinatra—is another mixed mood, with Baker fully capturing a wistful, melancholy atmosphere. For "I Get Along Without You Very Well," however, Baker anticipates Sinatra's more famous treatment by well over a year. The song has a rather complex backstory, but the upshot is that this is virtually the only instance when Hoagy Carmichael wrote a song based on an existing poem, and as a result it doesn't sound like any other song by Carmichael or by anyone else. Rather than merely being out of touch with his emotions, Baker is in denial here, trying to assure himself that he's getting along just swell even after the end of an important relationship—and there's an unspoken, underlying understanding that this relationship has been ended not by a breakup, but by death.

"There Will Never Be Another You," the Harry Warren–Mack Gordon standard (from the Sonja Henie movie *Iceland*, 1942) is more like a typical contemplation of a post-breakup scenario. Baker, both playing and singing, is at once wry and reflective. With the last three tunes from the February date, we're up to full-fledged-masterpiece level again: "Look for the Silver Lining" by Jerome Kern and Buddy DeSylva (associated with Marilyn Miller in the 1920 *Sally*) is a particularly strong example of the sympathy between Freeman and Baker, both of their solos fairly burst with invention and optimism, and make it clear that the song is still fresh and vital, particularly relevant to the bop era, though it's considerably older than Baker

or Freeman. (There's more overdubbing, with Baker playing behind his own vocal.)

At 2:20, "My Funny Valentine" is at once the shortest and the most iconic track in the collection, a song that would follow Baker around for the rest of his life—and which he had already played with Mulligan. Since being introduced in the 1937 *Babes in Arms*, this Rodgers and Hart standard had been almost completely overlooked for the first fifteen years of its existence, until Baker and Sinatra (within a few months of each other) almost simultaneously put it on the map. Even this early in his career, there are already almost half a dozen versions of "Valentine" in Baker's discography, mostly from various live appearances, although this is the first documented instance in which he sang it. Baker's February 1954 version is a very direct extension of the earlier instrumental treatments, particularly the slow and stark live version with Mulligan from 1952. Melancholy almost to the point of despondency, with none of the uplifting qualities you hear in, say, the classic Sinatra record, the song is mostly down but still affectionate. Sinatra's is remarkably moving, no doubt about that, but Baker is the one who makes us think about the funny valentines in our own lives—and ofttimes, it's us ourselves. There are dozens of cases where Sinatra is in the lead, but this time Baker is the one who moves us more quickly to tears.

The February 1954 session consisted of so many songs partially because the last two tunes, "My Funny Valentine" and "I Fall in Love Too Easily" (a remake of the first song Baker did in the studio, six months earlier) were already very familiar to Baker and Freeman. The quartet did seven tunes on this date, which, combined with "The Thrill Is Gone" from October 1954, gave Bock enough material for the first Baker vocal album, titled simply *Chet Baker Sings* (Pacific Jazz PJ LP 11). The cover boasted an especially attractive image from photographer William Claxton: Baker and Freeman in a studio, with Baker perched behind a music stand, mouth opened in mid-vocal. (As already mentioned, Bock even stretched five of the February tracks into part of a second album—titled *Pretty/Groovy*—when he removed Baker's vocals and replaced them with instrumental solos by two different reed players, tenor saxophonist Bill Perkins and clarinetist Jimmy Giuffre.)

At eight tracks, this 10-inch LP was a fairly perfect album. But better was to come.

Between May and August 1954, Bock recorded the Baker-Freeman Quartet live on the road, in three excellent concert tapes from Ann Arbor, Santa Cruz, and Los Angeles. The trumpeter doesn't sing on any of these dates. Apparently not enough of his fans had heard the LP at that point for there to be any demand for his vocals just yet. In the fall of 1954, Bock and Baker experimented with a sextet session (trumpet, trombone, and baritone sax, released as part of the album titled *Chet Baker Big Band*) and one of several reunion dates with Stan Getz.

In spring 1955, Baker would hit the road again, heading for the East Coast (New York, Newport) and then an extended stay in Europe. There would be a major gap in his Pacific Jazz studio sessions between March 1955 and July 1956. Before he left, Bock had enough material for two more 12-inch LPs that involved Baker's singing, although the producer would wind up repeating four tracks between them. In February, Bock produced Baker's second session with strings, this time with him singing as well as playing. This being perhaps the most elaborate enterprise that he ever had to subsidize out of his own pocket, Bock quickly released those same four string-and-vocal tracks on two different albums. *Chet Baker Sings and Plays with Bud Shank, Russ Freeman and Strings* contained the February string tracks plus an additional six tracks, from March, of vocals with the quartet featuring Freeman. The vocal/strings tracks were also used on an album called *Grey December*, which was filled out by the eight septet instrumentals from December 1953.

Thirty-five years later, those six quartet-only vocals from March 1955 were collected on the CD *Let's Get Lost: The Best of Chet Baker Sings*. None of the participants, Baker, Freeman, or Bock, who worked on all twenty tracks in the quartet vocal series (all collected on that 1989 CD), ever appear to have been asked about how the songs were picked—it seems to be mostly songs that Baker liked, with occasional input from the others.

The second song on the session was "Just Friends," which had been a jazz standard ever since it was first heard in 1931. Baker takes what started as a torch song and swings it in the manner of Louis Armstrong and Ella Fitzgerald. It's not the least bit sad, but if you listen closely, you might smell the faint aroma of remorse, as if Baker is partying as a means of "pretending / It isn't the ending." "Just Friends" was the kind of song he would have picked up in jam sessions, and certainly through his associations with Charlie Parker (who made a classic recording of the song with strings) and Mulligan. (Actually, the only notable singers who did it before Baker were Mildred Bailey and Sarah Vaughan. He recorded it before Billie Holiday and Anita O'Day, to name two.)

Now here's something interesting: all five of the other songs from this session were from the World War II era, songs that Baker heard when he was first learning the trumpet and, in his own casual way making a de facto study of the popular song: "Daybreak," "I Remember You," "Let's Get Lost," "Long Ago and Far Away," and "You Don't Know What Love Is." (All but the first are from wartime movie musicals.)

Baker undoubtedly knew "Daybreak" from the famous 1942 Tommy Dorsey record with Frank Sinatra. It wouldn't have mattered to him that this was a song based on an earlier melody, adapted by lyricist Harold Adamson from "Mississippi Suite," a semiclassical concert piece by Ferde Grofé. Where the Dorsey version was only slightly less symphonic than the Paul Whiteman original, Baker may be the first to have put Grofé's melody entirely into a jazz tempo. Baker's vocal is way less contemplative than Sinatra's, and his trumpet solo is bright and punchy, like the sun fighting its way through the clouds as the rain ends.

"I Remember You" boasts a famous lyricist (Johnny Mercer) and a composer (Victor Schertzinger) who had a much bigger career as a Hollywood director; in fact, he served in that capacity for *The Fleet's In*, the 1942 Paramount picture in which Dorothy Lamour introduced this future standard. There are relatively few major jazz vocal versions before Baker's in 1955; Sarah Vaughan didn't do her treatment (usually regarded as the definitive one) until 1962. Both Baker and Vaughan start with the verse in rubato, but where Vaughan stays out of tempo for the whole track, Baker and quartet pick up the pace at the start of the chorus. The verse is actually very expressive, with Baker stressing and caressing key words like a real crooner ("I recall that I sawwwww you smile"). The coda has Baker playing with the words and notes as he repeats them, as if he were singing a trumpet cadenza.

"Long Ago and Far Away" is the major collaboration between Jerome Kern and Ira Gershwin, a composer and a lyricist both better known for working with other partners. Originally done as a romantic pas de deux between Gene Kelly and Rita Hayworth in *Cover Girl* (1944), Baker does it with a beat—very playfully—and a snappy verbal coda ("Our love started long ago"). His opening two choruses of trumpet are as cheerful as it's possible to be, as is Freeman's single chorus of piano after the no less exuberant vocal. Baker splits the last chorus with himself, playing the first sixteen bars on trumpet and singing the last, with another clever closer ("It seems now our love started long ago . . ."). It's hard to believe that so much joy, optimism, and ebullience can be contained in a four-minute track.

The mood slows dramatically for the more somber "You Don't Know What Love Is," a harmonically stylish torch song written for Carol Bruce in the 1941 Abbott and Costello comedy *Keep 'Em Flying* (but dropped from the movie) and the longest number on the CD. The five-minute track starts with the vocal, and it's immediately one of Baker's best ballads, one that highlights a key distinction between his playing and singing. As a vocalist, he merely hints at the pain and the anguish that the lyrics express. When he plays, he's a lot more directly emotional—he actually goes to those peaks and valleys with his trumpet that he only suggests with his voice. "You Don't Know What Love Is" is also the earliest extant TV clip of Baker that I know of, a two-minute excerpt from a longer performance from Europe (possibly Switzerland) in 1955 or 1956.

Which brings us to "Let's Get Lost." This 1943 song also originated in a Paramount wartime musical (*Happy Go Lucky*, 1943), and is one of the last important songs by Frank Loesser strictly as a lyricist. (He reemerged after the army as a composer and book writer as well.) Introduced by Mary Martin, the song was done by only a few dance and swing bands in summer 1942 just before the American Federation of Musicians declared a strike on record labels and it was virtually impossible to make a recording of a new (or any other) song for two years. It's fair to say this is a lovely song that would have been totally forgotten if not for Baker; especially since Bruce Weber used it as the title for his 1988 documentary about Baker, it became inexplicably associated with the trumpeter—virtually the only time you ever hear "Let's Get Lost" is in some kind of tribute to Baker.

It was an astute choice for a title, and it was somewhat prophetic that Baker recorded it on his last date before departing from California. He was about to head east, and wouldn't be back in the Golden State for almost a year and a half. Russ Freeman remained with him for the East Coast dates, notably New York and Newport, but when the quartet headed for Europe, the pianist went back to Los Angeles. He was replaced by Dick Twardzik, an outstanding modern jazz pianist from Massachusetts whose keyboard prowess was an open secret among Boston beboppers.

In those pre-jet days, a "tour" of Europe by an American performer was rarely more than a few weeks or months. Even the most famous touring unit in jazz, Norman Granz's Jazz at the Philharmonic troupe, had just broken through to overseas venues. For Baker to stay in Europe for almost a year was unheard of. Baker was setting the pattern for the rest of his career: He would remain overseas the great majority of the time, only returning occasionally to his native country when a major gig beckoned. His life became an endless round of circling from one gig to another; the very idea of "home" would become an increasingly abstract and irrelevant concept. Soon enough, he would also be traveling from one high to another, an unrepentant drug user in spite of the example set for him by Charlie Parker and Dick Twardzik, who died as a result of heroin usage within a few weeks of each other in 1955. (The pianist was, in fact, working in Paris with Baker at the time of his death.) The career trajectory and the narcotics addiction paralleled each other, almost frighteningly: Baker had, very deliberately, fixed his life into a permanent pattern of getting lost.

His music, fittingly, also changed in Europe. Twardzik was one of those wonderboy martyrs strewn across the history of jazz—he was only twenty-four when the overdose overtook him in a French hotel room. He was an exceptional pianist, and very different from Russ Freeman. In the music Baker made with Twardzik, he still sounds like Chet Baker, but the quartet in general makes a noise that's much more easily categorizable as regulation modern jazz. Twardzik is much more beboppy than Freeman, also more blues-oriented, and his playing has more of an intellectual edge; had Twardzik returned from Europe, he would have likely settled in New York, and worked in parallel to Horace Silver as one of the major pianist-leaders of the hard bop movement.

Twardzik was not, however, a better pianist for Baker. The music Baker made with Freeman is, on the whole, entirely superior. The Baker-Freeman quartet is much lighter, more whimsical and capricious, with more of a dancing quality. Twardzik's direction was the direction the whole jazz world was shortly to go in, but it was by no means an improvement. Somehow the harder-edged music that Baker began making in 1955–56 aligned itself with the directions his career was taking, and complemented the ongoing sense of "lost." (Baker also fell increasingly under the influence of the music of Miles Davis during the European trip, which resulted in the loss of some of his own identity.)

But not all at once. When the trumpeter, at long last, returned to California and resumed his ongoing relationship with Pacific Jazz Records, Bock wisely reunited the Chet Baker–Russ Freeman Quartet for two distinct projects. The group cut six vocal titles in July 1956, Baker's first session after the trip, and then in November they recorded an entire instrumental album of eight tracks. (The latter was titled simply *Quartet,* and for the only time Freeman was billed first.) It's those six vocals from July that concern us here, and it's hard not to divine from a few of the titles some kind of message about how the two men felt about each other:

"That Old Feeling," "It's Always You," "My Ideal," and, yes, "My Buddy." The first tune from the sessions (there were two, July 23 and 30) could not have been better picked. "That Old Feeling" is a snappy, peppy, danceable piece in the tradition of Baker and Freeman's "But Not for Me" and "Long Ago and Far Away." Baker starts by playing the verse on trumpet, and does it so eloquently that the words would seem superfluous.

That old feeling continues with two Burke and Van Heusen numbers from wartime musicals, the all-time jazz standard "Like Someone in Love" (from the 1944 *Belle of the Yukon*) and the lesser-known but equally deserving "It's Always You" (from *Road to Zanzibar*). The latter was introduced by Bing Crosby, but it makes more sense that Baker glommed it off Dorsey and Sinatra. "Like Someone in Love," at 2:26, is short and sweet, with no wasted motion, Baker's singing having matured to the point where he really seems to be thinking up the lyrics as he sings them, as if they're really just occurring to him. In another signifying point of artistic evolution, this is one of the few tracks in the series where Baker just sings, and leaves his horn in the case. "It's Always You" seems even more like an internal monologue: even though he addresses the object of his affection as "you," there's no doubt that he's talking (i.e., singing) to himself.

Walter Donaldson and Gus Kahn's "My Buddy," an oldie from 1922, opens with a very capricious muted trumpet solo. There's no mistaking Baker from any other muted player, even such Harmon mute specialists as Sweets Edison and Miles Davis. The following vocal and Freeman's piano solo are much more straight-ahead, and Baker returns to singing for the coda, ending on a high note for the final "you." "I've Never Been in Love Before," from Frank Loesser's 1950 *Guys and Dolls,* is the newest tune in the stack, and Baker starts it so abruptly that you're almost afraid you've missed something. This is a very relaxed and laid-back track (at 4:39), yet it still has the urgency of the shorter, perkier numbers; Freeman's harmonies behind Baker are particularly lush and lavish here.

"My Ideal" is the last vocal that Baker recorded with Freeman, and it's a fine closer to the series. Here, the keyboardist switches just this once to celeste; Baker intones the verse lovingly, making this one of the most perfect interpretations ever of the Richard Whiting standard (successfully revived after the composer's death by his pop star daughter, Margaret). When Baker sings about looking for his ideal, he makes it sound as if he's already found it.

My personal collection of Baker includes roughly 180 different albums recorded under his own name over a thirty-five-year period that ended with his violent death in Holland in a fall from a window, and only a handful of these are vocal albums. Some are very fine, yet there's nothing to compare with the sheer magic that he and Russ Freeman created together between 1953 and 1956. The twenty songs that Baker sang with Freeman and his original quartet are like nothing else in jazz, a perfect body of work. They're a great reminder of the best work of an artist who found himself well before he ever got "lost."

4

Tony Bennett and Bill Evans

The Tony Bennett / Bill Evans Album and *Together Again*

(1975, 1977)

n 2011, Tony Bennett turned eighty-five, and as part of the international celebration of this big-numeral birthday, the singer did a TV special and concert in London, for part of which he was accompanied by the Royal Philharmonic Orchestra. At one point, during a break in the filming, he was approached by a group of members of the

ally made several other outstanding piano-centric albums, including *Tony Sings for Two* and *When Lights Are Low*, both with his longtime accompanist Ralph Sharon. In 2015, on the eve of his ninetieth birthday, Bennett released *The Silver Lining: The Songs of Jerome Kern*, a collaboration with pianist Bill Charlap.) It's not entirely a coincidence

orchestra, string players mostly, who wanted him to sign some albums from their personal collections. The album they had all picked as their favorite was the one that meant the most to Tony as well: *The Tony Bennett / Bill Evans Album*. For the last forty years, Bennett has grown accustomed to all sorts of knowledgeable people—particularly jazz musicians and fans—citing that album as his best, but he was especially impressed that so many classical players knew about it. He said, "I thought, 'Wow! The symphony.'"

To a certain extent the album stands out because it's so different from the rest of Bennett's recorded canon. (Or so most casual listeners assume: he actu-

that most of the great jazz albums by male singers are team-ups, like *John Coltrane and Johnny Hartman*, Sinatra with Count Basie and Antonio Carlos Jobim, *Louis Armstrong Meets Oscar Peterson*, Nat Cole's meeting with four outstanding soloists on *After Midnight*. These are all special occasions for these artists in that these projects took them, if not out of their comfort zones, at least away from business as usual.

These albums have cast a disproportionately large shadow: jazz deejays who consider themselves hip who would never play anything else by Cole, Sinatra, or Bennett in particular, play these albums all the time. And those jazz fans who generally avoid male singers will even admit to loving them; aspiring music students, both vocal and instrumental, of either gender have committed every note of them to memory; one isn't surprised to see the contemporary jazz singer Allan Harris paying tribute to Bennett and Evans in the company of a Japanese piano prodigy, or to find John Pizzarelli teaming up with Jobim's grandson Daniel to re-create the Sinatra-Jobim sessions.

Even in this rarefied company, the Bennett-Evans albums stand out. The songs on these two records have penetrated the musical bloodstream to an unprecedented degree. Generations of jazz fans know "Young and Foolish" from Tony Bennett and Bill Evans, whereas only a handful of theater geeks even remember *Plain and Fancy,* the Broadway show that introduced it. In those songs where Evans altered the chord changes as part of his interpretation, most contemporary pianists will know the Evans changes and not the originals. It's thanks to Bennett and Evans, in fact, that "Some Other Time" has become an all-time jazz standard, one of the most heard songs in clubs over the last forty years, and easily Leonard Bernstein's best-known song in the jazz world.

There had been other voice and piano pairings before, notably Ella Fitzgerald's amazing sets with Ellis Larkins and Paul Smith, Bennett's own 1959 *Tony Sings for Two* with Ralph Sharon, and the excellent Stan Kenton–June Christy *Duet* of 1955. But the Bennett-Evans combination took things to a whole other level, so much so that any other singer-pianist duo is automatically compared with these two albums of 1975 and '76.

The difference between the Bennett-Evans albums and their predecessors is keenly illustrated by a comparison of *Tony Sings for Two* and *The Tony Bennett / Bill Evans Album.* The 1959 album is a clear-cut example of a pianist accompanying a singer in the classic tradition; Sharon rather brilliantly gives him the harmonic and rhythmic support that he needs while staying out of his way. Architecturally, it would be like the foundation of a building that you would never see—the skyscraper stays up without its support structure ever being apparent. *Tony Sings for Two* differs from other vocal albums merely in the intimate nature of the accompaniment; it was unusual enough for a star of Bennett's level to appear without an orchestra, let alone without a bassist or drummer, and the voice was exposed to a much greater degree than on your typical jazz or pop vocal performance.

On the Bennett-Evans collaborations, instead of the singer being accompanied by the pianist, with one in the spotlight and the other comprising a supporting cast of one, the two participants are equal partners. Bennett even chose to underscore this fact by opening the second album, *Together Again,* with a piano solo by Evans—so no one would have the false idea that this was simply a vocal record with piano accompaniment. Indeed, the way that voice and keyboard interact here seems to have no antecedent in the whole history of jazz; this is more like an American idea of lieder.

I've always resisted the notion, expressed in much of popular culture, that individuals in relationships somehow "complete" each other. Artie Shaw, writing from his own considerable experience, once espoused the opinion that it was insane to think that there are all these "half" people running around out there. Rather, only individuals who are whole to begin with, in and of themselves, are in a position to bond with other people.

And that's the way the Bennett-Evans sessions work: Evans, not surprisingly, plays like a complete entity unto himself—something he proved with his various solo albums over the years. Bennett too is the rare singer (outside of the folk music tradition, perhaps) who has performed a cappella, most notably on "Fly Me to the Moon," which he has sung countless times not only without musical accompaniment but without benefit of amplification.

They are each complete; fortunately, Bennett and Evans didn't record in isolation booths, but if there were some way to listen to one without the other, I expect you would hear that neither the pianist nor the singer needs the other to form a complete statement. Yet they are still working together in such a way that two elements, which are wholes in themselves, become an even greater whole when they join together in concert (in every sense of the term).

• • •

Tony Bennett has a generous habit of giving credit to others for ideas that had already occurred to him. He thanks Frank Sinatra, his primary role model, and Tony Tamburello, his vocal coach, for steering him toward his career-long search for high-class songs. He credits accompanist and partner Ralph Sharon for encouraging him to record jazz concept albums. It's hard to imagine that Tony hadn't already thought of taking these steps long before others came along to encourage him in these directions. Likewise, I've always harbored the suspicion that Tony had dreamed about cutting an album with Bill Evans even before Annie Ross did history the favor of serving as the catalyst for that collaboration.

The collaboration was not completely unprecedented in either career: as mentioned, Bennett had earlier cut two piano-centric albums with Ralph Sharon, *Tony Sings for Two* and *When Lights Are Low* (1964). Evans, also, did one notable album with a singer when, in the middle of a European tour in 1964, his trio teamed up with the Swedish vocalist Monica Zetterlund for an album called *Waltz for Debby.* (In addition to the title song, sung in Swedish, the album also included the two Bernstein *On the Town* songs that he would later play with Bennett.)

The two first appeared in the same concert—although not together—in 1962. That March, President Kennedy threw a special jazz party on the White House lawn, and among the dignitaries who performed were Bennett and Dave Brubeck (who performed together in a concert that was issued in 2013) and Evans. Bennett had long been a fan of Evans, having first become aware of him (as so many people did) during 1958 for the few months when Evans worked with the Miles Davis Septet.

"I met Bill backstage [at the White House]," Bennett recollected, "and he told me that he liked the songs I picked throughout my career, and that he admired me for sticking with quality songs." It wasn't merely that Bennett and Evans shared a predilection for quality material, but that they often happened to be the same songs. Over the years both gentlemen recorded "Young and Foolish," "Who Can I Turn To?," "My Foolish Heart," "So Long Big Time," "On Green Dolphin Street," "The

Shadow of Your Smile," "For Heaven's Sake," "Stella by Starlight," "Yesterday I Heard the Rain," "Emily," "Alfie," and many others. Bennett was also the most important pop star—if not the only one—to sing "Waltz for Debby," Evans's most notable effort as a writer of popular songs with lyrics.

In November 1968, Bennett celebrated his twentieth anniversary in show business, an occasion commemorated with a special edition of the record-biz bible *Billboard.* Like all such dedicated issues, this one was heavily laden with testimonials, by everyone from showbiz legends (Sinatra, Judy Garland, Louis Armstrong, Fred Astaire), jazzmen (Count Basie, Gil Evans, Stan Getz, Dizzy Gillespie, Duke Ellington), intellectuals (Gunther Schuller, Alec Wilder), industry leaders (Mitch Miller and Clive Davis of Columbia Records, music publisher Howard Richmond), composers (Cy Coleman, Harold Arlen), and representatives of the past (Ted Lewis) and future (Barbra Streisand).

One of the more eloquent such tributes was paid by Bill Evans, who said, "Like many instrumentalists, I never was a great vocal fan. But Tony's development has been fantastic, and for the past few years he's been my favorite singer. Tony really has knocked me out more than anybody. The reason is that he has developed through a long, hard process of pure dedication to music and to his own talent. The end result of this type of development is more precious; it has a depth and a quality and a purity that appeal to me."

Tony was spending a lot of time in England in the early 1970s, around the time he parted company with Columbia Records (his home base for his entire career until then). Among his closest friends in these days were the brilliant jazz singer Annie Ross, whom he already had known for over fifteen years at that point, and her then husband. Annie had known Bill Evans for just about as long; they were introduced in the mid-1950s by one of Evans's own mentors, the clarinetist Tony Scott.

Then, at one point in the early 1970s, Bill Evans and his trio appeared at Ronnie Scott's Jazz Club in London. Annie, Tony, and Tony's pianist at the time, the gifted John Bunch, all sat at a table ringside. Years later, Ross recalled, laughing: "I get these ideas, like sometimes I'll hear a song and I'll bring it to Tony or another singer, I'll say, 'Why don't you do that? It would be very good for you.' I loved Bill and the way he played and of course I also loved the way Tony sang. I just thought it would be a perfect combination." For a brief moment, Bennett pondered the idea of singing with two pianos, Bunch and Evans, but Bunch insisted, "I didn't feel that I was in a class with Bill Evans, and frankly, I tried like hell to discourage him from that."

Evans later told writer Leonard Lyons that a team-up with Bennett "was one of those things that was in the air for years. I always figured that if Tony would do one of my tunes, I'd be overjoyed. In fact, he did record 'Waltz for Debby' once." He continued, "Tony and I have always had a mutual respect and a distant acquaintance with each other. It so happens that my manager and his manager are good friends."

In the mid-1970s, Bennett was recording for Improv Records, a company that he co-owned with a partner. Throughout the 1950s and '60s, the singer had been frustrated by what he viewed as the debilitating commercialism of the major conglomerates (especially Columbia). Improv, however, would be committed to preserving and popularizing the highest-caliber music Bennett could possibly record. At this point, what had been a loose concept—a duo album with Bill Evans—now took concrete form. Since the pianist was then under contract to Fantasy Records, Bennett worked out an arrangement with Evans's manager, Helen Keane, whereby the pair would actually cut two LPs, one for Fantasy and one for Improv. Both were taped in San Francisco, the city by the bay where Fantasy was based and where Bennett had left his heart. They taped the Fantasy package, *The Tony Bennett / Bill Evans Album* first, in June 1975, and then did the follow-up, *Together Again,* in September 1976.

There was no actual preparation for the first album—unlike, say, what happened with Johnny Hartman and John Coltrane, who at least sat in together on a gig somewhat informally before recording. Evans and Bennett went into the studio with only Keane, who was officially credited as producer, and the engineer. They didn't even

discuss possible song choices beforehand. One of the pair would just think of a song, then the two would work out a routine and a key, go over it a few times, and then put it down on tape. As Bennett recalled, "I would name a tune, and Bill would say, 'That's good, let's do that.' We'd find a key and then the two of us would work it out. For about forty-five minutes, we'd work out the arrangement, he'd say, 'Do you wanna modulate here? How many choruses do you want?' And then we would play it through and work out all the changes and all that. We spent three days doing that, until we had nine songs in the can."

In retrospect, it might have been preferable for the first album, *The Tony Bennett / Bill Evans Album,* to have opened with "Some Other Time," not only given Evans's long history with the song but with the way his treatment of the Bernstein classic opens—the famous two-chord ostinato vamp. There is almost no better way to begin anything, whether it's a song or an album. In 1958, Evans was recording his second album as a leader, *Everybody Digs Bill Evans,* and he started to play his version of "Some Other Time" with an imaginative though very simple introduction; he kept playing with the thing, and eventually a figure that had started life merely as an intro had evolved into a wholly original composition. He titled the new tune "Peace Piece," a reference not only to the tranquil nature of the tune, but also, possibly, to how "Some Other Time" was a product of the World War II era, when any piece of peace was not to be taken for granted. Evans recorded both "Peace Piece" and "Some Other Time" (with Bernstein's melody) at that 1958 session, but "Some Other Time" wasn't released until some other time many years later. He also played it on his classic 1961 live recording *Sunday at the Village Vanguard.*

The Bennett-Evans version uses the "Peace Piece" ostinato to lead into the Bernstein melody. Of course, it might not have made an ideal opener since it's a song about saying goodbye, yet unlike many goodbye lyrics there's an undercurrent message of hope. This is a World War II song about fighting men saying goodbye to their loved ones, but it's a farewell song with a silver lining—the idea that "we'll catch up some other time" isn't merely a false promise. Bennett and Evans manage to brilliantly capture the contradictions, they bring out the marvelously sad-happy quality—pure melancholy—that makes the song so rich both emotionally and musically.

The album actually opens with "Young and Foolish," one of the many numbers that both men had previously recorded independent of each other. Evans was only twenty-nine when he included it on the same *Everybody Digs* album, and Bennett was thirty-six when he sang it on his 1962 LP *I Wanna Be Around.* But by 1975, when the two were forty-five and forty-eight, respectively, they were both better able to tap into the song's larger meaning.

The classic duo performance conveys immediately that Bennett and Evans now realize that "Young and Foolish" is not a song about being young and foolish, it's a song about having been young and foolish, in the past tense, and that's a key distinction. In the show *Plain and Fancy,* it's sung by a middle-aged couple who are nostalgically reminiscing about their youth, and wanting to be, as Arnold Horwitt's lyric goes, "young and foolish again." Like many classic songs, it's all about wanting rather than being, and Bennett and Evans both show that they are well aware of the gap between the two. Importantly, Bennett's 1962 version uses the verse ("Once we were foolish children . . ."); Bennett and Evans experimented with the verse in 1975, and it is heard on an alternate take, but ultimately decided not to use it, and the issued master take is verse-less (and is a full minute shorter than the alternate).

One of the key aspects of their mutual artistic maturity is the use of space; Evans was capable of cramming every measure with more notes than there are fish in the sea, and Bennett, as his earliest records proved, could hit notes that were louder and longer than Mario Lanza's. But by this point in their artistic evolution they were keenly aware that they didn't have to fill every space—in fact, that an empty space could communicate as much as a note or a word could. The trick with interpreting such an intensely emotional text as "Young and Foolish" is to sing as little as possible, the bittersweet nature of the lyric is better expressed with a light touch rather than an iron fist. Rather than dishing out a

million notes at once, like so many young and foolish musicians, they know well it's more effective to make every note count.

Ray Noble's "The Touch of Your Lips" is also about expressing deep emotions with the lightest possible touch; it's not your Aunt Gertrude kissing you with a big heavy mouthful of gooey lipstick, it's the lightest imaginable butterfly kiss from a lover. Other songs in the American repertory may more explicitly describe an amorous interlude, with more explicit details, but Bennett and Evans make the simple touching of lips into the most erotic experience anyone could wish for.

Bennett once famously cited the team of Cy Coleman and Carolyn Leigh as his favorite contemporary songwriters, and Evans too recorded no fewer than a half dozen Coleman tunes. (Evans learned many of these both from Bennett and from Blossom Dearie, one of his favorite pianists.) More than anything else by Coleman and Leigh, "When in Rome" is a patter song—a clear descendant of Cole Porter and Noël Coward. Yet it was the rare patter tune that, as Evans had acknowledged in a 1973 solo recording, could stand on its own, without the lyric. With Bennett singing the lyrics, it only gets better; generally, comedy is almost entirely dependent on timing and rhythm, yet Bennett and Evans get the point across (and the laughs come through) even without the assistance of bass and drums—no rimshots necessary here. This is a tale of continental (not to mention serial) infidelity that Bennett animates entirely through the nuances of his voice—for instance, the way he caresses the word "fundador" (which turns out to be a Mediterranean brandy, but you knew that), and the way he shoots up to the final "*do* as the Romans do" in an exaggerated high note.

"We'll Be Together Again" and "My Foolish Heart" arrive in what could be described as reverse order, since they depict the end and then the beginning of a relationship. "Together Again" is partly the work of pop star Frankie Laine (a friend of Tony's), and I always find it hard to believe that the iron-throated belter could come up with something this tender (something he rarely managed in his own singing). One of the classic songs by composer Victor Young and the even more underappreciated lyricist Ned Washington, "Foolish Heart" had been made into a jazz standard by Billy Eckstine (another of Tony's closest colleagues). Prior to this recording, the verse ("The scene is set for dreaming . . .") was fairly rare, but it's been much more common in the last forty years, thanks to this album. The lyric postulates the idea of the protagonist's heart as a separate, parallel entity ("My heart and I are reluctant to start"), and it almost seems as if Evans is taking the role of the "heart" in this story; both players demonstrate that they well know where the line falls between love and fascination.

"Waltz for Debby" is the best known of Evans's many original compositions, debuting on his first album, the 1956 *New Jazz Conceptions*. Gene Lees, the journalist and lyricist and friend of both Evans and Bennett, later wrote the moving and appropriate lyric. Bennett sang it in 1964 on his album *Who Can I Turn To;* Evans played it many times on both studio and live albums. As we know from dozens of tracks by Mabel Mercer, the waltz is an old-fashioned time signature that composers often utilize to depict youth and innocence. Evans's original melody was inspired by his three-year-old niece, his brother's baby daughter, and around the time of the Bennett sessions—nineteen years later—the pianist told an interviewer that he had just been to Debby's wedding. Bennett sings it (in both takes) as if he's thinking of his own daughters, Joanna and Antonia, who were very little girls at the time; his ending diminuendo, "But then *sooo* will I" is touching without overdoing it.

"But Beautiful" is by Tony's close pal Jimmy Van Heusen, and like a lot of that composer's classic songs (most famously, "I Thought About You") is built on an ABAB pattern. Bennett's singing amounts to a master class in the craft that some people call "phrasing," the way he articulates all the contrasting adjectives—happy vs. sad, good thing vs. bad, tearful vs. gay—Johnny Burke's whole lyric is essentially one pair of these after another, set up in a repetitive pattern that totally depends on a master interpreter like Bennett to give it resonance. Burke and Van Heusen were both keenly aware that you don't have to include everything in the printed music to a song, you have to leave something for the interpreter to do.

The ninth track, "Days of Wine and Roses," ends the first album somewhat cryptically—but beautifully. The phrase comes from a poem by the English poet Ernest Dowson, which became the title of a television play by JP Miller about an alcoholic couple, which then led to both a film adaptation (1962) and finally a classic title song for said film by Henry Mancini and Johnny Mercer. Mercer's lyric uses deeply poignant imagery that, as we now know from recent biographies of the songwriter (including one by "Debby" lyricist Gene Lees), expresses his own experience as a habitual drinker. It's the shortest track of the collaboration, and essentially consists of one all-keyboard chorus by Evans, followed by a vocal chorus by Bennett in which Evans sticks to the sidelines. More than anywhere else in the first album, Evans and Bennett keep it as simple as possible, and again one can't help reveling in Bennett's emphasis of phrases like "just a *passing* breeze, *filled* with memories." Tony has often said that you can bring out the inner meaning of a song by stressing what seem to be the least important words of a line, and this is a stunning example. You can almost literally feel the breeze passing, and the song is indeed crammed to the brim with memories—even Mercer's mixed metaphors seem vibrant and vivid.

"Days of Wine and Roses" is a song that's simultaneously about endings and beginnings. In placing it at the end of their first album together, Tony Bennett and Bill Evans were clearly indicating that there was more to come.

Over the next year, Bennett and Evans worked together quite a bit: they opened the 1976 Newport Jazz Festival in New York, played Washington, D.C., in November, and made television appearances together. The combination kept getting better and better. As Tony told the *New York Post*'s Peter Keepnews that June, "Bill's a great guy. We really get along good. It's just two guys goin' and doin' it." He later told me, "My one regret is that they didn't get down all those rehearsals and run-throughs. Unfortunately the engineer was afraid of running out of tape. But it was fascinating to hear Bill work on tunes like that." They taped the second album in September, once again crafting the material on the spot, but probably also utilizing songs they had developed in live appearances together.

The release of the first album, on Fantasy, caught a lot of people by surprise. Not that Bennett hadn't already made a habit of collaborating with the greatest jazz musicians around, like Count Basie (with whom he made two albums in 1958–59) and Duke Ellington (with whom he toured extensively in 1968). Rather, it might have seemed like an unlikely pairing in terms of the personalities of the participants. Bennett was and is one of the most outgoing performers in all of music. One of his favorite words of praise for a musician is "gregarious," and the qualities he prizes in other performers can be taken as a description of his own work, specifically his conviction that reaching the audience, getting his message across—communicating—is the most important thing.

Evans, on the other hand, is generally characterized as one of the most introverted players in the history of jazz. The most celebrated image of this virtuoso is with his head almost buried in the keyboard, not caring a fig about what he looked like to the audience, completely consumed with ingesting every single nuance of sound emitting from his instrument. Hell, Evans could take "Santa Claus Is Coming to Town," as he does on his first solo recording, from 1963, and make it sound moody and introspective. As Joe Cocuzzo, Bennett's drummer at the time, put it, "If ever there was an understated man in the world, it was Bill."

Yet across both albums, the two more than met each other halfway. Bennett also possessed a reflexive, inwardly directed quality that he allowed to come to the fore at the right moments. Likewise, Evans, when he wanted to, could play as dynamically extroverted as anybody. That was part of the purpose of "The Bad and the Beautiful." As Tony Bennett's longtime friend and vocal coach, the late Tony Tamburello, once said, this David Raksin movie theme is a helluva baptism of fire for any piano player. Not only was Evans playing it more outwardly than might be expected, the mere fact of it opening the album raised many eyebrows. Which is precisely what Bennett and Evans intended.

"I've learned a lot of ways to keep the public's interest," Bennett explained. "One of them is to do the unexpected, so they don't know what's going to happen, or when. When I did the album with Bill Evans, the first thing I had him do was play 'The Bad and the Beautiful' as the opening track, before I started singing. It was just unexpected. You're mentally prepared to listen to a Tony Bennett record, and all of a sudden you hear just the piano for the first tune."

Evans herewith steps up to the plate first to show us all every little thing that the solo piano is capable of. On his early solo sessions, Evans sounds almost frighteningly alone; the bass and drums are very conspicuous by their absence. It's almost as if he wants the listener to think about the trio when he's playing solo. Not here, however. With Bennett, and on the second album in particular, he plays much more outwardly, and more orchestrally, taking his solo instrument and making it completely surround the listener.

It also surrounds Bennett, without overwhelming him, on "Lucky to Be Me" especially, but also the remaining eight tracks. Bennett's voice brings a whole other texture to the proceedings. Bennett had long since established his bona fides as far as swinging was concerned (listen to his *The Beat of My Heart* album if you have any doubt of that), and he finds no need to "jazz" up these performances. Bennett approaches the material on both albums with the confident air of the jazz artist who knows he has nothing to prove. The routines are neither overtly fast and swingy nor slow and dramatically draggy, but somewhere right down the middle (although they're also not, in one of Louis Armstrong's favorite expressions, "half-fast"). Even the verses that precede many of the tunes have lots of rhythmic feeling. "Lucky to Be Me" sets the mood by establishing a swing feeling that doesn't necessitate a fast tempo.

Both this and "Make Someone Happy" give Bennett and Evans the opportunity to examine the melancholy underside of two traditionally peppy show tunes. Evans doubles the time on his improvisation on the former, and Bennett's outchorus is one of many trademark examples of the singer's mastery of dynamics; he knows exactly when and how to gradually turn up the volume on the climactic "Build your world around her" and he can take a nondescript phrase like "stuff of life" and invest it with so much feeling you know exactly what lyricists Betty Comden and Adolph Green were thinking. He does the same with all of Alec Wilder's somewhat cryptic lyric to "A Child Is Born," turning the abstract into the concrete. Dynamics are even more crucial here, since the lyrics don't say much. He increases the impact of the last word ("born") by whispering it at the end of the first chorus, belting it on the second.

The "bonus" track (about which, more later) "Who Can I Turn To?" and the effectively simple "You're Nearer" (the oldest tune here, from the 1940 film version of *Too Many Girls*) are the only other show tunes. "You're Nearer" has Bennett returning after the main vocal only for a single concluding line (rather than a whole chorus or even eight bars). Two further back-to-back selections, "A Child Is Born" and "The Two Lonely People," come from jazz sources, the latter by Evans himself. Though Evans first recorded this piece on the 1971 *Bill Evans Album* on Columbia, the Bennett album represents the only time he performed it with the sumptuous lyric written by Carol Hall, who later made it on Broadway with a somewhat more commercial venture titled *The Best Little Whorehouse in Texas*. Conversely, Bennett is the more withdrawn partner here, ending his first chorus almost passively, signifying that the story isn't over, that there's more to be said.

All the remaining songs are, perhaps coincidentally, from films, although not movie musicals. Long associated with Billie Holiday, "You Don't Know What Love Is" had been written for Carol Bruce in the Abbott & Costello comedy *Keep 'Em Flying*. Here too, Bennett's tone is deliberately ambiguous, as if to say, Not only do *you* not know what love is, but *I* wouldn't care to hazard a guess as to what it is either. His voice goes way up near falsetto range on "the thought of reminiscing," in the bridge, and he shoots skyward for a big note at the end, not coming down for a landing until sometime afterward.

"Maybe September" and "Lonely Girl" are movie themes with lyrics by filmland's Jay Livingston and Ray Evans. They had already won three Oscars with their own words and music, but in the 1960s they did some very successful work as lyricists for various composers, such as Henry Mancini's "Dear Heart." Both of these are very beautiful songs from very trashy movies, and both are tunes by two famous arranger-bandleaders in widely varying genres, respectively, easy-listening mogul Percy Faith and jazz giant Neal Hefti. Bennett had introduced "Maybe September," both on his classic 1965 LP *The Movie Song Album* and in his only film appearance, *The Oscar*. Here, he positively soars on "little boy *lost*" and still keeps the conversational flow of the line moving. Evans then takes a very full and moving thirty-two-bar chorus, before Bennett returns with a special coda not included in the basic chorus, which begins with the words "A taller tree . . ." "Lonely Girl" (from *Harlow*) is a rare lyric written in the second person—"Lonely girl / In all your silks and satins . . . love has never known you"; the lonely girl clearly is both philosophically and grammatically, a descendant of Duke Ellington and Mitchell Parish's "Sophisticated Lady."

The concluding "You Must Believe in Spring" (yes, also from a movie, the 1967 French flick *Les Demoiselles de Rochefort*, in which it was known as "Chanson de Maxence") is a song that's unnecessarily complex and tuneless in the wrong hands, but intricately magnificent in the right ones. So far, Bennett-Evans and, more recently, Freddy Cole have waxed the definitive interpretations. Our twin protagonists have found a way to take a subtle collection and end it in a fashion that's subtler still, an ending that's downright stealth.

That was all that was believed to exist from the Bennett-Evans sessions, until in the mid-1990s, when a random package from Holland, a three-CD set on the Disky label, titled *As Time Goes By*, happened to contain—apparently by accident—a hitherto unheard version of "Who Can I Turn To?" by Tony Bennett and Bill Evans.

Bennett already had a long history with the song, and was, in fact, part of its history. *The Roar of the Greasepaint—The Smell of the Crowd*, with book, music, and lyrics by Leslie Bricusse and Anthony Newley (and starring the latter), was a British production that never made it to London. Even though their previous effort, *Stop the*

World—I Want to Get Off, had been a hit both in the U.K. and the U.S., *Greasepaint* was relegated to playing the provinces.

Then, a curious thing happened: Tony Bennett recorded the show's big ballad, "Who Can I Turn To?" The singer not only put the song on the charts, but he created a demand for the show itself. Even though *Greasepaint* had never made it to London, thanks largely to Bennett it went straight to Broadway, where it ran a respectable 231 performances. Tony's 1964 record of "Who Can I Turn To?," with its famous opening oboe obbligato and descending swoop of strings, led to an album with the same title and quickly became a Bennett signature.

Eventually, other previously unknown tracks emerged. Most notably, a second complete and brand-new track, an excellent reading of Cole Porter's "Dream Dancing," turned up. Then there was an alternate take of "Young and Foolish," from the 1975 album, which was so different it might as well have been a whole new song. In this respect, the Bennett-Evans sessions further strengthened their parallels to Nat King Cole's *After Midnight* and the Sinatra-Jobim collaborations; in both of those cases as well, valuable extra material turned up many years after the fact.

Those September 1976 sessions hardly represented the end of Bennett's association with Evans. Two months later, they worked a duo concert together at the Smithsonian Institution in Washington. A highly capable visual artist, Bennett drew a sketch of Evans that was included by Fantasy on the back cover of the original *Tony Bennett / Bill Evans Album,* and later made the front cover of *Blue in Green,* a 1991 release of a 1974 concert. In 1998, when

Tony was working on an album of children's songs, I played him Evans's composition "Children's Play Song" (from his 1969 album *Left and Right*). With the help of Alan and Marilyn Bergman (lyricists on "You Must Believe in Spring" and a zillion other classic songs), "Children's Play Song" became the title track of Bennett's album *The Playground.*

Bill Evans died at the age of fifty-one in September 1980. Shortly before, Evans talked to Bennett for the last time that summer. The singer was playing a small town in Texas when the phone rang in his hotel room and it was Evans. Tony was amazed that Evans had taken the time to get his itinerary and track him down to this obscure locale. Obviously, Evans had something to tell him, and it couldn't wait until they were both home in New York. As he talked, it became clear to Bennett that Evans knew he wasn't long for this world, that the drug addiction that had ravaged his life for so many years was about to claim him permanently. He said, "I wanted to tell you one thing: just think truth and beauty. Forget about everything else. Just concentrate on truth and beauty, that's all."

To this day, Tony remains especially proud of the two Evans albums, often citing them as the most satisfying projects of his long career. "If you can get to a pure, simple thing, it always, it lasts forever. The best records that Nat Cole ever made were with his trio, and the best records I ever made are the duos with Ralph Sharon and Bill Evans. We just went in there at two-thirty in the morning and went to work. Just piano and voice, that's all we needed. You wouldn't believe how many well-educated people come over to me and say, 'Oh my God, the album you made with Bill Evans!' That's the most prestigious thing I ever did."

5

Ray Charles

Modern Sounds in Country and Western Music

(1962)

The most amazing thing about *Modern Sounds in Country and Western Music* is that it actually surprised people when it was first released in 1962. In hindsight, all the various facets of this breakthrough album make perfect sense—Ray Charles's lifelong love of (and early professional experience with) country music, the christening of his new full-scale touring orchestra, the contractual relationship with ABC-Paramount Records, and his overwhelming acceptance from the Nashville community—but at the time it seemed shocking.

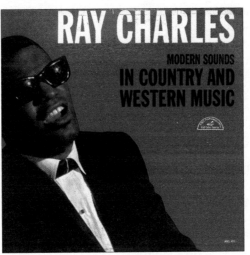

For some so-called sophisticated urbanites, country music was something akin to the way Gene Wilder describes the people of the town of Rock Ridge in *Blazing Saddles:* "These are just simple farmers. These are people of the land. The common clay of the new West. You know . . . morons." That, at least, is how denizens of both the East and the West Coasts thought of country and western—music for morons. Some fans of Dave Brubeck, Frank Sinatra, or *My Fair Lady* could pardon rock 'n' roll, because it wasn't making claims to anything other than being music for kids, and the folk music boom at least had some kind of social relevance (even if it wasn't particularly challenging intellectually or lyrically), but grown-ups listening to Conway Twitty? There's a famous story about Charlie Parker listening to country music and loving it (telling his friends to "listen to the stories"), which was long held up as an example of the jazz giant's perversity.

It's believed that about 300 million years ago, there was only one land mass on the earth—a "supercontinent" now referred to as "Pangaea," from a Greek word meaning "entire." Over the course of the millennia, Pangaea gradually broke off into Africa, South America, Eurasia, North America, etc. *Modern Sounds in Country and Western Music* exemplifies one of the great Pangaea moments in American musical culture. If American music is a series of subgenres—jazz, blues, country, Broadway—then there are moments when the various strands multiply and separate, like a paramecium, and other instances when they come back together, merge, and re-form. Throughout the 1920s, jazz musicians both black and white would play on blues and country record dates; no one considered it especially shocking to see a big band like Paul Whiteman or George Olsen onstage in a Broadway show. (Try imagining that in 1960.) In 1930, the two crucial founding fathers of two of the major strains in American music, jazz (Louis Armstrong) and country (Jimmie Rodgers), collaborated on a classic recording session. In 1930, it didn't surprise anyone, but thirty years later, many scholars refused to believe it had actually happened.

The 1950s were an era of Pangaea as well: the music of Elvis Presley was equal parts R&B, C&W,

and "mainstream" pop, which were all the strands that went into what was thereafter called rock 'n' roll. Ray Charles's career was also all about the aligning of continents: in the 1930s, Thomas A. Dorsey created modern gospel music by bringing the messages of the traditional African American spirituals to the musical form of the blues; in the 1950s and '60s, Ray Charles created soul music by reinfusing R&B with the spiritual energy (and specific musical forms) of gospel. In reinfusing the two forms—which were already closely inter-twined—Charles created something entirely new: a point that was driven home by the reaction of a great many conservative churchgoers at the time, who acted as if Brother Ray had scandalized their name by singing "baby" instead of "Jesus."

Yet the concept of Pangaea means different things in different generations: for the last forty years, music industry writers have employed terms like "crossover" and tried to retrofit them to earlier decades. I can't imagine Charles himself ever once used the term "crossover" in his entire life, even though he consciously crafted ways to weave these various strands of American music together. By 1970, artists like Sinatra and Ella Fitzgerald were try-ing to reach the young generation by singing with a go-go beat and donning bell bottoms. A decade earlier, however, the crossover was extending in the opposite direction: Ray Charles and Bobby Darin, to name just two major hitmakers of 1959–60 (between "Mack the Knife" and "Georgia on My Mind"), who already had the youth market in their pocket, were trying to catch the greater rewards that they perceived as coming from appealing to parents of the kids who were then buying their singles. This was an era when even Berry Gordy of Motown Records ("Young America's Favorite"), the man who was probably responsible for more hit singles than any other industry figure, had set his professional sights on the goal of bringing an act to the Copacabana—not Woodstock.

Thus Ray Charles's efforts at the turn of the 1960s, as he entered into a new contract with ABC-Paramount Records, were driven by the idea of catching the ear of the older generation: he began to concentrate on the album format, while the still-lucrative singles market became, increasingly,

an afterthought. And as far as content for those albums went, Charles relied for a few years on the Great American Songbook, content that was also designed to appeal to listeners of the singer's own age (he was born in 1930). And then, in a move that seemed amazingly both forward and retro at the same time, he expanded his touring ensemble from eight pieces to a full-sized big band—it was now Ray Charles and His Orchestra, as if it were 1941 (and he were Earl Hines or Lionel Hampton) rather than 1961. There had always been a jazz element to his work—Charles's 1950s and '60s saxophone sec-tions were widely praised for employing two of the best players on alto and tenor, respectively, in Hank Crawford and David "Fathead" Newman—and now he emphasized the jazz component more than ever, especially when he began playing jazz festivals.

Overall, the gambit worked—Ray Charles was perhaps the first artist from the R&B (or even rock 'n' roll) sphere, even more than Louis Jordan, to be taken seriously by the mainstream establish-ment. Even Sinatra himself famously declared Ray Charles to be "the one true genius we have"—it's impossible to imagine Sinatra saying that about Louis Jordan, Charles Brown, Stevie Wonder, or James Brown.

The use of standard songs and big bands was perceived by the mainstream establishment as an attempt by Charles to grow more "sophisticated." (In truth, Charles's R&B concoctions were remark-ably profound—in terms of tempo, harmony, orchestration, on a level comparable to the best of Sinatra and his number-one collaborator, Nelson Riddle.) What then confounded those mainstream supporters of Charles was his decision to go in what they then perceived as the opposite direction: instead of getting more sophisticated, Charles was now making an album of country music, which some saw as the very antithesis of coastal erudition.

Among those who felt that way, apparently, were the executives at ABC-Paramount. In the bio-graphical film *Ray*, released several months after Charles's death in June 2004, there's a scene where Charles (played by actor-comic Jamie Foxx) is shown signing his initial contract with the corpo-ration, and said executives are telling him, "Frank Sinatra doesn't have a contract like this." In November 1959, that was indeed correct: Charles was able to insist upon having total artistic freedom and ownership of his masters. According to Daniel Cooper, in his excellent notes to the 1998 four-CD package, *Ray Charles: The Complete Country & Western Recordings, 1959–1986*, the C&W suggestion was partly a means for Charles to test the faith of his "partners" at ABC. Would the label be willing to truly stand behind Ray, no matter what he came up with? Apparently, the C&W idea was so far out that Charles figured that if they stood for this, they'd stand for anything—and that they truly meant what they said.

Yet Charles had grown up in the original Pangaea era—when he was a struggling young blind pianist in Georgia and Florida, the main factors separating the blues from country music were racial and political rather than musical. He grew up listening to *Grand Ole Opry* on the radio and loving it, and in his teens one of his first professional gigs was with a local country band called the Florida Playboys. Ironically, it was his blindness that facilitated the engagement. At that point in our cultural development it was assumed that certain women were willing to throw themselves at capable musicians and singers, even if it meant crossing the color line to do so (which, owing to segregation laws in most states, was technically illegal). A black man—a performer especially—merely had to look at a white woman to risk a lynch mob, but, as Charles later wrote, "Since I couldn't see, and they saw that I couldn't see, I wasn't much of a threat."

Charles recorded a country song for the first time in June 1959: "I'm Movin' On" by the Canadian cowboy Hank Snow. Where Snow's lyric mentions "a big eight-wheeler rollin' down the track," the two-four rhythm of the piece suggests that he's moving on by means of stagecoach or some other horse-drawn conveyance. Charles's more aggressively swinging version has much more of a locomotive feeling, including the horns imitating a train whistle and the Raelettes chanting behind him in what suggests a train rhythm. As Charles reimagines it, it's more or less a follow-up to his most recent mega-hit, "What'd I Say," with the genius squealing and yelping over the band and

the backup group in much the same way. And it's also an ingenious prequel to Charles's C&W series, a bonus track for an album that wouldn't be recorded for another two and a half years.

Ray Charles was indeed moving on. That June 1959 date would be his last for Atlantic Records; he next entered a studio in November of that year on behalf of ABC-Paramount. The relationship was sainted from the beginning, with Charles landing hit after hit in both the album and 45 rpm single formats. The biggest of these was a thirty-year-old standard by Hoagy Carmichael, "Georgia on My Mind," which justified his faith in adding the traditional American Songbook to his arsenal; all four of his albums from 1960 to 1961 were built around standards and jazz, *The Genius Hits the Road, Dedicated to You, Ray Charles and Betty Carter*, and *Genius + Soul = Jazz*.

As far as everyone could see, he was increasingly headed toward more and more jazz and standards. The country and western project represented an abrupt and unforeseen change in direction. At this point, Sid Feller, who was already serving as Charles's unofficial co-producer and musical co-director, got involved. He started gathering country songs from over a period that went back roughly twenty years, back when the genre was known variously as western swing or just plain "hillbilly" music. "I called all of the country and western music publishers, most of which were in Nashville at the time," Feller told Cooper, "and they sent me hundreds and hundreds of songs, and I went through every one of them until I found about 40 that were really good music. I put 'em on one big tape, and I sent it to Ray in California."

Charles whittled it down to twelve selections, which he recorded over three or four sessions in early February 1962. Prior to 1962, Charles had already done two of the best albums ever of big band jazz, *The Genius of Ray Charles* and *Genius + Soul = Jazz*, the first done with an all-star studio band conducted by Quincy Jones, the second with what was essentially Count Basie's orchestra. The first date of this project, February 5, was also the studio debut of the new Charles touring band: four trumpets, four trombones, five saxophones, and a four-piece rhythm section, including the leader/star on piano, and arrangements by Gerald Wilson and Gil Fuller, two big band veterans with considerable jazz pedigrees. The first tune on that first date—also the opener of the album—wasn't "One O'Clock Jump," "Take the A-Train," "Flying Home," or "Sing, Sing, Sing" but "Bye Bye Love," a 1957 hit by the Everly Brothers.

"Bye Bye Love" is the sole song on *Modern Sounds* that originated with a pair of artists that were significantly younger than Charles, and who were as much a part of the world of rock 'n' roll as they were of country. The 1957 single has elements of rock and rockabilly (country-tinged rock, or the other way around) and the burgeoning folk music—the sound of a high-voice male duo that would soon be heard in a million coffeehouses. But the major difference is that in 1957, Don and Phil Everly were twenty and eighteen years old, respectively, and they were singing for a teenage audience. (The Everlys had already recorded a much more youth-y, folkabilly treatment of "This Little Girl of Mine," one of Charles's earliest hits.)

"Bye Bye Love" was both the first tune recorded on the *Modern Sounds* sessions and the opening number on the album. Following a ferocious yelp by the leader-star, the Gerald Wilson arrangement of "Bye Bye Love" treatment opens with the Raelettes singing the opening section of the song; Wilson and Charles have essentially changed the entire complexion of the piece: from two little white boys singing for other teens to four grown-up black women. The treatment is jazzier, blacker, and decidedly more adult—you're thinking about anything but a twenty-year-old and his kid brother. By starting with the Raelettes, Wilson is heightening tension for the star's entrance, and he comes in at the second section—what in the jazz world would be called the bridge, although that's not really the proper name for such a section in an ABAB construction. There's a driving piano solo and a brass interlude before Charles returns with the second "bridge"; it ends with Charles musing ("Well! What you say?") over the Raelettes chanting "I think I'm gonna die" over and over, like a mantra.

Charles and Feller set up the sessions and the resulting album symmetrically: two sessions with the big band, the first arranged and conducted by Wilson and the second by Gil Fuller. The third date was a string orchestra, presumably not involving any members of Charles's touring group, under the direction of Marty Paich (who had already done notable string arrangements for Mel Tormé, Sammy Davis, Gloria Lynn, and others). In the final album, there were six tracks with the big band, three by Wilson and three by Fuller, in addition to six ballads with strings. There were two leftovers, "Move It on Over," by Fuller, which was issued a few months later as part of *Modern Sounds Volume Two*, and "Just a Little Lovin'" as arranged by Wilson, as opposed to the version on the album arranged by Feller. (Wilson's version appeared forty years later on a Dunhill CD titled *Ray Charles Greatest Country & Western Hits*, but according to the Tom Lord *Jazz Discography*, it's not anywhere in Rhino's *Complete Country & Western Recordings* box.)

Wilson's other two orchestrations on the first album are "Careless Love" and "Hey, Good Lookin'." The first sets the folk song to a distinctly funky two-beat—one can easily imagine dancers in Memphis or Detroit shuffling back and forth first on the right, then the left. Although numerous versions of this traditional piece were adapted and copyrighted by various composers, most famously W. C. Handy, this treatment features "Ray's own original lyrics," which thus entitled him to copyright it. Then, when "Careless Love" went on the B-side of the blockbuster hit "I Can't Stop Loving You," it's fair to assume that Charles made more money from this track than anything else on the album.

"Hey, Good Lookin'," which concludes the original album, is one of only two Hank Williams songs on *Modern Sounds Volume One*. This time Wilson heightens suspense by delaying the entire band's entrance for ten seconds while we hear drummer Bruno Carr lay down the beats—ten whole seconds, mind you. Which sets us up for a rather perfect transformation of a two-beat hillbilly song into a smooth groove 4/4 big band swing number in the manner of Wilson's once and future employer, Count Basie. "Hey, Good Lookin'" is a romper and a stomper (in symmetrical contrast to the other Williams song, "You Win Again," one of the cowboy poet's most touching ballads) that charges ahead, also with an exceptional solo by the leader.

Of Gil Fuller's charts, "Half as Much" was a hit for Hank Williams, but was actually written by an unrelated cowboy crooner-composer named Curley Williams. This is just about as close as the brass sections get to a ballad; it's got all the heartbreak of the iconic Hank Williams recording but set to a medium-slow, undeniably danceable 4/4 groove—a ballad à la Basie. "Half as Much" is emblematic of an early country/mainstream crossover, since it also was a number-one hit for Rosemary Clooney in 1951, and likewise, Floyd Tillman's "It Makes No Difference Now" speaks to a still earlier crossing over, as it was successfully recorded by Bing Crosby in 1940. Fuller's arrangement starts with a piano intro, and then Charles sings Tillman's melody mostly straightforwardly, with steady drumming and a repetitive, choreographic pattern from the saxophone sections.

"Just a Little Lovin'" is one of two numbers from the canon of the longest running of western music giants Eddy Arnold, though in terms of both the heights of passion and the depths of despair (on the other Arnold composition, "You Don't Know Me"), this very laid-back and even-tempered cowboy Como could scarcely compare with the exaggerated emotional approach of Ray Charles. The beat is bouncy here; you can imagine dudes in cowboy hats, string ties, and three-piece suits two-stepping to it at the Peppermint Lounge.

Which brings us to the six ballads. It's often been said—by myself among others—that Ray Charles was the undisputed master of nonverbal sounds. "What'd I Say" has nonsensical lyrics, similar to those devised by square-dance callers in such a way as to fill the beats, "See the girl with the red dress on / She can Birdland all night long." It's not exactly Cole Porter. But the most eloquent parts of the "text," as it were, are the carefully orchestrated grunts and moans and other nontextual sounds that he emits throughout—particularly when they're delivered back and forth with the Raelettes, at which point these guttural noises take on an erotic subtext. Yet the title of "What'd I Say"

is a question, and the answer is—well, the words as such don't say a hell of a lot, but the statement has remarkable force and power just the same and the meaning is crystal clear.

Charles's moaning and groaning is pure eloquence, somewhere in between Ella Fitzgerald scatting "How High the Moon" and her doing one of her great ballads, like "Summertime." Yet the slow love songs here all show that Charles was also a lyric interpreter to contend with Nat King Cole or Frank Sinatra. The first and the last of the six country ballads, all with string charts by Paich, are the most iconic: "You Don't Know Me" was written and introduced by Eddy Arnold, but immediately became one of the few country standards recorded well beyond the borders of Nashville, as when Carmen McRae taped a lovely version in 1956. Charles sings it with an authority that Eddy Arnold could scarcely imagine. (This is one of several songs from the album that Charles sang in a televised concert in Rio in 1963, where it proved highly effective even without strings.)

Charles and Sid Feller were drawn to the team of Floyd Tillman and Ted Daffan, who had worked together at the beginnings of their careers, although the four songs from them here were written long after they had gone their separate ways. They're all archetypically sad and direct country ballads: Tillman's original 1948 hit record of "I Love You So Much It Hurts" opens with a plaintive solo fiddle that sounds diametrically opposed to the very slick string section that commences Marty Paich's arrangements. As a singer, Tillman had his own quirks for pronouncing words and bending notes, although Charles is much further out in this area as well. Tillman's record has a classically country-esque piano solo—from the era before another Floyd (Cramer) redefined Nashville piano—of the kind that Charles himself might have played with the Florida Playboys back in the day. Even more than Tillman, however, Charles is adept at showing both the "love" and the "hurt" with his voice.

On most CD issues of the album, there are two Daffan songs with Marty Paich string orchestrations in a row, as "Born to Lose" goes directly into "Worried Mind"; however, on the original LP, the two songs had a changeover between them, as

"Born to Lose" was the last track on Side A and "Worried Mind" was the opener of Side B. In both Daffan songs, again, the directness of the lyrics seems in direct contrast to the grandiosity of the strings and choir, but Charles's voice and delivery insure that the meaning will be anything but obscure. Ted Daffan's original singles of "Born to Lose" and "Worried Mind" are both in a country-style two-beat dance tempo. As a singer, Daffan sounds so resigned to losing and worrying that he seems to feel it isn't even worth crying and moaning about it; he goes ahead and loses and worries without making hardly any kind of a fuss about it, almost completely matter-of-fact. Charles, conversely, goes through a much more gut-wrenching experience; for him, being born to lose or left with a worried mind as a parting gift from a departing lover is worth crying and moaning about.

"You Win Again" would seem a logical follow-up to "Born to Lose"—somebody wins, somebody loses. However, the one original country and western singer-songwriter whom he doesn't try to mess with is the great Hank Williams—who actually anticipated Ray Charles in terms of the creativity with which he used his voice, the moans and deliberately distorted pitches. Here, Charles doesn't try to out-moan the originator, now it's his turn to sound resigned and defeated, without putting up a struggle. Yet his comparatively laid-back vocal finds all sorts of colors that Williams doesn't suggest in the original—not necessarily better or worse, but different. In that way, Brother Ray is glorious even in defeat.

The last of the ballads on *Modern Sounds in Country and Western Music* is Don Gibson's "I Can't Stop Loving You." Sid Feller, who sequenced the album, later told Cohen that he more or less buried it as the eleventh track on the album, the last song before the closer, Hank Williams's exciting "Hey, Good Lookin'." More than any other tune on the first Ray Charles C&W album, Charles's "I Can't Stop Loving You" comes closest to Don Gibson's original: same medium-slow (yet still danceable) tempo, close harmony with voices behind. The major difference, as with every country song that Charles did—with the exception of those by Hank Williams—Charles just cuts a whole lot

deeper than the cowboy composers who wrote the songs to begin with. But then, Ray Charles also cut it a whole lot deeper when he sang songs by Harold Arlen, Johnny Mercer, or Hoagy Carmichael as well.

On the whole, there's no obvious reason why "I Can't Stop Loving You" should have been the breakout success from the album that it was—not to mention such a blockbuster hit. Like "Georgia on My Mind" from three years earlier, "I Can't Stop Loving You" was another hit ballad with strings that just somehow conquered the world. The song would be omnipresent in Charles's subsequent career, a hit that he included in more future concerts—with the Raelettes taking the place of the Caucasian choral group—than even "Georgia" or any of his breakthrough, classic R&B hits. Willie Nelson later said—very generously—that "with his recording of 'I Can't Stop Loving You,' Ray Charles did more for country music than any other artist."

The single was a juggernaut of a hit, and so was the album. Charles's very next project, in fact, was *Modern Sounds in Country and Western Music, Volume Two*, recorded and released well before 1962 was over, and very much cut from the same cloth. It eventually led to a boxed set containing nearly eighty tracks of country music released in 1998. The third album in the series, roughly, was *Country and Western Meets Rhythm and Blues* in 1965 (it was also released as *Together Again*). In the opinion of some, that would have been a better title for the first two country albums, from 1962. And yet it wasn't. One point that Cohen (in the notes to the *Complete Country and Western Recordings* package) raises is that neither the R&B stations nor the C&W deejays were keen to play the original *Modern Sounds in Country and Western Music* when it first came out—the R&B guys weren't into country music or enormous Caucasian choirs, and the country guys, Willie Nelson notwithstanding, were not initially crazy about an outsider coming along and "modernizing" songs that they felt were sufficiently modern enough to begin with.

The R&B and C&W stations were the gatekeepers of those traditions, working to keep the boundaries alive and meaningful rather than break them down, as Charles was doing. Eventually, both factions saw the light and realized how brilliant the music was. But from the perspective of the period, it seems clear that Charles wasn't aiming his music at the relatively small African American R&B market, or even the country audience. Instead, he was aiming for everybody else; by merging the two ampersand musics, R&B and C&W, and along the way throwing in techniques from big band jazz, gospel, and other genres, he came up with something that everybody had to love—if not the very first time they heard it, then very soon thereafter.

Generations who were raised on Charles's country music have justified their love: for the rest of the 1960s, there were even more traditional pop stars (like Frank Sinatra and Nancy Wilson) who sang "I Can't Stop Loving You" than country singers. Within a few years of Charles's death in 2004, Jazz at Lincoln Center mounted a three-way tribute to Charles with a trio of superstars in various fields, Wynton Marsalis, Willie Nelson, and Norah Jones, and the bulk of the repertoire from the concert came from Charles's first two country albums. In 2013, Madeleine Peyroux released a jazz/country hybrid album that started life as a homage to *Modern Sounds in Country and Western Music* and was eventually released as *The Blue Room.*

Musing over several decades of his country "explorations" close to the end of his career, Ray Charles said, "'Born to Lose' . . . man, that's the blues."

6
June Christy
Something Cool
(1955)

You notice her in a dimly lit corner. She wouldn't be sitting at the bar itself. No, her type never is. She's at a table, looking very proper—right down to her little white gloves—and at least a little out of place. That look is impeccable: her makeup is as it should be, the seams of her stockings are perfectly aligned, and she's a beautiful woman, if slightly past her prime, with blond hair, not a single strand of which is out of place, and blue eyes. You go up to her—after all, that's what both of you are here for—and ask her what she's having. There's a pause before the answer comes. "Something cool," she starts, not quite looking at you, not quite looking at the bartender, then repeats it: "I'd like to order something cool." You're intrigued, you let her keep going and you don't say anything. She starts with small talk ("It's so warm here in town / And the heat gets me down"). As she continues, it becomes increasingly apparent that she's not quite cognizant of exactly where she is and what she's doing. She seems determined not to admit, even to herself, what's actually happening here, that she's in some cheap joint allowing a strange man to buy her a drink. She pretends that she's met you before but can't remember your name—in fact, she's had so many she's lucky if she can remember her own goddamned name. Even in her more lucid intervals there's still a certain level of denial. ("I don't ordinarily drink with strangers / I most usually drink alone . . ."—yeah, right!) The more she drinks, the more she talks,

and the more extravagant her tales become—and the deeper she descends into delusion. She's full of excuses for points that you haven't even called her on: She wants you to know that she owns an expensive fur coat, but avers that she isn't wearing it because she's saving it "for the cold." She wants you to know that she doesn't smoke "as a rule" but is only accepting your offer of a cigarette because "it might be fun." It isn't long before she's rambling on about what a high-class dame she used to be: how her mansion had so many rooms she couldn't even count 'em; how rich and eligible bachelors would take a number and get on a waiting list for the privilege of escorting her to a fancy-dress ball (the line forms to the right, dear); how she used to spend her fall seasons in Paris. By now you're quite sure she's lost it, except perhaps when she starts talking about the man she used to love ("quite so handsome, quite so tall . . ."). Here, she sounds so honest and so thoroughly convinced of it herself that it's impossible not to believe her. It's a sobering thought, quite literally, and as she reflects on it, she gradually returns to the current time and place—with you, in this dingy little dive. Perhaps you'll go home with her right then and there; maybe you'll even be the next big event in her life. God knows, she's had plenty. But, chances are, you're just a guy who stopped to buy her something cool.

And . . . scene.

Fade out.

It sounds like a screenplay, right? But imagine putting all that detail, all those nuances, into a popular song—the kind of song that is normally thirty-two bars (sixteen lines) and deliberately vague. This one is approximately sixty bars long, and the form is roughly AABACDDEAA. What kind of songwriter (or even a playwright) would compose such a song? What kind of artist would not only sing it but make it the signature song of her entire career? Julie London's signature was "Cry Me a River," which was a downer, yes, but torchy and sultry, more defiant than vulnerable; Sinatra sang "One for My Baby," "Angel Eyes," or "Guess I'll Hang My Tears Out to Dry" at virtually every show, but was careful to balance such saloon songs with more upbeat and life-affirming fare, like "My Way" or "New York, New York." Who else would base their entire career on a complicated, highly nuanced ode about a barroom pickup and a delusional alcoholic staring into the abyss of despair?

There's nothing else in all of American popular music quite like "Something Cool"—it has more in common with theater and film than it does with the usual American Songbook. It's not quite noir, since there's no crime involved (except crimes of the heart, perhaps), and it reminds us of those tales of impaired and dysfunctional lovers as told by the era's greatest playwright, Tennessee Williams. The unnamed female protagonist of "Something Cool" is about as Blanche DuBois as you can get. (The songwriter, Billy Barnes, later wrote an affectionate homage and parody titled "A Tennessee Williams Note" in his 1962 *Billy Barnes Summer Revue*.)

The closest thing to a precedent for "Something Cool" is Billy Strayhorn's "Lush Life," and it's not a coincidence that the arranger and conductor Pete Rugolo orchestrated the most iconic recordings of both songs. Yet the narrative of "Something Cool" describes an altogether different kind of lush life. Somehow you feel the guy in "Lush Life" actually has the resources to spend "a week in Paris" to "ease the bite of it," whereas the faded demimondaine of "Something Cool" is merely delusional; she's lucky if she can get as far as New Jersey. "Something Cool" is a song that's entirely sui generis, a cool jazz "Soliloquy" rather like Billy Bigelow on bourbon-and-soda. And the album that it titled is one of the all-time greatest.

Something Cool, both as an album and as a song, was a breakthrough for June Christy (born Shirley Luster, 1925–1990). "Something Cool" was not her first claim to fame; that would be serving as the band canary with Stan Kenton's orchestra, which she did from 1945 until he temporarily disbanded in 1949 (and thereafter continued to reappear with Kenton occasionally as a guest star). Nor was it her first record as a solo artist; she had been making singles for Capitol Records (Kenton's label) since 1947. Nor was it her first chart hit—that would be "My Heart Belongs to Only You," a far more conventional Eisenhower-era anthem that made it to number 22 on the *Billboard* chart in 1953.

But "Something Cool" was the first song in which Christy—whose name was well known to big band and jazz fans for a decade by 1955—found her own unique persona. This was where she established an identity for herself as distinct from Kenton's band. With "Something Cool," Christy showed that she was a distinct musical entity unto herself. Up until this point, many in the music world regarded her as a road-company version of the original cool canary, Anita O'Day. Kenton had originally hired her as O'Day's successor in his band because of her overt sonic similarity to the older artist. (It was O'Day herself—in her own story—who brought Christy to Kenton's attention.) Both women (as well as Chris Connor, who sang with Kenton a few years after Christy left) had an impeccably dry sound; it was unique and free of vibrato, the vocal equivalent of what Paul Desmond and Miles Davis, for instance, were doing with the timbres of, respectively, the alto saxophone and the trumpet.

In much music, vibrato was taken as a sign of warmth and emotional involvement. It was Christy's task, however, to establish that she was a warm and emotional singer even without the crutch of vibrato, that she could connect with a song lyric and with an audience even without it. O'Day took great pride in functioning as a musician and turning her voice into an instrument (she also had a lyrically sensitive side, but she didn't crow about it); it was up to Christy, and to a lesser extent Connor, to use the sound that O'Day pioneered to a greater extent in service of the words and the narrative. O'Day built up her musicianship to the point where she, no less than Ella Fitzgerald, was capable of doing a full-length scat solo—a track that was a wordless improvisation from beginning to end ("Malagueña" and later "Four Brothers" and "Slaughter on Tenth Avenue," among others). Christy, conversely, went in the opposite direction, not only to employ that sound to amplify the inner meanings of classic texts by Porter or Hart, but to help create a more ambitious Great American Songbook, a songbook of new tunes (many written for her) that were longer, more lyrically profound, and more harmonically challenging. Christy could sing lieder-like works such as "Something Cool" and "Lonely House," but also such joyful, carefree fare as "I Want to Be Happy." *Something Cool* was the album—and the song—with which she opened the door to a whole new musical world.

It was, apparently, a stroke of random luck that she connected herself so directly with the term "cool," which was becoming a major buzzword in the popular side of the jazz world—the Miles Davis album *Birth of the Cool* would be released a few years later. When the *Something Cool* album was released, "cool" folk all over the nation made it a point to own a copy, as much for the title and the attitude it conveyed as for the remarkable music it contained.

"I don't know who called [the album] that," said musical director Pete Rugolo in an interview in the mid-1990s. "I guess they felt that would be an interesting title, to indicate that the album was on the cool side. In those days that was kind of a jazz word [as in] 'Everything's cool, baby!' I produced the Miles Davis *Birth of the Cool* sessions, but I didn't name those either. Talk about hip talk—that was the word in those days. If it was cool, it was good."

While Rugolo was Christy's preferred arranger and conductor, most of her recordings were produced by Lee Gillette (who had helped make Nat King Cole into a superstar) and then Bill Miller (no relation to the pianist of the same name). In all likelihood, the company A&R men had more to

do with picking songs for Christy's 45 rpm singles. The making of the *Something Cool* album in particular seems to have been guided almost entirely by Christy and Rugolo, with little interference from the production or marketing side of Capitol; in my interviews with Rugolo, he barely mentions Miller at all. (Without chart success like "My Heart Belongs to Only You," it's altogether unlikely that Capitol Records would have considered letting Christy make an album.)

As Rugolo noted, most of the songs on Christy's albums were found by the singer herself, by her husband, the tenor saxophonist and fellow former Kentonite Bob Cooper, and, to a degree, by Rugolo. "She had a lot of friends who wrote songs," said Rugolo, "and they were all after her, and they would give her these songs." Somehow, "Something Cool," words and music by Billy Barnes, wound up in her lap.

Barnes (1927–2012) was a Los Angeles–based songwriter who generally specialized in humorous, or at least ironic, material; his regular employment was writing witty musical bits for Danny Kaye and other stars to sing on TV variety shows. He was virtually the only composer in Hollywood at the time whose primary interest was theater, rather than film or television. And even then, unlike most theater-oriented composers of his generation, Barnes seems to have been exclusively interested in the revue format, as opposed to the book shows of the post–Rodgers and Hammerstein world. Following the success of Christy's *Something Cool*, Barnes wrote a series of fully mounted Broadway-style revues, most of which were produced in Los Angeles with the idea of making it to New York—and in two cases they actually did.

The most successful of these productions was the 1959 *Billy Barnes Revue* (featuring such future TV perennials as Bert Convy, Ken Berry, and Ann Guilbert), which opened Off-Broadway at the York Theatre, then moved onto Broadway proper. It played a total of 199 performances; considering the economics of the day and its modest budget, this qualified it as a success, particularly as Decca Records released an original cast album of the production. That score produced Barnes's only other notable individual "hit," namely "I Stayed Too

Long at the Fair." This was another song about an urbane worldly woman who was not quite as happy as she ought to be; Barbra Streisand popularized it in 1963, exactly ten years after June Christy and "Something Cool."

When you examine the session listing for August 14, 1953, "Something Cool" looks as if it was originally an afterthought for Christy and Rugolo. The rest of the date was all singles, intended for play on jukeboxes and AM radio, whereas "Something Cool" was not merely too long but too involved and complex for most of the music mediums of its day—it was still relatively rare for a pop or jazz artist to record something expressly for an LP at this point. The other songs on the date were breezy and unchallenging, easily digestible fare like "Whee Baby" and "Why Do You Have to Go Home?" A week or so later, Christy left on a tour of Europe with the Kenton organization.

Yet Capitol was already leading the charge toward the album format. As early as 1950, the label had produced Mel Tormé's ambitious song cycle *California Suite*, the first important jazz or pop vocal 12-inch LP. In 1953, it released two absolute breakthroughs of the long-playing medium (both 10-inchers), *Nat King Cole Sings for Two in Love* and Frank Sinatra's *Songs for Young Lovers*. "Something Cool" was obviously intended for that format.

Back from Europe in December 1953, Christy joined Rugolo at the studio (this was still two years before the construction of the landmark tower), and this time they laid down only two tracks, "Magazines" and "Midnight Sun." Both were new songs with the potential to make it as singles, but clearly "Midnight Sun" was something special—an imaginative, expansive melody written by arranger Sonny Burke for Lionel Hampton's vibraphone as well as his big band. Burke (1914–1980) was already a storied veteran of the music industry. His "Black Coffee" became a jazz-pop perennial thanks to Sarah Vaughan and, most famously, Peggy Lee, who made it the title of one of her greatest albums, and he then collaborated very successfully with Lee on the score to the Disney classic *Lady and the Tramp* (1955). In 1960, Frank Sinatra hired him as

his producer and all-around general factotum at Reprise Records, where he worked on nearly all of the Chairman's classic albums of the 1960s. Hampton introduced Burke's tune in 1947, and six years later (after the song had also been recorded instrumentally by Harry James, Les Brown, and others), Johnny Mercer happened to hear the Hampton version on his car radio and was inspired by the song's title to write a love lyric depicting an Arctic scene. Although Mercer was no longer actively involved in Capitol Records, that label was still where his heart lay, and, so far as I can tell, Christy, in December 1953, was the first to record the lyric, which would be officially published a few months later.

Christy made "Midnight Sun" into an instant jazz standard with the album that became *Something Cool*. In fact, the first two songs recorded for the project were a literal declaration of coolness: "Something Cool" and this snow-covered love song. Mercer's text, with its mixture of icecap imagery and erotic warmth, provides a perfect vehicle for Christy's stylistic expression. There are other stunning readings, such as those of Jo Stafford (*Jo + Jazz*) and Ella Fitzgerald (*Like Someone in Love, The Johnny Mercer Songbook*), two singers who, like Christy, present an intriguing mixture of heat and coolness. Still, to me at least, Christy's is the definitive treatment. When I feel like listening to "Midnight Sun," *Something Cool* is the album I reach for.

By the end of 1953, this future album was off to a roaring (and yet icy) start. Two songs were in the can, and then, on January 18 and 19, 1954, Christy and Rugolo recorded five more (as well as another single), which would provide the balance of the original album. The first tune from the two-day session would be "Lonely House," and it extended the mood that had already been established. This was still another "art" song, a moody, wordy piece that no one would ever dance to or sing along with in the car; Count Basie and Glenn Miller wouldn't have played it—though Stan Kenton might have. "Lonely House" derives from the score to *Street Scene* by Kurt Weill and Langston Hughes, a work that, like *Porgy and Bess* earlier and *Sweeney Todd* later, split the difference between Broadway musical and grand opera. The Christy-Rugolo treatment is at once grandly theatrical and sublimely hip: the chart is full of haunting dissonances that bring out the forlorn quality of the text. Like "Lush Life," it's a moody tone poem, and Christy's contralto perfectly captures the haunted mood. It's nothing like a Sinatra saloon song; rather, this is the kind of tune that gives you the creeps. Throughout, Rugolo interjects discordant brass that makes it sound like a nightmare montage sequence in a film noir like *Murder, My Sweet*—maybe this "Lonely House" is actually a psycho ward.

The next two songs from the January 18, 1954, session bring us back into more familiar realms of jazz and pop: "I Should Care" and "It Could Happen to You" are among the most-recorded standards in the literature of jazz and related vocals. Both are from the swing era, but Christy and Rugolo go well out of their way to insure the arrangements sound like anything but your typical World War II–era big band fare. "I Should Care" (Cahn, Weston, Stordahl) is somewhat moody and melancholy, with Christy's bittersweet vocals laced with string bass and flutes. The interpretation is inseparable from the arrangement, it's almost as if the orchestra is part of her voice, as if she's expressing the brass, reeds, and rhythm vocally. It's hard to tell where the singer ends and the orchestra begins—Rugolo's arrangement supports the words as much as the notes. "It Could Happen to You" (Burke, Van Heusen) is the first out-and-out swinger in the recording sequence. Christy's second chorus, following a Harry Edison–esque muted trumpet interlude (not sure who—Maynard Ferguson, Conrad Gozzo, or Shorty Rogers) is wonderfully playful.

"A Stranger Called the Blues," by Mel Tormé and his songwriting partner Bob Wells, is the third four-minute art-song epic on the original 10-inch LP. (Curiously, Tormé himself doesn't seem ever to have recorded it, though Sammy Davis Jr. later did in an album of Mel's songs.) "Stranger" is so ambitious that, like "Something Cool" and "Lonely House," it takes the whole extended length of the track for Christy to get through a single chorus. "A Stranger Called the Blues" is even more cinematic and noirish than "Lonely House"; as in both "Good

Morning Blues" and "Good Morning Heartache," the blues itself has anthropomorphized into the physical form of a human being, one that the first-person protagonist of the song can actually converse with.

"Stranger" sounds like lyrics to a main title theme of a film of a novel by Chandler or Hammett, except that in Hollywood at that period few of those themes actually had words (Mercer's famous lyric to "Laura" was written after the fact) and, until the 1950s at least, those themes tend to be more semiclassical than bluesy (more Miklós Rósza or Dimitri Tiomkin than Duke Ellington or Benny Carter). Christy's vocal is trailed throughout this track by a searingly shadowy alto saxophone obbligato by Bud Shank. The song's form is roughly ABAB, and as Christy moves into the first bridge, Rugolo interjects a brass fanfare reminiscent of "Blues in the Night" (the "My mama done tol' me" line). The lyrics on that bridge, or B section, spell out the word "blues" in the tradition of the older "M-o-t-h-e-r" and the later "L-o-v-e," as in "B is for the bitter tears I've tasted . . ." It's a very subtle lyric, probably by Wells (who was usually the lyricist of the team): the blues is personified as a human being, but the protagonist is speaking to the guy who done her wrong ("Thanks to you our love became / A stupid little game"). Yes, the mood is very much like an early 1950s tale of love, crime, and betrayal, but the song wouldn't work as a movie theme because it tells too much of a story in itself—the movie itself probably couldn't compete. Christy and Rugolo make it seem much more vivid than most actual film noirs.

Following all that bitterness and blues, "I'll Take Romance" is a welcome breath of optimism. It swings like crazy, but there are enough tempo changes to link it as much to Broadway and operetta as to the big band tradition. It's a song from Oscar Hammerstein's underappreciated Hollywood period, written with Ben Oakland as the title theme for a 1937 vehicle for opera soprano Grace Moore. Oakland was a prolific journeyman composer who wrote everything from semiclassics (like this 1937 waltz) to jive ("Beau Night in Hotchkiss Corners") and novelties ("L'il Abner")—not to mention jivey novelties ("The Java Jive"). "I'll Take

Romance" was written as a waltz, and that's how Christy starts: The first eight bars are in slow, tentative 3/4 time, with just guitar backing; then she unexpectedly launches into swing, and the time shifts from three to four. The brass comes in, and though it gets excitingly loud, it's never tacky. Christy and Rugolo repeat the pattern, the last bridge in a slow three, before switching back to a fast four. It's a truly brilliant arrangement, using the big band vocabulary to create a work that's much more than dance music.

And that was that—for the time being. "I'll Take Romance" was the final tune recorded for the original package. Between August 1953 and January 1954, *Something Cool* had evolved from an afterthought to June Christy's first full-fledged album—and one of the major success stories of the early days of the album medium.

Christy was out of the studio for most of 1954; that was the year she and Bob Cooper gave birth to their daughter, Shay. Just as momentous, one imagines, was the birth of what would ultimately be her greatest accomplishment, the *Something Cool* album, which Capitol released as a 10-inch LP (Capitol H-512) on August 2, 1954. Within two weeks, *Billboard* (August 14, 1954), the music industry bible, had chimed in with an overwhelmingly positive review: "The unique song stylings of June Christy have been delighting Kenton ork [orchestra] followers and other members of the hip set for many years. On this new release the thrush gets a chance to show off her special, rather cool singing style on this new, rather cool album. The title tune is a long story-ballad that will interest some, but she gets a chance to swing out with 'It Could Happen to You' and 'I Should Care.' The Pete Rugolo ork backs her in this collection of cuttings, and the ork supports her in modern fashion. Good wax, especially for jazz fans."

Something Cool surprised everyone by turning into something nobody anticipated that it ever could be—a bona fide hit. Said Rugolo, "It sold, and Capitol realized who she was and what." At that time, singles were the bread and butter of the pop music field, for bands as well as singers—Duke Ellington had done some experimenting with lon-

ger works, the classic Sinatra Capitol series had only just begun, and the Ella Fitzgerald songbook series on Verve (anticipated by an early experiment with Gershwin) was still in the future. Elsewhere, a few specialist jazz producers like Bob Weinstock and Norman Granz were recording long-track jam sessions.

Capitol could see the benefit of getting in on the ground floor of a new technology before the foundation was even laid; in contrast, Columbia Records, long the industry leader, was still poohpoohing the entire long-playing format. Mitch Miller, majordomo of the label's wildly successful pop division, told me (on many occasions) that back in 1953–54 it would have been a waste of time to think about making pop albums, since virtually no one owned a long-playing turntable at that point. Tony Bennett told me he was dying to make an album in 1953, but because of Mitch, he had to wait a while. When *Something Cool* broke through, it was a double surprise that such an esoteric, off-beat concept would catch on at all, let alone in the new medium. "It was the albums that did it for her," Rugolo pointed out. "*Something Cool* really did it."

By the end of 1954, it was apparent that the 12-inch LP was going to be the next big thing in the music business, and certain earlier albums—famously, *Nat King Cole Sings for Two in Love*—had to be expanded to fit into the longer format. Capitol was sure that *Something Cool* had "legs," as they used to say, and, in sessions in December 1954 and May 1955, Christy and Rugolo recorded an additional four tracks. In between those two sessions, in early May, Christy recorded her second album. This was *Duet*, a project that might be seen as taking her backward, since it was a reunion with longtime collaborator Stan Kenton. Nonetheless, Christy and Kenton were breaking new ground here, in that this was one of the first times a disc had been made of just voice and piano duets (the major predecessor was the original Ella Fitzgerald and Ellis Larkins Gershwin collection).

The last tune of the original seven for *Something Cool* was "I'll Take Romance" and the first tune cut in the December 1954 12-inch sessions was "Softly, As in a Morning Sunrise," both with lyrics by Oscar Hammerstein II. There was a long-standing tradition of swinging "Softly," starting with Artie Shaw's famous swing band treatment of 1938. Still, one suspects that Hammerstein wouldn't have been thrilled with either of these "serious" songs being revved up and utilized for jazz purposes. "Softly" came into its own in the high modern jazz era, and it was heard on dozens of 1950s albums, both vocal and instrumental. In that context, Christy's "Softly, As in a Morning Sunrise" is hardly radical. It retains much of Romberg's brooding minor key and bittersweet attitude, yet it's totally swinging at the same time. Her vocal here occupies the same sonic register as Artie Shaw's clarinet, which may have been a model for both singer and arranger. (Abbey Lincoln, on one of her seminal Riverside albums, *Abbey Is Blue* (1959), reprised two songs from *Something Cool,* "Lonely House" and "Softly, As in a Morning Sunrise," suggesting that Christy must have been an influence on her. Where Lincoln leaves in Hammerstein's original 1929 line "The passions that kill love / And let you fall to hell," Christy was apparently importuned by Capitol to change it to "Let you fall to earth.")

"This Time the Dream's on Me" is a Johnny Mercer–Harold Arlen song from the score of the 1941 film *Blues in the Night,* in which it was completely overshadowed by the boffo success of the title song. Jazz musicians (including Charlie Parker) kept it alive, but there aren't many vocal versions from before 1955—even Chet Baker played it rather than sang it. It's quite the zippiest tune on *Something Cool,* packing a lot of drive in a brief minute and a half. Rugolo speeds Christy along with piano block chords and staccato phrasing—which gives the piece even more of a feeling of movement. The use of a modulation upward makes the piece seem even more positive—so does a brief scat (three notes, really) before the final line.

"I'm Thrilled" obviously occupied a special place in Christy's heart. This is perhaps the only tune on *Something Cool* that isn't regarded as any kind of a standard, but it's a lovely song from the pinnacle of the swing era that Christy must have heard as a youngster and loved. Collaborators Sidney Lippman and Sylvia Dee were collectively responsible for a disproportionate share of

the novelty hits of the 1940s: "A You're Adorable," "Chickery Chick," "My Sugar Is So Refined," "Laroo, Laroo, Lilli Bolero," "The Pushcart Serenade," and other songs that historians often cite when they want to list goofy novelties. Their two most notable "serious" songs are "I'm Thrilled," which in 1941 was recorded by Ella Fitzgerald, Glenn Miller, and Claude Thornhill (all of whom would have been heard by Christy and Rugolo), and the Nat King Cole hit "Too Young." Christy had previously recorded "I'm Thrilled"—twice, actually—not for commercial release, but on semiprivate transcriptions, which were not sold to the public but distributed to radio stations. The 1955 "I'm Thrilled" is more of an event—Rugolo begins with a dramatic sting, and Christy then uses the first half of the bridge ("It's like the magic of springtime / When you enter the room") as an introduction. The 1955 performance is moving, but in this case I have to admit I prefer the smaller-scale 1949 reading done for Thesaurus transcriptions.

The last of the extended epics is "The Night We Called It a Day," written by singer-pianist Matt Dennis and lyricist Tom Adair for Tommy Dorsey's orchestra, introduced brilliantly by Jo Stafford with that band, but also associated with ex-Dorsey vocalist Frank Sinatra, who recorded it twice, memorably. The Christy-Rugolo version is dark and brooding, although the melancholy nature is offset by sheer musical beauty. In five minutes, there are only two choruses, and the second begins with sixteen bars without lyrics—but not entirely instrumental. Christy hums in harmony with the orchestra (and, again, Bud Shank) in what could be called a vocalese in the classical sense of the term. Even at the slow tempo, it feels so perfect that you would never guess it's almost twice as long as nearly every track on other vocal albums (most cuts on Peggy Lee Capitol albums are well under two and a half minutes).

The 12-inch *Something Cool* (Capitol T 516) was released almost a year to the day after the 10-inch, on August 1, 1955. By that time, *Duet* was already in the can; however, by the fall of 1955, *Something Cool* was selling so well that Capitol made the obvious move of green-lighting further albums by the Christy-Rugolo combination, starting with *The*

Misty Miss Christy, released in the summer of 1956. *Billboard* described *Misty* as "a good follow-up to her smash *Something Cool* package. Jocks will like it and the color photo portrait on the cover will add impetus." Next came *Fair and Warmer* (1957), about which *Billboard* said, similarly, "June Christy's previous album *Something Cool* was a smash. In a sunny mood, the thrush is equally appealing." *Something Cool* was indeed a smash. In October 1956, when *Downbeat* did a feature on Christy, the magazine estimated that *Something Cool,* presumably in both of its two formats, had sold a walloping 93,000 copies.

"*Something Cool* was a big hit for us," said Alan Livingston, then president of Capitol Records, "but that was the only thing that she did that really amounted to anything sales-wise." *Fair and Warmer* was followed by *Gone for the Day* (1957), *The Song Is June!* (1958), *June Christy Recalls Those Kenton Days* (1959), *Off Beat* (1960), all with Pete Rugolo; *June's Got Rhythm* (1957) and *Ballads for Night People* (1959) with Bob Cooper serving as musical director; and *The Cool School* (1959) with the Joe Castro Quartet.

Then, at the end of 1960, there came *Something Cool* again, this time in stereo. Like the LP itself at the dawn of the previous decade, and the compact disc a quarter century later, stereo was the technological McGuffin (to borrow a term from Alfred Hitchcock) that was helping the record companies move a lot of product. Many singers re-recorded their old hits in the new medium, singers like Nat Cole, Kay Starr, and Frank Sinatra (who had the added incentive of redoing them this time for his own label). In the case of *My Fair Lady* and most of the others, most fans agree that the original mono takes are superior—the voices are younger and more enthusiastic, and the material fresher than it would be a few years later. With *Something Cool,* this is not always the case. The title track is slower, almost a minute longer, but it's a deeper, more finely tuned "Something Cool" than the former Miss Luster could muster at the age of twenty-eight in 1953. (The phrasing is different in some spots, as when she describes her dress as being "very, very old.") At times, as on the new "Midnight Sun" and on the faster tunes, her voice at age thirty-

five sounds a little more weatherbeaten. Unlike the heroine of "Something Cool," Christy wasn't alone in the world—she had a family (a husband who stayed by her side through thick and thin, and a supportive daughter)—yet she had her own demons to battle. Tormé's "A Stranger Called the Blues" is far more harrowing in 1960 than in 1954, and Bud Shank's new alto obbligato is even sharper and more probing. In the case of the last track, "I'm Thrilled" (actually her fourth studio recording of this eternally thrilling lament), the 1960 version is preferable to the 1955.

In short, the 1960 *Something Cool* in stereo was not a half-assed remake but one that fully used all the resources—technical, orchestral, vocal, and personal—that were newly available. The tip-off was not only a special disclaimer ("All that has been added is the magic of stereo") on the back, but a new illustration: The original cover painting featured an ice-cold drink in the foreground with Christy smiling, head rested on chin and eyes closed, in the background, all rendered in cool monochromatic shades of greenish blue. The 1960 painting had Christy in full color, eyes wide open, polished fingernails, and the drink in the foreground now not only has a slice of citrus but a bright red cherry. Brother, can you spare a lime?

Apart from the mono and stereo recordings of the song "Something Cool," there are also two visual versions worth mentioning. In 1954, Christy appeared in a Universal Pictures two-reel short subject entitled *Miss Universe;* Tony Curtis was the host, and for the most part it was a poolside talent showcase for beauty pageant contestants—zaftig beauties parading about in vintage bathing suits—with special guests Rose Murphy and Christy, along with Pete Rugolo's orchestra. Christy sings "Something Cool" in what looks like a classy restaurant, and she looks beautiful, like one of her album covers come to life in vivid Technicolor. Yet Universal substantially altered both the mood and the impact of the piece: the song has been truncated from four minutes down to two, and in the process they cut out all the darker, deeper moments. Christy is smiling joyfully throughout the whole number, holding a cocktail and a cigarette as she gazes at a Hollywood hunk in a white dinner jacket. It's completely bereft of both irony and profundity, but indeed it's something to see.

In 1959, Christy appeared on Hugh Hefner's late-night TV series *Playboy's Penthouse,* on which Hefner entreats her to sing that song "which tells such a very unusual story." Hef at least trusted the intelligence of viewers in allowing Christy to sing the full four-minute song, which she does partly seated next to her pianist. She takes her time and gets the full value of the song; it's a more intimate performance, with no orchestra or even a rhythm section, just piano. She's in an alcoholic environment again—everyone is holding a martini glass, including the singer. It seems more like an illustration of the heroine's delusions rather than her downfall; everyone is immaculately dressed—the women are coiffed to the nines, the men have on razor-sharp tuxedos. We don't think for a minute that she's off her nut when she says she lived in a mansion or spends the fall in Paris. And, true, one misses the orchestration, but damn, it's moving. Christy makes it more touching and bittersweet precisely by not letting it get completely dark.

The stereo *Something Cool,* along with a few classic Sinatra, Peggy Lee, and Ella Fitzgerald albums, actually weathered the sea changes in the music industry in the 1960s and stayed in print for decades. Long into the twilight of the LP era, in the late 1970s and early 1980s, one could just walk into King Karol, for instance, near Times Square, and find it for $3.99, the way I did, about 1980. It worked in the album's favor that it had only eleven tracks; Capitol kept it in the catalogue at a budget price. In its various editions, the *Something Cool* LP had reportedly sold as many as a quarter of a million copies.

In 1981, the Japanese were the first to reissue the original mono *Something Cool* on vinyl (with the monochrome cover), and Japanese EMI issued it on compact disc not long after June Christy died at sixty-five in 1990. The original CD, subsequently issued in the United States, was perhaps the oddest issue of them all. For starters, it featured the 1953–55 mono material, but used the 1960 full color, stereo cover. The 1990 edition very generously provided thirteen additional songs not on the origi-nal album, but for some reason known only to the Japanese, the extra cuts were not placed at the end, where God meant bonus tracks to go. Instead, the CD producers took all twenty-four tracks that were produced over the six sessions and two years that it took to record the complete original album and presented the whole works in chronological order, thereby tossing Christy's carefully considered sequencing to the winds. Now the title track, "Something Cool," no longer even opened the album. Some of the thirteen bonus tracks are good (like the appealingly rhythmic "Kicks"), others, not so much—and none of them belonged in the middle of *Something Cool.*

In 2001, Capitol at last brought out what is likely to be the final edition of *Something Cool;* this contained both the 1953–55 mono and the 1960 stereo editions in full, and utilized the original blue green-ish, eyes closed cover painting. The only caveat with this latest and probably last "physical" version of the album is that, once again, the sequencing is off. Instead of the songs being in the order determined by Christy and company, now they're heard in recording sequence. This is far from a deal-breaker, it's still a great album (or pair of albums), no matter what the sequence, especially since "Something Cool" is still the lead-off track on both the mono and stereo halves of the disc. (Listeners who want to hear the tracks in the original order are encouraged to resequence the CD using iTunes or Apple Music.)

Although nearly all of Christy's subsequent albums, even the heart-wrenching *Interlude* of 1977, were terrific, *Something Cool* was the one that everybody remembered. The irony is that June Christy was always something more than cool. She was a poet in a nightclub, or, in pioneering jazz critic Martin Williams's memorable description of Billie Holiday, a great actress who never had an act. "Something Cool" is an amazing piece of musical acting: Christy uses the microphone like a subjective camera—Philip Marlowe in *The Lady in the Lake*—and makes the listener see the world through the eyes of her "character." The character herself is always completely believable, even as she slips over the thin boundary between reality and delusion. I'll drink to that.

7
Rosemary Clooney
Blue Rose
(1956)

Don't think of yourself as someone sing-ing with an orchestra," Billy Strayhorn instructed Rosemary Clooney. "Just pre-tend you're a girl getting ready for a date, an important date with someone you love, and you're really looking forward to it. And as you're brushing your hair, you hear Duke Ellington on the radio. Almost subcon-sciously, you start hum-ming along with the band, not thinking at all about what you're singing."

That was the direction that Clooney needed to make it work. Up until this point, she was convinced there was no way it was going to happen. Here she was, on her feet and work-ing, when she should have been taking it easy during the most trying part of a very difficult pregnancy, attempting to sing with an orchestra that wasn't

within three thousand miles of her—something that virtually no one had ever tried before.

But then, it was amazing that *Blue Rose* ever got made at all—physically, culturally, technologically, economically, and logistically. The most incredible thing about *Blue Rose* is the simple fact that its two principals, Rosemary Clooney and Duke Elling-ton, were in the same place—conceptually and professionally, though not geographically.

Supposedly, at one point Columbia Records was going to title the Clooney-Ellington album *Inter-continental*. Much of the backstory of how the album was conceived and produced is tied up in

the greater concept of travel, both literally, from one coast to another, and metaphorically. In 1956, both Rosemary Clooney and Duke Ellington were in a state of transition; in fact, both were undertak-ing a parallel journey from pop music to art music. Ladies first.

Under the stewardship of producer Mitch Miller, Clooney had, for roughly half a decade, reigned as one of the supreme hitmakers at Columbia Records: begin-ning with "Come On-a My House" in 1951, she was constantly on the jukeboxes. She was most famous for a series of novelty songs that might be perceived today as somewhat demeaning—both to the singer herself, in that these songs were hardly Oscar Hammer-stein (even though some fairly respected theatri-cal types like William Saroyan and Bob Merrill were involved), and also in that they seemed to be ridiculing anyone who wasn't from a major North American city. "Come on-a My House" was derived from an Armenian folk song, but was delivered in mock Italian-American, as was "Mambo Italiano." "This Ole House" was a legitimate country song with a somewhat spiritual message, but by the time Mitch Miller and the gang got through with it, Clooney's hit single came off as a rather mean-spirited put-down of what was then still known as "hillbilly" music.

Clooney began making the transition to other kinds of music as early as 1953. That was the year she married actor José Ferrer; the first of their five kids arrived in 1955. Around that same time, Mr. and Mrs. Ferrer arrived at the idea of moving from New York to Hollywood. There were potential opportunities for both Ferrers in the movie capital: it seemed like a good bet Mr. Ferrer could make the transition from Broadway actor to Hollywood leading man, and that Mrs. Ferrer, with her outstanding looks, superlative singing, and vivacious personality, would follow in the high-heeled footsteps of Doris Day, from band canary to hit-making headliner to Hollywood heroine. The couple purchased a house in Los Angeles, which, coincidentally, had previously belonged to short-lived crooner Russ Columbo and was next door to lyricist Ira Gershwin.

Mr. Ferrer, who had already won a Best Actor Oscar for *Cyrano de Bergerac* (1950), continued to land high-profile movie roles, as in *Deep in My Heart* and *The Caine Mutiny* (both 1954), but Mrs. Ferrer's picture career never really got off the ground. Paramount Pictures quickly shoved her into five major musicals in the 1953–54 season, but only one of these releases, *White Christmas,* was regarded as anything like a success. Her film career was severely curtailed by her maternal responsibilities (five kids is a lot, even with nannies and nurses); in the mid-1950s, she would host her own variety show series (and make other TV guest appearances), but there were to be no more movies, and fewer and fewer hit records.

Even if the pictures no longer wanted her, Clooney chose to remain and bring up her brood in Los Angeles; it had become home to her, more than any place she had ever lived before, not Kentucky (where she was born), Ohio (where she grew up), or New York (where she became a star). "This ole house," as she called it, on Roxbury Drive, was where she lived with both of her husbands (the second was a former dancer named Dante DiPaolo) and all five of her children.

Rosemary was overwhelmingly devoted to her kids and the idea of family—they were more important to her than anything else, even music and singing—but her marriage to Ferrer was not a happy one. George Avakian, who ran the jazz and pop albums division at Columbia Records, was

well aware of what was going on. "I just thought she was the most delightful person. But her husband, José Ferrer, was a pretty abusive SOB. She had some pretty sad stories to tell."

On the positive side, Ferrer exerted an uplifting influence on his wife's professional career. As Clooney later related, at this point in her life, she felt sandwiched between two strong-willed men, Ferrer and Miller, who both knew what they wanted from her. Miller interpreted the couple's move to Los Angeles as Ferrer's attempt to extract the singer from his influence, and he began acting increasingly like a jealous ex-lover. The last straw came when Miller mouthed off to an interviewer that Clooney, without him, would never have any more hit records again. When she read the interview, she was furious. Miller denied that he had actually criticized her husband, and claimed that the reporter misquoted him, but Rosemary (as she later told me) was so upset that she called the journalist and had him play the interview tape for her.

But Mitch, for worse and for better, was right. One of the main aspects that Ferrer nurtured in his singing wife was a love of good music; he was a sophisticated connoisseur of the arts, with tastes that were substantially more highbrow than mambos Italiano. From the beginning, he was encouraging her to expand her horizons. He never tried to get her to sing Mimì in *La Bohème,* but he appreciated jazz and the better sort of popular song. A man of the theater, he was well acquainted with the best songs being written for Broadway—and there was something better out there, he insisted, than come on-a my ole house. Rosemary was also mindful of Tony Bennett, a virtual big brother to her, and how he was constantly fighting with Mitch Miller over material. And she saw how Frank Sinatra, who was one of her original inspirations, was bringing his already iconic career to even greater heights by recording entire albums of superior songs.

Partly by following her own instincts, she had already been successful with at least a couple of first-rate songs, namely "Tenderly" and "Hey There." Even by 1956, it was clear that Bennett and Sinatra were showing the way to a higher level of popular artistry than most of Miller's charges, like Johnnie Ray and Guy Mitchell (or, among women, the now forgotten Mindy Carson and Joan Weber). "I didn't want limits," she later wrote. "I wanted horizons."

At this time, Miller had little faith in the concept of the pop album. Still, the market was changing quickly in the wake of postwar prosperity, the economic boom, and the technological boom that went with it. Capitol Records took the lead as far as pop LPs were concerned, and the gamble paid off handsomely.

Yet even before 1955–56, Clooney had already participated in a few album projects: the upper management of Columbia Records was of the opinion that one of the major justifications for an album by a pop singer (as opposed to a symphony orchestra or a Broadway cast) was the team-up, and their favorite approach was to combine a star vocalist with a famous band or instrumentalist. Clooney's earliest sessions recorded directly for album release were done with Harry James's orchestra and heard on a package called *Hollywood's Best*. The next few years would also see Jo Stafford with jazz accordionist Art Van Damme, Frankie Laine with Buck Clayton, Tony Bennett with Count Basie.

With Ferrer's encouragement, Clooney, who had been nurtured by the swing band tradition, was increasingly eager to work in a jazz context. While playing in New Orleans in 1952, she recorded a session with a Dixieland group fronted by local trumpet hero George Girard. In 1955, she sang on three tracks with Benny Goodman—one of which, Cole Porter's "It's Bad for Me," was actually a duet with the clarinetist himself—which were released on a 10-inch LP titled *A Date with the King*. And at around the same time, she happened to hear an old voice that was new to her. Columbia reissued an album of classic, thirty-year-old recordings by the Empress of the Blues, Bessie Smith.

And that started her thinking.

Even as a number of forces were conspiring to edge Clooney away from ephemeral songs on 45 rpm singles and toward classy songs on full-length albums, Duke Ellington was undergoing a transition of his own. As with Frank Sinatra, the early 1950s are regarded as the maestro's most fallow period. He had temporarily lost two of his most significant voices, alto saxophone star Johnny Hodges and arranging and composing partner Billy Strayhorn. His contract with Columbia Records had expired, and though he did some interesting work for Capitol Records (including a solo piano album), on the whole Ellington seemed rather directionless. In retrospect, we can see that he was also making a gradual transition from pop music to art music, from dancing crowds in Harlem to concert audiences all over the world. Up through the war, he was thought of as an entertainer, a flamboyant bandleader with flashy suits and flowery speech, who had more in common with Cab Calloway (the two shared the same manager, and both came to fame in the old Cotton Club) than he did with Toscanini.

When Ellington "came back," he was regarded less in a purely pop vein and increasingly in a category all his own. He still played ballrooms and dances, but now the focus was increasingly on sit-down concerts and festivals; instead of devoting his energies to pop songs with lyrics, now he concentrated on the suites and other longer-form works—a move that was also encouraged, technologically, by the development of the long-playing album. (Ellington quickly realized that any album's worth of new and original compositions was, essentially, a suite.)

It makes perfect sense that the chief vehicle for this combination of "comeback" and transition was the 1956 Newport Jazz Festival. Jazz, as a whole, was slowly sticking its head up out of the smoky nightclubs where it had primarily existed up until then and being heard in more formal venues. Producers like Norman Granz (of Jazz at the Philharmonic) and George Wein (of the Newport Jazz Festival) and attractions like Ellington (who already had the composure and deportment of a concert artist), along with such newcomers as Dave Brubeck and the Modern Jazz Quartet, were leading the charge.

The market was essentially forcing jazz upstairs. Big bands were no longer the most commercial entities around, a fact of which Mitch Miller was well aware. As Avakian explains, Columbia had a policy of releasing only two singles a week and Miller, who was always hungry for hits, was reluctant to give one of those slots to an instrumental jazz artist. The two major jazz acts on the label who were most likely to benefit from a singles release were Ellington and pianist Erroll Garner, and they both wound up leaving Columbia over this issue. "They felt that they had to have singles," Avakian reports. "They couldn't believe that disc jockeys would actually play albums." Avakian adds, "Duke had the last laugh, because he left Columbia and went to Capitol Records, where the first thing he recorded was 'Satin Doll,' which was a big hit single for him."

Around this time, Clooney discovered Bessie Smith, thanks to a Columbia LP that Avakian had produced and compiled. "Rosemary had never really listened to Bessie Smith before, and she was just blown away," the producer reports. "Her first idea was to do a whole album of Bessie Smith–style blues. I had to tell her, 'Rosemary, I just don't think that's you.'"

But Rosemary's next idea turned out to be a winner. Listening to the Empress of the Blues interacting with musicians like Louis Armstrong, she began to consider the possibilities of doing a team-up with a major band. "She asked me if it might be possible to do an album with Duke Ellington, and I liked that." Avakian approved of the idea, but was pessimistic about Ellington agreeing. "He had never showed an interest in such a project before. I had once proposed an LP with Sarah Vaughan, which he shrugged off politely. [He said he was] 'Too busy.' . . . I asked Duke about it, and slightly to my surprise—Duke agreed. I think that he appreciated the purity of Rosie's voice."

Although *Blue Rose* seems like a natural from the vantage point of sixty years later, at the time it was hardly a done deal. Ellington was not, at this point, a Columbia contract artist (he was about to cut an album for Bethlehem Records), and Clooney was hardly thought of as a jazz singer. Ellington had never cut a full album with any vocalist, even those who were on his own payroll.

Even so, the biggest issue was logistics. Ellington was then playing Café Society in New York and Clooney was virtually bedridden in Los Angeles. According to Avakian, her second pregnancy was

especially difficult because it came so quickly after the first. It was decided to use overdubbing: to record the orchestral tracks with the big band in New York and add the vocals later in Columbia's Hollywood studio.

In retrospect, this makes absolutely no sense. Why was Columbia in such a hurry? Ellington was constantly on the road, and he was bound to be back on the West Coast sooner rather than later. Couldn't they have found a spot on the schedule when the band would be closer to California? While he did stick to the East Coast for most of early 1956, the orchestra would play Las Vegas in May and then San Francisco in June (before coming back east in July for what would prove to be a historic concert at Newport). Besides, Clooney's pregnancy was—obviously—not going to last forever. Rather than waiting, it seems as if they wanted to strike while the iron was hot, before somebody changed their mind. "Once we got talking about it, we kept saying, 'Well, Rosemary has a big family and who knows when Duke will go out there again, so let's just do it this way.'"

Supposedly, at one point Columbia gave the album a working title of *Intercontinental*, which would indicate they were attempting to utilize the overdubbing process as a selling point for consumers. Multitrack technology was a novelty then and not yet viewed as the enemy of spontaneity (and therefore of jazz). But plans changed. The corporation decided not to play up the overdubbing angle, and the LP packaging avoided all mention of it. (The cover, however, displayed separate and unconnected images of Clooney and Ellington, without even attempting to make it look as if they were in the same place at the same time.)

By now, Avakian was running Columbia's entire pop album division—and jazz and international music—and needed to delegate the production of specific albums to producers on his staff. Once the broader outlines were in place for the Clooney-Ellington project, he let his new staffer Irving Townsend take charge of the hands-on production. Townsend was a dedicated amateur clarinetist and a pro-level writer who had been recommended to Avakian by none other than Benny Goodman. *Blue Rose* would be his first assignment as producer.

Ellington, Avakian, Townsend, and Clooney were all in agreement on another point: that Billy Strayhorn should serve as musical director. Strayhorn was the other major composer and orchestrator who wrote for the Ellington orchestra more or less continually from 1939 to 1967. Among his many other gifts, he was an extremely sophisticated and sensitive orchestrator for vocalists, and his presence on *Blue Rose* was a further guarantee that it was going to be a special project. Strayhorn had arranged a lot of vocal tracks for the band since joining the organization in the 1940s, but the opportunity to take charge of Ellington's first collaboration with a major star vocalist was a challenge that was truly worthy of him.

It was decided to make the whole album an Ellington songbook, which was also unprecedented. However, Strayhorn was too canny to turn it into a set of "Rosemary Clooney Sings Duke Ellington's Greatest Hits" or something along those lines. That same year, Ella Fitzgerald launched her songbook series with the first session for *Ella Fitzgerald Sings the Cole Porter Songbook;* in September 1956, Fitzgerald would begin work on her *Duke Ellington Songbook.* The general idea throughout the Fitzgerald songbook series was to canonize the best-known songs by the most celebrated songwriters. Producer Norman Granz wasn't looking to dig up any neglected gems or obscure delights; it was only the most famous of the famous that he wanted.

Strayhorn, however, was doing precisely the opposite: he was only picking songs from the catalogue that he felt were uniquely suited to Clooney's sweet, deep vocal timbre. He included a few of Ellington's very best known songs: "Sophisticated Lady," "Mood Indigo," "It Don't Mean a Thing (If It Ain't Got That Swing)." Yet he left out a great many of the band's biggest breadwinners; there's no "Don't Get Around Much Anymore" or "I Didn't Know About You," among many others. In their place, he dusted off three lesser-known items from the Ellington-Strayhorn backlist: "Grievin'," "I'm Checkin' Out, Goom Bye" (both from 1939), and "If You Were in My Place" (1938)—all had been recorded once and pretty much forgotten since then. Clearly, he was considering the singer first and the songs second, rather than the other way around.

To that end, a few weeks before the orchestral sessions in New York, Strayhorn flew to Los Angeles to work on the charts with Clooney at her house on Roxbury Drive. Strayhorn was widely loved in the world of jazz and African American music for his warmth and his thoughtfulness; he tended to make long-lasting friendships, as he did with Lena Horne, and Clooney quickly grew close to him. Although the singer was suffering from what seemed like terminal morning sickness, she remembers the ten or so days Strayhorn spent at her house as one of the most enjoyable experiences of her career.

"In the early stages of it we would work at the piano, picking songs and going over cues. But some days, I was too sick to even come downstairs, so he would come up to my room and we'd just talk about the record. Or if I was too sick even to do that, he would just sit on the end of my bed and comfort me, or we'd watch TV together. We got to be very good friends way before the record was finished—once he even baked me a pie and brought it upstairs." Before long, Rosemary gave him the key to the house, and when she wasn't feeling well enough to leave her bedroom, he would let himself in through the back door and bring crackers (or anything else she felt capable of eating) upstairs to her.

Having finished the planning, Strayhorn returned east to complete the arrangements and supervise the recording of the orchestral tracks, which transpired in New York on January 23 and 27, 1956; Ellington himself played the piano. The band's star trumpeter Clark Terry later told Strayhorn biographer David Hajdu, "I didn't know what to expect, picking up a part for one more version of [the oft-performed] 'Sophisticated Lady.' Then I played it, and I told Strayhorn, 'That arrangement of "Sophisticated Lady" is really the most fantastic chart I have heard in a long time.'"

With the orchestral part now in the can, Strayhorn and Townsend rejetted to Hollywood to steer Clooney through the recording of her vocals on two sessions, on February 8 and 11. While all the charts are believed to be Strayhorn's work, Ellington did compose one new piece of music expressly for the album. This was "Blue Rose," the wordless tune for which Strayhorn's coaching proved so helpful. In addition to "Blue Rose," the partners also included "Passion Flower" on the album, which further illustrated their ongoing mutual fascination with floral subjects. This Strayhorn instrumental was already a famous feature for Johnny Hodges, who, like Strayhorn, had also returned to the band. Here, the saxophone giant "indulges himself," as Ellington would say, in earth-shattering glissandos as the orchestra behind him plays Prokofiev-like dissonances.

For all of Strayhorn's contributions, it's Ellington's own melody that carries the most resonance in the album. Clooney's superlative humming is supported by an especially rich set of Ducal harmonies, a chord progression that, as scholar Andrew Homzy has observed, anticipates the one John Coltrane would utilize in his jazz classic "Giant Steps." (Duke Ellington was the only major musician who would collaborate with both Rosemary Clooney and John Coltrane.) Ellington later tried out "Blue Rose" as an instrumental, an arrangement that wasn't released until long after his death. It should be noted that even without words, Clooney is a better storyteller than most singers who have the benefit of lyrics.

Strayhorn had a strong, distinctive personal style of writing for jazz orchestra, but he also served as a collaborator and even pinch-hitter for Ellington; when he wanted to, he could write so much like Ellington that only the bandsmen were aware who had written what. For the most part, the writing on *Blue Rose* (even Ellington's newly composed title song) is indistinguishable from Ellington's.

As Clark Terry noted, it's the Ellington perennial, "Sophisticated Lady," that sounds the most like pure Strayhorn. Lovingly rendered by Clooney, its elegiac harmonies and stately mood, particularly behind the last eight bars of the vocal, illustrate what fellow arranger Ralph Burns meant when he described Strayhorn (to David Hajdu) as "writing classical music for the Ellington Orchestra." Jimmy Hamilton's clarinet, though not necessarily strictly soloing, is the primary voice in the ensemble at several points, and Strayhorn cleverly brings out three of Hamilton's key sides: cool and semiclassical on "Sophisticated Lady," fiery and swinging on

"I'm Checkin' Out, Goom Bye," and knee-deep in the blues on tenor on "It Don't Mean a Thing."

Hamilton, Hodges, and Carney (on "Hey Baby" and "Grievin'") are the primary soloing reeds, although Paul Gonsalves also turns up briefly on "Grievin'." All four trumpets—mostly muted—also get into the act: Ray Nance on "Me and You" and "I'm Checkin' Out," Clark Terry on "It Don't Mean a Thing" (on which he alludes to "Azure Te") and "Just A-Sittin' and A-Rockin'," Willie Cook on "Mood Indigo" and "If You Were in My Place," and Cat Anderson on "Grievin'."

The album opens with "Hey Baby" in which Clooney sings the line "You're just the type to bring out my attributes and my good looks" so directly and personally that she might as well have been talking strictly to Strayhorn. It's to her credit, as well as the arranger's, that she's never overshadowed by any of these venerated veterans. The lyrics of Strayhorn and Ellington have also never received a better hearing, and she even intones some slightly obtuse samples of "Dukespeak" in a way that makes them perfectly clear, as in such cryptic slanguage as "Goom Bye" and "As long as there's three heavens above." (What in the world could that possibly mean?) It's hardly surprising that the singer on *Blue Rose* would resurface years later to begin a long history of jazz albums with small groups and major soloists.

In many ways, *Blue Rose* was a project driven by economics—the idea of teaming Clooney with Ellington to show the diversity of both artists, as well as to stir up a little excitement for Ellington's first new Columbia project. It also was the result of technology: not just in the overdubbing process, but, as we've seen, in the 12-inch LP format itself was still nothing to take for granted at Columbia in 1955 when the project was planned. Ellington, Strayhorn, and Clooney demonstrated an ambition beyond even the time limits of the 12-inch format by recording a total of thirteen tracks, two of which, "If You Were in My Place" and "Sittin' and A-Rockin'," didn't make it onto the original release. These were issued at the time on a 45 rpm EP and later turned up on a French LP issue, before they were at last included on a Sony Music Legacy CD edition in 1999.

Still, what makes *Blue Rose* great has nothing to do with either money or machinery. There is such a thing as an Ellington mood, rich with passion yet slightly muted emotionally, expressive but cool at the same time, and Clooney latches onto it no less perfectly than any of the soloists, some of whom, like Hodges and Carney, had already been with the Duke for more than twenty-five years. She captures the precisely perfect mood throughout: defiant but not melodramatic on "I'm Checkin' Out," grieving but hardly suicidal on "Grievin'" and "Just A-Sittin' and A-Rockin'," and jubilant but not hysterical on "Hey Baby" and "Me and You." She also displays a rare talent as she turns in earthily sensual non-verbal vocals on "Blue Rose" and the opening of "Mood Indigo."

As noted earlier, Strayhorn gave Clooney very specific philosophical guidance regarding the title song, "Blue Rose." There was one additional number for which Rosemary remembered Strayhorn's instructions. "When you sing 'I'm Checkin' Out, Goom Bye,' don't sing it angry. Just because you're leaving the other person, it doesn't mean you're mad. You're in charge." The tune was first recorded by Ellington in two very different treatments—and under two very different titles—in June 1939. First it was heard as "Barney Goin' Easy," in a medium-tempo, minor-key treatment, with composer credit going to Bigard. Then, four days later, the full Ellington band recorded it as "I'm Checkin' Out, Goom Bye," in an extravagantly swinging chart with lyrics sung by Ivie Anderson, Ellington's non-pareil band singer of the 1930s, and now credited to Ellington and Strayhorn. Clooney has an appropriately defiant and empowered attitude throughout this lyric (possibly Strayhorn's), although it's not known if "goom bye" was a short-lived slice of Harlem slang circa 1939 or just an invention of the songwriters. Clooney swings especially hard when the melody picks up speed in the bridge (the words are highly quotable: "I'm in the know / You got to go / The cake is all dough").

As Strayhorn told her, "You're leaving because you're the strong one—possibly you may even come back!" Where both the 1939 recordings feature Bigard, the 1956 treatment spotlights his suc-

cessor, the smooth and dynamic clarinetist Jimmy Hamilton.

Of all the older Ellington chestnuts in the album, there was perhaps the most life left in "Mood Indigo." Introduced in 1930, this was Ellington's first hit song with lyrics, the maestro's earliest composition to enjoy a long and healthy life as a popular standard. He—and everyone else—performed it frequently over the years, but in the 1950s "Indigo" was enjoying a new lease on life. Ellington made it the lead-off track on one of his first and most successful albums, the 1950 *Masterpieces by Ellington,* in a rather amazing fifteen-minute band arrangement that climaxed, almost literally, in an amazingly sensual vocal by one Yvonne Lanauze. In 1957, an even more erotically charged all-instrumental treatment took pride of place (even in the title) on the band's most romantic album, *Ellington Indigos.*

Strayhorn's arrangement is of that same caliber; it opens with a stark, dissonant piano intro, full of minor seconds, which in this context sound both musically and sexually kinky. The opening melody of the original arrangement of "Mood Indigo" was stated by a unique combination of muted trumpet, clarinet, and valve trombone; Strayhorn's variation is to have Clooney introduce the first melody wordlessly, humming in harmony with Hamilton's subtone clarinet. "Mooing" is perhaps a pejorative way to describe a singer, but Clooney is indeed "moo-ing" indigo. She doesn't start singing words until she gets to the second half of the song (which begins "Always get that mood indigo"). Even when she sings the lyrics, however, Clooney sounds as if she's holding back, phrasing tightly, more like a carefully controlled muted trumpet than a singer. Strayhorn follows her with an expressive muted trumpet solo by Willie Cook, and he, in turn, sounds more like a human voice than a horn. The trombones then take over, restating the melody on what's got to be the most languid, positively torpid unison trombone passage you've ever heard.

In 1938, Ellington collaborated on the score to the fourth edition of *The Cotton Club Parade,* with lyricist Henry Nemo, one of the more colorful characters of the swing era; their union resulted in two excellent songs, "I Let a Song Go Out of My Heart" and "If You Were in My Place (What Would You Do?)." Both were recorded by the Ellington orchestra as well as a Ducal small combo (under the titular leadership of Johnny Hodges) and, coincidentally, also by Mildred Bailey, a singer who had a deep influence on Clooney. Although both seemed equal at first, "I Let a Song" was instantly recognized as a classic, but "If You Were in My Place (What Would You Do?)" had more in common with "I'm Checkin' Out" in that after being introduced by Ivie Anderson, it too was rarely heard from again over the next two decades.

After a brief, tantalizing Ellington piano intro, Clooney jumps right in with the melody on "I Let a Song," as if a song were literally jumping out of her heart. She's not exactly "letting it go," it's more as if she can barely contain it. Strayhorn positions her against wah-wahing brass, and the horns collectively soar in the instrumental break. Both of the Ellington-Nemo songs are structured more in terms of a traditional singer-band relationship, the orchestra very much in the background—as opposed to "Mood Indigo," where Clooney sounds like an essential part of the band itself. The ABAB "If You Were in My Place" has Strayhorn taking the piano intro, and his touch is immediately distinctive from Ellington's. Clooney's vocal is reflective and introspective (offset by more lower-register reeds), as if she's pondering a conundrum internally—when she sings "you," she really means "me." In the sixteen-bar instrumental break, the reeds are more outgoing, but Clark Terry, playing muted, is more withdrawn, like a trumpet parallel to Clooney.

Of the more familiar Ellington songbook items—the ones that would be called "canonical" in twenty-first-century speak—"I Got It Bad (and That Ain't Good)," with a lyric by Paul Francis Webster, comes nearest to the original recording. The 1941 "I Got It Bad" was as close to an out-and-out vocal record as Ellington ever made in that period, featuring Ivie Anderson throughout, except for two brief spots by Johnny Hodges. The Clooney version features the singer all the way through, except for Ellington's piano intro, and the most that the band can do is stay out of Clooney's

way—nothing else is required. Clooney sings both sets of lyrics to the bridge, the one that begins "And when the weekend's over . . ." as well as the one that starts "Though folks with good intentions . . ." Like Anderson (who belongs with Mildred Bailey and Maxine Sullivan in the school of outstanding 1930s swing singers with small voices but remarkable rhythmic placement), Clooney's vocal is restrained and laid-back, a classic example of showing by not showing.

From 1932, "It Don't Mean a Thing (If It Ain't Got That Swing)" has been heralded over the decades as one of the first pop songs to include the word "swing" in the title, thus helping to introduce an era; in retrospect, it's equally noteworthy for the way Ellington's own lyric incorporates scat phrases into the actual text. In the more famous versions of "It Don't Mean a Thing (If It Ain't Got That Swing)," such as Ella Fitzgerald's, the singers vocalize the scat portions—the famous "doo-wot, doo-wot, doo-wot, doo-wots"—themselves. Strayhorn, however, wisely has Clooney sing the real words and lets Hodges play the doo-wots on his alto; this is more of a band-and-soloist feature than any other track on the album, and we hear from tenor saxophonist Paul Gonsalves, Clark Terry (in an especially tasty solo, again muted), and baritone saxist Harry Carney.

"Just A-Sittin' and A-Rockin'" was also first recorded in 1941, although unlike "I Got It Bad," it was played for the first few years as an instrumental. In 1945, Lee Gaines, of the Delta Rhythm Boys, added a lyric, after which it was played and sung by many of the major bands of the early postwar period, among them Stan Kenton, Woody Herman, Charlie Barnet, Buddy Rich, Earl Hines, and so on. Clark Terry introduces the vocal and, later, returns for the coda. Clooney shows her developing sense of time, particularly in the way she clips the notes at the end of the lines in the main section, then, in contrast, relaxes and sings the lines of the bridge much more expansively legato. The central refrain is short and punchy and confident; the bridge is more introspective and expansive.

The remaining tracks amount to very worthy odds and ends from the Ellington catalogue, which Clooney was virtually the only major non-Ellington vocalist ever to sing. "Hey Baby" was earlier done by Ray Nance with the Ellington big band in 1946 and then by Al Hibbler backed by an Ellington spinoff group. Both Nance and Hibbler sing with signifying machismo—a braggartish attitude that, they convey to us, is obviously a put-on. Paradoxically, the Ellington–Nance and Hibbler versions both begin with the vocal, but the Strayhorn-Clooney chart sounds more like a regulation Ellington band record, in that there's only a single chorus of vocal surrounded by an Ellington instrumental, framed by the Duke's piano intro and outro. The first chorus is wah-wahing muted brass, followed by a slow, memorable baritone bridge from Carney. Clooney enters stealthily, with a long low note that almost sounds like she's trying to emerge unnoticed from behind Carney. From the start, she's much more erotic than Nance or Hibbler; they both sound as if they're kidding to a degree, but Clooney gives you the impression that she means it.

The blues-laced "Grievin'" is just about the most obscure tune in the set: credited to Ellington and Strayhorn, it was only in the band's book very briefly in late 1939 and early 1940, and then just as an instrumental; the song wasn't heard from again until *Blue Rose,* which marks the debut of the lyric, quite possibly by Strayhorn himself. There's a live aircheck from the Southland Cafe, Boston, in January 1940, in which the tune is played much more aggressively; Clooney's relaxed, four-minute treatment (which opens with twelve bars of Harry Carney) is much more grievous. The phrasing of the key word, "Grievin'," as set up by Strayhorn, seems very much in the style Ellington and Strayhorn wrote for Al Hibbler; they stretch the single syllable over two different pitches ("Gri-ev") for no reason other than that it sounds good—this is surely what Ellington referred to as "tonal pantomime." This time Clooney and Gonsalves reverse roles: she sounds like a saxophone, he sounds like a singer.

The 1940 "Me and You" is still another lesser-known jewel from Ivie Anderson's crown. Both the original and the 1956 version begin with the Ducal piano and muted trumpet to state the melody before the vocal entrance. Both words and music are credited solely to Ellington, and the line "as long as there's three heavens above" seems characteristically Dukish. After the instrumental intro, Clooney takes over. It's her lightest vocal on the set, she just touches each note lightly and moves on—as if she were skipping rocks on a pond. There's also the only instance here of her using singspiel, as she lingers on the word "consolidate," and speaks it, a gesture which makes it sound as if she's reinforcing its meaning even as she ponders it.

The overall reaction one has to *Blue Rose* is frustration that Ellington didn't enter into enough other full-length collaborations with singers of Clooney's stature—Ella Fitzgerald and Frank Sinatra would be the only others. In her second memoir, Clooney reports that she was too busy working on the album to take note of a new singer named Elvis Somethingorother who created a national sensation when he appeared on *The Ed Sullivan Show* around the same time as the sessions for the album. By this she means that not only was *Blue Rose* not a world-beater in sales, but soon the entire music industry would be heading off in a whole other direction.

But *Blue Rose* would have serious and positive ramifications for both the two key collaborators. George Avakian explains, "The album didn't sell very well but it did bring Duke back to us. He was interested in getting back to Columbia Records, and that's when I brought up the idea of doing a new piece, a long piece, at the Newport Jazz Festival. And so the rest is history, you know?" The 1956 live LP *Ellington at Newport*—the best-selling original album of Ellington's lifetime—would officially launch the Ellington resurgence, and lead into his highly productive and very visible elder-statesman period.

When *Blue Rose* was finally released, Clooney commemorated the occasion by presenting Strayhorn with a watch, which she had inscribed, "Love, Trilby," in honor of Svengali's famous protégée. Among *Blue Rose*'s many admirers was Clooney's more frequent collaborator Nelson Riddle. Riddle, who was then establishing himself as the greatest orchestrator ever of the American Songbook, told her that *Blue Rose* contained some of the finest writing for singer and orchestra he'd ever heard.

And now that well over sixty years have passed, it's still hard to think of anything that surpasses it.

For Rosemary Clooney, *Blue Rose* meant that she was now a genuine artist, someone whose name might be mentioned in the same breath with her idols Ella Fitzgerald and Billie Holiday. She was now officially something more than just a hitmaker chirping ephemeral ditties that would be forgotten even before the checks were cashed. Near the end of her life, she told me that it was Duke Ellington who first gave her a glimmer of her own value as an artist. As she once said, the experience of working with Ellington "validated me as an American singer. My work would not fade with my generation. I had now moved into a very exclusive group."

8

Nat King Cole
After Midnight
(1957)

Trumpeter Harry Edison was widely known around Hollywood for three things. The first was his skill at getting the most out of a few choice notes, which was a key factor in his specialty, a unique ability to play behind singers, and to fill very small spaces with a lot of music. The second was his high squeaky voice, which occasioned Lester Young to nickname him "Sweets," and which was often echoed in the sound of his muted trumpet and widely imitated by nearly everyone who knew him. (The arranger—conductor Billy May, who worked with Edison on many sessions—did a great impression of Sweets.) And the third was his love of baseball. There's a famous if possibly apocryphal incident in which Edison had been driving to a recording 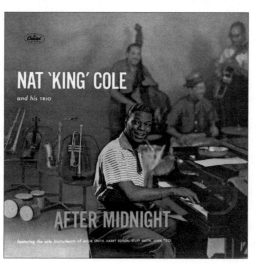 date with Frank Sinatra, but en route was paying too much attention to a game on his car radio and not enough to driving within the speed limit. He was pulled over by a patrolman, and then pleaded for mercy, explaining that no less a personage than Sinatra was waiting for him. "Sure he is!" the officer said, and to prove he was telling the truth, Sweets dragged the cop to the studio with him and introduced him to the Chairman.

Around Hollywood, Sweets was somewhat infamous for interrupting sessions—keeping two dozen violinists and a big star waiting—while he took out a portable radio to get the latest scores. However, Edison never had to apologize for his obsession with the national pastime to the two most famous male singers whom he worked with, Sinatra and Nat King Cole—they both were, if anything, even bigger baseball buffs than he. Sweets and Cole were frequently found at the games together, particularly after the Dodgers relocated to Los Angeles in 1958. As Freddy Cole, the singer-pianist's younger brother, remembered, "Nat and Sweets loved to go to the games together and root for 'Dem Bums.'"

Nat and Sweets were at a game in August 1956 and they were overjoyed when the team that they were rooting for won, so much so that they had to let off steam by playing. Four calls were then made, first to Cole's producer Lee Gillette to arrange for studio time at the Capitol Tower, and then to the three regular members of his working trio, guitarist John Collins, bassist Charlie Harris, and drummer Lee Young.

Upon arrival at the tower, Cole, Edison, and the trio quickly and exuberantly laid down five masters on songs they already knew very well. At that point, Cole and Gillette were so delighted with the results that they scheduled three more sessions in roughly the same format: King Cole and his trio plus a different guest soloist, alto saxophonist Willie Smith, trombonist Juan Tizol, and Stuff Smith, dean of hot violinists. The finished album was titled *After Midnight* to convey that loose, relaxed mood.

Although *After Midnight* contained no hit singles, in the sixty years since it has been released it has become one of Cole's most beloved albums, especially in the jazz community. Innumerable attempts have been made by singers of varying degrees of ability to re-create the *After Midnight* sound. *After Midnight* has been memorized from beginning to end by millions of contemporary jazz singers, who place it on the same level as *John Coltrane and Johnny Hartman, The Tony Bennett / Bill Evans Album,* and the *Sinatra-Jobim* collaborations. Like those albums, *After Midnight* is a de facto collaboration as well: this is the only one of his original albums where Cole both sang and played all the way through, the most significant meeting of Cole the vocalist with Cole the pianist.

In the jazz world, Cole's move from jazz pianist to pop superstar was viewed with a mixture of suspicion and envy: Cole and longtime friend and producer Norman Granz supposedly had a falling out over it, and even Stuff Smith opined, shortly after Cole's death, "Nat didn't really want to sing. He wanted to have a group. Nat wanted to play piano, I think. I might be wrong! Commercially speaking, it was a good thing he sang. You know, to make some loot. Well, loot's great."

It's true that Cole had first made his mark as a pianist who also sang, and the selling point of his early career, which lasted until roughly 1950, was both his playing and singing, as well as the amazing interplay of his trio, which during its peak years costarred bassist Johnny Miller and guitar virtuoso Oscar Moore. In the early 1950s, as Cole became known more and more as a popular vocalist and less and less as a jazz pianist, he nevertheless used the long-playing medium to document his piano playing. This was consistent with the idea that the album format was primarily to preserve history, rather than to showcase what was current, and it would be some time before Cole finally got around to recording a whole album of pop vocals—that was, in the mind of everyone concerned, what singles were for. Right before *After Midnight,* he released an album of piano and rhythm instrumentals titled *Penthouse Serenade* and another of piano solos accompanied by full orchestra, titled *The Piano Style of Nat King Cole.* By the summer of 1956, the only kind of piano album that Cole had not made was one where he both played and sang,

in the approximate tradition of the classic King Cole Trio.

Yet not exactly. From the beginning, there was always a duality to Cole's music, not merely manifested in his ability to both play piano and sing, but in the way he was at once a perfectionist maestro, a pianist-arranger if not a true conductor in the classical sense, and a reckless, hell-for-leather improviser. For roughly a dozen years, Cole worked almost every night with the trio, and he had the same two sidemen for very long stretches of time—Oscar Moore was with him for a full decade, from the first date played by the trio in 1937 onward. Thus the interplay between the three men was incredibly tight, as were the arrangements that they jointly worked out. Their playing especially suited the 78 rpm single format: they could make more music in three minutes than most orchestras could play in an hour. The trio's success was predicated not only on Cole himself, his expert playing and singing, but in the closeness of the unit. They were sometimes referred to as "The Chamber Music Boys" because unlike, say, most of the small groups that came from the ranks of big bands, they were anything but a jam session group: the trio played solos, but each solo was part of an integrated whole, it was never just three guys blowing for themselves.

After Midnight never tried to replicate that closeness. Where the pre-1950 trio sessions were tight, *After Midnight* was loose and casual. Although hardly as free-wheeling as a Jazz at the Philharmonic concert, *After Midnight* was a jam session—in direct contrast to the classic King Cole Trio recordings which had more in common with chamber music. More than anyone else, Cole was well aware that he could never re-create the astonishing, telepathic interplay that was the Trio's signature; that legacy had passed to the other groups he had directly inspired: the Oscar Peterson Trio, the Modern Jazz Quartet, the Ahmad Jamal Trio, and, later, the Bill Evans Trio.

The classic trio sound was driven largely by the close collaboration of Cole and Moore. But by 1956, while the guitar was still an essential part of Cole's sound, it no longer played the crucial role that it once did. In fact, John Collins, Cole's guitarist in the latter part of his career, once told me that he was disappointed that the guitar was no longer a key player, he had hoped to do what Oscar Moore and Irving Ashby had done, but instead, during his tenure with Cole, the guitar was just there for rhythmic support—a supporting player rather than a costar. The backup on *After Midnight* was essentially a conventional rhythm section, with piano, bass, and drums; which is the way the world was going: two years later, Oscar Peterson also decided he would no longer keep the Cole trio format, and replaced his guitarist with a drummer.

In the Trio, the interplay was the thing. Cole himself was keenly aware of this, which is one reason why he made the 1956 album sessions deliberately different from the earlier singles. The oversimplified version of Cole's career trajectory is that he modulated from jazz pianist to pop singer, but the more complicated truth is that he switched from team player and captain to visiting fireman and star. Cole's piano playing itself is just as good on *After Midnight* but the strength of the album is that he's playing and singing like a man on a lark rather than a man whose life's mission was to raise the bar as far for the possibilities of small ensemble playing. Cole was smart enough to realize that re-creating the Trio would have been a patently meaningless exercise: the times were different, Cole himself was no longer the same artist he had been, the musicians were different, and the medium and the rules had changed. Yet on its own, and in the context of Cole's later work, *After Midnight* is a masterpiece, one of the great jazz vocal albums of all time, completely deserving of its classic status and influence on subsequent generations.

The first session held "after midnight" on August 15, 1956, was the purest in that it genuinely seems to have been completely spontaneous, with Cole only playing and singing songs that were already in his repertoire—he wanted to capture the feeling of the moment. That's what a jam session is: playing extemporaneously on songs everybody knows, rather than taking the time to learn something new. Three of the songs were long-standing signatures of the King Cole Trio: "Sweet Lorraine" and "It's Only a Paper Moon," which were both

standards that Cole obviously had been playing for many years even prior to the Trio, and "(Get Your Kicks On) Route 66," the Trio's first big postwar hit, from 1946, which he helped make into something of a national anthem for musicians who were taking a shot at singing (it was recorded quickly by Wingy Manone, Buddy Rich, and Georgie Auld).

In my opinion, the three remakes of the Trio perennials are, overall, among the least satisfying moments of the album. It's annoying when a radio station, for instance, plays these 1956 remakes instead of the originals; all three were also reremade in 1961 in stereo recordings that directly utilize the Trio format and arrangements (for *The Nat King Cole Story*) without Edison. On "Sweet Lorraine," Edison joins on the famous intro as if he really knows it, but both he and drummer Lee Young seem somewhat superfluous. Remaking Trio classics seems entirely inapposite to the point of the album, however; if you weren't familiar with the originals, you would probably think this judgment was absurd. The Cole Trio classics are herewith expanded with more solos (and longer ones)—not necessarily improved, but changed. Cole and Edison are in top shape on "Sweet Lorraine" and "Route 66," and while these versions just lack the sense of purpose of the originals, it's hard to argue with such outstanding playing.

"It's Only a Paper Moon" is the most different from the classic King Cole Trio version. Since at least 1943, Cole had used a block chord intro that was, to listeners, as much a part of the tune as Harold Arlen's melody. (The 1961 stereo recording restores the classic arrangement.) For *After Midnight,* Cole did not use that familiar intro but created a new one that was, surprisingly, just as good, and better suited to Edison. It's amazing to think about all the piano music that Cole still had left in him.

Cole began the date with two songs that were not generally regarded as part of the Trio's history, even though he had recorded them both before, and these are both among the album's highlights. "You Can Depend on Me" is a standard by Earl "Fatha" Hines, whom Cole repeatedly cited as his original inspiration as a pianist. Cole had previously recorded it as his feature with the Capitol

International Jazzmen in 1945; he opened that record with a piano solo in a Hinesian manner, although *After Midnight* represents the only time that he ever sang it. Slow and relaxed, even with a few hints of guitar intermingling with Cole's piano intro (a Trio trademark), it shows that Cole was a whole other artist making a whole other kind of record than he had in the 1940s. His singing throughout is even more nuanced, he never seems like he's just throwing away a vocal, the way he occasionally did earlier on.

"Candy" is equally tasty. The song was one of the big hits of the World War II era, as recorded by Johnny Mercer and the Pied Pipers, one of the more successful songs by Alex Kramer and Joan Whitney, whose tunes were on the charts consistently in the war years. Cole had sung "Candy" in 1945 on a V-Disc, and this is the major instance where the 1956 version is unquestionably superior. Cole's vocal is much more intense and full of details (like when he bites down on "*I* wish that there were four of her . . ."), the piano solo is fuller and more luxurious, and overall the vibe is much sweeter in a "Candy" sort of a way.

Following the August date, Cole and Gillette moved forward with the notion of turning Cole's spontaneous desire for a jam session into an actual album project. He would lay down an additional twelve songs over three more sessions about a month later, each of which featured a different guest soloist. (The pianist apparently had a vision of Jacob Marley's ghost: "You will be visited by three guest soloists.")

The first, on September 14, was William McLeish Smith. Professionally billed as Willie, Smith was a swing era alto saxophone master second only to Johnny Hodges. He was the blues and ballad soloist supreme with the great Jimmie Lunceford band, then enjoyed a renaissance in a long-term association with Harry James and His Orchestra, and for a time replaced Hodges with Duke Ellington. He was a long-term associate of Nat Cole's: they recorded together for Keynote (as "The Keynoters" in 1946) and on several live sessions (on a "Just Jazz" concert and Armed Forces Radio Service Jubilee).

By now, Cole and Lee Gillette, the officially credited producer, were taking it seriously, to the

extent that Cole was learning new songs. This was a curious decision—I can only assume it was Gillette's idea, because the jam session format was much better suited to familiar standards. For one reason or another, Cole attempted most of the newest material on the Willie Smith date, starting with "Don't Let It Go to Your Head," co-credited to Hollywood studio pianist Charlie LaVere (a Gordon Jenkins regular who plays on, among many other recordings, Cole's *Love Is the Thing* album); it's a slightly awkward lyric that Cole makes sound better, perhaps, than it actually is.

The other two new songs are "You're Lookin' at Me," and "I Was a Little Too Lonely (And You Were a Little Too Late)." Of the three, only the last, the one fast novelty number in the batch, truly amounts to a King Cole classic. The others are decent songs that Cole makes sound great, but on some level they're a waste of a valuable opportunity that Cole could have taken advantage of to sing a few of the really great songs he never recorded, like "Sophisticated Lady" or "Come Rain or Come Shine." Bobby Troup's "You're Lookin' at Me" is not in the same class as his "Baby All the Time" or "Come to the Party," but is a solid enough effort and worthy of Cole's attention. It achieved some cachet when Carmen McRae made it, rather surprisingly, the title of her 1983 tribute album to Cole. One might assume that it was a Cole classic or signature, but in reality he only sang it this once—obviously the song meant more to Carmen than it ever did to Nat.

"I Was a Little Too Lonely (And You Were a Little Too Late)" is by far the most satisfying of the new songs on *After Midnight*. It was written by a pair of old pros, Ray Evans and Jay Livingston (authors of Cole's breakthrough hit "Mona Lisa" and his classic "Never Let Me Go") for Cole to sing in a rather minimal film called *Istanbul*, essentially a B-level knockoff of *Casablanca*, with Erroll Flynn and Cole as Technicolor equivalents of "Rick" and "Sam." At first, there were big plans for this song: Cole was to sing it in the movie, and Capitol hedged their bets by having him make what appear to be two very different versions of it. One was here, at the second *After Midnight* date, and the other was in the middle of a session for the album *Love Is the*

Thing with Gordon Jenkins (although it's impossible to imagine how this rhythmic tune might have been done by Jenkins with his massed army of fiddles). It was a terrific song for Cole, absolutely in the tradition of such swingingly funny comedy KC3 classics as "The Trouble with Me Is You," "Now He Tells Me," and "The Best Man"; no wonder Cole had high hopes for it.

But then, everything seemed to go terribly, horribly wrong for "I Was a Little Too Lonely." First, it was all but cut from the film—you hear just forty seconds in the released print, and the movie itself was also far from a roaring success. In the end, both the movie and the song felt like a mere throwaway. At that point, Capitol declined to release either of Cole's recorded versions of the song—and the *After Midnight* track wasn't heard until the CD of the album thirty years later. The song has become, in a sense, a posthumous Cole classic, recorded in tribute to him by John Pizzarelli, among others.

There was only one standard on the Willie Smith date, but he and Cole make the most of it. The 1929 "Just You, Just Me" had long since been established as a jam session favorite by Lester Young and others; in 1946, the Cole Trio had recorded an instrumental version for a commercial radio transcription. Just by including it here, even with the rarely sung lyric, Cole was signifying that this was a jam-driven album. Cole hardly throws away the words, but delivers them with the sensitivity and attention to detail that characterizes his mature work—like his colleague Sinatra, he can now be romantic, even at swingin' tempos. All the solos are framed by an attractive riff that also serves as an intro and coda, and put one in mind of how Thelonious Monk transformed this song into his own classic, "Epistrophy."

Cole had been an early advocate of Pan-American rhythms, including calypso as well as rhumbas and congas, and for the third session (September 21) he brings in two guest stars to help create an exotic, Latino kind of mood: the Puerto Rican trombonist Juan Tizol and the Cuban percussionist Jack Costanzo.

Like Willie Smith, Tizol was known for his years with both Duke Ellington and Harry James and,

later, in various Hollywood recording studios. Tizol was a highly unique musician. Unlike Cole's other guest stars, Tizol was not primarily an improvising soloist: his main contribution to jazz history was as the composer of such exotic jazz standards as "Caravan," "Perdido," "Pyramid," "Bakiff," and others. He was a key factor in the Ellington success story, both as a player and composer, and he also contributed mightily to the James band, and, more recently, Nelson Riddle—among other things, he takes the memorable valve trombone solo on the Sinatra Capitol version of "Night and Day." Tizol was an unusual choice for this jam-session-flavored album, since Tizol was most definitely not a jam session kind of guy; rather arrangers and bandleaders called upon his unique valve trombone sound to provide exotic atmosphere and tonal color.

The main order of business is "Caravan," one of the all-time jazz standards, co-credited to Tizol and Ellington, a rare tune from the big band era that grew even more popular in subsequent decades among modern jazzmen (thanks to Art Blakey, among others). Cole had been playing "Caravan" at least since he cut a transcription of it in 1938, when the song was relatively new, and "Caravan" had been a chart hit twice since then: vocally by Billy Eckstine in 1949 and orchestrally in 1953 by Canadian bandleader Ralph Marterie (a recording that seems much in the spirit of Les Paul and Mary Ford). The combination of Tizol's ethereal trombone, Costanzo's bongos, and Cole's understated vocal makes for a highly convincing treatment: it was Eckstine who first put "Caravan" on the map for vocalists, but, with all due respect, more contemporary singers clearly know it from Cole.

"The Lonely One" was composed by saxophonist Lenny Hambro, who for much of his career was associated with the Cuban composer and bandleader Chico O'Farrill. The playing of the Cole-Tizol-Costanzo composition makes it a perfect companion piece to "Caravan," equal parts Latin and Middle Eastern, music for a Havanese belly dancer. Lyrically, the song seems like an attempt to create a sequel to Cole's 1948 hit "Nature Boy"—it's practically "Nature Boy" spelled sideways.

Then Costanzo sits out, Cole and Tizol deliver the best two slow ballads of the album. "Blame It on My Youth" and "What Is There to Say" were composed by members of George Gershwin's inner circle, respectively, Oscar Levant and Vernon Duke. Cole's "Blame" is less profoundly tragic than the Sinatra-Riddle version (from *Close to You*), which had been taped a few months earlier in that same Capitol Tower studio, but altogether convincing just the same. "What Is There to Say" is the other side of the coin, slow but vaguely optimistic rather than melancholy. Duke and E. Y. Harburg wrote it for the posthumous 1934 edition of the *Ziegfeld Follies,* but it quickly became a jazz perennial rather than a pop hit, embraced by the swing bands and then modernists like Gerry Mulligan. These two ballads show that the small group format isn't only suited to a JATP-style jam session, but that the intimate format also uniquely supports Cole as a crooner of love songs; both are exquisitely bittersweet. Cole has never been more convincingly romantic, and he's brilliantly supported by both Tizol and his own piano playing. As an interpreter of the great love lyrics, the King takes a royal backseat to no one.

It turns out that Cole was saving the big guns for last: Hezekiah Leroy Gordon "Stuff" Smith (1909–1967) had been one of the major stars of New York's Swing Street in the mid-1930s, leading his own small band in a small club rather than leading a big band in a ballroom. Smith was generally regarded as the greatest of all swing violinists; as the Danish jazz violin superstar Svend Asmussen told me, "I thought that Joe Venuti was the greatest, but then when I heard Stuff for the first time, I forgot about Joe!" Smith's celebrity had faded somewhat after the war, but ten years later he was enjoying something of a renaissance: Norman Granz was recording him extensively as a leader and also employing him on dates with Dizzy Gillespie and Ella Fitzgerald, and he even turns up on a few dates with Nelson Riddle.

Smith was a brilliant choice for the project. Like the violinist, Cole had also been nurtured on Fifty-second Street. In the early period, before the Trio hooked up with Capitol Records and gradu-

ally became the most celebrated small group of the 1940s, they first became famous on L.A.'s Central Avenue, but they also paid their dues on Swing Street. It's easy to imagine Cole and Smith jamming together at Kelly's Stables or the Famous Door at the dawn of the 1940s.

"Ah, there was a session!" As Smith exclaimed in his 1965 interview with Anthony Barnett, "There's a boy, man. He can play all the piano you want to hear." He continued, "Nat King Cole was one of the finest piano players in the country, I mean for swinging, man." Smith continued, "Yeah, he played beautiful, I mean to me, some guys just kind of fit you, and other guys don't. But he fitted me." The violinist was right: he and Cole "fitted" each other beautifully, and their four tracks are easily the album's highlight. Even apart from the rest of the album, the four Cole-Smith tracks represent a sainted collaboration, two masters at their absolute pinnacle, bringing out the best of each other.

This fourth and final date (September 24) starts out with a subtle salvo, "Sometimes I'm Happy," in which both the principals are laid back in a blissfully bittersweet fashion. Clearly, both Cole and Smith are inspired heavily by Cole's occasional collaborator, Lester Young, and his iconic 1943 interpretation of the Vincent Youmans classic. (The thought of which provokes one to speculate that it's too bad that apparently nobody thought to put in a call to the Pres himself for this album. His brother Lee was Cole's usual drummer, as he is on this album. Lester was still active in 1956, and occasionally playing brilliantly, although his work was often inconsistent in the years leading up to his death at the age of forty-nine in 1959.) "Sometimes I'm Happy" is set in an ABAB structure: the violinist and pianist alternate on each eight-bar section, with Cole taking the two bridges.

"I Know That You Know" is perhaps the fastest tune in the album. Here's another jam session standard delivered at horse race tempo—again, very much in the Jazz at the Philharmonic spirit of a bunch of soloists trying to outplay and even outrun each other. (JATP was so named because it brought jazz, for the first time, into the concert hall shrines of classical music, but it could have just as easily played sports arenas—and many compared it to ancient Roman gladiatorial combat—"Jazz at the Colosseum.") Smith plays gloriously here, full of warmth and swing, showing that the jazz violin, in the right hands, can easily compete with the saxophone or trumpet for sheer soul. The piano-violin exchanges, in the intro and the instrumental break, are the finest "trading session" on the album. Further, while Lee Young is rarely included on anyone's list of jazz's greatest drummers, his playing here is perfect.

Considering that "When I Grow Too Old to Dream" was written by Oscar Hammerstein and Sigmund Romberg for a Hollywood opera (*The Night Is Young*, 1935), the song has a surprising pedigree in the African American musical community: Putney Dandridge, The Cats and the Fiddle, Helen Humes, Dizzy Gillespie (with The Tempo Jazzmen), Rose Murphy, Sheila Jordan, and many others; some of these incorporate a jive routine that had apparently become a favorite on both Swing Street and Central Avenue. Most jazz versions are breathtakingly fast, Cole's and Smith's, contrastingly, gives the song space enough to breathe. The singer pauses luxuriously between the first few words: "When . . . I . . . grow too old to dream . . ." Smith responds with that same phrasing in his solo, emphasizing the first note and then pausing before continuing with the phrase. Guitarist John Collins also takes his best solo on the album, and, collectively, they show that one doesn't have to play at a breakneck tempo to truly swing.

"Two Loves Have I" represents the nexus of two major African American icons, Josephine Baker and Nat King Cole. The great transcontinental diva's theme song was titled "J'Ai Deux Amours" in French, and it was originally imported into the U.K. in 1932 as "Give Me a Tune" (as recorded by Ray Noble and Al Bowlly). After the war, it washed up on American shores as "Two Loves Have I," and was sung by a wide variety of mostly male pop singers, Buddy Clark (again with Ray Noble), Frankie Laine, Dean Martin, Perry Como, Alan Dale, Dick Haymes, and, the version that probably most inspired Cole, Billy Eckstine, in 1947. Cole's treatment is relaxed, with a prominent bass vamp by Charlie Harris, and still with enough urgency to

make the "switch ending" in the lyric seem almost like a surprise. Rather than a highlight, "Two Loves" is a kind of low-key contrast. It sounds more Paris, Texas, than Paris, France, and Smith gives it something of a hillbilly feel. "Two Loves" was also one of five tracks that were left off the original 1957 LP release of *After Midnight* and first released on the CD edition roughly thirty years later.

In January 1957, presumably just as the album was coming out, Smith appeared on Cole's TV show and backed him on "I Know That You Know." Later in the spring, Cole promoted the album by bringing out Tizol, then a regular member of Nelson Riddle's studio orchestra, on the show, and reprising their treatment of "Caravan." In October of that year, Cole's somewhat estranged old friend Norman Granz brought an entire Jazz at the Philharmonic lineup onto the Cole show, which gave the pianist a chance to reunite with such colleagues as Stan Getz and Coleman Hawkins. (Interestingly, however, not one of the songs on *After Midnight* was featured on the JATP episode.)

Cole never stopped playing piano: he included a keyboard feature in most of his personal appearances, and he occasionally recorded on piano. He also re-created six signature King Cole Trio arrangements in stereo in March 1961, and in November of that year he played organ on six tracks of the album *Let's Face the Music and Dance*, along with Billy May's orchestra. Around this time, Cole was in contact again with Stuff Smith, who interested him in a song he had written. (Cole asked the violinist to demonstrate the tune for him, and Smith said in a letter, "He is a nice guy, but he wants everything perfected. Which is great. I will drop by his house when he gets to town and show him how 'Miracles' [Smith's song] should be played.") But he never worked with a small jazz combo of the *After Midnight* variety again.

After Midnight's great strength is its spontaneity, which also insured that the circumstances that produced it would have been difficult to repeat, making it virtually impossible to replicate the album and especially to surpass it. "And, you know," as Stuff Smith said of Nat King Cole, "he had so much music in his heart, man!"

9

Nat King Cole
St. Louis Blues
(1958)

By 1958, Nat King Cole had so successfully conquered "mainstream" show business that even NBC's decision to cancel his highly popular TV show could hardly slow him down. He was continuing to sell records in amazing quantities—he left Sinatra far behind in terms of record sales, and only that upstart Elvis Presley challenged him in the hit singles department. Cole was such an unimpeachable part of the pop music firmament that the majority of his listeners had no idea that he had begun his career doing jazz and the blues.

Cole himself, however, never forgot where he came from: while his singles were mostly pure pop (and, mostly, great pop music) many of his early 12-inch albums were highly jazz-oriented. In 1955 and '56, he recorded three outstanding albums centered around his piano playing (*Penthouse Serenade, The Piano Style of Nat King Cole,* and *After Midnight*), all of which challenged him by placing his keyboard skills in new and different contexts. In 1958, he got back in touch with two aspects of his roots: it's sometimes said that the church and the blues represent two different sides of the coin of African American music, and this was the year that Cole addressed both. At the end of the year, he returned to his spiritual origins in *Every Time I Feel the Spirit,* but well before that, in January, Cole recorded a classic album that easily established how much the blues were an ongoing and profound part of his musical makeup.

The album that we know as *St. Louis Blues* (one of the few Cole projects to be recorded in New York) revealed exactly what Cole had in common with his contemporaries Joe Williams and Dinah Washington. All three were born (the two men just a few months apart) in the Deep South and grew up in the Northern cauldron of jazz and blues known as Chicago in the interwar years. All three were capable of singing all kinds of music, from Jerome Kern to Thomas A. Dorsey, but they each had a distinct grounding in the blues.

Although the blues is often referred to (sometimes derisively) as a "roots" music, at its highest peak, which is where Cole, Williams, and Washington all took it, it is an incredibly sophisticated form. All three found a way to sing a modern, mid-twentieth-century blues, a highly refined jazz-club kind of blues that had more in common with Charlie Parker than it did with those singing guitarists, who were even then deserting the Mississippi Delta for the greener pastures of the North.

The musical roots of Cole, Washington, and Williams were more in Lonnie Johnson than Robert Johnson. They could sing the blues and make it sad and mournful, but brought to it the same meticulous attention to lyrics and storytelling skills that they applied to the songs of Cole Porter. In singing the blues, they showed a stylistic allegiance to Frank Sinatra and Ella Fitzgerald rather than Lead Belly. The Chicago school of the blues was urbane and subtle, highly nuanced, and belonged more in a tuxedo or an evening gown than a pair of overalls.

Whether he was playing piano, singing, or doing both, Cole performed essentially two kinds of blues. When they were slow, and usually sad, he brought to it all the tenderness and sincerity of a great love song. And conversely, when he sang a fast blues, it was with unbridled exhilaration and swing. The approach to the blues perfected by Cole and his major collaborator, arranger Nelson Riddle, is so exciting (even when Cole sings a quiet or contemplative song, it can be described as exciting) that *St. Louis Blues* qualifies as quite possibly Cole's strongest statement as a stand-up vocalist. Cole, Washington, and Williams were all in a unique category in terms of blues, jazz, and the standard American Songbook, and one has to wait another generation, for Ray Charles, Sam Cooke, Nina Simone, and Aretha Franklin, for more artists who could match them.

Cole's greatest blues album, *St. Louis Blues,* was originally released as *Nat King Cole Sings Songs from St. Louis Blues* (Capitol Records SW 993). As the title indicates, it was a tie-in to the film *St. Louis Blues,* which, unfortunately, was Cole's only starring role in a major feature film. The mid-1950s were the years of bandleader biographies (Glenn Miller, Benny Goodman, Gene Krupa), which had followed a series of songwriter biographies (Gershwin, Rodgers and Hart, Porter, Kern, Romberg). These had, in turn, succeeded a generation or so after a strain of "Jazz Singer" variations from the very dawn of talking pictures, in which members of an ethnic group struggle with the cost of cultural assimilation. When Paramount Pictures produced *St. Louis Blues* in 1958, they drew on all these standard tropes and biopic clichés.

But the one thing that they did not draw upon was the actual life of the composer, W. C. Handy, that the movie was supposed to be about. *St. Louis Blues* was, essentially, yet another variation on *The Jazz Singer* (which had recently been remade with Danny Thomas and Cole's friend Peggy Lee) with real black people. (The 1927 *Jazz Singer* starred Al Jolson as a Jewish entertainer who finds success by emulating black musical styles; the epically dreadful 1952 *Jazz Singer* involved Danny Thomas, a Catholic Lebanese playing a Jewish entertainer.) Most notably, as in the case of pictures like *Words and Music* and *Till the Clouds Roll By* there's an all-star cast of singing actresses doing the composer's songs, which included Pearl Bailey and Eartha Kitt, and portraying the women in Handy's life, while Mahalia Jackson and Ella Fitzgerald make cameo appearances in all-singing, nonspeaking roles. (Cab Calloway gets a few lines of dialogue, but, alas, wasn't given the chance to sing.)

Of all the biopics of songwriters and bandleaders produced by the Hollywood studio system, this was the sole film depicting an African American artist. Alas, *St. Louis Blues* was a first-class disappointment. He isn't very good in the film (except when he's singing), but then he wasn't particularly well directed and wasn't given a very good script to work with. There's every reason to believe that he could have done much better in a better vehicle.

The sole redeeming aspect of the movie was the music and the way that, as with the Miller and Goodman stories, *St. Louis Blues* kindled new interest in the music of its subject. Previously, the one major new 12-inch LP of Handy's music had been by Louis Armstrong and his All-Stars in 1954. (Interestingly, Cole and Armstrong did very few of the same songs; I would have loved to hear Armstrong do "Joe Turner's Blues" and equally so to hear Cole sing "Aunt Hagar's Blues.") The Paramount picture led to three new albums of the Handy songbook by the film's three principals, Cole, Bailey, and Kitt, and all three albums were first-rate. (In 1959, New Orleans trombonist Kid Ory also recorded an all-Handy album, as would Ellingtonian trumpeter Cat Anderson in 1977.)

Cole's album, however, was more than that: it was the climax of his professional relationship with Nelson Riddle, the greatest of their few full-length projects together and a unique statement, unmatched anywhere in the jazz-pop spectrum, even the aforementioned other Handy albums by Armstrong, Bailey, and Kitt. The Cole album, in fact, did the job that the movie was supposed to: it dramatically and entertainingly conveyed the full importance of Handy's music while making a case for its ongoing relevance. Following *After Midnight,* this is also Cole's most rewarding work with trumpeter Harry "Sweets" Edison, who seems to have come east for these and several other sessions around the same time. Edison's distinctive "beeping" muted trumpet contributions can be heard all over the album.

Working primarily in the second and third decades of the twentieth century, W. C. Handy (1873–1958) would devote his life to the cause of moving vernacular black music into the mainstream of American popular culture. Handy, who was known as the "Father of the Blues" (also the title of his autobiography), was widely successful, and proved himself a role model for successive generations of African Americans both from a musical and a business standpoint. The Cole album illustrated how well those ideals had been carried out since the period covered in the film, the years when Handy debuted his classic blues. The album was a testament to black and white solidarity, between a black star and a white musical director, a black composer and a thoroughly mixed ensemble of section players and soloists. Handy died at the age of seventy-four in March 1958, which means that he might have lived to hear the Cole album; if that was the case, I can't imagine he ever heard his music sound better.

The first track is an opening title-style overture-medley. *St. Louis Blues,* the album, opens with the famous opening strain of Handy's 1912 classic, treated in a semiclassical fashion, but not pompous like the old "symphonic jazz" of the 1920s but with overtones of Aaron Copland. From there, the familiar opening blues theme goes into an instrumental passage identified as "Love Theme" (not by Handy but by Riddle), the transition suggesting a Broadway overture, but rendered with more sensitivity than most pit bands could play it.

The first track ends by introducing Cole the vocalist with something listed as "Hesitating Blues." There are two very similar early jazz pieces which are both undoubtedly derived from earlier folk sources: Handy's "Hesitating Blues" and a slightly different blues called "Hesitation Blues," which Jelly Roll Morton claimed to have written. The Handy version wasn't recorded much, but the "Hesitation" variation caught on with early coun-

try bands, like Milton Brown and His Musical Brownies and Bill Boyd and His Cowboy Ramblers (who called it "Must I Hesitate?").

However, the "Hesitating Blues" that Cole sings would seem to be completely different from both songs; it's not Morton and it doesn't sound like any earlier version of the Handy song either. Both of those songs pivot around a blues wherein a colored gentleman argues with a telephone operator, he wants to talk to his high-brown girl, but the operator explains that "a storm last night blew the wires all down." As the gentleman gets impatient, he sings the hesitatin' blues. That "Hesitating" was sung by Armstrong, Bailey, and Kitt, but it's nothing like the song that Cole sings here at the end of the first track, which begins with "Procrastination is the thief of time . . ." It could be that the piece that Cole sings is an obscure section of Handy's song (many of his compositions have all kinds of unexpected strains, some of which are rarely performed) or more likely a new concoction by either Riddle (à la "Love Theme") or Mack David (à la "Morning Star," as we shall see).

Whatever the origin of Cole's "Hesitating Blues," it's a stunning sample of the artist's unique way of blending the idioms of blues and love songs. Cole's knack for "crooning the blues," not just on this album but going back at least as far as his 1943 "Gee Baby, Ain't I Good to You" is one of the major innovations of his career, and a substantial influence on a whole school of followers that included Charles Brown.

Cole's first full vocal is heard on "Harlem Blues," circa 1926, one of Handy's later and lesser-heard works (recorded memorably by one of the composer's own favorites, the singer-pianist-bandleader-composer Willard Robison). Cole and Riddle do a swinging version of what Handy conceived of as a moody piece; in which, as originally written, the lyrics comically protest the transition in Negro life from the rural South to the urban North. It's a twist on eighty zillion Tin Pan Alley tunes by post–Stephen Foster composers singing the praises of a Southern paradise, but this one rails against Harlem life without quite celebrating home sweet home in a little shack back in Alabammy or Georgia or wherever. One can readily understand why producer George Avakian didn't choose this one for the Armstrong album, but Cole and Riddle swing it into good health.

Considering that Handy's world-famous blues classics describing the towns of Memphis and St. Louis helped make those cities famous—especially outside the United States—it's a surprise Handy wrote so little about New Orleans, the birthplace of jazz. "Chantez Les Bas" was inspired by a Louisiana Creole tune, with lyrics in both English and Creole-French *patois*—it means "Sing 'em low." It's another later Handy work, originally published in 1931 but not widely heard until Artie Shaw recorded a classic big band treatment. Shortly afterward, in 1944, it was included on a 78 album of Handy's music by pianist James P. Johnson and Handy's daughter Katherine, as well as Armstrong. The Cole-Riddle treatment is a laid-back, bluesy folk song, with the singer every bit as relaxed as an old man puffing on his pipe and rocking back and forth on his porch in the middle of the Louisiana swamp. The only regret is that Cole left out the song's equally marvelous verse.

"Friendless Blues" was listed on the cover of the second issue of this album as "Friendliness Blues"; no, that's not exactly the same thing. Whatever the title, it's a regulation twelve-bar blues; Riddle deploys a vaguely Basie-like brass obbligato off and on throughout, and there are also prominent trombone, clarinet, and piano obbligatos. Unfortunately, since the sessions were done in New York, and that branch of the American Federation of Musicians has refused to open its files to researchers, we have no idea who the soloists are.

"Stay" (which is not to be confused with an entirely different song that Cole recorded in 1955) is another minor mystery. The only other well-known recording is by Fats Waller in 1935, in which he duets with the composer's other daughter, Elizabeth Handy (her only known recording). However, in the Capitol files, the song is credited to Andy Razaf, who obviously wrote the lyrics, and "E. Handy"—apparently meaning Elizabeth—not W. C. This is one of the few songs associated with Handy that doesn't even allude to blues form, sounding more like a regulation song of the era—it could be by Eubie Blake, Don Redman,

Waller himself, or any of Razaf's other regular collaborators. (The bridge melody is especially tasty.) The Cole track opens with very solid Sweets Edison, beeping away as brilliantly as ever, backed by a descending reed line. Cole interprets the song as a sort of a predecessor to "Baby It's Cold Outside." The instrumental break is deliberately unbluesy, with eight bars of prominent celeste.

"Joe Turner's Blues" (most famously recorded by the blues giant Big Joe Turner in 1940, but also beloved of early country and hillbilly musicians) is the big butt-kicking swinger here. If the arrangement sounds different from the rest of the album, it's because it's the work of producer-orchestrator-Capitol-employee Dave Cavanaugh. (A discovery made recently by Cole discographer Jordan Taylor.) It lacks the sophisticated Debussy-ian harmonies of Riddle's "St. Louis Blues" and the self-aware, wise-guy sense of humor of "Beale Street Blues," but it compensates with a raw and groovy directness. Apparently Cole wanted at least one simpler chart that he could use on the road, and Cavanaugh's "Joe Turner," which doesn't require any string section, is much more transportable.

Cole swings this one with glorious aggression, and takes us right to the heart of the blues. Handy explained that this song was about black families in the post–Civil War era being torn apart when their men were carried off involuntarily and forced to live and work far away from their loved ones. In the best tradition of the blues—and African American music in general—that tragedy has been turned around: the looming threat of the breadwinner being forced away from the family has been transmuted into the message, "you better appreciate me now, woman, because I'll soon be gone"—the same idea that can be found in most songs of the "classic blues" era. Cole defuses a potentially tragic situation and responds by vigorously swinging it—true to the blues ideal of smiling in the face of trouble and making light of catastrophe. Cole would swing it even more exciting almost exactly two years later, when he re-recorded the chart on his *Live at the Sands* album. This is my personal favorite track on the set, and, I think, one of the all-time masterpieces of Cole's comparatively short but incredibly productive career.

"Beale Street Blues" offers Riddle's comment on the way the blues were traditionally rendered by big bands, with lots of blaring brass and dramatic stop-time breaks—"If Beale Street could talk," at which point the horns come in with a great big "WHAMP!" When Cole finishes his choruses, Edison just keeps going in what amounts to an extension of Cole's vocal, expressed on a highly vocalized trumpet solo, on top of the same backdrop. This 1916 classic was kept alive for many years by trombonist and singer Jack Teagarden, who made it almost as important a part of his act as "Basin Street Blues."

"Careless Love," from 1921, offers more old-codger-style mock ranting, in this case, inspired by a soap opera orator Handy heard railing against mass-produced products and foodstuffs. Handy himself transposed that sentiment into a comic protest against the liberated sexuality of the 1920s, which he comically characterizes as "loveless." He argues that since the government has levied a "pure food law" to protect us from unhealthy additives in groceries (sound familiar?), why shouldn't the legislation also protect the often equally unsavory ways of thoughtless lovers? Along with "Yellow Dog Blues" and "St. Louis Blues," "Careless Love" was one of the three major Handy classics immortalized early on by the great Bessie Smith. Again, Cole's crooning, and Riddle's Ellington-influenced mixtures of brass and reeds, emphasize the love song aspects of the text. Cole sings of "Loveless Love" as if he were doing a twelve-bar torch song, with an "Angel Eyes"–like diminuendo at the end.

"Morning Star" is a new song by Mack David, written for the film, borrowing only the title of an older, more spiritually oriented Handy piece. While I do regret that Cole didn't sing the actual Handy composition (which Pearl Bailey sang quite wonderfully on her Handy *St. Louis Blues* album), the new Mack David tune is also excellent, very much in the vein of Judy Garland's "Friendly Star." Where the movie itself was about strained parent-child relations, this new piece is a clear-cut anthem of maternal love. This is Riddle's most ambitious string section orchestration on the package.

One of the few things the film does get partially right is the origin of "Memphis Blues," Handy's first notable composition and the second most famous work of his career. As the picture shows, "Memphis Blues" famously was written as a political campaign jingle; but in the interest of not igniting interracial hostility, Paramount Pictures does not show us how the song was swindled away from Handy by a pair of conniving white publishers. Had the movie been made in 1968 rather than 1958, that plot point would surely have been depicted differently. This is the only lyric to one of Handy's major compositions that's not by the composer himself, being the work of George Norton (also the lyricist on "Melancholy Baby"). Handy got cheated out of his royalties, but, almost as if to make it up to him, Norton used the text as a kind of promo for the bandleader-composer, in lyrics that sing the praises of the remarkable Memphis maestro. Cole's treatment is both traditional and literal, as when he sings of "the trombone's croon." The unknown trombonist (sounding something like Bill Harris) also plays in the break, trading fours for a twelve-bar chorus with an open-bell trumpeter and he winds up with a Teagardenesque coda.

The 1914 "Yellow Dog Blues" is, like "Joe Turner," based closely on traditional folk-blues sources. "Yellow Dog" also makes light of a sad situation—men packing up and heading north, joining the Great Migration to Chicago, Detroit, and Harlem, but leaving their women behind. "Where the southern cross(es) the dog" refers to the meeting of the train line and the Yellow Dog River in the Mississippi Delta—"Every cross-tie bayou, burg and bog." In 1925, Bessie Smith established "Yellow Dog" as one of the archetypical women's blues, which laments how the menfolk are free to jump on the rails and ride, but the unliberated women of the day are forced to remain at home—tied down by their own apron strings. The train itself becomes a kind of mechanical rival, the instrument of desertion. Some of the same ideas (and musical material) later evolved into such blues classics as "C. C. Rider" and "I Wonder Where My Easy Rider's Gone."

The three most famous vocal performances of "Yellow Dog" are by Smith, Armstrong, and Cole, and the first two treated the material as cautionary tales of love and loss; contrastingly, Cole and Riddle swing the "Yellow Dog" with a vengeance.

Cole expresses the rapture of the man who may be leaving his woman, but more importantly, is hoping to leave the oppressive, Jim Crow ways of the Old South, for the freedom and dignity he hopes to find up north. Cole's adaptation includes part of the verse the relocated lover writes his girl back home but leaves out Handy's original line "*Uncle Sam has rural free delivery*" (which Smith famously delivered as "*Uncle Sam is the ruler of delivery*").

"St. Louis Blues," one of the most famous songs of all time, climaxes the album and elaborates on the semi-symphonic snippet that began the opening overture, this time expanded into a full-length treatment with a Cole vocal. "St. Louis Blues" is essentially a woman's song—she sings of how the man she loves was seduced away from her by a St. Louis hussy with a powdered face and store-bought hair. All male versions are somewhat strained (including Bing Crosby, on his famous recording with Duke Ellington); the Armstrong All-Stars album solved the problem by having Velma Middleton sing it, rather than Armstrong. Cole and Riddle seem to be distracting from the issue by playing up the concerto grosso aspects of the arrangement, and by making it relatively short—just one chorus of all four famous strains. It's dramatic and it's great, but like many tracks on the album, one wishes there were more.

• • •

The film *St. Louis Blues* tanked, but the album was a success, and, eventually, a classic. The original 1958 *Nat King Cole Sings Songs from St. Louis Blues* (SW 993) stayed in print long after the movie had been forgotten, and, around the time of Cole's death in 1965, was reissued as *Nat King Cole Sings the Blues* (SW 1929).

In an odd way, what works best on the *St. Louis Blues* album is the same element that destroys the movie: the film was absolutely inauthentic and took virtually nothing from Handy's actual life. But what's great about the record is the way Cole and Riddle take chances with the Handy canon and both modernize and personalize it, adding overtones as they saw fit from sources as varied as Maurice Ravel and Count Basie. The Cole-Riddle partnership was never more inspired, particularly in the climax of the remarkable "Yellow Dog Blues."

The repeat of the last line in the coda provides an appropriately mythic ending to this tale of the legendary Joe Turner, while Cole himself imbues the vocal with autobiographical relevance. You can't sing about Joe Turner this convincingly unless you've *been* him. He was here last night, that rascal, but by the time the rooster crowed, he had left me, gone where the southern cross' the dog.

10

Bing Crosby

Bing with a Beat

(1957)

like making records even more than making movies," Bing Crosby told critic George Simon late in his life. "That's because you're constantly creating. And it's especially fun when you're working with great musicians. And the good thing about it is that when you're finished recording, you've got something that's really your own." He could have been talking about *Bing with a Beat,* that remarkable album that he made in 1957 with Bob Scobey's Frisco Jazz Band. This was not only the singer's best all-original LP, but a shoo-in on any respectable list of the Top 10 greatest jazz vocal albums ever recorded. *Bing with a Beat* is the album— more than any other— where Crosby sounds like he's singing for the sheer joy of it, with a degree of warmth and emotional involvement that exceeds everything else he recorded in his long and incredibly prolific career.

Crosby (1903–1977) was in the middle of the fourth decade of what was quite possibly the most remarkable career in American music. More than any other entertainer, actor, singer, or comic, Crosby defined twentieth-century vernacular pop culture: he was pop music, and pop music was him.

This isn't just after-the-fact hyperbole, but rather the result of a carefully cultivated career strategy worked out by the singer with the astute Jack Kapp. It was no accident that well before World War II, Crosby was known as the ultimate musical Everyman. During the years of his reign— which encompassed at least two complete decades, the 1930s and the 1940s—he was expected, even morally obligated, to sing anything and everything that could be conceivably regarded as pop music. His greatest strength was sheer diversity, and he covered every conceivable genre of popular song from "White Christmas" to "Sweet Leilani" to "San Antonio Rose." Musicians from as far afield as Louis Jordan, Jascha Heifetz, Xavier Cugat, and Woody Herman defined crossover success as the opportunity to work with Bing Crosby, who had come to be regarded as a walking symbol of mainstream American taste. In these years, there was no such thing as a generation gap—rather, entire families, from Granny down to Junior, would nestle 'round the Philco and listen to Bing.

By the mid-1950s, there were signs that the Champ was ready to relinquish the title. Nineteen fifty-four brought forth the resurgence of Frank Sinatra, who, ten years earlier, had come closer than anyone to dethroning Crosby. Nineteen fifty-five marked the first year that rock 'n' roll, then defined as pop music aimed strictly at teenagers and younger, dominated the singles market, and then 1956 brought along Elvis Presley. By 1957, Crosby was able to retire undefeated, but it's worth noting that it took two remarkable successors, Sinatra and Presley, to reign over the kingdom that Crosby had once ruled all by himself. Now over fifty, Crosby seemed to be happy that he no longer had to compete for hits, not that anyone else ever gave him much competition. The albums he made in the Eisenhower era offer some of his greatest singing, both exuberant and relaxed at the same time—none more so than *Bing with a Beat*.

No longer the embodiment of the collective taste of the nation, the singer was sufficiently self-liberated to indulge in what was his personal favorite music: jazz. Most listeners to Crosby's records and radio shows over the previous twenty years knew well what a jazz fan the singer was, but it occupied little more of his professional time than Hawaiian, cowboy, or Christmas songs. Crosby had apprenticed with the great hot players of the Jazz Age, working with many of them in Paul Whiteman's orchestra, and gleaning from them the solid, swinging rhythmic foundation that was the basis of everything he sang.

While Crosby had crossed paths (not to mention cadenzas) with many of the major figures of the swing era at one time or another—including Ellington, Basie, both Dorsey brothers—and even actually recorded a bebop novelty (the 1949 "Bebop Spoken Here"), the style of jazz that most excited him was the brand that he was not ashamed to refer to as Dixieland. When traditional, New Orleans–style small group jazz underwent a revival of interest in the late 1940s, Crosby was one of its champions, and he helped to give multimedia exposure to old friends like trumpeter Red Nichols and to newer bands like the Firehouse Five, and especially to his hero, Louis Armstrong.

It was inevitable that Crosby's immersion in what he called "The Dixieland Cult" should bring him to San Francisco—ground zero for the Dixieland Revival. That was where the living legends of New Orleans like Bunk Johnson and George Lewis found their most appreciative audiences, and where even before the war the music had found a spokesman in cornetist Lu Watters. The Lu Watters Yerba Buena Jazz Band had attracted thousands of fans and eventually launched the careers of two bandleaders who would become even more popular on a national level, trombonist Turk Murphy and trumpeter Bob Scobey.

Scobey (1916–1963) was one of the most gifted practitioners of the neo-Dixie style (soon to blossom all over the world, and have a particularly profound effect on the development of British pop music). Born in Tucumcari, New Mexico, Scobey played in dance and swing bands as a young trumpeter, and eventually wound up working with Watters in San Francisco. Scobey was part of the Yerba Buena Jazz Band from the very beginning—and stayed with the group for most of a decade. As a featured player in the Yerba Buena, Scobey got in on the ground floor of the postwar Dixieland boom and also formed a long-lasting musical partnership with singer and banjo player Clancy Hayes. In 1949, the two formed their own group, briefly known as "Alexander's Jazz Band," before adapting the longer-term title "Bob Scobey's Frisco Jazz Band." With the bands of Watters, Scobey, and trombonist Turk Murphy all based in the city by the bay, "Frisco" had indeed become New Orleans on the Pacific.

In addition to being an outstanding trumpeter—one of the very best in his field—Scobey was a good-looking, charismatic bandleader and a dynamic figure, a perfect face to put on the movement. Nineteen fifty-seven may represent the height of his popularity: even by February, when he recorded *Bing with a Beat*, the trumpeter had already cut two albums, *Swingin' on the Golden Gate* (RCA) and *Music from Bourbon Street* (Verve). Said Crosby, "Bob reminded me of Red Nichols in his style and his approach. He played good jazz and had a good sense of humor in his attitude towards his music." Scobey is a bit more fiery than Nichols: Scobey's solos (particularly on "Whispering," on which Crosby voices his approval) have the same kind of aggressive, crackling tone that one associates with the mighty Armstrong.

Both traditional jazz and swing were flourishing on recordings during the early album era. RCA Victor in particular was busily making mostly excellent new hi-fi sessions with all manner of veteran bandleaders (Larry Clinton, Red Norvo, Jay McShann, Erskine Hawkins), soloists (Coleman Hawkins, Red Allen, Bud Freeman), and vocalists (Helen Ward, Jimmy Witherspoon, Cab Calloway). When Crosby came up with the idea of *Bing with a Beat,* it obviously was received as a no-brainer: the still sizable audience for swing and Dixieland would conjoin with the millions of Crosby fans out there.

A few months earlier, in August 1956, Scobey and Hayes had cut an album titled *Beauty and the Beat* for RCA; apparently the corporation had the idea of making the phrase the "Beat" a trademark for the trumpeter when they reused it on *Bing with a Beat.* The Verve albums seem to have used Scobey's working Frisco band, whereas most of his sessions for RCA employ a combination of regular Scobey-ites and well-pedigreed studio jazz players. Only two of the personnel on *Bing with a Beat* were regular band members, one of them the formidable Clancy Hayes, who was apparently content to take a backseat to Crosby in that he merely plays on the album rather than sings. (Although a Crosby-Hayes duet would have been highly welcome.) Pianist Ralph Sutton (as he later told Crosby's biographer, Gary Giddins) had joined Scobey the previous year when the band's keyboardist declined to leave San Francisco to go on the road; he would go on to become one of the most important latter-day stride and traditional jazz pianists. The versatile bassist Red Callender, who played on most of Scobey's RCA dates, was a hero of the Central Avenue scene and a regular presence in the Los Angeles recording studios.

Most of the remaining men on the two February 1957 dates already had a long history with Crosby, and among these clarinetist-arranger Matty Matlock and trombonist Abe Lincoln would play on most of Scobey's RCA sessions as well. Tenor saxophonist Dave Harris was a CBS session player who became well known as soloist with Raymond Scott's groups of various sizes; percussionist Nick Fatool won his wings in Benny Goodman's great band of 1939–41, and while he subsequently played with many major swing bands, in the 1950s he was much in demand as a drummer on Dixie-centric dates. All four men—Lincoln, Matlock, Harris, and Fatool—frequently appear on Crosby's sessions (particularly the jazz-oriented projects) from the 1930s to the 1950s.

After Crosby and Scobey, the key man on the project was Matlock, who played clarinet and

wrote all the expertly crafted, deceptively simple arrangements. The Kentucky-born Matlock (1907–1978) spent much of his career in the shadows of others. When he joined Ben Pollack's reed section in 1929, it's no surprise, in hindsight, that he would attract less attention than Pollack's star clarinetist, Benny Goodman. When Matlock became a founding member of the Bob Crosby Orchestra in 1934–35, he found himself overshadowed by the band's brilliant (if unhygienic) clarinet star Irving Fazola. Still, Matlock was a major talent, and he was increasingly the man whom the elder Crosby turned to when he wanted to do a traditional jazz-oriented project. Matlock played on and arranged most of Crosby's highly successful Dixie-driven hits, like "Sam's Song," "Play a Simple Melody," and "In the Cool, Cool, Cool of the Evening." During the Dixie gold rush, Matlock at last became a leader in his own right; with producer George Avakian, he cut albums for Columbia and then Warner Bros. (On the latter label, Matlock's band was billed as "The Paducah Patrol," after his hometown in Kentucky.)

The idea of Dixieland-backed vocals was not, in 1957, a done deal. At the height of the Jazz Age, when small-group-style, post–New Orleans jazz was simply known as "jazz," there were relatively few singers who recorded in such a setting: Ethel Waters, Cliff Edwards, and Annette Hanshaw come to mind. By the time vocalists started to become important in bands, the swing era was well upon us. In the late 1930s, Bing Crosby and Connee Boswell, singing together and separately (both were under contract to Decca), made jazz dates utilizing a hybrid of swing and traditional jazz backings, which often as not involved units from the Bob Crosby band (and also trombonist Abe Lincoln). Bing recorded enough of these titles over the years for Decca eventually to collect them on an early LP titled *Bing and the Dixieland Bands.* It's worth noting that these were not separate and distinct from Crosby's "pop" sessions; he didn't make a point of singing older songs on small group jazz dates but did contemporary pieces like "You Must Have Been a Beautiful Baby" and "When My Dreamboat Comes Home." As a result, he was able to offer genuine jazz content on a fair number of chart hits.

The paradigm had somewhat shifted by 1957—nearly all the songs on *Bing with a Beat* were actually from the Jazz Age—but now Crosby and Matlock were modernizing Dixieland for the purpose of accompanying singers much the same way that Sinatra and Nelson Riddle were concurrently doing with the big swing band. Fortunately, Matlock and Crosby had twenty years of experimenting behind them, because the questions they had to ask did not have obvious answers. Traditional jazz was generally perceived to involve minimal preparation: the most that was worked out beforehand were only imprecise routines—who solos when? When does everybody play together? The "arrangements" were loose and approximate, unlike the high-precision style later popularized by taskmaster bandleaders like Benny Goodman and Jimmie Lunceford. The bands of the 1920s—even to a degree the eleven-piece jazz-flavored dance bands—were like those chorus lines you see in early musical movies, with girls kicking only more or less in unison, nothing like the super-tight coordinated movements of the Rockettes. In the swing era, the arranger would ascend, and in the modern era, full-fledged jazz composers would take charge—but in the Jazz Age, so the perception goes, it was every man for himself.

The other key step in the evolution of *Bing with a Beat* occurred less than a year before it was made. Over a three-year period, from 1954 to 1956, Crosby recorded an extensive series of studio transcriptions for a daily show on CBS Radio. The total output was 160 songs, the bulk of which were issued commercially for the first time in 2009, in a seven-CD boxed set from Mosaic. Although nearly all these tracks were recorded with pianist Buddy Cole's quartet, Crosby sang twelve selections (all recorded on one date, apparently) with a jazz combo that featured both Matlock and Lincoln. These tracks could easily be released by themselves in an album titled *Bing Before the Beat—The Prequel*. (In fact, it's altogether possible that Crosby was contemplating releasing them at some point, since some of the CBS quartet transcriptions were released commercially at the time.)

The mood is overall very similar to *Beat*—the songs are all from the 1920s—but Crosby and Matlock haven't got the balance precisely right yet. The band sounds a little too controlled and well arranged, it never really cuts loose; overall, it lacks the energy that Scobey and Sutton and company brought to the *Beat* album. The singer's own level of inspiration doesn't reach the pinnacle it would attain a year later; he shows energy and enthusiasm but not to the degree he would in the company of Scobey. In terms of the *Beat* album, the most interesting 1956 track is "Yes Sir! That's My Baby," which starts with the same off-beat percussion introduction between Bing and Nick Fatool that would later open "Let a Smile Be Your Umbrella" (and begin the *Beat* with a bang).

The beauty of Matlock's arrangements for *Bing with a Beat* is that they're nearly completely transparent; you're never conscious that you're listening to an "arranged" performance. The whole thing appears to be completely spontaneous; like Nat King Cole's *After Midnight*, it sounds like a gang of jazzbos in an informal after-hours hang. What it doesn't sound like is a band of studio musicians huddled around music stands, putting on their glasses and reading notes off a printed page while the union contractor stares at his watch and worries about overtime. More than any other of Crosby's collaborators, Matlock has translated Bing's personality into an instrumental sound: casual yet committed, emotional yet off-the-cuff, full of heartfelt feeling but no sign of sentiment. These aren't corny old songs to Bing; rather, they're vital texts, full of essential truths.

It's telling that Crosby avoided songs that became over-roasted chestnuts, and even, for the most part, the major canonical composers of the era. There's no Cole Porter, no Rodgers and Hart, no Gershwin brothers, no Jerome Kern—but there is a lesser-known song by Irving Berlin ("Some Sunny Day"), and one well-known jazz standard by Jimmy McHugh and Dorothy Fields ("Exactly Like You"). There's also "Mack the Knife," but "Mack" was still years away from becoming a pop perennial. Likely this was a deliberate strategy to keep everything fresh: maybe "Someone to Watch over Me" was already overdone by 1957, but "Along the Way to Waikiki" hadn't been heard in forty years. In the words of a Peter Allen song later sung by

Bing, the songs on this album were so old that they were new again.

To make the songs sound fresher still, Crosby begins a great many of them with the verse. Verses were just being rediscovered in the postwar era. Vaudevillians and Broadway singers insisted on singing the verse to songs in the 1920s and earlier—it gave them more to work with, another tool with which to reach an audience. Swing bands tended to eschew verses, and so did the singers who came up in that era—verses were usually out of tempo, and therefore were of no use to dancers. For all of his service to the popular song, Frank Sinatra almost never sang them, particularly on his swing albums (although when he did sing one, as on "When Your Lover Has Gone" or "I Can't Get Started," it was all the more effective for it). Decades later, younger artists who sought out the older songs—like Mel Tormé and Bobby Short (and other cabaret-oriented singers)—began restoring them. But Crosby always was a proponent of the verse.

Crosby's joy, humor, and enthusiasm are unmistakable throughout *Bing with a Beat;* he sings every word as if he's going for the gusto.

The album starts on an incredibly fresh note, or rather, not a note but a beat. We begin with a few telling rimshots from Nick Fatool before Crosby enters with the verse to "Let a Smile Be Your Umbrella." ("Once I met a happy little bluebird . . .") He starts nearly a cappella, accompanied by Fatool only. This brand of Dixieland is both a heterophonic and a polyrhythmic music, and while Fatool is playing one beat, Crosby is singing to another. The vocalist and the drummer aren't exactly together, they're sort of circling around each other, like boxers waiting for the best moment to land a punch. In the midst of all the rimshots and woodblocks we're soon up to the verse to "Umbrella," which might not have been heard since J. C. Flippen (a singer decades before he became a western movie character actor) recorded it when the song was new in 1928. Crosby establishes a lot of his game plan here on the opening track: this album will make heavy use of verses and of a remarkable level of interplay with the band. Said interplay is heightened by

the use of spoken asides and special lyrics, all of which sound completely ad-lib. Scobey solos in the instrumental break (as does Dave Harris, briefly), after which Crosby's second chorus is even looser and more swinging than the first—a general pattern that he most likely, like the rest of the world, learned from Ethel Waters.

Verses are supposed to be out of tempo—they are on most 1920s and '30s recordings (including Crosby's own), but the verse to "Umbrella" is peppy and danceable. "I'm Gonna Sit Right Down and Write Myself a Letter," however, uses the verse more traditionally, as a rubato intro. Where much of the album, between Crosby and Scobey, is saturated with the spirit of Satchmo, this particular track is strongly inspired by Fats Waller—Fats didn't write it, but he made it into a stride piano signature; Ralph Sutton could have probably played it in his sleep by 1957. (Written in 1935, "Sit Right Down" is also the newest song on the album.) Sutton quotes a few famous phrases from the classic 1935 recording by Waller and His Rhythm, and Crosby's asides with the band are also definitely in a post-Fats frame of mind. When he returns, after Sutton's solo, he praises the ensemble, "The way you fellahs play, I swear I'm feeling better . . ."

The mood gets mellower for "Along the Way to Waikiki," a 1917 song by Richard Whiting and Gus Kahn (who were both based in Chicago—a long way from Waikiki). This was part of the first wave of Hawaiian-styled songs in American pop, which would come and go in cycles, and was far from over in 1957. It's easy to imagine the fourteen-year-old Crosby listening to "Waikiki" by The Peerless Quartet on the family Victrola, but he also could have been exposed to the song in a mid-1930s recording by Harry Owens and His Royal Hawaiian Hotel Orchestra, the composer-bandleader responsible for Crosby's mega-hit "Sweet Leilani." Owens's instrumental version is a bouncier little-grass-shack-style fox-trot, while Crosby's is a slower and more romantic dance, and the solos by Sutton and Scobey completely capture the mood. (Blogger Dave Whitney points out Matlock's use of the combination of clarinet and tenor in the arrangement, a sonic device associated with the Bob Crosby band.)

"Exactly Like You" was written by Fields and McHugh for the 1930 *International Revue* (which also included "On the Sunny Side of the Street"). Dorothy Fields's immortal lyric notwithstanding, it wasn't Bing's mother who taught him to be musically true but Louis Armstrong, who immediately immortalized "Exactly" on one of his earliest big band sessions. Crosby doesn't directly imitate Armstrong here, but he was the obvious inspiration, particularly in that this track contains the closest thing to a scat solo on the album: during the instrumental break, he hums back and forth with the horns for sixteen bars. The band drops out behind Bing at key points in the first bridge, which has the feeling of a stop-time break in a blues record, the kind of thing that Armstrong perfected, and Scobey's solo here (preceding Sutton's eight bars) is particularly Satchelmouthed.

"Dream a Little Dream of Me" was also written in 1930, but enjoyed less of a direct path to pop immortality. Most of the great standards were born on Broadway, others in Harlem, and more in Hollywood, but "Dream" is one of the few that hailed from Wisconsin. It was originally written by Fabian Andre and Wilbur Schwandt, two musicians who played in a local dance band billed as "The Midnight Serenaders" led by one Glen Lietzke (which may not be the correct spelling). This band cut the first recording of the song in Grafton, Wisconsin, circa August 1930, with the leader singing; the song was then titled "Stars" and boasted a thoroughly putrid lyric. Somehow the melody or the record reached Gus Kahn, a major hitmaker of the era, who was usually based in Chicago—which is closer to Grafton than to Tin Pan Alley. Kahn gave it a whole new title and lyric, keeping only the first word, "Stars shining bright above you . . ." Gus's Kahn-tribution made all the difference: "Dream a Little Dream of Me," as it was now known, is one of the all-time great pop songs. It was widely popularized in an early recording by Ozzie Nelson's orchestra (and other period dance bands), but then, like a lot of songs, it was pretty much forgotten after its initial burst of popularity and was rediscovered in the 1950s.

For his part, Crosby is extremely frisky throughout: during the instrumental break, he cheers Scobey on with Bert Williams-esque Ebonics: "Yeah Bob! You ain't just dreamin'—you is awake!" In the second bridge, he keeps the speaking mode going even while he sings; he shows a little sign of strain the last line ("All I keep sayin' is this"), but then he gets even more resonant and mellifluous in the last eight bars, ending on a note that's practically basso profundo ("of me"). The song has a built-in nostalgic quality that must have been apparent even in 1931, and is musically ingenious in the way it modulates up a minor third from the central refrain to the bridge (from G to B flat in the published music) and then back again.

"Last Night on the Back Porch," introduced in *George White's Scandals of 1923,* was one of Paul Whiteman's most memorable early records; the prolific and talented Lew Brown wrote the lyrics, while the music is by the little-known Carl Schraubstader. It's all about horny kids making out where no one can see, and could have only been produced during the lusty, sexually liberated spirit of the Roaring Twenties. "Back Porch" also made an impression on Johnny Mercer, who recorded it in 1937 in a special arrangement for which he wrote a whole mess of new choruses, verses, and patter sections.

"Back Porch" is also one of the highlights of *Bing with a Beat,* with Crosby at his most exuberant, starting with the original verse (which Mercer didn't include in 1937). Scobey is heard over the ensemble, but then Lincoln takes over with just the rhythm section and offers his best solo of the date. Crosby's second chorus is even more animated, and he starts to ad-lib "the first time I dug this chick it was true love at first sight" and he ends it as if reminiscing about his own college days circa 1923: "last night gave her my frat pin." He seems to be having so much fun that he surprises both himself and us by returning unexpectedly for a spontaneous coda: "Last night Maw went shopping / and I loved her best of all!" This extra tag, obviously, had to be predetermined in the arrangement, but it has the feeling of being completely ad-lib.

Irving Berlin's 1919 "Some Sunny Day" is quite possibly the album's signature: it's the track that everybody remembers. While Crosby was certainly familiar with the records by Marion Harris, Paul

Whiteman, and, more recently, Lee Wiley, he sang this lesser-known Berlin song out of a more personal connection. As he told Simon, "I used to hear the Brox Sisters singing it.... One of the Sisters [Lorayne] was married to [Whiteman trumpeter] Henry Busse. And that's how I happened to hear the song." The Broxes had made a famous early recording of "Some Sunny Day," which had been heard in the 1919 Broadway musical *La-La-Lucille!* What Crosby didn't mention is that in 1930, Whiteman's band worked with the Brox Sisters in the film *The King of Jazz*, and for a time Crosby was involved romantically with sister Bobbe Brock (who later married songwriter Jimmy Van Heusen).

Thus, "Some Sunny Day" was a song that he associated with both an old girlfriend and going home—two good reasons why it was perfectly appropriate for *Bing with a Beat*. The Berlin ballad itself is cast in ABCA form—highly unusual for Berlin or anybody else. (The B section, musician and scholar Dan Levinson notes, is actually the same melody as the first A, but in minor, which is even more uncommon, although Jelly Roll Morton used the same form for "Someday Sweetheart," from 1923.) "Sunny Day" also has two verses (neither of which was sung by either Crosby or Wiley, but both were done by Marion Harris in 1922), which both concern themselves with the act of going home to mammy in Alabammy. The melody is slightly reminiscent of Franz Lehár's 1907 "Vilia" (from *The Merry Widow*), but the setting of "Some Sunny Day" is considerably less cosmopolitan than old Vienna.

"Some Sunny Day," like so many songs of the immediate post–World War I era, is about a nostalgic return to rural roots. It isn't enough that the old redheaded hen in the barnyard is happy to see him come home, rather, she's so overjoyed about his return that she will immediately "go back to the hay / and lay me my breakfast." Then, in the second chorus, Bing spontaneously modifies it to, "back to the hay ... a couple over easy." The reeds take over in the instrumental break, with solos by Harris and then Matlock himself. Crosby has never been more irresistible than in the second chorus, which he ends on an exuberant high note—you get a clear visual image in your head of the Groaner throwing

his arms up in the air on the final "... some sunny day!" (Crosby remade the song on a 1975 British session, a track that included Berlin's first verse but regrettably set the whole thing on top of a faux-funk beat that must have seemed dated by 1976.)

"Whispering" had been one of Pops Whiteman's breakthrough hits in 1920 (and was later reworked by Dizzy Gillespie into the bebop anthem "Groovin' High"). Crosby begins by whispering the count off to the musicians, then sings the verse in tempo while Sutton plays with amazing subtlety, literally whispering via the keyboard. The brass enters doing anything but whispering on the refrain, as Crosby glides over the beat. He's also incredibly effusive in his asides to the band here: while Scobey turns on the heat in a Satchelmouthed fashion, Crosby exhorts him in a manner that would have done Fats Waller proud: "Nice whispering, Bob ... you're reachin' me! ... Just barely gettin' through ... Murmur, murmur!" There are also two additional ad-lib comments whose meaning is not entirely clear: while Scobey solos, Bing observes "This sounds like a beef!" (Does he think the trumpeter is complaining about something?) Then, in the coda he exclaims, "Whisper to me, dearie / Put me on the ear-ie!" (My best guess is that he's saying, put me in your ear, in other words, "listen to me.") The specific meaning is unimportant, what matters is that the high spirits here, as on "Some Sunny Day," are once again completely contagious.

Time for a slow-down. In 1919, "Tell Me" (sometimes listed as "Tell Me [Why Nights Are So Lonely]") had been one of Al Jolson's most poignant early recordings. Jolson's treatment is very touching, even though he takes it at what seems today like a breakneck tempo (those World War I–era fox-trots were relentlessly peppy, even the ballads), and he makes use of the same kind of spoken asides later done on records by Armstrong, Waller, and Crosby. Composed by Max Kortlander and J. Will Callahan, it's a fine illustration of how keeping a song uncomplicated can heighten its overall emotional impact. Every line in the main refrain is, essentially, a question that begins with the words "tell me," a brilliantly simple and effective construction. "Tell Me" never became a standard, but other people remembered it fondly too, and it turns up in a couple of period movie musicals, *For Me and My Girl* (1942) and *On Moonlight Bay* (1952), in which it was beautifully sung in a slow tempo by Doris Day. Crosby seems determined to out-poignant both Day and the late Jolson, while maintaining a dance tempo (faster than her, slower than him) all the while. Like Crosby's vocal, Dave Harris's tenor solo is warm and effusive.

By an apparent coincidence, *Bing with a Beat* includes two old songs that became new hits in the rock 'n' roll era: "Dream a Little Dream of Me" would be a biggie for Mama Cass in 1968 (she was quite a biggie herself) and "Mack the Knife" would become a blockbuster for Bobby Darin in 1959. Darin, like Crosby, would learn the opening song from *The Threepenny Opera* from Louis Armstrong, who made the first notable jazz or American pop recording in 1956. Crosby is way more relaxed than either Armstrong or Darin, as he shows when he commences the piece by exhaling in tempo. He literally just exhales the count-off, and then warns the bandsmen to "bivouac" (entrench themselves and prepare for an onslaught). He's mellow and understated as he enumerates the atrocious acts of the *über*-criminal Macheath with something like begrudging admiration. Scobey's trumpet solo comes almost as close as anyone has to nailing Armstrong, and Crosby's final vocal is accompanied by a close paraphrase of the great one's "Coal Cart Blues."

Both Crosby and Scobey on "Down Among the Sheltering Palms" are even more Satchelmouthed; it almost sounds like the singer and the trumpeter were trying to imagine how Louis Armstrong and His All-Stars would have recorded this 1915 song. "Palms" (recorded most famously when it was new by The Lyric Quartet on Victor) originally washed ashore as part of the same wave of Island music as "Waikiki." (Composer James Brockman later went on to write the even more successful "I'm Forever Blowing Bubbles" in 1919.) Crosby later told George Simon that "Sheltering Palms" was "one of the numbers I used to sing while I was playing drums back with the little band we had back in Spokane." That little band was somewhat ahead of its time: the song enjoyed a full-scale revival in 1932, led off by Crosby's close friends The Boswell

Sisters—and other Crosby associates who swayed to it over the years include Johnny Mercer, Eddie Condon (with Jack Teagarden and Pee Wee Russell in 1947), and future All-Star Earl Hines, in a stunning piano solo.

Crosby once again starts with the verse—a completely different verse than the one sung by The Lyric Quartet in 1915. The verse enables Crosby to make the song pensive and nostalgic at the same time it's romantic and exotic—I met you and fell in love with you beneath the sheltering palms, and now I yearn to go back there and see you again. Like all great interpreters, he makes the song into something bigger and deeper than it might otherwise be—a simple tale of sandy beaches and palm trees has now been seasoned with a hint of melancholy. In Crosby's interpretation, it's a proper tale of lost innocence to rank with "When the World Was Young" and "Last Night When We Were Young." Scobey's solo is perfectly in tune with that contemplative mood. As with the Gershwins' later "Fascinating Rhythm," the syncopated accents and breaks are part of the actual tune, as is the slang utilized in the text ("spoonin', croonin', sweet honey-moonin'"), and Crosby elaborates on them.

The interjection, "Oh so contented," is written into the song itself, as a kind of jazzy "break"; then in the second chorus Crosby changes it to "Oh, so *Shangri*!"—a reference to *Lost Horizon* and Shangri-La. For years, Michael Feinstein and I have had an ongoing debate regarding the merit of these minor lyric changes and ad libs by Crosby and especially Sinatra, but here it's clear that they illustrate the depth of Crosby's involvement with the material. These ad libs show that he's really feeling the song, he's so deep in the spirit that he can improvise new words which capture the original intentions just as well as the actual lyric. At the very end he makes a joke out of formalizing the slang, British-style: "Mater loves Pater and everything's jolly now!"

Twelve songs and that was it. *Bing with a Beat* sounds just as fresh now as that some sunny day in Los Angeles nearly sixty years ago when Crosby recorded it.

• • •

To repeat what Crosby said to George Simon, he loved making records, because "when you're finished recording, you've got something that's really your own." The broader truth is that a lot of his records weren't really his own—it was his voice, and his personality, but when you sing thousands and thousands of songs, it would hardly be possible to create a personal connection with every one of them, to make "Onward Christian Soldiers" just as personal as "Your Socks Don't Match." Crosby later used Dixieland-style accompaniment on his long-awaited album-length collaboration with Louis Armstrong (*Bing and Louis,* 1960) and his second meeting with Rosemary Clooney *(That Travelin' Two-Beat).* But nothing comes close to *Bing with a Beat.* It's the album Crosby later said that he "always wanted to make" and it stands alone as the single most amazing example ever of the Great American musical Everyman for once just being himself.

11

Bing Crosby and Louis Armstrong

Bing & Satchmo

(1960)

For years, it was thought that Louis Armstrong was born in 1900 and Bing Crosby in 1904; the truth, it turns out, is that they were closer in age than was previously realized; as Gary Giddins has pointed out, Armstrong was actually born in 1901 and Crosby in 1903. The two men were also mutually involved in new technology: it was through Crosby's patronage that recording tape was developed after the war; then, when tape recorders went on sale a few years later, mostly to professional engineers in the beginning, Armstrong became a pioneering home-recording enthusiast with his own private studio. The Mighty Satchmo, as Crosby referred to him, was always a technophile—if he were alive today, he would be all over Facebook and YouTube (of course he al-

ready is, albeit posthumously). Yet Armstrong was making personal recordings well before the advent of audiotape. The earliest private recording that survives is a disc that he cut at the Decca Studios in 1939, in which he sends birthday salutations to his dear friend Bing Crosby (as well as "Madame Bing and all the little Bingies!") and then plays and sings a chorus of "Happy Birthday to You" more ebullient than any version of that song has a right to be.

Prior to 1960, Crosby and Armstrong sang together on only one commercial recording, "Gone Fishin'," in 1951. In the middle of that number, Crosby ad-libs to Armstrong, "Man you taught me!," and he wasn't just whistling "Dixie." Armstrong taught Crosby—along with every other singer—and he also learned a few things from him as well. The two men defined the term "mutual admiration society"; theirs was a love-love relationship. Between the two of them, they revolutionized the way that American music is both played and sung—and had more to do than anyone else with the way that pop and jazz have sounded for the last century—and going forward into the future.

Bing Crosby once famously described Louis Armstrong as "the beginning and end of music in America," but he did more than pay Armstrong lip service. Rather, to extend the oral metaphor, Crosby put his money where his mouth was: over a period of decades, Crosby recruited Armstrong as a musical partner at every opportunity, and in every one of his mediums—at Crosby's instigation they worked together on recordings, radio, and even motion pictures—and this at a time when the sight of a black man and a white man performing together, as equals, would practically guarantee an uproar in the American South.

Famously, Crosby had opened the door for Armstrong to make his first appearance in a mainstream Hollywood feature film (the 1936 *Pennies from Heaven*), and the two shared space on a Decca medley of the songs from that score. Over the years Crosby also pressed Armstrong into service for three more feature films: *Doctor Rhythm*

(1938), *Here Comes the Groom* (1951), and, most famously, *High Society* (1956). Armstrong was a frequent guest on Crosby's long-running radio series, especially in the 1949–51 period, and one of these appearances led to "Gone Fishin'." Although *High Society,* which also costarred Frank Sinatra, Grace Kelly, and Celeste Holm, was already rich in musical and dramatic talent, everyone agrees that Armstrong's amazing contribution helped make that 1956 production into a veritable blockbuster, both as a movie and as a top-selling soundtrack album.

On the strength of "Gone Fishin'" and "Now You Has Jazz" (their classic duet in *High Society*), Crosby and Armstrong were well established as frequent musical partners; a whole generation grew up seeing them together on the big screen and small. Trumpeter Jimmy Owens vividly remembers enjoying them on TV as a little kid and aspiring musician in the 1950s, and he remembered being struck by how intrinsically cool Crosby was, in contrast to Armstrong's hotness—sometimes literally, puffing his cheeks and mopping his brow.

Then, in 1960, Crosby and Armstrong made their major full-length project together as a team, the remarkable *Bing & Satchmo.*

Both participants had long since established themselves as sturdy duet partners. Crosby was quite probably the duet-ing-est man in recording history; this aspect of his influence has only grown, rather than waned, in the twenty-first century, an era when it sometimes seems like almost every new CD being released by a legacy artist is another set of duets—Frank Sinatra, Ray Charles, Barbra Streisand, Tony Bennett. Armstrong had also sung with a wide array of collaborators, both male and female, including Jack Teagarden, Louis Jordan, his own band vocalist, the underappreciated Velma Middleton, and Billie Holiday. In the 12-inch-album era, Armstrong launched a widely heralded series of boy-girl duo albums with Ella Fitzgerald *(Ella and Louis, Ella and Louis Again, Porgy and Bess),* even as Crosby was doing the same with Rosemary Clooney *(Fancy Meeting You Here* and *That Travelin' Two-Beat).* The two Crosby-Clooney albums—and *Bing & Satchmo* as well—were produced by Simon "Sy" Rady, an independent A&R

man whom arranger Billy May described as having a proclivity toward duo projects. All three were arranged by May, and all benefited from special material written for them by an ace songwriting team.

Through these albums, Billy May became established as the number one go-to guy for vocal duet projects in the 1950s and '60s: he would also helm the baton on the 1961 *Two of a Kind* by Bobby Darin and Johnny Mercer, as well as a series of duet singles involving various combinations of Nat King Cole, Dean Martin, Sammy Davis Jr., and Frank Sinatra. Whenever two mega-stars wanted to sing together, it seemed like May was always the man on the podium. When I interviewed him in the early 1990s, he insisted that this turn of events "was just an accident"—he never intended for it to turn out that way.

May's strength was that he was capable of working within virtually any style of music that a given project called for, from Dixieland to Broadway to big bands to gospel, and making it sound both authentic and highly musical. Since all of those sounds come into play on *Bing & Satchmo,* it's hard to imagine anyone else who could have done nearly as well; he came up with a large-format traditional jazz sound in the same vein as Bob Crosby, but thoroughly drenched in May's characteristic musical humor. May pointed out that he brought in the right players for the project: "We had a lot of musicians there, old friends. I used some guys that had worked with Bing a long time ago—Matty Matlock and guys like that."

As with the Crosby-Clooney albums, and unlike the first two Ella-Louis albums, *Bing & Satchmo* would be a full-scale "production." One thing it isn't is a couple of vocalists sitting around a rhythm section, swapping standards back and forth (or "crossing cadenzas," as Crosby would put it). The first two Ella-Louis sound more like that; Crosby and Armstrong's radio duets were also generally done in such a loose, informal fashion. *Bing & Satchmo,* however, sounds like an incredibly hip original cast album, or, more to the period, like the soundtrack of an elaborate TV special (the only thing that's missing is the June Taylor Dancers), complete with a full orchestra, a large mixed chorus singing special lyrics, and, through it all plenty of space for Armstrong's celestial trumpet.

All three of the Crosby–Billy May duet projects employed a well-known songwriter (or team thereof) writing what Sammy Cahn referred to as "special material." On *Fancy Meeting You Here* it was Cahn and Jimmy Van Heusen; on *Travelin' Two-Beat* it was Ray Evans and Jay Livingston. For *Bing & Satchmo,* no less a personage than the legendary Johnny Mercer himself eagerly wrote much of the script for two of his personal musical heroes. Mercer not only wrote special lyrics (as on "[Up a] Lazy River"), he contributed two wholly original songs, "Rocky Mountain Moon" and "Little Ol' Tune" (two of the few for which he wrote both words and music) and added a fresh set of words to The Original Dixieland Jass Band chestnut of an instrumental, "At the Jazz Band Ball." Mercer also made an unbilled vocal cameo appearance (also on "Lazy River"), and if that wasn't enough, he wrote the album's liner notes.

Crosby initially bankrolled the recording through his own production company, and he owned the finished masters. Alan Bergman, then an aspiring young songwriter, was at the time a protégé of Mercer's, and he remembered that although Sy Rady was present at the sessions, most of the artistic decisions were being made by Mercer. Mercer was directing the session, and he had also picked all the tunes, nearly all of which were pre-swing jazz standards or had come from the Armstrong canon. Mercer, had, in effect, put the whole package together. "Johnny Mercer wrote a lot of special lyrics to some numbers while we recorded it in the studio," said Billy May. "He was really interested in getting it going."

Mercer contributed special lyrics for ten out of the twelve songs (the other two were by Bergman); between the tailorings of Mercer and May, all the songs became elaborate vehicles for two star singers, solo trumpet, and in roughly half the songs a chatty chorus. Although the idea of a large background vocal group suggests a kind of pop music that some might regard as diametrically opposed to the language of jazz, this chorus is amazingly hip: in both words and music, they sound more like Lambert, Hendricks & Ross than they do Mitch Miller.

In one notable instance, Mercer pulled a real Jon Hendricks in that he took Armstrong's classic solo from his 1931 "Lazy River" and set it to lyrics for the vocal group, which is heard after Armstrong enters singing a variation on his own solo and the proceedings modulate rhythmically into double-time.

For years it was rumored that the recording process on *Bing & Satchmo* utilized overdubbing. Hans Westerberg's discography of Louis Armstrong, *Boy from New Orleans* (published in 1981), states that the orchestral parts were taped on three dates in June (28–30), the vocals of the two principals were added on July 5, and then Armstrong overdubbed his trumpet solos on the 7th. When I asked Billy May about it, he said, unequivocally, that it wasn't so: that the whole album was taped "live," with all the elements recorded together.

"That was all done live," Billy told me, although he later clarified, in correspondence with his discographer, Jack Mirtle, that "Bing and Louis sang it live but improved it later," meaning, presumably, that they came in and polished up a few rough spots here and there. May vividly remembered the date, he recounted to me, not least because it was his only commercial recording with Armstrong. "Everybody was falling down laughing, because Louis was so funny, and Bing, he likes a joke too, and Johnny Mercer was there writing special material, and he's coming up with one-liners—and jeez, it was really funny." Going by May's recollections, the album was probably recorded on June 28, 29, and 30—most pop albums were done as twelve tracks in three sessions as per union rules at the time—and the two stars made their fixes on July 7.

The high spirits that May describes are apparent from the first track, "Muskrat Ramble." This is the New Orleans jazz standard generally attributed to Armstrong, which he bequeathed to his longtime colleague, trombonist Kid Ory. After lyrics were added by Ray Gilbert in 1950, the song became a pop hit for the McGuire Sisters in 1954 and, in a rockabilly style, for the Matys Brothers three years later. Mercer wrote a new lyric around Gilbert's earlier text, which sets up the proceedings rather like the opening scene of a Broadway musical:

Crosby and chorus are waiting for Armstrong and the All-Stars ("his Dixieland Five") to arrive at the train station; Crosby assists Armstrong in making a grand entrance, and one can easily visualize a Mardi Gras parade, with Armstrong as a King of the Zulus, as they sing together. The ensemble sounds especially jazzed by Armstrong's presence—these are all stellar soloists, not a bunch of faceless studio hacks—and they all play with May's characteristic exaggerated dynamics in a dramatic style that sounds like an ensemble of Armstrongs. (Trumpeters Dick Cathcart and Shorty Sherock in particular were of the generation that learned to play through the process of Satchmosis.) Crosby starts it, but the whole track (indeed the whole album) is highly Satchmo-centric.

The second tune and the last one on side one, "Sugar" and "Let's Sing Like a Dixieland Band," both involved Alan Bergman, who continues to regard Mercer as his mentor. "Johnny told me he was producing an album with Bing and Louis and asked me if I wanted to write something for them," Bergman remembered in a recent phone conversation. Mercer also asked Bergman, and his two partners, Marilyn Keith and Lew Spence, to come up with a countermelody for the 1920s jazz standard "Sugar" with original lyrics. Spence worked out the tune itself, and Alan and Marilyn came up with the text, in which the chemical components of sugar (dextrose, glucose, etc.) are analyzed from a rather charming perspective. The overall outline is similar to Armstrong's classic treatment of "Rockin' Chair" with Jack Teagarden: Crosby sings the melody first, with obbligato by Armstrong; then, when Armstrong sings the words and music, Crosby provides the asides re: complex carbohydrates (liquid, solid, or powdered). Armstrong sings at the end, "Sugar raises cane with my darling" and briefly quotes from "Bess, You Is My Woman Now" ("morning time and evening time . . .").

For his own original song, Bergman thought that he had a terrific idea. "Since Louis and Bing were both great improvisers, I thought why not write a song where they both get to scat? That's how I came up with 'Let's Sing Like a Dixieland Band.' Then, when I got to the date, Bing took me aside and said, 'Listen, I love this song and it's great

for us, but you don't expect me to scat with Pops do you? He's the Dean—I couldn't ever keep up with him!' I had to rewrite it—right there on the date. Bing was very nice about it, but that was the first time I ever had to do that—I was nervous enough just thinking about Bing Crosby and Louis Armstrong doing one of my songs! I told Johnny about it, and he said, 'Welcome to showbiz, kid!'" "Let's Sing Like a Dixieland Band" is another delightful duet, done by just the two principals without benefit of choir, trading phrases both verbal and otherwise. As Louis scats, Crosby sings a simple raplike set of words around him, which were apparently the lyrics hastily scribbled down by Bergman only minutes before they were recorded.

Horace Silver's "The Preacher" shows that either Mercer or Crosby—or someone—was keeping up with the latest thing in modern jazz. This 1955 tune had already been widely recorded by bop bands, big bands, and even a few Dixieland groups, but this was certainly the first time it was done by a pair of mainstream star vocalists. It almost sounds like Silver wrote it for the two voices in 2/4 time. Crosby often referred to Armstrong as "The Reverend Satchelmouth," and here Armstrong directly essays the role of a musical minister and righteous reverend. His interaction with the male choir (particularly the basses) makes "The Preacher" sound like a bonus track from his 1957 album of spirituals, *Louis and the Good Book*.

"Dardanella" indirectly derives from the Crosby canon; it was a very early hit (by Fred Fisher, of "Chicago" fame) for Crosby's longtime boss, bandleader Paul Whiteman, although that was at a time when Bing was still a teen in Spokane. May uses a minor key clarinet (probably played by Matty Matlock or Wilbur Schwartz) as a way of infusing the atmosphere with Eastern exoticism in this tale of a Turkish titwillow, a demimondaine from the Dardanelles. (It's a logical follow-up to "Hindustan" and "Calcutta" from *Fancy Meeting You Here*.) Crosby and Armstrong trade off lead and supporting roles, with one singing the original words and the other singing Mercer's witty counterpoint text, which is audaciously topical, especially when the choir informs us that Dardanella "looks so dreamy in her *Maidenform* bra."

Hard to believe, but true: Armstrong had never previously recorded either of the New Orleans jazz perennials, "At the Jazz Band Ball" or "Way Down Yonder in New Orleans" (although he had played the latter with his All-Stars at many concerts). On "Way Down Yonder" the musical banter between the two principals is especially priceless; utilizing Mercer's special material, the piece is a veritable three-way conversation between a trio of musical savants. Armstrong gets most of the best original lines, to Crosby's delight: "way back yonder these poor old chops / had an embouchure that was tops . . . Pops!" The triple rhyme during the habanera excursion in the center is classic:

We would dig the cognoscenti,
King Oliver and [Tony] Parenti,
Swingin' the "Tiger [Rag]," "That's A Plenty."

When Armstrong refers to a parade, the band quickly quotes the famous circus march "Entrance of the Gladiators."

As a composer, Armstrong had a predilection for novelty and rhythm tunes, famously "Ol' Man Mose Is Dead"; his 1939 "Brother Bill" could have been a black vaudeville tune of the sort that Bert Williams might have performed. (It's very similar to such black vaudeville and minstrelsy fare as "The Preacher and the Bear.") Even Armstrong's chuckle is incredibly musical, he almost seems to laugh on key. Crosby refers to the dual protagonists (the song is sometimes listed as "Me and Brother Bill") as "two nimrods," which is at once a reference to an Old Testament monarch and to Sir Edward Elgar (his famous "Nimrod" variation). (As we also know from Bugs Bunny cartoons, by the 1950s "nimrod" had become an affectionate term indicating an individual of substandard intelligence.) Armstrong must have been pleased with Mercer's supplementary lyrics, in which the two nimrods are likened to a "four-legged jet" that is "still running yet."

"Bye Bye Blues" (another tune that Armstrong recorded only on this one occasion), from 1929, is credited to dance band leader Bert Lown (and three other collaborators) and eventually became a favorite among traditional jazz bands. Crosby's

baritone is especially ripe, rich, and mellow, as Armstrong once described his singing, "like gold being poured out of a cup." Mercer brings back the big choir here, and the choral music and text are rife with all sorts of references to the blues both real and ersatz, famous and obscure: "Ev'ry Day I Have the Blues," "Stumbling," "Tickle Toe," "I Ain't Mad at You," "River, Stay Away from My Door," and even "Pop Goes the Weasel."

In addition to the seven specialty jobs (not counting the two by Alan Bergman), *Bing & Satchmo* contains three original all-Mercer lyrics that are so rare that they might as well be unique to this album. "At the Jazz Band Ball" is an incredibly hip and happening new libretto to the ur-jazz classic (originally recorded by The Original Dixieland Jass Band in 1917). It's an evocative tableaux of Storyville-era New Orleans, which could have been taken from the text of *Mister Jelly Roll*, describing honky-tonk piano professors in the process of inventing ragtime, even down to a *soupçon* of French expressions—like "man it's strictly *bon-ton*."

The title of "Little Ol' Tune" sounds literally like it was taken from one of Armstrong's onstage introductions; it's a fanciful depiction of the songwriting process, opening with the male choir mimicking a barbershop quartet (referring to "melodies and diphthongs"). The songwriter-singer eventually recorded it himself, but while "Little Ol' Tune" is a cutie, "Rocky Mountain Moon" is a hidden Mercer masterpiece. It's a lovely waltz that country singers who occasionally gravitate to the songbook, like Willie Nelson and Crystal Gayle, should consider. The choir is relatively subdued, and the mood is similar to "I Love You Samantha" from *High Society*, with Crosby making melancholy while Armstrong plays marvelously muted obbligatos behind him. It's the quietest and most intimate moment on the album, and the twosome wind it up in exquisite harmony.

Crosby originally licensed the masters to MGM Records, who released eleven songs as the original *Bing & Satchmo* LP in 1961. For some reason, "Lazy River" was withheld from the original release, but turned up a few years later on a special anthology

LP released to raise money for the United Nations. (The first commercial release was on a double LP of rarities issued by DRG Records in the 1970s.) Crosby eventually sold the rights (along with a few other projects, including *Travelin' Two-Beat* and a Christmas album) to Capitol Records. In the 1970s, Capitol issued ten of the twelve tracks on a budget LP, which to the annoyance of Alan Bergman did not include "Let's Sing Like a Dixieland Band" and "Little Ol' Tune." (This is the edition that I grew up with.) In the early CD era, Australian EMI very briefly released *Bing & Satchmo* along with *Travelin' Two-Beat* on a twofer CD together—a rather rare disc issued only in Australia. Surprisingly, *Bing & Satchmo* was not readily available on a domestic American CD until DRG licensed it from Capitol in 2009.

Billy May made a comment about *Bing & Satchmo* that I almost never heard him say in all the many times I spoke with him, and with regards to all the many projects I asked him about. "It really worked out good. That's a good album. I mean, I'm proud of that album, of my efforts." I'm sure everyone involved would agree. *Bing & Satchmo* was the culmination of the lifelong mutual admiration society between two giants of twentieth-century music. If it ever gets any better than this, I'm not sure I want to know about it.

12

Doris Day

Day by Day (1956)
and *Day by Night* (1957)

ight has weight. It was Albert Einstein who first put forward that particular scientific theory, and it's since been proven: sunshine has mass and is affected by the force of gravity.

The popular arts could use an Einstein of their own. In music, film, and theater there's a tendency to think of the brighter, sunnier moods and

Herman is a composer with just as much craft—and certainly more melody—than Sondheim. The famous line "dying is easy, comedy is hard" notwithstanding (Edmund Gwenn? Edmund Kean?), a performer is much more likely to reap a certain kind of reward by dying than by slipping on a banana peel.

a more upbeat attitude as having so little weight as to be entirely frivolous—it's the darker moods that are somehow perceived to have significance. Nearly everyone agrees that comedy is harder to do than drama, yet the Academy Awards, infamously, almost never go to comedies, and in England, Laurence Olivier is knighted relatively early in his career while Noël Coward and Rex Harrison have to wait until they're old men for the same recognition. In the musical theater, the big awards and the major accolades go to the dark brooding dramas of Stephen Sondheim rather than the diva-driven comedies of Jerry Herman, even though

Doris Day, traditionally, has on the whole been taken a lot less seriously than singers of comparable stature who happen to have a lot more turbulence in their careers, like Edith Piaf, Billie Holiday, and Judy Garland. All three of them sang no shortage of upbeat, cheerful songs, but they all were tragically self-destructive in their personal lives. Somehow, it's easier to regard a diva as a great artist if she's always on the verge of doing herself in—paging Amy Winehouse.

In terms of musical/cultural physics, the converse of the theorem that sunshine has no weight is the equally erroneous notion that slow tempos invariably convey heaviness and dark drama. Yet any kind of slow tempo in pop music was a relatively new idea in Doris Day's era; during the 78 rpm dynasty, nearly every record was a danceable fox-trot; even the slow blues of Bessie Smith or the most romantic song by Bing Crosby were a lot faster than those same genres in later generations. It was Billie Holiday and Frank Sinatra who pioneered the concept of the slow ballad in twentieth-century pop, which they both extended into the era of the long-playing album. In the mid-1950s, Sinatra's classic "concept" albums were coming in two distinct flavors: they were either slow and sad or fast and ecstatic.

Then, in 1956–58, a new kind of slow was brought forward by Doris Day and Nat King Cole, in such albums as Day's *Day by Day* and *Day by Night* and Cole's *Love Is the Thing* and *The Very Thought of You*. These releases showed that "slow" no longer had to be automatically heavy and sad. Slow could be sexy and romantic. A song could now be upbeat philosophically, even cheerful, no matter what the tempo was.

There might be a slight hint of melancholy here and there, but nothing about *Day by Day* or *Day by Night* is the least bit depressing; pensive, perhaps, or maybe anxious, but not melancholy or squirmy. These songs are all positive and romantic. Some are slightly faster than others, but tempo is not an indicator of the mood, the slower songs are not necessarily the saddest. It's more like the rhythm of slow lovemaking, as if these songs are trying to extract as much pleasure as possible with every note. You want it to last longer for maximum enjoyment. You want to savor every second of it, and not miss a moment.

The album format was a boon to Day for many reasons, not least of which was that it afforded her the means to move beyond the limitations of 150-second singles. In the immediate postwar years, Day (born Doris Mary Ann Kappelhoff in a year that's still being debated, but is probably 1922) graduated from big band singer to a solo career and, from there, quickly into the movies. She would be the only female equivalent of Sinatra and Bing Crosby in following their trajectory out of the dance bands and into the upper heights of

solo stardom, a career achievement that Rosemary Clooney, Ella Fitzgerald, Peggy Lee, and many other former band chirps surely envied. In both her movies and her music of the early 1950s, Day established a consistent personality: upbeat, sunny, optimistic—innocent—so much so that Oscar Levant's infamous wisecrack ("I knew her before she was a virgin") resonated with Day the way it would have with no other actress or singer.

She sang mostly snappy, peppy, upbeat songs; most were actually good for what they were (although she also sang her share of insipid novelties); you can say what you like about "Mr. Tap Toe," but I defy you to stop humming it. Simultaneously, she was also playing snappy, peppy upbeat characters in family-oriented musical comedies. Many of these were period-costume pictures set in bygone days that were offered by Warner Bros. as a kind of an escape out of the more complex values and fears of the age of anxiety and into a simpler, more innocent era—a time before hydrogen bombs and Senate hearings.

By 1955–56, Day was ready to reach out for something deeper: while she had previously played supporting roles in a few dramas (*Young Man with a Horn, Storm Warning*), 1955 saw a rather abrupt break with her earlier "frivolity." This arrived in the form of a harrowing true-to-life showbiz drama titled *Love Me or Leave Me*, a "backstager" with elements of a crime drama and psychological thriller that allowed Day to go to the limits of what she could do both as a singer and a dramatic actress. Throughout these years, her music was also growing proportionately, and it would attain a parallel pinnacle with *Day by Day* and *Day by Night*. The songs were of the sort that were gradually being acknowledged (in the wake of Sinatra and Fitzgerald) as classics: instead of "Mr. Tap Toe," "Sugarbush," and "The Purple Cow," she was now singing Jerome Kern and George Gershwin.

Day by Day and *Day by Night* were profoundly enriched by the contributions of musical director Paul Weston, the best arranger-conductor then working with Columbia Records in Los Angeles. Weston (1912–1996) had recently switched to Columbia from Capitol Records in tandem with his wife and longtime musical partner, Jo Stafford.

Weston's writing for singers was uniquely suited to both Stafford and Day—it was subtle, understated, and contained a lot of craft and technique without exhibitionism. Like Day and Stafford, Weston glorified the song itself above everything else, never calling attention to the arranger.

The twelve tracks of *Day by Day* were taped at Columbia's most frequently used Hollywood studio, Radio Recorders, at 7000 Santa Monica Boulevard, on September 17, 21, and 26, 1956. Weston maintains a perfect balance of consistency and diversity on the three dates: on the first and third, he uses instrumentation close to that of a standard big band. On the 17th, there are four saxophones, two trombones, one trumpet, and a very full rhythm section (piano, vibes, bass, drums, and, uniquely, two guitars); on the 26th, there are four trumpets, four trombones, four saxes, and the same two-guitar rhythm section (sans vibes, however). For the middle session, he all but gets rid of the horns—the only one present is Day's close friend, Ted Nash, on reeds and saxophones—but has a full string section with twelve assorted fiddlers. As with the transition between the quartet numbers and the full ensemble on Sinatra's *In the Wee Small Hours,* one is never fully conscious of the difference in the backings on the three sessions. (In 1995, the tracks on both of the *Day by* albums were issued in chronological order, as part of the Bear Family boxed set *Qué Será.*)

How better to start, then, than with "The Song Is You"? Oscar Hammerstein's lyric famously sets up love and music as parallels to each other, putting them both on the same page. Frequently, lovers might share a song, or a song might remind you of him or her, but Hammerstein takes the interrelationship of love and music several levels deeper: your lover *is* the song, the song *is* her; the two are one and the same, interchangeable. The melody and the text are a perfect fit for Day, who, here especially, sings like she's making love.

"Hello, My Lover, Goodbye" was written by the "Body and Soul" team of composer Johnny Green and lyricist Edward Heyman. The text is at least as good, if not better, although the melody and harmony aren't quite as complex as those of that iconic standard. It's the first mixed mood song on *Day by Day,* delineating the dilemma of the inconsistency of love; as soon as she decides she likes somebody, he's already packing his bags. The ending of the bridge is especially poignant: "Yet like the ever-shifting sands, I drift away." Ted Nash, here playing alto (over the full string section), seems to be flirting with her as she sings, as if he were saying hello and goodbye in the same breath.

"But Not for Me" (the Gershwin brothers' *Girl Crazy* standard) uses the big band—though here, as elsewhere, even though the instrumentation is almost identical, the charts don't sound like anything Weston would have written for Tommy Dorsey or that Day would have sung with Les Brown. Descending woodwinds lead into the verse, which Day sings with the appropriate sense of self-deprecating irony. As with many Cold War recordings of the song, the lyrics in the bridge refer to "more skies of grey than any Broadway play can guarantee" instead of "any Russian play," as per Ira Gershwin, though Broadway plays, unlike Russian ones, are not synonymous with skies of grey. The change seemed hardly logical even at the height of the Eisenhower era—the Gershwin lyric could hardly be construed as pro-Soviet. The chorus is slightly faster than the refrain.

"I Remember You" opens with a George Shearing–like combination of vibes, guitar, and piano, playing an introductory riff that reoccurs throughout (it's briefly reminiscent of the opening of Nat King Cole's "Unforgettable"). Day's vocal is backed by the strings and one of the guitars inserts a few obbligato-style fills. You might think that someone forgot to remember to include the verse, but she doesn't need it, the chorus is a perfect entity in itself in Day's interpretation. Even without its verse, this is still the longest track on the album (four minutes), a long, luxurious delineation of the very process of memory itself. Said memory is rather hazy; in light of what we know about Johnny Mercer, one can easily imagine the text is at least partly inspired by the thought processes of a drunk stumbling around in the morning, with hazy memories of the night before: "A distant bell / And stars that fell like rain out of the blue . . ."—she puts an emphasis on the word "distant" to make it sound even more distant. In reality, waking up with someone you barely remember from the night before is more like a nightmare than a dream, but Day and Weston make the song sound supremely romantic. The coda is especially effective: singer and orchestra ritard, but only slightly—to do so in a big dramatic way would be to defeat the purpose of the album, so they slow down in a manner that's subtle, even "stealth."

A vibe riff also opens Ray Noble's "I Hadn't Anyone Till You"—but this is much closer to upbeat, and the mood is considerably more cheerful. The song is usually done wistful and sad, but Day is blissfully in the moment—she has someone now, the "you" of the title—and, in fact, like a virgin on her wedding night, she's glad that she never "had" anyone until him.

"But Beautiful" is a song about contrasts, "Love is funny, or it's sad / Or it's quiet, or it's mad / It's a good thing, or it's bad." Weston sets these up by opening with a sonic contrast between high trumpets and low reeds. It's worth pointing out that this is done understatedly—without the extreme exaggerated contrast between high and low, brass and reeds, that you would hear, for instance, in an arrangement by Weston's friend Billy May. Day is especially relaxed and sensual here, focusing more on the funny than the sad, the quiet rather than the mad. She tightens up the "sad" and the "bad" and luxuriates on the "beautiful," stretching it out to make the word itself sound all the more beautiful.

The contrast in "Autumn Leaves" is between strings and a solo flute (sounding rather Asian)—one would guess the first is a metaphor for the wind, while the second symbolizes the falling leaves themselves. What chance do dead leaves have against the collective force of the wind? Not much, so fall they do. In the instrumental break, the strings take the melody, and Day hums—"scats" isn't the right term—an obbligato so as to suggest that she herself were a falling leaf; throughout, in fact, the way she stresses and elongates certain words, as opposed to others, seems to suggest the rising and falling of the wind—as if the words were being blown about without any conscious input on her part.

Henry Nemo was one of the more extravagant characters of the swing era, as an entertainer and philosopher (and educator—Anita O'Day cites him as one of her key "instructors"), but his lasting legacy is as the lyricist and occasionally composer of such songs as "I Let a Song Go out of My Heart," "Blame It on My Last Affair," and " 'Tis Autumn." Introduced by Mildred Bailey in 1940, "Don't Take Your Love from Me" is the most durable ballad by "The 'Neem," as he was known. Weston here backs Day with the four-reed, three-brass ensemble, and the undulations of the collective saxophone suggest the reed rapture of Woody Herman's Second Herd. Day sounds as if she's making an urgent request, but never pleading or begging.

"There Will Never Be Another You" supports the notion that Harry Warren's most lucrative period was his early 1940s tenure at 20th Century-Fox. The songwriter turned out even more hits and standards in these years than earlier at Warner Bros. or later at MGM, even though the Fox films themselves aren't nearly as good as the earlier Busby Berkeley musicals or the later Arthur Freed Unit productions. "There Will Never Be Another You" was written for *Iceland,* otherwise only remembered by Sonja Henie fans and ice-dancing buffs. Throughout his entire career, Warren composed one classic song after another, with barely time to take a breath in between. Abetted by vibes, guitar, and low-moaning reeds, Day isn't pleading here or being blown about by the elements but stating her feelings from a position of confidence and security.

Day is back to contending with the elements—more leaves being blown away—on "Gone with the Wind." As indicated by vintage original 78 rpm record labels, the title of this 1937 hit song was directly inspired by the best-selling Margaret Mitchell novel, even though it had nothing to do with the subsequent film (the lyrics, notably, do not mention Scarlett, Rhett, or even contain so much as a "fiddle-de-de"). The song was the first tune on the first session (with the full violin section). Day sounds less in control here, more as if she's merely gliding on the winds of emotion.

"The Gypsy in My Soul," which originated in the University of Pennsylvania *Mask and Wig Show* (1937), is one of only two major songs that were written for college shows (the other being "East of the Sun," written for the Princeton Triangle

Club's 1935 production *Stags at Bay*). Like a Gypsy who roams far from his place of birth, "Gypsy in My Soul" was at first much more widely popular in England than the United States, although it later more than made up for lost time by becoming a major jazz standard in the album era. Day's "Gypsy" is the zingiest track on *Day by Day,* opening with the catchiest and the most insistent vibes riff yet. As if to illustrate the danceability of the arrangement, Day, ever the hoofer, indulges in some fancy terpsichore with the reeds, who dance around her—and she around them. (Ted Nash also gets a brief saxophone solo.)

The closing track, "Day by Day," has a deep personal connection for both Day and Weston. He composed the melody in collaboration with his friend and occasional collaborator, fellow arranger-conductor Axel Stordahl, and it was their single most notable effort as songwriters. (A third companion, the prolific and resourceful Sammy Cahn, wrote the lyrics.) Day's ties to the song are less straightforward. In 1938, the singer began working under the professional name of "Doris Day." The nom-de-bandstand was suggested by bandleader Barney Rapp, under whose employ she was working at the time. It's reported in many sources that the name was inspired by the song "Day by Day." It makes a great story, but the Cahn-Weston-Stordahl standard wasn't written until 1945, by which time she had been known as "Day" for seven years. (The song that actually inspired the name change was undoubtedly "Day After Day," recorded by Artie Shaw in 1938.)

However, Day did have a fruitful relationship with the Weston song: she sang it with Les Brown in 1945, and it would remain one of the very best sides she made as a band singer. It was only fitting that she should return to it in 1956, with the composer himself conducting. The comparison of the two recordings is in itself a vivid illustration of Cahn's message (in the lyrics) that people grow and the love between two people can get better over a long period; in 1956, Day somehow sounds both much more confident and, at the same time, more tender and vulnerable than she did in 1945. Our relationship with her has only grown stronger over the dozen years since the song was new. Placing it

as the closing track on the album was an inspired notion, making the clear-cut promise that her love for us and ours for her will continue to grow, even as we go through the years, day by day.

Day by Day was released three months after it was recorded, on December 17, 1956, and the follow-up, *Day by Night,* arrived less than a year later. The cover of the first album has Doris looking with her full face into the camera, bright and perky. The cover of *Day by Night* shows her from the right profile, in front of a black backdrop, staring off into the night.

The second album was taped in three dates in August 1957: on the 23rd and the 30th, Weston brought in saxes, strings, and rhythm; in between, on the 27th, it was again a big band instrumentation with four trumpets, three trombones, four saxes, and rhythm. (Thus there were two dates with strings, rather than one, doubtless to the annoyance of her manager and husband, Marty Melcher, who would have gladly recorded Day with a harmonica and banjo if he thought it would save a buck.) The two *Day by* albums are more than similar enough to be sequel-and-original; they even sound as if they were planned simultaneously—even more so than *Songs for Swingin' Lovers* and *A Swingin' Affair,* or *Love Is the Thing* and *The Very Thought of You.* Sometimes, the *Night* album sounds even more shimmeringly romantic than the *Day* album, sweeter and more tender, if such a thing were even possible—and there are more strings on more tracks. In truth, however, in a blindfold test I would have a hard time distinguishing between the two.

"I See Your Face Before Me" comes from a 1937 Broadway show called *Between the Devil,* which is generally described as a story about a bigamist. In *Wee Small Hours,* Sinatra had anointed the number as one of the most moving of all torch songs. Sinatra's version is much more sad, but even though Day's track—and the album—begins with a dramatic sweep of the strings (for a second the arrangement almost sounds like Gordon Jenkins), the singer is much more optimistic: she may be separated from her lover, but she's actually encouraged by the way she sees his face before her: it gives her hope, and strength to continue.

However, if you happen to be tired of seeing someone's face before you, the logical thing to do is to "Close Your Eyes." (From 1933, it's one of two notable songs by Bernice Petkere, the other being "Lullaby of the Leaves." Yes, she evidently had a fondness for minor keys.) Minor though it may be, it's not at all bleak; using the big band format, this is more in a fox-trot tempo and is in something closer to a Riddle-Sinatra mode—the muted trombone intro is especially Nelsonian. Weston again has a trombone and a saxophone paraphrasing each other in what amounts to a conjoined solo in the break. This is a classic song, one of the shining highlights of what we call the Great American Songbook, yet no other interpreter ever made it as clear as Day does. Petkere's lyric wasn't telling listeners to close their eyes and lay themselves down to sleep (when the word "sleep" appears in the lyric, it's strictly metaphoric); it's about girls on the dance floor who trust their partners so implicitly that they can close their eyes while dancing, knowing that their men will protect them from harm.

"The Night We Called it a Day" was written by Matt Dennis and Tom Adair, who were then working for bandleader Tommy Dorsey, just at the point when Weston was leaving. It's a song about a faded love affair, but rather than wallowing in regret, Day seems pleased to be reminiscing about a relationship that once made her happy: she remembers April, and she's smiling.

Bing Crosby recorded "Dream a Little Dream of Me" on *Bing with a Beat,* and, as we've seen, it's a song that originated with a dance band in Wisconsin before a lyricist from Chicago (the legendary Gus Kahn) got ahold of it. Day seems to be focusing on the idea that lovers don't necessarily have to be parted by the sandman—they can still see each other in their dreams (in fact, she had already made a movie called *I'll See You in My Dreams* detailing the life story of the self-same Mr. Kahn).

There's a joke about Cole Porter and Irving Berlin having a drink together and teasing each other with the question "Can you believe that it sometimes takes two guys to write a song?" There were, in fact, several units of three-man songwriting teams working on Broadway and Tin Pan Alley, most famously the highly successful trio of Buddy

DeSylva, Lew Brown, and Ray Henderson. The threesome of Jerry Livingston (originally known as Levinson), Al J. Neiburg, and Marty Symes had a lesser but still significant track record that also includes "When It's Darkness on the Delta" and "It's the Talk of the Town." "Under a Blanket of Blue," the first tune recorded at the first session, is a slightly offbeat title concept for a song about the night—usually songwriters, including but not limited to Irving Berlin, describe the daytime skies as being blue—but make no mistake: this is a song about a nocturnal encounter, hence the blue blanket of stars—as embodied by the warm blanket of strings. Day's voice may not be as big or as overwhelming as Judy Garland's or Sarah Vaughan's, but she can easily envelop you like a blanket—not merely with her chops but with her entire personality.

We're back to romp tempo for "You Do Something to Me." This is vintage Cole Porter (*Fifty Million Frenchmen,* 1929), and up until this album it was characteristically rendered super-fast (both by the early dance bands and Sinatra in 1950). Day's interpretation is gentler, sweeter, and sexier. Weston just hints at the big band tradition in tempo and instrumentation (with brief muted trumpet solo), employing just enough decoration. Weston's particular brilliance, like Riddle's, was to have the song unfold without it seeming like just a cycle of choruses; the piece progresses straightforwardly without ever appearing to repeat itself.

"Stars Fell on Alabama," like several other of Mitchell Parish's nocturnal love songs (especially "Deep Purple"), seems like a sequel to "Star Dust," what with romantic notions heightened by the shooting stars and dust from the moon. In his songs with fellow Irving Mills contractee Frank Perkins, Parish also leaned toward Southern-centric love songs, like "Down a Carolina Lane" and "Emaline," which are so drenched in the antebellum atmosphere that you can practically smell the honeysuckle hanging on the vine. Both Day and Sinatra learned "Stars Fell on Alabama" from Jack Teagarden and, coincidentally, Sinatra recorded his version around this time as well (in November 1956). Day sings it so rapturously that although I have my personal doubts that she was ever in Alabama (the place is hardly what you or I would call a "fairyland") I have no trouble imagining her floating through the sky, one heavenly body amidst others.

In the latter part of her career, Kate Smith became iconic for belting out patriotic anthems like "God Bless America," but earlier she had been known for melancholy songs of love and loss that often involved the moon. Both her theme song, "When the Moon Comes over the Mountain," and "Moon Song" (her key number in her only starring film, the 1932 *Hello Everybody*) were lunar-centric songs of separation, lyrics about being alone in the night—alone with one's memories, with only the moon for company. While "You Do Something to Me" is the perkiest song on *Day by Night*, then "Moon Song" is the saddest; it's a moon song that wasn't meant for her, and Day knows better than to try and invest it with her trademark optimism. She finds some joy in the bridge, as she goes backward to describe how her "sorrow ended" and her big affair was a "rhapsody of love," before arriving at the inescapable conclusion that the moon song, sweet as it may be, just wasn't meant for her.

Most of us assume, I think, that the dreams referred to in "Wrap Your Troubles in Dreams" are hopes, ambitions, desires, aspirations. Day, however, makes it clear that the song is explicitly about nocturnal dreams, and highly sensual ones at that. At less than two and a half minutes, this "dream" barely amounts to a catnap, but frequently the most enjoyable dreams don't require any more time than that.

Marty Melcher was undoubtedly responsible for the inclusion of "Soft as the Starlight," the work of Joe Lubin and Jerome Howard. The latter was one of the songwriters in Melcher's stable who was obviously willing to work for cheap, or to give Melcher (and his partner in crime, attorney Jerome B. Rosenthal) a kickback of the proceeds from the publishing rights. Working together and separately, Lubin and Howard wrote a dozen or so songs performed by Day for her records and films, of which this is the most substantial. (There's also the unforgettable, not to mention unforgivable, "Rickety Rackety Rendezvous" and the title song from *Move Over, Darling*, which has Melcher's name on it as a coauthor.) "Starlight" is derived from a traditional folk song, "Hush Little Baby." Even though the song itself is hardly a benchmark of originality, it's exquisitely orchestrated by Weston and sung by Day, who renders it with supreme tenderness, the sort that could be directed at either a child or a lover.

"Moonglow" is clearly a standard of the first rank, composed by arranger Will Hudson; Eddie DeLange, who multitasked as lyricist and bandleader, wrote the words, and publisher Irving Mills cut himself in for a piece of the authors' action. Nearly four minutes long, Day sings it with a lot of alto saxophone around her. It introduces her at the start, finishing her sentences for her in the coda, and in general fills in the empty spaces whenever she's not singing. Her phrasing is mostly staccato, and yet she somehow still makes the song and the moonglow itself exquisitely romantic.

"The Lamp Is Low" brought Maurice Ravel onto the pop record charts just shortly after his death in 1937; the adaptation is by the songwriter Peter DeRose (who wrote lots of dreamy tunes during this period) and Bert Shefter, who never wrote anything else of note, but with this one exceptional song certainly earned himself a legacy. There's no overt reference to French Impressionism in Weston's orchestration, but his writing and Day's singing come with an added measure of high class. Day has never sounded more relaxed, sensual, tender. She's very low-key on "watch the shadows," and then there's what seems like an excruciatingly long pause before "come and go," as if she were animating the very shadows themselves. She gets deeper and heavier and more serious when she needs to be on "while you linger in my arms"— she makes the word "while" seem like time passing. The ending suggests a fade-out as in a clinch in a movie; in vintage Hollywood, the only time you know something intimate is happening is when they don't show it to you; if the camera lingers on a love scene, it's a sure sign that it's about to be interrupted. Here, you really feel as if the love scene is just beginning as the orchestra comes up and the visuals in your mind's eye slowly fade to black.

Day by Night was issued on November 11, 1957. Throughout the recording of the two *Day by* albums, the artist was busy shooting two very important films in her career: Warner Bros.' highly ambitious adaptation of the Broadway smash *The Pajama Game*, and the comedy *Teacher's Pet*, in which she starred opposite Clark Gable. Day doesn't seem to have given much thought to either album in the following fifty-five-plus years. On all the occasions I've spoken with her—and in other interviews—she never acknowledged these or any of her other recordings as anything particularly noteworthy. She remembered the recording of *Duet*, her 1962 collaboration with André Previn, merely because the circumstances were more unusual for her, but to this day Doris refuses to be impressed by anything in her own catalogue. She went for decades without listening to any of her records, and when the German label Bear Family began issuing a complete set of her Columbia sessions in the 1990s, she literally had to force herself to listen to just the smallest part of that voluminous package. Day's slightly younger contempo-

raries, like Tony Bennett and Rosemary Clooney, could both be described as humble, yet they had more of a sense of their worth. In other words, they realized that at least some portion of their recorded output was extraordinary.

But Doris worked for her entire career—for hundreds and hundreds of tracks, singles, albums, films, TV shows—at an extremely high level, without thinking anything of it. Is she merely being modest? I don't think so. She just can't find anything to crow about in her own work—quite possibly she thinks that everybody can sing this well.

Doris is more proud of the things she really had to work at, such as running her animal-related charities and winning her legal battles over the years. And most of all, there was her loving son, Terry, who gave her more happiness than all the songs, movies, and husbands in her life put together. Singing was always the easy part, and it shows. You don't get to be this great by working at it.

13

Doris Day and Robert Goulet
Annie Get Your Gun
(1962)

At first glance, this 1962 album may seem like the sonic equivalent of a domestic house cat. *Felinus domesticus,* or whatever it's called, serves no useful function whatsoever (my own apartment aside, relatively few are expected to catch mice), they're only expected to be cute, purr, lick themselves clean, and, in the process make humans happy. There's a similar concept among very serious cinema scholars, who use the term "scopophilia," which, kinky as it sounds, merely means "the pleasure of seeing"; in other words, a movie (or an element therein, from Lassie to Ava Gardner) that just looks pretty—there's no greater value to it than the attractiveness of the image. Even if the 1962 *Annie Get Your Gun* album fell into that category it would be worthwhile: it's a beautiful album, with two outstandingly beautiful voices, a luxurious chorus (more than one, actually), lush orchestrations, and state-of-the-art hi-fi stereo.

But this album is, in fact, much more than that; the 1962 Columbia Records *Annie Get Your Gun* can only be described as a great album, with two great voices singing the great songs from a great score of a great show. Granted, that's a lot of "greats" to bandy about. Most of the time even one is too many, but this is an exceptional piece of work.

Coming away from this recording—more than any other treatment of the score—one is firmly convinced that *Annie Get Your Gun* is Irving Berlin's finest hour. This was the composer's first foray into the new postwar world of musical theater, wherein plot, song, story, and character were firmly integrated, intertwined, and interconnected; it was no coincidence that *Annie* was produced by the two key innovators of the genre, Richard Rodgers and Oscar Hammerstein II. It was a bold step forward for the songwriter, who was up until this time firmly associated with what are often described as "frivolous revues." It's true that not all of his work could be so characterized: a great many of his earlier productions, like *The Cocoanuts* (1925–26) and *Face the Music* (1932), were actually full-length book shows (although these were more like extended comedy sketches with songs), and he had also written *As Thousands Cheer,* a 1933 revue with considerable social significance. Berlin was also a pioneer of musical political satire, as in *Louisiana Purchase,* but there was nothing in his canon before 1946 to compete with *Show Boat* or *Oklahoma!* Thus, *Annie Get Your Gun,* which premiered on Broadway in 1946, was a breakthrough for Berlin. It was the first time he was expected to write songs that needed to carry a story or helped define a character.

The result: who says you can't teach an old dog new tricks? It surprised no one that the old master totally thrived in this brave new world. Berlin was a highly competitive man, and one suspects that the participation of Rodgers and Hammerstein egged him on to do work even better than anybody was expecting, just for the satisfaction he would derive from beating them at their own game. The rivalry of Berlin and Rodgers is well documented. The two men were among the most successful Jewish composer-producer-entrepreneurs of all time. But Berlin came from the generation of Jews that just barely made it over here, escaping from the persecution of the Old Country by the skin of their teeth; Rodgers was a child of privilege, the comparatively pampered son of a wealthy doctor and a thoroughly assimilated family. Berlin had to teach himself to write music, even when he couldn't actually play it, whereas Rodgers had the benefit of attending the school that eventually became Juilliard.

They first crossed paths on the 1926 show *Betsy*. The score was primarily by Rodgers and his lyricist Lorenz Hart, but the producer recruited Berlin to contribute one single song, "Blue Skies," which became the runaway hit of the show—much to Berlin's delight and Rodgers's consternation. Likewise, right after Annie Oakley's first song ("Doin' What Comes Natur'lly"), the local hotel owner ("Foster Wilson") sets up a shooting match between Annie and Frank Butler, whom he describes as "a swollen-headed stiff from the wild west show." In this competition, Annie is the underdog, and that she wins the match sets the events in motion that form the basic trajectory of the story. It's not hard to imagine Berlin identifying with Annie.

Yet *Annie* is more than the show that proves how well Berlin could compete with R&H, it's the show that reaffirms his place in the pantheon of great songwriters. All the songs are as thoroughly integrated into the plot as the best of Rodgers and Hammerstein. "You Can't Get a Man with a Gun" shows that Berlin could throw tricky internal rhymes around to the same hilarious degree as his great friend Cole Porter. "They Say It's Wonderful" and "The Girl That I Marry" are romantic ballads that soar with the opulent brilliance of Jerome Kern (the producers' first choice to write the score; he died suddenly before he could get started). "Who Do You Love, I Hope" resounds with the same taut sexual tension one finds in the best songs by Dorothy Fields (whose participation in the show

as book writer also almost certainly inspired Berlin to do even better than his best). "Anything You Can Do" is a comic duet unmatched anywhere in the musical theater or popular song of that time—the benchmark against which later such songs would be measured.

Twenty years after *Betsy*, Berlin was still trying to get one-up on Rodgers. In 1943–45, Rodgers had decidedly taken the lead in this de facto competition: while he and Oscar Hammerstein were creating the breakthrough works *Oklahoma!* (1943) and *Carousel* (1945), Berlin was busy with his role in the war effort, writing, producing, and appearing in his traveling all-soldier production *This Is the Army*. When Berlin returned home from the war—the international tour of battlegrounds that had preoccupied him for three years—he found himself playing a very different game from the one he had left.

Annie Get Your Gun was his turn at bat, and he scored a home run on every level. He came up with a seamless book show (no small thanks to book writers Dorothy and Herbert Fields), which would be by far his most revived property and one that holds the record for introducing more great songs than any other show or even film; the agreed-upon total is that eight numbers from the score are standards and classics, a record that no other show approaches. (By way of comparison, *Show Boat* has six.) Pushing sixty, Berlin, who was perhaps the most successful songwriter in the entire American idiom, approached *Annie* like someone who still has something left to prove. And he proved it many times over.

The Day-Goulet album (which was recorded in 1962 and released in 1963) is a key part of the development of the show: it's worth pointing out that when *Annie* enjoyed its most important revival, from 1999 to 2001 (which ran almost as long as the original), I saw it with at least three different leading ladies, among them Bernadette Peters and Reba McEntire, and all of them sounded a lot more like Doris Day than they did like Ethel Merman, Mary Martin, or Betty Hutton. While Goulet is a near-perfect leading man who more than holds up his share of the musical load, it's Day's treatment of the Annie songs that makes the album sparkle.

Where the earlier Annies all belong to a specific time and place, Doris Day's "Annie" seems totally timeless.

Well before 1962, *Annie Get Your Gun* had been a smash on Broadway (Merman) and in a touring company (Martin), on London's West End (Dolores Gray, amazingly), and in Paris. (And in the 1950 MGM film version, it was Betty Hutton who got a man with a gun.) In 1957, there had been a new tour with a new cast (or semi-new, in that Mary Martin, who had played Annie in the 1947 road company, was back), which culminated in a television production and a new cast album. It obviously hadn't escaped the attention of Columbia Records that both the 1946 Broadway cast album and the 1957 touring cast album were huge sellers for, respectively, Decca and Capitol.

Can it be a coincidence that the long-playing album was, for all intents and purposes, introduced just as two essential forms, the Broadway musical and jazz, were reaching a new plateau in their artistic evolutions? Even though jazz and Broadway were no longer as directly connected to each other as they had been in Gershwin's time, they were nonetheless developing along parallel pathways. Both jazz and the musical were in a position to benefit from the long-playing medium; it made total sense to listen to a jam session that was longer than the three minutes of a single, and it also made sense to want to listen to forty to fifty minutes of the score of a Broadway show in a single sitting.

The technology was a key part of the way that the music was heard, and eventually affected the content as well as the delivery system. The integrated book show and the modern cast album both have roots going back over the decades, but they were established as permanent givens within a few years of each other. One big step in the evolution of the cast album was that the cast didn't have to come from an actual production, that a cast could be assembled just for recording purposes. Most "studio cast albums," as they came to be called, featured two stars, like Decca's *Porgy and Bess* which costarred Sammy Davis Jr. and Carmen McRae. But the most aggressive producer of cast album variations was Columbia Records, under the stewardship of Goddard Lieberson. In the 10-inch era, he sanctioned a series of one-woman cast albums with Mary Martin of shows from the pre-*Oklahoma!* era (*The Band Wagon, Girl Crazy,* etc.). When in 1956 he steered Columbia to a gold mine with *My Fair Lady* (Columbia not only did the album but owned a piece of the show itself), the label got even more enthusiastic. More than other labels, Columbia, under Lieberson, seemed determined to release a recording of every major show, and they continued to produce all kinds of studio cast albums—at least eight with the reliable, charismatic baritone Jack Cassidy (with sopranos Portia Nelson and his then-wife Shirley Jones as his leading ladies). Columbia also produced studio casts with Broadway-type people (Barbara Cook in *The King and I* and *Show Boat,* the latter with John Raitt, who also did a memorable *Oklahoma!* with Florence Henderson) and others with more pop-oriented artists.

The 1962 *Annie* was a combination of all of the above. It was a particularly appropriate role for Doris Day, who'd spent many of her earlier films playing the world's sexiest tomboy, a sequence of costume pictures that culminated in *Calamity Jane,* a 1955 Warner Bros. film that was essentially a new production of *Annie Get Your Gun* with slightly different character names. Howard Keel was the leading man in both—"Frank Butler" in one and "Wild Bill Hickok" in the other, not that it made any difference.

Robert Goulet, Columbia's "Frank Butler," was ten years younger than his Annie, but he was an ideal choice. The compatibility of the two leads is spelled out in their individual opening numbers, Frank's "I'm a Bad, Bad Man" and Annie's "Doin' What Comes Natur'lly." The two songs are perfect counterparts to each other, in that they first present their characters as archetypes but then, in the course of thirty-two bars or less, the personalities of the two emerge, not just as silhouettes but fully developed, flesh-and-blood individuals. In "Bad, Bad Man," Frank paints a portrait of himself as a womanizer and vainglorious blowhard, and in "What Comes Natur'lly," Annie likewise tells us she's nothing but an ignorant backwoodswoman. It just takes a little listening to realize that neither character is exactly what he or she first seems to be;

for all of his bad-bad-ness, Frank is a sentimental pussycat at heart, who puts up a big front to avoid seeming vulnerable (even the chorus of trilly little debutantes who sing back at Frank inform him that he's "making too much fuss"); Annie's purported ignorance, we soon see, is just a front, a facade calculated to put her adversaries off their guard.

"Bad, Bad Man" is actually the third track. We open with Fritz Allers conducting the studio orchestra in the overture; it's a vivid performance —as far as I know, the first time the *Annie* overture had been recorded in stereo. Then there's the usual opening number, "Colonel Buffalo Bill" by "Charlie Davenport" (in this case, a studio singer named Leonard Stokes) and mixed chorus; in fact, in the first three numbers we hear three different choral groups: a mixed adult chorus on "Colonel Buffalo Bill," a girls' chorus on "I'm a Bad, Bad Man," and a children's chorus on "Doin' What Comes Natur'lly." The 1999 revival omitted "Colonel Buffalo Bill," which is, to a degree, understandable—it is about Buffalo Bill saving a stagecoach from savage Indians (although they could have made them into "bandits" just by changing a word). Both the 1950 film and the revival omit "I'm a Bad, Bad Man," which is more regrettable, because it sets up the Frank Butler character so perfectly, especially as sung by Goulet. Berlin does something he rarely if ever did before, which is to use the rhythms and repetitive patterns of a folk song—the melody is essentially the same line going up and down, and the words repeat in a nursery rhyme-ish kind of way.

Virtually all the recordings leave out the more salacious lyrics in Berlin's score, though they're in the *Complete Lyrics* book as collected by Robert Kimball, such as "send your mothers on Wednesday / Because Wednesday is old hens' day." Berlin's melody is perfect for Goulet, it brings out his beautifully resonant lower register and then allows him to go up for a dazzling high note on the title words, "I'm a bad, bad man!" For all the apparent folksiness of Berlin's melody, it requires a baritone with an extraordinary range to pull it off properly. Goulet's combination of egocentrism, naïveté, and sheer charisma is perfect for the character: he plays Frank like Lancelot, his breakthrough role

in *Camelot*. There were even more risqué lyrics to "Doin' What Comes Natur'lly," and again, a lot of these aren't in most of the cast albums. ("You don't have to mix with the Vanderbilts / Not to take off your panties when you're wearing kilts." Berlin apparently enjoyed hearing Merman sing about her "panties"; he also wrote a reference to said undergarment for her to sing in *Call Me Madam*.) Day sings solidly on the beat, but never squarely; she uses the rhythm to heighten the key points of Berlin's jokes; Berlin's placement of the rhymes is a key ingredient in the entire set-up/punchline format. Day's performance is full of wry humor, and she gets more of the "off-key" notes of "Sister Sal" ("who's mus-i-cal") than any other Annie.

The next two songs further heighten the dichotomy between the two characters. Unlike "I'm a Bad, Bad Man," Frank's next song, "The Girl That I Marry" must be sung without irony, at least on his part. Even when the curtain went up on the show for the very first time in 1946, the audience was well aware that Annie and Frank were going to end up lost in each other's arms—so for Frank to sing it with even the slightest hint of irony would be counterproductive. The audience has already seen Annie, thus when Frank sings of how the girl that he marries will have to be "soft and pink as a nursery," we're completely aware that his leading lady is anything but. Thus, he's got to sing it utterly straight, and this is something Bob Goulet does better than almost anybody. He can make the honest sentiment of the song sustain interest—he doesn't need any spice or special sauce to give it seasoning. "The Girl That I Marry" is a classic Berlin romantic waltz, fully as beautiful as the wonderful waltzes ("All Alone," "Remember," "The Song Is Ended") he was turning out regularly twenty years earlier. (One of Betty Hutton's funniest moments comes later in the film's "second act," when she does her impression of Butler bellowing the song in a blustery mock baritone, imitating Keel's mellow bellow, which comes after a dynamite bit where she acts out her idea of a reconciliation scene with Frank, playing both parts.)

"You Can't Get a Man with a Gun" is one of Berlin's all-time funniest songs. The words put one in mind of Cole Porter's description of his lyric-writing process as something like doing a cross-word puzzle, finding precisely the right word to go in the right spot for maximum impact. Day's version is hysterical, although at first listen it seemed a trifle too cartoonishly fast—I kind of expected her to linger over the one-liners a little as if to savor them; but as the two and a half minutes reach their end, it becomes obvious that she's snapping out Berlin's witty rhymes with the same tempo as Annie Oakley shooting at clay pigeons: Bam! Bam! Bam! Bam! You get the idea. One wishes Columbia had let her do all three verses. Day is especially funny on Berlin's line "They don't buy pajamas / For pistol-packin' mamas." "Pistol Packin' Mama" was the most popular country and western song of the World War II era, and the reference remains in *Annie* to this day, even though when contemporary audiences hear it, most of them probably don't realize that Berlin is goofing on the title of a song that was famous seventy years before.

So far the show's structure is symmetrical; one solo each for the leading man and lady. So far Annie has been funny and Frank has been earnest. The first big duo is "They Say It's Wonderful" and it has to be admitted that the duets aren't as magical as the solos, which is largely because Day and Goulet recorded their tracks separately, on different coasts even: she was in Hollywood, apparently working with just a piano or rhythm section; the orchestra and Goulet were recorded in New York. Of course, knowing that makes all the difference, and when you listen to "They Say It's Wonderful" it's hard to put it out of your mind; once knowing it, you can't un-know it. "They Say It's Wonderful" reminds me of the climactic love duet in *Kismet*, wherein the two lovers are in different parts of the city, singing at the same time, knowing that the other one is out there, returning their feelings in kind. In "They Say It's Wonderful" we have no trouble believing that Annie and Frank are on the same page, but we do have a hard time believing that they're in the same room. Even so, the song's overall message still rings clear—falling in love *is*, in fact, wonderful—and that's the important thing.

"My Defenses Are Down" is one of the great leading man songs; as it was for Ray Middleton, Keel, and Raitt before him, it's a chance for Goulet

as the big "swollen-headed stiff" to admit that he's human. Everyone in the audience already saw in "I'm a Bad, Bad Man" that there was a big chink in his armor, but at last he's ready to admit it to himself: that with his defenses down, he's as vulnerable as any other gullible guy to Cupid's arrows and/or a gal with a gun. It's a moment of self-awareness, the kind of song that would become common currency in the postwar musical theater, an archetype almost, "Billy Bigelow" discovering he can care for something beyond himself in *Carousel*, "Bobby" learning to appreciate "Being Alive" in *Company*. Berlin's line comparing Frank to "a knight without his armor" turned out to be prophetic, since that's exactly what Goulet was in *Camelot*, and how he portrays his role here. Still, the way he savors those big battleship notes in "Yes I must confess that I *like* it" shows that, vocally at least, he's anything but defenseless. If chops were a weapon, he'd be a black belt.

"Moonshine Lullaby" works on many levels, especially as sung by Day. It's a seriocomic song if ever there were one; Berlin wrote it for Annie to sing as a comic turn with her little brothers and sisters on the train, penned with considerable tongue-in-cheek as a hillbilly's love song to the thing he loves the best—bootleg hooch. With Merman doing it, there's an inevitable element of camp and thus of comedy. Merman sings it slide-rule straight, side-splittingly exactly as Berlin wrote it, without any embellishments. Day sings it with a male quartet plus a small children's choir, but she intones it so tenderly that you have to take it at least somewhat seriously. The tempo is much slower than it is on the 1946 cast album, so much so that the track is an entire minute longer than Merman's. It's actually one of the prettiest ballads of Day's whole career; the two choral groups imbue it with an undeniable kind of a camp feeling, but other than that, this is a ballad performance worthy of inclusion on a "best of" Doris Day compilation.

Did Irving Berlin ever write another song like "I'm an Indian Too"? Pretty much the only ethnic group he usually made fun of was his own, as in "Yiddisha Nightingale." (Even "C-U-B-A" doesn't poke fun at actual Latinos; the subject of its satire are all the Americanos who were heading for

Havana in 1920 to wet their whistle.) The song was unfortunately but understandably dropped from the recent revival. I love the song, but I have to admit that I would cringe if I were watching a production while seated next to a Navaho. Likewise, I would have a hard time if I were sitting next to Gloria Steinem watching the show's climactic scene, wherein Annie throws the shooting match to prove her love for Frank—although I would feel obligated to point out to Ms. Steinem that the book was, in fact, written by Dorothy Fields, one of the great women of the American Theater. (Dottie never threw a shootin' match to any man!) I don't know how I would feel about listening to "Moonshine Lullaby" while sitting next to a hillbilly.

Whereas the music uses the instrumentation and tom-tom rhythm we find in all the mainstream "Indian" numbers (like "From the Land of the Sky Blue Waters"), the lyrics are a tongue-twister, more akin to Gilbert and Sullivan or what Ira Gershwin did for Russian composers in "Tchaikovsky." Since Betty Hutton was the most extravagantly comic of all Annie Oakleys, it should be no surprise that this was her single best number in the 1950 MGM movie; by contrast, the surviving footage of Judy Garland doing the number in the uncompleted early *Annie* movie is just excruciating. Hollywood stunt-dancer "Indians" drag her from place to place, and Garland looks as if she's really in pain. Doris Day is sort of in-between Hutton and Garland. This sort of wacky novelty isn't all that different from the goofball polkas and such like that Mitch Miller had her sing ten years earlier, but it's still not really her forte. Thus while Day does a yeoman job with "I'm an Indian Too," it's hard to call it a highlight.

On the other hand, "I Got Lost in His Arms" is by what seems like a very different Irving Berlin, the Berlin who, as a composer of romantic ballads, is easily in a class with Kern or Rodgers. It's also an instant Day classic, only two and a half minutes long but sheer heaven. Day's voice is positively radiant—it shimmers like sequins in the sunlight. There's only one verse and one chorus (the refrain is in ABAB form), but that's all that Day needs to make the most amazing magic.

One of the main ways that movies differ from stage productions is that live musicals almost always require a subplot, which usually takes the form of a secondary couple; their main functions are to inject the show with still more song-and-dance numbers while also giving the leading man and leading lady a chance to go offstage and catch their breath. In *Annie*, the secondary couple is "Tommy Keeler" and "Winnie Tate," but their part of the narrative is frequently dispensed with; they were dropped from both the 1950 movie and the 1966 Merman revival. But Tommy and Winnie were given a terrific, underappreciated song in Act Two: "Who Do You Love, I Hope." One wishes that Day and Goulet had sung that duet, but Columbia wanted to stick to the letter of what a cast album is supposed to be: the actors playing Annie and Frank do not sing Tommy and Winnie's song. Then again, since it would have been an overdubbed duet, it's possibly not much of a loss. The two singers here, Kelly Brown and Renée Winters, do a perky and respectable job; it's an excellent song, a perfect excuse for a dance number, an Irving Berlin gem that deserves to be heard more often. (In giving the song to artists other than Day and Goulet, Columbia was also further minimizing Day's workload and ensuring that she could record all of her vocals in a single session.)

Berlin was anything but stingy when it came to sharing his talent with his audiences, and, as a result, *Annie Get Your Gun* has two eleven o'clock numbers, "I Got the Sun in the Morning" and "Anything You Can Do." "Sun in the Morning" was a perfect song for Day—even the names are compatible; she was eternally as sunny and upbeat as this very bright Berlin bouncer demands. This was actually her third commercial recording of the song, the first time in 1946 as vocalist with Les Brown's Band of Renown, then much more recently on her 1960 album *Show Time*, a collection of Broadway numbers. The 1946 version is a solid big band swinger, the 1960 and the 1962 are both more relaxed—the charts are similar structurally and tempo-wise but they're far from identical; the *Show Time* version is about fifteen seconds longer, and the *Annie* album version begins with what sounds like a church chiming morning bells as the verse starts; also, the later version has a mixed choir behind Day, while the 1960 does not. In all instances, the song is a perfect one for Day. It's not surprising that she would keep coming back to it.

Where "Sun in the Morning" was the song-and-dance high point of the show—Annie performed it with a very colorful chorus line of dancing debutantes in white gloves and cowboys in towering hats—the comic climax is traditionally "Anything You Can Do." In the MGM version, it's almost anticlimactic—it's perfect for a leading lady like Merman or Martin who can be funny with a funny song, but for a comedienne like Hutton, it's almost overkill. (After hearing Hutton assume the mock-persona of Frank Butler at several points, you may well think that "Anything You Can Do" would be funnier with her singing both parts by herself.) Day and Goulet are perfect on paper for this highly competitive duet. Day is spunky and sexy and Goulet is exactly like Rock Hudson in his three movies with Day: a super-masculine stiff, but one blessed with an all-important and even fearless sense of humor, especially about himself. He's not exactly self-deprecating but he's self-deflating. Still, the comic duet would have worked better if they had actually recorded it in tandem rather than separately—although I do relish the way she spits out the punch line "in your hat" which was a barely disguised comic euphemism. (Back in the days when men actually wore hats, this was a code phrase for "up yours!") On the other hand, Doris's ultra-high note in the "any note you can sing, I can sing higher" bit could have used another take, it's one of the only questionable notes ever heard in her entire huge discography.

We end with another track on which the two principals don't sing, "There's No Business Like Show Business." Usually it's heard halfway through Act One, by Buffalo Bill, Charlie Davenport, and Frank Butler as they try to sell Annie on the idea of joining their troupe—and thus getting into show business. It is then reprised at the end of Act Two

as a sort of planned encore. In this audio-only production, essentially we just hear the reprise without having heard the song the first time around. It's the perfect way to end the show, but on this album it seems like a mere chaser, something to let us know that the album is over. That's an important purpose, yes. (Well, they couldn't have closed with "Anything You Can Do.")

The 1962 *Annie Get Your Gun* album was released when the musical theater was a feeder into Hollywood—the most popular shows were turned into movies—but those two newer media, television specials and long-playing albums, were also major tributaries of Broadway: shows were spun off into recordings and TV productions, but in a way that never challenged the supremacy of Broadway, any more than the Hudson River challenges the supremacy of the Atlantic Ocean. Robert Goulet did most of his best work after *Camelot* not creating new roles but in reprising classic leading man parts for TV—*Brigadoon, Kiss Me Kate,* and *Carousel*—and he was excellent in all three, all of which were also released as cast albums. It seems a shame that he would create only one classic role (Sir Lancelot in *Camelot*). Still, his career, which kept him in road companies and TV sitcoms for decades, was long and profitable. For her part, this is as close as Doris Day would come to playing in a classic musical comedy—she would have made a great Julie Jordan, Nellie Forbush, or even better, Sister Sarah (better still, opposite Dean Martin as Sky Masterson—that's my fantasy football casting for *Guys and Dolls*). I can see Day in her forties as a very different Auntie Mame or Dolly Gallagher Levi (although admittedly not Golde in *Fiddler* or Fanny in *Funny Girl*).

In a sense, the Doris Day–Robert Goulet *Annie Get Your Gun* album is a window into what might have been. Not that it needs to be to justify its existence. It's a terrific recording of two of the best voices in popular music singing one of the greatest musical theater scores ever written, and that's quite enough, thank you very much.

14

Blossom Dearie

My Gentleman Friend

(1959)

Personally, Blossom, as they say, was a piece of work; she could be pleasant, but (as the guitarist Tiny Grimes once said about playing with Art Tatum) dealing with her was always a privilege, rather than a pleasure—especially at the end of her life. Once, in 2001, when I wrote a liner note for a CD reissue of one of her Verve CDs, I referred to her as having been an "expatriate." When the CD was released, shortly after the 9/11 tragedy, Blossom hit the roof—she had somehow thought the term "expatriate" meant someone who had renounced the country of their birth, a former patriot, and she was livid, demanding that Universal Music withdraw the CD and change the booklet. Nothing as pedestrian as a dictionary could convince her that she was misunderstanding the word.

Then there was one occasion a few years later—close to the last time I ever spoke with her. She had already stopped performing, and a contemporary Broadway star was paying homage to her as part of a big concert at Town Hall. The star made a big speech about what a great artist Blossom Dearie was (true), and what an influence she was on a whole generation of singers (also true) and then she proceeded to sing one of Dearie's signature songs. You know that moment, in between when the singing stops and the applause begins? Usually you can hear a pin drop, but not this time—in that brief instant, the entirety of Town Hall heard the diminutive, immediately recognizable voice of the honoree, Miss Dearie herself, saying clearly, "That was terrible!" Everyone in the hall roared with laughter—including the star herself, who knew to expect the unconventional from Blossom.

To a lesser degree, Blossom's fate in recent decades parallels that of Nina Simone, in that both artists have proved to be much more influential in the digital era than they were when they were at their own professional peaks, the years when they were actually recording the LPs that would become so inspirational to Millennial singers. Dearie's first major album, the 1957 *Blossom Dearie,* was reissued on CD fairly early in the game, and for a while it seemed like every singer in New York owned a copy and memorized it.

Even today, when I hear a young singer like Marissa Mulder do "They Say It's Spring" or "Everything I've Got Belongs to You" I have no doubt but that they learned them from Dearie.

For years, I would have said that that first album was her best. However, upon listening to them all again, the album that falls upon my ears to best capture the brilliance of Blossom is her final Verve album, *My Gentleman Friend,* from 1959. It's not nearly as popular with contemporary singers as the earlier album—mainly because Verve's corporate heirs waited much longer to put it out on CD—but to my mind it's unquestionably her single best. This is the one that captures her remarkable gifts for vividly animating the most intricate lyrics, the one where she conveys the most emotion and passion with her distinctive baby voice, and the one that best documents her superior skill as a pianist, both as a self-accompanist and a full-scale keyboard soloist.

Just as she was a unique personality—and not always in a good way—when she wasn't playing, as a performer Blossom totally stood out for many good reasons. More than almost anyone else, she was halfway between the jazz world and what became known as the cabaret world; she could work in a room where Anita O'Day or Ella Fitzgerald worked, and she could work in a room where Mabel Mercer or Bobby Short worked—she was a major interpreter of lyrics while at the same time being one of the most gifted pianists in the American idiom. She was both Tony Bennett and Bill Evans at the same time (no exaggeration: Evans was a major fan of hers, and learned many songs from her, as we shall see). Yet her singing was as minimal, whispery intimate as her keyboard technique was prodigious.

Dearie's reluctance to be labeled an "expatriate" is ironic in the big picture of her career. Her Parisian experience was absolutely crucial to her development as an artist, and she returned from her travels with considerably more than she had left with: apart from the many hours of valuable experience in playing before club audiences, she now had a very tangible connection to a major American producer (Granz) and a unique repertoire of Franco-American material. And, oh yes, she also came back with a husband, namely, the excellent Belgian jazz flautist Bobby Jaspar (1926–1963). She brought all of these elements to bear on a recording session in 1959.

My Gentleman Friend was recorded over two "dates" in April and May 1959; it was Granz's habit to log recording sessions over multiple days, thus the dates for this album are April 8 and 9, and May 21 and 22. These sessions employ her trio of the period, with guitarist Kenny Burrell, bassist Ray Brown, and drummer Ed Thigpen. The two-day April session began with Dearie recording all the twelve songs that would go on her album *Blos-*

som Dearie Sings Comden and Green. Then, after the Comden and Green album was finished, she still had enough energy left to put all of the elements present to good use when she recorded three French songs, with Jaspar joining the trio. She then finished this very productive two-day session with the song that would be the title of the next album, "Gentleman Friend."

As an album, *My Gentleman Friend* offers a contrast between very familiar standards (it closes with a Gershwin mega-classic) and more obscure but worthy songs ("Hello Love," "You've Got Something I Want"). Along the way, there are several songs by Blossom's close friends—and also those French chansons.

The title track would have been better known to Dearie's audience in the 1950s than it is today. "Gentleman Friend" (there's no "my" in the song title) derives from the Broadway revue *Make Mine Manhattan*, a successful show that ran a year in the 1948–49 season; it starred Sid Caesar, and thus illustrated the close connection between the Broadway revue and the television variety show in the postwar period. "Gentleman Friend" was introduced by juveniles Sheila Bond and Hal Loman with the dancing chorus—one can only imagine that it was a cute and perky boy-girl number. It became one of the more popular songs by Richard Lewine (who was, much later, described in his *New York Times* obituary as "a Broadway composer and television producer, and a custodian of the legacy of Richard Rodgers, a second cousin"). Arnold Horwitt, who wrote book and lyrics for *Make Mine Manhattan*, enjoyed a prominent career in revue: *Pins and Needles* (1937), *Call Me Mister* (1946), *Make Mine Manhattan* (1948), *Inside USA* (1948), *Two's Company* (1952), and *The Girls Against the Boys* (1959), almost all of which were successful. He also occasionally branched off into full book musicals, such as *Are You with It?* (1945) and *Plain and Fancy* (1955), but the revues were his specialty.

"Gentleman Friend" is a perfect Dearie song—light and breezy, yet full of honest feeling and genuine charm. As with Doris Day's, Dearie's is the kind of sunshine that, in its overall excellence, carries weight and profundity without being heavy. Both verse and chorus are eminently swinging, but not in an aggressive way (the way that most big bands swing—with the huge exception of Count Basie, who knew better than anyone how to swing lightly). Dearie brings out the ways in which even the lyric conveys this approach: This isn't "Body and Soul"—"my life a hell you're making"—or "Yesterdays," all dark and gloomy. This is a cute song about a young girl being happy to be wearing "a hat with cherries, and a brand new yellow dress." Dearie perfectly captures the mood, and communicates it to all of us. Horwitt's lyric is a perfect mixture of formality and sheer exhilaration: sixty years later, the singer's beau would be described as "a cute guy" or "a hot dude" rather than a "gentleman friend," but both the lyricist and the singer are having fun playing with what was even then an antiquated expression.

It's not clear why Granz didn't make the obvious choice of using "Gentleman Friend" as the opener. Instead he begins with an obscure song by a pair of very famous songwriters, George and Ira Gershwin. (He would conclude the album with one of the most famous songs by the brothers, "Someone to Watch over Me.") "Little Jazz Bird" was introduced in the 1924 *Lady Be Good,* the first full-length collaboration by the brothers, but was vastly overshadowed by both the title song and "Fascinating Rhythm"—there were virtually no 78s of "Little Jazz Bird" when the show was new. It was more or less unheard on records until singers started doing Gershwin songbooks in the late 1950s, and even then it was never on anyone's A-list, being overlooked by both Fitzgerald and Vaughan, for instance, although Chris Connor recorded a memorable version.

But the song is perfect for Dearie; in fact, she's a "little jazz bird" herself. "Into a cabaret, one fatal day, a little songbird flew. / Found it so very gay, he thought he'd stay, just to get a bird's eye view." Rather than "updating" the song, she keeps it in a two-beat fox-trot, although slightly slower than it would have been played in 1924. It's the narrative that drives Dearie: the little bird is so inspired by the jazz band that he goes out and tells the other birds that they're out of date unless they "syncopate" and emulate the "warbling of a saxophone." It's easy to see how Dearie could relate, especially

as a little jazz bird who had spent years of her life proselytizing for the cause of American music overseas.

After "Little Jazz Bird" and "Gentleman Friend," we arrive at the first of the two Cy Coleman–Carolyn Leigh songs. "It's Too Good to Talk About Now" is track three, while "You Fascinate Me So" is track five. At this point, Coleman—the former Seymour Kaufman—was transitioning from a saloon pianist to Broadway composer, and, in addition to receiving an early vote of confidence from Sinatra (who sang "Why Try to Change Me Now" and "Witchcraft"), he was continually supported and encouraged by, among others, Tony Bennett, Peggy Lee, and Blossom Dearie, who consistently performed his music. Dearie's endorsement was of particular importance in regard to spreading the word of Coleman's wonderful songs throughout the jazz community. Bill Evans, generally regarded as the most important pianist of the 1960s and '70s, was exposed to Coleman's songs mainly via Dearie. He was especially enamored of Dearie's piano playing (particularly, as he put it, her unique way of stacking chords on top of other chords), and as a result began playing a lot of Coleman songs, and dozens of other pianists, in turn, learned Coleman's songs from him.

However, that wasn't the case with "It's Too Good to Talk About Now"—a pleasant enough song whose entire history seems to begin and end with Dearie. Like a number of Coleman-Leigh songs, it seems to belong to two worlds at the same time: you can imagine a hip piano trio at Birdland running rampant over its chord changes, and can also picture a boy-and-girl team of song and dancers hoofing like a pair of vaudevillians circa 1915, with the coda extending the ending in the best variety show tradition. Apart from that, it's a snappy tune that didn't deserve to have disappeared so abruptly. From any other team, it would have been a gem, but from Cy and Carolyn, it's not even the pick of the litter.

"You Fascinate Me So," on the other hand, went on to great things, becoming one of the team's most performed standards. (They wrote it for a projected musical show called *13 Daughters,* which eventually made it to Broadway for a few weeks in

1961, although without Coleman and Leigh. The composer himself introduced the song on one of his own albums in 1958.) Along with "Witchcraft," "Playboy's Theme," and "The Best Is Yet to Come," "You Fascinate Me So" is also blessed with a vamp and a countermelody, which is better than the main melodies of most other songs.

The two Coleman-Leigh songs are complemented by three French chansons, two of which ("Chez Moi," "L'Étang") are the work of Paul Misraki, a songwriter closely connected with his more famous collaborator, Charles Trenet. Dearie obviously encountered all of these during her expatriate phase (you should forgive the expression); in those days, French songs were generally regarded by Americans and the rest of the world as something light and fluffy and frou-frou—and that's the French music that Dearie taught us all to love. (Even Edith Piaf, no less than Billie Holiday and Judy Garland, often sang songs that were snappy and fun, like "Pauvre Jean.") Later, the more modern generation of French songwriters, such as Charles Aznavour and Jacques Brel, gave French songs a reputation for being dire and bleak. The three lightest and airiest songs on *Gentleman Friend* are the Parisian imports: "Chez Moi" (a Misraki composition that was also recorded in a cool jazz treatment by visiting tenor saxophonist Zoot Sims). Also by Misraki, "L'Étang," a lovely, placid contemplation of a pond, is a stunning ballad with Debussy-ian, Impressionistic overtones. Bobby Jaspar's contributions on flute form a key part of the overall atmosphere even though he doesn't take a whole solo.

A prolific singer-songwriter, beloved all over the French-speaking world, Trenet would write three songs that became all-time classics, widely heard across the globe, and well known in English: "Boum!" (from 1938, and an ironic hit for Frenchmen a year before the start of World War II), and, after the war, "La Mer" ("Beyond the Sea" in America), and "Que reste-t-il de nos amours?" ("I Wish You Love"). "Boum!" was Trenet's earliest song to catch on internationally; he recorded it in both French and English while in America, and the song's booming, bouncy rhythm was a natural for radio sweet bands. At 2:10, Dearie's version

has no choice but to be fast and snappy—short, sweet, and delightfully swinging. The tempo is similar to that of all those 1930s sweet bands, but Dearie is infinitely hip, even when playing a businessman's bounce. Even though there's a perfectly serviceable English lyric, she sings it in French, in a clipped, staccato fashion, and there's even time for a full solo from Jaspar. (There's also a tangible connection between two of Dearie's faves, Trenet and Coleman and Leigh: in their 1962 Broadway musical *Little Me*, Sid Caesar played, among other characters, a French song-and-dance man named "Val du Val" whose signature song was titled "Boom-Boom.")

Along with "It's Too Good to Talk About Now," there are two other songs that are unique to *My Gentleman Friend*, "Hello Love" and "You've Got Something I Want," both of which are by friends of Dearie. The first is credited to Michael Preston Barr and Dion McGregor, who also wrote an equally obscure song ("Try Your Wings") that turns up on another Dearie album (*Give Him the Oo-La-La*). "You've Got Something I Want" is by Bob Haymes, a Dearie favorite. The younger brother of crooner Dick Haymes, Bob sang with dance bands (Bob Chester) and starred in at least one film but had a more durable career as a songwriter: Nat Cole made his "That's All" into a standard, but Dearie did at least five of his songs in her Verve series ("You for Me," "Now at Last," "A Fine Spring Morning," "They Say It's Spring," and "You've Got Something I Want"). Through most of the last sixty years, the 1952 "That's All" was by far Haymes's best known song, but in the contemporary era, Dearie's recordings have proved so popular with younger singers that in New York nightclubs one hears "They Say It's Spring" at least as often. "You've Got Something I Want" is a coy, zingy little number, whereas "Hello Love" is a tranquil ballad that's mostly Blossom and her own piano; the other instruments are more felt than heard. These two very unfamiliar songs sound wonderful when Dearie sings them; in a way, it's an unfair advantage—to fully access whether these songs themselves are really good, we should hear them sung by someone less talented.

Following "L'Étang" and "Hello Love," the album concludes with "Someone to Watch over

Me." It's slow—at six minutes, the longest track here. One might question the wisdom of ending with what appears to be a whimper as opposed to a bang. It's hardly a big climax, and I can't imagine that Blossom ever ended a show like this, I certainly never knew her to do so. Yet the quiet, understated conclusion seems brilliantly Dearie-licious. You can do certain things on an album that you can't do in a live show; Sinatra, for instance, filled entire LPs with nothing but slow ballads, but he would have never done a concert that way. Maybe the reason Granz and Dearie ended like this is, simply, because it works: Dearie is so exposed, open, and vulnerable, and this long, slow, introspective treatment of the 1926 standard (from *Oh, Kay!*) is so perfect, and such a complete statement unto itself, that nothing could possibly follow it. And if there's one thing that Dearie consistently achieved, it was the complete absence of superfluousness. Anything following "Someone to Watch over Me" would be positively un-Dearie-like.

Unlike many of the entries in this book, *My Gentleman Friend* has never been singled out as a classic album or even a high point of Dearie's career—it features the same mixture of songbook standards, songs by friends of the artist (both famous and obscure), and chansons as do most of the others. *My Gentleman Friend* deserves to be here because it is the Dearie album with the most of the best songs, and the one on which Dearie gives her most consistently excellent performances.

Blossom was much too subtle to overwhelm you; she delivers everything sotto voce, there's never anything that would amount, in comparison to another singer, as a moment of belting. But even though a contemporary singer like Cassandra Wilson would be quicker to say that it was Nina Simone who inspired her, the influence of Dearie is unmistakable—Wilson's device of using a soft dynamic and even silence to command a crowd's attention comes straight from Dearie; like Blossom, when Cassandra wants to emphasize a point, rather than getting louder, she has the band play softer—just as Dearie has the bass and drums drop out in those moments.

Bobby Short had a sense of drama and a range of facial expressions and onstage personas to complement his music; her other major contemporary, Barbara Carroll, continues to interpret the American Songbook with a surplus of classical technique (and the taste to employ it only as necessary) that makes her piano solos often breathtaking. Yet Dearie had something no other pianist or singer ever had, an abundance of charm. A sweet, little-girl voice, and a perpetual sense of wonder that went with it, accompanied by a piano style that was profoundly rich in an advanced knowledge of harmony, but which impressed the listener with its beauty and simplicity rather than complexity.

15

Matt Dennis, *Matt Dennis Plays and Sings Matt Dennis* (1954)
Bobby Troup, *Bobby Troup Sings Johnny Mercer* (1955)

Matt Dennis and Bobby Troup were small but significant exceptions to a major rule. Prior to the mid-1960s, there were only a handful of important singer-songwriters in the land: the basic equation was to keep the two pursuits separate (even in country music, blues, and early rock 'n' roll). The major exceptions were,

singer-songwriters and the idea that performing artists are expected to write their own material. But for the fifty years before that, beginning with the emergence of the modern popular song (usually dated to "Alexander's Ragtime Band" and "They Didn't Believe Me" in 1911–12), pop music was built around a model in which the guy who sang the

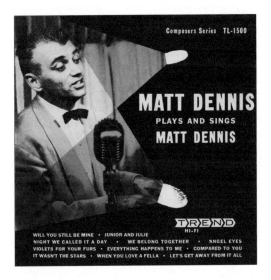

roughly in order of appearance, Hoagy Carmichael, Harold Arlen, and Johnny Mercer, who were established as fixtures in the pop music firmament by the start of the swing era. Between that time and the coming of The Beatles and Bob Dylan, there were only two other singer-songwriters who arrived at the party, and they did so in rough parallels to each other: Matt Dennis (1914–2002) and Bobby Troup (1918–1999).

The American popular music of the last hundred years can be divided into two distinct periods. From the moment the Beatles landed at JFK in 1964 to today, pop has been dominated by so-called

song and the guy who wrote it were almost always two different guys.

Both Dennis and Troup were first heard from as songwriters during the late big band era: Dennis wrote most of his early hits (and the majority of his best-known works) under a publishing arrangement with Tommy Dorsey; Troup launched his career with a flirty novelty song titled "Daddy" that became an unlikely but huge hit for the sweet band of Sammy Kaye (an ensemble not generally known for its sex appeal). After the war, both Dennis and Troup settled in Los Angeles, where they became part of the Hollywood community, writing music for movies and television, and, in Troup's case, enjoying a significant on-screen career as well.

Troup and Dennis played a key part in a major transition that occurred around the end of the war. The big band era had been focused on ballrooms, which, never more so than in the Depression, were a populist venue, within the economic range of practically everybody. But around 1945–46, when the government imposed a tax on dancehalls, the ballrooms began closing, and more and more smaller, intimate club venues began springing up that featured singers and small groups rather than big floors for social dancing. Singer-pianists had an obvious advantage, and both Troup and Dennis were among the earliest nightclub institutions on the West Coast; all of a sudden there were many more opportunities for them to perform than had been possible just a few years earlier.

The arrival of the LP coincided with the rising prominence of the small nightclub, and by the mid-1950s Troup and Dennis were prominent in both. It's easy to imagine stars and directors catching them at the Crescendo on the Sunset Strip or Billy Berg's, particularly on a Saturday night when they weren't shooting in the morning. Both were recording regularly—the long-playing disc suited their relaxed, laid-back styles much more than the three-minute single. These were gratifying years for the two of them—seemingly every show business and music medium welcomed their input. Appropriately, Johnny Mercer expressed his implicit approval of both of his stylistic descendants in that both Troup and Dennis at one time or another recorded for Capitol during the period when Mercer was still in charge.

Both men recorded only sparingly, unfortunately, but in their brief but vital careers they each made several classic albums: Dennis reached his pinnacle with a live collection of the best of his own songs, *Plays and Sings Matt Dennis,* and Troup's overall best album was a homage to his original inspiration, titled *Bobby Troup Sings Johnny Mercer.*

Recorded in 1954, *Plays and Sings Matt Dennis* speaks to several musical trends of the era. Not only is it an early example of the 12-inch LP, but it also documents the era in which both little road-

house "nite spots" as well as independent record labels briefly dotted the landscape. Dennis taped the album at a long-forgotten club called the Tally-Ho and for a short-lived company named Trend Records. Trend was owned and operated by veteran producer Albert Marx, who, among other things, was responsible for recording the legendary 1938 Benny Goodman Carnegie Hall concert. (Trend was also eventually absorbed into Decca and then MCA and is currently buried in the best catalogue of the Universal Music Group.) For the album, Dennis is accompanied by bassist Gene Englund and drummer Mark Barnett, while his wife, Virginia Maxey, also sings on several tracks.

Throughout, Dennis's voice is surprisingly deep and profound—much more so than shown on his earlier recordings—with a lithe autumnal quality to it. No question, the man had authentic chops. He could have easily succeeded as a performer even if he hadn't written a single tune.

"Will You Still Be Mine" was one of the ten or so pivotal songs that Dennis had originally written while on the payroll of Tommy Dorsey, nearly all of which had lyrics by his longtime collaborator Tom Adair. Where most of these were famously introduced by Sinatra, "Will You Still Be Mine" was a standout for the young and perky Connie Haines, who recorded it at the same 1941 Dorsey session that included the Dennis classic "Let's Get Away from It All." More than most dance band records, the original Dorsey disc featured the vocalist surprisingly extensively; she gets the verse and two whole choruses, it's almost more like a vocal or personality record than a dance band disc.

But as perfect a tune as it was for Haines and the Dorsey band, it's an even better opener for the singer-songwriter-pianist himself thirteen years later. Here at the Tally-Ho, Dennis rolls out chorus after chorus, only the first of which corresponds to what Haines sang in 1941. Since some of the original lyrics were too dated thirteen years later ("when FDR declines to run ... will you still be mine?"), Dennis instead came up with an entirely new set of words for everything after the first chorus. As always, the lyric is loaded with topical gags and one-liners, and a song that's amusing enough to begin with is made even more so with sideline commentary by Dennis himself, as well as deliberately misspoken lines. One of the funniest is "When Miss Monroe is old and flat . . ." he then corrects himself, "FAT!" This is a particular combination of music and comedy that pianist-singers do better than anybody—it requires the accompaniment and the foreground vocal to be in perfect coordination—and pianist-singer-songwriters do even better than that.

The second song, the far more obscure "Junior and Julie," is a real charmer. The phrase "dated" is generally understood to be pejorative, but "Junior and Julie" could have only been written in the immediate postwar era, and is all the more adorable because of it. A married couple sings with a kind of "nostalgia for the future" about the wonderful life that's going to be lived by their two kids, and that's why they're ecstatically happy to be "saving their pennies for Junior and Julie, the two greatest kids in the land." You don't have to be a feminist to find it objectionable that their expectations for their son (who will "be a great doctor") are somehow more inflated than that for their daughter (who "will be a great lady, asked to the White House for tea"). Spoiler alert: like a lot of period songs, it has a wonderful twist ending— what Scott Fitzgerald would call a *Saturday Evening Post* windup: this time the gag is that the couple singing the song "just got married today." Even the existence of those two swell kids, Junior and Julie, is part of their optimistic dream of the future. Dated as the song may be, the contemporary singer Erin Bode did a marvelous record of it, and to her credit without changing any of the lyrics.

"The Night We Called It a Day" has the distinction of being perhaps the first song ever written at the specific request of Sinatra, who asked Dennis to come up with something special for him to record on his first solo session, in 1942. Also published by Dorsey, and over the years was also closely associated with the Sentimental Gentleman's other most famous "graduate," Jo Stafford, who sang the lead vocal with the Pied Pipers on the Dorsey band's own version of the song. It's one of the sadder and more serious songs here, beginning with what can only be described as a classic "cocktail piano" (you can practically taste the martinis) intro.

This is another brilliant selection for a singer-pianist with a light, almost casual voice. Up to the mid-twentieth century, it was assumed that to convey sad emotions in a meaningful way, it was essential to have a big heavy operatic voice. But this song brilliantly conveys deep and profound emotions while being comparatively light itself; the song is ineffably sad even though the chords aren't dark and morose. Even the title, which contrasts between the literal "night" and the phrase "call it a day" (which already had been used for a 1933 song, titled "Let's Call It a Day"), is somehow playful. It's hard to imagine that anyone could sing it more movingly than Sinatra or Stafford, but Dennis's understated treatment—incredibly minimal though it may be, using just a trio and taking up only two minutes of time—comes closer than anyone else.

The next track, "We Belong Together," which is co-credited to Dorsey saxophonist Don Lodice (and is not to be confused with an earlier Jerome Kern song and a later early rock doo-wop hit, both with the same title), introduces guest vocalist Virginia Maxey. She had sung with almost half a dozen major bands in the 1940s, Charlie Barnet, Tony Pastor, Ziggy Elman, Jimmy Dorsey, and was also at one time a member of Mel Tormé's Mel-Tones. She's an excellent though somewhat generic female band singer, perhaps a half step beneath the Helens (Humes, Forrest, O'Connell, Ward), albeit indistinguishable from many other perky canaries of the World War II and postwar years, but that's a pretty high standard right there.

This is the second list song on the album, a songwriting conceit that's particularly effective for boy-girl duets, and Dennis, both as singer and songwriter, makes the most of it. To give you an example, they sing, "we belong together,"

He: "like Fibber McGee and Molly"
She: "Kukla, Fran, and Ollie"

Eventually they climax the lyric with:

He: "Vanderbilt and his moolah"
She: "Bankhead and Tallulah"

at which point they both sigh *"Dahling"* in an exaggerated Tallulahesque purr.

It's a cute duet, if hardly a song for the ages, and it's not a major loss that this particular Dennis song was apparently never heard from again.

"Angel Eyes" is just the opposite; this is the one later Dennis song, from a decade after his huge rush of hits and standards from the Dorsey-Sinatra-Stafford period, that became an all-time classic. (Eternally associated with both Sinatra and Nat King Cole, the first singer that the composer presented it to was actually Ella Fitzgerald.) It's also the most significant of Dennis's songs with a lyric by someone other than Tom Adair; the words are credited to Earl Brent, a lesser-known songwriter who was hanging around the fringes of Hollywood, and, disappointingly, never wrote anything else nearly as worthwhile.

In a more equitable world, Brent would have enjoyed a major career both as a songwriter as well as a screenwriter. "Angel Eyes" is incredibly cinematic, especially when presented in this stripped-down trio version, and Dennis's vocal is much more understated and noirish. Brent's lyric reads like a monologue from a Raymond Chandler novel or could easily be from a musical adaptation of Nicholas Ray's *In a Lonely Place*. The use of the first person when telling the story, with all the cryptic clues that contains, becomes a counterpoint to the subjective camera in *The Lady in the Lake*. Dennis knows exactly what words to emphasize, which ones to linger over, and which ones to rush past; he's not interested in making his own melody (or his collaborator's text) sound glorious, he's interested in telling the story, and this he does better than almost anybody.

Where Dennis is profoundly disillusioned in "Angel Eyes," he's remarkably optimistic and upbeat in "Violets for Your Furs," a Dennis-Adair-Sinatra-Dorsey classic that's much more innocent and considerably less dark as a narrative. At two and a half minutes, it's a very quick little tableau, almost more like a greeting card—an urban winter scene, New York in the holiday season—than a full landscape. Dennis sings it simply and directly, with no unnecessary embellishment, just the verse and one chorus. It's 150 seconds of intimate imagery, as

the lyric states, "just a little simple magic that I'd heard about somewhere."

Dennis has highly personalized the next Dennis-Adair-Sinatra-Dorsey classic, "Everything Happens to Me," perhaps too much so. The first chorus is on the same level as "Violets for Your Furs," but then he launches into a newly written second chorus, which arrives in four eight-bar sections (AABA). The first is about how, as an entertainer working in supper clubs, he often has to screech over the noise of blenders, nose blowers, and other distractions; the second is about how he lands a small part in a movie but is then edited out; then he tells us that when he gets his picture in a magazine, "here I sit with gravy on my chin"; and lastly, when he writes a new song, he has high hopes for it until he learns that the record label has placed it "on the back of Jimmy Boyd," the thirteen-year-old child singing sensation whose single of "I Saw Mommy Kissing Santa Claus" was a huge hit in 1952. Needless to say, these are not common garden-variety problems that most of the people listening to Dennis can readily identify with. These new lyrics are charming but only to a degree; you really had to be there in the room with him for them to be totally effective; they don't hold up as well on a recording, especially not sixty years later.

We then get a run of four songs (cowritten with three generally unknown credited coauthors) that are essentially unique to this album. By any standards, they're all superior samples of the songwriter's art, but they're also easy to overlook, precisely because they're in such august company. Even a good song sounds second-rate compared to "Angel Eyes" and "Everything Happens to Me." Still, even Dennis's B-level songs are better than the best efforts of most other songwriters.

"Compared to You" is our third list song (following "Will You Still Be Mine?" and "We Belong Together"); this one is more witty and romantic, where the others are more outrageously comic and upbeat. (The collaborator here is one Paul Herrick Young, who had two other songs that got out there, "Can You Look Me in the Eyes" and "Where in the World?"). The list conceit is also very reminiscent of "These Foolish Things" especially in lines like "a half-remembered love song with its long-remembered thrills / Are little things compared to you."

"That Tired Routine Called Love" is a sardonic riff on the various conventions of a relationship, in the spirit of Rodgers and Hart's "I Wish I Were in Love Again." The general underlying message is that love may be tedious and repetitious—but what the hell, bring it on, baby! Dennis sings earnestly and plays it with plenty of zip and zing. (Especially in witty rhymes like "Me thinks it . . . smells!") It was written by Dennis and someone credited as "Louis Ted Steele"; there was a studio conductor named Ted Steele, but it's not known if this is the same guy. Dennis sings wonderfully as always, and his percussionistic piano work is especially compelling here.

The final two songs in this stretch are co-credited to one David S. Gillam. "It Wasn't the Stars That Thrilled Me" also seems to depend upon the listener's knowledge of other songs—the song mainly makes sense when you hear other songs about how thrilling the moon and the stars are. This is a prime example of what might be called an "un-list" song, of which the template might be "The Nearness of You." As you can see, it's a small step from "it's not the pale moon that excites me" to "The stars were very bright, but it wasn't the stars that thrilled me . . . last night." "When You Love a Fella" is a cute and frisky vocal duet between Mr. and Mrs. Dennis, and the last appearance here of Maxey, but it's not a song that you ever need to hear more than once.

While the preceding batch of tunes isn't particularly memorable, the album then concludes brilliantly with a Dennis-Adair classic, "Let's Get Away from It All." We're accustomed to hearing the famous Tommy Dorsey version, with Sinatra and a cast of thousands, but Dennis's own solo reading (no Maxey here) is both intimate and swinging, and his piano work is again exceptional as he puts his own tune through some Chopinesque paces.

Even though not every song is one of his best, *Plays and Sings Matt Dennis* is by far his best overall album. Of his subsequent albums, the best are those in which he primarily concentrates on playing and singing the works of other authors and composers besides himself, such as his excellent

Rodgers and Hart songbook, *She Dances Overhead.* (There's also a big band album with Sy Oliver titled *Welcome Matt,* and *Play Melancholy Baby,* an excellent small group set of standards.)

But this first album is the most essential, the one that most clearly illustrates why Dennis belongs in the same sentence with such predecessors as Mercer, Carmichael, and Arlen, as well as the leaders of the more recent singer-songwriter movement, like Bob Dylan, Joni Mitchell, Tom Waits, and James Taylor. As a singer, songwriter, pianist, and bandleader, he proves that it is indeed possible for one man to do everything, as long as that one man is Matt Dennis.

Great albums that never were: *Bruce Springsteen Sings Bob Dylan. Joni Mitchell Sings Carole King.* How about *Paul McCartney Sings Willie Nelson?* No, you can't possibly imagine any of those, can you? And neither can anyone else. And there's a good reason why: because they would never happen. Not ever, in a million years. The mid-1950s were the only time when the singer-songwriters that were then active were likely to actually perform each other's work. But *Bobby Troup Sings Johnny Mercer* is more than a historical accident; it's a unique example of two major talents who normally wouldn't have crossed paths who in a sense collaborated on a fantastic album. And yet, to use such loaded words in describing *Bobby Troup Sings Johnny Mercer* almost defeats the point; the album is wistfully light and swinging, just the opposite of big and heavy.

In the mid-1950s, Troup was, like Dennis, busy with a breathlessly wide range of professional activities, not least of which was cutting albums of his own for two start-up labels, Bethlehem Records and Liberty Records. He had already been an active participant in the postwar recording boom, appearing as a band vocalist with Count Basie, pianist Freddie Slack, and Jerry Gray's Glenn Miller spinoff orchestra, as well as recording singles of his own. His first album as a leader and featured attraction was done for Capitol in 1953 with a California-cool-style jazz backup group led by valve trombonist Bobby Enevoldsen, a 10-incher titled simply *Bobby Troup.*

In January 1955, Troup cut his first 12-inch LP, *Bobby Troup Sings Johnny Mercer,* for the newly launched Bethlehem Records. For the sessions he accompanied himself on piano, abetted by an all-star Los Angeles rhythm section of guitarist Howard Roberts, bassist Red Mitchell, and drummer Don Heath. Trombonist Enevoldsen made a cameo appearance on this album as well, playing his valved instrument on four tracks.

We know just from the selection of the songs themselves that Troup really knows and loves the Mercer canon—more than that, that these are some of the songs that inspired him to become a songwriter to begin with. This is so early in the game—the tradition, then solidifying, of doing vintage standards in the album format—that it was impossible for him to tell which songs would be Mercer's overall most popular. Troup had no way of knowing at this point that he was picking the two songs that would become Mercer's most frequently sung standards, "Come Rain or Come Shine" and "Skylark." In 1955, "Come Rain or Come Shine" was still thought of as the major survivor of Mercer's first big Broadway show, alas, and a history-making flop.

Like *Bobby Troup, Bobby Troup Sings Johnny Mercer* is an outgrowth of Troup's saloon piano act. One of the key differences, however, is that on the earlier album Troup's presence as a lyricist is all over the place, even on standards that he didn't write—many, like "Chicago," have special, customized lyrics that he wrote for his live performances. ("I saw a blonde with an old roue / He looked kind of cute in his crew-cut toupee.") On the 1955 album, he doesn't mess with Mercer's huckleberry poetry. Both albums, however, emphasize Troup's spare, minimalist style, never holding a note for two beats when one will do, emphasizing the lyrics and drawing out the inner meaning of the songs rather than showing off his own chops.

Troup telegraphs his intentions by beginning with "Jamboree Jones," a narrative song concerning football and music. This is a rather atypical song in Mercer's output: whereas the other tunes in the stack show what Mercer could do when he was writing for Bing Crosby, Fred Astaire, Judy Garland, or Lena Horne, to name just a few. "Jamboree

Jones" illustrates the kind of song that Mercer liked to write for himself—as well as one of the comparatively few for which he wrote the music as well as the lyrics. "Jamboree Jones," first published in 1936, is a highly detailed story song of the kind that scarcely exists in the Great American Songbook. In both its structure (three choruses and a coda) and its content, it has more in common with many a traditional folk song, or to be more specific, such genres identified by folklorists as the "Child ballad" or the "murder ballad."

In its melody and rhythm, "Jamboree" is very much a part of the swing era. As Mercer said, he wrote it with Benny Goodman in mind; however, "Benny never played it much, because I don't think he liked it," which, he implied, lessened his own enthusiasm for the song. However it's hardly the kind of thing that Goodman would have played. This is not exactly dance band fare: when Paul Whiteman recorded it in 1938, it was essentially a vehicle for his vocal group, the Four Modernaires. Mercer might have meant that the character the song describes was directly inspired by Goodman, an obsessive musician who practices on his clarinet "day and night"—if he's not talking about Benny, it's someone mighty close. And as for not liking it himself, Mercer actually recorded it twice—unusual, in that he didn't record the vast majority of his own songs even once. The song spoke directly to Troup because it was essentially a "party piece," demanding storytelling abilities as opposed to raw chops; it's in that vein that Troup excels, no less than Mercer. (And so too when John Pizzarelli sings it.) Troup's version is highly intimate—he sings it without a vocal group—and yet he puts the story over no less convincingly.

"Midnight Sun" is a song that also depends on delivery—which is why Mercer recorded it himself (much later, nearer the end of his life) and also why it appealed to Troup: you don't need big chops to put it over, it's all about style and conviction. Where "Jamboree Jones" is pure narrative, "Midnight Sun" is all description—painting pictures rather than telling stories, yet the images themselves constitute a story in the listener's head. The song's remarkable construction, the triple rhyme scheme, doubtlessly also did much to endear it to Troup, whose version here, from January 1955, may only be the second recording of the lyric. (The earliest vocal version that I know of is June Christy's, on *Something Cool*.) While Mercer's presence echoes throughout the performance, so too does that of credited co-composer Lionel Hampton, whom Troup pays homage to both in the staccato nature of his piano intro as well as his breathless vocal. Enevoldsen's brief, eight-bar solo enhances the intimate mood.

Next to "All the Things You Are," "Come Rain or Come Shine," with a melody by Harold Arlen, may be the most frequently cited example of a classic song from a flop show. Jazzmen and hip singers picked up on it immediately, and thus "Come Rain" never went through a dormant period when it was scarcely heard—the song has been recorded without a letup since 1946. Troup's quartet reading is short, simple, and direct, with the singer dwelling on the contrasts: "*I'm* going to love you, like *nobody's* loved you—come *rain* or come *shine*" and likewise, "*high / deep*" "*in / out*." The song was originally written for Lena Horne (who had been replaced by Ruby Hill by the time the show opened) and Harold Nicholas in *St. Louis Woman*. Thus it was always part of the African American experience, and the only downside of that is that from the 1960s onward it was done by a lot of artists who mistook it for a gospel song. Although there are allusions to the overwhelming forces of the universe, this is not what the song is all about—it's about the contrast between the personal and the universal, the intimate more than the all-encompassing, as Troup demonstrates that he understands.

"Laura" is a departure, a modern jazz piano instrumental of the 1945 film score by Tinseltown theme-smith David Raksin, which had become a hit record for Woody Herman (and subsequently a standard) after Mercer added the lyrics. In the 1955 Troup recording, we listen for the artist's voice, and we also listen for the valve trombone, but we hear neither; he has decided to feature his own piano. Troup has clearly studied Nat King Cole's 1952 instrumental (on the album *Penthouse Serenade*), a rather brilliant, far-sighted interpretation that might pass for the work of Bill Evans in a blindfold test. Troup's intimate instrumental—like his sing-

ing, quiet and understated—seems somewhat like a direct extension of Cole's.

Johnnie Johnston, a long-forgotten crooner who enjoyed a brief vogue during World War II as a Hollywood leading man, introduced "That Old Black Magic" in *Star-Spangled Rhythm* (1942)—singing while Vera Zorina, then the wife and muse of George Balanchine, danced a snow ballet. Troup's low-voiced, spare style does indeed suggest a magical incantation, and the riff leading into the vocal (which suggests "One O'Clock Jump") may be part of that spell. At four and a half minutes (the longest track here), there's ample time for an extended solo by Troup, one of his fullest keyboard statements on record, as well as by Roberts.

For the last half century, we've all grown up with Mercer and Arlen's "One for My Baby (And One More for the Road)" via the epically sad masterpiece reading by Sinatra (on *Only the Lonely*). Yet as originally conceived, the song was at least as much comic as it was tragic; in all the early interpretations, including those by Fred Astaire (in *The Sky's the Limit*), as well as Mercer and Arlen themselves, the song is much less dark and much more humorous. "Baby" is pure saloon fodder, even more so than most so-called saloon songs: it actually takes place in a dark bar in the middle of the night, and Troup writes and sings about it like he knows it, like he's experienced it firsthand. Understated humor and all, he sounds like he's talking directly from his heart and soul, and one quickly forgets that he's actually singing and playing the piano, the communication is so direct. His playfulness actually makes the song even more touching.

Mercer wrote "Cuckoo in the Clock" for himself to sing with Goodman on *The Camel Caravan*, and he also sang on the band's Victor recording. (Mercer was in something of an ornithological phase during the swing era, what with "Cuckoo in the Clock," "Bob White," "Mr. Meadowlark," and "Skylark" all hatching from the same nest.) "Cuckoo in the Clock" was a successful and swinging novelty in 1939, with recordings by the orchestras of Red Norvo (Mildred Bailey singing), Glenn Miller (Marion Hutton singing), and Kay Kyser (Sully Mason singing), in addition to Goodman and Mercer. It was well-crafted nonsense, with a solid dance beat. Troup's recording is highly affectionate; he's clearly reflecting on wherever he was in 1939, and who he was trying to score with while being interrupted by a kvetching cuckoo.

"Cuckoo in the Clock" has a melody by Broadway and Tin Pan Alley veteran Walter Donaldson. In that same year, 1939, Mercer wrote at least two other songs that can handily be considered classics, with two other collaborators: "Day In, Day Out" with Rube Bloom and "I Thought About You" with Jimmy Van Heusen. Yet though both of these songs were highly successful, neither of these musical relationships turned out to be lasting ones. "I Thought About You" is inexplicably not on the Troup album (it's hard to imagine a Mercer songbook that doesn't contain it) but "Day In, Day Out" is here. One line in the lyric anticipates the title of "Come Rain or Come Shine," but Mercer wasn't rehashing ideas from one song to the next. (In his album notes, he chides himself for having used the phrase "come rain or shine" in two different songs.) "Day In, Day Out" was frequently heard in the 1950s, all over LPs and TV variety shows, but it's become much scarcer in recent decades—as opposed to "I Thought About You," which is omnipresent. Troup starts out rather wistfully before he quickly snaps into more of a fox-trot dance tempo; again, it's much more understated than most performances of the song, the numerous versions by both Sinatra and Cole were considerably louder and more literal in terms of "the ocean's roar, a thousand drums." His ending too, a nightclub equivalent of a board fade (in which he simply plays and sings softer and softer), is also especially effective.

"Jeepers Creepers," one of Mercer's first of many standards written with Harry Warren, is the second instrumental on the *Mercer* album. Enevoldsen is back for this one, and everyone gets a solo, including Troup, who quotes "Stormy Weather." The early part of his piano statement is mostly single horn-like lines, then he revs it up by getting much more orchestral and playing considerably louder—it almost sounds like two different musicians. All this reflects what he had learned on the job working in saloons—how to sustain interest with just his own playing. Bassist Red Mitchell doubtless remem-

bered the chord changes for "Jeepers Creepers" from his tenure with Woody Herman, where he knew them as the foundation of the Herd anthem "Four Brothers."

"(Love's Got Me in a) Lazy Mood" is one of the gems of the Troup album. The melody was written by the outstanding saxophonist Eddie Miller, a New Orleans musician best remembered as a key member of the original Bob Crosby band. He first recorded this melody as his feature with Crosby's Bobcats in 1938; the title then was "Slow Mood." In 1943, after that Crosby band broke up, Miller started his own orchestra, using the tune as his radio theme song, now outfitted with a new title and an excellent lyric by Mercer, which the two authors recorded together in 1944. From the start, we know we're in rarefied country: "I'll tell you why the days go by like caterpillars do . . ." No one could capture a bucolic Southern countryside more vividly than this son of Savannah. It was a clearly special song to Mercer: out of fewer than half a dozen major recordings of "Lazy Mood," two were produced by Mercer himself: the Eddie Miller disc, with his own vocal, and an equally lovely, slightly later 78 by Paul Weston's orchestra with Matt Dennis singing. (It's the only song I can think of recorded by Mercer, Troup, and Dennis.) Troup's staccato phrasing is even more convincingly lazy than Mercer's.

From one of Mercer's most unjustly neglected songs, Troup moves on to one that possibly even exceeds "Come Rain or Come Shine" as his most over-sung. In recent decades especially, "Skylark" has come to rival "Over the Rainbow" and "Summertime" as one of those songs that's done so often, especially by so-called jazz singers, that my first impulse is to run from the room screaming whenever I hear it—even the greatest song ever written ceases to be a delight when you hear it too often. That's an unfair criterion to apply to Troup, since the song wasn't nearly so overfamiliar in the mid-1950s. For both lyricist Mercer and composer Hoagy Carmichael, the song grew out of personal relationships, and not necessarily with each other. Musically, the melody was inspired by Carmichael's close friend, the iconic and long-deceased jazz trumpeter Bix Beiderbecke; the two notes that comprise the main melody were said to be derived from a characteristic Bix phrase. Lyrically, the narrative was supposedly a reflection on Mercer's love affair with Judy Garland. Neither claim is 100 percent verified, but they both have a certain truthiness about them (as Stephen Colbert would say). For his part, Troup certainly sounds as if he's expressing something deep and personal; the opening eight bars, in which he's only accompanied by very subtle commentary from Howard Roberts, are so intimate and understated that he's completely crossed over the bridge between singing and speaking. He's coming from a time when the song wasn't being taken for granted, and singing from a place in the heart that's uniquely his.

"I'm with You" is, in fact, literally his—it's the only song that Mercer and Troup wrote together; both, apparently, contributed to the music as well as the words. There's only one other major recording, and that's by Anita O'Day on a 1956 Verve single. (That is, until 2014, when John Pizzarelli, a major fan of both Mercer and Troup, included it on his own Mercer songbook album.) The tune sounds very West Coast cool as it opens, with Troup scatting in counterpoint to Enevoldsen's valve trombone. It's a short and perky affair: after a full chorus of wordless vocalizing, he sings the lyrics, swinging and again staccato, then his piano and the trombone take eight bars each before Troup sings the last half chorus—with bonus lyrics. The coauthors doubtlessly intended it as a song of romantic love ("Ain't with the upper crust / The Stork Club is not a must / But baby, I'm with you"), but somehow it's hard to hear it as anything other than an expression of solidarity between the two singing songwriters. Mercer writes, "We wrote it, I hope I'm correct, / Out of our mutual respect."

Mercer made a final contribution to the album—the liner notes, delivered in rhyme. He offers some kind of a comment or perspective on all twelve songs, ending with "I like the men with whom he works / I like each crummy room he works," and, finally, "At any rate, I'm deeply thankful / I hope that Bobby makes a bankful."

There were two collateral benefits to *Bobby Troup Sings Johnny Mercer*, both unanticipated at the time. In 1955, Troup was actively shepherding the

career of his future wife, Julie London. As mentioned, the singer-songwriter and now also producer was involved with two fledgling West Coast labels, Bethlehem Records and Liberty Records. In March, roughly five weeks after the Troup-Mercer session, London and Troup (playing piano) cut four sides that were released as an EP by Bethlehem, and then a month or so after that London recorded an entire album under Troup's supervision but with only the accompaniment of guitarist Al Viola, for Liberty. By the year's end, Liberty had released two successful albums by London, the second of which contained "Cry Me a River," the song that would be her biggest single and signature.

From that point on, London was the star singer in the relationship, and Troup would devote much of his energies to her career—a consequence that seems to have given him enormous satisfaction. London's own singing, with what she called her "thimbleful of a voice," closely paralleled Troup's, but where he was supremely intimate, London was sultry and openly erotic in a way that Troup never was—in a way that only a woman who looked like a va-va-voom movie star in that Marilyn Monroe era of pulchritudinous movie stars could be. Where Troup was cool, London was hot, vocally as well as visually.

To listen to Troup's own recordings in the context of London's much bigger career as a singer is to see how he did the groundwork and laid out the blueprint for her, which becomes especially clear when comparing Troup's "Midnight Sun," from here in 1955, to London's (on the 1958 album *Julie*). Although London made many memorable albums that were enhanced considerably by Troup's input, it seems a shame that he apparently lost interest in making albums of his own singing. He made a few albums of standards, of which the Mercer album is the best, but, regrettably, never laid down a definitive album of his own songs, something like *Bobby Troup Sings and Plays Bobby Troup*.

The careers of both Matt Dennis and Bobby Troup—as well as Chet Baker, Blossom Dearie, and Julie London—were essentially made possible by the advent of the new recording technology of the era: the kind of sound that could only be captured by tape, the kind of low-key mood that was best suited to the long-playing format. (Likewise, London's sales were greatly boosted by the brilliant use of a sexy album cover.) Nearly all pianist-singers in the 78 era tended to be loud and rambunctious—more friends of Fats (as in Waller), such as Nellie Lutcher and Julia Lee, than subjects of the King (as in Cole). Even Cole himself was quieter and more intimate in the era of tape and LPs than he had been earlier in the age of shellac and 78s. Apart from the ability to better capture softer voices, it was a particular benefit to be able to listen to as many as six songs by them in a row; you could relax more when you didn't have to get up and change the record with every song—you could concentrate on, well,

other things, the very same sort of activities that these soft, sensual voices actually suggested.

The moment when the likes of Matt Dennis and Bobby Troup could be presented as stars and recording artists in their own right was a brief one. They always were what would today be known as "niche" artists, but as traditional pop became more and more marginalized, they then had to squeeze themselves into what seemed like a niche within a niche. We're lucky, then, that they took advantage of the moment, and left us with a small but valuable group of albums that offer a unique perspective on the Great American Songbook, what it is, and how it should be sung.

16

Billy Eckstine

Billy's Best!

(1958)

Never was an album more appropriately named, and, alas, never was such an excellent album so little known.

When we talk about other great albums, we (and by "we," I mean "I") tend to use phrases like "widely influential" or even "life-changing." But once in a while you come across a remarkably outstanding album that's almost completely unknown, one that no musician or singer has ever cited as an influence. Recorded in 1957, *Billy's Best!* came at a point in Billy Eckstine's career after he had already reached his pinnacle of success and fame, and was already in what should therefore be considered a decline—although almost no one, least of all Eckstine himself, would have been aware of that at the time.

The only really important thing that anyone needs to know about *Billy's Best!* is that it features the greatest voice in popular music singing twelve absolutely magnificent and brilliantly selected songs. Eckstine's other albums of the period had some sort of theme or other distinguishing characteristic to them, such as his collection of songs from Broadway (*Broadway, Bongos, and Mr. "B"*) and Hollywood (*Now Starring in 12 Great Movies*), his meeting with Count Basie, his duet album with Sarah Vaughan (which was also an Irving Berlin songbook collection), his small group jazz album (*Imagination*), his live album (*No Cover, No Minimum*), his album of French songs (*Mr. B in Paris*). If you haven't actually heard the album, *Billy's Best!*

actually stands out by process of elimination: by 1957, nearly every project released by every major singer had some kind of a theme to it—but the only thing that this set had going for it was the fact of its being, as the title promised, *Billy's Best!* Like I say, in this context especially, the title becomes especially significant, and appropriate.

Billy's Best! was Eckstine's first solo project for Mercury Records. From 1948 to 1955, he had been one of the premiere hitmakers of the postwar era. Eckstine had been the first African American male to become a superstar singer of love songs, at a time when even his close friend and counterpart Nat King Cole was still largely known as a purveyor of novelty and "rhythm" tunes. Almost single-handedly, Eckstine transformed MGM Records from a start-up to an industry force. (His success transformed the industry on multiple levels, and even helped launch a vogue for Hollywood studios to enter the record business: by the end of the decade, Warner Bros., United Artists, and Paramount Pictures all had record labels.)

Following his eight-year association with MGM, Eckstine switched to RCA Records. This proved to be a disastrous move: the best that RCA could do with him was a handful of singles distinguished only by their abundant mediocrity. The only upside to the RCA contract was that it was short, and, after only a year, he switched to Mercury Records. The steadily emerging Chicago-based label was clearly on the rise: Eckstine's "Little Sister," Sarah Vaughan, was the reigning star of the jazz line (which was overseen by Bob Shad) and, paralleling Ella Fitzgerald at Verve, was enjoying tremendous success with live albums as well as Broadway-driven songbook packages. Dinah Washington was easily the industry leader in the R&B field at the time, and their major white pop act was Patti Page, a supreme force to be reckoned with at the cashbox. Mercury's chief musical director at this point was arranger-conductor-composer Pete Rugolo, for a long time Stan Kenton's number one aide-de-camp, now establishing himself as an important composer for film and television.

In New York, in April 1957, Eckstine recorded his first sessions for Mercury; a set of duets with Vaughan for the album that would be titled *Billy Eckstine & Sarah Vaughan Sing the Irving Berlin Songbook*. Then, over three days in August in Los Angeles, he taped the twelve songs for *Billy's Best!* Eckstine's longtime accompanist Bobby Tucker was credited as the conductor, but the bulk of the charts were done by Pete Rugolo. (Some discographies also list Henry Mancini as one of the arrangers, which is certainly possible.)

I formally interviewed Eckstine only once— about 1991—I wish now that I had thought to ask him about *Billy's Best!* However, I might not have yet heard the album, at that point, while Eckstine was alive. The same goes for Rugolo, I talked to him several times about June Christy, Nat King Cole, and Stan Kenton, among other subjects; it never occurred to me to talk about his collaboration with Eckstine. If there is any particular backstory to this project, which is unlikely, it died with the two of them. (The closest thing to a unifying concept to *Billy's Best!* is that a surprising number of these songs had a parallel history of being favored by jazz and African American artists, like "A Sunday Kind of Love," "Trust in Me," and "You Don't Know What Love Is." Then again, some of the tunes here are completely out-of-the-box, especially "Babalu.")

In 1964, Eckstine's final album for Mercury was titled *The Modern Sound of Mr. B.*, and it was all contemporary numbers. The *Billy's Best!* album, which was taped seven years earlier and features

naught but exceptional standards composed between 1930 and 1950, could have easily been titled *The Classic Sound of Mr. B.*

On listening again to *Billy's Best!*, the one thing that strikes me is the contrast between the power of Eckstine's voice and the vulnerability he conveys with it. His is the kind of instrument that, at surface value, would seem to be appropriate for big songs, be they about a man and a woman, like "How Deep Is the Ocean," or man and the universe, like "Ol' Man River." It's amazing how warm and intimate he sounds with such a huge, superhuman voice, as on songs like "I Got Lost in Her Arms," "Where Have You Been?," or to sound so truly interested in such simple, homey pleasures as in "A Sunday Kind of Love" is a major accomplishment; the voice itself sounds so strong as to be imperious, but the man behind it is warm and human.

It's a familiar tactic among singers: you start a song with a verse, particularly one that's not widely known, as a means of creating suspense. The crowd invariably applauds at the moment when the verse gives way to the chorus, and the unknown becomes the familiar. In the hands of a master like Eckstine, listeners will pay especially close attention— they've been down this path before, and know that an unfamiliar verse will often lead to a classic song that they know and love. Traditionally, some verses (like that of "But Not for Me" or "Over the Rainbow")—are almost as well known as their choruses. But some verses are so obscure that it's no exaggeration to say that nobody knows them, they exist on the original sheet music but have almost never been sung.

Billy's Best! gets under way with what is perhaps the most extreme example I've ever heard of a major artist opening not just a song, but an entire album, with a verse that almost certainly no one listening to the album would possibly recognize. We hear a flute intro, playing a lovely but generic phrase that offers no hint of the song to come. The woodwinds are lovely and pastoral, and convey a sense of innocence, which is similarly conveyed in the lyric of the verse. After the intro, we then hear the amazingly mellifluous voice of Eckstine singing:

Nightly, lights are shining brightly,
Feet are tripping lightly,
While the music plays.

It's safe to say that everyone who bought the LP—and, for the most part, ever since—would be surprised and delighted by the very dramatic transition from verse to chorus into "Boulevard of Broken Dreams." In 1957, most listeners to Eckstine's album would have remembered the song as Tony Bennett's breakthrough hit of 1950. But as Tony himself would be the first to acknowledge, at twenty-four years of age, he was hardly in a class to compete with his friend Mr. B, who, at forty-three, has the experience and seasoning to deliver a considerably more nuanced and powerful performance.

Harry Warren wrote "Boulevard" as what might be called "a Hollywood tango" (they refer to it in the movie as "the Argentine number") for the 1933 Fox musical *Moulin Rouge* (which was no connection to the 1952 *Moulin Rouge* or the 2001 *Moulin Rouge*). It was introduced by actress Constance Bennett (no relation to Tony, and not usually a singer) with an almost comically exaggerated French accent. The tango is not only the rhythm of the piece, it sets the tone for the lyric as well: starting with the idea of dancers in an exotic café (the tango originated in Argentina, but by the 1930s was widely heard all over Europe, particularly in Paris), the lyrics revolve around the notion of the kind of characters who might be found dancing the tango in a Parisian café during the Depression. (Hence the word "Boulevard," which is French.) Al Dubin's lyric describes them with "gigolos" and "gigolettes"—the latter apparently an invented term by the librettist himself; a female *gigolo* would appear to be a kinder, gentler euphemism for a prostitute.

In *Moulin Rouge*, the song is staged as if it were a sequel to "Remember My Forgotten Man" in *Gold Diggers of 1933*. Torn from today's headlines, the underlying motif is to show how harsh realities—made even harsher by the Great Depression—have corrupted an innocent youth from the French provinces. Like a lot of songs in old musicals ("Ol' Man River" in the 1936 *Show Boat* for one), the scene takes the lyrics rather literally. After Ms. Bennett sings the number (verse, then chorus) with a line of near-naked (and very pre-Code) chorus girls, she is then shown engaging in a dialogue with an old reprobate—obviously a wealthy, elderly man gone slumming in a seedy café in search of young female flesh. He asks her how she wound up where she is—kind of a stupid question, this being the Depression, you'd think the answer would be obvious enough. What impelled her to transition from an innocent country girl from "the waterfront of old Marseilles" (the lyrics refer to "an old cathedral town") into a painted gigolette—a fallen woman—in a Montmartre café. She's nobody's sweetheart now.

Harry Warren and Al Dubin could have titled this song "Remember My Forgotten Woman"—harmonically, the minor-to-major mood is similar in both songs, except that "Forgotten Man" is a march and "Boulevard" is a tango. (They'd employ a similar trajectory in "Shanghai Lil" from *Footlight Parade*.)

By including the verse, Eckstine shows that he apparently remembered the movie, and he seems to be heightening the Parisian references—as opposed to Tony's version, which has nothing explicitly French in it other than all those gigolos and gigolettes. Eckstine's tango rhythm is slightly less exaggerated than Bennett's, and overall his singing is much more intimate and less belt-y; even Eckstine's big ending, while sufficiently big, is much less of a mega-blast than on the 1950 hit single.

After opening with a song about the darker side of love (among other things), Eckstine follows "Boulevard" a few songs later with Irving Berlin's comparatively idealistic "I Got Lost in His Arms" from *Annie Get Your Gun*. The song was written for Ethel Merman as Annie Oakley, and as such it's one of Berlin's most successful attempts at expressing emotions directly from the perspective of a female character. This is one of his most touching, tender songs overall, and Eckstine's reading is, likewise, one of the most warm and intimate vocals of his career. The voice is still there in abundance, but it's always there to enhance the narrative, rather than call attention to itself. Rugolo's background is all celestial strings and twinkling stars, with Nelson Riddle–style polytones, suggesting an outdoorsy, nocturnal setting, as if the singer were still in the middle of a romantic interlude rather than describing it after the fact.

Eckstine was probably the first major male singer to tackle Annie's big love song (Tony Bennett followed suit thirty-three years later). But if "I Got Lost in *Her* Arms," as he revised it, was a slightly unexpected choice in 1957, then "Babalu," a few tracks later, comes from way, way, way out of left field. The piece—"song" isn't precisely the correct word—was first published in 1939 and is the work of Margarita Lecuona. While this is the only notable work attributed to Ms. Lecuona, she was a cousin to the most famous Cuban composer of that era, Ernesto Lecuona. Lecuona primarily composed classical piano works, as well as pieces with a sung text, but all of his music can be described more like chamber works rather than songs.

"Babalu" emigrated from Havana to America courtesy of the extremely popular Spanish bandleader Xavier Cugat, who made a successful recording featuring his star *cantante* Miguelito Valdez. Even after leaving Cugat, Valdez continued to use the song as his signature. It would still be associated with Valdez, except that he was little known beyond Latin audiences, and thus it remained for Desi Arnaz, another Cuban national and Cugat veteran, to claim "Babalu" as his own. Arnaz, who crafted a much more successful career among mainstream audiences, widely popularized "Babalu" in nightclubs, motion pictures, and especially on television, where he played "Ricky Ricardo" on *I Love Lucy*. In 1941, a version of the song was published in the United States with an English lyric by Bob Russell, who would write many successful texts of Latin American songs, but after Valdez and Arnaz, no one thought an English lyric was necessary. Like the equally famous "Hawaiian War Chant," the song is a battle cry, written in the form of a prayer in the Santería religion, a musical offering to the god of war, Chango (sometimes spelled Xango). In many ways, the most memorable part of the song is its dramatic opening, a loud and dramatic incantation of the war god's name.

The most surprising thing about "Stella by Starlight" is that Eckstine had never recorded it before 1957. First heard in 1944 as a movie theme for the spooky thriller *The Uninvited*, Victor Young's melody almost immediately became a jazz and pop standard after Ned Washington added his equally iconic lyric two years later. The song was instantly taken up as one of the key anthems of the postwar era, both in terms of modernism (Claude Thornhill, Charlie Parker) and romanticism (Harry James, Frank Sinatra). It's precisely the kind of thing that you would have expected Eckstine to sing in the mid-1940s with his own orchestra, or, a few years later, as one of his early singles for MGM Records. Victor Young's melody is soaringly operetta-like, and yet well suited for Fifty-second Street, a combination that suggests that Young, in that aspect, might be seen as a successor to Jerome Kern. Dick Haymes gave vent to the song's romantic side, Anita O'Day expressed its modernistic side (it's one of the few songs that she sang on two different Verve albums), but Eckstine is one of the few singers capable of reflecting both aspects of "Stella" at once. With his remarkably deep bass-baritone, Eckstine starts low and gets progressively higher: the first chorus stays relatively in the same range, but then he returns in an out-chorus (the last eight bars only, starting with "A great symphonic theme . . .") and shoots for the stratosphere, from basso almost to an Italian tenor high note—the low to high trajectory was hardly a new idea in 1957, but his voice itself and his harmonic sense are nothing if not progressive.

Likewise, Harold Arlen's "When the Sun Comes Out," with its hint of the blues, is still another perfect song for Eckstine. For Arlen, the song was a reunion with his first major collaborator and lyricist, Ted Koehler. For the team, "When the Sun Comes Out" was clearly a return to their Cotton Club style of a decade earlier and completes the trinity of blues-tinged "weather songs," which already included "Stormy Weather" and "Ill Wind." Rugolo's arrangement begins with growling dissonant brass subtly alternating with dramatic strings; likewise, Eckstine's vocal encompasses both a jazzy side and a ballad side; the bridge, for instance, sounds a lot less bluesy and more like a traditional love song.

"Nobody's Heart" (which is frequently listed as "Nobody's Heart [Belongs to Me]" or "Nobody's Heart Belongs to Me") is from Broadway rather than Harlem, originating in Rodgers and Hart's last original show, *By Jupiter* (1942). Eckstine sounds "sad at times" as Lorenz Hart's touching lyric goes, as if he's resigned to defeat but somehow trying to make the best of it. Despite a voice that sounds as powerful as a hurricane, Eckstine sounds somehow vulnerable. The lyric ends with the line "Nobody's heart belongs to me today," and the last word is especially potent, like the singer is trying to trivialize his pain, as if the words were about something insignificant, like "I don't think I'll shine my shoes today."

"Where Have You Been?" was not included on any of Ella Fitzgerald's *Cole Porter Songbook* albums, which therefore immediately qualifies this 1930 song (from the book show *The New Yorkers*) as a comparatively obscure Porter song. Like the Gershwins' "How Long Has This Been Goin' On?" it's an essentially cheerful lyric, expressed by someone who has just fallen in love and is still not sure whether or not to believe it; the questions— "Where Have You Been?" "How Long Has This Been Going On?" "What's the deal, see?"—convey a lingering element of doubt; pinch me, I can't quite believe it. Sinatra never sang it, alas, but he and Eckstine are among the few singers who could convey the precise cocktail of emotions—euphoria tinged with trepidation—that Porter's multidimensional lyric requires.

The songwriting team of Don Raye and Gene de Paul also represented two different kinds of songs: there was a folk blues aspect of their work, shown in many successful pop hits at the time that astutely encased boogie-woogie rhythms in song form, like "Beat Me Daddy, Eight to the Bar" and "The Boogie-Woogie Bugle Boy of Company B." Yet they also wrote some of the most sophisticated and sensitive ballads of the World War II period, like "I'll Remember April," "Star Eyes," and "You Don't Know What Love Is"—which Eckstine sings here. Eckstine had first recorded the song in 1941 when it was new, while still a member of the Earl Hines Orchestra. The 1957 version (taped a few months before Billie Holiday's on *Lady in Satin*) is deeper and much more sonorous, more resonant musically as well as lyrically. The *Billy's Best!* reading sounds much more confident than Holiday's (which could justifiably be on an album called *Billie's Best*) . . . but then again, Holiday was never what you'd call a paragon of emotional stability.

"A Sunday Kind of Love" is another astute choice, a song that spans many different genres. Starting in 1953, when it was done by the early doo-wop group The Harptones, it had been associated with R&B performers—so much so that it's generally forgotten that "Sunday Kind" goes back to the big band era. It was composed in 1946 by two relatively unknown songwriters, Anita Leonard and Stan Rhodes, and it was published by Louis Prima's publishing company, which was run for him by one of his general managers, a woman named Barbara Belle. Prima put the song in the hands of an old friend, pianist and bandleader Claude Thornhill, who recorded a best-selling version of "A Sunday Kind of Love" with the young singer Fran Warren. At this point, the better-established publisher Lou Levy stepped in and offered to take over the song for his company, Leeds Music. The composers, Leonard and Rhodes, were eager for this to happen, so a deal was worked out: Leeds Music would take over the publishing, and Prima and Belle would give up their publishing rights in exchange for being cut in as coauthors. Thus, the song has four names—Leonard, Rhodes, Prima, and Belle— only two of whom actually wrote it. Long into the R&B era, the song remained widely popular among African American entertainers, especially after Etta James cut it. Eckstine's interpretation is exquisite, a perfect balance of intensity and relaxation— the Sunday kind of a mood—that the lyric talks about.

"Trust in Me" has a similar history. It was introduced by the big bands (the first notable recording was by Mildred Bailey and Her Orchestra) and almost immediately picked up by African American, jazz, and blues artists. Introduced in 1937, "Trust in Me" is the work of two veterans, Jean Schwartz ("Chinatown, My Chinatown"), Milton Ager ("Happy Days Are Here Again"), and the lesser known Ned Wever. "Trust in Me" had the good fortune to be revived and re-revived in the 1950s, when it was sung by Louis Jordan and Eddie Fisher, as well as The Orioles, Clyde McPhatter, and Hadda Brooks. Two of the greatest R&B singers ever, Dinah Washington and Etta James, both recorded "Trust in Me" in 1961. Eckstine's voice is soothing and reassuring; he's nothing if not completely trustworthy. We trust him implicitly in all he does.

Doris Fisher, who wrote "That Ole Devil Called Love," didn't have quite the career enjoyed by her father (Fred Fisher of "Chicago" fame) or her brother (Marvin Fisher of "When Sunny Gets Blue" fame). Still, she landed at least three or four substantial hits and standards, of which "That Ole Devil Called Love" may be the best. It was immortalized by Billie Holiday, and since then is mainly heard in tribute albums to Lady Day (such as those of Chet Baker, Tony Bennett, Etta Jones, and Rebecca Kilgore). Eckstine is one of the few to sing Fisher and her collaborator Allan Roberts's lovely verse ("someone's whispering in my ear . . ."). Eckstine shows how even a superman with super-chops trembles at the thought of the old devil called love, who puts rain in his eyes, tears in his dreams, and rocks in his heart.

After this sequence of medium-slow ballads, Eckstine ends the album with something brighter and more cheerful. "Zing! Went the Strings of My Heart" is a 1934 pop song from a Broadway revue titled *Thumbs Up!* It was almost completely ignored in its native country when it was new (although recorded by several British bands); the only important domestic artist who seems to have noticed it was the young Judy Garland. She sang it throughout her early career, in vaudeville, on the radio, and at auditions, and then ultimately immortalized it for posterity in the 1938 film *Listen, Darling*. Even when Eckstine sang it in 1957, it was understood that he was, essentially, borrowing it from Garland; it may well have been her ultimate up-tempo song just as "Over the Rainbow" was her signature ballad. Eckstine takes it at a medium-fast clip; when he gets to the first, all-important "Zing" he takes his time with an especially pronounced pause before he gets to the next phrase, ". . . Went

the Strings of My Heart"—while all of the song's major interpreters (including Garland and Sinatra) emphasize the break, none take it as far as Eckstine. Otherwise, he's jaunty and affable, swinging and relaxed—it's a perfect closer.

In retrospect, *Billy's Best!* seems like a classic: at the time it was fairly unnoticed. The year of 1957 was an incredibly rewarding one. In the field of jazz and pop vocal albums alone, the following were all either recorded or released (or both) within that twelve-month period: Louis Armstrong—*Satchmo: A Musical Autobiography, I've Got the World on a String, Satchmo Under the Stars, Louis Armstrong Meets Oscar Peterson;* Tony Bennett—*The Beat of My Heart, Tony;* Connee Boswell and the Original Memphis Five—*In Hi-Fi;* June Christy—*Gone for the Day, Fair and Warmer, June's Got Rhythm;* Rosemary Clooney and the Hi-Los—*Ring Around Rosie;* Nat King Cole—*Just One of Those Things, After Midnight;* Perry Como—*We Get Letters;* Bing Crosby—*Bing with a Beat;* Sammy Davis Jr.—*It's All Over but the Swingin', Mood to Be Wooed, Boy Meets Girl;* Billy Eckstine and Sarah Vaughan—*Sing the Irving Berlin Songbook;* Doris Day—*Hooray for Hollywood;* Ella Fitzgerald—*At the Opera House, Like Someone in Love, Get Happy!, Ella & Louis, Ella & Louis Again;* Judy Garland—*Alone;* Eydie Gormé—*Swings the Blues;* Woody Herman—*Songs for Hip Lovers;* Eartha Kitt—*St. Louis Blues;* Lambert, Hendricks & Ross—*Sing a Song of Basie;* Peggy Lee—*The Man I Love;* Abbey Lincoln—*That's Him;* Julie London—*Make Love to Me, About the Blues;* Carmen McRae—*After Glow, Carmen for Cool Ones, Mad About the Man;* Rose Murphy—*Not Cha-Cha but Chi-Chi;* Anita O'Day (with Oscar Peterson)—*Anita Sings the Most;* Jackie Paris—*The Jackie Paris Sound;* Della Reese—*A Date with Della Reese at Mr. Kelly's in Chicago;* Annie Ross—*Sings a Song with Mulligan!;* Bobby Short—*Bobby Short;* Frank Sinatra—*Where Are You?, Close to You, Come Fly with Me, A Jolly Christmas;* Keely Smith—*I Wish You Love;* Jeri Southern—*When Your Heart's on Fire;* Jo Stafford and Art Van Damme—*Once Over Lightly;* Dakota Staton and George Shearing—*The Late, Late Show;*

Sylvia Syms—*Songs of Love;* Mel Tormé—*Meets the British, Live at the Crescendo;* Sarah Vaughan—*Sings George Gershwin;* Dinah Washington—*Sings Fats Waller;* Lee Wiley—*A Touch of the Blues;* Julie Wilson—*At the St. Regis.*

All of the above could be described as albums that are, at the very least, well worth owning and listening to more than sixty years later, and more than a few of them might indisputably be rated as classics. For the most part, some are so-called concept or theme albums, others are live albums, but they nearly all have some sort of unifying factor, even if it's only tempo, mood, or at least the vaguest sort of programmatic idea, a live album or a songbook album, a collection of swingers or of ballads. *Billy's Best!* is the rare classic album from that period built only around great songs and no other signpost of an idea.

Yet themes and concepts only get you so far. I've easily listened to *Billy's Best!* at least as many times as any other album on this list, probably a lot more than most. It features one of the greatest artists of his or any other time singing twelve of the most wonderful and singularly appropriate songs ever written. To ask for more than that would be to seem ungrateful.

17

Ella Fitzgerald
Lullabies of Birdland
(1955)

Sometimes, exceptions can prove rules. Take, for instance, the musical technique known as "scat singing." On the whole, scatting is, at its best, a minor annoyance; at its worst (which is more often than I'd like), it's a crime against humanity. Applied judiciously, scatting can be like seasoning to a meal: it's fine to sprinkle a dash of it here and a pinch of it there, but who would want to eat an entire dish of salt? Eight bars of scat can spice up a performance, or, if I'm in an indulgent mood, maybe sixteen. But a whole chorus is probably something that few vocalists should even be legally permitted to attempt. The contemporary scene includes no shortage of purely "instrumental" singers, who certainly have the chops, the technique, and the musical know-how to pull off extended, wordless improvisations. Still, no matter how musically hip the singer thinks he or she is, no matter how well the chord changes are navigated, nearly all scatting starts to get unbearably boring very quickly.

Of the thousands of vocalists who have attempted it, there have been, at the very most, perhaps a dozen who could sustain an audience's interest while scatting at any length. The technique was, for all intents and purposes, perfected by Louis Armstrong (who had the good sense to use it only sparingly) and, a generation or so later, was brought to new heights by Leo Watson, Martha Raye, Anita O'Day, Mel Tormé, and Sarah Vaughan. There are also a small handful of top-drawer scatters in the twenty-first century, such as Dee Dee Bridgewater and Dianne Reeves, who all make effective use of moans, groans, chanting, and other nonverbal means of expression.

Even so, there can be no argument that Ella Fitzgerald still reigns as the all-time greatest scat singer; it was she who brought the craft of wordless vocalizing to an Olympian zenith, matched by no other artist. Even before 1945, there was no doubt that this was the case; but it was over the course of ten tracks recorded between 1945 and 1955 that Ella vanquished all other potential contenders to oblivion. The release of *Lullabies of Birdland* in 1955 established that no other singer in history could even come within miles of her—for any other artist to do one whole track of scat (Mel Tormé's "That's Where I Came In," Sarah Vaughan's "Shulie a Bop," Anita O'Day's "Malagueña," among others) was impressive enough, but to come up with ten, and have them all be unequivocally brilliant—is an achievement of superhuman proportions.

Generally speaking, human beings tend to do the impossible—climbing Mount Everest, tightrope-walking between the Twin Towers of the former World Trade Center, bungee jumping off Niagara—if for no other reason than to prove that it can be done. The human spirit is as indomitable as it is foolish. *Lullabies of Birdland* ranks with that kind of an achievement: and in showing that she could do it—a whole album of scatting—she proved conclusively that no one else should dare attempt it. Kids, don't try this at home.

Lullabies of Birdland derives from the imagination of Milt Gabler (1911–2001) as much as from the endless wellspring of creativity and invention that was Ella Fitzgerald (1917–1996). Gabler, who was Fitzgerald's producer for the first part of her "solo" career (the years after her breakthrough with Chick Webb and subsequent period of leading the Webb band after his death) had been the one to encourage her to do scat features to begin with. Then, in 1954–55, as she was in the midst of preparing to leave Decca after twenty years, Gabler had the even more brilliant idea of collecting all her "bop numbers," as he called them, onto a single, remarkable album. As we've seen, there were generally two types of albums released from the 78 rpm era onward: compilations of previously released material and "new" albums of material recorded directly for the specific album. There were, very occasionally, albums that were a combination of both. These would be instances when a producer or catalogue director would realize that they had, for example, almost enough Bing Crosby travel songs to fill out an LP, so they would then ask Crosby to go back into the studio and cut a few more to fill out that particular project.

At some point in late 1954, Gabler began to conceive of an all-scat album for Ella, and it was a happy twist of fate that a brand-new song titled "Lullaby of Birdland" just happened to come his way. In a sense, that's what all of these scat features were—rather literally. The term "lullabies" was ironic, since for the most part these weren't soothing melodies to sing babies to sleep; rather than lull the little brat off to Dreamsville, these were vigorous, loud, and fast up-tempo numbers that would wake Junior up—along with half the neighborhood. Yet the "Birdland" part of the title was somewhat more direct; in that sense, it could be taken to mean that Fitzgerald was singing like the birdies sing, with nonverbal noises rather than words.

By 1954, Gabler had accumulated enough of these "bop things"—in fact, he had so many that

he could leave a couple out. Her 1951 single of Duke Ellington's "Love You Madly" has an extended scat sequence and would certainly qualify for the album. In 1952 she recorded "Preview," a bluesy riff by one of Count Basie's current saxophonists, Paul Quinichette (who actually called it "Prevue" on his recording). Ella's treatment is scat all the way, no lyrics, and could easily have fit on the *Lullabies* album. However, even though he had more than enough material, Gabler still decided to add a few more tracks, which he had specifically recorded for the *Lullabies* project, making it a true hybrid of concept and compilation album.

Although there apparently are some pressings that include "Preview," making it the eleventh track, every copy that I have ever personally encountered includes only ten tracks. The series of Ella's wordless epics begins in 1945, when the Great Lady recorded her premiere all-scat extravaganza, "Flying Home," on October 4. "Flying Home" was the ideal vehicle with which to establish the concept of "full-length" orchestrated scat solo—in other words, one that occupied an entire track, not least because it had already helped define the idea of the full-length horn solo. The original song was credited to Lionel Hampton and introduced by the vibraphonist while he was still a member of Benny Goodman's orchestra. In Hampton's account, the Goodman band had been booked in Los Angeles one night and Atlantic City the next, which seems improbable, in the context of the period, but is hardly impossible. The only way to get across the country overnight was to fly, which was a new experience for most of the Goodmanites. Aloft for the first time, Hampton began nervously humming a new riff in his head without even thinking about it; when Goodman happened to notice the tune and ask him about it, he spontaneously titled the piece "Flying Home."

"Flying Home" was already well established when Hampton made his second and most iconic recording of it, in May 1942 on an early session as the leader of his own big band. This classic version included other solos, beginning with an introduction by the vibraphonist-leader, but it quickly became renowned for the tenor saxophone solo by Illinois Jacquet, which took pride of place among such relatively recent saxophone spectaculars of the era. (These included Coleman Hawkins's "Body and Soul," Ben Webster's "Cottontail" with Duke Ellington, and the various Lester Young features with Count Basie). By the end of the war, "Flying Home" was a virtual swing anthem—it was famously jammed on by Louis Armstrong and an all-star group featuring Hampton and Hawkins at an early all-star jazz concert at the Metropolitan Opera House. Chances are that anyone who heard Ella's recording—cut in October 1945—already knew the tune.

Fitzgerald's take on it follows the rough outline of the Hampton-Jacquet version, although it's not a literal vocal adaptation of that already classic side (the kind of thing that would be done later by Lambert, Hendricks & Ross). Significantly, the Fitzgerald arrangement, which was recorded in two closely matching takes, is even more of a featured solo than Jacquet—she's the only solo "voice" on the side, and her vocal corresponds to the solo sections by both the saxophonist and vibraphonist. Fitzgerald's wordless vocal mostly follows the path of the tenor solo in, for instance, the famous start where Jacquet plays a phrase that sounds inspired by "Ah! So Pure" ("Ach! so fromm, ach! so traut") from Friedrich von Flotow's opera *Martha* (which Fitzgerald might have also known from a popular recording of the aria by her hero, Connee Boswell).

The quote from *Martha* is only the first of many. Fitzgerald throws in her own quotes—some of these are closely followed by the orchestra, which suggests that at least these parts of her solo were worked out in advance: the fragments "Merrily we roll along / on the deep, deep, deep, blue sea" and "horses, horses" are completely mirrored in the orchestration. The latter is a phrase—two notes separated by an octave leap—that goes back at least as far as the 1926 pop song "Horses," most successfully recorded by George Olsen and His Orchestra. (The Canadian scholar David Lennick believes that this phrase also originated in classical music—in this case with Tchaikovsky, in the "Troika" movement of his piano suite "The Seasons.")

This business of semi-spontaneously quoting older music is something that had already been around (in the scatting of Leo Watson, for one, and,

more instrumentally than vocally, by Louis Armstrong); still, the practice was perfected and raised to the level of a fine art by Fitzgerald. Her quotes became part of the jazz literature: at the close of her 1960 record of "Jingle Bells," she quotes "I'm just crazy 'bout horses" (the direct lyric from the Olsen record), thus riffing on her own legacy. (More recently, Diana Krall directly referenced Fitzgerald and her now famous "horses" in her 2005 big band version of "Jingle Bells," a song that admittedly has more to do with horses than does "Flying Home.")

Chronologically, the next item that would go into the *Lullabies* collection was "Oh, Lady Be Good" from March 1947. The title of a 1924 show, "Oh, Lady Be Good" had originally been the first notable success by the Gershwin brothers, George and Ira, as a team; it wasn't Fitzgerald's first Gershwin song (that honor goes to "I Was Doing All Right" recorded a decade earlier) but it would be the Gershwin number most closely associated with her over the course of her long career. "Oh, Lady Be Good" came five years before "I Got Rhythm," and had that *Girl Crazy* number never been written, "Lady Be Good" most likely would have been Gershwin's best known jam session vehicle. The 1947 version teamed her with a big band under the direction of bassist and orchestrator Bob Haggart. It's one of the few tracks on the *Lullabies* set with an actual lyric, which Fitzgerald races through and summarily dispenses with. She thereupon lunges into one of her fastest and most dazzling wordless extravaganzas, in the midst of which she introduces what would quickly become one of her signature devices: a hummed, lower register simulation of a bass solo. The quotes include fragments of "Raggin' the Scale," "Star Eyes," Dizzy Gillespie's "Oop Bop Sh'Bam," and "A Tisket, A Tasket." Fitzgerald would sing this up-tempo scat version of "Oh, Lady Be Good" many times (including at the Hollywood Bowl, Carnegie Hall, and the Shrine Auditorium in Los Angeles) and also include a ballad treatment, including all of Ira Gershwin's lyrics and verse, on her 1960 *Gershwin Songbook*. But as many times as she performed it, acolyte Mel Tormé possibly sang it even more frequently in her honor, changing the title to "Ella Be Good."

Six months later, in December 1947, Fitzgerald recorded "How High the Moon," the next of her increasingly celebrated wordless specialties: like "Oh, Lady Be Good," "Moon" had begun life on Broadway in the revue *Two for the Show* (1940), in which it was sung by Alfred Drake and danced by Eunice Healy. Fitzgerald's accompaniment consists of four musicians associated with Dizzy Gillespie, namely trumpeter Leonard Graham (better known as Idrees Sulieman), pianist John Lewis (later the force behind The Modern Jazz Quartet), bassist Ray Brown (whom Fitzgerald had married ten days earlier on December 10), and drummer Joe Harris (who was virtually the only member of the early Gillespie orchestra still alive sixty years later).

The Fitzgerald arrangement of "Moon" begins with the Broadway lyrics (but not the verse); the tempo is only medium-fast, which, considering what Fitzgerald is capable of, is comparatively slow. It turns out she's waiting for the right opportunity to double the tempo, and that occurs, heralded by a drum break, right after the traditional lyrics. We're expecting the scat to begin right away, but instead at this point there's a special lyric, which despite the way it contains a built-in apology ("though the words may be wrong to this song . . ."), which the singer almost certainly wrote herself, that prepares the listener for the wordless vocal. Self-effacing as the special lyric may be, Fitzgerald actually heightens expectations to the point that no singer other than herself could possibly live up to them.

Two alternate takes exist (both issued on the 1994 CD package *The War Years*), and in all three the scat opens with a paraphrase of the melody of the Cuban song "Poinciana." Almost twenty years later, after several decades of establishing "How High the Moon" as one of her all-time great scat jazz classics, Fitzgerald returned to it as a slow ballad (and with the verse) on her 1964 album *Hello, Dolly!*

The next "lullaby," "Basin Street Blues" wouldn't arrive until almost two years later, in September 1949. Where many of the so-called "Lullabies" were what we might describe as "lateral salutes," to contemporary musicians whom Fitzgerald regarded as her peers (like Hampton and Jacquet on "Flying Home"), "Basin Street" was more of a vertical salute upward to Louis Armstrong, who was, in a phrase he liked to use, one of her original "inspirators." She picked an interesting, even curious song to honor the great man; though he sang "Basin Street," it was never a Satchmo signature. Rather, most jazz fans would associate "Basin Street" with Jack Teagarden, Armstrong's frequent collaborator. The narrative, such as it is, of the lyrics depicts jazz activity in the music's ground zero, New Orleans, and for that reason it's often thought of as going back to the beginning of jazz, but actually it was written by the New Orleans–born songwriter Spencer Williams in 1926.

Fitzgerald had sung "Basin Street Blues" at Carnegie Hall, as part of a Jazz at the Philharmonic concert, on September 18, 1949, two days before recording it for Decca. Sy Oliver's arrangement opens with a guitar intro, appropriate for a Southern-style blues, before Fitzgerald launches into the melody; she sings with an especially smooth, pretty voice, which is contrasted by the somewhat bright and even jagged edges of Oliver's brass section. When the song reaches its bridge, the backing switches from brass to reeds, both singer and accompaniment become more harmoniously matched to each other. The song is not in twelve-bar blues form, but has traditionally been treated like a blues—and, by Armstrong and Teagarden in particular—phrased like one, with stop-time breaks and other blues devices.

The great moment is the second chorus, in which Fitzgerald does a full-scale, no-holds-barred impression of Satchmo; it's one of the most moving homages by one great artist to another that has ever been documented. It's also a miracle of singing—that she could sustain that gravelly voice for a full thirty-two bars without damaging her throat. Sammy Davis Jr. famously said that whenever he did vocal impressions, he would save Satchmo for last, because it left his voice unable to do anything else.

Apart from Armstrong, Fitzgerald's greatest inspiration was Connee Boswell—also from New Orleans—and "Basin Street Blues" gave Fitzgerald the chance to honor her as well. In 1937, Crosby and Boswell had recorded the song as perhaps the most memorable of their many duets. When Fitzgerald made a guest appearance on Crosby's radio show on November 4, 1949, the crooner revived that arrangement, this time for a duet with Fitzgerald. It opens with an unnamed trombonist playing a slow, bluesy phrase, in obvious emulation of Jack Teagarden. The live performance has a lot of patter between Fitzgerald and Crosby, but still she takes advantage of the opportunity to work in her Armstrong impression.

The next two lullabies in the series, "Smooth Sailing" and "Air Mail Special," return Fitzgerald to the nexus of Lionel Hampton and Benny Goodman—as well as to a contemplation of transportation. "Smooth Sailing," by saxophonist Arnett Cobb (a veteran of the Hampton orchestra who also played "Flying Home"), had been a jazz/R&B crossover hit in the fall of 1950. Fitzgerald's 1951 record does a superior job of focusing and stating Cobb's blues melody better than the Cobb original; Cobb's tune has no phrase that could be sung to the words "Smooth Sailing." The Fitzgerald disc employs Bill Doggett on organ, and a vocal directed by the choral arranger Ray Charles; surely, both were intended as pop ingredients, but both sound incredibly hip now, with Fitzgerald scatting this sexy, medium-tempo blues melody over a combination of organ and choir. Like virtually every track on *Lullabies,* "Smooth Sailing" was so successful for Fitzgerald that she kept singing it for years to come in concerts: in the famous Tokyo 1953 Jazz at the Philharmonic show, she sings it with a standard piano-based rhythm section (no choir or organ) and twenty years after *that,* she reprised it at her landmark Carnegie Hall "lifetime achievement" concert, this time with a new arrangement for full jazz big band.

Credited to Charlie Christian, "Air Mail Special" was originally introduced by the Benny Goodman Sextet in 1940 under the title "Good Enough to Keep"—and the first soloist on the original record, even before Goodman or Christian, was Lionel Hampton. Like "Flying Home," "Air Mail Special" was an instant swing-era anthem. Who knows how many times Fitzgerald had heard it between 1940 and 1952—by various bands in ballrooms, on records, on the air—when she cut it, once again

with Bill Doggett on organ and the popular choral group The Ray Charles Singers (no relation to the later superstar Ray Charles). Her improvisation is transcendently beautiful: once again she is completely aloft for three glorious minutes. Her feet never touch the ground. It too stayed in her repertoire for years: the best live version is an absolutely hysterical reading from the 1957 Newport Jazz Festival, using a small group but a much longer improvised sequence.

After flying and sailing comes "Rough Ridin'." This "instrumental" was taped on the same 1952 date as "Air Mail Special" and also features Bill Doggett's organ and the Ray Charles Singers. It's a lighter and bouncier riff affair—less frenetic than "Air Mail Special"—and apparently was a tune that Fitzgerald and pianist Hank Jones concocted for the date. It's one of only two tunes that Fitzgerald gets credited for on *Lullabies,* and it qualifies as one of her more successful works as a composer. She liked the melody enough to return to it ten years later, on her 1962 album *Rhythm Is My Business,* this time with Doggett both playing and conducting a full orchestra, and, surprisingly, with a full set of lyrics, that, like the tune, were also apparently by the singer herself. Now boasting words like, "You are givin' me rough ridin' / And you know you're makin' me blue," suddenly it was a wordless specialty no longer.

A few months later, in June 1952, Fitzgerald and Sy Oliver went back into Decca's New York studio for more *Lullabies.* The session was polarized between the highbrow and lowbrow extremes of the singer's output, in terms of both jazz and the Great American Songbook. She laid down three scat extravaganzas, "Ding Dong Boogie," "Mr. Paganini," and "Preview," all of which made heavy use of scat singing and thus could have easily gone onto the *Lullabies of Birdland* album. Yet none of them did. Oddly, the one tune from the date that did make it, "Angel Eyes," was one of Fitzgerald's all-time best interpretations of a classic ballad, with words.

Obviously, Milt Gabler chose it to go on this album for contrast: this is one of Fitzgerald's most heart-wrenching ballads, and one of many tracks that puts the lie to the notion that Fitzgerald never really sang lyrics, or couldn't make you cry. Composer Matt Dennis told me that he brought it to Fitzgerald in 1951, at a time when they were both performing in Reno. He played it for her on a Monday, two days before she was due to open, and on Wednesday she made it her first number. Dennis attended the opening; Fitzgerald introduced him from the stage, and announced she was going to record "Angel Eyes" for Decca. Gabler's out-of-the-box thinking paid off: although it's the only slow ballad on *Lullabies*, it's no less a jazz performance than "Flying Home." Sy Oliver's orchestration opens with a haunting, minor intro phrased by the brass (emulating strings) and, in general, recalls the work of his Decca colleague, ballad master Gordon Jenkins. Over the years, Fitzgerald would sing it hundreds of times, and more than a dozen live recordings have been documented; it may well be her most celebrated ballad.

What was left on *Lullabies of Birdland* were Ella's contributions to the blues. Between 1952 and 1955, she recorded at least three more blues numbers, of which two—the ones with the fewest words—made it onto the album. "Later" is a fast blues that originated with bandleader-composer-vocalist Tiny Bradshaw. When Fitzgerald recorded it in 1954, she didn't transform the whole record and solo into vocal terms, as she did on "Flying Home." Essentially, she scats up a storm on the head rather than the sax improv; the only words are the phrase "Later for the Happ'nings, Baby." In a live aircheck from Birdland, 1954, she introduces the tune as "Later for the Happ'nings," a title that may have been invented by Henry Glover, the prolific R&B songwriter who shares credit for the song with Bradshaw. Fitzgerald's disc includes a wailing solo by Sam "The Man" Taylor, and a wordless choir singing behind both Fitzgerald and Taylor that makes it even more exciting. "Later" is an amazingly exuberant track, leaving no doubt why Gabler included it in the *Birdland* album.

The major thing the album still didn't have was a slow wordless blues, and Gabler found one in the movie *Pete Kelly's Blues*. This was one of Fitzgerald's very few feature film appearances: a melodrama set in the Roaring Twenties with Jack Webb walking around like a hardboiled dick even though he's supposed to be a jazz trumpeter. He stops in at a road house at one point, where the entertainment is one "Maggie Jackson," a singer, played by Fitzgerald, working with a Dixieland band. She sings parts of two songs ("Hard-Hearted Hannah" and the title song, "Pete Kelly's Blues") on-screen, and then does "Ella Hums the Blues" (in which she's credited as composer) off-camera. All three songs were included on the *Pete Kelly's Blues* soundtrack album, and then Gabler quickly reused "Ella Hums the Blues" on *Lullabies*. It's probably her single most famous—and best—performance of the blues, in any tempo, with or without lyrics. She's so full of the spirit of the blues that the presence or absence of words hardly matters; as with Louis Armstrong's masterful scat on "Basin Street Blues," lyrics would only trivialize the singer's deep emotional impact. Coincidentally, in another album released as a tie-in to the movie, Jack Webb reads a line of narration that goes. "[Here's] what all good blues numbers should say: things used to be good, and they'll be good again, the only trouble with the world is that it's right now." Fitzgerald without words is just as powerful and moving as Sinatra singing Lorenz Hart: full of longing for the past and hope for the future, but most of all dealing with the right now. She surely doesn't need lyrics to move us profoundly.

It was at the same June 1954 session with Fitzgerald and Sy Oliver that yielded "Later" that Gabler recorded her doing the song that would tie all the other scat epics together—and serve as the title of the album: "Lullaby of Birdland." This would truly be, once and for all time, the mother of wordless extravaganzas.

In 1949, the music entrepreneur Morris Levy opened a high-profile jazz club, just north of Times Square, that he named "Birdland," after Charlie "Bird" Parker, then widely heralded as the leader of the modern jazz movement. In 1952, Levy and Birdland were sponsoring the most famous of all jazz deejays, "Symphony" Sid Torin, whose theme song was "Jumpin' with Symphony Sid," composed by tenor saxophone colossus Lester Young in 1946. This apparently inspired Levy to commission the very popular British pianist George Shearing to compose a theme song specifically for the club itself. Shearing based his new tune on the familiar chord changes to the 1927 standard "Love Me or Leave Me." Over the next fifty years, he would tell a million audiences what happened next: when he was asked to write the song, it took him exactly ten minutes to work it out. "But," as Shearing always said, "it really was ten minutes plus umpteen years of experience." Shearing was then recording for MGM Records, and the original MGM single of "Lullaby of Birdland" went by fairly unnoticed in 1952; it was far from the bravura success that Shearing's "September in the Rain" had been three years earlier.

In 1954, however, two music publishers, one of whom owned the rights to "Lullaby," were having lunch. The other publisher remarked to the first what a lovely tune "Lullaby of Birdland" was, and that it was a shame it had never been a hit. That he had noticed it at all was surprising, since, at this point, it was just another modern jazz instrumental of the kind that were then being recorded by the dozens on labels great and small. The first publisher told him that approximately ten different lyricists had submitted texts for the melody, all of which had been rejected. But, he said, if you like the tune so much, why not put your money where your mouth is? The second publisher had a lyricist under contract with a good track record, named George David Weiss, who had already written, among other hits, "Confess," "Oh What It Seemed to Be," "Rumors Are Flying," and "Wheel of Fortune."

The two publishers then agreed that Weiss should be given a crack at the "Birdland" lyric, and he was actually able to come up with a lyric that both the publisher and Shearing liked. And, fittingly, the first artist slated to record the new vocal version of "Lullaby of Birdland" was Ella Fitzgerald. This was no surprise, but it would be Weiss who received a rude surprise roughly a week before the Fitzgerald disc was to be released. "The publisher came to me and said, 'What name do you want to put on the song?'" Weiss was shocked to learn that because of the publishing situation, he had no choice but to use a pseudonym: Shearing and Weiss were contracted to publishers that

were represented by the two major rights organizations, BMI and ASCAP, respectively, that were fiercely competitive with each other, making this a line in the sand that no one dared cross. For an ASCAP songwriter to collaborate with a BMI man would have then meant instant excommunication from the music business. "I said I'd rather throw the song away than see it come out with another name on it," said Weiss, "but my publisher and my agent and my lawyer all got together"—in a kind of intervention—"and tried to convince me that it would be a shame to deny the world the opportunity to enjoy such a great song, blah, blah, blah, and I fell for it." The song was published by Patricia Music, with "words by B. Y. Forster," a pseudonym that Weiss had extrapolated from his wife's maiden name; he thought that it sounded British enough to complement Shearing's name. Many years later, Weiss sought an audience with the upper brass at BMI and was finally granted the right to put his real name on the song. (Weiss, who told this story to radio interviewer Michael Anthony, may have been exaggerating when he said he was shocked by the situation—in those days all kinds of songwriters published their work under all kinds of pseudonyms.)

Fitzgerald started her June 4, 1954, session with "Birdland" (followed by "Later"). The opening is ostentatious, to say the least: it starts with a dramatic introductory cadenza, expressed simultaneously by saxophonist Sam Taylor (at his most florid) and a wordless choir. The backing choral group here almost sounds like a hybrid of a church service and "Nessun Dorma." The combination of the small group backing (basic rhythm section plus tenor sax) and the organ and choir makes "Birdland" feel both loose and formal at the same time.

Ella sings the minor key melody at a medium clip, deliberately and with great expression rather remarkable for a song that isn't really a love song or a torch song but a meditation on the state of being in love. When we're in love, we're like the birds in the skies "flying high above / all because we're in love." But "if you should tell me farewell and goodbye" (Lord only knows why he'd feel compelled to tell her both), then, she says, she would cry "like the weepy old willow." Fitzgerald instantly established the new lyric as a vocal jazz classic: within the next eighteen months, it would be further immortalized by Chris Connor, Sarah Vaughan, and many others.

With the exception of "Ella Hums the Blues," which Gabler recycled (or even pre-cycled) from *Pete Kelly's Blues*, "Lullaby of Birdland" would be the final piece in the LP puzzle, providing the album with both its title and opening track. It was the perfect song to hang the whole theme of the album on: all of the other ten tunes, which were mostly also jazz instrumentals that Fitzgerald had transformed into vocal classics, using a combination of lyrics and scatting, were, in their own way, also lullabies of birdland. Indeed, virtually everything Fitzgerald ever sang could now be considered a lullaby of birdland.

Over the years, Fitzgerald recorded other full-length scat solos, many with orchestral accompaniment: in 1947, she included an extended scat on a live performance of "Blue Skies," partially in duet with drummer-singer Buddy Rich, which was released on V-Disc as "BudElla." She later developed this into a mostly scatted "Blue Skies" for her 1958 *Irving Berlin Songbook*. That same year, Roy Eldridge's "Little Jazz," in an orchestration for Fitzgerald by Marty Paich, became a wordless highlight of Fitzgerald's *Ella Swings Lightly*. In 1959, she scatted an ingenious orchestration (by Russ Garcia) of Tadd Dameron's "Cool Breeze," and in 1970 did the same for another early bop classic, Dizzy Gillespie's "Manteca" (on *Things Ain't What They Used to Be*), arranged by Gerald Wilson.

When the single of "Lullaby of Birdland" was originally released in June 1954, *Billboard* missed the point (and the boat). "Later" was enthusiastically received ("Here's some of Miss Fitzgerald's great, modern scat singing. It should please her many fans. The gal is as wonderful as ever on this one."). But regarding "Lullaby," all the anonymous reviewer had to say was "The Birdland jazz joint's theme now has a lyric. Not much, though, of interest to the mass market." It would be her last major collaboration with Gabler; following "Ella Hums the Blues," there would only be two more singles dates for Decca in the summer of 1955. In January 1956, she began the next phase of her career with producer-manager Norman Granz's new Verve label.

If Weiss, Shearing, and Gabler were disappointed in the reception of the single, the album exceeded all expectations. *Lullabies of Birdland* would be Fitzgerald's most elaborate statement as a vocal improviser: as such, it may be her single most emulated album—more young singers have learned from it than any of her well-known live albums or *Songbook* collections. She herself kept singing numbers from it in her personal appearances for decades to come. By that standard, certainly, this was by far Fitzgerald's most successful album project.

There never was an official package titled "Ella Fitzgerald's Greatest Hits," but *Lullabies of Birdland* could appropriately be retitled *The Absolute Best of Ella Fitzgerald*, for that is surely what it is.

18

Ella Fitzgerald and Louis Armstrong
Ella & Louis
(1956)

One reason I'm often reluctant to refer to myself as a "critic" is an overwhelming sense of embarrassment over what the critics wrote about Louis Armstrong for most of his life. In the 1950s in particular, the years when Armstrong was at his most popular, the critical fraternity seems to have had one primary agenda: they wanted jazz to be taken seriously as an art form, and therefore anything that made jazz seem too populist was somehow suspect. In the 1950s and '60s, the most horrendous hand grenade of an insult that you could lob at a jazz musician was to say he was "too commercial."

That can be the only reason why Louis Armstrong was routinely regarded as a pariah—for the mere fact that he made the music seem entertaining. And the better he became at pleasing crowds ("I'm in there," he famously said, "in the cause of happiness"), the more the critics seemed to dislike him. You would think that they would have cut him some slack, since if it hadn't been for Armstrong, there's no way that jazz would have ever reached the level of any kind of an art form—it would have stayed at the level of a folk art, like, say, basket-weaving, and have been heard mostly in New Orleans and a few other towns in the Deep South. (The jazz fad launched by The Original Dixieland Jass Band in their visits to Chicago, New York, and London probably would have been just that—a fad that would die out a few years later, much as ragtime had done.)

Yet even the late Artie Shaw, quite possibly the biggest snob I ever met in my life, told me, "Louis was an entertainer—as opposed to an artist—but he was so great at what he did that it didn't make any difference." To read the criticism of Armstrong from those years is to get a sense of the jazz press setting the stage for the twenty-first century, in which jazz has become something more like the symphony or opera, depending on foundations and patrons for support rather than the love of the general public. Armstrong was pilloried for not conducting himself like Dave Brubeck or the Modern Jazz Quartet—now those were jazz musicians you could bring *mater* and *pater* to see and not be embarrassed. But Armstrong viewed himself as an entertainer more like, say, his colleague Bing Crosby, who was perfectly content to sing a classic song by George Gershwin at one session and then do "MacNamara's Band" at the next, or even a popular actor like Cary Grant, who could do heavy drama in one vehicle and then be silly enough to wear a dress in another.

To read the critics of the 1950s on Armstrong is to cringe; he knew what he was and what he wanted to be, while they wanted him to pretend he was Bach or Mozart. *Down Beat*'s review of Armstrong's 1956 performance at the Newport Jazz Festival is particularly galling: "He demonstrated with finality that it takes more than the old rolling eyes, handkerchief on head and chops, and the same old Paramount Theater act to warrant time at a festival of jazz." The elitist attitude and just plain snobbery is overwhelming, as is the total disdain for anything popular. Clearly, the audiences at the Paramount Theater are merely hoi polloi, the Joe Sixpacks of the world, who will accept any gimmicky crap you throw at them, whereas the Newport attendees, both those who are rich in taste as well as material wealth, deserve something better.

The assets of *Ella & Louis,* taped just about a month after Newport 1956, are obvious: here are the two greatest voices of jazz sharing the microphone on eleven of the greatest American popular standards ever written. The combination of the two sonic worlds is in itself remarkable: the satin and silk of Ella Fitzgerald's voice intermingling with the smooth-as-number-twelve-sandpaper voice of Armstrong. Armstrong described himself as having a "sawmill voice," and one of his favorite stories involved the judge who presided over one of his three divorces. His Honor assumed that Armstrong had a cold, but when Pops explained that this was his natural speaking voice, the requested divorce was immediately granted. Yet there was a million miles between the natural sweetness of Armstrong's chops, "sawmill" as they might be, and the scabrous sound of a blues singer like Howling Wolf—now there's a truly frightening voice, one that's all badass attitude and zero tenderness. (Or for that matter, Blind Willie Johnson, who sang gospel songs like "Nobody's Fault but Mine" with so much fire-and-brimstone in his voice that he could literally scare sinners back into church.)

Armstrong made many other duet records, and for general entertainment value my own favorite is the series of eight sides he and Ella recorded together for Decca Records between 1946 and 1951. But the 1956 *Ella & Louis* is unique for reasons in addition to the thrill of hearing Ella and Louis together. This is also the single most notable recorded example of Armstrong giving a performance that is entirely free of what *Down Beat* dismissed as "the old Paramount Theater act." One can't imagine that he would have ever given a performance intended to please the reviewers rather than the audience, but in this exceptional album

he delivers just as much for the critics as for the mere listeners. The main reason, as we shall see, is because he was compelled to leave his comfort zone and work in a wholly different musical universe.

Adding a level of irony, the album was produced by Norman Granz, who at that time was best known for his series of Jazz at the Philharmonic concerts, which also roused the ire of the critics for having the unmitigated gall, as it were, to make jazz entertaining. The circumstances of the recording of *Ella & Louis* were such that Armstrong didn't have the opportunity to prepare any "act"—he just showed up and sang and played. And that, it turned out, was plenty.

The grandfather of *Ella & Louis* was Jack Kapp, founder of Decca Records, who was the music industry's original instigator of the duets trend that continues to this day. Working extensively with Bing Crosby, Kapp proved conclusively that if one star can sell X number of records, then two stars singing together will sell not just 2 x X but more like X squared: sales increase not incrementally, but exponentially. It was under Kapp's watch that Milt Gabler released a series of duet discs for both Louis Armstrong and Ella Fitzgerald: they both were teamed with The Mills Brothers and Louis Jordan. It was only a matter of time before Gabler brought Armstrong and Fitzgerald together in that series of eight classic sides from 1946 to 1951. (The most celebrated of these is "Dream a Little Dream of Me.") These are highlights in the careers of both artists; the two are instantly the most simpatico duet partners that either of them ever worked with.

Granz undoubtedly had those eight excellent sides in mind when he reunited Armstrong and Fitzgerald in 1956. He had obviously wanted to make such an album for a while. "The logistics were always difficult, on almost all of Louis's sessions, because he traveled so much," said Granz. Fitzgerald was on the road constantly as well, but at least she then resided in Los Angeles, so Granz would have access to her when she was off the road: "I didn't have that much time, I might have [had] only a day or two days to do an album." Granz elaborated that record dates were generally a secondary concern to Armstrong's manager, Joe Glaser, who, as we discussed in our essay on *Louis Armstrong Meets Oscar Peterson*, booked such sessions around (and often after) more lucrative concert dates.

Granz more or less solved his own problem. On August 15, 1956, he produced a spectacular concert—a full edition of the Jazz at the Philharmonic troupe, plus Oscar Peterson's trio and Art Tatum playing solo, as well as complete sets by Ella Fitzgerald and her quartet, and, the biggest headliner of them all, Louis Armstrong and His All-Stars. For a climax, Fitzgerald joined Armstrong's All-Stars on two numbers, "You Won't Be Satisfied Until You Break My Heart," which had been the first of their recorded duets in 1946, and "Undecided," which was in the working book of both artists.

It's a highly plausible argument that the Fitzgerald-Armstrong relationship reached its all-time apogee on that night: "You Won't Be Satisfied" is a luminescent duet that begins with Armstrong enthusiastically introducing Fitzgerald (as "the darling of song and our little sweetheart"). He then gags up the title by starting to announce it as "You Won't Be *Sausage*-fied." Fitzgerald sings the words slowly and luxuriously, with lots of warmth and feeling; even when she blows a lyric and apologizes (without departing from the melody) we can't help but love her. Armstrong's vocal chorus is also remarkably warm and emotional, you can tell he's looking straight at her—doing the whole "Paramount Theater act." After a brief trumpet solo, the two sing together, and the love between them is overwhelmingly palpable. Following "Satisfied," the All-Stars launch into "Undecided," playing more or less the same arrangement that they had already been using for a few years. Fitzgerald finds her place in the chart, fitting comfortably into Armstrong's musical domain, and while she sings angelically, he blows one of his strongest solos of the night.

Granz had initially booked Armstrong's All-Stars just for the Hollywood Bowl concert, but was delighted to be informed by Glaser that Armstrong was available to do a record date on the following afternoon. Granz requested just Armstrong himself, not the whole band. Having now tested the two stars' appeal as a power duet in front of the JATP audience, Granz proceeded with his plan to

have the two of them cut a full album together and brought them into the studio on that following afternoon, August 16, 1956.

On the two live numbers done at the Bowl, the twosome had the advantage of working with familiar material, including a duet they had already recorded. The way most record companies and producers worked, the tunes would have been decided upon beforehand, as well as keys and arrangements of some kind. Granz often worked this way with his big band projects, but in this case he had only a day or two to put the session together.

Everything we know about the album tells us that the two singers (with Armstrong occasionally taking a trumpet solo) recorded all eleven tracks in this one day, and with no advance preparation. Obviously both were consummate professionals— that wasn't the problem; the potential problem was that Armstrong was so overworked that he occasionally sounded tired, especially since, as we have seen, most recording sessions came after what was already a hard night's work.

This was already a highly productive season for Armstrong: in addition to the usual nonstop touring and TV appearances (including *The Ed Sullivan Show*), there were two other key projects, the Newport appearance (which, the reviewer to the contrary, was an excellent performance, shortly thereafter released on LP by Columbia) and his famous collaboration in Lewisohn Stadium (which at the time was New York's equivalent of the Hollywood Bowl) with Leonard Bernstein and the New York Philharmonic barely a week after Newport (also recorded by Columbia and included in the documentary *Satchmo the Great*), and then the Hollywood Bowl. Yet Armstrong and Fitzgerald are not only both in excellent shape, chops-wise, but especially turned on by each other—each pushing the other to achieve greater heights than they might have achieved individually.

The casualness of the session is the album's strength and its weakness. Even with minimal preparation, we're talking about a couple of superhumans here, and their casual is better than anyone else's best (and most carefully prepared). Two amazing artists, with a rhythm section for the ages, and eleven of the highest-caliber standard songs.

Who could ask for anything more? And viewed from another perspective, who could ask for anything less—because the album is so spontaneous, Armstrong hasn't had the opportunity to develop any of that so-called Paramount Theater shtick that the critics so objected to.

The downside is that while the album is a true collaboration, sometimes it doesn't seem like a real set of duets. In the previous eight Armstrong-Fitzgerald Decca duets, there is constant interplay, the two continually bantering back and forth. In the 1956 Verve album, there's frequent interplay between the two principals, but for the most part she'll sing a solo chorus, then he'll sing a solo chorus; it's rare for them to sing more than sixteen bars together in harmony—that would have taken more time and the input of a musical director or arranger. (In that sense, the album that Armstrong made with Bing Crosby in 1960, *Bing & Satchmo,* is a more accurate extension of the 1946–51 Armstrong-Fitzgerald duets.) But even without continual interplay, we still get a distinct sense that the two are singing directly to each other—and clearly each is thoroughly jazzed by the presence of the other.

As far as the production of the album goes, we have some testimony from Granz, but it seems like everything he said was completely disingenuous. In Granz's telling, "When [Ella] made the album with Louis, she insisted that he select the tunes, and she sang them all in his keys even if they were the wrong keys for her." It's hard to believe that could be the case; Ella sounds completely comfortable with every song in every key, there's nothing that's too high or low or just plain wrong for her.

At the Hollywood Bowl, Fitzgerald essentially guested with Armstrong's band; in the studio the next day, Armstrong essentially became a guest star in the musical universe of Fitzgerald and Granz. The band consisted of four musicians with whom Fitzgerald worked regularly; this was Oscar Peterson's trio, with guitarist Herb Ellis and bassist Ray Brown (also Fitzgerald's ex-husband), with the addition of superstar drummer Buddy Rich.

Despite Granz's recollections, the selection of tunes is clearly by Granz himself. There are four songs that had been written for Fred Astaire, which is a sure indication of the producer's personal taste. One thinks that if Louis had been picking the songs, there would have been more favorites from his childhood—traditional songs from New Orleans, and early pop tunes from the teens and twenties. Louis's taste went beyond the American Songbook classics that Granz favored: he loved the blues and he loved comic songs and novelties, and there are none of these on the album.

The idea of beginning with "Can't We Be Friends?" (the 1929 jazz standard by Kay Swift and her husband, Paul James Warburg) seems clearly like a producer's choice. (It was the fifth tune recorded at the session.) Fitzgerald sings a chorus, then Armstrong sings one (using a different set of lyrics), then the third chorus is sixteen bars of trumpet, followed by a bridge in which they sing alternating lines, and then they sing the last eight-bar section together. The answer to the titular question is obviously "Yes, we can be friends."

The pace slows down for "Isn't This a Lovely Day?" (Irving Berlin, from the 1935 film *Top Hat*), which was introduced by Astaire in a fox-trot dance tempo but becomes a slower and more meditative ballad here. It opens with Fitzgerald singing the verse (which, like many of the verses written for Astaire, is not rubato but in a definite dance beat) followed by Armstrong luxuriating in the chorus, throwing in the occasional "baby" and other Satchelmouthed asides. Fitzgerald then sings another chorus, at her warmest and most romantic, while Pops plays behind her. Armstrong then plays half a chorus in the foreground before Fitzgerald joins him at the bridge, and they sing together briefly in the last eight bars. It fills up six minutes and change, but it's worth every second.

Compared to that intimate epic, "Moonlight in Vermont" (John Blackburn, Karl Suessdorf, published in 1944) is a quickie. In a tempo that's slower still, Ella sings a chorus, and Armstrong plays sixteen bars that are positively magisterial, before she returns and takes it out, with Armstrong entering for a line or two.

Another Astaire classic, "They Can't Take That Away from Me" (George and Ira Gershwin, from *Shall We Dance,* 1937), is a natural choice for a duet. Armstrong plays muted behind Fitzgerald for the first chorus and then he sings a second chorus, but his scatted intro is worth the price of admission all by itself, as is the way he ends by declaiming "swing it, boys," under his breath, almost like Bob Hope understating a punch line to make it funnier. He plays sixteen bars open, then joins Fitzgerald intermittently on the last half chorus—they sing the last line together, the first time so far on the album that we've heard any vocal harmony.

"Under a Blanket of Blue" (Jerry Livingston, Al J. Neiburg, Marty Symes) wasn't a hit or a notable number when it was introduced in 1933, but became a jazz standard years later, being recorded by Doris Day among others. This time Armstrong sings it before Fitzgerald, and plays an open-bell trumpet solo after her, and there's more brief interplay and harmony in the last few bars.

"Tenderly" (Walter Gross and Jack Lawrence) is mainly distinguished by a beautiful open-bell trumpet solo at a very slow tempo; the pace picks up when Fitzgerald then sings it with Pops playing behind her. Armstrong then sings a chorus of his own at the same tempo; his own vocal is perhaps more rambunctious than tender (one rewritten line goes "You took your chops / Away from Pops!"). Then, surprisingly, the tempo slows back down again, with Armstrong playing exuberantly and Fitzgerald scatting over him, ending in a Satchmo impression. (Which was one of her signature bits in concert.)

The second side of the original LP opens with Pops singing the verse to "A Foggy Day" (the Gershwins again) at a much slower tempo than by Astaire in *A Damsel in Distress* (1937). The tempo again picks up after the verse, and both Armstrong and Fitzgerald sing a whole chorus each. Armstrong plays sixteen bars (the song is in ABAB format), and Fitzgerald sings the last half chorus with Armstrong providing an obbligato behind her, this time using his voice rather than his horn.

It's easy to believe that Armstrong selected "Stars Fell on Alabama" himself; he would have known the song from his longtime colleague and collaborator Jack Teagarden. Teagarden made the first classic recording of the song in 1934, and then used it as his solo vehicle for a while during his years with Armstrong's All-Stars. The melody is by

the relatively obscure Frank Perkins and the lyrics are by Mitchell Parish, who made it part of his cycle of "cosmic nostalgia" songs, along with "Star Dust" and "Deep Purple." Thanks to Armstrong (and, indirectly, to Teagarden) the song became more important as a jazz standard in the 1950s than it had been to begin with, and there were also classic, Armstrong-inspired recordings by Frank Sinatra (*A Swingin' Affair*) and Doris Day (*Day by Night*) in 1956–57. Pops begins with a gorgeous trumpet intro before deferring to Ella for the first chorus, occasionally joining her in something roughly like a vocal duet; to my ears, he's a tiny bit tentative, as if this were a first run-through, but no matter, they both sound glorious. The lyric reading is saturated with the mixed emotions that Ella and Louis would have felt about the American South—something that Day and Sinatra wouldn't have necessarily felt. The sweetest portion is the second chorus, wherein Armstrong mostly sings the words and melody while Fitzgerald scats around him.

The last of the four Astaire songs is "Cheek to Cheek" (by Irving Berlin, from *Top Hat*, 1935), and it's one of the more competitive takes of the session, in a very friendly way. Peterson plays a brief but tasty piano riff by way of an intro, and Pops leaps right in; the words "Heaven, I'm in Heaven" seem especially appropriate when we consider the combination of Armstrong, Fitzgerald, and Peterson. Armstrong sings the first chorus with overwhelming, incandescent warmth and remarkable sympathy with the lyrics, and inserts a little of his customary business (like "Now, Mama, dance with me" and "take it, Ella" at the end) before Fitzgerald takes over for the second chorus; there's a very subtle change of time-feel-change between the two, they're both in 4/4, but Armstrong's feels more like New Orleans–to–swing and Fitzgerald like swing-to-bop. The two get really aggressive in their third chorus together; for the first time we feel a slight healthy rivalry and competitive edge, which is a good thing, as it takes their interaction to a higher level than most tracks; there's a lot of frisky energy in this chorus.

"Cheek to Cheek" feels like a pas de deux, a dance between two principals who are at points trying to outdo each other, but "The Nearness of

You" (by Hoagy Carmichael, one of the trumpeter's favorite songwriters, with a lyric by the brilliant Ned Washington) is a pure love song. This track captures Fitzgerald at her considerable pinnacle of romantic feeling, and Armstrong as well, and those feelings are expressed equally strongly by both his sixteen bars of trumpet and his voice. Fitzgerald sings the last half of that chorus by herself, and does it wonderfully—but one can't help but be a little disappointed. Their affection for each other is immediately visceral, even though they actually sing little of the song together. One wishes that they had taken even twenty minutes to work out some kind of genuine duet routine instead of just singing around each other and trying not to step on each other's toes.

"April in Paris" and "The Nearness of You" were the last two of the eleven tunes recorded on the date, although they were taped in reverse order from the way that they appear on the album, which ends with "April in Paris." Did Granz plan to make this the climax, which is why he let it run on to over six and a half minutes? He doesn't seem to have planned anything particularly carefully, but, in a case like this, the semi-spontaneous results were remarkable. It starts more like a love song between Ella and Oscar, you've never heard either of them sound this rapturously romantic before. Then, Pops comes in and sings another full chorus, and he really turns on the understated emotion—when he sings, you're not thinking about the song, or the melody, the lyrics, or whatever, you're thinking about April, you're thinking about Paris, and you're wondering what has it done to your heart? His trumpet solo is even more like this. No wonder all the major style setters of the next generation—Sinatra, Fitzgerald, and Billie Holiday—all learned so much from him. After the trumpet solo, Fitzgerald sings the last eight bars, with Armstrong playing the coda; it's a quiet ending, but a spectacular one.

Ella & Louis was very well received (it reached number 12 on the *Billboard* album charts), so much so that Granz reunited his principals a year later. This time he had enough clout with Joe Glaser to request Armstrong's services for two sessions, in July and August 1957. During the two 1957 dates, Granz recorded the two stars doing twenty semi-spontaneous duets, issued in various forms over the years as *Ella and Louis Again.* ("I've Got My Love to Keep Me Warm" is notable as one of the few to actually open with the two singing in harmony.)

For their third project together, Granz at last organized an actual framework around them, using them as the two solo voices for a unique interpretation of George Gershwin's *Porgy & Bess,* with musical director Russ Garcia conducting a full studio orchestra with strings. At another interview, Granz elaborated, "I always got [Louis] under the worst possible conditions. We'd work for months to set everything up—like on the *Porgy & Bess* LP with Ella—at the last minute we'd find he'd have a concert somewhere that evening. Everything would have to be rushed." Still, that 1957 team-up, the last of their major collaborations together, would be a classic. (The final occasion when "Ella and Louis" worked together seems to have been the 1959 Playboy Jazz Festival in Chicago.)

But perhaps the greatest collateral benefit of the first *Ella & Louis* wasn't even the duet concept, but the idea of Armstrong singing jazz standards with a state-of-the-art contemporary jazz rhythm section, helmed by the brilliant Oscar Peterson; this led to what was possibly an even greater album, the 1957 *Louis Armstrong Meets Oscar Peterson.* Had Armstrong ever paid attention to critics, he might have taken particular satisfaction in the words of *Down Beat,* the same publication that thoroughly trashed his 1956 Newport performance only a few months earlier. Even they had to admit that *Ella & Louis* was a great album—no "Paramount Theater act" here. The reviewer proclaimed it "one of the very, very few albums to have been issued in this era of the LP flood that is sure to endure for decades." At least they got that right.

19

Ella Fitzgerald

Mack the Knife: Ella in Berlin

(1960)

Clearly, it's a kind of black magic. Ella Fitzgerald's classic concert album *Mack the Knife: The Complete Ella in Berlin* (the expanded 1993 CD edition) opens with "That Old Black Magic," and it's something more than just a random choice.

In the first years of the 12-inch LP, Ella Fitzgerald quickly established herself as the supreme master of two kinds of albums, the songbook and the live recording. (Frank Sinatra, conversely, took control of the "concept" album—a format that Fitzgerald exhibited little interest in.) Perhaps not by coincidence, in 1956 Fitzgerald had begun working with the producer Norman Granz, who had been her personal manager for some years before then. Granz had negotiated her switch from her previous record company affiliation, Decca, to his own new outfit, Verve, just as the industry as a whole was making the transition into the brave new world of 12-inch LPs. Granz aggressively advocated for both songbook and live albums, and he would use Fitzgerald as a sort of test case to prove to the world that both new formats were capable of inspiring some legendary music. Granz was especially bullish on the idea of live performance recording; he had been taping Fitzgerald as a participant in his Jazz at the Philharmonic shows well before he had the contractual rights to release any of those performances. From 1956 on, he would tape her live

concerts consistently for roughly twenty-five years, and then cherry-pick the tapes for what he wanted to release.

Throughout the 1950s and early '60s especially, even after Granz sold his interest in Verve Records in 1961, there continued to be an ongoing stream of Fitzgerald releases: live albums alternating with songbooks and other studio projects. While nearly all the songbooks were considerable successes, it's interesting to ponder why certain live albums were hits in their day and others were all but ignored. In 1960, Fitzgerald's Berlin concert, released as *Mack the Knife: Ella in Berlin,* was a blockbuster, but then her next live album, *Ella in Hollywood* (1961), was all but completely ignored until, curiously, fifty years later the Hollywood set was re-released in a considerably expanded CD edition that was proclaimed far and wide as a masterpiece.

Both the 1960 Berlin and the 1961 Hollywood shows (as well as the 1961 German concert eventually released as *Ella Returns to Berlin*) were examples of Fitzgerald at her absolute best, but in retrospect we can see that the Berlin album had several clear-cut advantages. This was the height of the Cold War, and the idea of the jazz world's greatest singer bringing American music to Germany, former enemy of the United States, and laying it on the doorstep of the Kremlin was irresistible—as if Fitzgerald were striking a blow for freedom by zinging both the Nazis and the Communists in one fell swoop. In 1962, Benny Goodman (whose parents had been Russian-Jewish immigrants) would become the first high-profile American jazz or popular performer to tour the USSR, but in 1960 Ella singing in Berlin was as close as anyone had come. Listening today, one has to wonder how many East Germans and Soviets were in attendance in the Deutschlandhalle as Fitzgerald sang, this being well before the infamous Berlin Wall was erected in 1961. It's also hard not to hear a foreshadowing of President Kennedy's iconic 1963 speech from the same city, with its much repeated tagline, "Let them come to Berlin."

It didn't hurt either that "Mack the Knife" was by far the biggest pop song of the 1959–60 period: Bobby Darin's single was quite possibly the last pan-generational hit in American pop music, being beloved by the younger generation who dug Elvis as well as their parents who grooved to Sinatra. Louis Armstrong had already warmed up jazz fans to the song, particularly internationally; like Fitzgerald (much more than Sinatra or Elvis), Armstrong was continually on the road across the globe and continually singing "Mack," which, having been written in Germany in 1928, already had a multi-continental, multigenerational flavor to it. In 1960, practically everyone in the world was singing "Mack," and Fitzgerald's live recording, made in Germany, showed that the song could be done by women as well ("we've never heard a girl sing it," as Fitzgerald says in her introduction), and even by, in her case, a woman who didn't happen to know the words.

Apart from those advantages, the Berlin concert was one of Fitzgerald's truly blessed hours: she was riveting from start to finish. It was a night when she could literally do no wrong. Even with an artist as talented, dedicated, and consistent as Fitzgerald, there are some nights that are more magical than others, when absolutely everything seemed to click. On any given night of her life, Fitzgerald was magical, but on the evening of February 13, 1960, she was transcendent.

Early in 1960, Paul Smith (who turned ninety in 2012), who had played piano on most of Fitzgerald's studio dates since 1956, was recruited by Granz to travel with the singer on her 1960 European tour. "Norman liked the way I played, so I took a leave of absence from my staff job at NBC," Smith told Fitzgerald biographer Stuart Nicholson. "We did a European tour early in the year. In Germany, Norman had them record us. We recorded in Hamburg, Stuttgart, six or eight cities in all, just our usual set. But when we opened in Berlin, it was Ella's version of 'Mack the Knife,' the first time we played it in the Deutschlandhalle, that made the album *Ella in Berlin,* and that was the version that Norman put out." The rest of Fitzgerald's quartet included future guitar star Jim Hall, who was apparently on the road with her only for this one tour, as well as bassist Wilfred Middlebrooks and drummer Gus Johnson, who would work with her for considerably longer.

The original 1960 LP *Ella in Berlin* opened with "Gone with the Wind"; the CD release, issued in 1993, gets under way with two previously unissued tracks, "That Old Black Magic" and "Our Love Is Here to Stay." Often, when sifting through his live tapes looking for material to issue, Granz would try to avoid songs that Fitzgerald had recently released on other albums. "Our Love Is Here to Stay" had been heard on Fitzgerald's epic 1959 *George and Ira Gershwin Songbook,* but "That Old Black Magic" had not yet been issued on any Fitzgerald Verve release. Possibly, Granz was holding it aside as he was already planning Fitzgerald's Harold Arlen Songbook, which would be recorded a year later.

While Deutschlandhalle audiences in 1960 were delighted, record buyers in that same year were cheated: there could be no better opening number than "Black Magic." (For the purposes of this discussion, we are following the track listing of the 1993 CD edition rather than the original 1960 LP.) It's a fast boppy arrangement, with Fitzgerald singing rings around the tune and lyrics but still maintaining their essential meaning. She opens with a riffy paraphrase of the song's last four notes, "Black magic called love," sung in harmony primarily with Jim Hall. Fitzgerald would sing at least three different arrangements of "Black Magic" in a six-year period, among them a big band chart by Benny Carter in 1955 and Billy May's very different *Harold Arlen Songbook* arrangement from 1961. This modernistic yet swinging combo treatment was documented on a number of concerts in the 1958–61 period, although none of those tapes was released at the time.

After the fast "Magic," Fitzgerald ritards down into a slow dance tempo for "Our Love Is Here to Stay," the first of four Gershwin numbers heard in the set; she had spent much of the previous year recording her epic *George and Ira Gershwin Songbook* and the music of the brothers was clearly very much on her mind. "Our Love Is Here to Stay" is in a tempo that's perfect for dancing at a wedding, but Fitzgerald's vocal, particularly in the second chorus, is full of Fitzgeraldian colors that no mere wedding singer could begin to approximate.

"Gone with the Wind" is very much in the vein of "Black Magic," being a twenty-plus-year-old standard reanimated with a modern jazz vamp and considerable melodic license. Fitzgerald gets all the lyrics precisely right (except at one point she sings "flown apart" rather than "flown away") but plays around with the tune, injecting new life into it with various riffs. She's singing the lyrics here, make no mistake, but with far less seriousness than one might expect to hear in a classic torch song.

By way of comparison, the next number, "Misty," is treated more like a genuine ballad, in a slower, more romantic tempo. Yet she's also frisky and playful here. She reconfigures every melodic line and every phrase as she goes along, at times going up where you'd expect her to go down, often landing on a different part of the beat from what you'd expect. She also stretches various words unexpectedly ("That's why I'm follow-ow-ow-ing you / O-o-o-o-on my own . . ."). Her approaches to the two songs are differentiated primarily by tempo: "Gone with the Wind" could just as easily have been treated as a purer slow love song and "Misty" could just as easily have been bopped up.

On the other hand, Rodgers and Hart's "The Lady Is a Tramp" could never be anything other than an up-tempo swinger in the Fitzgerald universe. In hindsight, it seems surprising that she didn't sing it at all until her 1956 *Rodgers and Hart Songbook*. "Tramp" was introduced in the 1937 Broadway musical *Babes in Arms*, another surpris-

ing fact since the song is better remembered as a key number for Frank Sinatra in his 1957 film of Rodgers and Hart's *Pal Joey*; lyrically, the song seems to belong in a story about a lowlife juggling the various ladies and tramps in his love life rather than a more wholesome story about stagestruck kids putting on a show. "The Lady Is a Tramp" easily belongs on anyone's short list of the greatest of all entries in the Great American Songbook. Lorenz Hart's lyric is driven entirely by irony—the woman thus described is not a tramp in any sense of the word but is a free soul and an independent spirit who simply refuses to conform to conventions. This is the kind of irony you rarely get in other kinds of songs such as the blues, country music, or post-1970 singer-songwriter pop. Ella Fitzgerald was later criticized by some for allegedly not fully understanding the words to the songs she sang, but "Tramp" puts the lie to that accusation; no other singer—even Pope Frank—has been as savvy as she was in conveying the deeper meaning of Lorenz Hart's intricate, multilayered, and highly ironic text.

In 1956—August and then November, respectively—"Tramp" became a career signature for both Fitzgerald and Sinatra. Sinatra sang it from a personal perspective, in the third person, as if he were describing the kind of woman that he respected; Fitzgerald did it even more intimately, in the first person ("I get too hungry . . ."), as if it were an anthem of personal liberation. Unlike Sinatra's, Fitzgerald's love life was never headline news, and it always seemed as if she were using Rodgers and Hart to playfully explore and celebrate her sensual side—and what's more, she was doing it at a breakneck tempo. Certainly, "Tramp" is one of the most consistently joyous lyric readings in Fitzgerald's canon. She liked it so much that she even wrote a special coda to end it ("She's a hobo, she's a scamp"), indicating that, like "How High the Moon," it occupied a special place both in her heart and in her repertoire.

On the studio recording, highly appropriate for a *Songbook* album, Fitzgerald started with the verse ("I've wined and dined on Mulligan's Stew . . ."), which had been largely unsung in the two decades since *Babes in Arms*. What's unusual is that as

"Tramp" entered her live shows, she continued to sing the verse. Perhaps the verse was Fitzgerald's way of distinguishing her version from Sinatra's increasingly iconic renditions (for much the same reason that both Fitzgerald and Sinatra did the verse to "Over the Rainbow" to distinguish their versions from Judy Garland's). The other key difference between the 1956 big band version and the many live trio and quartet performances is the different lyrics: on the studio version, Fitzgerald sang the verse and the first two refrains (which begin "I get too hungry for dinner at eight . . ." and "I Go to Coney—the beach is divine," respectively). In concert, she went directly from refrain one to refrain four ("girls get massages, they cry and they moan"), thus skipping refrains two and three. Another Fitzgerald tradition was to insert the name of a local eatery into Hart's line "The food at *Sardi's* is perfect, no doubt"—here it's "The food at the *Kempinski* is perfect, no doubt," in a reference to a well-known European hotel chain still in operation, and, also no doubt, where Fitzgerald was staying in Berlin in 1960.

Fitzgerald's and Sinatra's interpretations also differ in tempo: Sinatra's is more in his classic "heartbeat" tempo, fast enough for an exuberant dance but slow enough for all the words to come through, whereas Fitzgerald relies on the audience already knowing the words, so she can shoot them out as quickly as possible—and with as much clarity as possible, although there's no guarantee that everybody will get every syllable. Sinatra's is more like a Jimmie Lunceford–style two-beat, Fitzgerald's is in a solid four in 1960, although in the mid-1960s, as in her 1964 Juan-les-Pins concerts, she gave it an entirely different four-beat time feel. Yet at the same time, she obviously wasn't trying to escape Sinatra's shadow, but rather to dance around it. Near the very last line, where Hart originally wrote "For Robert Taylor I whistle and stamp," Fitzgerald instead sings "For Frank Sinatra I whistle and stamp," and as the crowd applauds, she giggles, "Thank you, Frank Sinatra fans!" Fitzgerald and Sinatra would ultimately consummate their love for the song—and each other—in the Chairman's 1967 TV special, *A Man and His Music + Ella + Jobim*. Their most memorable duet by far was "Tramp," which, in a characteristic display of graciousness by the host, was performed by the two titans in an arrangement that was much closer to hers than to his.

The next batch of songs on the Berlin CD alternate between the Gershwins and Cole Porter, starting with the ballad "The Man I Love" done slowly and romantically in acute contrast with "Tramp." Of the three Cole Porter songs on the CD, two were actually mistakes owing to an error on the part of the reissue producer. "Love for Sale" and "Just One of Those Things" were sung by Fitzgerald at the Hollywood Bowl in 1956, and it's the Hollywood Bowl tapes that somehow wound up here on the Berlin CD. ("Too Darn Hot," which arrives a few tracks later, is genuinely from Berlin 1960.)

Following the two erroneous entries, we find ourselves back in Berlin in 1960 with more Gershwin and Porter. "Summertime" provided the highlight of Fitzgerald's masterpiece recording of *Porgy and Bess* done in collaboration with Louis Armstrong. Pops isn't around to open this "Summertime" with his majestic trumpet solo, but it begins equally auspiciously with Fitzgerald at her most emotional. I've long theorized that Fitzgerald may have been more inspired by stories of mother-child love than she typically was about most songs which tell of man-woman romantic love—although, as we've seen, both "The Man I Love" and "Misty" on this very same Berlin concert prove that she could sing your basic love song as movingly as anybody. In any case, her "Summertime" is as powerful as always—and hearing it again, I was struck by the thought that had Fitzgerald come to maturity in a different time or place, she might have sung more spirituals, blues, or "traditional" African American "roots" music; instead, she brings her considerable technique and her emotional wherewithal to a song that's at once a spiritual and a lullaby, written by a Jewish songwriter for a Broadway show. Yet the feeling she generates is no less profound than any genuine gospel song or blues could produce.

"Too Darn Hot" is considerably more exciting than the rather pedestrian arrangement on Fitzgerald's 1956 *Cole Porter Songbook*. Ella starts comparatively cool, starting a cappella and rubato, and gradually increasing both the tempo and the temperature. "Lorelei," however, is even hotter. The inclusion of "Lorelei" on the 1960 tour was a surprise: compared with "The Man I Love," "Summertime," and "Love Is Here to Stay," "Lorelei" is hardly an all-time Gershwin standard. Rather, this is a comparatively minor number from a flop show, the 1933 *Pardon My English*. It seems likely that Ira Gershwin would have introduced Fitzgerald to the song when he served as an unofficial consultant on *The George and Ira Gershwin Songbook*—I can't imagine that she would have heard it any other way. "Lorelei" was a well-placed comic turn in *Pardon My English,* and had comparatively little life traction beyond that short-lived show. "Lorelei" may be at once Fitzgerald's sexiest and funniest song. Here, as with "Tramp," she taps into her sensual side, albeit largely in jest. As with Louis Armstrong, who was eternally one of her guiding lights, sex was always an opportunity for humor with Fitzgerald. Even though, unlike in "Tramp," the lyrics never make it explicit that the woman singing about the "Lorelei" isn't truly a tramp, it's an especially funny piece of material for Fitzgerald because she has deliberately distanced herself from the siren of whom she sings; could be this was her way of directing barbs at those singing sexpots who proliferated in the 1950s, like Julie London and Dorothy Dandridge. She emphasizes the erotic humor of the text when Paul Smith plays a bluesy, barrelhouse phrase near the end of the number, and she announces to the crowd, "Now strip tease!"

"Lorelei" leads into "Mack the Knife," thus connecting two songs with reference to German culture: "Lorelei" is based on a Teutonic legend and comes from a show set in Germany, thus explaining Ira Gershwin's inclusion of the phrase "Ja! Ja!" "Mack," is, famously, a Weimar show tune that had, over a thirty-year period, evolved into an American pop tune. Kurt Weill, who idolized Gershwin, would have been honored by the juxtaposition.

"Mack the Knife" underscores Fitzgerald's unique status in the music world of 1960: she was an internationally known figure, and though a jazz singer was more popular than most female pop singers. Her market, unlike Patti Page's or Peggy Lee's, was almost entirely driven by album sales—

even in the pre-LP period, she was rarely thought of as a singles artist—but she sold eighty zillion records just the same. In her spontaneous asides throughout the concert, Fitzgerald seems acutely aware of where she stands in the cultural hierarchy, and she's constantly acknowledging other singers—in "Black Magic" it's Billy Daniels, in "Tramp" it's Frank Sinatra (which is especially obliging of her, since she sang it before him), and she dedicates "Mack" at one point to "the Louis Armstrong fans and the Bobby Darin fans."

She lets us know more than once that she's only singing "Mack" because "it's a surprise hit," yet she sings it with commitment, conviction, and sheer dynamic energy that's extreme even for Ella Fitzgerald—obviously her personal excitement had been mounting over the hour or so that the concert has been transpiring. Listening fifty years later, it's hard to believe the evidence of our own ears that she spontaneously forgot the lyrics and improvises most of what we hear on the Berlin recording (as Louis Armstrong supposedly did on "Heebie Jeebies," one of the first scat masterpieces). Still there are endless Fitzgerald concert recordings extant, and she never sings anything like the Berlin "Mack" lyrics anywhere else, so there's no direct evidence to undermine her claim that these lyrics were anything other than what she said they were. (When she sang "Mack" on her 1961 concert in the same city, she introduces it as "the song that started right here in Berlin," and she gets all the words right.)

"Mack the Knife" was originally written as an exceptionally plain, sing-songy melody in C major: it's essentially just eight basic bars that repeat and repeat. Bobby Darin's arranger, Richard Wess, injected excitement by making the melody modulate upward with practically every eight-bar segment, but Fitzgerald gooses the song by intermingling the published lyric (Marc Blitzstein's English language adaptation of Bertolt Brecht's original German libretto), her spontaneous words, which primarily describe her in the act of forgetting the actual lyric and making up her own, and her own scatting. For four and a half glorious minutes, she swerves among the three. The result is one of the most involved, intimate, and emotional pieces of singing she ever delivered—an amazing moment that fortunately was documented by Granz's recording equipment. What could better illustrate international solidarity and the Brotherhood of Man than Fitzgerald improvising on a German American song in Berlin?

More proof that the word-forgetting episode on "Mack" was genuinely spontaneous: "Mack" is followed by the evening's climactic scat number, "How High the Moon" and Fitzgerald would not have deliberately planned two such epic wordless numbers back to back. "Moon" was already established as a virtual anthem of the swing-to-bop transition when Fitzgerald introduced her specialty arrangement in 1947 (issued on the *Lullabies of Birdland* album); it had been a Fitzgerald concert perennial for many years before and since. The seven-minute Berlin version follows the traditional outline: she starts with the basic chorus (as introduced on Broadway in *Two for the Show* in 1940), followed by her own specialty chorus ("though the words may be wrong . . .") leading into the scat sequence. It is unquestionably one of the greatest pieces of improv that Fitzgerald—or anybody else—ever committed to tape.

A quick inventory of the references the singer drops into the scat sequence will convey some idea of its frenetic quality, though not its matchless majesty: 1:23 "Poinciana"; 1:35 "Deep Purple"; 1:40 "Love in Bloom"; 1:52 "Ornithology"; 2:24 "I Cover the Waterfront"; 2:39 "Rockin' in Rhythm"; 3:29 "The Irish Washerwoman"; 3:41 "Hawaiian War Chant"; 3:47 "The Peanut Vendor"; 3:55 possibly several notes of "Salt Peanuts"; 4:10 "Peter, Peter Pumpkin Eater" (see below); 4:13 "Whatta Ya Say We Go?"; 4:16 "Stormy Weather"; 4:36 "Yes, We Have No Bananas" (in minor); 4:38 possibly "Flight of the Bumble Bee"; 4:39 possibly another few notes of "Deep Purple"; 4:50 "Did You Ever See a Dream Walking"; 4:57 "A Tisket, A Tasket"; 5:00 "Heat Wave"; 5:01 "Christmas Night in Harlem";

5:06 "On the Trail" (from the *Grand Canyon Suite*); 5:20 *William Tell Overture;* 5:35 "You're Getting to Be a Habit with Me"; 5:38 "Mop Mop"; 5:58 "Gotta Be This or That"; 6:00 *Rhapsody in Blue;* 6:03 "Idaho"; 6:20 unknown minor key melody, possibly an improv; 6:35 "Smoke Gets in Your Eyes."

The Berlin "How High the Moon" testifies to a capacity for melodic invention that the rest of us—who don't happen to actually be Ella Fitzgerald—can barely imagine.

The combined force of the album—not least because of Granz's wise decision to title it *Mack the Knife* (a rare occasion when the producer used someone else's hit song as the title of a Fitzgerald concert album) and the Cold War angle combined to make the Berlin concert album a blockbuster hit, easily the most successful of all of Fitzgerald's many concert albums. Granz also released what *Billboard* called "Ella Fitzgerald's happy, live-performance version of 'Mack the Knife'" as a 45 rpm single, and the trade paper further described it as "a runaway sleeper hit." The album won two awards from NARAS at the 3rd Grammy Awards in 1960: Best Female Vocal Performance (Single), for "Mack the Knife," and Best Vocal Performance, Female (Album), and received what amounted to a third Grammy when it was inducted into the NARAS Hall of Fame in 1999. (The sequel, *Ella Returns to Berlin*, her follow-up concert from the same city in February 1961, wasn't issued until thirty years after the fact.)

It's hard to imagine that after even one listening of *Mack the Knife: Ella in Berlin*, anyone could doubt that Ella Fitzgerald was the greatest female vocalist of all time. If there be any such doubters reading this, then to them I say: let them come to Berlin, and relive that glorious evening in 1960, when Ella Fitzgerald made Berliners of us all. Well before President Kennedy went to Berlin, Ella Fitzgerald had already been there and gone.

20

Judy Garland

Judy at Carnegie Hall

(1961)

The classic 1939 film of *The Wizard of Oz* ends with Dorothy and Aunt Em arguing over whether the Marvelous Land of Oz is "a real truly live place" or merely something that the girl just imagined in an especially vivid Technicolor dream. Likewise, Keats's even more classic poem *Ode to a Nightingale* ends with the narrator wondering whether he is awake or asleep. In both cases, the lines are blurred at the point where reality ends and dreams begin. This dilemma occurs over and over in the life and career of Judy Garland; with such a larger-than-life figure, boasting a talent much bigger than reality, it's hardly surprising that rumors and half-truths have surrounded every stage of her life, every element of her mythology.

For instance, one "fact" that Judy Garland fans have bruited about for fifty years is the idea that, in 1961, the legendary singer was on the way out and becoming increasingly unreliable. However, she still owed one album to Capitol Records from an old contract and the label, despairing of ever getting her into the studio, opted instead to record her forthcoming Carnegie Hall show. They were desperate, the story goes, and it was the only option open to them. This notion is still repeated all over the Internet and in many documentaries, but it just isn't so.

In fact, probably the opposite was true: Garland had fully emerged from a period of decline, and was approaching what is sometimes described

as her "comeback." As Garland historian Lawrence Schulman points out, Capitol actually had a surplus of releasable Garland material in the vault by early 1961. The label was sitting on two complete, unreleased albums: *That's Entertainment!*, taped in June 1960, followed by her London sessions, done during her August 1960 tour of the U.K. (and eventually issued in 1972). Capitol held back on releasing the British material as they realized that a live album from Carnegie Hall was a possibility.

She had already been working in formal concert halls; unlike Frank Sinatra and Ella Fitzgerald, she had never sung with dance bands or in supper clubs, so the idea of playing big rooms, at least the size of a Broadway theater (such as her famous shows at the New York Palace), was already a fait accompli. In fall 1960, the revitalized Garland played a series of dates in Europe, and between January and April 1961 had done eight big concerts across the United States. She had, indeed, been regularly playing large halls since the mid-1950s. But at that point, those were closer to variety/vaudeville shows, with Garland headlining a bill that included dancers and other acts. By 1960, she was working in a more formal concert format, with no other acts on the bill.

Clearly, she was ready—and Capitol Records was well aware of it. Before 1961, the most important artist to record live was Ella Fitzgerald, who had done several excellent concert recordings, and whose 1960 *Mack the Knife: Ella in Berlin* in particular was a blockbuster. There were also successful live albums by Sarah Vaughan, Mel Tormé, a classic Carnegie Hall album by Billie Holiday, Sammy Davis Jr., and Tony Bennett.

Singers of the Great American Songbook, be they on the jazz or pop side of the fence, were being shoved upstairs, out of the pop singles market and into the concert halls. There had almost always been scattered appearances here and there by pop singers in a formal setting: even Al Jolson had appeared in something like a formal concert hall, and in the summer of 1943 both Sinatra and, coincidentally, Garland herself sang in symphonic situations (Garland with radio conductor Andre Kostelanetz). Ella Fitzgerald had sung at Carnegie Hall as early as 1947, as a special guest on a concert by Dizzy Gillespie's big band, and then repeatedly as a member of the Jazz at the Philharmonic troupe. Billie Holiday gave a historically important recital at Carnegie in November 1956 in conjunction with the publication of her memoir, *Lady Sings the Blues.* Harry Belafonte did two celebrated Carnegie concerts, in April 1959 and May 1960, both of which were released on LP by RCA Victor. In between the two Belafonte concerts, in May 1959, the young pop star Joni James did a Carnegie show that was released on MGM Records. Sinatra had also occasionally appeared at Carnegie, inevitably for political or philanthropic events. (Just a few months before Garland, in January 1961, Sinatra brought the Rat Pack and Tony Bennett into Carnegie as a part of an all-star benefit for the Reverend Martin Luther King.)

Thus, the idea of a Garland at Carnegie album must have had great appeal to Capitol, and was far from an act of desperation.

Garland's opening salvo (following the overture) on April 23, 1961, makes it clear that she comes from a theatrical background rather than a jazz or big band one: "When You're Smiling," the 1929 pop-jazz standard, is a typical rousing opener. The song was written by Mark Fisher (no relation to Fred, Marvin, or Doris Fisher), a celebrated bandleader of the era who played at the Edgewater Beach Hotel in Chicago and recorded for Columbia. "Smiling" was closely associated with Louis Armstrong, who recorded it commercially three times and, equally important, inspired other singers to do it, especially such immediate Armstrong disciples as Billie Holiday, Frank Sinatra, and Bing Crosby—in fact, Garland had already done it about a decade earlier as a solo feature on Bing Crosby's radio show.

She takes "Smiling" in mid-tempo—certainly bright, but not terribly fast—and not anywhere near as fast as most Vegas-style opening numbers, like "I'm Gonna Live Till I Die." You might say it's noncommittally fast—the next number could be either fast or slow and there would be effective contrast. What makes this "Smiling" notable is that after the opening chorus, Garland unexpectedly launches into a "patter" section, prepared for her by long-term mentor Roger Edens. The new section delineates the virtues of smiling in the face of adversity, in a low-key kind of a way. The special lyric includes the line "If you suddenly find out you've been deceived / Don't get peeved. . . . and for Heaven's sakes, retain a calm demeanor / When a cop walks up and hands you a subpoena." After the patter, she goes back to the familiar melody, but this time with a new Edens lyric: "But when you're crying, don't you know, that your make-up starts to run . . ." She delivers it in her signature, "vaudeville"-style half-time, making it more exciting by first slowing it down, then getting gradually faster and building to a big belting climax.

Sinatra and Fitzgerald and most singers from a big band background would consider it enough of a personalization to do their own arrangement, by Nelson Riddle or whomever, but Garland has to take it a step further: by adding new lyrics and that whole other spoken / comedy section, she's made it into something more like a number from a movie or a TV variety show. We'll see Garland doing this several times more during this concert—most famously, perhaps, on "San Francisco."

She has effectively turned an old pop standard into a contemporary show tune, and follows it with two comparatively swinging arrangements of vintage Broadway numbers—neither of these, not coincidentally, describes the specific state of being in love, but both are about being adjacent to it: "Almost Like Being in Love" (from *Brigadoon*) and

"This Can't Be Love" (from *The Boys from Syracuse*). Garland doesn't quite swing like Fitzgerald or Sinatra, but the charts are in a swinging four and she more than keeps the beat going. Putting the two numbers together—and adding in more original lyrics ("love to love, glad I'm alive / Love to live, think I'll survive")—transforms the material into a completely new, wholly original setpiece. From the basic swinging dance beat of "Can't," when she returns to "Almost," she again goes into something like vaudeville half-time—the drummer (one Bill Lavorgna) plays a consistent set of rolls behind her. The percussion plays a key role in Garland's climax—fully as important, for instance, as the drummer would in a number by, say, Dizzy Gillespie.

Most editions of the *Carnegie* album have this medley running for six and a half minutes, but in actuality it ends in less than four minutes, and the rest of the track is Garland telling a funny story about a French hairdresser. This is one more reason why she's so sympathetic: in moments like these she's the opposite of a self-entitled diva; rather every story she tells casts her as the *schlmozzle*, the one whom bad things happen to. She goes around expecting everyone to dump on her, rather than kowtow to her.

The mood slows down for the evening's first real ballad, the 1922 "Do It Again." This might be described as coming from late in George Gershwin's early period—one of his last notable songs before he entered into a full-time collaboration with his lyricist brother, Ira. This lyric is by show-biz mainstay Buddy DeSylva, who later enjoyed a career as film producer. DeSylva was quite a talented lyricist—indeed, "Do It Again" is fully the equal of any of the hundreds of George and Ira classics from 1924 on.

Garland's interpretation makes it better still; she completely reimagines "Do It Again" in her own image. In 1958, she sang it with Nelson Riddle on her best studio album, *Judy in Love*. That Riddle arrangement opens with the original 1922 verse ("Tell me, tell me, what did you do to me?"), sung slowly, but when she gets to the chorus, the tempo picks up into something more like swing time. Less than two years later, she recorded her perfected

interpretation at her 1960 London studio session (released as *Judy in London* on LP and *The London Sessions* on CD). This much improved version is in slow, romantic-ballad-time all the way, stately, elegant, and amazingly sexy. It opens with an entirely new verse ("You really shouldn't have done it, you hadn't any right / I really shouldn't have let you kiss me . . ."), and she sings the chorus achingly slow—Billie Holiday has nothing on her. The strings are barely audible, the bass fiddle emphasizing the beats is considerably more prominent. The song is about conflicting moods: it fully captures the mind-set of a young flapper-to-be at the start of the Jazz Age (like those in Fitzgerald's *This Side of Paradise*): she wants to be if not sexually, at least romantically liberated, to kiss boys, but also to be a good girl who doesn't disobey her mother, who told her "it is naughty." This conflict between being naughty or nice is what drives the lyric. No one has better captured these conflicting impulses than Garland, raging hormones on one side balanced by an equally raging sense of propriety on the other. (In my mind's eye, I visualize Garland as Esther Smith in *Meet Me in St. Louis* singing this song. I know that's roughly twenty years earlier, but try telling that to my mind's eye.)

The tension between propriety and erotic release is heightened by different, new lyrics in the out-chorus (which starts with "turn out the lights"), in which she sings, "I know tomorrow morning you will say 'goodbye and amen' / But until then, please do it again." This takes the scenario to a whole other level—not a sixteen-year-old girl debating whether or not to be kissed, but an adult woman, wary, from experience perhaps, of being seduced and abandoned. Garland conveys mountains of emotion without so much as raising her voice; the track is over six minutes (there's a ten-second spoken apology for a frog in her throat), well over twice as long as the 1958 studio version, and it fully justifies every second.

Judy Garland singing "Do It Again" is a concert highlight—as well as a career highlight—and what follows, in carefully cultivated contrast, is deliberate and willful kitsch. Under ordinary circumstances, Garland doing "You Go to My Head," the classic 1938 ballad of love and lush lives—would also be a highlight. But someone thought to have Garland do the song in a mock-mambo style— this is what she would sing if she were a guest on *I Love Lucy*, dueting with Desi at the Tropicana. She recorded this arrangement in the 1960 London sessions, and there it almost works: the tempo is relaxed enough for her to capture the feeling of the song—and rather exuberantly at that. After the first chorus, the clave beat more or less disappears and the whole thing eases into a more relaxed basic 4/4, then ritards down to rubato for a characteristically Garland climax. This is one of the few examples where the studio version is better than the live. At Carnegie, she sings it much faster (the track is a whole minute shorter), and everything gets away from her: the mood, the beat, and even the lyrics ("I forgot the goldarned words . . .")—she gets flustered and starts making up nonsense syllables that aren't quite worthy of the term "scat."

The next five songs all derive from what was then Garland's current album, the still unreleased *That's Entertainment!* arranged and conducted by guitarist Jack Marshall (best known as the nominal musical director on Peggy Lee's mega-hit "Fever"). "Alone Together" brings us the dark, heavy, and "serious" side of Garland at its most convincing, building consistently toward an epic climax. (After the song is finished, she says, "If I'm known at all, I'm known for singing sad, tragic songs.") For decades, all kinds of conspiracy theories have swirled about this number—the most repeated of these was that this song was not recorded at Carnegie this night, but in the studio months afterward, and inserted into the *Carnegie* master tape with overdubbed applause.

The more prosaic truth, as Schulman has determined, is that two things happened: Garland started the song standing slightly too far away from the microphone, and then the tape ran out mid-song on Capitol's main recorder. Both problems were easily solved: on Capitol's definitive CD issue (released at the time of the fortieth anniversary in 2001), the volume level was adjusted, and a backup tape with the complete performance of "Alone Together" was utilized. "Alone Together" is one of the more dramatic numbers at the concert, even when shorn of such brouhaha—and it's also part

of the larger sphere of drama that Garland continually inspires: if the same thing had happened at a concert by Ray Charles or even Elvis, no one would have bothered to make up stories about it.

Speaking of conspiracies, Garland then confides in the crowd, "I do like to sing jazz, but they won't let me," and then, in a moment of self-parody, adds, "I don't know who 'they' are," as if implying that there's some unnamed force of Judy police out there patrolling Carnegie, who only want to hear her singing those "sad, tragic songs." She announces that she's about to join forces with "nine men in the band." Among his other talents, Jack Marshall had a knack for arranging light, swinging orchestrations using fewer musicians than the full studio contingents generally heard on Capitol vocal albums, and the three charts that follow feature Garland in a deliberately—but never self-consciously—jazzy vein.

The Gershwins' "Who Cares?" lunges forward in a way that allows Garland to act as if she's not sure what's supposed to happen next: "I lead, right?" She counts off and then adds, to the crowd rather than the band, "Oh! It works!"—acting as if she's genuinely surprised. Marshall's arrangement is fast and boppy in the manner of the California cool jazz of the period, and such midsized combos as Shorty Rogers and His Giants or Shelly Manne and His Men. The bop tempo hardly puts a damper on the Garland pizzazz: she quickly brings the brief chart to an exciting and satisfying finish, then announces that the next tune is in "a striptease tempo," adding "we don't do it, we just talk about it." When someone in the crowd apparently makes a suggestion that Garland do more than "talk about it," rather than being offended she comes right back with "Ah heck! Nah, not in Carnegie Hall, it wouldn't look right." A "moaning" clarinetist (in Garland's phrase) launches Irving Berlin's "Puttin' on the Ritz" in a vigorous traditional jazz two-beat—her so-called "striptease tempo."

The jazz portion continues with the Gershwins' musical inquiry "How Long Has This Been Going On?" Garland is overheard telling pianist Mort Lindsey to count off the tempo—evidently she has little faith in her own ability to do so. She delivers it slow and sultry, rather like Lee Wiley or Billie Holiday, full of intimate feeling, backed only by rhythm section—prominent piano and guitar; even when she modulates and gets considerably louder and belty-er, she doesn't compromise the intimate mood. Then she counts off and the jazz segment concludes with another bright bouncer of a jazz standard, "Just You, Just Me." Technically speaking, she still isn't swinging, not like Ella Fitzgerald or Sarah Vaughan, but, to quote the title of the song that launched the segment, who cares? (Garland came close enough to swinging so that she was invited to headline at the Newport Jazz Festival a few months later.)

After having left her comfort zone for eleven minutes, Garland closes the first act with two signatures, "The Man That Got Away" and "San Francisco"; she sang both a thousand times, but these performances are extra-special. Calling "The Man That Got Away" a torch song is like calling the San Francisco Fire a wienie roast; it's a great roaring bonfire of a torch song. Garland's performances are typically described as big and dramatic, but "Man That Got Away" is incredibly subtle, conveying the idea that she's holding back as much emotion as possible, rather than deluging listeners in it. There are moments when she seems about to break loose, as on about 1:50, on the line "It's all a crazy game," but then she de-crescendos again, barely murmuring "good riddance goodbye" as quietly as possible. She does this repeatedly, building up, then paring down, like one lover teasing another, delaying the climax for what seems like a torturous, erotic eternity.

"The Man That Got Away" had been written by Harold Arlen and Ira Gershwin for Garland in *A Star Is Born* (1954), although the melody was originally composed in 1941 as "I Can't Believe My Eyes," with a lyric by Johnny Mercer, a "trunk song" dropped from the score of *Blues in the Night*. (Mercer, who had an intimate relationship with the young Garland, must have viewed this as the song that got away about the gal that got away.) No one else could make the song such a classic; Sinatra sang it wonderfully in both the 1950s and the 1980s in many concerts, but Garland has the magic. Arlen, who composed many a Judy signature, provided her with an appropriately expanded

canvas to accommodate her expanded dynamic and emotional range: the song is sixty bars long, and though it's in AABA format, each A section is extra-long and extra-intense. The bridge, however, is much briefer and quieter—as if Arlen and Gershwin intended it to be meditative respite, a lower volume contrast to the rest of the song. Garland almost talks part of it, and her phrasing here is endearingly awkward, she breathes and pauses in unnatural places. Sinatra wouldn't have approved, but in her case it works, it makes her overall performance seem more spontaneous and heartfelt, as if she's blurting the words out in the only way she can, completely bereft of any kind of artifice or even craft.

The track is a full five minutes, one of the longest in the Garland oeuvre, including thirty seconds of applause on both sides—but notable in that it's only a single chorus of the song straight through, with no repeats. She finally brings us to the climax at the end of the bridge, an emotional peak that she sustains through the first part of the last A. But then, she ends rather quietly, tapering off to a quiet finish in a manner that actually suggests Sinatra more than Garland—which partially explains why the Chairman felt the song so suited him.

It's a canny move to make the ending of "Man That Got Away" not anticlimactic but truly preclimactic, because the lull allows her to end the first half with a huge wallop. "San Francisco" is a slice of turn-of-the-century Americana written by three Jews (Walter Jurmann, Bronislaw Kaper, and Gus Kahn), the first two of whom were relatively recent refugees from Hitler at the time they composed this song for the 1936 Hollywood historical epic *San Francisco*. It's technically a movie song, but Garland makes it into a true show tune; in fact, in her hands it's probably the greatest Act One closer that ever was.

She begins with not so much a verse as a prologue, a piece of special material written by Roger Edens, and she sings it with comically exaggerated mock drama, describing how the song was introduced in the movie. After the opening line ("I never will forget Jeanette MacDonald . . ."), there's a long pause where the crowd reacts. She grumbles and grunts on the word "ruins" and then the technology echoes her when there's the sound of a microphone mishap right after "and sang . . . and sang . . ." From the slow, portentous prologue she snaps into the chorus, delivered in the fast and peppy 2/4 of a classic show tune. At the end of the first chorus, she ritards again, in vaudeville half-time, a unique Garland device, a way of using a slowed-down tempo to increase excitement, in another new patter section written by Edens. In the last few bars, she seems to be doing everything at once, the tempo is at once fast and slow, the mood at once silly and serious. It's an epic conclusion, and it's only the end of the first half of the evening.

Better still was to come.

After the audience has been doing "whatever it is you do at intermissions," as Garland says, she returns with "That's Entertainment!" This has the punch and power of an Act Two overture—the instrumental break has a heavy bass drum and overall the piece has the energy of a circus parade, in very fast 2/4 time. Garland sings it like a July Fourth flag-waver in support of everyone who ever told a joke or sang their heart out, or rather as if it were the national anthem of her country, which is the land of pizzazz, and she is the greatest patriot who ever lived. ("That's Entertainment!" is nearly seven minutes, but ideally it should have been divided into two tracks, since three minutes is a spoken anecdote detailing her misadventures with the English press during her recent appearance in London.)

After that humorous tale, the crowd is in a very merry mood indeed, and Garland hits 'em with two absolute zingers. These are a pair of masterpiece orchestrations written for her by the greatest of all pop music orchestrators, Nelson Riddle, the first one slow ("I Can't Give You Anything but Love," from the 1958 album, *Judy in Love*), the other fast ("Come Rain or Come Shine," from the 1956 album, *Judy*).

"I Can't Give You Anything but Love" begins with another original prologue. The song actually did have a verse, which virtually no one since Ethel Waters ever sang. (It began with the line, "Gee but it's tough to be broke, kid . . .") The verse

that Garland sang is completely original in terms of both words and music (it begins "Now that it's your birthday . . .") and bears no similarities to the actual verse by Dorothy Fields and Jimmy McHugh. Once again, my money's on Edens, but why anybody felt it was necessary to come up with a new verse remains a mystery, except that the uniqueness of it all makes Garland's interpretation even more special. (Postscript: it should be noted that the "Garland" verse is sung much more frequently by singers in the twenty-first century—Rufus Wainwright, Marilyn Maye, and many others—than the "real" one by Fields and McHugh.)

"I Can't Give You Anything but Love" offers Garland at her most maternal, her tenderest, and most compassionate. For most of the first chorus Riddle backs her with prominent support from the bass as well as shimmering strings that suggest stars glittering in the distant heavens—which become even more celestial at the end of the bridge (behind the line "all the things you've always pined for"), a Riddle-ism that anticipates the famous shimmering stars background he later wrote for Sinatra's "Lost in the Stars." (This is the sound that Bill Miller, Riddle's frequent pianist, described as "Nelson-style polytones.") As with the studio version, the Carnegie includes a rhapsodic, romantic tenor sax solo in the instrumental break.

"Come Rain or Come Shine" is a wildly exciting quasi-Latin arrangement that had roots in an earlier chart that Riddle had written for Rosemary Clooney's TV show. As the arranger said in an interview with NPR's Robert Windeler more than twenty-five years later, "It had the same general feel to it, not note for note but close enough. I remember Joe Shribman, who handled [Clooney] at the time, said 'I think we're in trouble.' [I said,] '*We're* not in trouble, Joe—*I'm* in trouble. You're fine.' I went back there and [Rosemary] gently reprimanded me. Don't rub two girl singers together. It was very tempting sometimes when you had something that was successful to use it again."

The Clooney arrangement sounds more like one of Stan Kenton's Cuban fires, with a distinct Afro-Latin jazz accent; the Garland version makes greater use of dynamics, and builds gradually from soft to loud, going from just bongos in the intro to a loud, almost screaming orchestra. And though there's also a Pan-American element to it, the Garland chart has more of a showbiz (rather than jazz) groove overall. Both are somewhat inspired by Peggy Lee's infamous Pan-American take on "Lover," but Riddle has a lot more skill and subtlety, in both versions. We actually hear the intro twice at Carnegie Hall: following prolonged applause, there's what seems like a false start on "Come Rain or Come Shine," the percussionist plays the bongo-drum introduction, but Garland doesn't enter—there's a pause, he plays the intro again, and this time she starts. Expertly she builds to a fever pitch: she hits the climax at the end of the second chorus bridge, whereupon she reaches the words "I'm gonna be true, if you let me." She then repeats "let me, let me, let me . . ."—she teases and torments, like delaying a lover's sexual climax. Music just doesn't get any more exciting than this.

Following "Come Rain or Come Shine," she introduces composer Harold Arlen in the audience, encouraging him to take a bow. (He would also be similarly introduced from the stage roughly a year later when Tony Bennett did his own landmark concert at Carnegie Hall.) "I think after all that insanity, we should calm down," she says, introducing a comparatively quiet segment where she sings with just the piano of musical director Mort Lindsey. Rodgers and Hart's "You're Nearer" gets the intimate treatment, followed by the Gershwins' "A Foggy Day," with verse, and then, surprisingly, Noël Coward's "If Love Were All," which is probably the best of all. She promises the crowd that she'll get the full band back if they find the voice-piano idea boring, and then apologizes for not remembering the words, which also makes the segment seem more spontaneous. All three, especially the last, are simple, direct, plaintive. She sings the bridge to the Coward number in a manner that really seems as if she's thinking to herself, louder and more aggressive at the start ("but then if somebody splendid"), hushed and reverent at the end ("wanted to have me near"). In the last eight bars she sounds self-assured, even defiant, while still maintaining the intimate vibe—it's at once a musical conversation between singer and pianist and a woman reason-

ing things out in her own head; a dialogue that's at once external and internal.

Following the three Garland-Lindsey duets, there's a fade down and a fade back up, as if there had been some sort of edit (even though all evidence points to the current CD editions being the completely complete concert). Without any spoken intro, we then hear her launch into "Zing! Went the Strings of My Heart." She'd been singing that song ever since it was written, at the start of her career; apparently it was part of her original audition for MGM, who later had her reprise it in the 1938 picture *Listen Darling*. The 1961 performance takes its cue from Nelson Riddle's arrangement from the 1958 *Judy in Love* album. Garland's singing is exuberant, but here the orchestra assembled at Carnegie is noticeably inferior to the standard of playing by the Capitol studio musicians three years earlier. The tempo is faster, and where the studio version is much more rhythmically subtle, something like a South American batucada rhythm, at Carnegie, drummer Lavorgna sounds like he's playing for a burlesque show. It's a much heavier beat. Garland's energy, however, is exceptional, and the crowd responds in kind.

"Stormy Weather" is the third Arlen song on the Carnegie program; the biggest, however—the big one—is still ahead. "Stormy" shows that Garland wasn't the only fabulous diva for whom Arlen supplied the all-time signature song, since "Stormy Weather" is forever associated with Garland's onetime MGM colleague Lena Horne. As much as the song is indisputably Lena's property (she actually sang it twice in *The Lady and Her Music* on Broadway), I've personally always preferred Garland's version. (In fact, Garland had been singing "Stormy Weather" since it was first written in 1933—when she was eleven—although she didn't record it until 1960.) Horne was generally sassy and defiant on "Stormy Weather," but Garland is fragile and vulnerable. When she repeats the word "Love" four times, she gives each utterance a completely different intonation—and implication. On the final section, starting with "Can't Go On," she sounds exaltedly downtrodden, as if she were somehow glorious in her misery, magnificent in defeat.

There follows a section of four familiar Garland chestnuts, known as her "olio medley" in a reference to minstrel show tradition. All but one of which were vintage songs from World War I or earlier, and the fourth is one that expertly evokes the turn of the twentieth century: "You Made Me Love You" (sung by her in *Broadway Melody of 1938* (1937), although here without the famous "Dear Mr. Gable" monologue), "For Me and My Gal" (another old-timer, which she sang in *For Me and My Gal,* 1942), and there's also "Rock-a-Bye Your Baby" (about which more below). Lastly, "The Trolley Song," which had been expressly written for Garland (in *Meet Me in St. Louis,* 1944) evokes the pre–World War I era just as evocatively.

"Rock-a-Bye Your Baby (With a Dixie Melody)" belongs to this section, but it's a stand-alone, not part of the medley. The song is an anthem to the whole concept of singing, drenched in the traditions of minstrelsy, Broadway, and showbiz in general. It was long associated with Al Jolson (who introduced it in the 1918 *Sinbad*), and perhaps it's no coincidence that Garland waited for about a six-week mourning period after Jolson's death in 1950 before she sang it for the first time in public. Also not coincidentally, that performance occurred on the Bing Crosby radio show: where Jolson was Garland's spiritual rabbi, Crosby was an actual benefactor who supported her during a lean period.

As it happens, "Rock-a-Bye Your Baby (With a Dixie Melody)" is a fitting anthem for Garland to sing in honor of musical mentors and parental figures. As sung by Jolson, the narrative is roughly that Mammy's little sonny boy is home again, and as he walks through the cabin door he pleads for Mammy to sing to him like she did when he was a little pickaninny. "Sing 'Old Black Joe' just as though you had me on your knee." It's a song that sings the praises of the act of singing, and in its own way it's bigger and more all-inclusive than all the individual "mammy songs" that Jolson ever sang because it celebrates the entire genre of mammy songs. Jolson's best documented performance of the song is in his first film, the breakthrough 1926 all-talking, all-singing short subject, *Al Jolson in a Plantation Act;* here, he introduces it with a coyly defensive speech arguing for the validity of "mammy songs." The lyrics (by Sam Lewis and Joe Young) are a veritable orgy of mammy-isms. Garland makes it a song about the glories of singing being passed down from Jolson's generation to hers—the "Mammy mine" that she refers to is obviously Jolson himself. The gender issue is insignificant—Jolson is the Mammy of us all.

The Carnegie performance of "Rock-a-Bye" is probably Garland's finest. Jolson did his famous shtick in the middle—he talks directly to his mammy in a spoken monologue; and Garland does hers as well, she delivers the entire song in vaudeville style half-time, as if the whole song were one big sustained climax from beginning to end. Garland's performance, in the old-school showbiz parlance of *Variety,* is totally "socko" and the crowd goes wild.

Appropriately, this is the formal close of the concert—everything that happens after falls under the heading of an encore, whether planned or otherwise. Garland takes her bows over the orchestra's instrumental rendition of what is clearly her theme, "Over the Rainbow." Rather than leave the stage, as might be expected, we hear her talk back and forth with the audience, uttering the most quoted line of patter from the concert, "I know, we'll sing 'em all and stay all night. I don't ever want to go home. I never . . ." (In subsequent concerts, fans would be chanting these lines to her from the audience.)

In Garland's hands (and tonsils) "That's Entertainment!," as we've seen, becomes the national anthem of anyone who's ever stood on a stage and belted a number to the kids in the balcony. Likewise, "Rock-a-Bye Your Baby" is now a universal salute for anyone who's ever sung a song on a more intimate level to a loved one, a sweetheart or a family member, and, yes, even to one's mammy or sonny boy.

But "Over the Rainbow" is now something even bigger and more spectacular: it's the rallying cry for everyone in the whole wide world who's ever dared to dream—about anything. You can't help noticing how much her rendition has grown and matured since it was introduced by her in 1939 (in *The Wizard of Oz,* as everyone knows)— it's matured, but not necessarily become older-sounding: she actually sounds younger and more innocent than she did at age sixteen, and thus more invested in the deeper meaning of the text. In her earlier treatments, Garland sang it like a little girl in search of refuge, "a place where there isn't any trouble"; a generation later, it seems more like Garland is expressing a dream of international peace and brotherhood. It's no longer a song about a childhood fairyland, it's now an anthem of universal hope and solidarity, a forerunner and close relative of John Lennon's "Imagine" or Bernstein and Sondheim's "Somewhere." It's an understated prayer for all of humanity.

Following which, she takes more bows (to the "Rainbow" instrumental), and finishes with three more standbys, two of which, following "San Francisco" (and, in a way, "Over the Rainbow") are songs about places: "Swanee" a gangbuster number (also from the Jolson canon as well as George Gershwin's biggest hit within his lifetime) that climaxes in the longest-held note of the evening. (There's about five minutes of "Rainbow" bows afterward, which also should have been edited into a different track.) She addresses the crowd again: "'Chicago'? All right. . . . We don't have an arrangement of 'Liza.' We have Liza here" (at 5:45), indicating her fifteen-year-old daughter, Liza Minnelli herself, "but we haven't got an arrangement." After several waves of applause, it is decided that "After You've Gone" would make a good immediate pre-exit number, as the musicians look for a chart they hadn't expected to play. Garland wryly observes, "Now they'll shuffle their music—like a poker game!" "After You've Gone" brings back more ragtime-vaudeville era hijinks: once again she modulates into half-time, and then unexpectedly snaps back into full speed ahead at the very end.

At least a full minute of "Rainbow" music again follows. And then "Do you really want more? Aren't you tired? . . . We've only got one more. We'll do, we'll do, we'll do 'Chicago'!" Fred Fisher's "Chi-

cago" is a companion piece to "San Francisco," both of these historical homages to celebrated cities were rendered by Garland in epic-level production numbers with arrangements and special lyrics by Roger Edens (and both were officially recorded, for the first time, at the 1960 London session). The chart of "Chicago" is at once archaic, in a jaunty, syncopated 2/4, and modern, with modish bongo drums heard throughout. At any other concert, it would be a showstopper, here it's almost anticlimactic. But not quite—it's just a closer that could hardly be expected to eclipse "Rock-a-Bye" and "Rainbow."

In various chronicles, Garland is sometimes described as having a fall-and-rise, similar to Sinatra's career pattern of ten years earlier. The April 1961 Carnegie concert thus takes the place of *From Here to Eternity* in the Garland saga, although one could say that the 1954 *A Star Is Born* was also a "comeback" vehicle. The *Carnegie Hall* recording was a huge hit, a sensation even—placing number one on the pop album charts and staying there for an unbelievable 199 weeks—which, for a double LP set especially, was no small accomplishment. *Carnegie* did foreshadow a second—or third—wind in the Garland career: it led directly to her 1962 TV special with Sinatra and Dean Martin, and from there to her 1963–64 CBS TV series, as well as to an ongoing run of concert appearances in major halls across the world up until her death in 1969. Garland's concerts sparked a career, in much the same way that renewed touring would later do for both Sinatra and Elvis Presley. Both of these men would create amazing moments in concerts in the last phase of their careers, but neither of them achieved what Garland did on April 23, 1961. It was that rare moment in the cultural firmament when pop music became something like Henry V's victory on St. Crispin's Day: you'd give anything just to be able to say that you were there.

Johnny Hartman

John Coltrane and Johnny Hartman

(1963)

With the possible exception of Lee Wiley and *Night in Manhattan,* there's no other major artist whose reputation rests so firmly on one single album. On the strength of this one work alone, Hartman is a great singer, beloved of fans, critics, aficionados, and, perhaps, most importantly, entire generations of singers, most of whom have never heard more than six tracks by him. But those six tracks are indeed miraculous; it hardly seems like a waste that he would have spent his entire career up to that time building up to this one masterpiece.

Both Johnny Hartman and Lee Wiley were among the most gifted singers of jazz and the American Songbook who ever drew breath, yet circumstances, and in some cases their own foolishness, conspired against them. Their total output is about ten CDs each. (At least released in their lifetimes; some other live and unissued material was issued posthumously in both cases.) I remember in the 1980s, a few years after Hartman's death in 1983, that when some hi-fi company invented a CD player that could hold ten CDs at a time, thinking that such a device could easily accommodate the complete works of either Hartman or Wiley. In the second decade of the new century, their total combined output could more than easily fit on the smallest flash drive or iPod that has ever been sold.

And not only is their output small to begin with, but it could actually be further reduced to one album apiece—it's impossible to think of Wiley's legacy without *Night in Manhattan* or Hartman's without his classic 1963 meeting with tenor saxophone icon John Coltrane. In fact, to the extent that anybody has even heard of Hartman at all, it's usually because of *John Coltrane and Johnny Hartman.*

It's hard to imagine why he isn't better known; as a singer, Hartman seemed to mark the perfect halfway point between Frank Sinatra and Billy Eckstine, the deep resonant voice of Eckstine combined with the subtlety and attention to lyrical detail of Sinatra, as well as the intelligence and musicianship that both icons shared. Musically, he seemed to have everything, including career breaks at the right points—a berth with Dizzy Gillespie's orchestra at the height of the trumpeter's fame, a contract with RCA Victor just at the very moment after Eckstine had increased the visibility of black baritone balladeers (and the combined efforts of Eckstine and Sinatra had made all their careers possible), and influential supporters like Steve Allen, Tony Bennett, and Sammy Davis. Yet somehow, even with all those elements in place— the most important of which were his talent and sublime musical taste—Hartman never seemed to make it. He attained the upper brackets of artistry, but not of the music business. He kept going, which was achievement enough, when rock and then soul threatened to put his entire generation out to pasture, but he never had a hit single or became anything like a household word, even in black households.

And yet, even by the time of his death at age sixty in 1983, this album from twenty years earlier had already become a widely appreciated "turntable favorite"—and certainly after it was reissued on compact disc a few years later, for the first of several occasions, he would have been able to retire on the royalties. Even if his overall career was not the success it deserved to be, this album was, on every conceivable level, a major accomplishment, artistically and even commercially.

The considerable gaps in our knowledge of Hartman's career are filled by the long-awaited full-length biography, *The Last Balladeer: The Johnny Hartman Story,* written by Gregg Akkerman and published in 2012.

In 1962, John Coltrane released *Live at the Village Vanguard,* recorded at that lower Seventh Avenue jazz shrine a few months earlier. The second side of the original LP was taken up in its entirety by an original composition by the saxophonist titled "Chasin' the Trane." Ostensibly a blues, this sixteen-minute track was, at the time, probably the scariest, most ferociously avant-garde recording yet released by a major jazz star. To 1962 ears, it was a harrowing experience—and, even in retrospect, it remains that way, except, quite possibly in comparison to some of Coltrane's later, even more avant-garde far-out works. Many of the saxophonist's listeners were shocked by what they heard, including longtime supporter Ira Gitler. Both Coltrane himself and his producer, Bob Thiele, who ran Impulse! Records, were anxious to show that there was another side of Coltrane, and this, Akkerman feels, led to Coltrane's three highly celebrated, comparatively "inside" studio albums of 1963: *Ballads, Duke Ellington & John Coltrane,* and *John Coltrane and Johnny Hartman.* All three albums consisted primarily of standard material, mostly slow love songs (perhaps Coltrane's single most moving treatment of a standard ever is, in

fact, on the Ellington album: "In a Sentimental Mood"), and two were album-length team-ups— the only two of Coltrane's career.

It's not known who proposed the idea of Coltrane doing an album with a vocalist. Such a thing was, in fact, very rare—at this particular point there were very few team-ups even between a star pianist and a singer; the meeting of Doris Day and André Previn, taped in late 1961, had probably just been released at the time Coltrane and Thiele were discussing ideas. (*Duet,* the 1955 meeting of June Christy and Stan Kenton, was probably not on anyone's mind, excellent though it is.) When the idea of a tenor/singer album was discussed, Thiele's first thought was to approach one of the great female jazz vocalists, specifically Sarah Vaughan. But Coltrane wanted a male singer; he had come of age, musically, in the era of the great black baritones, like Billy Eckstine, who was a key figure in the new era of both romanticism and modernism. Eckstine helped nurture the birth of modern jazz, and as a singer was a central influence in the way ballads would be played from the mid-twentieth century onward, especially by tenor saxophonists of Coltrane's approximate generation. Coltrane had already recorded Eckstine's 1944 song "I Want to Talk About You" and, in fact, would help make it into a jazz standard. He was playing the song a lot in 1961, further indicating that the great black baritones were on the tenor's mind.

At the start of their respective careers, Hartman (1923–1983) and Coltrane (1926–1967) were both part of Dizzy Gillespie's band. Although they weren't in the group at the same time, they surely were aware of each other. At the start of 1963, Hartman had not recorded in four years, and that previous album, *And I Thought About You* (1959), was incredibly obscure—it had only been in print for roughly a minute and a half, noticed by no one. If they wanted a singer with name recognition, Hartman, who had primarily been working overseas at that time, would have been the last name on their list.

Coltrane, who was obviously familiar with *Songs from the Heart* (Hartman's classic album of 1955), may have likely viewed Hartman as a kindred spirit; Coltrane himself was virtually unknown until Miles Davis tapped him for his quintet at almost the age of thirty—comparatively old for either pop music or jazz at that time—and he might have regarded Hartman as another potential late bloomer. Coltrane said of Hartman, "He's a fine singer, and I wanted him to make a comeback." This is in itself a funny comment, since Hartman had never been a headliner—this album would make him bigger than he had ever been previously.

It seems to have been Coltrane who pushed the idea forward; both Thiele and Hartman himself had to be talked into it. In retrospect, it was a brilliant idea: Coltrane was aware early on that he and Hartman were a match made in heaven—the timbres of their instruments suited each other remarkably well. The family of saxophones was designed to correspond to sonic ranges of the human voice, both male and female: soprano, alto, tenor, baritone (and there are more obscure instruments at either end, the much higher sopranino and the lower bass saxophone). Yet the relationship is slightly askew: the tenor saxophone corresponds most accurately with the male baritone voice, and in this equation Coltrane and Hartman were especially simpatico. In listening to the finished album *John Coltrane and Johnny Hartman,* one almost never notices, for instance, that "My One and Only Love" opens with the melody stated by the tenor saxophone, rather than the baritone voice. Coltrane's phrasing of the love song here and throughout is so mellow, so sensitive, and so thoroughly influenced by his collaborator that it's almost as if Coltrane is trying to be his own Hartman—and doing a remarkably thorough job of it. The two are not only on the same page, they're on the same paragraph, the same sentence, the same word, the same comma.

Hartman was well aware that Coltrane was developing a reputation as one of the "furthest out" players in jazz, and thus when Thiele called him, his first reaction was that this was not the kind of guy that he wanted to make a record with. "I didn't think we'd fit too well, but [Thiele] told me to go to Birdland when I got back to the states and listen to him." The singer was highly trepidatious. "I didn't know if John could play the kind of stuff

that I did. And so I was a little reluctant at first," he said. "After hearing him play ballads the way he did, man, I said, 'Hey, beautiful.' So that's how we got together." Hartman didn't sing as part of the formal show at Birdland, but they tried a few tunes together afterward.

Akkerman guesstimates that this Birdland encounter transpired on Friday, March 1, 1963. On Wednesday the 6th, Coltrane brought what would later be known as his "classic quartet" (pianist McCoy Tyner, bassist Jimmy Garrison, drummer Elvin Jones) out to the Rudy Van Gelder Studio in Englewood Cliffs, New Jersey. Van Gelder's was the studio—and the engineer—of choice for all the major jazz labels of the period; all of Coltrane's albums for Prestige, Blue Note, and Impulse! would be recorded there. The March 6 date turned out to be an odd duck of a session: as of fifty years later, only one single track from this date has seen the light of day, and this is hardly typical Coltrane fare. The tune was "Vilia" (aka "Vilja" in the original spelling), one of the hit tunes from Franz Lehár's 1905 operetta *The Merry Widow.*

Coltrane was clearly in a ballad frame of mind: most of the *Ballads* album consisted of songs that he had learned from Frank Sinatra, including a few ("All or Nothing at All," "Nancy [With the Laughing Face]") that were overt Sinatra signatures. The Ellington album, in addition to the heartbreakingly beautiful "In a Sentimental Mood," also contained "My Little Brown Book," a Billy Strayhorn song that Ellington vocalist Al Hibbler (another member of the Eckstine-Hartman black baritone continuum) had already made into a classic. And then there was that mysterious "Vilia." None of these have any direct connection to the Hartman session, except that it does show that, at this particular point in time, Coltrane's mind was traveling down a track that was many rail yards away from "Chasin' the Trane."

Coltrane was clearly enamored of Hartman's *Songs from the Heart,* the singer's first album and his best thus far. Although not as famous as the 1963 session, this 1955 album remains an absolute masterpiece on its own terms: the combination of the singer's rapturous baritone, his sensitive but robust delivery, his amazingly intelligent interpretations, and the support of trumpeter Howard McGhee and pianist Ralph Sharon. (The first was an acolyte of Dizzy Gillespie, the second was the long-term musical partner of Tony Bennett.)

So, work on the Coltrane-Hartman album proceeded: between Saturday, March 2, and Tuesday, March 5, six tunes had been selected and rough arrangements worked out. Truth to tell, the "arrangements," so to speak, weren't much (compared with a typical singer–big band album of the period at least), all were set in slow ballad tempos, most starting with Hartman and then followed by a solo by Coltrane. The routines, such as they were, were mainly a matter of setting the keys with pianist McCoy Tyner.

The day after "Vilia," Thursday, March 7, Coltrane and the quartet returned to Englewood Cliffs, this time joined by Hartman. The saxophonist and the singer rode out together from Manhattan, and even that drive itself has become legendary. Six selections had been planned on, but somebody happened to turn on the car radio, and there was the voice of Nat King Cole singing Billy Strayhorn's "Lush Life." The singer and pianist had made the first commercial recording of this future jazz standard in 1949, and in 1961 he recorded the song again, utilizing the same original Pete Rugolo orchestration, but this time in stereo (for his career retrospective album *The Nat King Cole Story*). It's likely that this new stereo version was the one being played on the radio in 1963. The story goes that upon hearing "Lush Life," Hartman exclaims, "Man! This is one of the great tunes of all time." Coltrane then responds with a question, "Do you know it?" Indeed he did.

The first tune on the date was "They Say It's Wonderful" (from the 1946 hit show *Annie Get Your Gun*); we can be reasonably sure that Hartman learned it from Sinatra's contemporaneous single. The first sound we hear is neither Hartman nor Coltrane, but pianist McCoy Tyner, who plays Irving Berlin's classic tune with a gentility and harmonic acumen directly reminiscent of Ralph Sharon's accompaniments on *Songs from the Heart*. On this track, especially, the way that Coltrane plays lightly and politely around Hartman's

vocal directly suggests Howard McGhee's trumpet, with Coltrane holding his sound back to imply the saxophonic equivalent of a trumpet mute. In fact, the feathery, light sound that Coltrane gets when he circles Hartman sounds more like McGhee than any of the major tenor obbligato specialists already famous for accompanying singers, like Lester Young or Stan Getz.

As delicate and restrained as Coltrane is, Hartman is even more so—like Sinatra, he puts in exactly the correct amount of emphasis for each note, nothing more, nothing less. After Hartman's first chorus, Coltrane enters only slightly more forcefully, with an entrance that's at once relaxed and yet dramatic, enhancing Hartman's mood rather than calling attention to itself. After a full chorus, the tempo slows down, and Hartman reenters at the bridge ("you leave your house one morning . . ."), singing it rubato, as if it were a verse rather than an out-chorus. He sings the last eight bars ("to hold a girl in your arms is wonderful"). He slows down again for the coda, with a descending pitch that Gregg Akkerman describes as "a beautifully dissonant penultimate note," an ending reused from "Moonlight in Vermont" on *Songs from the Heart*, further playing up the connection with the 1955 LP.

The second of the six tunes cut at the session was the one they heard on the car radio, "Lush Life." This is a completely classic, even archetypical reading, which uses the Cole version as a template in terms of tempo and overall format, although without the large-scale orchestra and strings—and bongos!—that accompanied Cole in both 1949 and 1961. Hartman follows the general path of Cole's vocal, but with key differences, the overall phrasing is reminiscent of Cole (especially in the opening section, sometimes thought of as the equivalent of the verse), as in the way he puts the emphasis on the opening line, "I *used* to visit all the very gay places . . ." but still, he's clearly worked out his own way of singing it; for instance, he doesn't repeat Cole's infamous mistake, bowdlerizing Strayhorn's line "your siren song" as "your siren of song" (which doesn't even make sense), Hartman, unlike Cole, gets the lyric right. He's also more inclined to play with the time than might be possible in a full-scale orchestration, as in the line "*Ahhhh* yes I was wrong . . ." Coltrane's solo also finds a remarkable balance between the ballad mood and modern jazz aggressive; it's romantic without in any way being mere make-out music.

As we've seen, Coltrane, who had already recorded "Lush Life" as an instrumental on one of his first sessions as a bandleader, in 1958, was, in 1963, in an Ellington-Strayhorn kind of a mood. He was also thinking about Nat Cole; the 1962 *Ballads* album included many nods to Sinatra, but Coltrane also played "Too Young to Go Steady," an obscure Jimmy McHugh song from a flop show that he could have only learned from Cole.

Then too the March 6, 1963, "Vilia" session, from the day before the Coltrane-Hartman date, included Coltrane's first attempt at "Nature Boy," a Cole signature that Coltrane would return to in 1965. The curious thing is that, because of corporate shenanigans of various kinds, the Hartman-Coltrane "Lush Life" is the recording that exposed the most people to Strayhorn's song over the last fifty years: the 1963 album has been perennially in print, whereas Cole's version was hard to find throughout the 1960s and '70s, when only the singer-pianist's pop mega-hits were easily available, and wasn't widely heard again until the compact disc era. Strayhorn himself disavowed the Cole recording (in spite of all it did for him), and he also told Ellington scholar and pianist Brooks Kerr that he disliked the Coltrane versions because the saxophonist played an incorrect chord change (in both 1958 and 1963). Yet the composer himself congratulated Hartman for his vocal, telling him, "you made my whole song come alive."

Of the seven songs recorded on March 7, "My One and Only Love" has the strongest connection to Sinatra (although he also recorded "They Say It's Wonderful" and "You Are Too Beautiful"). It was Sinatra's 1953 single that made "My One and Only Love" a jazz standard almost instantaneously, although, curiously, Sinatra virtually never sang it again. (The melody has a long backstory; composer Guy Wood originally titled it "Music from Beyond the Moon" before Bobby Mellin, usually a publisher, came up with the now classic title and lyrics.) The 1963 recording opens with a plaintive

reading, highly lyrical and romantic, sensitive to every nuance of the text—by Coltrane, however, rather than Hartman. In fact, when Hartman enters, his phrasing is such that he suggests he's singing a second chorus, he takes more liberties, slight though they may be, as if he knows well that the audience is already well familiar with the tune.

"My One and Only Love" is five minutes, giving Coltrane and then Hartman each a full-length go at Wood's melody; it could literally be two sides of a single: Coltrane plays the tune and then ritards at the end, giving it a full coda, then the proceedings start all over again at about 2:20. (I'm sure that many a deejay accidentally interrupted it at the midpoint.) Hartman later said that he was so blown away by Coltrane's solo that he forgot to make his entrance, and thus another take was necessitated. Yet the beautifully bisected nature of the arrangement works so well that one can hardly believe the whole thing wasn't planned in advance in exactly this way.

The most obscure song on the album is "Autumn Serenade," written around 1944 by composer Peter DeRose and lyricist Sammy Gallop, and the only one of the six Coltrane-Hartman tunes that's not well known enough to be described as a standard. DeRose belonged in the same category as Lewis Alter, Matty Malneck, and Rube Bloom; all were post-Gershwin-ites who composed semiclassical instrumental works as well as popular songs. (In all of their cases, a number of their formal works were later adapted into songs with lyrics, such as Malneck's "Stairway to the Stars" and Alter's "Manhattan Serenade.") With its moody, noir melody, "Autumn Serenade" was popular with a wide range of bands and instrumentalists in the immediate postwar era: Hal McIntyre made a beautiful treatment, featuring the leader's distinctive alto saxophone, Claude Thornhill played it as a feature for his piano, even Art Mooney made one of his more serious (less novelty-oriented) recordings of the piece. Other jazz players made it clear that they also loved the sound of this tune coming through their horns, like Bobby Hackett and Jack Teagarden. The closest thing to a hit version was by Harry James in 1945; the trumpeter used the piece as a chance to show off his orchestra's jazz as well as classical chops, in a stunning Billy May arrangement that contrasted the leader's hot horn with a soaring string background.

"Autumn Serenade" is a natural baritone song, one assumes it was Hartman's choice—hearing Hartman sing it, you can't believe that Sinatra, Crosby, Eckstine, Cole, and the others somehow missed it. Tyner opens with a dark, minor but catchy intro, and Hartman gently lunges in. Compared to a masterpiece like "Lush Life" or something as monumental as "You Are Too Beautiful" or "My One and Only Love," two songs that contemplate the very nature of relationships, "Autumn Serenade" is a comparatively trivial piece of business. It's not all that distinct from other melancholy songs about the ending of love and the changing of the seasons, leaves falling like tears and all that. It's easy to forget that it's on the album—but, as must be obvious, Hartman's and Coltrane's throwaways are better than most artists' A-list items. The tune closes the album, and as such seems like an encore or a bonus track. There's a vague hint of a Brazilian rhythm here, one amplified on subsequent recordings, like those of June Christy and Mel Tormé. Coltrane's solo is deliberately staccato, even choppy, he enters with two-note phrases somewhat reminiscent of his playing on his Sonny Rollins–inspired original tune "Like Sonny."

Written by three Jewish songwriters (the young Sammy Cahn, Saul Chaplin, and Hy Zaret), "Dedicated to You" is one of those songs like "A Sunday Kind of Love" and "Trust in Me" (both discussed in the essay on *Billy's Best!*) that were picked up by black bands and singers. "Dedicated" was first recorded by Andy Kirk's orchestra with falsetto Pha Terrell, following which dozens of African American icons sang it: Ella Fitzgerald and the Mills Brothers, Sammy Davis Jr., Billy Eckstine and Sarah Vaughan (one of their four classic duets from 1949), Al Hibbler (who also made collaborator Hy Zaret's "Unchained Melody" into an African American standard), Nat King Cole, Dakota Staton. Both Carmen McRae and Ray Charles made entire albums titled *Dedicated to You.*

The 1963 recording opens with an intro that's identical to the team's "Lush Life"—or rather a lack of same. There's just a very brief glissando by

Tyner, that's all, before we hear the voice of Hartman, in this case singing a rubato version of the melody, almost as if the tune itself were its own out-of-tempo verse. Hartman sings the first eight bars as an ad-lib intro, followed by a full and especially plaintive chorus from Coltrane. Unlike "My One and Only Love," there's no break between the two choruses, Coltrane's solo flows seamlessly into Hartman's vocal, although again he plays with the phrasing, treating his vocal more like a second chorus. He gets especially playful at the end, stretching it out for a memorable coda. The singer and the saxophonist are truly a two-headed hydra here. In fact, Coltrane played few actual obbligatos behind Hartman at the session itself, the obbligatos that are there were generally added later on in overdubbing, even as Louis Armstrong and Chet Baker occasionally did when they wanted to play trumpet behind their own vocals.

From the sublime "Dedicated to You" (which would become the title of Kurt Elling's 2009 tribute to Hartman and Coltrane), we proceed not to the ridiculous but to the extremely bizarre: "Afro Blue." Mongo Santamaria, the Cuban percussionist, composer, and bandleader (famously referenced by Mel Brooks in *Blazing Saddles*), introduced this piece, which would be his best known composition, in 1959, with his own ensemble in a track recorded in Los Angeles that featured jazz as well as Latin musicians. Before the year was out, the brilliant Chicago-based performer Oscar Brown Jr. (virtually the only figure of the time who, with the exception of Jon Hendricks, could be called a "jazz singer-songwriter") had written lyrics to this memorable theme, and it was soon sung on recordings by the young Abbey Lincoln as well as Brown himself. By 1963, Coltrane "had eyes" for the song—as Lester Young would say, an ambition to play it—and the Hartman date represents his first attempt.

Akkerman explains in considerable detail the complicated fate of this orphan track: it was left off the original album (with considerable justification), and the tape of the unissued take wound up in the hands of the saxophonist's in-laws. The unissued recording was finally heard by jazz scholar Barry Kernfeld in 2005, and based on Kernfeld's report it was hardly worth the wait. Rather than singing Brown's excellent lyric—which might have at least theoretically made sense—Coltrane had Hartman merely chant the words "Afro Blue" over and over. Three months later, Coltrane would start playing "Afro Blue" live on his working sets, but this concept of chanting a title like a religious mantra would later form the basis of one of the Jazz Messiah's most celebrated works, his 1964 extended masterpiece *A Love Supreme*. (This version of "Afro Blue" would seem to be the only time Coltrane played the Santamaria tune on a studio date; all issued versions of it are from live performances. Coltrane was also playing soprano here, the only tune on the date where he left his tenor in the case.) Thus the mystery is twofold, why he involved Hartman at all in the song, and then, why, once Hartman was involved, he didn't want him to sing the actual lyric. (And, finally, why he didn't ask Hartman to sing on "Nature Boy" instead, which would have been a much more appropriate song for the two Johns.)

"You Are Too Beautiful" is the last song recorded on this amazingly productive date; it became the second-to-last tune on the album, followed by "Autumn Serenade." Coltrane's tenor intro is among the warmest, most romantic things he ever played. So too is Hartman's vocal, although it engenders a rather curious by-product. Lorenz Hart and Richard Rodgers wrote this very unusual song in 1933 for an extremely unlikely project, *Hallelujah, I'm a Bum*, a highly ambitious and entirely original movie musical vehicle for Al Jolson. In the context of the story, the Jolson character is a homeless man, a victim of the Great Depression who cheerfully accepts his lot, that is, until he falls in love with a girl and becomes determined to go to work and make something of himself, rather than being a "bum" sleeping on a bench all day. (In a plot that recalls *The Threepenny Opera*, Jolson is the leader of the homeless, the "Mayor" of Central Park.)

Needing a love song for Jolson, Rodgers and Hart, who already knew all there was to know about writing love songs, came up with "You Are Too Beautiful." It functions in the movie narrative on several levels: as a man who really is literally a

bum, he feels unworthy of the love of this beautiful woman. Secondly, in the plot, the audience knows one key point that Jolson's character doesn't, the woman is an amnesia victim, who doesn't remember that she's actually the fiancée of the mayor of New York. (Okay, I didn't say it was a believable plot.) In the context of the picture, and in Jolson's larger-than-life personality, the song plays beautifully—but if there's a reason the song has been heard less in the last eighty years than other Rodgers and Hart songs, it's perhaps because the lyric just sounds so odd, as if Hart was reaching for a philosophical point that somehow exceeded his formidable grasp.

There's a famous schoolboy prank parody version of the song, sung at live appearances by such strange bedfellows as bebop saxophonist James Moody and Dean Martin, which goes, roughly, "You are too beautiful for one man alone / So I brought along my buddy . . ." Infantile as it is, I have to admit, every time I hear the song, my mind races to that gag. The only logical conclusion of Hart's lyric is that the woman so described is so beautiful that she should get some kind of dispensation to be poly-amorous—as she actually is, inadvertently, in the movie. It may well be a song alluding to an alternative sexual lifestyle—considering the lyricist's own personal life, who knows? Like I say, apart from the film itself, in which Jolson sings it incredibly movingly, the lyric is just kind of, well . . . odd. The way that both Sinatra (in 1945 and 1946) and Hartman sing it, one is forced to pay ultra-close attention to the lyrics, and I, for one, am left scratching my head.

"You Are Too Beautiful" was the final tune recorded—and the end of Hartman's involvement with the project. Coltrane changed and added some of his solos and obbligatos, but the Rodgers and Hart song marked the end of the productive March 7 date with Hartman, in which they laid down seven masters. Coltrane and Hartman placed "You Are Too Beautiful" as second to last on the original Side B, thereby ensuring that it would get the least attention. How very sensible of them then to end with "Autumn Serenade," a song that, if it's about anything, it's about conclusions. The hero is recalling "autumn kisses" he knew "as beautiful serenades," and in lyricist Sammy Gallop's beautiful, poignant lines, like "Silver stars were clinging to an autumn sky / Love was ours until October wandered by," everything is clearly in the past tense. This is a song about things being over, love is experienced in reflection only, a remembrance of things past.

Although it seemed like more and more of a classic over the passing decades, *John Coltrane and Johnny Hartman* was anything but neglected from the moment it was released, a few months later in July 1963. (In 2009, jazz singer Kurt Elling would release—and win a Grammy for—*Dedicated to You,* a contemporary contemplation of both Coltrane's *Ballads* and *John Coltrane and Johnny Hartman.*)

The most tangible, immediate benefit of *John Coltrane and Johnny Hartman* was that it was well received enough for Thiele to produce four additional albums with Hartman: two more on the jazz-oriented Impulse! Records, *I Just Dropped By to Say Hello* (1963) and *The Voice That Is!* (1965) and two others on the more pop-driven ABC-Paramount label, *Unforgettable* (1966) and *I Love Everybody* (1967). Yet if *John Coltrane and Johnny Hartman* couldn't make Hartman into a superstar, it was clear that none of his other albums would, either. It was apparently the wrong time to try and promote a singer of standards and occasionally jazz into stardom; the only way it could work is if such an artist had at least a tinge of soul and/or Motown to his work, as was the case with Lou Rawls, a baritone of comparable vocal register who might be described as, in some senses, a stylistic descendant of Hartman. On his live albums, in particular, Rawls did as much talking as he did singing, and he only sang standards at the beginning and end of his career, but, with the arguable exception of Barry White, Rawls could be considered the last of the line of black baritones that began with Eckstine, Herb Jeffries, Al Hibbler, Arthur Prysock, and reached an apex with Johnny Hartman. Twenty years earlier, at the start of his career,

all black singers were stereotyped as blues singers or, at best, jazz singers; now, with Hartman's own ballad style reaching its pinnacle, all black vocalists were expected to be soul singers. Ray Charles had very recently established that it was okay for black singers to do modern sounds in country and western music, but there never did seem to be a point, even in the wake of Nat King Cole, when African Americans were encouraged to sing Rodgers and Hart or Irving Berlin.

Earlier, I expressed the wish that Coltrane and Hartman had thought to do "Nature Boy" on the 1963 album. Hartman did eventually record the song, almost ten years later, on a dedicatory album to Coltrane taped in Japan and eventually released in the United States as *For Trane.* Listening to that performance only underscores why Hartman's albums of 1955 and 1963 are such masterpieces: at forty-nine in 1972, Hartman is still in excellent voice, and the Japanese musicians are totally world-class, there's no fault with their playing. But the 1972 "Nature Boy" is a disaster from the git-go, someone, apparently the producer, instructed Hartman to bebop it up, as if he were Ella Fitzgerald or Anita O'Day, rather than singing the melody in his straight-ahead, incredibly beautiful fashion, as he doubtlessly would have done in Coltrane's company in 1963.

Perhaps that's a key to both the blessing and the curse of Hartman's unique talent. He had an incredible gift—at his best, he was as good as anyone, even his heroes, Sinatra, Eckstine, and Cole. But his art was so specific, and it required precisely the right circumstances: Sinatra and Eckstine had the forceful personalities to control their own destinies, and Cole's brilliance as instrumentalist meant that he would never be stuck for long with an inferior musical situation. But Hartman had nothing to fall back on. In retrospect, it's amazing that he was able to leave us with as many masterpieces as he did. Without *Songs from the Heart* and especially *John Coltrane and Johnny Hartman,* the world would be a poorer place indeed.

22
Dick Haymes
Rain or Shine
(1956)

During one of his mid-1950s sessions at the famous Capitol Records tower, Frank Sinatra was frustrated at the difficulty he was having at trying to hit a particular note. "I wish that I had those low notes that Dick Haymes has!" he announced to all who would listen. (Or so it was reported by Sinatra's producer, Voyle Gilmore, who remembered the incident for his son, John, many years later.)

This was likely at the same time that, briefly, Haymes joined Sinatra as a singer contract artist on the Capitol label, and to listen to the two marvelous albums that Haymes made at that time is to know what Sinatra was talking about. Haymes's voice is indeed mellifluous and beautiful, the low notes especially. But while the voice is outstanding, the interpretative skills are perhaps even more so—there's no doubt that he has grown and matured as an artist in the ten years since he had made it to the top—or at least very near to the top, in the age when people were dropping his name in the same breath as Sinatra and Bing Crosby. Throughout he sings with uncommon tenderness, making every word count, and not missing a single possible ounce of feeling anywhere in the lyrics or music. It's the kind of detail that Sinatra brought to works like *In the Wee Small Hours,* but without aping Sinatra in the slightest—it's as different from Sinatra as Sinatra is from Billie Holiday.

As Haymes himself said decades after the fact, "When you sing a song, you don't just sing it with your throat and your head. It was probably a lot of things that were coming through—like Sinatra's *Wee Small Hours*—vocally, he has been better, but the truth, the feeling was there." It's also there in *Rain or Shine* and *Moondreams,* Haymes's two albums for Capitol, from 1955 and 1956, respectively, both of which are collaborations with the arranger-conductor Ian Bernard. The tragedy of these two albums, in fact, is precisely that they are so good. They are the works of a major artist at the peak of his powers. Yet they both amount to swan songs. If only he hadn't been able to sing anymore, if he had no more chops left, then the rest of his life and career wouldn't seem like such a waste.

There's more to being a singer than knowing how to sing. Or even to having good luck. Sometimes an artist has to know when the time is right to reinvent himself, even if he has to learn that lesson the hard way. Consider Louis Armstrong, Frank Sinatra, Nat King Cole, and, perhaps most of all, Louis Prima, on one hand, and Louis Jordan and Dick Haymes on the other. The first group all caught the change in the weather and rode it, thereby extending their careers to the ends of their lives and their ability to perform. Jordan and Haymes, however, had been so good at doing what they did, and so popular for what seemed like an entire generation, that they couldn't see the necessity of changing and adapting into the next thing—or even creating the next thing.

In their cases, the failure to adapt to changing times is particularly ironic. It makes no sense that Louis Jordan's career should be over just at the time that rhythm and blues, the genre he had pioneered, was changing its name to rock 'n' roll and was poised to become the dominant mode of pop music. As for Haymes, he was somehow washed up during an age when romantic crooners singing love songs were still all over the singles charts. In fact, by the mid-1950s, traditional crooners were expanding their base of operations to conquer new media like television and long-playing albums, two media in which Haymes wasn't near as active as he should have been. Why was Louis Jordan finished when second-rate imitators, both black and white, were mimicking his style to great success? Why was no one buying Haymes records the way they were still buying his approximate contemporaries Sinatra or Como? The dramatic answer is that the music-loving public is a great monstrous beast with an insatiable appetite for novelty. The idea, apparently, was to find a new sound, as Sinatra did; a new medium, as Como did; or a new audience, as Nat King Cole did. Such newness was the only way to reach that much desired "second act" that F. Scott Fitzgerald so famously alluded to.

Haymes was only thirty-seven when he made *Rain or Shine,* only a year older than Cole and younger than both Como and Sinatra. His early career had been approximately parallel to Sinatra, who had preceded him in the orchestras of both Harry James and Tommy Dorsey. He seemed to have everything necessary to be a major star, being a baritone with a mellow, rich romantic sound and movie star looks—he seemed tailor-made for the role of both big band singer and movie musical leading man. He's a singer who might well have prevailed over Sinatra in 1939–40, given the smoothness of his voice and the Hollywoodness of his face. It would take a most discerning eye and ear, like those of Tommy Dorsey, to see that it was Sinatra who already had that extra something special that none of the other singers of the period could match.

Sinatra and Haymes also broke out of the big bands within a short time of each other, and both followed the all-media trail (radio, record-

ings, films) blazed by Crosby a decade earlier. Using broadcasting as a home base, they both also recorded prolifically and successfully, and made it into the movies. Then, at the start of the 1950s, the careers of both singers took a rather abrupt nosedive, in such a complete parallel that it almost seemed they were going in for the Olympic synchronized swimming team, a swan song that was driven by questionable personal decisions and changing musical tastes. Through his own fortitude and artistic vision, Sinatra was able to turn his circumstances around and engineer the greatest comeback in history; his was the comeback against which all others would be judged.

In 1945, Haymes was probably the number three male singer—after Crosby and Sinatra. Come the 1950s, those positions were reversed, when Como parlayed his low-key charisma into a TV career that was the envy of all other singers. Vocally, Haymes's voice was at least as beautiful as Como's, perhaps even deeper and richer, but after that first flurry of fame, it was evident that he wasn't the long-distance runner that Como was. His sound was especially suited to the World War II era, rapturous and romantic—you needed something a bit more subdued in the Eisenhower era, and that was Como's strength. In the 1950s, Sinatra was hot, in the Marshall McLuhan sense, and Como was "cool"—full of understated charm—but Haymes was simply Haymes.

Sinatra also was a victim of the cruel hand of fate, but, unlike Haymes, he proved able to play those cards that fate dealt him and parlay them into a winning hand. He turned the notion of "the comeback" into a career strategy: he didn't plan his nosedive of 1950–53, but he was able to use it in retrospect—the same with his self-imposed retirement of twenty years later. Dick Haymes became a model of the opposite kind of trajectory, the emblem of the talented artist who can't rise above those same circumstances—and who also couldn't conquer his personal demons. Rather than being a role model, Haymes's career was a cautionary tale. In the mid-1950s, it was as if both Sinatra and Haymes had a date with destiny. Destiny, alas, skipped out on her date with Haymes halfway through and left him behind to pick up the check.

Yet the two albums of 1955–56, *Moondreams* and especially *Rain or Shine*, are tantalizing reminders of what might have been.

This pair of 12-inch LPs, both recorded for Capitol, showed that Dick Haymes had the musical talent to compete with anybody who was singing then, including Sinatra and Cole. He had parted company with Decca in 1952—a further parallel to Sinatra's departure from Columbia in the same year—and then, like Sinatra, he wound up on Capitol. According to his biographer, Dr. Ruth Prigozy, the singer's career seemed to be on a slight upswing in 1955: he'd enjoyed a very successful run at the Dunes in Las Vegas, where he first worked with Ian Bernard, and Capitol Records made him an offer. His agent worked out a deal for two albums. Haymes was probably happy to be on Capitol, which, as Sinatra, Prima, and Judy Garland were all proving, was the home of second chances. It's also important to note that the Capitol deal focused on long-playing albums, which he had not yet done. He would eventually make a couple of singles for the label, but label and artist alike seemed to have believed that his future lay in the new format.

This being Capitol, Haymes could have asked for either Nelson Riddle or Billy May as his musical director, but he had another idea. Perhaps there was part of him that wanted to keep some kind of musical distance between himself and Sinatra—had he worked with either of those great arrangers, the resulting record would have sounded highly Frankish indeed. Then too he also could have asked for his former collaborator at Decca, Gordon Jenkins, who also was about to sign with Capitol, but that he didn't do so indicates that he also wanted to put some distance between himself and his past. Instead of replicating anyone's past achievements, even his own, Haymes's idea was to go forward by bringing in Ian Bernard, thus continuing the good work that they had done together in Vegas.

For the first of the two albums, they relied primarily on the arrangements they'd used at the Dunes, some of which were by Johnny Mandel, then a young trumpeter recently out of Count Basie's band, and which included a number of the singer's signature songs. The first album, *Rain or Shine*, was taped over four sessions from December 20 to 23, 1955, at Capitol's new studios in the already famous "stack of pancakes" tower on Hollywood and Vine.

Indeed, even when addressing his own past, Haymes took the high road—no shortcuts here. The first words we hear on the album are "I'm as restless as a willow in a windstorm / I'm as jumpy as a puppet on a string," one of his best known songs, "It Might As Well Be Spring," from his 1945 film *State Fair*. Rodgers and Hammerstein meant it to be sung by a nervous young girl or boy in anticipation of their first real crack at the opposite sex, which is how Haymes sang it in 1945. Ten years later, he digs into it considerably deeper—he sounds seriously restless and jumpy, not merely teeming with the pent-up energy of puberty. The baritone sounds mellow and smooth as usual, but Haymes manages to convey just the right note of angst, a feeling that is underscored by Bernard when he includes a somewhat dissonant but very subtle string line in the opening eight bars of the vocal. The mood relaxes in the bridge ("I keep wishing I were somewhere else . . .") but the restlessness and jumpiness never completely let up.

Occasionally the richness and attractiveness of Haymes's deep baritone are at odds with the overall mood of the texts and the emotions they allow him to convey. "The More I See You," which he made into a classic love song when he introduced it in *Diamond Horseshoe* (also from 1945, surely the climactic year of his film career), isn't about nervousness so much as codependence. He's not calm or stoic here, he's telling someone how much he needs and loves her, how much he depends on her—for all the robust manliness of the voice, the overall mood of his message is one of overwhelming vulnerability. He later said, "When I sang 'The More I See You' [on *Rain or Shine*] I could have been thinking of the peak of my career, when I was working with Betty [Grable], walking around like the kingpin of 20th Century Fox."

Ray Noble's "The Very Thought of You" opens with a mix of brooding lower strings and clarinet, the overall orchestral texture being much like Sinatra's series of string quartet plus rhythm section dates of the mid-1940s, as heard on Sinatra's

Columbia album *The Voice* (the predecessor of the Chairman's 1957 album *Close to You*.) The use of a small ensemble, with just a few strings, rhythm, and subtone clarinet helps Haymes's voice sound amazingly intimate. It's entirely appropriate for a song about processing a message internally—in other words, thinking. Although the lyrics are addressed to a "you," the overall mood that Haymes puts forward is that he's not actually communicating with another person, but running these words over in his head, as if he's working on what he's going to say to his inamorata when he's lucky enough to be with her again.

Famously, Harry Warren was inspired to write the melody of "You'll Never Know" by a bugle call he heard at the race track. However, it was Mack Gordon's opening line ("You'll never know how much I miss you") that transformed this number from a period costume musical (*Hello, Frisco, Hello*) set in 1915 into a song of separation that perfectly captured the prevailing mood of the wartime era and won an Academy Award. This was shortly before Dick Haymes arrived at that 20th Century-Fox—he would have made a good leading man for star Alice Faye. After a brief piano introduction, Haymes states the opening notes in a manner as unlike a bugle call as possible, in a model of understated, subtle delivery. The key word isn't "you'll" or "know" but, importantly, "never." He sounds as if he's come to the end of all possibilities, that the girl he wants to reach is just beyond the range of his ability to communicate with her. She cannot be reached; she will never know.

We then come to another key moment in the album. In 1934, Arthur Schwartz composed two similar and excellent songs, which can be regarded as being of a piece, even though they have lyrics from two different collaborators and are from two different shows: "If There Is Someone Lovelier than You" (lyric by Howard Dietz, from *Revenge with Music*) and "Then I'll Be Tired of You" (lyric by E. Y. Harburg, from *Ziegfeld Follies of 1934*). Haymes sang them both on his Capitol albums, the first one here and the second one on the follow-up, *Moondreams*. Taken together, we might call them the Schwartz-Haymes "If/Then" song cycle. Philosophically, the lyrics complement each other

surprisingly well, and both are soaring melodies that feature Schwartz in a vaguely Jerome Kern-ish mode. Even though Sinatra sang "If There Is Someone Lovelier than You" several times on CBS broadcasts, he never recorded either one of these songs, making this a little corner of the Great American Songbook that was unique to Haymes.

The general mood of the music and qualities of the text seem almost operetta-like, deliberately old-fashioned in their construction. They're both rather rhetorical productions in which the protagonist just says no: no, there is no one lovelier than her and also, no, he is not tired of her. He creates a clear image of what she is by telling us firmly what she is not; by telling us how he doesn't feel, he indirectly, but brilliantly, shows us what he does. Even with the somewhat conservative nature of the texts (as with Kern, the lyrics tend to date faster than the music), Haymes sings with considerably greater depth of feeling and attention to lyric detail than anything he ever did in his Decca–20th Century-Fox period a half decade earlier.

Which answers the question that Irving Berlin poses in the next song, "How Deep Is the Ocean?" We can't respond with a specific mileage count, but we can say that, in the way Haymes sings it here, the ocean is substantially deeper than it's ever been before. The song is, famously, one of several from the early 1930s that are among the few that Berlin didn't write for a specific show or film. There's a slight jazz backbeat behind Haymes, just enough to allow him to phrase the melody more interestingly—it's far from completely straight. Most vocalists tend to sing this song as if it were a simple series of questions, one after the other, all unanswered. Haymes, however, phrases it as if he were somehow answering one question with another. Question: "How many times a day do I think of you?" Answer: "How many red roses are sprinkled with dew?"

Turning the LP over, we come to "The Nearness of You," a stunning collaboration by the brilliant Hoagy Carmichael and the undervalued lyricist Ned Washington. This amazing ballad arrived in 1940, in time to become another signature song of the World War II era (Haymes's pinnacle)—a time when many lovers were separated, and thus "nearness" was nothing to be taken for granted. (Which proves that the key factor in a love affair is location! location! location!) Haymes had sung a rather different-sounding medium-tempo big band arrangement on the air with Harry James when the song was new—a version that is lovely in its own way—but this 1955 treatment is the charmed one. In a sense, it's also a song about what isn't—not the pale moon, not the sweet conversation, and he doesn't need soft lights, etc. The lyric is essentially a process of elimination, and it brings out Haymes at his tenderest. And that, take my word for it, is mighty darn tender.

If it seems like we can't go two songs without a comparison to Sinatra, you can imagine that this is probably also the way that Haymes was feeling at this point in his life (and probably for quite a while before and after). Sinatra recorded "Where or When" three times, but never the verse, as Haymes does here. In fact, Sinatra's slow, stately 1958 Capitol recording was possibly influenced by Haymes's slow, stately 1955 Capitol recording. Like Sinatra, Haymes starts small and builds, but Haymes starts even smaller, with the verse, which he delivers not internally, as if he was thinking it aloud to himself, but intimately, as if he were communicating directly with a lover. Although this is, famously, Lorenz Hart's rather remarkable meditation on reincarnation, the mood is more specifically romantic than metaphysical. The idea of building to a climax well before the finish and then gently tapering off seems vaguely Frankish, but on the whole, Haymes is his own man here.

"Little White Lies" is probably Haymes's single best known song. He originally recorded it for Decca in November 1947, just a few months after the death of Walter Donaldson, who had written it (both words and music, which was unusual for him) in 1930. The Decca single was a blockbuster for Haymes in 1948, his last really big hit, and the one that's lingered the longest in our collective consciousness. (It was, by the way, particularly popular in England, where it was a favorite of the very young John Lennon and Paul McCartney.) The 1947 hit used a sizable orchestra and a full mixed choir, who surround him in more or less the same way the Pied Pipers do on his and Sinatra's Dorsey

ballads. But whereas his 1955 "Where or When" was heavier than most versions, this "Little White Lies" is delivered on a much smaller scale, with the singer emoting tenderly over a background of mostly guitar, vibes, and bass. Because Ian Bernard apparently feels that a full piano is too heavy, we hear a very spare, tinkly celeste (in the verse at least). As with the best of Haymes's colleague Doris Day, just because it's light doesn't mean it isn't deep.

It's probably a coincidence that the next two songs, "Our Love Is Here to Stay" and "Love Walked In," were both written by George and Ira Gershwin from the score of *The Goldwyn Follies* (1938); this was the brothers' final project and "Here to Stay," ironic as the title may be, is the last song George Gershwin ever worked on. "Our Love Is Here to Stay" (listed as such on the Haymes album, though the official Ira Gershwin lyrics compendium insists that the word "our" isn't actually part of the title) is one of the most romantic songs ever written; like "The Way You Look Tonight," it always seems especially appropriate for a falling-in-love montage in vintage rom coms or for the first dance at weddings.

Haymes likely had already heard the Sinatra "Our Love Is Here to Stay," taped at the same Capitol studio just two months earlier for *Songs for Swingin' Lovers*. He seems determined to make his treatment less jazzy (less "swingin'" if you will) and perhaps even more erotic than FS, starting with a very slow, almost completely singspiel verse (the phrasing of which directly anticipates Johnny Hartman, especially on the Coltrane album). The last two words of the verse "I mean in the way we care"—are amazingly expressive, confident yet tentative, and they lead very organically into the chorus, in a way that I've never heard any other vocalist achieve. He keeps the entire refrain at a dance beat—it never drops out of tempo—but exquisitely romantic. Some couples may want to rush home from the ballroom to hop into bed, but these two are enjoying moving around the dance floor in each other's arms. He stretches it out as if to indicate he doesn't want this love affair ever to end. He wants love to be here to stay.

"Love Walked In," at 1:41, is exactly half the length of "Here to Stay" (at 3:20) and both are precisely as long as they need to be. This is another small-group affair, stressing vibes and guitar plus piano, bass, and drums, like "Little White Lies" and "You'll Never Know." (All three were taped on December 23, 1955.) Phrasing lightly over a walking bass intro, Haymes is sure of himself and, on his own terms, swinging.

"Love Walked In" turns out to be a brief breather as Haymes builds to the big closer, *Rain or Shine*'s title track, "Come Rain or Come Shine." In 1955, this had yet to become one of the great "guy" love songs—this was well before Sinatra and Ray Charles created their famous interpretations; the most prominent version on Capitol before Haymes was by progressive bandleader Stan Kenton with June Christy. "Come Rain" is both the jazziest and the most robustly romantic vocal on the set; there's a prominent clarinet throughout, hitting lots of blue notes. This track is best illustrated by the cover, Haymes looking slightly older and wiser—he was a very mature thirty-seven—gazing intently over the photographer's left shoulder, his tie and collar loosened, a lit cigarette in his right hand. The vocal is slow and deliberate, intensely passionate yet cool at the same time—he's clearly in a class with Frank and Ray. He sounds deliberately tentative when he sings about how he's going to love her, but more solidly assured when Mercer reverses the pronouns at the line "You're gonna love me"—he's more confident regarding her commitment than he is about his own.

"Come Rain or Come Shine" ends with a big note at the end, long and strong, even as the clarinet comes in and guides us to the coda. The message is clear: Haymes is addressing us, as his audience, as much as he is speaking to the girl in his mind's eye, the unnamed female of his amorous intentions. In terms of his relationship with us, we've already endured both rain and shine together. But as he sings Johnny Mercer's lyric, rain and shine are more than symbols of good times and bad, but also

of the changing seasons, and thus of the passing of time; he clearly wants to stay in this relationship with us for as long as he can.

Alas, his commitment to us, those who love his music, wasn't compelling enough for him to give up the other relationship in his life, which wasn't to a woman but to alcohol. If he hadn't wasted so much of his mental capacity dealing with the after-effects of getting drunk, being drunk, and what comes after, he might have had enough brainpower left to be able to formulate a more effective career strategy for himself.

There's a lyric by the contemporary singer-songwriter Susan Werner that makes me think of Haymes: "I can be your girl through the best time and the worst time / But I can't be the girl that you notice for the first time. / There's so much that I can do, / But I can't be new." It's true that the rock 'n' roll thing was already happening, but as we've seen, people were still buying records by all the better smooth-voiced crooners. The tragedy is that Haymes in 1955 was a much greater artist than he had been in 1945, but to revive his career he needed to be something more than merely a better version of himself, which is, in effect, why other romantic singers and other hitmakers of the 1940s were reinventing themselves and flourishing.

Haymes followed *Rain or Shine* with *Moondreams*, which is just as fine an album, and contains a masterpiece reading of "The Way You Look Tonight." There also were a few oddball singles, including a pairing of tunes from Gordon Jenkins's *Manhattan Tower*. The subsequent career of Haymes was all dribs and drabs: a TV appearance here, a major Vegas appearance there, and once in a while a new album, none of which was as good as the two Capitol LPs of 1956 and 1957. But in the vast scheme of things, none of that makes any difference in terms of our appreciation of *Rain or Shine* and *Moondreams*. Sixty years later it doesn't matter that he couldn't be new. It only matters that he could be great.

23

Billie Holiday
Lady in Satin
(1958)

n the middle of 1957, a lawyer named Earle Zaidins contacted Columbia Records on behalf of
Billie Holiday. He managed to get through to a
relatively new A&R man named Irving Townsend,
who found his request somewhat surprising. The
great jazz singer, it seemed, wanted to do an album
with Ray Ellis, who at the time was a rising star in
the field of what was later
dubbed "easy listening"
music. Townsend later
claimed to have been
shocked. "It would be
like Ella Fitzgerald say-
ing she wanted to do an
album with Ray Con-
niff," he said, referring
to another extremely
popular "mood music"
maestro.

Townsend may have
been dramatically over-
stating his alleged sur-
prise for the benefit of
a good story. Both Billie
Holiday and Ella Fitzger-
ald had already done many recording sessions with
strings; in fact, most of Holiday's sessions of the
1940s had utilized an orchestra with "fiddles," as
she called them, and many of her signature songs,
like "Lover Man," "Good Morning, Heartache," and
"Crazy He Calls Me," were initially recorded in that
format. By the end of the 1950s, even very hard-
core rhythm and blues artists like Dinah Washington and Etta James were landing hit records with
strings. But if Townsend hadn't seen it coming,
Ray Ellis was even more incredulous. "I couldn't
believe it, because I had never met the woman,"
said the conductor. "I didn't know she was aware
of me."

Actually, for Holiday to have made any kind of
a record by 1957 was remarkable. Her career and
her life were at one of many low points. Especially
in the latter part of her life, she was almost continually down-and-out, due to her inability to stop
abusing drugs and/or stop letting herself be abused
by male playmates who liked to play rough. There
doesn't seem to be any
time when she was flying
high, except, of course,
when she was literally
high from using.

In January 1957, she
recorded her final stu-
dio session for producer
Norman Granz, who
had long been one of
her greatest supporters,
both for recordings and
concerts, and in these
years she was frequently
burning bridges, in front
of her as well as behind.
She had already cashed
in on her notoriety by
publishing *Lady Sings the Blues*, which brought in
some cash flow, but made it even harder for her, for
instance, to get an apartment. She was even separated from Louis McKay, one of the slimiest of her
lover men (who nonetheless got Hollywood to hire
Billy Dee Williams to play him in the Diana Ross
movie).

So in 1957, it looked unlikely that Holiday
would ever be summoned into a recording studio
again even with just a solo piano, let alone with a
string orchestra. Then she heard a new album on
Columbia Records titled *Ellis in Wonderland* and
decided that was what she wanted to do next. Fortunately, she had a close friend and supporter in

the lawyer Earle Zaidins, and he was moved to take up her cause with Columbia. It certainly helped that there were already Billie Holiday albums on the label, recorded during the years 1933–42, when Holiday recorded for them both as a "sideman" and as the featured star of her own dates. But what was an even bigger asset was the notion that CBS TV, surprisingly, was suddenly interested in her. Producer Robert Herridge wanted to include Holiday in an episode of the omnibus series *The Seven Lively Arts*, which would be titled "The Sound of Jazz." Zaidins and Townsend worked it out; CBS would secure Holiday's participation in the telecast, as well as on a new Columbia album tied in with the show (and also titled *The Sound of Jazz*), and Holiday would do one new album of her own for Columbia. We can thank Zaidins, Townsend, Herridge, and Ellis for the brief renaissance that Holiday enjoyed at the end of her career; due to them, her last eighteen months were among her most productive—her appearance in *The Sound of Jazz* helped to make this the single most impressive presentation of jazz that's ever been shown on television, and *Lady in Satin* would become one of the great albums of all time, not just of Holiday's career but of anybody's.

In 1957, Ray Ellis was a thirty-four-year-old arranger and conductor working under contract to Columbia Records, who was benefiting tremendously from a new genre of music inspired by technology. The recent development of the 12-inch LP had led to a boom in easy listening or "mood" music, and Ellis joined the ranks of such Muzak maestros as Ray Conniff, Percy Faith, and Paul Weston, who were considerably ahead of him in the pecking order at Columbia. The biggest name (and body) in that field was that of Jackie Gleason, the TV comedy superstar who actually conducted dozens of albums released under his name by Capitol Records.

Ellis in Wonderland, the album that attracted Holiday's attention, is a typical and very well-made product of the era: flawlessly recorded in hi-fi (this was the high point of the hi-fi and then the stereo boom), with strings that are by turns light and heavy, with some wit in the jazzier arrangements.

Ellis was certainly highly talented, though hardly as brilliant as Nelson Riddle or Billy May, and can't be said to have possessed the distinctive signature of a Gordon Jenkins.

All of which is precisely what Holiday wanted. According to Townsend, "She said that she wanted a pretty album, something delicate. . . . She wasn't interested in some wild, swinging jam session. She wanted that cushion under her voice. She wanted to be flattered by that kind of sound . . . she said this over and over." Townsend decided to give her what she wanted, and introduced her to Ellis. When, roughly twenty years afterward, Ellis was interviewed by researcher Linda Kuehl (who also is the source for the Townsend interview), he was remarkably frank. Ellis is so candid, in fact, that he drops whatever filter he might have had, and, in some comments at least, comes off both as a sexist and a creep. He rambles on at length about how unattractive Holiday had become, and how far she had fallen, a decline exacerbated by her bad habits, from the glamorous diva that "Lady Day" had been ten years earlier. At one point, he compares the process of writing orchestrations for a female singer to the act of making love to one, stressing that although he wasn't physically attracted to Holiday, he was inspired to write for her just the same.

He somehow pulled himself together and recovered from the shock of her appearance, and then they commenced picking the repertoire. "We went through a whole pile of music and she read the titles and the lyrics. More than half she'd only heard once or twice or hadn't heard at all. She just liked the lyrics when she read them. I showed her the melodies on the piano and she'd say, 'Yes, I want that.'" The number of new tunes (to her canon, at least) gives the album a sense of freshness, unlike some of her Verve releases, which were remakes of tunes she'd cut earlier in the 1930s and '40s.

The Holiday-Ellis relationship began inauspiciously and proceeded to go downhill from there: the singer constantly irritated Ellis by failing to show up for their meetings. "I was very busy in those days and at that point in my career I was the king of arrangers. Everything else I was doing, I could not have cared less about. I wanted to do *her,* and I wanted to do everything right, but we could not get together." Ellis describes himself as "evil" for losing patience with Holiday, but in this respect he seems entirely justified.

Ellis had anticipated that Holiday would be late—if she showed up at all—for the first date, so he told her to come at 10 a.m. while actually planning to be ready to go at noon. She didn't disappoint him. Yet Townsend remembered that she came all dressed up to the session, looking great, as if she were going to be performing in public. "Most [singers] don't give a damn and turn up looking like bums."

Alas, she didn't sound as good as she looked; she was badly prepared, as well as in her cups. "She was standing there with a bottle of gin," said Ellis. "I was so mad at her, I actually fought her during the session, I yelled, 'You bitch! You sing so great and you don't know what you're doing! You're blowing the whole God-damned thing!' It was an ego thing to me, because I'd slaved over the arrangements, picturing how she was going to sing it." Eventually, Ellis told her, "Look, baby, I'm going to give the band a fifteen-minute break while you learn that God-damned bridge.... I had to treat her like a school kid; she stood there and pouted."

Ellis can be forgiven, given all the personality conflicts that went into the project, for failing to recognize the overall greatness of Holiday's performance at that moment. (Later on, he would.) Throughout, the strings are heavy and melancholy, but never dour—likewise the choir. The settings are darker in pitch than anything on *Ellis in Wonderland* or any of his subsequent collaborations with singers (Johnny Mathis, Barbra Streisand, etc.), and perfectly suit Holiday's dark, low, croak of a voice.

The album would actually be taped on three consecutive days from February 19 to 21, 1958. Our appreciation of *Lady in Satin* is enhanced by a compact disc manufactured in France and issued semi-privately, containing what is apparently all the surviving additional material, including alternate takes both complete and otherwise from the February 1958 sessions. The phrasing and timing on all the additional tracks are completely different from the issued takes, even though the orchestral parts, the strings and the choir, are identical.

The first date begins with "You Don't Know What Love Is," composed by Don Raye and Gene de Paul in 1941, when they were on staff at Universal Pictures. It had already become a jazz standard, so much so that it's surprising that Holiday hadn't sung it before 1958. She makes up for lost time—"You Don't Know What Love Is" was immediately one of the highlights of *Lady in Satin*. There are three extant takes, the first a complete alternate that's as good as the issued one, but particularly different in the bridge. In the alternate, she pronounces the word "reminiscing" as "rem-O-niscing"; in the issued take, it sounds a bit closer to "reminiscing" and she spreads out the feel of the word completely differently. The second attempt is a breakdown, in recording studio parlance, in which she gets as far as the first line before something goes wrong; you can then hear her chuckling loudly, she sounds full of high spirits and good humor, as if she's fully enjoying herself. There's also a melodic trumpet solo in the instrumental mid-section, played by studio veteran Mel Davis. Like everything Holiday sings, her vocal is dripping with life experience. Every note sounds as if she means it because she lived it.

Billie Holiday and composer-iconoclast Alec Wilder were an unusual fit: Holiday's singing was direct and without artifice; most of Wilder's songs were, famously, just the opposite. He specialized in morose, gloomy ballads, yet she chose, paradoxically, "I'll Be Around," one of Wilder's comparatively least depressing efforts. There are six takes altogether, three of which are complete. Again, the differences between the issued take and the complete alternates are evident at the end of the bridge: in the unissued take, she spontaneously adds a few extra words, "Drop *me* a line, to say you're feelin' *mighty* fine...."; in the issued take, she doesn't include the extra verbiage, but makes the whole lyric sound immediate and personal using the words Wilder actually wrote. The breakdowns and chatter are rewarding: Holiday running over the tune at double-time just to get the melody in her head, Holiday cracking up when someone in the orchestra fluffs it, two false starts have her making improper entrances and apologizing.

"For Heaven's Sake" was already well on its way to becoming a standard when Holiday recorded it in 1958. "Heaven's" was written by Sherman Edwards, a songwriter who turned out mostly pop hits ("Wonderful, Wonderful," "Dungaree Doll," "See You in September"), and later composed the Broadway musical 1776. You might think that a song that begins "For Heaven's sake let's fall in love / It's no mistake to call it love" and continues "An angel's holding hands with me / How Heavenly Heaven can be"—which Ellis decorates with suitably cherubic flute-y filigrees—might be a little on the twee side for Our Lady of Despair. Apart from the notion that such imagery might have appealed to Holiday's innate spirituality (as on "This Is Heaven to Me" and "God Bless the Child"), she knew well the value of lighter and openly romantic numbers. Which is exactly how she sings it—in fact, the lightness of the song assumes a kind of profundity through Holiday. "For Heaven's Sake" survives in two generally indistinguishable complete—and excellent—takes, plus a few seconds of studio chatter, which have Holiday laughing and giggling, clearly in wonderfully good humor.

The last tune on the first day was "But Beautiful," the Burke and Van Heusen jazz standard written for Bing Crosby in the 1947 Road to Rio. Only one complete take is known to exist—which may indicate that Holiday was running out of steam—but it's quite beautiful. It's a song about emotional contrasts and gradations ("Love is funny, or it's sad / Or it's quiet, or it's mad") and Holiday gets every nuance exactly right; she makes every one of these adjectives sound completely distinct from all the others. Still, there's a minute of a breakdown take with some studio chatter that is absolutely priceless, featuring Holiday phrasing the opening line in lots of different ways; even though the key words ("fun-ny," "qui-et") are sung on the same, repeated, note, she sings them all in such a way as to give them lots of personality and variety.

The second date includes two songs from Sinatra's 1956 string album, Close to You, but the session begins with a nod to Nat King Cole: "For All We Know," heard in four complete takes (the issued take and three alternates). Written in 1934 by J. Fred Coots and Sam Lewis, this is the only song repeated from Ellis in Wonderland, but that instrumental version is much lighter and fox-trot-y. There's no one better than the Lady, in Satin or otherwise, at expressing a sentiment that's somehow sad and happy at the same time. We don't have a lot of time together, the lyrics say, but we have right now—"before you go, make this moment sweet again." At the end of take two, she announces quietly, "I can't make that ending, I'm telling you."

Rodgers and Hart's "It's Easy to Remember" (written for Bing Crosby in the 1934 Mississippi) is slow and exquisitely paced. Take nine is the issued take on the album, and playing it side by side with Sinatra's Close to You track is illuminating: both singers have a miraculous attention to detail that comes to the foreground in this all-string setting, and, for once, Holiday's string section is considerably larger than Sinatra's. There's also a lovely, melodic trombone solo by Urbie Green. The take identified as "Take One—Breakdown" has her getting through almost a whole chorus, but she gets lost in the bridge and skips to the final A, singing "Each little moment" about eight bars earlier than she should, and announcing quietly, "Uh uh, I lost the lyrics." Take two is complete, and close to the issued take nine. Take five breaks down half a minute in, at which point we hear Holiday saying, "I didn't do it," but on the next take, when it breaks down, she makes no such denial—and instead goes into something that sounds like a vocal warm-up or exercise.

"I'm a Fool to Want You" was already a Sinatra signature (co-composed by him); but Holiday isn't in the least bit competitive; just the opposite—she sounds resigned to defeat. Trombonist Urbie Green enhances that mood with an especially mournful obbligato behind her, genuflecting in the direction of Jack Teagarden.

A total of five takes were attempted, and take three is the one that was originally issued on the mono edition of the LP, while the stereo pressing utilizes a composite of takes two and three. The most recent Sony Music Legacy CD, produced by Phil Schaap, contains the hybrid of two and three (in other words, the original stereo track) plus the complete, unedited two and three. The additional material on the French CD includes some takes that sound like rehearsals, where Holiday is working over the melody; when she gets to the bridge on take one, she says, "once again these words I'd have to say . . . I hope!" As Ellis later recalled, "I would say that the most emotional moment was her listening to the playback of 'I'm a Fool to Want You.' There were tears in her eyes."

She's clearly having a very hard time as the session reaches the fourth tune, "The End of a Love Affair." There are two incomplete versions taped that day, one is a rehearsal run-through; at one point she tells her pianist Mal Waldron, "Mal, please play as loud as you can. . . . I don't know the tune." She seems to have given up at this point; Ellis then led the orchestra through the arrangement with no vocal, and an instrumental track was laid down.

Throughout the Kuehl interviews, both Townsend and Ellis repeatedly state that not only was Holiday completely at the end of her rope, but that it was a very short rope to begin with. This is certainly not borne out by the released album or even by the outtakes, on most of which she sounds full of high spirits and good humor. But, undeniably, she's exhausted at the end of the second date.

As the musicians are packing up, following the Thursday night (February 20, 1958) session, it is now well past midnight, making it Friday morning, and Ellis says to Holiday: "'Hey, Baby, we're doing another session tomorrow, and there's one [orchestration] that I still haven't written.' She said, 'All right, let's go to the Colony . . .'" This was at a period in history when the Colony was famously open around the clock to accommodate musicians who had to have a piece of music in the middle of the night. "It's three o'clock in the morning and she had been drinking gin—straight gin—through the whole thing. So I get into a cab. You know the whole black-and-white scene? So we get double takes. She really looks like a disaster. I'm trying to get her out of the cab and I'm trying to pay the driver. I'm thinking she's going to fall, so I'm holding her up. So I lean her against the lamp-post and I say, 'Hold it, baby.'"

Proceeding to the sheet music section, Ellis and Holiday began rifling through various songs. "She was out of her head. Cursing everybody in the joint. Cursing her mother. Nobody even recognized her."

Not so out of her head. The song that she selected was an absolute gem—"You've Changed." Even Ellis admitted it was a good choice, and later cited it as his favorite tune on the album.

Friday, February 21, 1958. The first priority was to get back to "The End of a Love Affair"; Holiday took care of this summarily. This song was omitted from the original stereo pressings of the LP: in the early days of the new medium, stereo tracks took up more room on the vinyl than mono, and, in this case as in others, one song proved too long—here, it was this final one on Side B. The song is the only one of note by Edward C. Redding, who wrote it for his friend Mabel Mercer. To my ears, it's not one of the highlights of *Lady in Satin*—it seems kind of trivial by Holiday standards, seeing as we already know that when Lady Day was feeling depressed at the end of a love affair, she did things a lot more destructive than walking a little too fast or smoking a little too much. Still, her phrasing is impeccable and full of feeling, especially the way she handles the word "little" and shoots for the high note on "the ones where the trumpets *blare*."

She seems to have recorded only one complete take of Rodgers and Hart's "Glad to Be Unhappy," along with seven breakdowns and fragments. The most difficult note is in the verse, on "and I'll say it was *grand*," but she makes it effortlessly. (Sinatra had a harder time, especially when doing it live.) On the take labeled ten, a breakdown, she rephrases the melody to the verse with amazing creativity, much the way she did for dozens of songs in the 1930s (like "I Can't Get Started"), but unfortunately she doesn't get much further on this take; at a minute and a half she stops and says, "I ain't makin' that verse!"

Carl Fischer, composer of "You've Changed," was pop belter Frankie Laine's accompanist, and the earliest versions of this future standard were by Laine and his close friend Nat Cole. Whereas there are a lot of short takes on "Glad to Be Unhappy," there are only two breakdowns on "You've

Changed"—and the complete take is a classic. This was a particularly astute choice by Holiday for herself; small wonder that it became Ellis's favorite. (The choir is especially well used here as well.) Her setup of the lyric is perfection, each time she gets to the word "changed," she stretches it to emphasize it—the first time she sings it as a single note; the second time she stretches it over two notes, twisting it like a knife. When she gets to the line "You've forgotten the words, 'I love you'" she sings those words "I love you" on a single breath, as if to make them into a song within a song all by themselves. She does the whole second chorus on a suitably higher pitch of emotion. This is not a broken-down singer who needs a lamp-post to prop herself up, this is a great artist at close to the peak of her powers.

Hoagy Carmichael's "I Get Along Without You Very Well," which is essentially a setting for a poem by one Jane Brown Thompson, is absolutely essential Billie Holiday. There's also a breakdown take where we hear her summoning pianist Mal Waldron, and at one point, having finished a take, she asks, "Can we make one more quickie?" She explains, "I said 'springs.'" (Meaning, instead of spring, singular.) It's clear she doesn't know the tune as well as, say, the songs she was still singing every night live, and there are obvious places where she seems to be rewriting the melody à la Holiday, if only because she hasn't fully been able to learn the melody Carmichael wrote. (Surprisingly, she only recorded about four songs by him.) But who cares? She is well ahead of Sinatra, Chet Baker, and everyone else on this one, and Ellis's string orchestration has never suited her better. Every little detail comes vibrantly alive, from the soft rains that fall or the laugh that sounds the same, the moon that refuses to be kidded, and, somewhere in all that imagery, the breaking heart. Maybe the lyric works for her because it's so anti–Billie Holiday: the protagonist of the song is going around trying not to show her true feelings, but Holiday is an artist who shows every emotion, and therefore the irony of the text becomes even more heightened.

Although she had only been able to get through three songs on the Thursday session, she does a full five on Friday, concluding with Matt Dennis

and Tom Adair's "Violets for Your Furs," another Sinatra classic (with a Dorsey-like trombone solo by Urbie Green). There's one breakdown, where Holiday tells Ellis that she doesn't like the tempo, "it's too fast, it sounds like it's swinging." There are three complete takes, of which the issued one is presumably in the tempo she prefers; when Ellis tells her where to come in, she says, "Okay, baby, I'll try to make it." With Holiday, the bad things are major disasters—being incarcerated, or worse, getting beaten up by some male companion—but the good things are the little details. When she sings Adair's lyric about flowers being pinned to a fur coat in the middle of winter, she sounds as if she fully appreciates such small things. We can't expect the big breaks, the really important things, but it's these almost inconsequential acts of kindness that make life worth living. She sings like a woman who likes to wear mink, and doubly so when her man gives her flowers to make her feel special. It's as if all the acclaim from all the fans, critics, and even fellow artists in the world doesn't matter as much to her as the attention from that one. The man doesn't even have to give her the fur itself. All he has to do is pin a violet to it to make her feel that life is worth living.

The session ends—not with bleak tragedy, or the profound depths of despair, or the dark night of the soul, but with an undeniable glow of human warmth. Just the way she had planned it all along.

In later years, Ellis tended to emphasize how difficult it had been to get the album made, and what a mess Holiday was. "Three sessions of torture" is how he described it. "[I was] completely disgusted, frustrated. I didn't want to hear that thing again. I can't stand the sound of her voice." When Townsend invited him to the mixing session, he emphatically declined. "I don't want to go to the mixing. I'm so bugged I wish I'd never got involved in the project. I'm up to here with Billie Holiday! I tell him, 'Mix it? Forget it! I'll destroy it!'"

A week later, Townsend called Ellis and said, "Hey, baby, I made a test of this thing. I think you should hear it." When Ellis actually listened with more objective ears, he couldn't believe what he was hearing. "I loved it. It was so sad. It didn't matter whether she sang the right note or the wrong note, because she sang twenty thousand notes on that thing. But she poured her heart out. What she ended up doing was a recitation to the music, although I hadn't realized it at the time." Ellis added that the music so moved him—freaked him out, even—that he couldn't sit still. He was at his home in Larchmont when he played the test pressing of the LP, but he immediately jumped in his car and sped to the city, just to avoid having to process the feelings that the music brought out in him. "I couldn't stay in the house by myself, that's how despondent the music made me."

Holiday herself was very pleased with it, and Ellis was so delighted with the results that when he heard from her again, in March 1959, he agreed to do another album with her. These would be her last sessions: they featured more of an all-star jazz lineup, including trumpeter Sweets Edison and pianist Hank Jones, as well as a smaller string section (but no choir). The 1959 tracks were released by MGM after her death in July 1959 as *Billie Holiday: Her Final Recordings,* and known to aficionados ever since simply as *Billie Holiday.* They are truthfully labeled as the Great Lady's final sessions, but, in truth, *Lady in Satin* was her real last hurrah.

Lady in Satin was championed by Holiday's peers (Miles Davis was a fan) and memorized by generations of disciples. It's regarded not merely as her best original album, but virtually her only one: *Billie Holiday: Her Final Recordings* also has its

merits, but does not truly challenge *Lady in Satin* for superiority. Some of the Verve LPs were actual albums, but it's hard to tell which (other than her famous 1956 Carnegie Hall concert, done to commemorate the publishing of her memoir, *Lady Sings the Blues*) were planned as albums, since Granz never made any attempt to organize them in any way.

Once again, Ellis is remarkably frank in his interview with Linda Kuehl, but totally repulsive. After already having said this many, many times, he further stresses that when Holiday came to meet with him at his office at MGM Records early in 1959, "Billie, by this time, looks like a real old, tired, black hooker—the type you really wouldn't want to go near. She looks terrible, a pathetic thing."

In the course of his long career, Ellis would make albums with Chris Connor, Johnny Mathis, and many other first-rank artists, including *Simply Streisand* (1967), one of that diva's most palatable offerings. But nothing else he would do would ever approach the beauty, majesty, and sheer perfection of *Lady in Satin.* He couldn't possibly have realized that this would be the project he would be best remembered for. But he did say, "She gave me the opportunity to be heard and look good. If you listen to the album, you can hear the orchestra very plainly." In hindsight, one hopes that he wished he could go back and tell the world, "Yes! This is the greatest singer of all time and this is the proudest moment of my career."

24

Lena Horne

Lena Horne at the Waldorf Astoria

(1957)

If any artist is the victim of revisionism—much of it self-administered—it's Lena Horne. By the 1960s, she was regarded as the most famous African American woman of her time, and was routinely accepted as a de facto civil rights leader. In the 1970s, with the release of *That's Entertainment!* and the long-after-the-fact deification of the MGM movie musical and the Arthur Freed Unit, Horne came to be regarded as the first great black movie star (in the same sense that Katharine Hepburn and Ava Gardner were movie stars). In the 1980s, after her one-woman Broadway musical became a huge hit (signaling neither the first nor the last career revival in her life) Horne radically retooled her style of singing, so much so that if you were hearing her for the first time, you might assume that she was the Grandmother of Soul, the one who taught Aretha Franklin and Ray Charles.

Lena Horne was, in fact, none of these things. Rather, she was a nightclub headliner who happened to be black. She was the most popular black woman of her generation to work in what were considered white mediums in front of white audiences, but unlike artists both older (Ethel Waters) and younger (Dinah Washington), Horne had been able to go the direct route: she wasn't a black superstar who crossed over; rather, she clicked with the white audience and the black at the same time. She sang relatively little of what was then considered black popular music, i.e., the blues or R&B, and unlike Waters and Washington, in their respective eras, she did not have notable hits on the race charts. Lena Horne's spiritual soul sisters were not Waters, Washington, or Billie Holiday, but Judy Garland and Edith Piaf, and like them, her stock-in-trade was a unique mixture of power and vulnerability. When audiences—almost exclusively Caucasian—flocked to see her at high-priced nightclubs like the Empire Room at the Waldorf, none of them were thinking of her as a racial symbol; nor were they lamenting the notion that her skin color prevented her from being offered any substantial movie roles. Fact is, as with Nat King Cole, at the height of his height, no one was thinking of her in racial or political terms—they were just thinking how great she was, and what a thrill it was to watch her at work.

By far her best album, or indeed, her single most substantial work in any medium, *Lena Horne at the Waldorf Astoria* shows us the artist that she wanted to get away from after the mid-1960s: a not very racially or socially conscious (or even particularly "black") nightclub headliner. It makes sense that Horne would make the first great live album, as well as land what was hailed for many years as the most successful album by a female vocalist in the annals of RCA Records. The singles chart was fairly divided, there was a mainstream market and a black market (as well as a country market); but in albums, Johnny Mathis competed for the same shelf space as Vic Damone and Lena Horne with Dinah Shore. (When the *Waldorf* album was on the charts, it was going up against Pat Boone, Nat King Cole, the *My Fair Lady* cast album, the *Around the World in 80 Days* soundtrack, vintage recordings by the Glenn Miller AAF Orchestra, and also the *Loving You* soundtrack album by Elvis Presley.)

Nineteen fifty-seven was probably the high point of Horne's career: she and Lennie Hayton, her husband and musical director, began the year by opening at the Waldorf on New Year's Eve (1956), then recorded the album while the run was still going strong in February, and ended with the Broadway show *Jamaica;* in between, she did *The Ed Sullivan Show* (twice) and other TV appearances. In other words, she was generally widely visible as one of the world's most popular nightclub headliners. Before the war, nightclubs and supper clubs ("nite spots," as the columnists called them) were generally dominated by dance bands, you paid the cover charge to fox-trot with your honey or your secretary and hold her tight; but starting in the mid-1940s, more and more you paid for the privilege of sitting down and listening to a name brand like Julie Wilson, Hildegarde, Frank Sinatra, or Lena Horne. As late as the mid-1960s, Midtown was awash in such clubs. The most recognizable (to later generations at least) were the Copacabana and the Latin Quarter, but by far the most prestigious at the time were those venues situated in hotel ballrooms, like the Persian Room at the Plaza and the Empire Room at the Waldorf. The great majority of the nonhotel clubs, particularly Birdland and the Copa, were generally under the control of what loosely could be called organized crime (though not always the traditional Italian Mafia); when you worked for the corporations or the very wealthy families that owned the Waldorf or the Plaza, that meant, at least, that you didn't have to deal with the mob.

Although the Empire Room already had a long history, with performers both white and black (though the audiences were almost exclusively Caucasian), Horne created a sensation at the Waldorf, so much so that other artists (like Tony Bennett) yearned to play there. One of the hoary truths about Horne's career thus far was that she never

amounted to much on commercial recordings—indeed, she scarcely competed in the hit singles stakes, as opposed to someone like Dinah Washington, who sold steadily and consistently on all kinds of material. At the start of her career, Horne was one of the few African American women signed as a solo singer by RCA Victor—surely a vote of confidence—but within a few years, even well within the MGM period, they let her contract lapse and she recorded for a time with the considerably less prestigious independent label Black & White Records.

Yet at the time of the 12-inch LP, RCA re-signed Horne. Clearly, they were prescient enough to realize that she could be much more meaningful in the album format than grinding out singles. Her first album under the renewed association was *It's Love* (1955), and then, at the start of 1957, when the rave reviews started pouring in, and it became apparent that her Waldorf run was being regarded as a historic, even legendary, event, RCA made arrangements to record her live. It didn't hurt that the company's offices were just a few blocks from the Waldorf; they certainly were in a good position to know what was happening in Midtown. It's easy to imagine RCA and NBC executives heading for the Waldorf after work for Horne's show, taking their wives and scarfing down multiple martinis on the corporate expense account.

Small wonder that *Lena Horne at the Waldorf Astoria* (which is often abbreviated to *Lena at the Waldorf*) was such a hit; it is an album of almost nothing but blockbusters; there are faster blockbusters, there are slower blockbusters, there are more extroverted blockbusters and more intimate blockbusters, but they're all, in the show-biz lingo of the era, "Boffo!" By the time I finally saw Horne live, in the 1980s and '90s, she wasn't doing a show like this anymore—partly because, as an elderly woman, she no longer had the wind power and the sheer chops necessary. (The show she was doing, particularly in her last few years of working, was appropriate for who she was at that time in her life—and excellent too, in its own way.)

I've seen artists do shows like Horne's Waldorf set only a few times in my life: Marilyn Maye, Ben

Vereen (old pro that he is), Tony Bennett, and a few others. This is the kind of show that's based on a foundation of constantly working, constantly tinkering, constantly perfecting. For most of the past few generations—say, since the reopening of the Oak Room at the Algonquin Hotel in 1980—what are known as cabaret shows tend to be built around a concept, such as the songbook idea (Cole Porter), a theme (World War II), a tribute (Hildegarde). They start with a premise and proceed, one hopes logically, from there. Conversely, there's no predictable logic in the Lena Waldorf show, other than that she starts with a bang—and it isn't necessarily the biggest bang in the show—and she just keeps banging away. The songs have nothing to do with each other, there's no logical progression that we can analyze, but everything just works—and the only way she knew it would work was by doing it. She constantly experimented with going from one song to another, figuring out what flowed properly and what didn't. The final result proves that experience is the enemy of logic: what works in front of an audience, night after night, can't necessarily be predicted—there is no formula—everything has to be proven by trial and error.

It's important that these are mostly songs that are unique to her. Apart from "Honeysuckle Rose," which was already recorded by a million jazz musicians and singers, the great majority of these are songs that nobody else was singing. The opener, for instance, is "Today I Love Everybody," which springs from her ongoing collaboration with Harold Arlen; like Judy Garland, she had a long and very specific musical relationship with Arlen, who wrote more signature songs for both divas than any other composer. "Today I Love Everybody" is a comparatively obscure Arlen song from the 1953 movie musical version of The Farmer Takes a Wife, hardly a classic of the genre, a picture that juxtaposed two unlikely couples, composer Arlen and lyricist Dorothy Fields (their only major project together) and leading lady Betty Grable and future TV western star Dale Robertson, not a notable song-and-dance man.

After an announcement ("Good evening, ladies and gentlemen, it's show time in the Empire. At this time, the Waldorf-Astoria is very proud to present . . . Miss Lena Horne.") She starts with a dramatic orchestral sting, leading into an out-of-tempo introductory verse ("You think the sky is blue / as far as I can see . . ."). This turns out to be the musical equivalent of an Olympic athlete running up to a long-distance jump or a pitcher cocking back his arm before a throw. She then launches into time, but as mentioned, she opens with a medium bang—by her own standards, "Today I Love Everybody" is more subtle and less predictable than a cookie-cutter opener like "I'm Gonna Live Till I Die," which was practically the national anthem for Vegas and hotel ballroom supper clubs in the 1950s. "Today I Love Everybody" is a virtual textbook definition of the words "bright" and "cheerful," bouncing as opposed to swinging, flirty rather than seductive.

The whole show is about energy as much as tempo, not so much about speeding up and slowing down as about the contrast between those numbers where she holds a little something back and those where she just lets everything go, and deluges the audience in emotion. She pulls back slightly for "Let Me Love You," a song much prized by cabaret artists of the time. (It was written by Bart Howard, accompanist for Mabel Mercer.) Guided primarily by a sure-footed bass line, she sings the first chorus more straight-ahead, and the second more serpentine, like the snake slithering around the apple tree and telling Adam where he can stick his rib; she teases out the melody as a way to entice the object of her seduction. For a temptress, she's remarkably direct, not making any promises to her intended but letting him know at the git-go that when she's done with him, she'll send him merrily on his way.

"Come Runnin'" is by Roc Hillman, a swing band guitarist who worked for years with the Dorsey Brothers Orchestra (probably a friend of Lennie Hayton's). Horne would also record it in her studio album Stormy Weather; the live version is brassy enough, even though it's somewhat less so than the studio version, which starts with a very noisy intro. The song perfectly matches Horne's sassy style, and she would keep doing it (as on the unreleased sequel to the Waldorf album as well as a live album from the Supper Club in 1994). It's a different kind of seduction and enticement, more playful and almost like a nursery rhyme in its repetitive, short, clipped phrases. She uses the minimal text as a point of departure "Come running / come flying / come laughing / come crying," the effect is rather like a superior dancer moving her way up a flight of stairs; she leaps up and down over the steps. At least once she twists her voice to sound more like a little girl (or is it an old woman?)—on lines like "*get here, baby,* just as fast as you can."

Track four is a medley of what she introduces as "the always surprising Cole Porter songs," four in total. Notably, all four are somewhat offbeat Porter pieces, the kind that a scholar and specialist like Bobby Short would do in a much smaller club like the Café Carlyle. The track lasts for over seven and a half minutes, but this isn't like a Steve and Eydie TV medley, where they race through the titles, and by the point where you've been able to recognize one song, they've already moved on to the next. Rather, Horne does virtually a full chorus of each, and even starts with the full verse of the first, the 1932 "How's Your Romance?" Porter, famously, wrote many French-inspired songs that spoke to his love of all things Parisian, but this is his only notable song to reference Italy. It was written for Erik Rhodes as "Tonetti," the Neapolitan gigolo, in *Gay Divorce;* the great character actor repeated the role in the 1934 film version, but alas, the song was cut. Here, Horne is feisty and sexy in two languages at once—even affecting the nasal twang of an Italian street vendor.

Another great song from *Gay Divorce* (and which also didn't make the movie), "After You" (aka "After You, Who?"), slows down the medley; it's Horne's most sincere moment yet, she sings one chorus with such directness and clarity that for her to add anything to it would seem redundant. She says everything that needs to be said in those thirty-two bars and roughly ninety seconds, with an especially plaintive ending. Very subtly, a beguine rhythm—reminding us of other Cole Porter songs that referenced his love of Caribbean music—is introduced, and all at once we're in the middle of "Love of My Life" (from the 1948 *The Pirate*). From there, we jump radically but smoothly into a nicely up treatment of the newest song in the medley, "It's All Right with Me" (from *Can-Can*). Horne is feisty and upbeat here, more defiant than seductive;

she's not trying to get anybody to do anything, but rather, as the other party expresses his intentions, she merely lets him know that whatever he has on his mind is all right with her. She's not the temptress but the one being tempted (". . . but they're such tempting lips . . ."). Even in passive mode, Horne is like a jungle cat, you can see her baring her teeth and her jungle-red fingernails.

One by-product of the live album was what became known as "bow music"—which means what it sounds like: when the artist makes an entrance, or takes a bow between songs, the orchestra plays a burst of fast and snappy music, something with a memorable theme, to amp up the excitement even further. At this point in Horne's career, her bow music was the song "How About You?" (On the CD, track five begins with the bow music—it might have made more sense to put it at the end of track four, or better yet, separate it into a track by itself.)

The bow music leads into an unaccompanied bass intro (it would be great to know the player—Milt Hinton would be my guess), over which Horne starts wordlessly moaning the words to "Mood Indigo." Duke Ellington had written several compositions to be sung wordlessly by the female voice, of which the best known was "Creole Love Call." By humming here, Horne is essentially rendering "Mood Indigo" as if it were "Creole Love Call." She then sings a whole chorus of the classic Ellington song with only bass. Track five soon reveals itself to be a composite, if you will, of two Ellington songs, "Mood Indigo" and "I'm Beginning to See the Light." Somehow that's a better word than "medley"—in the "Cole Porter Medley" she goes from one song to another, whereas here Horne makes the two songs into something more like one amazing mega-song. We keep expecting certain things to happen—for instance, the full band to come in and Horne to start blasting—but she continually defies expectation. She sings an exuberant but still understated chorus of "See the Light," and then returns to "Mood Indigo." Essentially, "See the Light" is nested within the middle of "Mood Indigo"—like a musical matryoshka doll.

This is some of the subtlest and most surprising singing Horne has ever done—just when we expect her to get loud and swinging, she gets soft and swinging. She isn't frequently described as a jazz singer, but this five-minute, two-song track is the quintessence of what good jazz singing is all about.

Back in the day, this was the end of Side A, and "How You Say It" was the start of the second side. This is the first of two songs here by the team of composer Harold Karr and Matt Dubey, and their presence in the Waldorf set—and on the album— may reflect the influence of RCA, which was then pushing the cast album for the team's then-running Broadway musical, *Happy Hunting*, universally regarded as a second-rate show with second-rate songs that ran longer than it should have because of the presence of a first-rate superstar, Ethel Merman. Both songs are somewhat curmudgeonly spoofs on Latin American dance crazes; they can only have seemed barely funny in 1957 and are far less so today. "How You Say It" is a comic Spanglish dialect number cut from the same cloth as Peggy Lee's "Mañana." (Either one could be sung by Mel Blanc in his mock-Mexican accent.) Embodying the role of a Spanish woman trying to describe the boy she adores in English, Horne expresses herself in three ways: pidgin-English, pseudo-Spanish, and nonverbal noises—grunts and growls and phrases like "Gee" and "Oy!"

The other Dubey-Karr song, "New Fangled Tango," is another goofball parody of a south-of-the-border dance extravaganza. (The chorus begins "A new-fangled tango / and there's nothing to it / You just sort of stand there / and just sort of do it.") Heard by themselves, the songs aren't bad, but they're hardly worthy of a place at the table alongside Cole Porter and Duke Ellington.

After "How You Say It," we get more "How About You" bow music and another bass intro leads to "Honeysuckle Rose"; again, Horne does the whole thing mostly with just bass and only minimal input from the piano. Her rhythmic dexterity parallels what Anita O'Day was doing with the exact same song at roughly the exact same time. As with the two Ellington songs, she plays "Honeysuckle Rose" very close to the vest. Her lithe alto has never sounded sweeter, she leaps from one note to the next as if she were playing hopscotch, but she keeps the narrative moving and the drama flowing

without ever raising her voice. Like Judy Garland, she does small just as well as she does big.

Again, this is outstanding jazz singing, and a perfect lead-in to the next number, a big, brassy, bouncy version of Rube Bloom and Johnny Mercer's "Day In, Day Out," which, as the title suggests, gives Horne the opportunity to exercise her acute capacity for contrasts, the difference between high and low, loud and soft, shouting and moaning. The track starts in a quasi-Cuban polyrhythm, light and romping at first. As the track continues, she gets progressively louder and more agitated; by the end, she's really blasting. But by starting small and building from there, she makes you feel she's earned the right to belt—she doesn't do it gratuitously, she uses the technique sparingly to add genuine excitement to the number. The belting is about the drama rather than the other way around. From slow start to big finish, "Day In, Day Out" is classic Lena.

So too is "I Love to Love," which follows "New Fangled Tango" as Side B, track five. "I Love to Love" is the most notable song by Herbert Baker, who spent most of his career writing and producing movies and TV shows, but, as this song proves, was also a first-rate songwriter (certainly way above Dubey and Karr). "I Love to Love" is a five-minute tour de force, and that term is appropriate since it begins with a verse that starts with a phrase in French. This is absolutely perfect Lena: simultaneously capturing her seductive and comic sides, each fueling the other. (Baker was, it seems, destined to tailor a great song expressly for a great diva: his mother was the vaudeville headliner Belle Baker and his father was Maurice Abrahams, a notable songwriter of the teens.)

Baker's song fits Horne as exquisitely as a Schiaparelli gown, clinging to every emotional curve, hugging every nook and cranny of her multidimensional personality; he has perfectly captured her simultaneous outpouring of eroticism and innocence, haughty imperiousness and self-deflating humor. "I Love to Love" was later done by such worthy constituents as Peggy Lee and Nina Simone, but neither of them can lay a white satin glove on her. (Although Simone, notably, changes the reference from "a Marlon Brando touch" to "a

Frank Sinatra touch.") Horne stretches the song out in a kind of musical striptease—drawing it, pulling it, like a burlesque dancer stretching her gloves as she slides them off. She also sings more of Baker's words, including some that the later interpreters don't bother with, like "Give me that real-life drama / Baby, this is sin-erama!" or "Just sit me on the couch where I can't resist / You don't have to be a psychiatrist." Singer and songwriter achieve an amazing synergy here, or, as she would say, "sin-ergy." Particularly remarkable is that this song, by a little-known songwriter, is perhaps the single most effective piece of material in Horne's repertoire—I'd much rather hear her sing "I Love to Love" than "Stormy Weather" anytime.

"I Love to Love" would be good enough to close, but she chooses to go out with a bigger bang, and that's "From This Moment On." She sings two choruses of the Cole Porter classic (dropped from the 1950 *Out of This World* and retrofitted into most productions of *Kiss Me, Kate* from the 1953 movie version onward): the first is bright, then she starts the second chorus at the bridge, but just when we expect her to get faster and louder, she gets slower and softer ("You've got the skin I love to touch"), dropping the orchestra altogether in the last line of that bridge ("You've got the lips to kiss me and kiss me . . ."). In fact, she gets so quiet that she drops the last words ("good night") altogether. The last eight bars are the big earth-shattering closer that we would expect. She belts the last line loudly—with dramatic pauses ("from—this—moment—on") and emphatically enough to be heard well over the orchestra, probably loud enough to be heard in Brooklyn.

We hear the voice of Lennie Hayton giving the orchestra the count-off into the bow music ("one-two!") and there's about sixteen bars of "How About You" before the fadeout. And that's all she sang.

Reviewing the album (June 10, 1957), *Billboard,* always looking for tips to pass on to record retailers, noted: "Horne's incendiary delivery and sultry, sexy cover photo make this package a solid stock item for dealers and a rich programming source for discriminating jocks." (With regard to the latter,

they also observed, "although some of the [songs] are too spicy for air consumption.")

The album was so successful for RCA—as mentioned, for years it was their biggest-selling LP by a female vocalist—that in 1960 they recorded another set by Horne at the Empire. The result—tentatively titled *Lena Returns to the Waldorf*—was just as good musically, but there were technical issues. The balance between the singer and the orchestra isn't good, and her microphone repeatedly pops and distorts. Strange that a major label, who knew what they were doing, should so fumble and drop the ball. (Obviously, this being the Mad Men era, the RCA staff had indulged in too many of those martinis.) Still, *Lena Returns to the Waldorf* documents an outstanding performance, one that quite possibly could be corrected by twenty-first-century digital means. Some songs are repeated from 1957 (and she continues to use "How About You" as bow music), but in place of the Porter and Ellington segments, there is a string of four classic songs by Hayton's buddies Johnny Burke and Jimmy Van Heusen, as well as an equally worthy sequence of three numbers by Rodgers and Hammerstein.

The original 1957 album, *Lena Horne at the Waldorf Astoria,* aka *Lena at the Waldorf,* is with a few possible exceptions we could argue about—*Mel Tormé at the Crescendo* (1954), *Matt Dennis Plays and Sings Matt Dennis,* taped live at the Tally-Ho in Hollywood (also 1954)—quite probably the first great live album by a major singer, and a true predecessor to *Mack the Knife: Ella in Berlin* and *Judy at Carnegie Hall.* Don't get me wrong, there was great stuff by Horne before this—generally more of it on the screen than in her recordings—and after as well, particularly the albums of the 1960s and her jazz-fueled renaissance of the 1990s. But more than anything else in her career, *Lena at the Waldorf* represents her best of the best. She was already known for both sexiness and sheer volume; now comes proof that she was an artist of nuance and power—rather than a mere symbol of something—who at her finest deserved to be mentioned in the same breath as Fitzgerald and Garland. Like them, she held nothing back, evidence of which is in every groove of *Lena at the Waldorf;* it's all there, right in front of you.

25

Barb Jungr

Every Grain of Sand: Barb Jungr Sings Bob Dylan

(2002)

When Bob Dylan sings "It Ain't Me Babe," he sounds like a young man (he was twenty-three at the time) trying to avoid commitment—to dodge a bullet, as it were. He introduced the song on his 1964 album *Another Side of Bob Dylan,* and whatever "side" the album title may refer to, it's a sure bet that the song does not reflect his sensitive side or "feminine" side. He sounds dismissive, he may not want to hurt the woman he's breaking up with, but he's clearly only thinking about himself. Conversely, when Barb Jungr sings "It Ain't Me Babe," she sounds much more compassionate— like she has something difficult to tell someone, something that he definitely doesn't want to hear, and she sings it as if she's thinking more about his feelings than she is about her own. It's the same words, more or less the same melody, and yet the meaning is so completely different as to be a whole other song. And that's exactly the point.

When *Every Grain of Sand: Barb Jungr Sings Bob Dylan* was first released in 2002, it was a revelation: the British singer (the most famous from Rochdale, Lancashire, since Gracie Fields) had achieved precisely what the lessons of the previous fifty years had proved to us was, literally, impossible to do. From the rock 'n' roll era onward, there were two kinds of popular song: the "traditional" kind, written by the likes of Irving Berlin and Cole Porter, which were meant to be performed in all kinds of different ways, from Al Jolson to Count Basie to John Coltrane to Rod Stewart, and the "contemporary" kind, in which the artist who wrote the song (both words and music, usually) was the same artist who sang the song—and no one else was allowed to sing that same song. It was the difference between "one size fits all" songwriting and "one size fits nobody."

Bob Dylan is the first major singer-songwriter of the current era. He is also the contemporary composer who can point to the largest number of "covers." But even so, there was nothing like Jungr before 2001—and precious little since. No one had ever taken songs by Dylan or any other songwriter from the folk-rock-contemporary genres and proven it was possible not merely to cover them but to reinterpret them—from the roots up. Jungr's treatments of Dylan songs, both famous and obscure, are textbook models demonstrating the very concept of interpretation. You wouldn't necessarily classify Jungr as a jazz singer (whatever that may mean), but she makes use of the jazz concept of taking a melody and casting it in a different form— say, adding percussion so that it sounds somewhat Pan-American, or adding a solo violin so that it sounds like Eastern European Romany music, or maybe taking a song in common time (2/4) and putting it into 5/4.

Yet what she did—and continues to do—with the lyrics was even more radical, and, at the same time, remarkably subtle. Irving Berlin wrote songs that reflected everybody's feelings and experiences, whereas Dylan's songs express his own almost exclusively—but when Jungr sings "Don't Think Twice," all of a sudden it's about her feelings and experiences, which might have nothing to do with the author's. Parts of the album *Every Grain of Sand* sound like smooth jazz, some sound like gospel music, but none of the songs sound the way they did when Dylan sang them; all of a sudden, they were no longer about Bob but about Barb. This was more than a breakthrough; this was, as I say above, a revelation. As high a regard as Dylan has been held in by those who think about pop music, Jungr showed that he was even greater.

As with what Sinatra did for Cole Porter—turning ballads into swingers and torch songs into bossa novas—Jungr heard possibilities in Dylan's music that the composer himself never even dreamed of. Nor was it his job to.

Recorded in October 2001, *Every Grain of Sand* consists of fifteen songs drawn from across the span of the first forty years of Dylan's career (and the thirty-one studio albums that he had released thus far). There are classic vintage Dylan songs from the height of his height in the mid-1960s going all the way through his latest album at the time, the 2001 *Love and Theft* (from which Jungr selected "Sugar Baby"). The set is almost evenly balanced between iconic Dylan songs (which are considered iconic mainly because they've been widely performed by other artists) like "Don't Think Twice, It's All Right" and, at the other extreme, such comparatively obscure works as "Things Have Changed." The latter is a 2000 song that was written for the main titles of a flop film called *Wonder Boys*. It was never even heard on a proper Dylan album, and in the mere act of including "Things Have Changed" on *Every Grain of Sand*, Jungr was loudly shouting out to Dylan diehards that she was one of them.

But in ranging from the familiar to the offbeat, the early to the recent, one criterion seems to stand out. For lack of a better term, Jungr is a cabaret singer—not that this is a dirty word (as multiple generations of clueless judges on *American Idol* would have you believe), but it doesn't

completely describe what she does. It is a term of convenience: in New York, almost any vocalist who does one-person shows of music written by other people (and accompanied by someone else on piano) is generally classified as "cabaret." In general, Ms. Jungr prefers those Dylan songs that come out of the classical narrative song tradition—songs with a beginning, middle, and end. Many of his most famous early songs are completely surreal and random. Consider "Mr. Tambourine Man," "A Hard Rain's A-Gonna Fall," and "Stuck Inside of Mobile with the Memphis Blues Again"—none has anything like a concrete narrative; rather, they pile one colorful image on top of another. In the psychedelic 1960s, it was widely understood that these texts utilized a Dada-like sensibility to rail against the establishment; they're anarchic in the sense that those other great Jewish poets, the Marx Brothers, are anarchic.

Likewise, Jungr also avoids those songs of Dylan that are pure narrative, folk-style songs, that take the form of traditional "ballads," the most famous of which is probably "The Lonesome Death of Hattie Carroll," for instance. The bulk of her Dylan songs are neither completely abstract nor completely concrete, but, in the fashion of most traditional Tin Pan Alley songs, somewhere in between. She obviously prefers those Dylan songs that travel a coherent path but without necessarily telling a complete story from beginning to end, songs that present characters, convey a mood, or get an idea across. A song can tell a story, or it can paint a picture, it can convey images, it can communicate ideas—and Jungr, like Dylan, is above all a master communicator.

The all-important title track on her breakthrough Dylan songbook album is the only one that comes from Dylan's three spiritually driven albums of 1979–81. "Every Grain of Sand" is the final track in Dylan's Christian cycle (that is to say, it's the last song on the last of the three spiritual albums, *Shot of Love*), and Jungr uses it as her closing number. Where the message of "Subterranean Homesick Blues" seems to be that existence is completely random and anarchic, "Every Grain" argues very convincingly that God is in complete control: "In the fury of the moment I can see The Master's hand / In every leaf that trembles, in every grain of sand." As sung by Jungr, even more than by the songwriter himself, it's a very sincere testimony to His supreme wisdom.

Jungr's "Every Grain" opens with a wind sound effect—used very subtly—at a very low volume; she sings Dylan's lyrics and melody over a churning, organlike pattern that sounds exactly like a harmonium in a religious service, played very effectively by the string section. Where Dylan's track is clearly a waltz, Jungr's is in a less distinct 2/4. Dylan intoned his own text somewhat introvertedly, as if it were a prayer or a mantra being voiced to himself, whereas Jungr speaks it much more extrovertedly, as if she were preaching to a congregation.

"Ring Them Bells" is not technically from Dylan's Christian period, having been introduced ten years later on the 1989 Oh Mercy, but it is a highly spiritual text that belongs with the 1979–81 albums stylistically if not chronologically. It's rife with religious references; the most obvious interpretation is that the ringing of the bells signifies a kind of salvation. Jungr sings it as a companion to "Every Grain of Sand." The title is similar to Duke Ellington's 1930 "Ring Dem Bells," but Dylan's song somehow sounds way older than that; older than water, even. Dylan's own record has a feeling similar to that of a traditional spiritual being sung by an ancient country blues singer or a very tired New Orleans parade band. Gospel music is often stereotyped as making rather too much use of decoration and embellishment, singers who will never sing one note when they can get away with belting ten. Yet "Ring Them Bells," in Dylan's rendition especially, is incredibly stark and pious, even ascetic. Jungr's interpretation is slightly more elaborate—she adds a vocal choir that's most likely three overdubbed Jungr voices. She also employs more gospel-style melisma, but in both cases these are tastefully and sparingly utilized. Despite the religiosity of the piece ("Ring them bells so the world will know that God is one"), one can't help wondering whether it's a companion piece to "The Time's They Are a-Changin'." Perhaps it's not talking about dying and going to heaven so much as the coming of peace and a new spiritual order on earth—the lion lying

down with the lamb and the end of "the distance between right and wrong."

"Not Dark Yet" is musically similar to "Ring Them Bells" but quite different philosophically. Where "Ring Them Bells" is heavy but optimistic, "Not Dark Yet" is nihilistic in the extreme; the lyrics speak of being afflicted by "scars that the sun didn't heal," and thus immersed in encroaching darkness. Dylan's version (from the 1997 Time Out of Mind) is enhanced by the darkness and cragginess of his own voice; he himself once said that he could sing "I Get a Kick out of You" and it would come out sounding like "Mule Skinner Blues." Some comparatively capricious lyrics leaven the profundity ("Well, I've been to London and I've been to gay Paree"), but the title aside, it's still as dark as can be imagined. Jungr's voice has more texture and shading to it, and more of an inherently positive feeling (it couldn't be any darker than Dylan's), but even in her vocal, if it isn't dark yet, it's incredibly bleak—and moving—just the same.

Not everything on Every Grain of Sand is so heavy or such a downer; "Tangled Up in Blue" (from 1975's classic Blood on the Tracks) is comparatively lighthearted. It draws on several Dylan traditions: it has the rambling, repetitive rhythm of "Subterranean Homesick Blues" and it builds over a long series of wordy choruses, but the song itself follows, for the most part, a logical narrative. The libretto gets a little poetic (or at least obscure) on lines like, "The only thing I knew how to do / Was to keep on keepin' on like a bird that flew," but, in general, the song makes sense. Jungr, to her credit, doesn't try to conventionalize it, or make it sound like a pre-1960 show tune. Nor does she change any genders; the person she's "tangled up" with in her story is referred to as "she" (as in "She was workin' in a topless place"). She stays true to Dylan's outlines, and, presumably, his vision of the song, but makes it her own just the same. Among other things, there's heavy use of the strings (it sounds like a solo cello playing pizzicato at the start) and accordion; Jungr and Simon Wallace jointly keep Dylan's minimal melody going and enhance it with several layers of elaborate polyrhythms and countermelodies—unlike the Blood on the Tracks original, this arrangement is not "spare" or "sparse" in any way.

Jungr also includes a goodly share of Dylan's more directly positive love songs, such as her two opening tracks, "I'll Be Your Baby Tonight" and "If Not for You." These are two of Dylan's most conventionally country-style songs—"I'll Be Your Baby Tonight" sounds like the work of any songwriter in Nashville other than Bob Dylan. (I imagine he would take this observation as a compliment, since it shows that he can write in more than one style, and that not all of his songs sound the same.) "I'll Be Your Baby Tonight" even has blue yodels written directly into the melody in the manner of country music pioneer Jimmie Rodgers.

"If Not for You" has more Dylan-y touches—in Jungr's treatment, the lyrics seem to say "If not for you, my life would be as bleak as the poor guy in 'Not Dark Yet.'" Compared to the more polished treatments by George Harrison and especially Glen Campbell (not to mention Jungr), Dylan's comparatively rough rendition of "If Not for You" sounds like nothing so much as a songwriter's demo. Whereas Jungr's "I'll Be Your Baby Tonight" finds Simon Wallace playing with a hint of slip-note style piano à la Floyd Cramer, her "If Not for You" isn't the least bit country. The use of soprano sax and strings gives it more of a Celtic feel; there's a subtle bongo rhythm heard throughout, and another very brief use of an all-Jungr choir. The bongos and strings return on the third track, "Things Have Changed," which Jungr and Wallace have reinterpreted as a rather aggressive tango.

Apart from "I'll Be Your Baby Tonight," there are two other Dylan babies: the 1965 "It's All Over Now, Baby Blue" (from *Bringing It All Back Home*) is a kiss-off song, and as in "Don't Think Twice, It's All Right," there's an ironic distance between addressing someone tenderly as "Babe" or "Baby Blue" and telling her goodbye—particularly if you're doing it in the same sentence. (Somehow that seems more poetic than saying, "So long, you jerk!") "Sugar Baby," as noted, is the most recent song on *Every Grain*, originating on the 2001 *Love and Theft*. Parts of both the music and words were directly inspired by the 1928 Tin Pan Alley spiritual "The Lonesome Road"; interestingly, the borrowing seems more obvious in Dylan's recording than in Jungr's—though in Jungr's treatment, the

strings play a background figure that's repeatedly reminiscent of "Ol' Man River," which, coincidentally or otherwise, was heard alongside "Lonesome Road" in the 1929 film of *Show Boat*. ("It Ain't Me Babe," on the *Man in the Long Black Coat* collection, has Jungr delivering a kiss-off aria with rather amazing tenderness.)

"What Good Am I?," the other song from *Oh Mercy,* is virtually the only clear-cut case where I would rather listen to Dylan's original version than Jungr's interpretation—the song sounds too stark, too personal, too *him* to be sung by anybody else. "Born in Time" is probably the least-known song from the least-known album here (the 1990 *Under the Red Sky*). It's also the most incomprehensible song in the collection: after listening to both the Dylan and Jungr versions, and reading the lyrics on Dylan's own official website, I still can't quite figure out how this particular deal is going down. I could tell you that Jungr heightens and accentuates Dylan's rhythms (the strings get very baroque here), giving the song more drive than on *Red Sky,* but as far as precisely what is transpiring in the lyrics . . . well, son, you're on your own.

In contrast, the larger meaning of "Forever Young" is absolutely crystal clear. Ostensibly dedicated by the songwriter to his children (on the 1974 *Planet Waves*), the song reads like a wedding toast, an appropriate salutation either to a young bride and groom, or a couple on their golden anniversary. It's one of the most covered of his songs, having been recorded by Joan Baez, Harry Belafonte (who once hired Dylan to play harmonica on a 1962 album), Johnny Cash (whose take is curiously dour), Diana Ross (in a rather breathless treatment), Rod Stewart (who essentially wrote his own variation on Dylan's song); many versions of Dylan himself doing it also exist, including early demos and concert performances drawn from over forty years.

Of all these myriad takes on "Forever Young," Jungr's is quite the best. It's the most rhythmic, the most exciting, the most dynamic and moving treatment; this is the one that I would play to toast someone I love. To me the song is so straightforward that it could be Dylan's answer to "More I Can Not Wish You," the wedding song from *Guys* and Dolls. As it happens, "More I Can Not Wish You" is the song into which Frank Loesser threw perhaps the most cryptic, almost indecipherable line in any traditional show tune—the one about "the sheep's eye and the lickerish tooth." Just this once, Loesser was more Dylan than Dylan.

Every Grain of Sand barely scratched the surface of the Dylan iceberg—if sand and icebergs even belong in the same metaphor. Ten years later, in 2011, Jungr released a CD titled Man in the Long Black Coat, which collected tracks from a cross-section of her albums from 2002 to 2008, as well as some new and previously unreleased songs. It's not exactly a sequel or a follow-up, it's more like a massive selection of bonus tracks. Once again, Jungr's Dylan scholarship is immediately apparent: there are at least three Dylan rarities here that were never heard on any proper Dylan studio album: "Tomorrow Is a Long Time," "Blind Willie McTell," and the extremely rare "Trouble in Mind."

As with the fifteen tracks on Grain of Sand, Jungr continues to favor songs that paint a coherent picture—as opposed to random imagery. "The Ballad of Hollis Brown" is notable as her major interpretation of one of Dylan's more literal folk ballads, and Jungr included it originally on her dedication to Nina Simone, Just Like a Woman (Hymn to Nina). (She also sang "Just Like a Woman" and "The Times They Are a-Changin'" on that 2008 album.) The arrangement borrows the avant-garde percussion approach of Steve Reich or Harry Partch, and Jungr keeps her voice at an even dynamic, flat and unemotional; she emphasizes the general point by intoning the words like an incantation.

"Trouble in Mind," sung by Jungr on the 2006 Walking in the Sun, is the rarest item here. It's officially part of the Dylan canon—the lyrics are available on his website—but the composer himself doesn't seem ever to have sung it, at least not while a tape was running; it's not on any studio album, any legally released concert, or even a bootleg that I can find. The title is directly inspired by the early blues classic credited to Richard M. Jones, recorded by dozens of jazz and blues singers, including Nina Simone. However, where Jones's tune is a basic blues about wanting the sun to shine on one's back

door, this is another deeply spiritual song, in the manner of "You Gotta Serve Somebody," offering instructions on how to avoid Satan when he comes up to you and whispers tempting things in your ear.

For all of its obscurity, "Trouble in Mind" is one of the gems of the Jungr-Dylan virtual collaboration. She starts with bass and finger snaps, à la Peggy Lee's "Fever," then keeps the beat going with heavy use of bongos in a way that suggests Nat Cole's "Calypso Blues," and also utilizes an electric organ somewhat similar in sound to that played by Al Kooper on Highway 61 and other mid-1960s Dylan albums. "Trouble in Mind" (not to be confused with "Trouble" on Shot of Love) is also one of Jungr's most rivetingly rhythmic performances; the snapping fingers don't make the rhythm feel forced in any way—you'd be delighted to snap your fingers to this even without being instructed to. Like a blues, "Trouble in Mind" seems like the same few bars of melody over and over, but Jungr and company keep it interesting, not least by varying the instrumental texture—a piano joins the organ about halfway through, and instead of making the proceedings too keyboard-heavy, it actually increases the swing quotient.

"The Times They Are a-Changin'" is a representative Dylan anthem where the lyric would seem to be much more important than the tune—however, when you hear an instrumental version (such as that by tenor saxophonist Joshua Redman) you recognize the song just the same. The line "The first one now will later be last" always reminds me of the Sermon on the Mount—how the order of things will reverse itself in the next world, and the meek will be the ones bossing everyone around, and all that. It's another rambling opus, once again more message than melody, but Jungr does it fast and swinging, with heavy bass and percussion. Surely no one, surprisingly not even a jazzman like Redman, had thought to do a treatment of the song that's primarily rhythmic. Nina Simone did it more like a prayer. But Jungr is the only one who's ever gotten me to snap my fingers to it.

At first "Just Like a Woman," the title track of Jungr's tribute to Nina Simone, seems a bit too rhythmic—personally I'd rather hear her slow this one down than speed it up. The choir of over-dubbed "Barbs" is somewhat heavy-handed here, especially at the start, but after a minute or so, the concept of Jungr doing this Dylan classic (from the 1966 *Blonde on Blonde*) over a quasi-reggae beat wins me over. The 2009 album *Just Like a Woman* falls into the category of "traditional" tribute albums, in that Jungr offers new interpretations—most of which are very fresh and original—of songs associated with or recorded by Simone.

Jungr's 2004 *Love Me Tender,* by comparison, is less of a tribute album than an essay in album form, a contemplation of the icon of Elvis Presley. Presley apparently was put off by Dylan's voice but intrigued by Dylan's lyrics: he famously recorded two Dylan songs, "Don't Think Twice, It's All Right" and the rarity "Tomorrow Is a Long Time." How-ever, there are private recordings of Elvis messing around with "Blowin' in the Wind" and "I Shall Be Released"—at the end of the latter track, Presley says, simply, "Dylan." Honoring both Presley and Dylan, Jungr includes startlingly fresh treatments of "Tomorrow Is a Long Time" and "I Shall Be Released"; the first utilizes a lot of cryptic images, but is basically a song about a relationship, and the second is even more abstract, but falls under the general heading of religious songs. At least Elvis, in his interpretations, makes us think that the songs are about love and God. Dylan apparently agreed: he supposedly once said that Presley's "Tomorrow Is a Long Time" is his favorite cover of one of his own songs.

Overall, that's quite a trifecta, or three-party parlay: Bob to Elvis to Barb. Both "Tomorrow Is a Long Time" and "I Shall Be Released" are achingly slow. "Tomorrow" has Jungr singing as minimally as possible, barely breathing the words out in a very low chest voice over a spare and even spooky background, in which a xylophone (or vibes or marimba) suggests a dancing skeleton (a rather seductively slow-dancing skeleton) or some kind of ghostly presence. "Released" uses the equally spare string section to give it a traditional religious feel-ing not quite a hymn, quite possibly a prayer, but a very down kind of prayer, filled more with resigna-tion than optimism, in which Jungr's singing grows increasingly anguished as the track proceeds.

A highlight of the 2003 *Waterloo Sunset,* "Like a Rolling Stone" is the interpretation that fans of the Jungr-Dylan interaction had been waiting for. For years it's been bruited about that "Rolling Stone" was directly inspired by Dylan's relationship with socialite-cum-stoner and 1960s icon Edie Sedg-wick. He has, not surprisingly, never confirmed this, but Sedgwick's biography corresponds fairly closely to the outlines of Dylan's song. Certainly, some of his own performances are so passionate that you would think he's singing about someone he knew and loved. There are live performances from the 1970s, in particular, where he literally snarls out his own lyrics, almost like a punk rocker; it becomes an even more vindictive update of such "you'll get yours"–type songs like "Goody Goody," "I Wanna Be Around," and "You'll Get Yours," as well as the Bessie Smith classic "Nobody Knows You When You're Down and Out." Jungr's reading is slower, softer, and altogether more sympathetic. Instead of blasting out "How does it feel" with an undertone of "J'accuse!" she virtually whispers it, without a trace of smugness or I-told-you-so. As with "It Ain't Me Babe," her reading can only be described as compassionate. Most singers, even Dylan himself, make this song about sheer atti-tude; Jungr's interpretation is about the lyrics and the story.

"Sara," from Dylan's 1975 *Desire,* is one of Dylan's most personal statements, sung directly to his then departing wife ("Sweet virgin angel, sweet love of my life"), and the composer's deci-sion to set it in three-quarter time makes it sound especially tender and heartfelt. The 1964 "With God on Our Side" is one of Dylan's most disap-pointingly didactic songs, a deliberate attempt to bait the right-wingers, both political and theologi-cal conservatives; it may be the only song on the two albums that I'd rather Jungr had skipped (I'd rather hear "Maggie's Farm," which is somewhat more nuanced), but Jungr sings it convincingly, like a populist anthem.

After *Every Grain of Sand* and *Man in the Long Black Coat,* much of which was previously released on earlier CDs, in 2014 Jungr released still another relevant CD, *Hard Rain—The Songs of Bob Dylan & Leonard Cohen*—the same way that Ella

Fitzgerald released at least three different Gershwin songbooks, Jungr will keep finding new Dylan songs to sing. The 2014 album contains eleven songs, six by Dylan and five by Leonard Cohen (often thought of as Dylan's Canadian counterpart, and, like him, inarguably one of the major songwriters of our time). It's hard to believe that Jungr had missed such iconic Dylan classics as "Blowin' in the Wind" prior to this, as well as "Masters of War" (a bit political for my taste), "It's Alright Ma (I'm Only Bleeding)," "Chimes of Freedom." There's also a reading of "Gotta Serve Somebody" (yes, we were waiting for that one) that's more seductive than spiritual—a very free interpretation—and the title song, "A Hard Rain's a-Gonna Fall."

When Jungr sings Dylan's songs about love (or the lack of it), like "It Ain't Me Babe" or "Like a Rolling Stone" (which, in her version at least, is clearly a love song or a post-love song), she tends to be more forgiving. When she does the political songs, like "Masters of War" or "With God on Our Side," she tends to be much harsher, more severe than Dylan himself—quite clearly, the subtext of her message is, "You've had fifty years since Bob wrote these songs to take care of this problem, and still you persist in this suicidal foolishness." She's anything but forgiving. The spiritual numbers tend to be even more transcendental, especially "A Hard Rain's A-Gonna Fall." The tempo and the tone would seem to be taken from one of those old preachers like the Reverend J. M. Gates whose sermons were released as recordings from the early 1920s on. Dylan's lyric is a veritable torrent of words, images, and verbal iconography, which Jungr barks out like a Baptist minister on a spree of spiritual, rhetorical invention—as if she were chanting the Sermon on the Mount—just one idea after another, advising listeners which moral paths to take and which to shun.

Two of the most compelling of the Dylan-Jungr songs are the songwriter's reflections of two mys-

terious, larger-than-life blues giants of the Jazz Age, Charley Patton and Blind Willie McTell, on the Dylan songs titled "High Water (For Charley Patton)" and "Blind Willie McTell." Jungr's voice sounds positively bone-chilling in both of these; she has unmistakably tapped into the creepy, scary side of the blues, like Victoria Spivey singing with a snake wrapped around her neck or Screamin' Jay Hawkins making his entrance being carried in a coffin. "High Water" first not only references Patton but also Big Joe Turner, Charles Darwin, and New Orleans clarinet great George Lewis, among others, plus a quote from Robert Johnson. (These fictitious "others" include "Fat Nancy," "Bertha Mason"—a reference to *Jane Eyre?*—and some unnamed woman who throws her "panties overboard.") Jungr's treatment is more starkly modern and compellingly creepy (perhaps more so in the post-Katrina world), opening with crashing, dissonant chords that suggest a levee breaking. It's kind of the blues on acid.

"Blind Willie McTell" (another rarity, a 1983 demo track first issued on a 1991 Dylan collection), is a meditation on the storied blues singer. The tune is similar to the traditional blues "St. James Infirmary," which itself is derived from the even more traditional "Gambler's Blues." Since there isn't an official studio recording, Jungr's sounds very polished in comparison to Dylan's, especially since she and her long-running musical director, Simon Wallace, made the decision to do her arrangement in a very off-beat (literally) 5/4 time signature—it's almost like Dave Brubeck meets Willie McTell.

I can't imagine that Willie McTell, Charley Patton, or even Dylan himself would have felt the need to perform anything in 5/4—he isn't Brubeck, and he isn't Gustav Holst—but authenticity isn't the issue, originality is. Just as Dylan's music itself frequently makes something new out of something old, Jungr will apparently never run out of ways to make us hear Bob Dylan's words and music with whole new ears.

26

Dave Lambert, Jon Hendricks, and Annie Ross

Sing a Song of Basie (1957)

Annie Ross

Sings a Song with Mulligan! (1957)

S ometimes you start off by trying to do one thing and end up achieving something beyond anything you could ever have imagined. When Jon Hendricks and Dave Lambert first started working together, their idea was to see what would happen if they could somehow attach words to famous jazz passages. It wasn't improvisation,

designer was obviously hoping that potential buyers would mistake the word "basic" for "Basie.") Since the two men's names were new to most record buyers at that time, the main focus was, indisputably, the sleek, well-proportioned form of Annie Ross perched on a piano in dancer's tights and a form-fitting leotard, snapping her fingers,

nor was it really interpretation in the traditional sense. Hendricks and Lambert, who were soon joined by Annie Ross, were surprised to learn, in hindsight, that they had created something entirely new: a complete musical genre unto itself.

When *Sing a Song of Basie* was released by ABC-Paramount in 1957, listeners had no idea what to expect. Did the cover offer any clues? The original LP cover credited the artists as "Dave Lambert and his singers, Jon Hendricks and his lyrics, featuring Annie Ross and the Basic Rhythm Section." (The

eyes closed, with an expression on her face that was not only sensual and hip, but somehow exquisitely musical. To her left was Dave Lambert, who had just turned forty and already looked like a college professor, even before he grew that distinguished goatee that made him look like the world's coolest garden gnome. To her right was Jon Hendricks— and this in itself was startling. As late as 1958, African Americans were not frequently shown mixing freely with Caucasians, in any medium; even the jazz world was not routinely integrated. It's hard to think of any other album cover of the period that shows black and white people intermingling so casually, including those from the hard-core jazz labels like Blue Note or Prestige. (Perhaps it's significant that while Lambert is shown gazing appreciatively at Ross, Hendricks is staring into space, as if he were well aware that he wasn't supposed to be looking at a white woman. Not long after, he thoroughly shattered that unwritten commandment by marrying one, and staying married to her for fifty-six years.) If you looked harder, or could tear your eyes away from Annie's legs, you might notice that Jon was holding an 8 x 10 glossy of Count Basie.

When you dropped the needle on the 12-inch LP, you heard the piano intro from the classic Basie version of "Every Day I Have the Blues." This was a widely heard single in the mid-1950s, if not quite an epic chart hit on a Nat King Cole/Johnny Mathis scale. And while it was a relatively new slice of Basieana (the most recent piece on the album), chances are that if you were interested enough to buy what was presented as a Basie tribute album, you would know the tune and recognize the intro. But where you next expect to hear the brass playing the lead-in to the melody, instead there's a female voice singing the brass part with words that go, "Dig Count Basie blow Joe's blues away." On the Basie record, this is the followed by the saxophones playing the basic blues melody; here, however, we hear two male voices singing those exact same notes, with their phrasing corresponding exactly to the way the reeds play it on the Basie record. As Lambert and Hendricks assume the role of the saxophones, we hear Ross continuing to echo the trumpets, blasting in at key rhythmic points around them; the "trumpet" (Ross) punctuates and supports the melody as played by the "saxes" (Lambert and Hendricks) with deliberately sharp shrill notes—in fact, listeners in 1957 were probably not fully aware that it was a female voice they were hearing. Ross is virtually indistinguishable from a trumpet here, or like amorphous stabs of sound, delivered perfectly on pitch and in time, exactly where the trumpet bleats were in the original record.

On the 1955 Basie record, the famous melody is first stated instrumentally by the reeds (as we've

just heard), and then sung by Joe Williams. In between there's a whimsical transition passage, wherein a muted trumpet plays a few capricious phrases and is answered by the trombones. On the Lambert, Hendricks & Ross track, Annie continues to sing the trumpet parts ("You're singing the blues, each time I see ya / You're singing the blues, those blues won't free ya"), and now the two male voices have become the trombones, answering back the words "Ev'ry day . . . ev'ry day . . ." in their lower register. When they performed this number live, Jon and Dave would mime air trombones at this point, a hip visual bit that helped make it even clearer to the audience exactly what was going on. The familiar blues lyrics, which are famously sung on the classic Basie record by Williams, are backed with a saxophone obbligato. Here, on the LHR version, those lyrics are sung by Hendricks. But since he's also still one of the saxophones, we hear two different Hendricks voices—one is the main vocal, the other is the sax obbligato—courtesy of the process of multitracking.

"Every Day I Have the Blues" is a world-famous, highly memorable melody—nearly everyone can hum it—but the lyrics of Jon Hendricks and the vocal arrangement by Dave Lambert reveal that the Basie chart (arranged for the band by Ernie Wilkins) is essentially a series of hard-swinging, interconnected riffs and licks. By putting words to these fragments of melody, LHR creates a rich tapestry of sound—one that's no less vital than the original Basie performance. So far, we have barely heard the first ninety seconds of the five-minutes-and-change track, and every second of the track is crammed to the brim with this same level of imaginative invention and unfettered creativity. The idea of following a classic instrumental was liberating for Hendricks as a lyricist and for all three members as vocalists. The roles played by vocalists and instrumentalists had suddenly been altered—all at once there were more possibilities in the world for both songwriters and singers. The ante had instantly been upped.

Hendricks's lyrics are almost always brilliant—he is the only writer to work in this field (which we call "vocalese," for the sake of convenience) who is truly an outstanding songwriter, who deserves to be mentioned in the same breath, for instance, as such lyricists as Sammy Cahn or Andy Razaf. On this particular piece, Hendricks does a great job of incorporating the lyrics from the familiar version of the song, and working around them. As we mentioned, here he sings the Joe Williams part—LHR performed other versions of the number where Williams himself sang his own part.

What Lambert, Hendricks & Ross did can be likened to the process of anthropomorphism: in the same sense that a Disney animator can make a mouse talk or a teapot dance, LHR took trumpets and saxes and endowed them with actual human voices and words—the solos and ensemble parts on the original Basie disc were now literally speaking to listeners, in English and with distinct voices. For instance, as we've mentioned, on the Basie-Williams disc of "Ev'ry Day I Have the Blues" (the song title of which is never consistent; on the LHR album it's listed simply as "Everyday"), there's a saxophone obbligato behind Joe; on the LHR record, the obbligato literally answers the singer up front. The sax assumes the role of a Greek chorus and when "Joe" sings "Every day, every day I have the blues," the "saxophone" answers him with "What are you gonna get but blue? Wish that I could help you. Baby, what can I do?" When the central voice laments "Nobody loves me, nobody seems to care," the "sax voice" responds by chiming in with "How're you gonna get her to care? / Got to be a millionaire!" The same way that *Mary Poppins* intensifies the relationship between live-action actors and animated characters, Lambert, Hendricks & Ross have fundamentally altered the very nature of the relationship between singers and instrumentalists—and done so in a way that's hip, swinging, and full of humor.

Annie Ross is far from the featured attraction here, but though she's just a side dish and not the main course, she pretty much steals the show. At this stage in her life, Ross, who was just twenty-seven, had a voice not unlike her physical presence—rich, full, and supple. You can't take your ears off her in the ensembles any more than you can take your eyes off her on the cover. She has amazing high notes—when she sings a trumpet part, you know it's supposed to be a trumpet; on other arrangements, she sings at the very upper range of the piano, and every note is clear and sharp, every word intelligible. Yet she can also dip down into the mezzo range. Ross is absolutely at the heart and center of everything the trio does, she's the filling of the pie, the other two are the crust: Jon and Dave are like a pair of Tom Ewells to her Marilyn Monroe in *The Seven Year Itch*. She couldn't do what she does without them; but without her, the other two would have no reason for even being there.

The early LP era—the second half of the 1950s—was an age of experimentation, in which there almost seemed to be an arms race going on as to who could come up with the most original and new things to do with old songs. Lambert, Hendricks & Ross amount to one of the most fascinating chapters of this remarkable era. As we've seen, the idea, as it evolved, was essentially to start with classic instrumental jazz recordings, by Count Basie, Duke Ellington, and others, and translate them into vocal terms, human voices singing. LHR were not the very first to do it, although earlier vocalese efforts were far less ambitious—pioneers of the genre like Eddie Jefferson and King Pleasure would take individual solos and put words to them, whereas LHR was doing this with entire orchestras, and with considerably better lyrics. Recordings like "Moody's Mood for Love" (sung by Pleasure and generally acknowledged to have been written by Eddie Jefferson) and Annie Ross's own "Twisted" were successful enough, but LHR raised the bar considerably by using three voices to capture the flair and energy of an entire big band. It was an ambitious notion and a tall order. The concept required singers with far-above-average vocal chops, rhythmic ability—not to mention memory skills—as well as a lyricist who could easily spin out the requisite words and an arranger/ringleader who could keep the whole thing together. This is what the world had in Lambert, Hendricks & Ross.

Sing a Song of Basie, written and produced over most of 1957 and released in early 1958, was one breakthrough among many in those years. No one had heard anything like it—and yet, unlike, say, breakthroughs like Ella Fitzgerald's *The Cole Porter Songbook* and *Ella in Berlin*, there wasn't a helluva lot that came after it. The LHR "formula" was so unique, so idiosyncratic that no one could copy it—even the originators of the idea were not together long enough to fully capitalize on what they had created. But although vocalese would hardly replace the more standard sources of material for jazz singers—swinging show tunes and the more familiar American Songbook—generation after generation of hipsters and swinging cats have been inspired and uplifted by what these three unique individuals had wrought.

Even before Jon Hendricks and Dave Lambert had ever crossed paths, they had been experimenting independently. Lambert had primarily been known as a scat singer, and also one of the first big band vocalists to explore the possibilities of modern jazz within the existing frameworks of the swing dance band, as he did with "What's This?" in 1945. A revolutionary record in its time, this single by Gene Krupa's orchestra featured two male singers, Buddy Stewart and Lambert, scatting a prewritten bebop melody in unison. Everyone paid attention: Mel Tormé later sang it with George Shearing, and Nat King Cole concocted an equally boppish sequel titled "That's What." "What's This?" had the most profound effect on Hendricks, who was at the time a law student in his native Toledo. It was "What's This?" that alerted him to the idea that there was more to be done in the way of utilizing voices within the framework of instrumental jazz than had ever been done before. Throughout his life, Lambert was a relentless experimenter; he was, fittingly, part of the inner "salon" of modernist musicians and composers who congregated around the arranger-composer Gil Evans. In many ways, he was a direct vocal counterpart to Evans; when, in 1953, Charlie Parker recorded a famous session with both orchestra and choir, Evans conducted the orchestra and Lambert put together the vocal group.

Throughout this climate of experimentation, the idea of vocalese was in the air. The term has different meanings: in classical music, Rachmaninoff's "vocalise" for instance, the word refers to a composition in which the human voice is deployed like an instrument, nonverbally. As far as anyone knows,

Hendricks was the first to use the term to describe the act of writing words to a famous jazz instrumental solo. Some of the more notable early examples of vocalese were Marion Harris's 1934 version of Bix Beiderbecke's all-time-classic cornet solo on "Singin' the Blues," and King Pleasure's hit single based on the James Moody saxophone solo on "I'm in the Mood for Love" (released as "Moody's Mood for Love"); another early success in the area was "Twisted" by Annie Ross. Whereas Hendricks was raised in the church (his father was a minister), Ross grew up onstage, all of her family (in the U.K.) were in variety and the British musical theater; her aunt was the famous Scottish entertainer Ella Logan.

Jon and Dave met around 1955; by then, following "Moody's Mood for Love" and "Twisted," the concept of vocalese was somewhat known, at least to jazz insiders. It was at that point that Hendricks had the idea to do a vocal version of Woody Herman's "Four Brothers" and reached out to Lambert through a mutual friend. "I really understood Dave, because I had all of his records, with Buddy Stewart and Gene Krupa, and when I heard him I heard what was in my own mind," Hendricks told me. "So, I went down to Dave's house [and] I said, 'I got this little thing I want you to hear.' So I sang 'Four Brothers,' and man! Dave jumped up and wrote the arrangement right then! It took him about fifteen minutes!"

Hendricks had already written several R&B songs that had been recorded, including one ("I'll Die Happy") by Louis Jordan, which led to a contact with Jordan's longtime producer, Milt Gabler of Decca Records. Gabler recorded Lambert and Hendricks, supplemented by extra voices, on a single of "Four Brothers" backed with "Cloudburst," a rhythm and blues instrumental by pianist Leroy Kirkland, released as by "Claude Cloud and the Thunderclaps." "That was a mild hit," Hendricks recalled. "Then, we didn't know what to do next, so Dave says, 'We both like Count Basie, so why don't we put some words to some Basie things and see if we can sell them to somebody—you know, get a date or something.' So, I said, 'Yeah, well, do you know how long it takes to write one lyric like that?' He says, 'You got something else to do, maybe?'"

Hendricks then wrote four lyrics to four Basie instrumentals.

This was 1956–57, when the 12-inch LP format was proving to be an enormous commercial success—what *Down Beat* described as "the LP flood"—and the rigid formulas for making jazz and pop LPs still had not yet been laid down. This was a time when labels and producers were willing to experiment in search of something that would sell, and thus Hendricks and Lambert eventually found a "rabbi" who was willing to take a chance. His name was Creed Taylor, and at twenty-seven—much younger than Jon or Dave—he had just joined the staff at ABC-Paramount, a brand-new company bankrolled by the broadcasting network in hopes of getting in on the long-playing gold mine. Taylor was willing to take a chance on the twosome, and, in the parlance of a later generation, green-lighted the album that became *Sing a Song of Basie*.

Their first idea was to approach the Basie project in the same way that they had done the single of "Four Brothers"/"Cloudburst," with Hendricks's voice up front backed by a small choir. But finding enough trained studio singers who could swing with the Basie feel proved difficult if not impossible. At this point they reached out to Annie Ross, whom they met through Jean Bach, one of the den mothers, so to speak, of the New York jazz scene. Jon and Dave would have known more about Annie than she knew about them; she'd already had a well-known record, "Twisted" (promoted by Prestige Records as the female follow-up to the huge King Pleasure hit "I'm in the Mood for Love"), and she had spent much of 1956 appearing in the successful revue *Cranks,* which played both the West End and Broadway.

Nearly sixty years later, Jon and Annie don't always agree on everything—in fact, they eventually found it difficult to work together, which led to the breakup of the group—but they do concur that the choir couldn't swing and their budget was shot. "When we got through with that date we were $1,250 in the hole and Creed was about to be fired," said Jon. Annie remembered, "It was Dave who came up with the idea of multitracking it—it couldn't have been me, I didn't even know what

multitracking was in 1957. We were desperate, and so Creed went along with it." Jon adds, "The engineer would be the only one that knew what was happening because we'd come in after the studio locked up at night," said Hendricks.

By now, Jon, Dave, and Annie were starting to think like a trio. The released album would be lightly overdubbed, and different editions with different remastering jobs fall differently on the ear. As we've seen, the original LP on ABC-Paramount was issued by "Dave Lambert and his singers," while the later vinyl reissue was by "Lambert, Hendricks & Ross" and showed the three, apparently performing live, singing into a single microphone (this was on Impulse!, the jazz label that Taylor founded in 1960). Some of the vinyl editions more heavily emphasized the multitracking, sounding like an echo chamber with the reverb button turned up to cosmic proportions, or the sonic equivalent of a roomful of mirrors. But the definitive CD edition, remastered and released in 2000, is a lot easier on the ears. The overdubs are there, but they've been minimized to the point where they're far less intrusive. Vinyl-purist audiophiles aside, this is a clear-cut case where the CD is a remarkable improvement over the LP—at least all of the vinyl pressings that I myself have heard.

Sing a Song of Basie contains ten tracks, all of which are based on instrumentals performed and recorded by Count Basie and His Orchestra; the only song that had featured lyrics prior to this project is the opener, "Every Day I Have the Blues." This was also the only one of the ten numbers that had a history pre-Basie: it's an ancient blues line that first surfaced in 1935 on a recording by Chicago singer-pianist Aaron "Pinetop" Sparks, and gradually made its way toward Basie via Peter Chatman, aka "Memphis Slim," and guitarist Lowell Fulson. Chicago vocalist Joe Williams was already using it as his signature well before he joined Basie; when the three elements—the song, the voice of Williams, and the Basie orchestra playing a masterful arrangement by Ernie Wilkins—came together, the result was an instant hit and all-time classic.

The second track is "It's Sand, Man!," a 1942 collaboration by two members of the trumpet section, composer Ed Lewis, and arranger Buck Clayton. The title is a play on the mythological figure of the Sandman, who whisks little kiddies off to Slumberland. In African American theatrical culture of the era, "sand men" were also vaudeville dancers—an offshoot of tap-dancing—who spread sand on the stage and slid across it, rhythmically, rather than tapping down on it. "Sand, Man" illustrates why Jon, Dave, and Annie were so insistent on getting the voices to swing: the vocal arrangement, the voices, and even the lyrics are completely at the service of the ideal of motivating and inspiring dancers. The rhythm is the most important thing, pushing everything forward. Certainly, Hendricks's words are driven by the beat, yet even with short, staccato phrases and highly clipped lyrics to go along with them, Hendricks is a complete poet, and the voices have the same kind of perfect timing as Basie's trumpets. In effect, the words become rhythms—he has the same kind of masterful torrents of verbiage that the better rappers aspire to. The words are as brooms, not only whisking dancers across the floor but sweeping up the sand in the process.

The most celebrated arranger of the 1950s "New Testament" band, which Basie himself described as "an arranger's band," was Neal Hefti, and *Song of Basie* includes two of his originals. "Two for the Blues" has a memorable melody, but its most salient feature is the playing of two saxophones in unison by the band's "two Franks," Frank Foster and Frank Wess, two tenor giants who were among the New Testament band's biggest stars. As such, Hefti's melody line, meant to be expressed by two horns together, is perfect for the LHR vocal group, with Hendricks and Ross making like the two Franks. Hendricks's lyric captures the spirit of the blues, the super-slick, high-gloss Basie-Hefti–style blues, perhaps, but no less blue and funky at its center.

Over almost fifty years on the road, Count Basie opened hundreds of broadcasts and thousands of sets—and closed even more—with "One O'Clock Jump," his self-composed theme song, which he introduced on records in 1937. One of the odder decisions in the *Song of Basie* album was to take this theme—possibly the single best-known Basie

number—and bury it in the middle of the album. This is one of Hendricks's most exacting jobs in terms of writing lyrics for a string of soloists on different instruments—as opposed to a feature for a single soloist, like "Little Pony" (coming next) or "Cloudburst" (on their original 1955 Decca single). An unexpected consequence is that the standout "solo" in the LHR version is Lambert singing the trombone part by George Hunt; Hunt was only in the Basie band a short time, and never became a legendary Basie-ite (unlike most of the soloists lyricized by LHR), and the LHR adaptation gave him a kind of immortality. Lambert's exclamation "What a party! What a party!"—inspired by Hunt's trombone solo—has been hummed and repeated by thousands of listeners who have never heard Hunt's name.

Hefti's other composition here is "Little Pony," one of his first pieces for the Basie band, introduced in 1951. This is part of the legacy of Basie features for individual virtuoso players—in this case, the luminous, short-lived Wardell Gray. Basie was always partial to tenor saxophones, and "Pony" is a Basie milestone in many ways. It comes from the first session by the revived Basie band, the first chapter of the New Testament, so speak. In his playing, Gray was equal parts Lester Young and Charlie Parker. In other lyrics, Hendricks turns instruments into characters; here, he depicts a saxophonist as a racehorse. The band's beat does, indeed, suggest a fast gallop, and the lyrics are crafted to describe both a wailing musician and a charging steed: "Little Pony went a-ridin' / Illustratin' what a horn is really for. / Had 'em comin' back for more. / When they added up the score: Joy Galore!"

Guitarist Freddie Green, more responsible than anyone else after the Count himself for the amazing Basie beat, composed "Down for Double" in 1941. "Double" never was a major staple in the band book—they played it only a few times in the 1940s—yet it caught the ears of Lambert and Hendricks as perfect fodder for the album, the easy-swinging, basic riff could certainly support a Hendricks lyric. It's one of Jon's most user-friendly texts—one can easily sing it as a straight lyric without all the vocalese verbiage, as Mel Tormé did. It's actually one of the most singable concoctions in the album, and ought to be done more often by contemporary jazz singers.

Like "Down for Double," "Fiesta in Blue" was a 1941 Basie record that happened to be a particular favorite of Hendricks—most people associated the composition (written and arranged by Jimmy Mundy) with Benny Goodman, who recorded it in March 1941 as a feature for trumpeter Cootie Williams well before Basie did it as a feature for trumpeter Buck Clayton. As Hendricks told me, it was the Basie-Clayton version that spoke to him. "I kept playing it over and over, and as I listened to Buck's horn, he seemed to be saying, 'Say, fellas . . .' And then as I got into the words I had to make a story." At first Hendricks was stymied by the contrast: a "fiesta" is one kind of thing, but the "blues" are another. "So how are you going to combine those?" Then he turned it around and became stimulated by that very contrast: "Well, you have a party for blue people and they all come because they've got the blues real bad. So what are they going to do? They're going to have a ball and it's going to be the party of all time. So, that's the way that was done." Apart from being a sterling example of Hendricks's lyrics, it's also a prime sample of Ross at her best: she sings Clayton's trumpet line beautifully, injecting her own personality into Clayton's solo lines, Mundy's composition, and Hendricks's words.

We next hear two blues compositions by tenor star and arranger Frank Foster, both introduced at the same August 1954 recording session. "Down for the Count" is a medium-slow blues that mainly features Basie's own piano and the trumpet of Joe Newman, on this occasion utilizing a Harmon mute, a metal device that attaches to the bell that jazz trumpeters (most famously Miles Davis) use to create an especially vocalized sound. The LHR treatment is half the length of the original; it's one of the few Hendricks lyrics here that seem to have had no existence after the album. Which is a shame; it's a good functional blues lyric, and one of the least complicated pieces here. Ross sings Basie's piano part; she would become the trio's primary voice for piano and trumpet, Hendricks for saxophones, and Lambert for trombones, though all with some exceptions.

"Blues Backstage" is a powerful Basie blues, with lusty solos by Foster and trombonist Henry Coker. The blues may seem to belong to a different continent than Italian opera, but when Hendricks studied the 1954 recording, he heard a "Vesti la giubba" story: "To me, it's *Pagliacci*." That's an admittedly heavy reference, but such is the general idea: a performer and his woman have just broken up, but the show must go on. "The curtain's up so I'm clowning / but when they ring it down I'll be frowning . . . underneath the funny makeup that I'm wearing / how much I'm caring / and she'll see how much it's killing me." For a three-minute track, Hendricks and Lambert especially create a remarkable rich texture of music and drama. "It's the *Pagliacci* story in the world of show business," said Jon, whose goal, he said, was nothing less than to "combine literature, poetry, theater, and drama all at one time."

The LHR "Blues Backstage" was also never heard from again after the 1957 album, but even so, Hendricks regards it as one of his signal achievements. Buck Clayton's "Avenue C," however, is a fast and furious, lindy-hopping riff number that Hendricks and Ross frequently used in their later reunions. The subject is that neighborhood on the Lower East Side of Manhattan that was already being called "Alphabet City," and in this instance Hendricks takes a string of short solos (trombonist Dicky Wells, tenor saxophonist Buddy Tate, trumpeter Sweets Edison, tenor saxophonist Lucky Thompson) and weaves them into a dialogue between boy and girl meeting cute on a certain New York avenue. Cute but explosive: this is perhaps the most exciting and incendiary number on the set, and it became even faster when the trio would perform it at live appearances. The album ends with "Avenue C," rather than "One O'Clock Jump," simply because nothing could follow it.

Before Annie Ross knew it, she was part of a vocal trio—something that she had never planned on. Less than two weeks after the final session for *Song of Basie*—and well before the album was released—she was embarking on another partnership and another album, this one with the celebrated saxophonist and composer Gerry Mulligan. Ross was both binational (she seems to belong to America and to England at the same time) and polyamorous, so to speak, in her career—she was perhaps the first major performer to be equally at home in both jazz and musical theater. Having spent most of 1955 and '56 as part of the revue *Cranks,* she switched to a jazz emphasis for a few years in 1957.

Sings a Song with Mulligan! was instigated by Mulligan. Even more than Ross, he was an artist who thrived on collaboration. The team-up with Ross was one of four albums he made in December 1957, all of which were unique combinations, including a reunion with Chet Baker, his first celebrated partner, and their extended reassociation led to Baker's playing on the first sessions with Mulligan and Ross.

To the extent that Ross and Mulligan had any template to work from, it was obviously the greatest singer-musician collaboration in jazz history, that of Billie Holiday and Lester Young. This wasn't merely because Holiday was one of Ross's mentors and Mulligan's hero was Young; rather, like Holiday and Young, Ross and Mulligan had a deep personal connection that stretched way back. As Ross once told me, she and Mulligan "dated for a while," but one could hardly say that this was the key—plenty of couples who dated (or even got married) were never on the same page, artistically or otherwise (I speak from experience), whereas Ross and Mulligan are instantly and immediately simpatico with each other to a remarkable degree.

Jazz is a music that often thrives on randomness; improvisation is not only the key to the best individual solos, but frequently to ensembles as well. That's why a saxophonist, pianist, bassist, and drummer who have never even met can sometimes work together spontaneously to produce something brilliant; try doing that with a classical string quartet. But still, musicians who know each other's "poker playing habits," in Duke Ellington's famous phrase, can often create something even more special. There's a very special synergy at work between Ross and Mulligan: they are instantly, to borrow the title of another Mulligan album, two of a mind. They think and feel and react and emote with the same mind and the same body, almost

as if they were playing the same instrument at the same time. Like Louis Armstrong as well as Chet Baker, they become a single entity who can both sing and play at the absolute top levels of jazz—or even, like Nat King Cole, who can do both at once.

Even in her prime, Ross never had a big, operatic voice, the kind that could hit the back of the theater, but she was endowed with tons of range, both musical and emotional; you won't hear any hint of an undernourished note on any of her classic albums. Billie Holiday was both a friend and an influence, and like her, Ross continually plays with the melody. She'll reshape a phrase here or change the rhythmic pattern there, hammering it into a whole new, entirely personalized form. Yet she never loses the thread of the lyric. Ross always gets the story across without feeling the need to stick to the exact letter of the written tune. And like Holiday, she swings unfailingly—she's every bit the musician that the best saxophonists or trumpeters are, but she's also a major interpreter and actress. "I've Grown Accustomed to His Face," for instance, finds her departing from the tune in a manner that's surprising for a relatively new show tune (as opposed to a song that was already a jazz standard), yet no Henry Higgins has ever sung it more movingly.

Mulligan apparently had Billie and Lester much on his mind during the making of this album. In between these sessions, he participated in *The Sound of Jazz,* the legendary telecast that would be the last hurrah for both of those jazz immortals. He wasn't the first great baritone saxophone player in jazz—that honor belongs to Duke Ellington's Harry Carney—but he was the first to play the supersized horn with the lightness and energy and fleetness of foot normally reserved for the tenor sax. Where Carney stressed the gravitas of the horn, Mulligan made it light and airy. Usually when the list of Lester Young acolytes is drawn up, the roster only includes the tenor players like Paul Quinichette and Zoot Sims, but Mulligan was no less an honorary son of Lester Young.

Released by Pacific Jazz Records in 1959, *Sings a Song with Mulligan* is, like the classic Lady Day–Pres sessions of the late 1930s, a collection of supremely hip love duets between two major jazz voices. Mulligan's quartet, with drummer (Dave Bailey) and bassists (Henry Grimes and then Bill Crow) is especially strong. The trumpet (Chet Baker on the 1957 sessions, Art Farmer on the 1958 date) is particularly dynamic, and there are many moments when the Ross-Mulligan love duet becomes a ménage-à-trois. But overall, the bass, drums, and even the trumpet are merely the supporting cast. This album is about Annie and Gerry, and the beautiful music they make together.

The Ross-Mulligan collaboration succeeds on multiple levels. What we have is a singer who knows how to use her voice like a horn, yet, when she takes off on a semi-improvised flight of fancy, doesn't leave the lyrics or the story behind—she makes the words mean something even while she's playing around with the tune. At the same time, we have a horn player who "sings" with the immediate identity, personality, and charisma of a human voice, a player who heeded Lester Young's dictum that jazzmen should know the words, not merely the notes, of the standards that they play. And as with Holiday and Young, Ross's low soprano and Mulligan's high baritone meet on a level playing field.

They recorded the bulk of the album on December 11 and 17, 1957. The group was Mulligan's regular bassist and drummer, Grimes and Bailey, plus special guest Chet Baker. Mulligan had conceived of the album and provided the opportunity through his relationship with Richard Bock; the singer and the saxophonist picked the tunes together and worked out the keys and arrangements. Bock had little interest in keeping an accurate discography; we don't know what tunes were recorded on what date (December 11 or 17), and we can't be sure that they're in the correct order.

The standard listing of the combined sessions begins with two songs by Harold Arlen, which document two very different sides of a romance: in "Between the Devil and the Deep Blue Sea" (from the 1931 *Rhythmania*, lyric by Ted Koehler) Ross (or Ross's "character") is mesmerized into remaining in a frustrating affair that she would just as soon be out of. "This Time the Dream's on Me" (from *Blues in the Night*, 1941, lyric by Johnny Mercer) is about

trying to keep a relationship going as long as possible, maybe even for a lifetime. She sounds genuinely frustrated in the first and warm and hopeful in the second.

While coming up with the general "routines," Ross, an experienced lyricist, made several lyric alterations, primarily for reasons of gender. "I Guess I'll Have to Change My Plan" (Arthur Schwartz and Howard Dietz, from *The Little Show*, 1929) was rarely, if ever, sung by a woman; thus she sings "Why did I buy that satin nightie" in place of "blue pajamas" and instead of "Why did I try to be a fly lothario?" she asks the question "Why did I try to be as clever as Monroe?" (Marilyn, not James).

The songwriter in Ross also inspired her to devise thoughtful extended original codas to two songs, "Give Me the Simple Life" and "You Turned the Tables on Me." The idea of adding to a song via an extended coda or "tag" was popularized in the postwar era by Billy Eckstine, and also became a favorite device of Mel Tormé. Ross originally thought of her tag to "Tables" ("Well, you said I had a lesson that I had to learn . . .") as an idea for her friend Billie Holiday. (She had completely forgotten that she recorded it herself on this album, and was fairly incredulous when I played it for her in 2011.)

"How About You?" (Burton Lane and Ralph Freed, from *Babes on Broadway*, 1941) is one of the harder-swinging numbers here, and the substitution of "Frank Sinatra's looks" for "Franklin Roosevelt's looks" may be a sign that she learned it from Sinatra. (In the second chorus, the reference is to "Billy Eckstine's looks.") Coming out of the first chorus, Ross repeats "I like it" three times, turning that passage into a riff for repeating; the instrumental break, with Mulligan and Baker running rings around each other, is particularly exciting. She doesn't miss any of the nuances of the text, and instills even the more boppish ballads with a sense of tenderness.

In fact, for a bop-centric album, Ross and Mulligan both achieve true poignancy on the slow love songs, especially "Let There Be Love," a British tune by Lionel Rand and Ian Grant. She swings strongly here, using the rhythmic momentum to enhance the lyric rather than detract from it. When Mulligan makes his entrance, following Ross's chorus, he truly has the presence of an outstanding vocalist, like Louis Armstrong following Ella Fitzgerald on their well-known duets. After the sax solo, Ross then sings a final chorus in something more like an ethereal "air" voice. This second chorus is more jazzy—she takes greater liberties with the melody—but it's also more personal and intimate; she makes the most of tiny details like "someone to bless me whenever I sneeze."

She may well have learned both "My Old Flame" (Arthur Johnston and Sam Coslow, from *Belle of the Nineties*, 1934) and "This Is Always" (Harry Warren and Mack Gordon, from *Three Little Girls in Blue*, 1946) from Charlie Parker. (She was close to Bird himself and also had a long relationship—and a son—with Parker's frequent drummer Kenny Clarke.) Again, Ross is both especially intimate and jazzy here. She didn't have the superhuman instrument of Ella Fitzgerald or the equally superhuman, lightning-fast rhythmic reflexes of Anita O'Day, but as a storyteller, there are few who are better; whether singing about a past relationship in "Flame" or an ongoing one in "Always," Ross is always sublimely believable.

By this point, Ross, Mulligan, and Baker had recorded seven tunes. Then, "Chet went into the bathroom," as Ross later remembered, "and we never saw him again." It's hard to escape the conclusion that Baker left early because he had to score (i.e., drugs). Ironically, during the 1952–54 period when Mulligan and Baker worked together regularly, Mulligan had an addiction and Baker was clean; by 1957, the situation had reversed. Perhaps it was with a sense of irony that Gerry and Annie recorded "You Turned the Tables on Me" after Chet left.

Yet it's equally possible that Baker felt that two was company and three was a crowd. This was Annie and Gerry's album, and Chet was merely a sideman, and not a particularly necessary one. His most effective ballad solo on the date is "My Old Flame," rendered in a very slow and "My Funny Valentine"–kind of a way, while his best up number is "How About You?," on which he plays brilliant counterpoint, first behind Mulligan, then behind Ross. He plays superbly here, but apparently it wasn't enough for him.

In any case, after he left, Ross and Mulligan (plus Grimes and Bailey) proceeded to cut an additional four "Chet-less" standards. "The Lady's in Love with You" (Burton Lane and Frank Loesser, from the 1939 *Some Like It Hot*) is a particularly stunning sample of vocal-instrumental interaction; most times when a jazz soloist plays behind a singer, you can hear the player reacting to the vocalist, but here you also catch the singer's reaction to the saxophonist, and shaping her own phrases around what he plays. Baker isn't missed here, nor on "You Turned the Tables on Me" (Louis Alter and Sidney Mitchell, 1936).

The one track we really wish Baker had hung around for is Duke Ellington's "It Don't Mean a Thing (If It Ain't Got That Swing)"; the number is more of a jam session than a proper song, and with just one horn to solo, there's not much point. Ross swings as much as always, and so does Mulligan, but you can't help wishing they'd picked some other Ellington song.

Yet "I've Grown Accustomed to Her Face"—or in this case, "His Face"—is one of the highlights of the project. We hear here how Ross's training in the theater was as essential to her evolution as all those years of working with the beboppers. The second chorus in particular includes a few exquisite moments of Mulligan singing the main melody of the *My Fair Lady* show tune, while Ross paraphrases the tune (while continuing to sing the actual words) all around him.

You could call it "emotional counterpoint." Scat singers take note: what Ross does here is much more musical, much more inventive, much more melodically inventive as well as dramatically and emotionally effective than any wordless improvisation. It's tracks like this that ensure that the Annie Ross–Gerry Mulligan team-up is worthy of being mentioned in the same breath as Coltrane and Hartman, Bennett and Evans.

Now they were up to eleven masters, all usable. That would probably have been enough, but for some reason Mulligan wanted more—or, possibly, he just wanted an excuse to spend more quality time with Annie. The following September, Mulligan and Ross reconvened for Richard Bock, this time on the producer's home turf, Los Angeles. The quartet again featured drummer Dave Bailey, but Bill Crow had joined on bass, and the new trumpeter was Art Farmer.

For some reason, the ensemble re-recorded two of the best ballads from the previous December, "This Is Always" and "I've Grown Accustomed to Her [His] Face." Re-recording the *My Fair Lady* song made sense, because the December version didn't have the trumpet, and possibly Mulligan wanted to provide Ross with more of a background. The new take of "This Is Always," however, with Farmer isn't any better (or worse) than the December take with Baker.

The good news is that there are three completely new tunes—"All of You" (Cole Porter, from *Silk Stockings,* 1954), "Give Me the Simple Life" (Rube Bloom and Harry Ruby, 1946), and "I Feel Pretty" (Leonard Bernstein and Stephen Sondheim)—all of which are prime Annie. "All of You" is medium-up; Ross's specialty, it seems, was seeming sexy even at tempos that other singers would have found much too fast for romance. The miracle of "Give Me the Simple Life" is that she makes us believe she could possibly be interested in anything that was "corny and seedy" even to the point where she underscores that statement with a "yes indeedy." Ross probably never said "yes indeedy" in her entire life, yet she makes it seem here like something she says every day, like it's the most natural thing in the world. (She supplements lyricist Harry Ruby's work with a few special lines of her own: "A penthouse on top of the Astor / with Marlon Brando inside!")

The best of the September songs was easily the *West Side Story* showstopper, "I Feel Pretty." Mulligan's highly contrapuntal treatment renders Bernstein's melody as if it were a Bach fugue; Ross not only sings it breathlessly fast, but in a highly staccato, baroque fashion. She also interlaces Sondheim's words with scat phrases rendered in harmony with Farmer (yes, the trumpet is fairly essential on this one). Here the tempo tells the tale, the rushed, super-fast pacing perfectly captures the mood of a young girl who's in love and therefore feels pretty. Only Ross could make the words resonate all the more strongly—even when she's not actually singing those words—

when scatting in support of the lyric and the narrative.

By the fall of 1958, when Ross and Mulligan recorded the last session for their album, *Sing a Song of Basie* had already been released and was proving to be, by jazz standards, a huge hit. To their surprise, Lambert, Hendricks & Ross began touring as a trio, and they also quickly returned to the studio for a follow-up album titled *Sing Along with Basie* in which they were backed by the Count himself and his full orchestra. At this point, Richard Bock realized that there was an opportunity here to work with the trio by themselves and individually, and he produced four more Pacific Jazz albums with the three vocalists: two solo albums by Ross, one by Jon Hendricks, and one with the full trio.

Lambert, Hendricks & Ross lasted for five years, until Annie left the trio in 1962, not only by playing clubs but as one of the first major attractions to support themselves playing jazz festivals. They worked the festival circuit all over the country, from Newport to the Playboy Jazz Festival in Chicago to Monterey. (In a sense, they were the first "supergroup," kind of a model for Weather Report or Crosby, Stills & Nash.) Along the way, they recorded three absolutely classic albums for Columbia Records, stunning examples of the jazz singer's art at its apogee.

Dave Lambert was killed in an automobile accident at the age of forty-nine in 1966. In the fifty years since then, the recorded legacy of LHR has continued to occupy a unique niche in the world of contemporary music—even beyond jazz: pop groups do Jon's songs and singer-songwriters like Joni Mitchell sing Annie's "Twisted." Annie and Jon, both named as NEA Jazz Masters, have grown comfortably into elder statesmanhood, Jon teaching as well as singing and songwriting, Annie maintaining a separate but no less impressive career as a film and stage actress.

Sing a Song of Basie was carefully prepared, whereas the chief virtue of *Sings a Song with Mulligan* is its raw spontaneity. *Sing a Song of Basie* has been more or less steadily in print for sixty years, sometimes with different covers, in the LP and CD era; *Sings a Song with Mulligan,* on the other hand, was never as easy to find as it should have been: Pacific Jazz was never as good at distributing its product as its East Coast counterparts. Which possibly explains why Lambert, Hendricks & Ross are regarded as the greatest jazz vocal group ever, but Ross herself—who is admittedly too difficult to pin down in any category or means of expression— isn't cited as often as she should be as one of the major jazz singers. How many singers, of her time or ours, could have stayed perfectly in tune with Mulligan's quartet without so much as a piano to guide them to the right notes? (Listen again to that remarkable high note that she nails, right on the money, at the end of "All of You.") Both albums prove that music conceived from solidly within the jazz tradition could appeal to everyone.

27

Eydie Gormé and Steve Lawrence

Eydie and Steve Sing the Golden Hits

(1960)

never heard them do reggae. Nor Hindu pop, or Balkan brass band music. Nor zarzuela. The idea of them doing hip-hop is also hysterical (although Mr. Lawrence has said, "I like rap as much as the next guy—but I'm still waiting for the third note!"). It's easier to catalogue the list of musical styles that Steve Lawrence and Eydie Gormé were not masters of than those which they sang to perfection. Yet listening to Steve & Eydie at their best, as on the 1960 album *Golden Hits,* the sensation is indeed multifaceted: you get the same kick that you do on a superior musical comedy album, like, say, the original cast recording of *Kiss Me, Kate,* as well as one of the best jazz-pop albums by any number of swinging singers—Bobby Darin, Kay Starr, Peggy Lee. And though Steve & Eydie were as squeaky

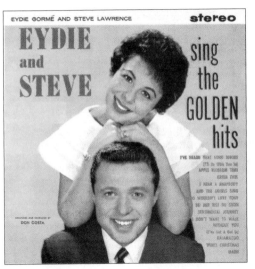

clean and optimistic as pop stars were expected to be at the start of the 1960s, they were hardly "white-bread." There was an unmistakable ethnic element to their work: they were completely comfortable performing anything in the Latin spectrum, from *mambo, chorro, tango,* and *fado canciones* to *mariachi* and *bossa nova,* and anything in the vast spectrum of Jewish music, including material in Hebrew or Yiddish.

At times, I feel sorry for Steve Lawrence and Eydie Gormé—it's like they were all set to inherit the keys to the kingdom, but just as they put said key in the door, the kingdom was starting to disintegrate. If the pop music of the big band era and the decade that came after (whatever we chose to call it) had kept going, without the sea changes of the late 1950s and the early to mid-1960s, then Lawrence and Gormé would have been even bigger than they were. But viewed from another angle, their timing was perfect—their ideal mediums were television and the long-playing record; they wouldn't have worked nearly as well in 1940s-style network radio nor 78 rpm singles—they were young enough to master the new technologies of the 1950s. If they had been significantly older or less attractive, then the camera wouldn't have loved them as much as it did, which is possibly even more than the microphone. (It's also tempting to speculate what it might have been like if they had been given another crack or two at musical theater—they would have made excellent leads in *Funny Girl,* for instance, and Eydie was even offered the part—or if Hollywood had ever actually built a movie around them.)

Television truly was their medium, and even their albums have the feel of TV specials: their performances were never just a bunch of songs, even a well-selected, carefully arranged bunch of songs, but there's always some kind of larger point to what they're singing. They had been married at the end of 1957, but Lawrence had served in the army for most of the next two years. In 1960, they were essentially working together full-time; there would be solo projects and appearances, but from then until Mrs. Lawrence's retirement almost fifty years later, "Steve & Eydie" were a permanent, ongoing attraction. They more or less announced that career move with two albums released that year: *We Got Us* and *Eydie & Steve Sing the Golden Hits*. (Yes, this is a rare example, early in the marriage, of Mrs. Lawrence's first billing, contrary to show biz tradition—i.e., Burns & Allen, Stiller & Meara, Nichols & May.) Those two albums were released around two additional solo albums by Lawrence, *The Steve Lawrence Sound* (1960, United Artists) and *Steve Lawrence Goes Latin* (1960, United Artists). (If Eydie had other things to do that year besides record a solo album, it's understandable: their first child, David Nessim Lawrence, was born in 1960.)

We Got Us is a fairly perfect set of boy-girl duets, but *Golden Hits* is even better. The title itself is both slightly misleading and not informative enough: in 1963, one of their peers released an album called *The Golden Hits of Billy Eckstine*, which was a collection of new recordings of the great crooner revisiting his best-known songs. But Steve & Eydie's "Golden Hits" were not their own hit singles; what the title doesn't tell us is that the album consisted of twelve songs from the big band era. It was a brilliant idea, one that gave them a coherent theme, one more original than, say, another Gershwin songbook (they would do a series of composer collections and TV specials years later) or a theme like songs about birds or the color blue.

Golden Hits is a spectacular album. The songs are perfect, the two singers are at their perkiest and most swinging, as are the arrangements by their longtime collaborator Don Costa. Like Riddle and Sinatra, Costa and the Lawrences had figured out how to arrange and sing these songs in a way that honored the spirit of the big band era while extending it forward and not re-creating anything.

The singers telegraph their intentions with "I've Heard That Song Before," a classic vintage hit from World War II and a song with built-in nostalgia for itself, which very directly illustrates how the act of hearing a familiar song is itself a kind of warm and homecoming voyage. The team starts with the familiar lyrics, as written by Sammy Cahn (the melody is by Jule Styne) for the 1942 B-musical

Youth on Parade; then, for the second chorus, S&E effectively announce the rest of the new album with a new set of special lyrics (quite possibly written by Cahn himself): "From the first song to the last / We'll sing some great songs from the past. / Plus a couple of up-to-date ones / All of them hits, all of them great ones."

"I've Heard That Song Before" was a huge hit in 1943 for Harry James and His Orchestra, but "I'll Be with You in Apple Blossom Time" (words by the little-known Neville Fleeson, music by the well-known Albert Von Tilzer) is more of a surprise. This waltz actually dates from closer to World War I (1920) and was a big number for the Andrews Sisters (who sang it in 2/4) during the lead-in to World War II (1940–41), a sentimental song that used the past as a way of looking forward to the future, more specifically, the end of the war. It was one of the first numbers that proved the Andrews girls could be effective with a ballad as well as a jive number or a comedy song, even though their arrangement included a chorus filled with satirical asides. The *Golden Hits* version is all Eydie—it's her main solo on this album. She sings in a relaxed yet highly danceable tempo, giving the song full respect and not camping it up. She sounds even better after a key change leading to the last half chorus, growing at once more playful ("what a *very, very* wonderful day for you and me") and more intense.

Although all twelve songs were hits in the big band era, some (including "Apple Blossom Time") originate from somewhat left-field sources, including two Spanish songs and two Yiddish songs—which arrive pretty much in a row. "Green Eyes" (originally "Aquellos Ojos Verdes" by the Havanese pianist Nilo Menéndez) was one of the very earliest Cuban songs to catch on in North America. It's perfect material for the Lawrences, especially considering Gormé's Hispanic background. It might be somewhat unexpected that this version opens with Mr. Lawrence rather than Mrs. Lawrence, but they're deliberately evoking the famous arrangement played by Jimmy Dorsey's orchestra. He croons it in a manner vaguely reminiscent of Bob Eberly, romantic and relaxed; then the tempo increases, and she sings more swingingly, evoking Helen O'Connell, but with considerably better intonation. Unlike what happens in the 1941 Dorsey record, in the last chorus they sing a highly spirited final half chorus together, with some special lyrics and spontaneous asides ("Love me, my pet brunette, love me!"). Like the rest of the album, it's sheer, exuberant fun.

"I Hear a Rhapsody" is lightly Latin by default, being the best-known composition of Richard Gasparre, a society bandleader who operated in the shadow of both Xavier Cugat and Guy Lombardo. It's a rapturously romantic song: if there ever were a Hollywood musical based on *Zorro*, this is what Don Diego would sing to his leading lady. The 1960 record is Steve all the way, opening with a dramatic piano introduction in contrast to the vocal, which is very relaxed and intimate—anything but grandiose.

Next is Eydie's solo "And the Angels Sing," which was Johnny Mercer's recasting of the melody that began life as "Fralich in Swing" by trumpeter Ziggy Elman (even as "Ziggy Elman" was a stage name for the musician who began life as Harry Finkelman). Transforming the piece from a klezmer trumpet exercise into a popular song was a considerable leap of faith for Mercer, who liberally adapted the source material. This was first a feature for Elman in the Carnegie Hall edition of Benny Goodman's band, and also was a major showcase for BG vocalist Martha Tilton. The Eydie-Costa version has virtually none of the direct Yiddishkeit of the Elman recording. She sings it more like a Mercer ballad than a *fralich* (or party song); she's especially compelling in Mercer's brilliant, distinctive bridge ("Suddenly, the setting is strange"), getting louder and more assertive but never quite belting.

After two solos, our young lovers reunite for "Who Wouldn't Love You?"—originally a hit for Kay Kyser's band, a hugely popular attraction during the 1930s and especially the war years (and even after), though unfortunately less well remembered than the Dorseys or Goodman today. (The lyrics and music are by Bill Carey and Carl Fischer.) The piece was a natural duet, originally for Harry Babbitt and Ginny Simms, and even more so for Steve and Eydie here. He sings the tune melodically and tenderly while she scats/hums a countermelody around him. When it's her turn to sing the melody, she comes on more loudly and aggressively. After a Lester Young–like tenor saxophone solo, they sing together, fairly brimming with spontaneous asides—they even quote the Andrews Sisters ("What's my name?" "Sonny Boy!"). The whole thing feels like live television.

In contrast to "And the Angels Sing," "Bei Mir Bist Du Schön" is about as Hebraic as you can get, being Sammy Cahn's English-language adaptation of a then-contemporary Yiddish song. The song was the first great hit—it launched their career—for the Andrews trio, but the Lawrences more faithfully recall the classic Benny Goodman version, starting the verse in a distinctive minor, introduced by a wailing clarinet dispensing blue notes by the score. They take most of the chorus in harmony, until he grabs the bridge in solo. Costa's studio orchestra takes a solid instrumental break, before the second chorus, where they alternate leading up to the release, and then it's time to sing that section in harmony together. The energy exchanged between the two singers and the band, as well as with each other, is palpable. The arrangement mounts in excitement at the ending, allowing the twosome to build to an even bigger climax than on any big band recording I've ever heard. Steve ends with a wiseguy ad-lib, ending this linguistics lesson by quoting Professor Henry Higgins, "By Jove, I think she's got it!"

Two solos follow. Irving Berlin's "Marie" is a rip-roaring feature for Mr. Lawrence. The piece famously began as a very old-fashioned waltz (even by 1929 standards) that Tommy Dorsey swung into 4/4 big band history. However, none of the singers who did it with the band, not Jack Leonard or even the young Sinatra, sounded as supremely hip as Lawrence does here. He is pure energy and testosterone, and it's a marvelous contrast to Gormé's solo ballad, "I Don't Want to Walk Without You," which follows. Written by Jule Styne (music) and Frank Loesser (who was then writing words only) and introduced in the 1942 musical film *Sweater Girl*, it was subsequently a major disc for Harry James and Helen Forrest. Although many of the numbers in this album are from World War II, this is the only major separation song here, and Eydie takes full advantage of that, delivering a touching ballad reading. She starts with a verse that's the most rubato (or least in tempo) of anything in the album. It's a very slow dance, and a highly romantic one at that (graced by a lovely tenor sax solo and obbligato).

If "Walk Without You" is the only heavy World War II ballad, then "(I've Got a Gal in) Kalamazoo" is the one genuine slice of authentic World War II nonsense, a lyric roughly built around the alphabet ("A B C D E F G H I got a gal in Kalamazoo!"). The song is a sequel, sort of. After Mack Gordon and Harry Warren's "Chattanooga Choo Choo" was such a blockbuster hit for Glenn Miller's Orchestra in the 1941 film *Sun Valley Serenade,* they followed it up with another semi-novelty song about love in a city with a goofy name, this time for the second Glenn Miller film, *Orchestra Wives.* Kalamazoo was obviously the next stop on the choo choo's railroad after Chattanooga. (In the same vein, Gordon and Warren wrote "Paducah" for Benny Goodman in *The Gang's All Here.*) Both Steve (who starts) and Eydie ride the rails with sheer swinging exhilaration. In the movie, the number reaches a climax with an exalted dance routine by the Nicholas Brothers, who address each other in the hepcat argot of the time as "Mr. Jackson." Here, the two singers interject references to Mr. and Mrs. Lawrence, and, as the lyrics state, it's a real pipperoo.

The only song that simply does not belong is "White Christmas," a Lawrence solo. It's technically part of the World War II big band experience, but in 1960, as now, more people naturally associated it with the holiday rather than the era. He sings it majestically, but even though it's a great song, it seems like a throwaway here—every time I play the album and reach this track, I want to skip past it—only because it's not the song I feel like listening to in the middle of a big band swing album, in between "Kalamazoo" and "Sentimental Journey."

"Sentimental Journey," however, is an appropriate capper, one of the last big hits of the war years, a song about going home that helped bring the era to a close. Taking it at much more of a romping tempo than the iconic Les Brown/Doris Day hit record, they start together in harmony, breaking it up into individual parts in the bridge. It's got a solid dance beat throughout, which doesn't compromise the thoughtful mood. As an ending, it's both sentimental and swinging.

With *We Got Us* and, even more importantly, *Eydie & Steve Sing the Golden Hits,* the couple was now established as something unique in show business: a full-time husband-and-wife duet team. There had been boy/girl comedy couples (from Burns & Allen to Nichols & May), but nothing like them in the music world. From that moment forward, they were among the most-recorded singers around, both doing two or three solo albums a year plus a continual string of duo projects. Though the pace decreased in later years, there were new albums as late as 1989's *Alone Together;* by that time, they were singing things like "I Dreamed a Dream." It was a long way—not necessarily upward—from Kay Kyser hits to the big ballad from *Les Misérables,* but they pulled it off with class and quality.

So much so that they were eventually absorbed into the orbit of Frank Sinatra; he frequently tapped them for benefits that he was hosting, among them a famous all-star fundraiser in support of Israel at the time of the Six-Day War in 1967. There also was one occasion, unfortunately unrecorded, when Mr. Lawrence was ailing and Sinatra (or so they said) actually took his place in the act with Mrs. Lawrence for a few shows—"Frank & Eydie." Toward the end of his life, Sinatra employed them as his opening act in his 1990–91 "Diamond Jubilee" tour, and also sang with them on his final album, the 1994 *Duets II.*

In 1992, Lawrence and Gormé appeared on one of the very first episodes of *The Tonight Show* under the new host, Jay Leno. NBC permitted them this particular sentimental journey because they had been frequent guests in every incarnation of the program thus far—under their original mentor, Steve Allen, Jack Paar, and Johnny Carson. (As far as I'm aware, the subsequent hosts, Conan O'Brien and Jimmy Fallon, never extended them that courtesy.) In 1992, Mr. Lawrence was only fifty-six (his wife was seven years older), but it seemed as if they'd been on television forever. That was the unfortunate by-product of having gotten their start in the new medium so young (when

Mr. Lawrence was about seventeen)—it made them seem older than they were. When Carson retired, it put the kibosh on the last vestige of traditional showbiz that Lawrence and Gormé represented. Eydie Gormé Lawrence died at age eighty-four in 2013, and it's hoped that Mr. Lawrence, who still has most of his chops, will continue to tour and record as a solo.

Roughly ten years before that, in the early to mid-1980s, I worked at a college radio station during the peak years of punk and New Wave rock—a period when attitude was everything. One of the other wise-asses who worked there took a vintage LP cover by Steve & Eydie (I recall it was the 1962 *It's Us Again*) and mounted it on the wall of one of the studios, for us to gaze at as we played the New York Dolls and Blondie. The message was clear: Steve & Eydie were old-time squaresville

and the rest of us were hip. Based on the cover to that album—which, apparently, was an advertising premium sponsored by a shampoo company—the two singers were indeed squeaky clean, like any of those generic pretty boy and girl cast members of *The Lawrence Welk Show*. Yet what distinguished Lawrence and Gormé was the amazing sophistication and depth of their interpretations, the songs they sang, even the arrangements—Don Costa's charts are full of interesting harmonic decisions; like the Lawrences themselves, they're anything but plain vanilla. And there's also the real feeling that they had for each other, something that I fail to hear in the work of, for instance, the Residents. For all the slickness of their image, Steve & Eydie brought a remarkable depth to pop music—and a collective legacy that few other singers can even touch.

28

Peggy Lee
Black Coffee
(1953 and 1956)

A good singer can—and should—make you believe the words. Peggy Lee doesn't even need words to move me; she can reach me at the bottom of my soul even with nothing more than the spaces in between the words. The song "Black Coffee" starts with "I'm feelin' mighty lonesome / I haven't slept a wink," and the third line is "and in between I drink..." Most singers don't think to pause at this point, but Lee does. She doesn't just pause, but she seems to end the sentence there, with the words "I drink."

At this point, you're thinking, "Well, if I felt that way, I'd be drinking too." To end the sentence with "I drink" implies drinking alcohol. But after that long, pregnant pause, she tells us that she's not drinking booze but rather "black cof-

fee," twisting those words with Billie Holiday–like inflections. And that's possibly the saddest thing of all. She's not imbibing anything that will soothe her pain, or, better still, knock her out. Instead, the black coffee will make her feel the hurt all the more intensely and make the sweet relief of sleep even more unachievable—black coffee will help her stay awake through every painful moment. Her pain is herewith intensified rather than ameliorated as she drowns her "past regrets / in coffee and cigarettes."

Even the album cover accentuates the discrepancy: it shows a scene out of *Good Housekeeping*, with a smartly arranged table featuring a fancy-looking coffeepot and cup, not to mention a rose. It's a proper table setting for power breakfast from the Eisenhower era, and whoever arranged for this particular setup to reside on the cover of this album obviously had no idea what the album or the song were actually about. Lee—or rather her character in the song—isn't drinking black coffee for breakfast, but rather in the middle of the night, as she waits for her man to come back home after he's finished carousing. Either that or the art director had a monumental sense of irony.

Possibly the placid domestic scene on the cover was intended to heighten the contrast, between what a happy home life should be, and the grandly dysfunctional scene that Lee is singing about. The lyrics are filled with references to a housewife's work: "Love's a hand-me-down broom," "I'm hangin' out on Monday my Sunday tears to dry." The bridge elaborates on how men are "born to go a-lovin'" while a woman is expected to "stay at home and tend her oven." The specifically female references make it clear that this is not a gender-neutral text. A few male singers have, in fact, tackled it: Freddy Cole and Bobby Darin both sang a revised male lyric; Ray Charles avoided the issue entirely by performing it as a piano instrumental. But no other interpreter, male or female, brings that raw edge of pain to the song, the bleeding, exposed wound that's omnipresent throughout Lee's performance.

No one besides Lee ever seemed so frail and so vulnerable.

Perhaps it's not a coincidence that *Black Coffee* was Lee's most important project in the aftermath of her divorce from her first husband, Dave Barbour, who, as Lee told us in interviews and her memoir (*Miss Peggy Lee: An Autobiography,* 1989), was an alcoholic. Lee always presented herself as a victim. However, in James Gavin's 2014 biography, *Is That All There Is? The Strange Life of Peggy Lee,* he offers a more realistic account, pointing out that it takes two people to break up a marriage and that Lee wasn't as blameless as she wanted everyone to think she was. But we're talking about a free interpretation of facts, which Lee didn't hesitate to do, whether she was turning her feelings into music or writing her book. For decades, it's been said that the personal pain that Frank Sinatra experienced during his relationship with Ava Gardner was the fuel that drove his great saloon songs; the same applies to Lee in her great tumult over Barbour. What made them great artists wasn't what they were feeling, but the way they used those feelings in their art, the way the profundity of their emotions was matched by their craftsmanship as professionals. "Black Coffee," then, is Lee's equivalent of "I'm a Fool to Want You" or "In the Wee Small Hours of the Morning."

Taped in 1953, *Black Coffee* belongs on any short list of the great jazz or pop albums. It also qualifies as Peggy Lee's first modern "concept" album, the first project that she planned from start to finish as an album. As such, it's part of a period when several of her peers—who, like Lee, could easily be described as both jazz and pop singers—used the album format to get away from the pop singles they were regularly turning out and create something special, something both jazzier and more intimate. On albums like Lee's *Black Coffee,* Sinatra's *Swing Easy* and *In the Wee Small Hours,* Nat King Cole's *After Midnight,* and Tony Bennett's *Cloud 7,* these pop-star artists were getting back to the jazz-and-pop-standards that they loved best.

Still, it's clear that no other singer, even among these heavyweights, puts so much of her heart and soul on the line as Lee, no one else is as warm and real and human. Lee is almost frighteningly exposed—every emotion ringing true—throughout the *Black Coffee* album, both the eight original tracks recorded in April and May 1953, and the four additional songs taped for the 12-inch edition some three years later.

Apart from being the first time she set about crafting an album project, *Black Coffee* represented a new beginning for her in two other key ways. "The early '50s were a heady time for her," said her daughter, Nicki Foster, who vividly remembered the recording sessions, even though she was only ten at the time. "She had switched labels [from Capitol to Decca], she was working for the first time without Dad [Dave Barbour], and she was entering the new world of the album-length format."

In other words, there were changes both professional and personal—and, to some degree, also geographic. The first was the dissolution of her ten-year relationship with guitarist Dave Barbour. They had been together since meeting in Benny Goodman's band, about 1941, but by 1951, Barbour was descending ever more rapidly into an alcoholic haze. He was unable to control his drinking, and he feared that he was becoming a danger to his wife and eight-year-old daughter: separating from them seems to have been the only way that he thought he could protect them.

Barbour had been a musical partner as well: her chief accompanist on most of her record sessions and personal appearances, a collaborator on nearly all of her many excellent original songs. Thus when she separated from Barbour in 1951, it seemed to portend that a career change was on the horizon as well. In the few years that followed, Lee not only made the break with Barbour, but also with Capitol Records by signing a five-year "pact," as *Variety* used to put it, with Decca in 1952. (As Lee herself told the tale, that switch was occasioned by her insistence on recording a rather unusual arrangement of Rodgers and Hart's "Lover," but that's a story for another time.) And, at the same time, she also began making the move toward becoming an albums artist, as well as continuing to release singles.

"She was being actively courted by Sonny [Burke] and Milt [Gabler]," of Decca, as Capitol's Alan Livingston told me, "so she wanted to go where she felt she was appreciated." Decca was also largely based in New York, which would give her an excuse to spend more time away from Los Angeles, thus enabling her to put most of the country between herself and her now ex-husband. She made her last session for Capitol in February 1952 and her first for Decca two months later in April.

Black Coffee was brewed a year after that. In the spring of 1953, her career was again on the upswing: she was featured on a biweekly radio show titled *Club 88,* and in March she enjoyed a well-reviewed run at the New York nightclub La Vie En Rose.

For the last sixty years, the song "Black Coffee" has been regarded as a Peggy Lee signature—although she rarely if ever sang it in clubs or concert halls. From the vantage point of history, "Black Coffee" seems like one of the all-time most perfect songs for Peggy Lee, no less than the later "Fever." But, for whatever reason, Lee seems not to have even noticed "Black Coffee" back when it was freshly percolated in 1949, the year it was successfully recorded by two other major jazz-pop divas, Sarah Vaughan on Columbia and Ella Fitzgerald on Decca. (Both of the previous major recordings of the song are surprisingly grandiose: Fitzgerald's uses the full Gordon Jenkins orchestra and strings, Vaughan's employs big brass and opens with chirping, birdlike flutes.)

"Black Coffee," with music by Sonny Burke and lyrics by Paul Francis Webster, seems to have been brought to Lee's attention around 1952 by the composer himself. By 1950, Joseph "Sonny" Burke (who would later become one of Sinatra's producers at Reprise Records) was already well known as a bandleader, orchestrator, and occasional songwriter ("Midnight Sun").

In 1947 and '48, Lee had, coincidentally, recorded two songs by Burke, the obscure "I Don't Know What to Do Without You, Baby" and the hit "You Was." In 1952, Lee and Burke began working together on songs, their first notable number as a team being the highly exotic "Sans Souci." Shortly thereafter, they collaborated on their most successful project, the score for the classic Disney feature *Lady and the Tramp,* released in 1955. In the middle

of that collaboration, Lee recorded Burke's 1949 "Black Coffee."

Burke's "Black Coffee" (which had had no connection with a 1935 British song with the same title) was fundamentally the blues. Yet, somewhere along the line, Burke was accused of not being entirely original. The legendary jazz pianist Mary Lou Williams charged that Burke borrowed the melody from her 1938 composition "What's Your Story, Morning Glory?" By a confusing coincidence, "Morning Glory" is co-credited to the African American trumpeter Paul Webster, then a member of Jimmie Lunceford's orchestra, which recorded a classic version of Williams's song in 1940. Paul Webster is no relation to the Academy Award–winning lyricist Paul Francis Webster, who wrote the words to "Black Coffee."

The two tunes, "Black Coffee" and "What's Your Story, Morning Glory?" are marginally similar, but only for a few crucial bars in the opening. The pianist tried to sue the publishers of "Black Coffee," according to Williams's biographer, Linda Dahl, who then settled $300 on Williams just to get rid of her. Undoubtedly, Williams was merely a nuisance. (Dahl reports that she also accused two old friends, Duke Ellington and Thelonious Monk, among others, of plagiarizing from her.) It's doubtful that she would have won the suit: both songs turn on an old blues phrase that also turns up in W. C. Handy's "Aunt Hagar's Blues," published in 1920 (which is heard most fully in pianist Art Tatum's recording), and the same phrase is heard in slightly different form on the 1956 blockbuster hit "Heartbreak Hotel."

As with "Fever" years later, "Black Coffee" is a perfect song for Lee because it allows her to combine elements of the Great American Songbook standards with the essential feeling of the blues. Lee is a far better blues singer than Fitzgerald, Vaughan, or anyone else ever to sing "Black Coffee." That title track, which opens the album, begins with Pete Candoli wailing on muted trumpet, in the best tradition of blues obbligatists. Lee's vocal is full of intimate innuendo, constructed of microscopic nuances, she's forever bending pitches, turning notes in on themselves in order to make them sound ever more blue: "Black *coff*-ee," "I'm hangin' out on *Mo-on*-day," "to stay at *home* and tend her oven . . ." She stretches and bends these notes for all they're worth, and winds up doing just one chorus all the way through, with no repeats. Virtually everything Lee does on this track makes her sound more like a blues singer than a pop star or a band canary. She's clearly got more in common here with Bessie Smith than Patti Page—and the trumpet obbligato makes it seem very much like the 1920s, the era when Louis Armstrong was playing behind the classic blues singers.

There are two other blues-related songs on *Black Coffee,* both, likewise, placed in strategic positions on the familiar 12-inch LP edition, and both by composers she admired and almost certainly knew personally. "Gee, Baby Ain't I Good to You," by Don Redman and Andy Razaf, is, for all purposes, a slow blues in thirty-two-bar AABA form (also with a bridge) but more erotic than depressing, a rare blues that celebrates the consistency of love. Deriving from the 1956 "addendum" session, "Gee, Baby," has a rather different feel from "Black Coffee" instrumentally at least, there's no trumpet on "Gee, Baby," instead, the track opens with a guitar intro, followed by a prominent bass break, and there's vibraphone throughout. Still, Lee's voice matches the mood of the earlier date remarkably well; she sounds just as exposed and emotional here, even if the lyrics are far from a depressing downer.

"A Woman Alone with the Blues" alludes to the blues without quite being the blues; the narrative and form are a bit too complex for the song to be classified as a true blues. However, it evokes a passionate interpretation by Lee, and couldn't be any more blue even if it were a straight-up twelve-bar blues. It's the work of Willard Robison, a recurring character in Lee's musical saga. In a 1948 interview with Leonard Feather, Lee remarked that Robison's songs travel "in the direction I'd like to see vocal music progress. They're sort of poems set to music, little character sketches. This is nothing new, I know, but it hasn't been done enough."

"A Woman Alone with the Blues" is also the most prominent example of Peggy Lee being influenced by Lee Wiley, in this case the older woman's 1947 recording. Lee has much less vibrato than Wiley, and sings with an even more intimate, burnished sound; somehow this Lee is even more believable and inspired than the previous Lee. Lee keeps it simpler than Wiley; the earlier recording contains an additional chorus that Lee excludes. Lee almost seems like she's deliberately trying to surpass Wiley, but, inarguably, the influence is there. When Anita O'Day did "A Woman Alone with the Blues" ten years later (on her album *All the Sad Young Men*), in all likelihood she learned it from Peggy Lee.

As mentioned above, those bent notes, or inwardly turned notes, in the song "Black Coffee" might be described as a nod to Billie Holiday—who, more than anyone else, specialized in singing sad, jazzy, and torchy songs with a small group. Later in her life, it was commonplace for know-nothing pundits to dismiss Peggy Lee as a mere Holiday clone; in truth, Holiday cited Lee as a favorite at least as much as the other way around. Yet in singing "Easy Living" and "You're My Thrill" Lee was well aware that she was selecting songs that Holiday had made into jazz standards and, it seems, deliberately inviting the comparison or at least paying homage. "Easy Living" is one of Holiday's more upbeat numbers (in mood if not tempo), and Lee's reading is more positive still, making no secret of its Holiday influence.

Introduced in 1933, "You're My Thrill" is the work of Sidney Clare and Jay Gorney, the only song by Gorney to become a standard other than his Depression anthem "Brother, Can You Spare a Dime?" "Thrill" is an unusual case where the lyric is potentially positive ("You're my thrill / You do something to me . . ."), yet it's Gorney's dark, minor melody that makes "You're My Thrill" into a torch song rather than an optimistic love song. Ultimately, "You're My Thrill" is far more of a downer than a thrill, and it was an inspired choice for both Holiday and Lee. Still, when Holiday tackled "You're My Thrill" in 1949, she made it into something even darker than it had ever been before. Lee's version is darker and heavier still; her vocal is stark and spare, her sultry low voice is closely shadowed by harpist Stella Castellucci (this is from the 1956 session). She sings it almost coldly, bereft of any emotion, letting the words speak for themselves and the notes just hang there in space—the harp accompaniment is so spare that the vocal might as well be a cappella for the most part.

More recent versions of "You're My Thrill," especially those of Shirley Horn and Joni Mitchell, draw equally on Holiday and Lee. Singer Jeannie Bryson (the daughter of Dizzy Gillespie), who recorded one of the first Peggy Lee tribute albums (in 1995, when Lee was still on the road), observed that the combination of melody and lyrics doesn't just depict someone who's merely preoccupied with someone else, but someone truly obsessed in a way that's psychotic and pathological: "Why this strange desire / That keeps mounting higher?" (In other words, it ain't "I've got a crush on you, sweetie pie.")

Apart from the blues-oriented tunes, the rest of the album is mostly classic show tunes, rendered in a swinging, jazzy fashion. "Love Me or Leave Me" originated in a Broadway show (introduced by Ruth Etting in *Whoopee*, 1928), and immediately became a pop hit and then evolved into a jazz standard.

The main focus is on the interplay of Lee, whose voice is harsher and more metallic here, with trumpeter Pete Candoli, using an especially vocalized tone; it's practically a duet for voice and trumpet. Nearly every jazz singer of the classic era sang it (including Holiday in 1941) but no treatment is jazzier or more rollicking than Lee's; here, Candoli is not so much playing a background obbligato serving as a full-scale partner. Lee makes the sad lyric into something defiantly upbeat—as instrumentalists were wont to do—she imbues it with the ethos of the blues, in which one sings of a sad situation with a smile on one's face, trying to chase away evil spirits with a smile and a swinging beat.

Although Lee might also champion offbeat songwriters like Willard Robison or Alec Wilder, and more than most pop or jazz singers of her generation had a genuine affinity for the blues, still, the basic meat of what she did was the essential American Songbook, and the bulk of the *Black Coffee* album consists of classic songbook standards from the Gershwins, Cole Porter, and Rodgers and Hart.

"It Ain't Necessarily So" from *Porgy and Bess* is done in a slow bluesy tempo with a rocking vamp, provided mainly by Stella Castellucci, which recalls the more famous opening rocking vamp in "Summertime," from the same *Porgy and Bess*. Lee's unique vocal bestows the Gershwin brothers opus with a combination of lightness and gravitas. Ira Gershwin's witty lyric is still funny, but now it's funny in a rhythm and blues kind of way, like a Louis Jordan comedy song, rather than in a Broadway kind of a way.

"I've Got You Under My Skin" was first heard as a grandly romantic song with a vague bolero rhythm (in the same vein as "Begin the Beguine") in the 1936 *Born to Dance*. Originally, "Skin" was never done as a swinger, even when performed by the big dance bands. On *Black Coffee*, "I've Got You Under My Skin" is set up very nicely by pianist Jimmy Rowles, who frames the melody with an ingenious vamp that makes Porter's tune somehow seem like it came out of left field. This is perhaps the only notably swinging version of "Skin" to predate Sinatra's, three years later.

Also written by Cole Porter (for the 1938 *Leave It to Me*), "My Heart Belongs to Daddy" was a sexy comedy song with a built-in opportunity for klezmer-style wailing; Lee is completely uninterested in those minor-key, Semitic aspects, but rather, she starts swinging and keeps swinging, without a second of respite. Just at the point where you think she might slow down, she pushes the tempo even harder, even yelling "yeah" at one point for emphasis. And yes, Lee is sexy even when she's swinging—her erotic appeal is not limited to slow and/or sultry ballads.

The two Rodgers and Hart songs are somewhat schizophrenic. "I Didn't Know What Time It Was" (from *Too Many Girls*) starts very slow with the verse ("Once I was young") and in the beginning is relatively faithful to the Broadway/cabaret tradition, but then it kicks into swing time with the refrain. Lee keeps the beat going at a fast clip but never remotely distorts either Hart's lyrics or Rodgers's tune. "There's a Small Hotel" (from the 1956 session and also from *On Your Toes*) alternates between waltz time, rendered wistfully and romantic, and a 4/4 swinger, with prominent piano solo by Lou Levy—it's a rare jazz or pop record from the period to repeatedly change tempos and time signatures.

Which brings us to one of the central conundrums of the album: the title song was an instant Peggy Lee signature, yet, as we've noted, she rarely sang it again. However, "(Ah! The Apple Trees) When the World Was Young" remained in her repertoire for the rest of her life. It was adapted by Johnny Mercer in 1951 from an older French chanson, "Le Chevalier de Paris (Les Pommiers Doux)" and the new English lyric was successfully introduced that year by Bing Crosby: at forty-eight, Crosby could more realistically approach the song from a middle-aged, somewhat jaded viewpoint—more so than Mercer, who wrote it at age forty-two, or Lee, who was only thirty-two when she recorded *Black Coffee*. Yet it's not a song about being old, it's about the contrast between innocence and worldliness, the jaded *boulevardier* of Paris reminiscing about his idyllic childhood. (Innocence was never Sinatra's strongest suit, and, probably for that reason, both Crosby's and Lee's versions of the chanson resonate more strongly.)

Curiously, when this track was played for the bandleader and composer Raymond Scott, his reaction was, "It must be Billie Holiday, but it's so accurate, precise, and artistic that I can't believe it." In a sense, Scott was insulting both Holiday and Lee: Holiday for generally not being "accurate, precise, and artistic" and, conversely, Lee for imitating Holiday. Scott to the contrary, it's hard to imagine a track where Lee sounds less like Billie Holiday. Rather than recalling Holiday's hard, sharp edge, as Lee does on "Black Coffee" and "You're My Thrill," her vocal here consists entirely of classic Peggy Lee smoke-and-pixie-dust, it's almost ephemeral rather than physical. When she sings about "seeing it all through a cloud," the images start to flash up in your mind, starting with a fluffy pink cloud—or the cinematic device of a flashback, where the picture becomes fuzzy as the scene slowly dissolves to another time and another place.

Lee is remarkably direct, and Mercer's text allows her to effectively reveal the two very distinct halves of a single character, the *distingué femme fatale* and "the schoolgirl that used to be

me." Pete Candoli sets it up with a quote from "La Marseillaise," but for the most part the show belongs to Lee and Rowles. Few American singers trusted the attention spans of their audience enough to do all three verses and refrains written by Mercer (Nat King Cole's 1963 version is a whole other matter), yet Lee's is pure magic for three and a half minutes. She is so superbly convincing that you quickly forget that thirty-two is rather young to be quite so jaded and world-weary. "That was a song," her daughter, Nicki, said, "that meant a lot to her."

The whole album meant a lot to her. It sold enough copies to justify an expanded 12-inch edition, so, in 1956, Lee recorded four extra tracks with a small group: "It Ain't Necessarily So," "Gee, Baby, Ain't I Good to You," "You're My Thrill," and "There's a Small Hotel." By now, her regular accompanist was Lou Levy, and the session featured vibraphone (Larry Bunker, doubling on trap drums), guitar (Bill Pittman), and harp (Stella Castellucci) in addition to piano, bass (Buddy Clark), and Bunker's drums. The 1956 tracks are compatible but slightly different; by that point she had already taped *Sea Shells*, an extremely high-concept album driven by poetry and Zen and very prominent harp by Ms. Castellucci. In 1956 she was also working on *Dream Street*, a set of mainly meditative songs with both large and small group backing, and then the superb *Miss Wonderful*, an excellent big band project with Sy Oliver conducting.

The four additional *Black Coffee* tracks came from an April 1956 session that actually yielded six cuts; she was likely considering all of them as possibilities for the expanded album, but ultimately held off on releasing two (Cole Porter's "Do I Love You?" and Willard Robison's "Guess I'll Go Back Home [This Summer]"), which wouldn't see the light of day until many years later. (Even now, it would be a blessing to see them released on an expanded, fourteen-track edition of *Black Coffee*.) Some of the 1956 tracks, particularly the sensual "You're My Thrill," sound like they would belong equally well on *Dream Street*.

Twenty-five years later, Miss Peggy Lee was working and living in London, and preparing for a series of recording and concert dates. The British music journalist Max Jones spoke with her at a party, and, as he reported, "Several people mentioned Peggy's old *Black Coffee* LP and [remarked upon] how popular it still was. The singer said how complimented she felt, particularly when artists such as Joni Mitchell praised it and said they'd listened to it. 'What higher compliment can you have than that?' she asked." Jones asked her if she planned to make any more albums in that general style. "Not especially, it seemed. Some jazz backings, yes, but what she sought and appreciated was variety."

Essentially, Miss Lee graciously demurred. Her attitude seemed to be that it had already been done, and how could she possibly improve on *Black Coffee?*

29

Peggy Lee
The Man I Love
(1957)

Quick: What's the first line of "The Folks Who Live on the Hill"? If you said, "Someday we'll build a home on a hilltop high," you'd be wrong. No jury would convict you, however. If you were to listen to the song the way most singers phrase it, or even to look at the published sheet music, you would get that impression. But you'd be wrong nonetheless.

Of the countless vocal versions of that Jerome Kern–Oscar Hammerstein II gem, the most notable artist to get it precisely correct is Miss Peggy Lee, who sang it in 1957 on her classic album *The Man I Love*, conducted (and essentially produced) by Frank Sinatra and arranged by Nelson Riddle. The opening line, as Miss Lee shows us, is not all nine words as listed above, but merely the first one: "Someday."

"The Folks Who Live on the Hill" is an extraordinary performance, even by Lee's standards. Her recording immediately became quintessential Peggy Lee, to the point where it almost has to be included on every possible Lee retrospective or collection. The redoubtable pianist George Shearing, who two years afterward teamed up with Miss Lee to collaborate on another classic album *(Beauty and the Beat!)*, told me that he regarded "The Folks Who Live on the Hill" as his favorite Peggy Lee track—and he isn't alone. Singer-pianist Shirley Horn also picked it as a favorite, and it was the song she sang in tribute to her at Carnegie Hall in 2003.

"The Folks Who Live on the Hill" symbolizes both an ending and a beginning: it is the closing track on *The Man I Love*, but that album would be the first project she embarked upon after launching a new association with Capitol Records. It was also the first and last project she would make in collaboration with Frank Sinatra, who conducted on only a handful of sessions on which he didn't sing. It was also the first of only a mere two albums she would make with Nelson Riddle, even then widely acknowledged as the greatest pop orchestrator of all time.

Lee interprets "The Folks Who Live on the Hill" with a miraculous balance of minimalism and maximalism, between what's directly said and what's merely suggested; the original song, the orchestration, and Lee's vocal fit together into a perfect equation. We know that Hammerstein and Kern wrote this song for leading lady Irene Dunne in the 1937 western movie musical *High, Wide, and Handsome* (in which she sings it superbly, in a quasi-operatic fashion), but in retrospect it almost seems like it could have been written expressly for Lee. In this instance, the goals of the lyricist and the singer are remarkably in sync with one another. Whatever Peggy Lee may be, she is always an artist of extreme subtlety, one who prefers to hint at something rather than explicitly state it.

"Folks" is a stunning example of Hammerstein doing the same thing; instead of painting a complete picture, he provides the listener with a few telling details, leaving us to put together the story from his clues. The first words, after "Someday," are "we'll build a home on a hilltop high," but he never says who "we" are—he just leaves us to realize on our own that "we" are a young couple in a new permanent relationship. First it's just "a cottage that two can fill." Then, in the second eight bars, he suggests that the couple will "make changes," meaning that the house will grow along with the family. The bridge takes the focus away from the house itself, and talks about what the couple or family sees when they sit on their porch ("the sort of view that seems to want to be seen"). In the final eight bars he talks about the couple growing old together; slyly, he never mentions their children directly until he talks about them moving out—"and when the kids grow up and leave us"—and the couple is "just we two" again. Hammerstein continually minimizes these salient points and thereby makes them more important.

Hammerstein's strength as a poet was his invisibility; the rhyme of "our *veranda*" and "*command a* view" is the only part of the song that could have been written by Cole Porter or Noël Coward. One line that puzzles post–World War II listeners is the reference to "Darby and Joan, who used to be Jack and Jill." In 1937, anyone listening would have understood that Hammerstein was contrasting two folkloric sets of English couples, the proverbial long-married, elderly Darby and Joan with the youthful Jack and Jill, who went up the hill, and, in this case, stayed there. The most disappointing moment in Lee's treatment of the song is the decision to change "Darby and Joan" to "Baby and Joe." (The only other part of the text she alters is to reverse the order of a "thing or two" and "a wing or two" in the second A.)

Still, the most crucial word of the whole song is that opening "Someday." The song is not a literal narrative of actual events that have transpired in this fictional character's universe; the whole text amounts to wishful thinking. In that sense, it's a dream within a dream—there are multiple layers of unreality and suspension of disbelief—but nobody has ever made this seem more vividly real than Lee. Even if the dream itself isn't totally real, the dreamer very much is. The way she sings "Someday," it becomes a phrase that points to an idealistic existence at some ambiguous point that is, hopefully, yet to come—a kind of nostalgia for the future.

She makes it clear that this is a dream—and a song—about two distinct concepts, love and home, that she brings together into a single package; you can't talk about one without talking about the other. In 1937 most people couldn't pay their rent on a tumbledown shack in Athlone or a shanty in old Shantytown, let alone build an ever-expanding home on a hilltop high. "Folks" extends the promise of a better existence: Someday we will be together. Someday things will be better than they are now. Someday life won't suck. Someday. Maybe soon. Both the Gershwin brothers and Rodgers and Hart were on a similar track when they used the word "Soon" as a song title. During the Depression and then the war, popular songs had a lot of "somedays" and "soons" in them.

With Lee, that "someday" is so potent and so powerful that you almost don't even need the rest of the song—she just says it all with that one word. Darby and Joan, who used to be Jack and Jill, might have been forgotten by 1957, but the rest of the song's message is, in Lee's hands, more meaningful than ever. "Someday" becomes a forerunner of "Somewhere over the Rainbow" and *West Side Story*'s "Somewhere." It's a signifier for wishes, hopes, and dreams.

The Man I Love is a unique effort for all three of the key collaborators, Lee, Riddle, and Sinatra. Most of Lee's albums tend to be light, intimate, and swinging, whereas the depth of the thirty-six-piece orchestra here suggests the Chairman's heavier efforts, like *The Concert Sinatra*. The orchestral textures are deeper than on most Peggy Lee Capitol albums, and the tracks are generally longer. Furthermore, Riddle is wearing his Aaron Copland hat, and the orchestrations are saturated with what pianist Bill Miller once described as Riddle's "polytonal" approach. The orchestral mode is more than slightly symphonic, even for relatively simplistic songs like "He's My Guy." Lee, following Sinatra's example, usually was in charge of her own musical destiny—she picked the songs she wanted to sing and told the arrangers how she wanted to sing them. But here, for virtually the only time in her pinnacle years, someone else is at the controls.

While the tonal textures of Riddle's background suggest Copland, the general tempos seem informed by Billie Holiday, especially her superslow recordings of standards in the early 1940s. The whole album is remarkably slow, achingly slow, almost slow beyond the call of duty—even slower than Holiday would have sung it. "The Folks Who Live on the Hill" is almost three minutes and thirty-five seconds long—very long for a track on a Peggy Lee album—there's only room for one chorus, which doesn't include the verse. Riddle very astutely elaborates on the more classical, impressionistic elements of Jerome Kern's compositional style. When you introduce classical elements into jazz or pop music you're usually courting disaster, but Riddle pulls it off without seeming the least bit grandiose or overstated.

Sinatra played a key role in almost everything: the selection of repertory, the tempos, the general structure of the arrangements, the orchestral colors, but not the singing itself. In her vocals, Lee is very much her own woman—Sinatra, to his credit, did not try to make her into a female version of himself. She sings and phrases every song like Peggy Lee. In his own singing, one of Sinatra's major musical strengths was his gift for getting down deep into the groove, rhythmically, in everything he sang, even the ballads; he was remarkably rhythmically specific. Not so with Lee: she deliberately floats over the beat, she drifts on top of the trenches rather than getting down into them. In this album especially, her approach is incredibly effective. Where Sinatra blends with the ensemble, both in the rhythm and the melody, Lee stands apart from it. Where the orchestra is big and symphonic, Lee's singing is even lighter than usual—her voice shines out like a flashlight in a cavern. At other times she seems like a butterfly in a thunderstorm.

"The Folks Who Live on the Hill" is the album's centerpiece and climax, but it's titled *The Man I Love* for a good reason. George and Ira Gershwin's "The Man I Love" has one of the more convoluted histories of any standard song: the Gershwins

tried it in several different productions of different shows, but it never made it to Broadway (not until many decades later, in pastiche productions). Along the way, they even toyed with the idea of having a male character sing it. "The Man I Love" became one of the most beloved songs of all time, but it was always sung by a woman. It was a song that Frank Sinatra loved, yet even with pronoun changes he could have never sung it himself (as Tony Bennett later did).

But unlike nearly every pop singer of his generation or since Sinatra had a musical vision that was larger than himself. His idea was to vicariously "sing" it through the mouth of another performer. And of all of his contemporaries, the one great singer of his approximate generation (male or female) whom he seems to have felt the closest to was Peggy Lee. Sinatra and Lee had been good friends—some say more—ever since late 1942, when they played on the same bill at the Paramount Theatre: he was making his debut as a solo act (not yet a headliner) and she was still the girl singer with Benny Goodman's orchestra. When she came down with a cold, he went out of his way to be nice to her; she never forgot it. She told Nancy Sinatra many years later that it was her Frank who became her de facto Jewish mother, filling her full of chicken soup.

The Man I Love, released by Capitol in 1957, is a milestone in both careers. It was Sinatra's first foray at producing and conducting for another vocalist. *The Man I Love* was a key step in his ongoing ambition to become something more than a performer himself. In several ways, the album was a dry run for Sinatra's Reprise Records: he not only produced and conducted, he went so far as to lure the star artist away from another label. For five years before 1957, Lee had been under contract to Decca; but Sinatra, who had come to Capitol in 1953, had determined to bring her back to Capitol, where he could work with her. In 1957, she and Sinatra were neighbors on Kimridge Road, way up in the Hollywood Hills, high above Coldwater Canyon, in the upper reaches of Beverly Hills. Lee had moved there around 1954, and two years later Sinatra built a house of his own nearby. Thus, "The Folks Who Live on the Hill" held a special significance for them. "We both shared quiet talks, funny jokes, and we planned a whole album together," Lee later wrote in her memoirs.

Pianist Lou Levy, who had recently begun his long tenure as Lee's accompanist, remembered the sessions distinctly because it was the first time he worked with Sinatra or Riddle. "Frank lived a few blocks away, right off Beaumont Drive, just down the hill," Levy told me around 1991. "He'd walk over and they'd have drinks. They'd hold parties and get-togethers. I think the idea started during an informal gathering at her house. Frank got the idea, and he suggested it to her. He got Nelson to write the arrangements, and he picked the tunes. I think it was one of his 'here's an idea you can't refuse' type of things."

Beyond her relationship with Sinatra, the song held a special meaning for Lee and her only child, her daughter, Nicki. "We were always the folks who lived on the hill," Nicki recalled not long after her mother's death in 2002, "When I was a child, the first house Mother and Dad had was on Blair Drive, in the Hollywood Hills. When they divorced, we lived in Denslow, in Westwood, on a smaller hill. But we always lived in houses on hills. That song was always our favorite."

"The album was totally his concept," Lee recalled, "he brought me a list of great songs from which to choose, and [Sinatra's longtime pianist] Bill Miller came over to set all the keys with me. Then, Frank hired Nelson Riddle to write all those lovely arrangements, and Frank conducted them."

Riddle was clearly aware from the start that *The Man I Love* would be a special project, even by Sinatra standards. Sinatra clearly encouraged him to create his most poetic, most classically inspired orchestrations—such as the luminescent, Copland-Americana-style intro to "Folks on the Hill"—but at the same time among the most intimate. In the end, Riddle achieved a nearly impossible blending of two contrasting ideals: the charts for *The Man I Love* are as grand as a sweepingly large symphony yet as personal as a great singer accompanied only by a solo piano player. (Like Ella Fitzgerald with Ellis Larkins, or Tony Bennett and Bill Evans.)

The title song—and opening track—was only

the beginning. Sinatra seems to have planned the album around songs he loved but didn't feel were right for him to sing himself. Gender was, of course, an issue. As for "Folks Who Live on the Hill," Sinatra seems to have viewed it as too homey for one of his own albums. Of the twelve tracks on *Man I Love,* Sinatra had previously recorded only one, Irving Berlin's "Just One Way to Say I Love You." (Note: for our purposes here, and in several other essays in this book, the songs are not discussed in album sequence.)

When Peggy Lee sings "Please Be Kind," it means what Cahn and Saul Chaplin intended. We know that at thirty-six Lee had lived, loved, lost, and suffered—she was in the middle of her third marriage (at the time, she was one up on Sinatra). But somehow she can do what Sinatra can't: become a doe-eyed innocent (aided considerably by Riddle and sultry sax soloist Buddy Collette). She absolutely makes you believe that this is her first affair, and that if you were to be anything less than kind to her, she would be absolutely devastated. No less than "The Man I Love," "Please Be Kind" demonstrates how Sinatra was using the voice and persona of his friend Peggy to do what he, as Sinatra, could not. And Sinatra would never attempt anything like it in his own albums. Some of his projects were more intimate (*In the Wee Small Hours* for one), while others were also more symphonically grandiose (*The Concert Sinatra,* which included his own breathtaking reading of "My Heart Stood Still"), but there isn't one that attempted to do both at the same time, as *The Man I Love* does so effectively. Her strength is her fragility.

The album's general tone is set by the opener: of all Gershwin's classic songs, "The Man I Love" is the one most explicitly crafted from the same cloth as the composer's concert works, especially the 1924 *Rhapsody*. Here, "The Man I Love" opens with an atmospheric intro, and throughout the combination of singer and orchestra outlines the simultaneous intimacy and grandeur that would apply throughout the remaining eleven tracks; the background, with harp, strings, and French horn, is very *Appalachian Spring.* Lee's singing is direct and specific—she's not singing about all men, or even every man in her life ("the men I love"), but about one particular guy. She takes the general and makes it personal; the objective becomes the subjective.

On "He's My Guy," the task at hand is precisely the opposite. The song is deliberately colloquial "He's My Guy"—not "He's My Man" or "He's My Paramour"—and, informal as it is, she makes it sound as if it belongs in this "concert" context. Lee is especially attentive to that strain of blues coloration which is not only essential to "He's My Guy," but to most of the songs from the collaboration of Don Raye and Gene de Paul. On some levels, it's rather chilling how easily she accepts to the inherent masochism in the text—"He's careless about me, I don't think he tries." But then, Lee was always keen to promote the image of herself as a victim, both in her songs and in her memoirs.

Even in a potentially excessive setting like a symphonic string section, Lee knows that the key to interpreting a text like "That's All" is knowing what to leave out. It's a song about giving everything, and it could be approached by overloading it with everything, both vocally and instrumentally. Lee and Riddle realize that to make the song work, you have to give it slightly less than "all." (There's an odd lyric change: the bridge ends with "a love time can never destroy," but she sings it as "a love only time can destroy." What was she thinking?)

"Just One Way to Say I Love You" (from the 1949 musical *Miss Liberty*) is also all about being as specific and direct as possible. Irving Berlin's message seems to be: you can dress up a love song a million ways, and use all kinds of fancy phrases, but the only thing that matters is those words "I love you." The bulk of the lyric is those three little words over and over, but Lee makes them sound different every time. As in "That's All," she's incredibly direct and free with her emotions here, especially as underscored by a supportive, masculine solo from the big-toned trombonist Ray Sims.

Lee makes "Happiness Is Just a Thing Called Joe" fit right in—like the music of Gershwin, that of Harold Arlen could sound suitably symphonic when necessary. Yip Harburg's lyric begins with a verse that's poetically Ebonic ("A certain man with eyes that shine / Voo-doo'd up this heart of mine"). As with "He's My Guy," Lee takes advantage of the hint of blues sensibility in the melody, and Riddle

amplifies it, even ensconced in all the strings and twentieth-century classical impressionism.

Oscar Hammerstein's text to "Something Wonderful" (from *The King and I*) is very different from "The Folks Who Live on the Hill," and much more literal. Yet both are songs about being in love with a man. Introduced by Dorothy Sarnoff—a proper soprano if there ever was one—this is one of Rodgers and Hammerstein's most operatic efforts: here, Riddle gradually escalates the use of Rodgers's countermelody, a two-note vamp that booms away in the background. Yes, that vamp is more than a tad grandiose, but it serves to make Lee seem even more diminutive and feminine by comparison. It makes her sound like a woman caught up in a situation beyond her control.

There's no overt narrative trajectory to *The Man I Love* that encompasses every track, but it's worth mentioning that the album opens with a song about the beginning of love—"Someday he'll come along, the man I love"—and ends with the ultimate ballad of romantic consistency, about love continuing and extending through the rest of one's life. One of the major songs about the arrival of love, "My Heart Stood Still," itself arrives nine songs in. The song (from *A Connecticut Yankee in King Arthur's Court*) was one of Rodgers's most classically styled melodies—in a sense, his answer to "The Man I Love."

The 1957 Riddle chart is refreshingly direct, with no intro or verse of any kind, but simply with one look at us. She phrases the first few lines in pointedly staccato fashion here "I—took—one—look . . ." as if more than her heart were standing still, but also time itself. The most compelling moment comes during the bridge; we go from the string orchestra to just Lou Levy's piano and, a few bars later, Lee singing completely a cappella. No strings, no orchestra, no piano; it's as if she's standing there naked and alone on a soundstage; she isn't trying to be sexy——or anything else—she's just naturally and completely vulnerable. The idea seems to be, rather than have Lee singing louder, to emphasize her by making the accompaniment behind her quieter—so quiet, in fact, that it disappears completely. Then, for the last section ("I never lived at all . . ."), the strings return in full force, rising behind her like a great crashing wave of sound. Rather than raising her voice, Lee seems to be merely riding that wave—it's an exhilarating moment.

"Then I'll Be Tired of You" and "If I Should Lose You" are about ongoing love, as opposed to new love. They use exaggeratedly fanciful—and specifically celestial—metaphors and imagery as avatars of commitment, as in "I'll be tired of you when stars are tired of beaming" and "If I should lose you, the stars would fall from the sky." Somehow lyricists assume that the most dramatic means of depicting the consistency of love is to bring "the stars" into the picture. (By an apparent coincidence, these two songs are also on Dick Haymes's Capitol album *Moondreams,* also recorded in April 1957.) She opens "I'll Be Tired" unaccompanied, sounding languid, rather than tired, un-rushed rather than forced. She sings like she's got all the time in the world, thereby underscoring the message of the text, which insists that love will last "beyond the years, till day is night, till wrong is right."

"If I Should Lose You" is a similar idea articulated slightly differently; apart from the way the stars behave in both songs, in "Tired" the "birds refuse to sing," in "Lose" they "sing a mournful refrain." But rather than merely being redundant, Lee and Riddle make them fit together like two pieces of a picture puzzle. Here, she creates a Zen-like world in which all things are in tune with each other; the birds and the stars and the cosmos all reflect her inner state. The second part of the lyric of "If I Should Lose You" is about bringing things together, as in "With you beside me, the rose would bloom in the snow / With you beside me, no winds of winter would blow." It's hard to miss how appropriately strong and affirmative Lee sounds on the "with you" lines of the song, but weak and passive on the parts of the lyric that are about losing. You could understand perfectly even if she were singing in Swahili.

From Billie Holiday's songbook and Isham Jones's pen, "There is No Greater Love" makes heavy use of French horns. Marty Symes's lyric doesn't use astrological metaphors, but the lover in question is repeatedly told by the speaker that he/she is the best, the greatest, the sweetest, in an effectively simple lyric that perfectly matches bandleader-composer Isham Jones's melody. Lee articulates all those adjectives; "greater" has a whole different feel from "sweetest." The text and the voice sometimes appear to be at odds with each other; the words seem to be about large, grandiose ideas, but Lee sounds humble and down-to-earth, and the song truly comes alive while being situated somewhere in between these two extremes. (There's some outstanding instrumental work here, a short alto sax obbligato by Buddy Collette and a very somber valve trombone passage by Juan Tizol.)

On the original LP, "He's My Guy" (track seven) opened side two, which closed with "Folks Who Live on the Hill." Where "Hill" is about noble, stable, and committed love, "He's My Guy" offers a kind of pre-rebuttal; it's a song about loving a low-life ("He's careless about me, I don't think he tries") and, as is typical of this particular species of torch song ("Jim," "My Man," "What Love Has Done to Me," "I Must Have That Man"), the scummier the "guy" acts, the more noble the long-suffering woman becomes. (It's a wonderful lowlife.)

The only way the album could possibly end is with that masterpiece "The Folks Who Live on the Hill" (a song she undoubtedly learned from one of her primary inspirations, the great Maxine Sullivan, who recorded it in 1937 when *High, Wide, and Handsome* was released). As noted, it's far from the album's only triumph; Lee sings, among others, "I'll Be Tired of You" and "My Heart Stood Still" with just as much sensitivity. There's no one other than Lee who could sing "He's My Guy" with, as we've seen, just the right mixture of blues and resignation, and there's also no one else who could have arranged it like Riddle, equal parts Debussy and Ellington. And no one could have put the whole package together as expertly as Sinatra.

Musicians distinguish between leading a band, the way most swing band leaders did it—just setting tempos at the beginning and then cutting it off at the ending—and real conducting, the way the major symphonic conductors would have to do it, in which the musicians have to be led very precisely through the most subtle changes in tempo and dynamics.

Lee described Sinatra as "a marvelously sensitive conductor, as one would expect"—which meant that he succeeded at almost anything he put his mind to. Still, no one would expect even the greatest of pop singers to be able to conduct (any more than, say, Nelson Riddle or Billy May could sing), particularly on the rubato passages where the musicians had no set tempo to follow. Lou Levy agreed: "Frank did a beautiful job, he was really there conducting. He had it all together, I don't know how he learned to do it, but he did." Levy insisted that Sinatra was doing more than just waving his hands around for show, but rather, "there were parts of it that actually had to be conducted, it wasn't all in tempo. I don't know if he was schooled off the premises, but he did fine."

Indeed, Sinatra was so thorough that, as Lee later wrote, he "designed and supervised the cover. He is a producer who thinks of everything—even putting menthol in my eyes so I'd have a misty look." For years, it's been rumored that Sinatra also posed with her on the cover, assuming the role of the man she loves with the back of his neck to the camera. However, Levy set the record straight: "She was married to [actor] Dewey Martin then, in fact, on the cover, where you see her face, that's the back of Dewey Martin's head. I heard her and Frank joke about it later, because the marriage didn't happen to work out, but the album did."

Which is an understatement. The album is an all-time classic that relaunched a long and fruitful association between Peggy Lee and Capitol Records. Tracks from *The Man I Love*, particularly "Folks," have been anthologized and reissued all over the world, although the entire album took a while to claim its proper place on CD. In 1997 it was included on a British import twofer (along with *If You Go*, an unrelated ballad album from 1961). Finally, in 2007, *The Man I Love* was issued on a domestic CD, licensed from Capitol to DRG Records, who added two singles from the period as bonus tracks. A more substantial addition is that of Nelson Riddle's name on the front cover; the original edition only credited Lee and Sinatra.

As its creators intended, *The Man I Love* blurs the boundaries between classical music and popular music in that it truly lives up to what has been called "classic pop." More than half a century after it was recorded, *The Man I Love* is still making hearts stand still.

30

Marilyn Maye

Meet Marvelous Marilyn Maye

(1965)

Going to hear Marilyn Maye is a lot like attending a wedding where the bride's family and the groom's family have never met. On one side of the room are the Broadway and cabaret people, who tend to like their singing big and theatrical, with a lot of drama and stage presence. On the other side is the jazz crowd, who want everything hip and cool and understated, and will split the scene, baby, if anything doesn't swing. Ms. Maye is the only pop-song diva working today who can satisfy both crowds at once, combining the projection and personality of Ethel Merman with the musicality and sheer swing of Ella Fitzgerald.

It's all a matter of timing. Ms. Maye's singing has such relentless drive that she literally rocks your world; so many feet start patting in time that you immediately fear for the foundation of whatever building you happen to be in. In the Maye musical universe, everything swings—even the ballads. She's so hip that basic scat singing is far too square for her; she'd much rather take a lyric phrase and stretch it into a run of syncopated, chromatic syllables. Even 4/4 swing itself is old-hat; instead, she'd rather take a familiar standard like "Come Rain or Come Shine" and repurpose it into a high-powered jazz waltz.

Unfortunately, her professional timing has never been the equal of her musical timing. By the time Maye made it to the big leagues, it was already very late in the day for the traditional American Songbook. She cut her first album for RCA, *Meet Marvelous Marilyn Maye*, in 1965, the same year as the Beatles' *Rubber Soul* and Bob Dylan's *Highway 61 Revisited* and *Bringing It All Back Home*. It was the eve of Sgt. Pepper and the Age of Aquarius, and not the best time to launch a career that revolved around songs like "The Song Is You" and "Happiness Is Just a Thing Called Joe."

Maye never followed the career trajectory of artists of comparable talent: both Maye and Rosemary Clooney were born in the Midwest in 1928, and were both in the right time and place to get in on the final phase of the big band era. Yet where Clooney earned early fame by traveling with a big band, Maye stayed mostly in her native Kansas City—and under the national radar—until she was almost middle-aged. Was she missing a beat, or just doing things her own way? She might have followed the familiar pattern: child entertainer, then big band canary, to hit-single maker (usually with Mitch Miller), to album artist, to widespread artistic acceptance as a singer of jazz and standards.

But if Maye had traveled any path other than her own, she might not have enjoyed the payoff that she's been receiving in her seventies and eighties. In terms of singers who concentrate on the traditional American Songbook—be they jazz or cabaret—Maye is probably the most influential artist currently active. She's revered not only as a singer but as a teacher and mentor, who directs shows for her various students and protégées. Like Mark Murphy in the 1990s, it sometimes seems like every young singer in New York tries to follow in her tiny footsteps. For such a small woman, she casts a giant shadow.

"I keep thinking that if I could have recorded earlier, my life might have been very different," Maye has told me. Recording is the key issue: between 1965 and 1970, RCA had enough faith in her to release seven albums of mostly traditional-style songs, this in an era of diminishing returns. In the forty-five years since then, she's released fewer than half a dozen new albums. Of all the artists in this book—with the possible exception of Lee Wiley and Jimmy Scott—Maye has the highest inverse ratio of both significance and overall excellence to recorded output; in other words, the most quality and the least quantity. That's only in terms of recordings; live appearances are precisely the opposite. In the first half of 2014 alone, Maye had performed over fifty shows in New York alone; kind of an amazing track record for an eighty-six-year-old.

Obviously, it's disappointing that her recorded output is so alarmingly small. She was thirty-seven when *Meet Marvelous Marilyn Maye* was released, and so it was hardly an apprentice effort; she had already been a professional singer-entertainer for nearly thirty years. All of her tricks, her stylistic mannerisms, are already in place—thus the first album is a highly representative sample of her best work, and she continues to sing many of these same songs and arrangements fifty years later.

It took a long time for the world outside Kansas City to finally meet marvelous Marilyn Maye. She was born there (on April 10, 1928), it's where she was raised, and it's still the city that she calls home. Her first professional experience—for several years beginning around 1939—was as a singing emcee in a kiddie revue every Saturday morning at the Jayhawk Theatre in Topeka. "I introduced all the other little acts, as well as the cartoons and *The Lone Ranger* [movie serial]," she said. "I sang 'God Bless America' more times than Kate Smith." It was the first of many long runs in her career.

It could be that Maye felt no need to tour with a swing band since she was already in the swingin'est part of the world—nothing she could find on the road could possibly equal what there was to be heard back home. Kansas City in the 1930s was to the swing era what New Orleans had been to early jazz: the home turf. Beginning during Prohibition and then continuing up through World War II, Kansas City was the party center of the Midwest, just as Harlem was to the Northeast; it was where you came to have a good time, to dance to swinging bands, to meet girls and get drunk, without anyone caring whether wet or dry was the law of the land. Rhythmically speaking, this was a city that knew where "one" was. There was no place better for Maye to learn the craft of a jazz-based singer-entertainer: how to get a crowd's attention, how to hold it, how to find the beat and lock it down. How to use rhythm to transform a song from a set of words, notes, and chords on a printed page into something unique, something personal, something entirely her own.

There was more to be learned in Kansas City than timing: most of the other singers who came from this time and place were more closely associated with the blues, like the pianist-singer Julia Lee and the blues shouter "Big" Joe Turner. The blues is a constant, ongoing process where interpretation and composition are closely aligned: when Turner sang the blues, he usually started with something he heard somewhere, then altered the words and reshaped the melody to suit himself. Marilyn has done this with the blues, notably on *Maye Sings Ray*, a relatively recent album-length tribute to Ray Charles, where she takes Brother Ray's signatures and refits them for herself while retaining the essence of the original.

It's one of Maye's more unique contributions to pop music that she can take this blues-inspired approach and apply it to show tunes and standards as well as the blues. "Put on a Happy Face" on *Meet Marvelous Marilyn Maye* incorporates a whole original patter section, where she interpolates both original lyrics and a new tune, to enhance what Jule Styne, Betty Comden, and Adolph Green gave her to start with.

Over eleven years, working five nights a week (ten months a year), Maye honed her craft in a

Kansas City nightclub called the Colony. In this period she was married to her accompanist, pianist Sammy Tucker (whom she describes as both "brilliant" and an alcoholic), and the two of them worked out many of her classic routines. Most of the standards on her RCA albums were based on arrangements that the couple fine-tuned at the Colony. They also cut an album together of original songs by a local writer named Carl Bolte Jr.; it was titled *Marilyn . . . The Most* and distributed on a local level, mainly in Missouri. Apparently, the project started as a demo for the songs, and there was hope that a national label would pick it up; instead, the singer, rather than the songs, got "picked up." (Which is how it should have been. The singer is very good—a lot better than the songs.) Released in 1961, *The Most* somehow reached the ears of Steve Allen, who was impressed enough to book her for multiple appearances on his prime-time variety show starting that same year. The guest shots with Steve Allen led to two equally important career developments: subsequent appearances on *The Tonight Show* and the ongoing support of Johnny Carson, and the attention of RCA Records. (To this day, Maye regularly dedicates concerts to both Allen and Carson; "They're both here tonight," she'll say. "They just have better seats.")

RCA veteran Joe Rene produced *Meet Marvelous Marilyn Maye*, while the orchestral charts were credited to Don Costa (probably the ballads and string numbers) and Manny Albam (the up-tempo and swing numbers); most of the actual "arrangements" were based on routines that Maye had been doing for ten years or more, going back to the Colony days. The album starts with a rather spectacular opening salvo in "Get Me to the Church on Time"; she began singing numbers from *My Fair Lady* from the time that show opened on Broadway in 1956, and there's still an extended medley from the score in her current act. (Her next album, *The Second of Maye*, included "On the Street Where You Live.") Frank Sinatra had already done a swing version of "Get Me to the Church on Time," but his was subtle, even minimal by comparison: Maye comes out blasting. She enters with all cylinders fir-

ing; this is a high-energy Vegas opening number on steroids. All her tricks are in evidence: she enhances the Alan Jay Lerner with brief scat lines as well as a taste of original lyrics over a syncopated original ("Though I'm always tardy / At everybody's party / On this occasion get me there in time"). Decades later, the performance artist Lypsinka incorporated this recording into her act; Maye was chosen as a generic, high-powered female swinger—he/she clearly didn't want the audience to recognize the voice, so Ella Fitzgerald or Peggy Lee wouldn't do. The choice of Maye as fodder for a drag queen illustrates how she swings so hard and so relentlessly that she approaches the edge of being a caricature herself.

Fully eight songs on *Meet Marvelous Marilyn Maye* originated in Broadway musicals, although one of them, "The Song Is You," is a case where people know the song but don't necessarily identify it with a show (the 1932 *Music in the Air*). All the others have clear-cut connections to well-known shows; when Maye sang "Put on a Happy Face" and "Make Someone Happy," listeners in 1965 would have been aware that they were part of the scores of, respectively, *Bye Bye Birdie* and *Do Re Mi*. Track ten, "Put on a Happy Face," is another big blaster—it could open any casino production or 1960s TV variety show. As indicated, the most salient feature is Maye's patter section. ("When your dog just growls and bites you while you're pattin' him on the head. / When your best friend starts an argument, winds it up like this: 'Drop dead!'") Like "Get Me to the Church," it's almost hysterically happy. You *will* put on a happy face.

Track nine, "Night of My Nights" (from *Kismet*) is the first recorded of Maye's many jazz waltzes. "I've always loved jazz waltzes," said Maye. "The idea doesn't lend itself to too many songs. It's swinging and yet it doesn't go so fast that you can't deliver the lyric." The jazz waltz, despite numerous predecessors, really began in the modern era in 1959 with Miles Davis and John Coltrane, and Maye is probably its most consistent vocal exponent. In *Kismet*, the young Caliph (Richard Kiley on Broadway, Vic Damone in the movie) sings "Night of My Nights" with a combination of youthful innocence and amorous anticipation ("Show her the way to my bridal chamber"), but Maye's interpretation is more mature—like a grown woman looking forward to spending quality time with a grown man. The time signature is an expression of that sophistication, at once exotic and erotic; 3/4 time is old-fashioned but also a little bit kinky. Maye's scatted second chorus, which incorporates a key change, has the feeling of a dance of rapture—also, like Rosemary Clooney in "Blue Rose," like a woman humming to herself as she primps for a hot date. This is also the track where she most clearly shows her links to Sinatra. No, he didn't sing a lot of waltzes, but he's the only singer besides Maye who's able to create a romantic mood at such a hard-swinging tempo. "Night of My Nights" is truly a song of "delight and delicious desire."

In addition to the songs from shows that were already regarded as classics, her producers gradually began to fill her recording schedule with numbers from new shows as an adjunct to their ever-growing original cast albums, much as Columbia Records had been doing with Tony Bennett. (There are many more brand-new songs on her subsequent RCA albums.) The two newest songs are the title song from *Hello, Dolly!* (1964) and "I Love You Today." The latter is from her "rabbi" Steve Allen's only Broadway musical, *Sophie,* which played eight performances in 1963. The show, a biography of showbiz icon Sophie Tucker (who was alive at the time), doesn't seem to have been particularly good, but this song is one of Maye's and Allen's loveliest ballads (especially in the Don Costa arrangement, which uses a hint of samba in the rhythm section, with Herb Ellis prominent on guitar), and another one that has been in her working repertoire for all these years.

"Hello, Dolly!" is a full-scale Maye extravaganza, one of many numbers where she incorporates so much invention, both vocally and arrangement-wise, that the four-minute, four-chorus track almost needs a flowchart to fully describe it. The general trajectory is quiet-to-loud, and not so much, as you might assume, from slow to fast—actually, it doesn't get that much faster, metronomically speaking, from beginning to end. She starts with the chorus rubato and piano (and with just a piano for accompaniment), as if it were a verse.

Halfway through the first chorus, the tempo picks up slightly, but more importantly the saxophones come in behind, giving the illusion of greater speed by playing a shuffle beat around her, and soon enough the trombones and trumpets also join in the dance. In the second chorus, it's again more of a matter of dynamics (getting louder) rather than tempo (getting faster). The third chorus is mostly a deep, growly voice impression of Louis Armstrong (a device that also seems like a nod to Fitzgerald). She climaxes with a big cadenza incorporating original lyrics and soaring up to a huge high note. As part of the album, the track is excellent, yet it pales in comparison with an album that she did sometime later, circa 1990, a one-woman cast album in which she sang the entire score to *Hello, Dolly!*

It made sense that RCA would launch a policy of having Maye introduce new show tunes, but what seems baffling fifty years later is her producers' penchant for giving her vocal versions of famous instrumentals. Some of these would be foreign songs, like the Franco-American song "Petite Fleur," which she sang as "A Time to Love, A Time to Cry" on her 1966 album *Sherry.* But more often these were songs that, in the best of all possible worlds, were not meant to be sung by anybody, in any language. The two of these instrumental-cum-vocals heard here on the first album fall on widely opposite sides of the dividing line. "Washington Square" was the major hit from The Village Stompers, an instrumental group that couldn't miss as a chart success in this era because, in a rather calculated way, they combined virtually everything that was popular in 1963: Dixieland, folk music, world music, and blues. The lyric version of "Washington Square," as sung by Maye, is a mildly diverting oddity, nothing more. (It isn't even the goofiest thing she would record for RCA; that would have to be the Al Hirt novelty hit "Java," also on *Sherry.*)

Conversely, "Take Five" is one of the album's high points, and another perennial that she's still goosing audiences with. This was the hit single off the most successful jazz album of the era, the 1959 *Time Out* by the Dave Brubeck Quartet, composed by the quartet's saxophonist, Paul Desmond. They envisioned the melody as a somewhat academic exercise, to show that jazz could be played in 5/4 time, but had no idea what an incredibly popular tune it would become. Brubeck and Desmond had already introduced the lyric (written by Mrs. Brubeck) in the company of Carmen McRae. You might think that one couldn't do better than McRae, and almost under any other circumstances, you'd be right, but Maye's version is second to none. Prior to 1959, 5/4 time had only been employed in classical music (famously in the "Mars" movement from Holst's *The Planets*), but far from sounding "classical," here the time signature serves to ramp up the exhilaration level even higher. Leading off side two, Maye charges into the tune in a euphoric, supercharged blur of energy; it seems hardly possible that any one singer could generate so much excitement. You lose your breath just listening to her, don't even try counting along with her—much less humming along with the scat solo that she delivers in rough harmony with an alto saxophone soloist (possibly Phil Woods).

Meanwhile, back in the workaday world of 4/4 time, there are four tracks that might be characterized as ballads, or, at least, somewhat slower love songs. Maye's ballads are unique; I've heard her go almost an entire set without slowing down to anything like traditional ballad time. The first few times I heard her live, I concluded that slow love songs were her Achilles' heel, the only thing that she didn't do. I was missing the point: Maye is not a slave to tempo. Rather than an obligatory slow-down into the predictable pattern of ballad time, like 99 percent of singers and musicians out there, she increasingly became a master of instilling emotion, romance, and even sentiment at all tempos. Just as she can thrill you with a slow tune, she can move you with a fast one, she can make you feel the weight of the whole human condition. The *Hello, Dolly!* album, with its matchup of her style with Jerry Herman's often surprisingly deep texts, contains some first-rate examples of this. When she sings "Put on Your Sunday Clothes," it isn't just about getting dressed and having a good time; she fully communicates the "down and out," the blue feelings that one needs to cure by putting on one's Sunday clothes. She gives you both sides of the coin at the same time, the "down and out" and the "Sunday clothes." By interjecting a note of

melancholy into a fast number, she makes the act of partying seem that much more necessary and even poignant.

This is the major area in which Maye has improved steadily over the last fifty years. Nearly every other aspect of her work is already perfectly in place here in 1965. The second track on *Meet Marvelous Marilyn Maye* is "Misty," and it benefits from a sumptuous string arrangement by Costa, heralded by a French horn intro; Maye's vocal has a strong emotion running through it, but I hear more vocal pyrotechnics than true feeling. It's thrilling from that perspective—especially in the breathless way she ascends chromatically on the opening of the bridge, and then stretches out the last note of that bridge. The final eight bars are a dramatic cadenza of flawlessly executed harmonic variations rendered with near-operatic chops. In other tracks she's out-Fitzgerald-ing Fitzgerald, but here she's out-Vaughan-ing Vaughan.

Track four, "Happiness Is Just a Thing Called Joe" (from the movie of *Cabin in the Sky*) is delivered slowly, but in a vaudeville/blues groove; it's more extroverted than intimate, but it's highly entertaining. In both choruses when she reaches the line "When he kisses me, it's Christmas everywhere," she throws in brief quotes from a familiar Christmas fare ("Jingle all the way . . . ," "Jack Frost nipping at your nose!"). Overall, the vibe is similar to Carnegie-era Judy Garland, but without the vulnerability. Track eight, "Where Are You?," is vaguely in the mode of Sinatra and Gordon Jenkins, plus a few cinematic devices: it opens with extra-echoey reverb on her voice, so she sounds like a character in a movie dream sequence. It's wonderfully arranged and sung, but again, the life lessons, the hard-worn experience that one hears in her more recent singing, just isn't there yet. She comes the closest on "Make Someone Happy"; this is the clearest example of a more mature Maye concoction that's happy, sad, and then happy again, a bittersweet rendition that's primarily sweet but with a hint of bitterness just the same. It's comparatively subdued; there's no boffo ending with a big cadenza. In this, the album's penultimate track, you do get a sense that Maye is thinking about the someone she wants to make happy. And more importantly, she makes you think about that someone in your own life.

Whereas "Get Me to the Church on Time" is an archetypical nightclub opener, "The Song Is You" is a closer for the gods. This is the future template for Maye's many "everything-but-the-kitchen-sink" extravaganzas; you can tell that she spent thousands of hours in Kansas City singing it over and over, honing it to perfection, before she was ready to take it into the studio. The song is, famously, one of Kern and Hammerstein's more operatic works, but had long since been transformed into a jazz standard, and Maye swings it with what can truly be called a vengeance. She tears into it with formidable ferocity, like a sacred monster of an actress chewing up the scenery; think Joan Crawford in *Mildred Pierce.* The first chorus is the original text comparatively straight, but at a racehorse tempo. The second is crammed with all kinds of variations, routines, bits of business that derive equally from jazz and vaudeville: new melodies, new harmonic variations, new lyrics ("let me repeat / How the notes come through . . ."), key changes, and then, out of nowhere, we hear an Afro-Cuban rhythmic pattern (possibly inspired by Nelson Riddle and Judy Garland's "Come Rain or Come Shine"). Maye then engages in what would be one of her trademark tricks, delaying the climax—and thus further heightening the suspense—by detouring through another song just when we least expect it. Just as she's building to the high note on "The Song Is You," all of a sudden we're in the middle of "I Hear Music," before she returns to the climactic line, repeating "The song is you" over and over. It's something more than merely a mantra, it's more like a kind of a spiritual affirmation. The song is her, the song is all of us.

With "The Song Is You," we can at last say that we have truly met marvelous Marilyn Maye. From this point on her career would be demarcated by different forums for her talent, starting when, in the late 1960s, she recorded seven full albums and numerous singles for RCA over the course of six years. The 1970s are best remembered for her frequent appearances (as many as seventy-six) on *The Tonight Show* with Johnny Carson (who also wrote the liner notes to her 1968 album, *The Happiest Sound in Town*). In the 1980s and '90s, she mainly did regional theater—she was the best-known Dolly Gallagher Levi in all of the Midwest, and a formidable Auntie Mame as well. (One still yearns to see her as Golde in *Fiddler on the Roof,* Fräulein Schneider in *Cabaret,* or Mama Rose in *Gypsy.*) From 1970 to beyond the millennium, she hardly recorded again (a situation that still has a long way to go toward being rectified) and barely appeared in New York.

In 2006, she played the city for the first time in fifteen years, in a run at the Metropolitan Room, an engagement that had been brought about for her by longtime supporters accompanist Billy Stritch and attorney Mark Sendroff. "I thought maybe eight people would show up," she said, and no one was more surprised than she was to see people waiting on line all the way down West Twenty-second Street, practically to Sixth Avenue. Over the last decade or so, she has become a twenty-first-century Gotham institution, having worked virtually every room in the city. There are times when I expect to see her singing at Whole Foods or the Fulton Fish Market. At an age when most of her contemporaries are, to put it charitably, either no longer active or in severe decline, Maye has lost nothing. In every way, she's a stronger artist than she was in 1965, which makes the dearth of new recordings (whether live or in the studio) all the more regrettable. She is a major influence on the current generation; even when she isn't herself singing, chances are the young vocalist onstage is one of her students (some of the most impressive of whom are, to name just three, Gabrielle Stravelli, Danny Bacher, and Deborah Silver); you can hear echoes of Maye all across the city. This too partly explains why her shows are always so crowded: on any given night the room is packed with dozens of singers. Ms. Maye always gives them the benefit of the doubt; she acts as if they're there to be supportive, to cheer her on. The larger truth is that they're there for their own benefit. They want to see how it's done.

31

Carmen McRae
As Time Goes By: Live at the Dug
(1973)

As a jazz singer, Carmen McRae was worthy of being mentioned in the same breath as Billie Holiday, Ella Fitzgerald, Anita O'Day, and Sarah Vaughan. Each of them had something amazing to bring to the table: with Fitzgerald, it was all about what she could do with the melody; for Vaughan, it was all about the overwhelming beauty and depth of her voice; with O'Day, it was all about the rhythm, the time, and sheer exhilaration—the thrill of it all; for Holiday, it was all about the way she injected her own life into every song she sang. For McRae, it was all of these things—she had something of the melodic gifts of Fitzgerald, the rhythm of O'Day, the vocal resources of Vaughan, and the capacity for autobiography of Holiday—but, more than for any of her peers, with McRae it was all about the song itself. If she is less well known, and less immediately identifiable than the others, it's because she doesn't "sound" like Carmen McRae, she sounds like the song she's singing.

The cover of McRae's 1973 album *As Time Goes By* shows a tight close-up of the singer's face in black and white, bathed in both light and darkness; the light obviously comes from a follow spot in a club. Her eyes are closed, as if to indicate that she's concentrating very deeply on what she's singing (a microphone is present). There's no shortage of glamour—she has long, fluttery eyelashes and properly applied makeup—but there's also an undeniable toughness. Her teeth are clenched and her rouged lips are firm and truculent—these are the kind of lips that aren't afraid to say what needs to be said.

You might assume she's thinking about the song, whatever it is, but in a way that's not entirely true. In a 1962 interview with Ralph J. Gleason, and in other interviews as well, she said that "three quarters of the reason that I choose a song is for the lyrics," adding, "I look for [a song that has] something to say." So it's not entirely accurate to say that she always concentrated on the song or even the lyrics specifically; what she's focused on is the actual story the lyrics are telling—the underlying meaning of the song, the idea that inspired the songwriter himself. Her goal is to communicate from the inside out.

It's beside the point to ask whether McRae was better than Fitzgerald, Vaughan, O'Day, or Holiday; the point is that she was on their level. If we don't know her as well as we know her peers, it may not be because of her music, but because of something in her personality. At the end of her long career, Carmen McRae began to develop a reputation for being, well, not to put too fine a point on it, a bitch. Or, if you'd prefer, an extremely difficult diva who was known to grumble at her musicians and was frequently testy in front of audiences. Even when she was onstage, there was always the fear in the house that she was about to jump salty, except for those moments when she was actually singing. In the 1990s, reviewers were inevitably talking not only about how well she sang but about how surly she could be between songs. Even the pianist and singer Diana Krall—one of her contemporary progeny, who only knew McRae through her reputation—spoke of her "Don't mess with me!" attitude, adding, "I wouldn't want to cross her."

So her attitude may be one reason why Carmen McRae is less known than her peers: evidently, she had a hard time making friends, and no one went out of his way to give her a break. She never had anything like a hit single, and did far fewer TV appearances than the other ladies in the pantheon. She was more worshipped than loved, and, among music industry gatekeepers who could have boosted her, far more feared than liked her. Of all the major artists in this book, McRae is the only one whose single greatest album, *Live at the Dug,* is, inexplicably, one of her most obscure.

McRae's much-discussed attitudinal issues may explain one highly unusual aspect of her career. In the early days, from 1955 to 1959, she recorded twelve studio albums for Decca and its subsidiary Kapp. This turns out to have been her golden age of studio albums; never again would she work so frequently and consistently in the studio. From 1960 on, she primarily cut live in-person albums—which could be taken to mean that producers just didn't want to mess with her. As a younger singer, McRae had made several albums that were obviously not her idea—there was a Noël Coward songbook album (1957), a set of songs about birds (1958), a collection of show tunes (1962), and several team-ups with Sammy Davis Jr. Obviously, these originated from a desire to increase her audience base. There was nothing like that after 1962; from then on, instead of planning an album around a concept of some kind—and go to the trouble of arguing McRae into it—producers found it much easier to simply send an engineer off to whatever club she was appearing at, the further away the better. It was a two-sided proposition: on the one hand, the producers couldn't sabotage her, but on the other they couldn't help her sell records either—she would spend the rest of her life appealing primarily to those who were already Carmen McRae fans, without much chance of making new ones. Probably she just didn't want to bother with people who would even buy an album of songs about birds.

Through most of her career, it seems as if she released at least two live, in-person albums, live-at-this-club-or-that-one for every one studio project—sometimes the ratio was even higher. Beyond that, the producers who had her under contract seem to have stayed up nights thinking of fresh ways to insure that no one would ever be induced to buy a Carmen McRae record. It wasn't merely that she released primarily live albums—Ella Fitzgerald released concert albums continually, but at least they were packaged in such a way that you could tell one from another. McRae's many live albums invariably seemed as if they were being spit out randomly, and they were impossible to distinguish from each other. Packaging was, in fact, key. Some of the album covers on Mainstream Records were downright hideous, as if the art directors searched high and low for the least attractive photos of McRae they could exhume. By contrast, she looks very fetching on all of her Decca and Kapp covers—and she still could later on, whenever anyone cared. There are two McRae albums on Atlantic Records, for instance, that were both taped live in different venues in Los Angeles: *Live at Century Plaza* (taped in 1968 but not released until years later) has her looking downright dumpy, with a face like a Muppet. What a welcome contrast is the cover of *The Great American Songbook* (recorded live at Donte's in 1971), where she looks positively majestic and even glowing.

The covers and packaging are hardly the end of the difficulties. The live tapes themselves—issued haphazardly to begin with—were further mangled over the decades. In November 1965, Mainstream taped at least seventy minutes' worth of excellent live material of McRae singing live in San Francisco, and they issued two LPs of those tracks, under the titles *"Live" & Wailing* and *Live and Doin' It.* Then, in the 1990s, when Sony Music controlled the Mainstream catalogue, it would have been a simple matter to release a perfect, seventy-minute CD, which could have been no less simply titled *Carmen McRae Live in San Francisco, 1965* (or even *Live, Wailing, and Doin' It in San Francisco, 1965*). Instead, Sony took one of the San Francisco LPs and combined it with another live album done in New York at the Village Gate—which made absolutely no sense. (But at least the cover of that CD release, titled *Alive!*, wasn't terrible. The music itself, as always, was excellent.)

By the end of the 1960s and the start of the 1970s, most of McRae's studio albums, such as *The Sound of Silence* and *Just a Little Lovin'*, were slated toward pop and Top 40 songs. These are, in fact, excellent records—McRae sings brilliantly on them. But her heart was in the classic jazz standards, as she consistently said in interviews. Her love of the traditional songbook is also manifested in that the vast majority of the songs she was choosing to sing in all those live sets were standards like "I Only Have Eyes for You" and "Easy Living."

So choosing one Carmen McRae album to write about requires a live set. Luckily, there's one that stands out from the others, and for multiple reasons—all of them the right ones. In 1973, she appeared at a club in Tokyo with the rather ungainly name of the Dug. It wasn't surprising that one show was recorded, but what's a surprise is that she chose to make the show a completely solo recital. McRae had started her career as a pianist-singer, and, like her colleague Sarah Vaughan, she had the keyboard chops to accompany her own singing on piano whenever she wanted to. This is the only time she ever recorded an entire set with just her own voice and piano. The album was released with the following words on the cover arranged in the following fashion:

As Time Goes By
Carmen McRae
Alone
Live at the Dug

Thus the album would appear to have three titles:

Carmen McRae—*As Time Goes By*
Carmen McRae—*Alone*
Carmen McRae—*Live at the Dug*

Likewise, the album's release history is not what one would describe as straightforward. *Live at the*

Dug, as we might as well call it for the sake of convenience, was recorded and issued on LP in Japan by the Japanese Victor Corporation. Then it was briefly issued in the U.S. on an LP released by the minor Catalyst label. Later, it was reissued on CD by JVC, again in Japan only; as of 2015 there is no easily available American CD release.

Carmen's voice is essentially the same as on the other albums she made in her early fifties and previously: bittersweet, melancholy, pungent. But from the first few notes of the piano and then of her voice, it's evident that this is a darker and deeper Carmen than we've ever heard before, not necessarily vocally but emotionally.

This is also a more profound interpretation of "As Time Goes By" than we're accustomed to. As time goes by, more and more people forget that this classic song (words and music by the little-known Herman Hupfeld) began life in a forgotten 1931 Broadway show called *Everybody's Welcome*, and not in 1942 in one of the most celebrated movies of all time, *Casablanca*. Along with "Over the Rainbow," this just might be the most famous song people know from classic Hollywood, and like that 1939 standard, this is a prime example of a song that is best known without its verse: Sam didn't sing this verse in Rick's Café Américain any more than Dorothy sang the verse to "Rainbow" in that black-and-white barnyard in Kansas.

After a few notes of piano introduction, McRae grunts approvingly, "Ah!" and then starts with Hupfeld's verse, altered somewhat to suit her personality: "No matter what the progress or what may yet be proved / The simple facts of life are such they cannot be removed" is now "No matter what the outcome or what might still be had / The dearest things in life are free, so how can that be bad?" You get the impression that the verse was so little known in 1973 that McRae felt few listeners would even notice that she had "personalized" it, and rather radically at that. She does indeed sound "a trifle weary," though not more than that, and on "relieve the tension," she stretches out the syllables with gospel-style melismas, as if the tension is truly being relieved.

She moves from the verse to the chorus without changing tempo, contrary to tradition; both verse and chorus are medium slow, but not rubato. Where the verse is ultra-personalized, via both lyric alterations and what McRae does with her voice, the chorus begins with her deliberately stepping back, making it a little less personal. For a line or two, she's almost like a lecturer giving sage advice: "You must remember this / A kiss is still a kiss . . ." but she quickly gets more and more involved in what she's singing, and even by the time she reaches "a sigh is just a sigh" there's no mistaking the audible sigh in her voice. Yet when she sings "the fundamental things apply," she's back to sounding terse and businesslike, phrasing those words squarely on the beat. The whole song progresses along those lines, McRae relaxing into the song and then pulling back. The second "as time goes by" just before the bridge has her minimizing the line, pushing it downward and understating it—delivering all four words in lowercase letters. She contrasts this by emphasizing every item in the list in the line "hearts full of passion, jealousy, and hate." Changing course again, when she reaches the end of the bridge, on the words "that no one can deny," she becomes warm and maternal, as if giving motherly advice to a dear friend rather than standing in front of a blackboard with a pointer.

At that point, there's a brief flourish of a few notes before she lunges into another half chorus, commencing with the bridge, which she sings in more of a clipped fashion, rather like a news anchorman recapping the day's headlines and quickly summarizing. This time she makes "passion, jealousy, and hate" seem merely like items on the list, or, in the long run, as if she's underplaying them in order to make the climax seem bigger. This time when she says "no one can deny," it's more definitive, like she's not about to let anyone deny it. In the last eight bars, she stretches the words more intensely than in the first chorus: "a fight for love and glory" becomes both more lovely and more glorious. She intones "a case of do or die" in such a way as to signal that we're coming to the end, as if we're driving down a road and see a stop sign looming on the horizon. What, you may ask, could follow a case of doing and dying? "The world will always welcome lovers" is declamatory, but she then repeats "as time goes by" three times: once

very minimally and understated; second, more emphatically; and, finally, conclusively. Time, she is telling us, is going to go by whether we like it or not. There are a trillion recordings of this iconic song, but McRae's is one of the all-time greatest; *As Time Goes By* is a very fitting name for this album.

The second track, "I Could Have Told You" (Carl Sigman and Jimmy Van Heusen), is a Sinatra song; other artists, like Shirley Horn and McRae, have recorded it, but it's clear that they all learned it from Sinatra and sang it, more or less, in his honor. McRae's self-accompanied reading is especially personal: Sinatra was eternally gregarious and outgoing, even when he was being suicidal. In his 1953 record of "I Could Have Told You," Sinatra sounds as if he's consoling his best friend in the world, who's in the middle of crashing and burning, the point being that he's communicating to another individual. But McRae sings as if she's looking in the mirror, or like John Raitt in *The Pajama Game,* singing back at herself—she could have told herself how to avoid all those romantic catastrophes, but she wouldn't have listened, not to herself . . . or anyone else. (We've all been there.) Her reading is almost beyond intimate. It sounds as though her deepest, most personal thoughts have been directly translated into words and piano notes; the thought process has been extracted directly out of her heart and soul, showing you more of anyone's inner self than you've ever seen before. When she sings "making promises he'll never keep," instead of stretching the last word the way you might expect, she cuts it off shortly, and follows it with a few minor notes for emphasis—as if to literally illustrate the sound of a promise unkept.

"More than You Know" is the major survivor of the 1929 all-black Broadway flop *Great Day,* which had the misfortune to open within a week of the stock market crash; Vincent Youmans wrote the music, Edward Eliscu the words, and Billy Rose, in all likelihood, contributed the title. "More than You Know" starts out more upbeat emotionally than the song that preceded it and slightly faster, something closer to dance tempo, although it slows down slightly and becomes more contemplative by the end; this is an advantage that pianist-singers have, that they can control every aspect of a performance and thereby make it mirror more fully their internal state. It must be said that none of the most celebrated full-time singer-pianists of McRae's approximate generation—Nat King Cole, Blossom Dearie, Bobby Short—took things to the extent that McRae does here. She seems to be communicating with no one but herself, even when she sings to "you," and we almost feel we're eavesdropping on a private conversation we weren't supposed to hear. You can easily imagine her singing to a photograph of her "man of my heart" rather than to the man himself in person. Even so, it's more optimistic than "I Could Have Told You," and she even allows herself the luxury of a brief piano solo.

Where "I Could Have Told You" speaks to McRae's allegiance to Sinatra, "I Can't Escape from You" (by Richard A. Whiting and Leo Robin) was something that McRae undoubtedly first heard sung by Bing Crosby, probably in his 1936 film *Rhythm on the Range;* she follows the basic shape of his Decca record (a common enough shape it is, verse and then chorus) in a slower tempo. McRae was the only major singer other than Crosby to favor this tune, and she had already recorded it in the studio with Ray Bryant's trio on her 1957 album *After Glow*. The earlier version is prettier, but the Japan performance is deeper and more internally driven, more contemplative. Here especially she sounds bemused by her inability to escape from whatever it is, whether it's a lover who haunts her or the inevitability of appearing at a place called the Dug in Tokyo and playing piano for herself. Her version is at once daydreamy and melancholy, as if she were by herself in an open field, the sun is shining, the birds are singing, but all she can think about is this person or idea or thing she can't escape from.

Even when "Try a Little Tenderness" was brandnew (in 1932), the Harry Woods song was generally regarded as lugubriously sentimental and oldfashioned. To Sinatra's credit, he was able to make people take the song seriously as late as 1945; by the mid-1960s, Dean Martin was singing a goofball parody and Otis Redding had recorded a very successful soul music reinterpretation, both of which are probably more entertaining than the song as originally written. (The song actually has a his-

tory with soul singers like Etta James, Sam Cooke, Gloria Lynne, and Aretha Franklin.) McRae's is the most moving of all. She again proceeds from verse to chorus almost as if she's thinking out loud, and her piano accompaniment seems like a direct extension of that. She's roughly in the first person and the third person at the same time: "I may get weary, women do get weary," but then, as a woman, she's offering advice to the men who love them, and personalizes it with little touches like "I won't regret it—neither will you—love is my whole happiness." She keeps it minimal yet highly emotional at the same time, and the end result is that nowhere else has she seemed so vulnerable, so exposed. I've heard few things more moving than the way she phrases, "I may be waiting, just anticipating, things I may never possess." There's an amazing sense of intimate mystery about the whole song, and about that line in particular. Who knows what she was anticipating, or what thing it was that she may never possess? It opens up an entire world of wonder.

"The Last Time for Love" is one of a very few songs composed by McRae herself. ("Dream of Life," recorded by Billie Holiday, is the best known.) Having her go from standards to a selfpenned song is instructive, and it tells us that, no, she's not necessarily any more open and direct on her own words and music than she is on those of Woods, Hupfeld, Whiting, and Robin, etc. It's a worthy song, though not an exceptional one, which she had recorded previously on one of her 1954 sessions for Bethlehem. Her piano solo, probably the longest in the set, is especially noteworthy, in the most literal sense of the word.

Written by Irving Berlin for Ethel Waters in the 1933 revue *As Thousands Cheer,* "Supper Time" is generally given equal footing with Andy Razaf and Fats Waller's "Black and Blue" as one of the first so-called "protest songs" on Broadway. Yet both songs have a dual meaning: "Black and Blue" was specifically about racial preferences within the African American community, and essentially became a civil rights song only in hindsight; "Supper Time" was specifically written about the widow of a victim of a lynching, but Berlin was commercially minded enough to leave a little wiggle room in the text, so that it can be sung from the point of view of any woman whose man has left her—not necessarily by dying—therefore including the numerous white singers who have sung it. McRae begins with what might be construed as a few lightly dissonant notes—which, to me, signifies that she has the lynching scenario in mind, rather than the idea that her man left her for another woman. No one else so adroitly underscores one brilliant point of Berlin's lyric in the way it starts with the woman calling to her kids, "supper time," and the way that it switches from an exterior call to an interior monologue. When she sings the words "supper time," she sounds as if she's barking out the back door to her kids, but the rest of each section gets progressively more and more introverted; by the point she gets to "ain't comin' home no more" she has completely modulated from exterior to interior—and then she does it all over again for the next eight bars. It's a masterful job of switching from spoken words to private thoughts. At 3:32, this is the shortest track in the set; no verse (as Berlin wrote it), and just one comparatively short—and unbelievably moving—chorus.

"Do You Know Why?" is another "remake," although it's really unfair to call it that. Like "I Can't Escape from You," this is a forgotten song from an obscure picture (the 1940 *Love Thy Neighbor*, remembered, if at all, as the only movie costarring those two famous radio feuders Jack Benny and Fred Allen). McRae likely learned it from the Tommy Dorsey/Frank Sinatra recording, and first recorded it on her outstanding 1958 album *Book of Ballads*. Otherwise forgotten though it may be, McRae shows that it's an excellent song, with characteristically outstanding music by Jimmy Van Heusen and lyrics by Johnny Burke. It's deliberately less intense than "Supper Time"—clearly, she and the Tokyo audience needed a breather, as do we, forty-plus years later. Here's a textbook example of a great singer pulling back and letting the lyrics speak for themselves, which is apparently an exceedingly difficult thing to do, given the scarcity with which it happens, especially in the contemporary era. The phrases tumble out, one after another, in perfectly logical formation and order: "We used to say . . . our love would stay . . . until the cows came home / And then the cows came home . . .

Do you know why?" She makes the words more poignant by underemphasizing them. It's entirely unornamented, no decoration, no embellishment, just pure song. Finally, in the very last line (again, just one chorus and no verse), she repeats the titular question three times, stretching it out for greater impact the last time.

If "Do You Know Why?" is an obscurity, the next song, "But Not for Me," is one of the most listened-to standards of all time, ever since the Gershwins wrote it for the 1930 *Girl Crazy*. Here, the verse is as familiar as the chorus—McRae is the first artist to make me notice how brilliant Brother Ira was to rhyme "try it" with "riot." It's a song about loving and losing, but with too much of a self-deprecating sense of humor to be classified as a torch song. She gets all the passion out of it that can be gotten, as well as all the irony, using each to underscore the other. (Unfortunately, she uses the 1950s update of the lyric, "more skies of gray / than any Broadway play"—rather than "Russian play"—"could guarantee." There's a brief lyric flub—"with love to rule the way" rather than "lead the way"—which further underscores the spontaneity of the enterprise. This time, she allows herself the luxury of a little decoration: as she comes out of the bridge, you almost literally hear her falling as she approaches the line "I was a fool to fall and get that way." There are even a few brief scat sequences here and there, mostly in the second chorus, all tantalizingly brief. (Mel Tormé famously described McRae as one of the great scat singers, yet she rarely indulged in the technique—at least not on recordings.)

"Somehow the thrill I feel is new, I must confess." The next track opens with a few lines of lyrics that we don't recognize at first. The opening to "Please Be Kind" is a genuine example of what is invariably described as "a rarely heard verse." The song is another reprise from the 1958 string album *Book of Ballads*, and, as with "Do You Know Why?," the solo live recording is both deeper and more intimate. Her major personalization is to repeat "oh oh oh!" before the last "please be kind" and her sixteen-bar piano break. She returns for half a chorus at the end, in which she stretches everything out more luxuriously, as if she were genuinely entreating a lover to treat her with kindness.

This 1938 number is a song about beginnings: "This is my first affair, so please be kind." The team of Sammy Cahn and Saul Chaplin wrote it in 1938, at the very start of their long careers as professional music-makers. McRae makes it the last song on the album. But who knows what beginning she might have had in mind? Maybe the start of a career in which she continued to work solo, as she does here? For her, that thrill was indeed new.

As far as we know, it never happened again, although there are later live recordings on which she plays her own piano accompaniment on a couple of songs. But never for the whole enchilada. Diana Krall once cited *Live at the Dug*—or whatever one might wish to call it—as one of her favorite albums by anyone. "She did a solo piano record of her own, *Live at the Dug*—that record kills me. Apparently she didn't like it." Krall adds, "She wasn't safe, you know. She brought some of her personal views in her music. Wasn't afraid to state her opinions. It took courage to do that at that time." And she concludes, "If you look at Frank and Nat, they're entertainers. But if you're going to say 'jazz singer,' I always think of Carmen McRae."

32

Anita O'Day

Anita O'Day Sings the Winners

(1958)

Picking a single album by Anita O'Day was difficult, if not impossible, for two reasons: first, because all of the dozen or so LPs that she made for producer Norman Granz between 1952 and 1962 are amazingly excellent. They represent the height of her career, and few if any artists ever enjoyed such a consistent track record—virtually any one of her Mercury, Clef, or Verve LPs could be cited as her best. But as it happens, the performance that was her most celebrated at the time—and still is today—was not an album but, rather uniquely, a live appearance that was filmed and then shown internationally.

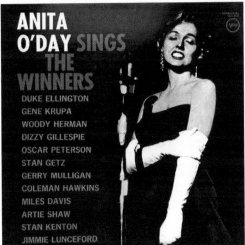

ANITA O'DAY SINGS THE WINNERS

DUKE ELLINGTON
GENE KRUPA
WOODY HERMAN
DIZZY GILLESPIE
OSCAR PETERSON
STAN GETZ
GERRY MULLIGAN
COLEMAN HAWKINS
MILES DAVIS
ARTIE SHAW
STAN KENTON
JIMMIE LUNCEFORD

This is *Jazz on a Summer's Day,* which, a decade before Woodstock, was the first major theatrical concert feature. O'Day's concert took place on July 7, 1958. According to various sources, she performed fourteen to sixteen songs, which were filmed with multiple professional cameras and sound equipment, very much a rarity at the time. Two of her numbers were selected for the final cut, both of which were her own highly original, imaginative interpretations of even-then-ancient jazz standards, "Sweet Georgia Brown" and "Tea for Two." Both are examples of O'Day using time in amazingly creative ways. She had a very attractive voice, but it wasn't a virtuoso voice (unlike Ella Fitzgerald's or Sarah Vaughan's); her main appeal was rhythmic. O'Day could do things with time that were almost less like a musician (like Fitzgerald) than a tightrope walker

or acrobat; one always felt as if she were taking all kinds of chances and balancing herself precariously. For all the bizarre choices that the filmmakers made (particularly with regard to the editing; there are many more shots of the crowd than there are of the performers), they made a wise decision in selecting two numbers in widely contrasting tempos: "Georgia" is slow and sensual, while "Tea" is fast and exuberant.

"Sweet Georgia Brown" is a textbook example of how a master jazz singer can be said to swing a slow, glacial tempo. Singing jazz, in the opinion of some, meant taking away the meaning of the words and the emotional content along with it, but not to O'Day. "Georgia Brown" was written as a comic song of praise for a heartbreaking vamp, a gorgeous hussy, and in O'Day's interpretation it remains a song of seduction, particularly in the first chorus, which she performs with only drummer John Poole for accompaniment. She not only sustains the melody without the help of a piano (Jimmy Jones was on duty for the rest of the set); the drum pattern feels distinctly Middle Eastern, and O'Day underscores the feeling with what sound like goofy pentatonic notes—she teases out the melody as if she were charming a snake. She stretches out all the vowels and squeezes and pleases all the consonants, like a playful partner; even the seductive way she holds her lips and teeth is a turn-on.

Like Vaughan and Fitzgerald, O'Day never had much of a personal life; none of her marriages was particularly successful, none of her love affairs was particularly loving. (Charlie Bourgeois, George Wein's associate, who probably booked her at the 1958 festival, once told me, "Anita didn't have affairs!") But in her high heels and little white gloves, summer sun hat and summer dress (she looks as if she's expecting one of the gentlefolk of Newport to invite her to a garden party afterward), she is damn sexy. One is tempted to say that she dominates the stage like a grand diva, like a Maria Callas, but hers is more the deportment of a master musician, in the same way that Chuck Berry, George Shearing, and Louis Armstrong all dominate the stage when the camera is on them in their segments of *Jazz on a Summer's Day*.

"Tea for Two" is even more playful. She races through the words and music like Secretariat or Man o' War, maintaining total coherence and control even at a breakneck pace. Again, the words "swinging" and "fast" shouldn't be confused with each other. There are plenty of Noël Coward patter songs and eleven o'clock Broadway numbers that are delivered at a God Almighty fast tempo without any attempt to swing; for anyone else, the tempo of "Tea for Two" would be too fast to swing. But Anita thrives at this tempo, she's warmer and friendlier and more lovable here. Something about singing faster than any racehorse or supersonic plane somehow seems more human.

Jazz on a Summer's Day was a major boost in O'Day's career. The movie featured no shortage of great singers, including Dinah Washington and Mahalia Jackson, not to mention Armstrong and Jack Teagarden. But somehow Anita was the one everybody remembered; the combination of what they saw and what they heard put her over the top. In retrospect, there was only one aspect in which O'Day and Granz fumbled the ball, in that they didn't immediately come out with an album titled *Anita O'Day Live at the Newport Jazz Festival*. This wasn't entirely their fault, as the festival would be recorded by a different label every year, famously Columbia in 1956 and RCA in 1963. Verve had recorded the festival the previous year, in 1957, and in 1958 it was Columbia's turn again. (The audio from Anita's 1958 set has thus far only been released on a bootleg—one wishes that the film footage of

the complete concert would somehow also turn up.) However, Granz was consistently bullish on the idea of live recording, and whether by coincidence or design, at the time of O'Day's triumph at Newport 1958 a live album was just about to come out. This was *Anita O'Day at Mr. Kelly's*, taped in Chicago in April 1958. Yet while *Mr. Kelly's* is an excellent album, it falls short of the amazingly high level that she attained at Newport.

Still, earlier that same month, in April 1958, O'Day had recorded an album that was even better, one that deserves to be classified among her absolute best, and that unequivocally cemented her status as a jazz artist. Normally, when a label wanted to shine a jazz light on a singer, they teamed him or her with a famous band (such as Count Basie's, with or without the Count himself). On *Anita O'Day Sings the Winners*, however, O'Day establishes her jazz bona fides by means of repertoire.

In a funny way, the album format was about moving forward and looking backward at the same time. The LP format was, first of all, a direct extension of the 78 rpm album. Just as there had been 78 album reissue collections of the legendary recordings of, say, Louis Armstrong and Duke Ellington, the same idea was then extended to long-playing vinyl: you could now hear an actual historical recording of, say, Bessie Smith or Bix Beiderbecke from thirty years earlier.

But the LP brought something new to the table as well. Some of the labels had deeper pockets than others; Capitol, for instance, only went back to 1942, and while they had many excellent recordings by, say, Benny Goodman, they didn't happen to own any of Goodman's swing era hits; the original masters of "Stompin' at the Savoy," "Let's Dance," "Air Mail Special," "Jersey Bounce," and other BG signatures were all owned by other corporations. In the past, from time to time, stars had re-recorded their biggest numbers for other labels, generally in superior fidelity, as Al Jolson did when he signed a contract with Decca Records in the last years of his life. Generally, though, the companies did everything they could to prevent this, and they frequently inserted a stipulation in contracts that expressly forbade artists from re-recording the same songs for other labels until a certain period of time had passed.

But in the mid- to late 1950s, many artists began the process—almost wholesale—of re-recording their most famous works in the new technology of high fidelity and longer playing time. Capitol Records inaugurated a new series of albums of swing era stars playing their best-known works in hi-fi, starting with Benny Goodman and including Harry James, Coleman Hawkins, the Casa Loma Orchestra, and Stan Kenton. (The latter case is significant because virtually Kenton's entire catalogue was already owned by Capitol.) Within a short time, the idea of simply reissuing vintage masters seemed less glamorous than re-recording signature hits in hi-fidelity and then stereo. RCA Records, among others, also launched an ambitious and inspired series of new albums by veteran musicians of the swing era and earlier, including Red Norvo, Helen Humes, Connee Boswell, the Original Memphis Five, Bud Freeman and "the Austin High Gang," Peanuts Hucko, Helen Ward, Larry Clinton, Jay McShann, Cab Calloway—these musicians did some of the best work of their long careers on these albums. A few of the most iconic performers even recorded full-scale "musical autobiographies": Louis Armstrong, Bing Crosby, and Ethel Merman, and slightly later, Nat King Cole and Frank Sinatra.

Those were the most favored options: re-release vintage masters or re-record historic arrangements. But, as we have seen, there was yet a third road to take, namely that of taking something old and doing something new with it. This option found its most visible expression in the "concept" albums of Sinatra and the "songbooks" of Ella Fitzgerald. These were not just new interpretations of songs that were now deemed to be classics, but the way in which the songs were connected from track to track was new—connecting songs by mood and by songwriter were both essentially new ideas, which had barely been explored on recordings, on the radio, or even in live performance in clubs and concerts. In fact, the whole of jazz seemed to be a perfect match for the new format: jazz musicians and singers reinterpreted old songs in huge quantities, whereas pop acts had to craft their potential hit singles one song at a time; from the beginning, stars like Ray Charles and Bobby Darin found that albums were a good excuse to sing vintage standards.

Some of the most creative ways to juxtapose old and new arrived between 1957 and 1959: in that period, the remarkable team of Lambert, Hendricks & Ross was launched with two breakthrough albums, *Sing a Song of Basie* and *Sing Along with Basie;* likewise, Gil Evans, in the midst of his epochal collaboration with Miles Davis, found time to create *New Bottle Old Wine* and *Great Jazz Standards,* two exceptional albums that combined new and old. The first two LHR albums treated the output of the Count Basie Orchestra as if it were a songbook (Basie himself was a casual composer, and by no means on the order of his compeer Duke Ellington), in a way that was at once faithful and yet highly creative: the idea was to attach words to big band instrumentals, and even, in one case, to write lyrics around lyrics that already existed. The original Basie recordings were re-created as closely as possible, but with the added dimension of verbal expression. Gil Evans also took a highly creative look at what was then being established as "the jazz repertoire"—the entire half century of recorded jazz as it existed up to that point—and turned in stunningly imaginative treatments of everything from modern jazz anthems like "'Round Midnight" to early jazz warhorses like "King Porter Stomp." (Other arrangers followed suit on their own albums; the very young Michel Legrand and Quincy Jones, for instance, came up with their own modernization of early jazz works, in ways very much inspired by Evans.)

Recorded in 1958, *Anita O'Day Sings the Winners* was all of the above. It was the climax of a very fruitful, decade-long professional relationship between the great jazz singer and the storied producer. O'Day's and Norman Granz's collaboration began in 1952, when Granz was an independent operator working through Mercury Records, and continued through the christening of his own more mainstream label, Verve Records, in 1955, which succeeded largely because of the releases by headlining singers like Ella Fitzgerald (and, to a lesser extent, O'Day); by the time Anita left the label in 1962, the company had long since been sold to a larger corporation. Though Granz benefited by their association, O'Day did even more so. At the height of the big band era, she landed several landmark hits with the orchestras of Gene Krupa and Stan Kenton, but by the end of the 1940s, although she kept working, she had not created anything notable recording-wise. She might have been regarded as too terminally hip for the room, sharing the fate of such obscure characters as Leo Watson, a brilliant artist little known beyond hard-core jazz fans.

Granz did very little of the actual work on O'Day's albums—he didn't have much to do with picking her material or her accompaniment, but he opened the door for her to achieve the same mainstream acceptance as Fitzgerald. Like Fitzgerald and Mel Tormé, also on Verve (and Carmen McRae, Sarah Vaughan, and Dinah Washington elsewhere), O'Day's work from 1952 to 1962, as I've said, is so consistently excellent that picking one album is almost arbitrary, but *Anita O'Day Sings the Winners* is certainly an obvious high point.

As with the LHR and the Evans albums, here O'Day is both re-creating the past and extending it, putting her own individual stamp on the material while, at the same time, remaining faithful to the originals. *Sings the Winners* is an arbitrary title; you might assume that the songs herein are the winning entries in some kind of songwriting contest or popularity poll. What they are is jazz classics going back roughly twenty-five years, neatly encompassing the swing years with the most famous works of the big band era.

The difference between *Winners* and the LHR and Evans albums is the amount of attention that went into them. The LHR and Evans albums seem to have been carefully crafted over a long period of time, the O'Day album seems to have been ground out as quickly as possible. It was done in two quick sessions of six tunes each, done in consecutive days, and even the decision to give it to two separate musical directors to write and conduct the charts seems like one calculated to speed up the production process.

Russ Garcia and Marty Paich were each given six selections, all of which were recorded during those two consecutive days, and then issued with the six Paich arrangements (from April 3, 1958) on side one and the six Garcia charts (from April 2) on side two.

A few of the song selections seem somewhat random: at the time, "My Funny Valentine" might have been identified with Gerry Mulligan, to give them the benefit of the doubt (although in retrospect it would have made more sense to do "Walking Shoes," Mulligan's best-known composition, which has at least two different sets of very singable lyrics). However, it's hard to imagine that anyone would have associated "Tenderly" with Oscar Peterson, although he could play with lyricism and sensitivity when the occasion demanded it. "Tenderly" is hardly the first word—or song—that comes to mind when we think of this high-powered pianist.

It hardly matters; this project is all about music, not scholarship. O'Day is one of those rare artists who are better served by a casual program than by a painstakingly crafted project like the Lambert, Hendricks & Ross albums—she's better off winging it as much as possible, and rather than inspire her, a concept that's too heavy or too specific would just get in the way. And Anita herself is in terrific form; at thirty-eight, her low soprano (mezzo? contralto?) has never sounded better. It never was a deep, rich voice, or a profoundly beautiful one, but it was a distinctive voice—there was no mistaking Anita for anybody else, even though by 1958 there were all kinds of singers making all kinds of albums who had been inspired by her. Possibly even more than Fitzgerald, whose voice was lovely and lyrical, or Vaughan, whose voice was operatic in its scope, O'Day had more in common with Billie Holiday in that the very sound of their voices was the epitome of pure jazz. There was something direct, unfancy, and unfrilly about her distinctive Chicago accent, a sound of getting down to business, of not wasting time or chops—a more formal soprano voice would have only gotten in the way of the swinging.

On April 2, 1958, O'Day and Garcia launched the first session with something familiar, Mary Lou Williams's medium slow blues "What's Your Story, Morning Glory." The Kansas City trumpeter Paul Webster (no relation to the lyricist Paul Francis Webster) came up with the title and Williams, then the musical director of Andy Kirk's orchestra, wrote the melody, and the New York–based lyricist Jack Lawrence wrote the words. The Kirk band introduced it in 1938 with a rather formal vocal by Pha Terrell. But O'Day and Russ Garcia are basing their treatment on the more successful instrumental from 1940 by Jimmie Lunceford's orchestra. The O'Day–Russ Garcia arrangement recalls the writing of Gerald Wilson, whose early work for Lunceford suggests a common ground between that orchestra and later, so-called progressive jazz ensembles like Stan Kenton's. The chart uses a lot of dissonance, and overall is more Kenton or Boyd Raeburn than Lunceford or Kirk; there's a lot of alto (probably the modernist Ronnie Lang rather than Benny Carter, who's also on the date). O'Day is a highly compelling blues singer, much more so than a lot of female vocalists in the jazz category. She captures precisely the right cadence throughout: in the second section, she clips the notes to the opening title phrase ("what's—your—story—morning—glory . . ."), then stretches them out in the next lines ("did you reeeeead it?," "might as well confesssssss it") and telegraphs them with big spaces between them ("oh . . . won't . . . you . . . tell . . . me . . . that . . . you . . . love . . . me . . . too!")

From the blues, O'Day and Garcia proceed to the uber-standard "My Funny Valentine." The arrangement, more Kenton than Mulligan, is highly dissonant, certainly more so than one expects for one of the greatest, and usually one of the most tender, love songs ever written. Arranger Garcia treats it in a very abstract, jagged fashion that almost sounds as if he wrote it as an audition piece for Stan Kenton. Garcia was using the 1954 recording by Gerry Mulligan and Chet Baker as his point of inspiration; although the song had been widely recorded between 1954 and 1958, the Rodgers and Hart classic was still mainly associated with Mulligan. Garcia knows what he's doing: the contrast between the arctic blasts of the orchestra and the cool heat of Anita's vocal makes for an effective contrast; like focusing our attention on something white by putting a black backdrop behind it, Garcia highlights Anita's warmth by placing her in a setting that's not just cool but icy cold—"Midnight Sun" would

have been a good number to orchestrate in such a fashion.

The larger truth is that O'Day, for all her visible toughness both on and off the stage, was a master balladeer; could be that she really related to the idea of a funny valentine because she was such a dysfunctional lover herself, and well knew what it was like to smile with her heart. Even in this context, she finds ways to be playful—when she sings "Are you smart" she goes up on the last note, twisting it at the end; then, the trumpet section proceeds to do the exact same thing, twisting the note exactly so, as if echoing her. (She re-recorded the song in a 1976 concert in Tokyo in an entirely different arrangement that's significantly softer and sweeter.)

"Sing, Sing, Sing," the third song of the first session, takes us to the very pinnacle of the swing era—Benny Goodman's historic Carnegie Hall concert of 1938. Originally scored for Goodman by Jimmy Mundy, this was a comparatively screechy piece for the era—it was much more futuristic than, say, Goodman playing "Don't Be That Way" or "Stompin' at the Savoy." Which is ironic, because Louis Prima wrote the piece as a very simple barroom singalong—the key part of the lyric is just everybody shouting "ohhh—ohhh" in unison, rather like a Cab Calloway–style audience participation number. This most inconspicuous of pop songs somehow evolved into one of the most complicated works in the jazz vocabulary, particularly with the interpolation of another riff number, "Christopher Columbus," by saxophonist Chu Berry.

Garcia suggests various elements from the classic Goodman Carnegie recording—Gene Krupa's drums, the leader's clarinet—but he doesn't re-create it literally; the "Christopher Columbus" riff isn't there, for instance. O'Day sings the melody, with plenty of scat embellishments, and then, re-creating the breathtaking clarinet-and-drums duo by Goodman and Krupa, she does a scat pas de deux with clarinetist Buddy Collette playing in a Goodman manner. Working with just drums—no piano, guitar, or bass—is a lot like playing in traffic, and it's something that would have given pause even to such virtuosos as Vaughan and Fitzgerald.

Yet O'Day is completely fearless, her scat sequence is brilliant and inventive, she never misses a beat (no surprise) or a note, even without any harmonic support. It's an exhilarating performance, one that justifies the premise of the entire album, and proves that a song with a minimal, even meaningless lyric can be an exceptional vehicle for one of the great jazz singers.

"Body and Soul" is indisputably a jazz classic, and the O'Day-Garcia arrangement is what we might call duplicitous—in several senses of the word. The album jacket credits the inspiration and dedication to the classic 1939 Coleman Hawkins solo (and there's a few bars of tenor cadenza at the beginning that shout out to Hawk), but the *Winners* treatment has much more in common with the 1938 Chu Berry–Roy Eldridge arrangement. O'Day and Garcia follow the general outline of Berry and Eldridge: she does the first chorus slow, in ballad tempo, as Berry did in 1938, but then doubles the tempo into a super-fast swing time, as Eldridge did on the famous Commodore disc. Finally, for a coda, O'Day reverts back into ballad mode, just as Berry and Eldridge did. What's amazing is that she does both things so well: she sings the ballad portions very emotionally and meaningfully, and she also swings harder and better than anybody else—this in particular is a performance that could be compared to Fitzgerald, or even Armstrong. (It also recalls the multi-tempo treatment of "Ol' Man River" by O'Day's number one fave, Martha Raye.) "Body" was one of several *Winners* arrangements that she kept in her personal "book": there's a wonderful appearance on the TV show *Art Ford's Jazz Party* from later in 1958 where she sings the same two-tempo chart, although when she recorded it again in 1975 in Tokyo, she stuck to ballad time all the way through.

The *Winners* album contains two Latin numbers that were both hits by "mainstream" (i.e., non-Latin) jazz orchestras, "Peanut Vendor" for Stan Kenton and "Frenesi" for Artie Shaw. The Cuban song "Peanut Vendor" ("El Manisero") was a surprising pop hit for Kenton in 1947, in fact, so much so that in 1956 he re-recorded it for his 1956 album *Kenton in Hi-Fi*. Garcia starts with Pete Rugolo's arrangement as a close template: he uses

O'Day to sing the melody, in place of the trombone solo that plays the first chorus in both Kenton versions. It's a goofy novelty lyric, not exactly the kind of thing that you'd want to hear Sir Noël Coward sing (or would you?), but then peanuts are precisely Anita's meat. Like Fitzgerald doing "A Tisket, a Tasket" or Armstrong singing "Heebie Jeebies" or "Ding Dong Daddy," this proves again that great jazz singers don't always need a great lyric, they can make incredible music with the goofiest and most minimal of novelties. Garcia re-creates Kenton and Rugolo's famous crashing, smashing, dissonant brass, which represent a rather playful kind of modernism—and which make a perfect foil for O'Day's impish sense of humor. Whether scatting or singing lyrics so nonsensical that they might as well be scatted, O'Day is perfectly adorable here; she's never been more charming or endearing. This track is a singular triumph for both the musical director and the singer; ever since I first heard it, whenever now I listen to the Kenton-Rugolo original, it always seems to be missing something.

"Frenesi" has more of a romantic component; between this song and "It Happened in Monterey" and "South of the Border," gringos are always going south of some border or other to get laid. In Anita's version, the object of her affection is a "handsome caballero" rather than a "lovely señorita," but she's again sweet and sincere throughout; her voice and entire manner are delightfully flirtatious. It's narratives like this that make it clear that one of O'Day's great strengths is her kinky, alpha personality—a trait that also puts her way in advance of such successors and sound-alikes as June Christy and Chris Connor. O'Day is not only a master musician like Fitzgerald (or, for that matter, Stan Getz) and a fearless improviser, she has personality like a movie actress or comedienne—she's like Celeste Holm or Eve Arden or Jean Arthur. You can practically feel Anita winking at you—her attitude leaps right out of the grooves.

The two Latin numbers finished the Garcia section, and O'Day returned the next day with Marty Paich at the podium. They started the second date, and the album, with "Take the A Train," which, in this context, is something of a throwaway. Compared to what has preceded it and what follows, it's easy to overlook. The combination of O'Day's voice and a reasonable facsimile of Billy Strayhorn's iconic composition for the Ellington orchestra is serviceable, and there's a surprising trade of fours between flute (Herbie Mann), trombone (Dick Nash?), and tenor saxophone (Bill Perkins). Still, the three-minute track is far from the tour de force it is on *Ella Fitzgerald Sings the Duke Ellington Songbook*. Oh well, not every track on an album can stand out, even on a classic album. This is the first track on Side A, the first we're hearing (and apparently the first recorded) of the six tracks arranged and conducted by Marty Paich.

There's a Kenton spirit to Paich's arrangement of "Tenderly"—apart from the rather gentle piano introduction (by Jimmy Rowles); most of the chart is at once warm and yet somewhat jarring, rather like some of the ballads that Paich arranged directly for Kenton, like "My Old Flame." There's nothing to suggest Oscar Peterson; the piano part makes me think of Walter Gross, the studio pianist who composed it. O'Day is again wistful and romantic in the middle of a rather harsh setting—she seems like the very human heroine of a contemporary science fiction movie, a flesh-and-blood character surrounded by an all-digital CGI background.

O'Day and Paich next addressed two "winners" inspired by Woody Herman. In 1947 Jimmy Giuffre took Harry Warren's "Jeepers Creepers" and regifted the harmonic sequence into "Four Brothers," a vehicle for Herman's saxophone section, and it became one of the band's signatures—an all-time classic work for jazz orchestra. Jon Hendricks wrote words to it in 1955, and while part of me wishes that O'Day had taken the trouble to learn that lyric, she's such an expressive singer that she doesn't even need words. With Anita, scat phrases are every bit as meaningful and expressive as lyrics are to a singer like Barbara Cook; the "sha-bop-de-bop" that she sings in one part of the song is completely different from the "sha-bop-de-bip" that she sings in another part of the song—and contains a whole other meaning. There are a few singers that can scat in such a way that you don't even miss the lyric, but O'Day does more even than that: she conveys a full sense of narrative. "Four Broth-

ers" has a beginning, a middle, and an ending, a sense of dramatic progression, and she does it all with "sha-bop-de-bop." Paich follows Giuffre's arrangement faithfully, placing O'Day in the role of all four original saxophone solos, at one point having her trade with one of the tenors. This was perhaps the most successful piece in the album, in that she kept doing "Four Brothers" for years to come. Often she would introduce it as a "jazz interpretation of 'Four Brothers,'" which is a quirky, curious way to describe it—it's impossible to imagine any other kind of treatment of this three-minute scatsinging tour de force.

"Four Brothers" was originally recorded by Woody Herman's Thundering Herd at a December 1947 session that also included Ralph Burns's concert work for the orchestra, "Summer Sequence"; "Early Autumn" began life as the final section of "Summer Sequence," and became the piece that catapulted Stan Getz to jazz superstardom even while he was still one of the Herd's Four Brothers. Much the same as he would do for "Midnight Sun," Johnny Mercer heard this big band instrumental and was moved to write a lyric, which Fitzgerald, Jo Stafford, and Billy Eckstine all recorded within a week or so of each other in 1952. It's one of Fitzgerald's best ballads, and even more so for O'Day. Buffeted by Four Brothers–like saxophones, she's at once both hip and vulnerable. Mercer's lyric brilliantly uses the descriptive imagery of summer changing into fall as a metaphor for the end of the relationship, and O'Day doesn't miss a detail ("May I ask you . . . Darling, if you care . . .") and conveys a vivid portrait of love and loss . . . and saxophones. It's another ballad triumph for the woman who always insisted she didn't care about singing ballads.

The last two pieces from the two sessions are bebop anthems, associated with the two most famous trumpeters of the modern jazz era, and both enjoyed, if that's the right verb, multiple sets of lyrics. The derivation of "A Night in Tunisia" is way too complicated to go into at any length, but even though composer Dizzy Gillespie always announced it and recorded it as "A Night in Tunisia," the melody was actually recorded for the first time as "Interlude" by Sarah Vaughan, with Gillespie playing behind her, in 1944. Later on a lyric was written to the "Tunisia" title ("The moon is the same moon above you . . ."), but the "Interlude" lyric is obviously the definitive one, and O'Day helps show us why. At times it seems like the lyric and the tune are inapposite, the song is about the end of love, or, rather, of love being "just an interlude" and the melody is almost relentlessly fast and loud. But O'Day makes it into an anthem of self-preservation, of looking love right in the face and staring it down. Even though love left her and only stuck around for an "interlude," she's not about to whine and moan about it. Take that, Mr. Love!

In the 1958 Newport concert, O'Day announces, "The next tune we've chosen is a tune we've been using as our theme, it's entitled 'Four,' from the Miles Davis musical school of thought, and it's in our new album—extra plug! And, I recently acquired lyrics on it, [which] I'd like to lay on you lightly, right now." First recorded in 1954, "Four" was popularized through the jazz world by Miles Davis, although it's generally believed to have been composed by the saxophonist Eddie "Cleanhead" Vinson. From 1954 onward, it was widely played as a jazz instrumental, then in 1958–59, two vocal versions emerged. Anita's version has a lyric by Bill Loughborough (who later wrote the jazz standard "Better Than Anything"), and she sang it on both the *Winners* album and at Newport. In 1959, Lambert, Hendricks & Ross introduced the Jon Hendricks lyric, which is much deeper and more philosophical, and that's the one that all singers for the last fifty-five years have favored. However, it terms of a simple, highly singable set of words, I personally prefer the Loughborough lyric. The Hendricks lyric, with all its profundity, would have never worked for Anita, whereas this text allows her to be cute and flirtatious again, as well as highly swinging. The Hendricks version almost makes you think too much, whereas this text propels the melody along—especially as Anita sings it—and never gets in the way of the swinging. Then again, Anita never let anything get in the way of the swinging.

That's the last tune on the *Winners* album, which represents O'Day at her best, not only in that it captured her swinging her hell-for-leather way through some of the most famous jazz standards of all time, but also in that it captured the best of her balladeering in tracks like "My Funny Valentine" and "Body and Soul." And, as we have seen, Anita's way with a love song has been sorely underappreciated, especially by the singer herself.

Winners is something of a very personal choice for me as well. That's the album I would always listen to whenever Anita became too exasperating. I formally interviewed her about a half a dozen times, between the 1980s and about 2001, by which time she was suffering from dementia and "old-timer's disease," and could only sing when someone held up gigantic cue cards for her to read. I saw her many times—but I only rarely talked to her after shows, mainly because you never knew which Anita you were going to get. Sometimes she could be pleasant, but more often she was surly, and she was rarely in the mood to sign autographs or exchange pleasantries. That wasn't what she was about.

On one occasion, I spent the whole of an afternoon and evening hanging out with her and her manager, Alan Eichler—talk about a long-suffering manager! She was in New York to sing at the JVC Jazz Festival, which possibly made her nervous and added to the already heavy tension. Anita was like a seventy-five-year-old six-year-old. She was petulant and moody and even perverse. If the conversation ever turned even briefly to a non-Anita subject, she would practically fly into a temper tantrum—she had to be the center of attention at every moment. We ate dinner, and she was constantly badgering the staff and the rest of us to wait on her hand and foot. The most significant moment—when I actually saw her devilish smile—was when she gleefully announced that she had never read her own autobiography, *High Times, Hard Times.* (Alan later explained to me that reliving those moments in her life was just too painful for her, but that night she acted like she deliberately didn't read it because she wanted to be able to tell everyone that she had never read it.) Overall, she reminded me of Gloria Swanson in *Sunset Boulevard,* a faded star acting ridiculously childish while her fans (including me) continued to kowtow to her every whim. For years afterward, I referred to her privately as "the Bebop Norma Desmond."

She frustrated and annoyed me to such an extreme degree that I vowed never to listen to her again—as God was my witness—which lasted only until I got home that evening and put on my copy of *Anita O'Day Sings the Winners*. Who wouldn't have preferred that Anita to the one I had just spent "quality time" with? The recorded Anita (even in her later albums) was swinging, upbeat, full of fun—and her work was rife with humor. That was the Anita that several generations of jazz fans fell in love with; in addition to everything else, there was an eroticism to her singing that attracted us. She was perpetually labeled the Queen of the Cool, but in reality she was much hotter than most jazz singers of her generation—with all the teasing and pleasing that she does in "Sweet Georgia Brown" she seemed downright kinky. With someone like that, you forgave a lot. It won't do to call the Anita who came to dinner the "real Anita," since the Anita on the Verve albums (especially *Winners*) is no less real. But that other Anita will die out with the memories of those of us who knew her, and the Anita who sang *Winners* will be around forever, which is how it should be.

33

Della Reese
Della Della Cha Cha Cha
(1961)

As the pop album began to evolve, certain trends gradually presented themselves: the live album (Ella Fitzgerald, Mel Tormé, Sarah Vaughan); the single-composer songbook album (Ella again); the tribute album (in the sense of *Mel Tormé Sings Fred Astaire*, Lambert, Hendricks & Ross paid tribute to Count Basie, Basie himself paid tribute to Sinatra); the duo album (Ella & Louis, Rosie & Bing, Billy & Sarah); the Broadway album (almost everybody, including Sinatra, Tormé, Ella, and Eckstine); and the international album (Bing Crosby did at least three around-the-world albums, as well as entire sets of French and Spanish songs; Connie Francis recorded traditional favorites in both Italian and Yiddish; Sinatra beckoned us to come fly with him).

The Latin album might be regarded as a subset of the international album, but there were more albums reflecting the Latin American countries (as well as *Madre España* herself) than all of the other nations (and musical traditions) of the world combined. By 1961, when Della Reese recorded *Della Della Cha Cha Cha*, there had been a Latin American dance craze for every decade: *tangos* and *habaneras* in the teens and 1920s, the *rhumba* in the 1930s (starting with "The Peanut Vendor"), *samba* and *conga* in the 1940s (an extension of Brazilian *choro* music, as in "Tico, Tico"), the *mambo* in the 1950s; in 1961, the *bossa nova* was already widely popular all over Brazil, and was just a season or so away from washing up on North American shores. (And, later, the 1970s would bring *salsa*.)

There were so many Latin albums (a trend that was launched in full force by Nat King Cole, who recorded three complete albums for Pan-American audiences) and, at the same time, so many Broadway albums, that for a time there was a subset that combined both. Peggy Lee launched a whole series that began with the wildly successful *Latin ala Lee!*—recorded in 1959 and released in 1960 (subtitled "Broadway hits styled with an Afro-Cuban beat") which was followed by, among others, Billy Eckstine's *Broadway, Bongos and Mr. B* (1961), Steve Lawrence's *Lawrence Goes Latin* (1960), and June Christy's *Something Broadway, Something Latin* (1965).

The glory of *Della Della Cha Cha Cha* (1961), arranged and produced by O. B. Masingill, is not that it's thematically different from at least a dozen albums in all three categories (Broadway, Latin, and Broadway-Latin). If you were listening to every new pop album as it came out in 1961, you might barely notice this one, or feel like you had heard it before. The glory is in the music itself, and Ms. Reese's exuberant, exciting singing: loud, brassy, and literally exploding with charisma and personality. Her voice is deeper than Dinah Washington's but has a similarly searing quality, it's the kind of sound that could cut through steel—no Peggy Lee she, all subtle and understated, no Blossom Dearie, whispering around the piano. Reese also has a quality that anticipates the slightly younger Nina Simone: her sound is right up in your face, her approach is, overall, confrontational. Unlike Simone, it's her voice, not her personality or her attitude, that's transgressive or threatening, but just the same, there's something about her singing that comes right into your personal space and invades your comfort zone.

Is *Della Della Cha Cha Cha* the single best album that Reese ever made? Not necessarily. She made some excellent straight-ahead jazz albums in the late 1950s (like *Della!*) and she made some terrific soul-inspired albums around 1970 (*Black Is Beautiful*). Reese aficionados might be concerned that we're representing her in this book with a camp album and a novelty album rather than what might be her greatest album, but, as Louis Armstrong would say, "it makes no neverminds." If *Cha Cha Cha* is supposed to be a lesser work, Reese, apparently, never got the memo. She only seems conscious that she's singing some of the greatest songs ever written, and delivering them as straightforwardly and effectively as possible. There may be camp in the packaging, in the album title, and in some of the orchestrations, but Reese herself is as outstanding as ever. No matter what's going on around her, she just stands and delivers.

With a personality and a voice that are as strong as Reese's, it doesn't matter that the idea is hardly original and the arrangements are just as gloriously tacky as the flamenco mermaid dress she's wearing on the album cover—those charts and routines are also just as tight and perfectly tailored to her as that dress. These charts are credited to Masingill, who is quite probably the most obscure musical director to work on one of these albums that we are herewith labeling as the classics. About all one can find out regarding him is that he was born Owen B. Masingill in 1920, and was initially a trombonist during the big band era, during which time he worked with the orchestra led by tenor saxophonist Sam Donahue, then those of Charlie Barnet and Claude Thornhill. By the album era, Masingill

had graduated from playing in orchestras to writing orchestrations for them. He turns up all over the map of pop music, writing for grown-up pop singers and big bands, as well as teen idols and doo-wop groups: Barnet and Donahue, Screamin' Jay Hawkins, Roy Hamilton, Dionne Warwick, Marcie Blaine. *Della Della Cha Cha Cha* is probably his best-known project; he died in Queens in 1979.

Eight of the twelve songs here came from musical shows; however, most were songs that had originated on Broadway some years earlier, and no one involved in this album in 1961 was probably thinking about their original sources (as opposed to, say, Mel Tormé and Margaret Whiting's *Broadway Right Now!*, where they deliberately picked songs from shows that were currently running). Neither the two principals nor anyone listening was particularly concerned with the fact that "Tea for Two" came from the 1925 musical *No, No, Nanette* or "Love for Sale" from the 1930 *The New Yorkers*.

Coming from the other way around, the song that opens *Della Della Cha Cha Cha* is almost exclusively thought of as a show tune—a song that's very well known, although it's rarely if ever performed outside the show it was written for and the subsequent film of that show. "Diamonds Are a Girl's Best Friend" was instantly a classic of the show music genre thanks to Carol Channing, who introduced it in the 1949 musical *Gentlemen Prefer Blondes*. For the last sixty years or so it's been the one song indelibly associated with Marilyn Monroe, best known as a comic actress and cultural icon but actually an underrated musical performer—at least, she's enormously effective in the movie musicals that she did make. "Diamonds" is quite a gem of a song, an archetypically perfect show tune. Jule Styne's melody isn't merely catchy and memorable, it's quite unforgettable, and inevitably linked to Leo Robin's letter-perfect lyric, which both establishes the character of "Lorelei Lee" and conveys a narrative filled with all sorts of wordplay and witty, unexpected rhymes (like that of "duels" with "jewels").

Della Reese's reading of "Diamonds" sets the tone for the rest of the album. She's delightfully audacious, with a searing, cutting sound, combined with a deep, chesty contralto—it's unmistakably part of African American vocal tradition, the kind of voice (the best kind, actually) that you'd expect to hear singing the praises of the Lord in a Harlem church or belting out rhythm and blues at the Apollo. It's not what you'd expect to hear doing a somewhat precious classic show tune— and yes, the *cha cha cha* beat makes the whole idea even more incongruous. The combination is much more transgressive, so to speak, than *Latin ala Lee!;* even Rosemary Clooney's team-up with Pérez Prado, the Cuban bandleader who did more than anyone else to popularize the mambo in North America, is just as good musically but not quite as outrageous. And yet Reese does an excellent job with the audacious lyric: the point of the story, and every twist and turn of Robin's witty wordplay, comes through—it's already clear that Reese is a singer with an exceptional flair for the dramatic. At one point she emphasizes, "But, Sweetheart, get that ice / Or else no dice!" At the end of the piece, she states directly, in a spoken tag, "It's been proven beyond a shadow of a doubt that diamonds are a girl's only friend."

Speaking of Rosemary Clooney, the second track here is her breakthrough hit—and probably the single song most associated with her—"Come on-a My House." Clooney herself was keen to point out that "Come on-a My House" was a rather extreme ethnic polyglot of a song: two Armenian Americans, playwright William Saroyan and composer Ross Bagdasarian, based it on a folk melody from their native land, while Clooney herself was a singer of Irish descent who sang it in a faux-Italian accent. (Not to be outdone, Louis Prima responded by delivering "My House" in a genuine Italian American accent.) The Masingill arrangement itself is too busy being exciting and danceable to stand still long enough to warrant any possible criticism. It's actually rather surprising that more Latin bands (and especially Cuban singers like Celia Cruz or La Lupe) didn't do their own versions. The multi-culti nature of the piece somehow makes Reese's delivery even more believable: when she says she's going to give us everything, no one could possibly doubt it.

"Why Don't You Do Right?" is also a polymath—

and one that launched the career of another iconic female singer. It started as a number about drugs (originally titled "The Weed Smoker's Dream") by a Chicago-based blues band rather curiously known as the Harlem Hamfats. From there, it evolved into a big band feature for Benny Goodman's orchestra that provided a career-launching point for Peggy Lee. The references to smoking weed were gone; instead, the better-known lyric concerns itself more generally with the archetypal failure of the masculine gender to do right. Reese, who was always highly conscious of the words, updates "1922" from the original first line to "1952" and "other women" to "other people." More logically, she punctuates the rather defiant text with "I'm not fooling!" and "I mean it!" The orchestra has some of the flashy brass fireworks we associate with mambo bands, but mainly the track is about Reese shooting the words out, and effectively at that, over the grinding beat of the Latin percussion section, particularly the shakers and the scrapers, and the staccato phrasing of the brass. There's also a wailing alto saxophone that assists in the transition from one melodic passage to another.

The album contains no fewer than three songs from Cole Porter, all of which empower Reese to enact the role of a sexually liberated woman. "My Heart Belongs to Daddy" had long since "graduated" from the 1938 Broadway show *Leave It to Me* to serve as a signature song for virtually every flirtatious, seductive singer for the next seventy-five years. I don't know what Porter would have made of the Latin background (yes, he was alive in 1961, but it was unlikely he heard it), but Reese sings the lyrics as well as anybody since the original, Mary Martin. In the first chorus, she modulates emotionally from flirty and flippant to sincere within just a few notes on the last few lines.

"Let's Do It" (aka "Let's Do It, Let's Fall in Love," from the 1928 musical *Paris*) is also saucy and mischievous, and Reese is exuberant throughout: she starts relatively small, with "Birds do it, bees do it," and we're more conscious of her sharp and, yes, high staccato phrasing, the way she carves out every syllable so precisely you might even feel she's overarticulating. Like Al Hibbler (one of her early mentors) she comes down on those consonants so hard that there's a noticeable residual after-effect, that sounds like "Let's do it-a!"—although at several points, she sings "Let's do it, let's *cha cha cha!*"

The third Porter song, "Always True to You in My Fashion," arrives a few tracks later. The *Kiss Me, Kate* (1948) classic delineates in lovingly voyeuristic detail the circumstances of the lady's numerous run-ins with persons in pants. Like that selfsame gal whose heart belongs to Daddy, she accepts fur coats and even checks from a variety of sugar fathers, all the while insisting that she's remaining faithful to her darlin'—of course, both her "fashion" and her "way" are highly subjective, and hence the humor of the text. Reese shows us that it's not only about sex, it's about language, and therefore her spontaneous interjections ("please believe me") and ("I swear") are both welcome and appropriate.

After "My Heart Belongs to Daddy" and "Let's Do It," we get a pair of songs in which Reese further embodies the very model of a flirtatious female. "Whatever Lola Wants" is the signature song of Satan's seductress in *Damn Yankees* (1955), Broadway's perennially popular tale of devil worship and baseball obsession, while "Daddy" is still another song about an attractive, avaricious young woman vamping a wealthy older man.

Songwriters Richard Adler and Jerry Ross gave the "Lola" number a hint of the mambo to begin with, which enabled Gwen Verdon to sing the song in a caricature of a Latino accent, as a Spanish Satanic seductress, which makes the Afro-Cuban setting all the more appropriate. The original show was about baseball, but the cover of the cast album showed Verdon in a sexy showgirl corset, hands on hips, obviously belting, with legs that go all the way to Hades—somehow audiences in 1955 found this more appealing than pictures of ballplayers. (Or, as Pseudolus says at the beginning of *A Funny Thing Happened on the Way to the Forum*, "for those of you who have no interest in pirates.") Reese's vocal here has that distinctly British edge that sometimes comes to the fore in her singing; it's not as subtle as that of Nat King Cole but also not as outrageously exaggerated as that of Al Hibbler (to name two men in her life). When Reese sings about a "coat and hat" as "cewt and hat," Professor

Henry Higgins would be aghast, but, fortunately, there are no songs from *My Fair Lady* here. Like Eartha Kitt, Reese is at once sexy and funny; in fact, she shows that the two qualities complement each other.

You can tell "Daddy" is an early effort by a comparatively inexperienced writer (the young Bobby Troup) rather than a master like Porter; his heroine is clearly also taking Daddy for all he's worth, but the text lacks that extra level of irony we find in nearly all of Porter's lyrics. Unlike a Porter heroine, this "baby" isn't patting herself on the back for being chaste and faithful even while she's taking "Daddy" to the cleaners. "Daddy" finds Reese playing with the time, continually stretching words and then running them all together; "won't-I-look-swell-in-clothes-with-Paris-labels" sounds as if it's all one very long word. Often, she imposes legato phrasing on top of the staccato beat. When she comes back with the bridge, "Here's an amazing revelation . . .," she finds other, even more exciting ways to play with the beat.

"Tea for Two" is one of the few songs on the album that's comparatively innocent; there are no sugar daddies, and no Satanic undercurrent—this is not one of those many songs where love is for sale. Reese tells us how she and her paramour are happy with just tea and each other. As usual, Reese is both funny and sexy here, as well as sweet and sincere, yet this track also captures her at her most exuberant: she's having more fun with the melody and the rhythm here than anywhere else. The song had been born a show tune (in the 1925 *No, No, Nanette*), then quietly became a jazz standard, but by 1961 was perhaps the best known *cha cha cha* of the period, thanks to a hugely popular arrangement by the Tommy Dorsey Orchestra, that was heard at a million proms throughout the land. No matter what the incarnation, Reese has plenty of fun with it.

Following "Always True to You in My Fashion" comes "It's So Nice to Have a Man Around the House," a 1951 pop song that might as well be a show tune; Dinah Shore made a well-known recording, and there was another famous version by the team of Ethel Merman and Ray Bolger. Lyricist John M. Elliott (1914–1972) was generally credited as Jack Elliot (the previous year, he enjoyed a runaway hit with the Bing and Gary Crosby duet "Sam's Song"), and in the decades following his death he tends to be confused with the film and TV composer Jack Elliott as well as the folksinger Ramblin' Jack Elliott. Composer Harold Spina (1906–1997) wrote hundreds of songs recorded by hundreds of bands and singers, mostly in the 1930s. Like a well-tailored dress, "It's So Nice" has a lot of specific material to it, more so than most thirty-two-bar popular songs—the mere fact of it dealing with sustained love rather than new love means that it's more adult-oriented than most nonshow songs of its day or any other: it's not about confessing one's love in a big dramatic way, it's about the little details that are both sexy and trivial at the same time, like helping your woman zip her zippers. Like an episode of *Ozzie and Harriet,* the song is ideally suited to the era of nuclear families. In singing collectively of the men she's known, Reese is both compassionate and forgiving.

Rodgers and Hart's "There's a Small Hotel" is also more about sustained love than new love, which, given the cultural climate of the two respective generations, was much more popular in the 1950s than in 1936, when the song was first introduced (coincidentally, by dancer Ray Bolger) in *On Your Toes.* Reese's interpretation is both intimate and sentimental, as well as rhythmic and tuneful.

After "Tea for Two" and "Small Hotel," all bets are off—we go back from sincere love to "Love for Sale." As the title of this, the fourth Porter song on the album, suggests, this is the ultimate anthem of romantic discourse as commercial commodity. Yet most jazz and cabaret singers who sing it rarely turn up on the stage in fishnets or spandex. Usually Porter's title is taken metaphorically; the woman

singing feels like she's been abused by love, and is so downtrodden that she might as well be putting her "wares" directly on the market, like fish (or the dope peddler in "Why Don't You Do Right?").

Unlike "My Heart Belongs to Daddy," there's no room for coyness or flirtation—everything is right there in front of you, right on the table (or wherever). Reese's version is more dramatic than personal, opening with a big, loud cadenza flourish before getting into the melody—in spite of the mambo beat, she sounds more powerfully Washingtonian than ever here. The lyrics are so intimate and personal that Reese decides it's best to belt them out loudly and dramatically; she doesn't need to reveal herself, the words themselves do it for her. Her personality and soul are in every note. In any case, it makes for a perfect closer—certainly no song of innocence (like "Tea for Two") or playfulness (like "Always True to You in My Fashion") could do the job so well. In fact nothing could follow it; it's a perfect conclusive statement, so the album appropriately ends here.

Ultimately, the charm of *Della Della Cha Cha Cha* may be that it's anything but significant. It can hardly be said to have changed the world, but it's a delight from start to finish—and it changes my mood and puts a smile on my face every time I play it. When I want to feel rapturously romantic, I'll put on *Songs for Swingin' Lovers;* when I feel the blues so bad that I'm ready for the river, I'll listen to *Lady in Satin;* and when I really want to drown in my own tears, it'll be *In the Wee Small Hours.* But when I want to do nothing more serious than enjoy thirty-five minutes of pure fun—or, better still, to dance around my apartment in a whirl of euphoria—I'll reach for *Della Della Cha Cha Cha.*

34

Jimmy Scott

The Source (1969) and
Lost and Found (1972)

oes it somehow seem like the jazz world engenders more than its share of archetypically underrated artists? Surely there are master choreographers or architects out there who deserved more recognition than they actually received, or novelists whose work isn't regarded as highly as some feel it ought to be. But the literature

Somebody's Fool." And you might think that the world might have listened when such supporters and devotees as Ray Charles and Nancy Wilson, as well as music industry types like songwriter Doc Pomus and producer Joel Dorn, all steadfastly beat the drum for Jimmy and constantly told the world what a great artist he was.

of jazz is a veritable litany of one underappreciated giant after another. In terms of jazz vocalists, perhaps the most chronically underappreciated master is James Victor Scott (1925–2014), who was billed for most of his career as "Little Jimmy Scott."

There were all kinds of reasons why Scott should have been better known than he was: you might have thought that jazz fans would have grown to love him through his association with Lionel Hampton and a classic live recording he made with Charlie Parker. You might think that the soul music audience would know him from his signature song, the classic soul ballad "Everybody's

So, Scott's career misfortune wasn't necessarily the failure of the music establishment to recognize him, nor a fault of the fickle finger of fate. Much of his misfortune was his own doing. He continually made the wrong enemies, and worse, the wrong friends. As Doc Pomus put it, "Fate hasn't always been kind to Jimmy. But Jimmy isn't always kind to Jimmy. Just when things are going smoothly, he'll come out of a trick bag, hook up with the wrong woman, get drunk, disappear— and wind up shooting himself in the foot." He added, "When you hear him sing, however, you forget all that, and you just fall in love with that voice."

But where many artists shoot themselves in the foot, as the good doctor put it, Scott continually shot himself in the face, metaphorically, even as he burned his bridges in front of him. One of the crueler tricks that unkind fate played on him was that he made his greatest album, the result of a short string of sessions for Atlantic Records (eventually released under the titles *The Source* and *Lost and Found*) just as he was about to do a disappearing act. This career move, such as it was, was hardly voluntary, just yet another case of bad timing. The wave of youth pop of the late 1960s was steadily forcing traditional pop singers—and older artists in general—out of the picture, and Scott had no choice but to pull a Houdini.

It was Scott's age, or, rather, his general lack of newness, not his musical style, that put the kibosh on his career. The musical sea changes of the era, which put nearly all of his contemporaries out of business, actually made Scott more relevant to the musical tenor of the times. (In exactly the same way that the arrival of rock 'n' roll a decade earlier should, by any reasonable standard, not have put Louis Jordan out of business.) The 1960s might have been Scott's most triumphant decade: he was the grandfather of all soul singers, and it was in this period that his influence was most keenly felt, as acolyte Nancy Wilson has put it, especially among female jazz-soul vocalists of that era. Scott was the direct inspiration for many younger and more successful artists, artists who, unlike him, didn't go around sabotaging themselves. Instead, this entire generation of African American artists was selling zillions of discs to both black and white teenagers. If they didn't pay lip service to Jimmy directly, they did by way of Ray Charles, who, like Wilson, was citing Jimmy Scott as one of his own inspirations.

Perhaps that's part of the brilliance of long-distance runners like Sinatra, Armstrong, and Ray Charles: by the time their imitators have caught up with them, they're already on to the next idea. Jimmy Scott, was, like Louis Jordan and Dick Haynes, just stuck with being himself.

One man who thought Jimmy could be relevant to the soul music audience was Joel Dorn, a producer who had recently started working at Atlantic. It annoyed him no end that the grandfather of soul couldn't get a record deal during what was, in fact, the golden age of soul. In David Ritz's thorough biography of the singer, *Faith in Time* (published in 2002), Scott is generally depicted as an outsider and a loner. As Dorn (1942–2007) told everyone he met, he began as a deejay on a Philadelphia station, where, spinning discs primarily for the African American market, he quickly learned how to gauge the broader tastes of the public. He gradually morphed from radio to album production, and by 1967 he was working at Atlantic Records as assistant to Nesuhi Ertegun, who had had run the label's jazz division from the beginning.

Why not a new, state-of-the-art album by the great Little Jimmy Scott (as he was still being billed) for Atlantic Records? It probably wasn't much of a hard sell. The Ertegun brothers, Ahmet and Nesuhi, had a great love for African American vernacular music and an attendant sense of history. As Dorn recalled, Jimmy happened to come into the Atlantic offices, accompanied by his then manager, one Duke Wade, with the idea of approaching Jerry Wexler, one of the label's senior producers. The Erteguns were already familiar with both sides of the Little Jimmy equation: first, that he was one of the great soul-jazz singers ever, if not the greatest; but, on the downside, that he was unreliable, to put it mildly. Plus there was the way he looked; it wouldn't be until very late in his life that one of his record labels felt confident enough to put Jimmy's actual picture on one of his own albums. They weighed the pros and cons and decided that he was worthy of a shot.

Contracts were drawn and plans were made for Scott to do an album for Atlantic produced by Dorn. "I named it *The Source*," as Dorn told Ritz, "because for modern singing—especially modern female singers—Jimmy is really the indisputable source."

The 1969 album is, in many deliberate ways, a direct extension of Scott's 1962 album, *Falling in Love Is Wonderful*. Because of extramusical circumstances that would also bedevil the Atlantic project, the earlier record is ridiculously rare—Dorn was one of the few who actually owned a copy.

Produced by Ray Charles himself (and released on his own label, Tangerine Records), the 1962 LP consisted of Scott singing slow love songs accompanied by a big string orchestra; Dorn decided the Atlantic sessions would do the same: Jimmy Scott, classic ballads, and a lush, romantic string section. It would be taped over three sessions at Atlantic Studios in New York in March 1969.

One Ray Charles element that informs the 1969 album is the presence of tenor saxophonist David "Fathead" Newman. Newman (1933–2009) had been the instrumental star of Ray Charles's bands for a dozen years from the mid-1950s onward, and anyone hearing his saxophonic sound would have immediately thought of Brother Ray. However, on the Scott sessions, Newman (whose colorful nickname was partially derived from tenor giant Gene Ammons, known as "Jughead" or "Jug" Ammons), plays rather differently than usual. Utilizing a broader and breathier tone, and playing in Scott's extremely slow tempos (so reminiscent of Billie Holiday), he seems to be deliberately evoking Ben Webster, one of the all-time giants of the tenor sax obbligato.

The rhythm section included some of the most simpatico players then to be found in the New York studios, starting with bassist Ron Carter, who was then gigging around after having recently returned from a career-making, five-year stay with the Miles Davis Quintet. The drummer was Bruno Carr, another veteran of the Ray Charles organization, and there were two well-known guitarists, Eric Gale and Billy Butler. The pianist was Junior Mance, a jazz player who was and is probably best known for his tenures with Dinah Washington and Dizzy Gillespie (as well as for being the uncredited composer of the jazz standard "Walkin'").

The string charts were done by Bill Fischer and Arif Mardin, two Atlantic stalwarts who gained a reputation early on for supplying string sections for jazz, funk, and soul artists; Mardin (1932–2006), who, like the Ertegun brothers, was Turkish, would be particularly successful in his long relationship with Aretha Franklin, being a major factor in her breakthrough success at Atlantic. It was all the more reason to be optimistic; as Dorn told Ritz, "Jimmy was especially pleased to be on the label

pumping out hits by everyone from Led Zeppelin to Aretha Franklin."

Dorn added that he couldn't wait to get started, but that on the first session a problem that he hadn't anticipated presented itself: the star singer was, literally, toothless. Scott had ordered a new set of dentures, but hadn't been able to pay for them. Dorn somehow delayed the session to later that night, and in the meantime "scrambled around and found the bread." It does indeed seem curious that Scott, who was only forty-three at the time, was faced with this issue, but his health was always precarious—even though Scott was still singing into his mid-eighties. (Scott outlived both of his greatest champions, Doc Pomus and Joel Dorn, even though the latter was many years younger.) "If you listen to those songs very carefully," Dorn said, "You can hear a small whistle. Those are Jimmy's brand new dentures."

There would be three dates, March 3, 4, and 5, 1969, consisting of three songs each; one song ("Yesterday," presumably the Paul McCartney number) has never been issued. The final album, as released in 1969, consisted of eight songs.

That already iconic—if seldom heard—1962 album *Falling in Love Is Wonderful* was a foundation for the 1969 *The Source* as well as a point of departure. All ten songs on *Falling* were from the golden years of pop, the years of Broadway, big bands, and World War II; the latest is "Why Try to Change Me Now" from 1952.

The sources of *The Source* are more diverse and contemporary: only three numbers are from classic (that is, pre-1955) popular music: "Day by Day" (by Sammy Cahn, Axel Stordahl, and Paul Weston), "This Love of Mine" (Hank Sanicola, Sol Parker, and Frank Sinatra), and "I Wish I Knew" (Mack Gordon and Harry Warren). Those three 1940s songs are all associated with great crooners, the first two with Sinatra (who cocomposed the second) and the third with Dick Haymes.

Three other numbers are from the 1960s, "Exodus" (Ernest Gold), "On Broadway" (Jerry Leiber, Barry Mann, Mike Stoller, and Cynthia Weil), and "Our Day Will Come" (Mort Garson and Bob Hilliard), all of which can be safely described as pop hits. (And, coincidentally, all three are grouped together, at the start of the album's side one.) "Unchained Melody" (Alex North and Hy Zaret) is kind of a bridge between the two generations; written in 1955, it was a breakthrough hit for the former big band vocalist Al Hibbler, and yet the song is best known from its many R&B, soul, and rock interpretations. The eighth song is a traditional African American spiritual; "Sometimes I Feel Like a Motherless Child" is a timeless classic that transcends, well, everything.

The 1969 sessions use the four-piece rhythm section, plus strings, and the only horn is solo saxophonist Fathead Newman. The most crucial difference between the 1962 and the 1969 albums is the matter of timing and those myriad considerations that are frequently lumped together under the umbrella term "phrasing." Both albums are roughly the same length in terms of time that clocks can measure, yet *Falling in Love* is ten tracks and *The Source* is only eight; obviously, then, the 1969 tracks are slightly longer, and take up more time to cover the same amount of musical ground. Scott stretches out more fully, in a manner that is indeed more like a jazz singer than a soul singer, a manner that has more in common with Louis Armstrong and Billie Holiday (and, especially, Shirley Horn) than with Mahalia Jackson or the many subsequent generations of members of Aretha Franklin's church.

In comparing the two albums, Scott himself elaborated on this key difference: the "kind of singing" that he did on *The Source* wasn't possible on *Falling in Love*. "It wasn't that Ray [Charles]'s supervision was strict, but those string arrangements restricted any extreme vocal movements. Going to a record session is like going to a dance. You dance with the girl you brought. You sing with the charts you're given. Dorn had the cats write charts that let me wander. I liked that and tried to make the most of that wide-open mood."

Indeed, he does. Marty Paich's arrangements on *Falling* sounded more like those that he was writing on most of Charles's own ballads-and-standards albums, in a definite tempo; it's easy to imagine Brother Ray's own voice coming through, instead

of Little Jimmy's. However, Fischer and Mardin came up with a completely different kind of background for Scott seven years later. When Scott sings "Time goes by so slowly" in "Unchained Melody," no man will say him nay.

This is made clear by the opening, the four-and-a-half-minute "Exodus." The first thing we hear is Scott's distinctive voice completely a cappella, stating the opening notes, "This . . . land . . . is . . . mine." It's not until the third note that we get a hint of the background, a shimmer of basses and low strings. It's dramatic in its subtlety, if such a thing is possible—the slowness of the timing, the understatement. "Exodus" famously originated with the 1960 film of the same name based on the 1958 novel of the same name. Composer Ernest Gold was a part-Jewish refugee from Austria, who, like Erich Korngold and Bronislau Kaper and others, wound up writing movie music in Hollywood. "Exodus," for which Gold also wrote the highly anthemic words, was his only notable song (as opposed to instrumental movie theme). Inspired by the founding of Israel, the song is one of several show and movie tunes (such as "Summertime" and "You'll Never Walk Alone") by Jewish composers that have seemed particularly relevant to the peoples of the African diaspora. Saxophonist Eddie Harris transformed the movie theme into a soul jazz instrumental classic, and Bob Marley liberally incorporated whole sections of it into his own song titled "Exodus."

For the black people no less than the Israelis, "Exodus" was an anthem of liberation and solidarity, in the Gold song no less than Marley's. Jimmy Scott sings it like both a prayer and a national anthem, yet it's almost too serious for him to throw in the gospel-style melismas that, for instance, Ray Charles used on his famous recording of "America the Beautiful." Rather, Scott makes his point with timing and dynamics—the way he stretches out the words "and waaaaalk this looooovely land with me . . ." He sings, "though I am just a man," he emphasizes the word "I" over multiple notes and syllables and a louder volume, but when he gets to "just a man," he says those three words quietly and humbly, thus conveying an ineffable sense of humility.

Like much of Scott's singing, he has it both ways—at times he sounds restrained, and yet he lets the volume rise and belts like a wailing banshee at others. "Exodus" sets the mood for what follows in that it's an exemplary slice of pop (jazz? soul?) singing and musical acting. He builds to the ending, "To make this land our home / If I must fight, I'll fight to make this land our own / Until I die, this land is mine." Those are only three lines and a couple dozen words, but Scott makes them seem monumentally significant—he stands firm, like he's planting those words into the fertile soil and building a synagogue in the desert.

"Our Day Will Come" and "On Broadway" were both hit singles in 1963. For some reason beyond my understanding, Dorn claimed to be dissatisfied with these two (I wish I had thought to ask him why). Suffice it to say that the producer is flat-out wrong: "Our Day Will Come" and "On Broadway" are as great as the rest of the album. (Likewise, biographer David Ritz is also wrong when he suggests that "Day by Day" leaves everything else on the album behind in the dust.) "On Broadway" represents the apogee of Brill Building pop, in that the song was conceived by one great songwriting team, Barry Mann and Cynthia Weil, and then finished by another, Jerry Leiber and Mike Stoller; this was in the climactic eleventh hour of the Brill Building era, just a few months before the Beatles would land at JFK and reduce the whole of 1619 Broadway to rubble.

Scott's interpretation of "On Broadway" is a much more intimate experience than the original hit by the Drifters, conveying the story of one man—a highly personal account. This is the opposite of those victory lap songs that were becoming so prominent in the 1960s (in the vein—and the "vain"—of "My Way," Anthony Newley's "Once in a Lifetime," and "Here's to Life"). He wants to make it, he's trying to make it, but the overall mood is pervasive melancholy, more of a catalogue of defeats, of trials and tribulations, of why it's impossible to succeed in show business, even when really trying. As sung by virtually everyone else, "On Broadway" has an undercurrent at least of life-affirming optimism, but not so much when Scott sings it.

"Our Day Will Come" is a unique slice of pop from the era between Elvis and the Beatles: it was the work of Bob Hilliard, an old-school lyricist probably best remembered for the Sinatra classic "In the Wee Small Hours of the Morning" as well as a few Broadway (*Hazel Flagg*) and movie (Disney's *Alice in Wonderland*) credits, and Mort Garson, better known as a pioneer of electronic music. The song was the only number-one single by Ruby & the Romantics, an African American vocal quintet consisting of lead Ruby Nash and four male backup singers. Although generally often classified as R&B, R & the Rs don't sound like any earlier doo-wop group or any later Motown soul unit; theirs is a very cheerful brand of pop, characterized by a brisk, danceable tempo, a shuffle beat, a very clean-sounding Hammond organ background, and a generally optimistic mood.

Nancy Wilson's 1964 record of the song is considerably slower than the 1963 hit single, but nothing could have prepared the listeners of 1969 for what Scott does with "Our Day." He so looks forward to the day that will come that he sings of it reverentially, it's a song of hope, optimism, and even faith in the future. In fact, as Jimmy sings it, "Our Day Will Come" has essentially the same message as "Exodus," although once again it's much more personal and intimate than most anthems. Fathead Newman's solo is most prominent here, sounding extremely Ben Webster–ish. It would be an exaggeration to dismiss the Romantics (no less than the Drifters) as mere bubblegum pop—they're at a much higher level artistically than, say, the Archies or the Tokens, but nonetheless Scott takes both of these songs, which are hardly forgettable to begin with, and makes them into something greater than they could have ever been without him, something moving, something profound, something classic, something for the ages. Where the Romantics single is essentially a dance track, and the Wilson track is a ballad, the Scott interpretation is a hymn. Both here and in "Exodus" Jimmy is singing what sounds like a personal prayer for himself, that his own day would come, that someday the bells would ring for him, that he would find his way into the Promised Land.

For some reason, songwriters often like to celebrate the lack of knowledge: "I Never Knew," "Nina Never Knew," "You'll Never Know," and "I Didn't Know What Time It Was." Dick Haymes introduced "I Wish I Knew" (in the 1945 film *Diamond Horseshoe*) and established it almost immediately as a standard. While there were prominent jazz interpretations from the 1950s (Chet Baker, Ahmad Jamal), it was John Coltrane's 1962 recording that made the Warren-Gordon ballad into a song that absolutely every jazzman of the last fifty years knows by heart. Scott's 1969 track starts with a prominent tenor fluttering around the tune as an intro, before Scott begins his plaintive ode, sounding remarkably downtrodden, even for Little Jimmy. The tenor sax is all over the place here, gaining a key solo in the instrumental break; Fathead is sort of a Hardy to Scott's Laurel, upbeat where Scott is melancholy, cheerful where Scott is morose; Jimmy is looking for an answer and Fathead is generally acting like he has all the answers. In the last line of the first chorus, he sings, "I wish'd I knew," but gets it more grammatically correct in the last line, which is big and dramatic, and, even more than most of the other seven tracks, achingly slow.

With "Our Day Will Come," Scott takes a potentially trivial tune and makes it immortal; with "Unchained Melody," he takes a grandiose text, full of monumental metaphors about time going by so slowly and rivers flowing down to the sea, and brings it back down to size. Even Al Hibbler, for all his highly personal approach to singing—you'd never mistake Hibbler for anybody else—had a big, booming, baritone voice, the kind that, like his colleague Billy Eckstine's, seemed designed to take on the big issues. Where those baritones are looking at the big picture, Scott finds God in the details—and, at almost six minutes long, there are a lot of details. (One detail he misses: he sings the opening line as "I've hungered for your kiss," rather than "your touch," which rather throws off the rhyme "time can do so much.") Scott stretches every syllable that can be stretched; when he starts with "ALLLL my love, my darling . . . a loooonnnng lonely time," you really feel the weight of his passion, not to mention his patience. His needs seem needier, his

lonely rivers seem lonelier, his open arms seem, well, opener. He sings the bridge with just the most minimal single string support from the guitar, providing a respite from the otherwise constant drone of the strings. When he builds to the climactic "are you stilllll mine?" he makes it sound like he's plunging a dagger into somebody's heart.

Which brings us to "Day by Day"; while I disagree with David Ritz's contention that the 1945 standard is the unchallenged masterpiece of the album, there's no denying that it's a total stunner. Again, Scott stretches words as far as they can be stretched, to the benefit of the lyric. He never sings "love," he invariably sings "loooooove." Taking a different tack than "Unchained," "Day by Day" purports to be about the small stuff, taking life one day at a time, but then lyricist Sammy Cahn—and thus, also Scott—get carried away by the ebb tide of huge emotions: he tells us his devotion is endless, stretching into infinity, and, like Irving Berlin before him, he compares it to the depth of the ocean. All of a sudden, the song is bigger and more dramatic than "Unchained Melody"; that was only about lonely rivers, whereas here the emotional journey encompasses an entire lonely ocean. Neither the lyric nor the melody, as written, has so much as a single sad note in it. Nothing the least bit unpleasant or tragic happens, opens, a gentleman is simply confessing his love—he even informs us that all his dreams are coming true. Yet Scott makes it somehow sound devastatingly sad. If he can make the days so dark and stirring, you shudder to think at what he might be able to do with the nights.

"Motherless Child" starts comparatively reserved and stays that way. Scott enters a cappella, and then is joined by guitar. For the second section ("This world out here . . .") a flute (apparently played by Newman) appears behind him. The strings enter dramatically behind him on the third ("Why did I leave . . ."). Everything is going by the fourth stanza, which repeats the first ("Sometimes I feel like a motherless child"), and it reaches its comparative climax. Yet it never gets big and belty the way that "Unchained Melody" and "Day by Day" do; if there were any one song where the knee-jerk reaction would be to use an overdone gospel-style technique, this would be it—yet, conversely, this is the song where he's the subtlest, the most restrained, and sounds the least like he's shouting in the Amen Corner.

You might have thought that nothing could follow "Motherless Child"—what could be bigger than God? Between the lonely rivers and the deep oceans, thus far he has dealt with the natural world (particularly the aquatic world), and with "Motherless Child" he has addressed the infinite and the spiritual. The only thing that's left is love, and not just any love, but "This Love of Mine." I have to imagine that both Scott and Dorn had Sinatra ingrained in their brains and were at least subconsciously aware that *In the Wee Small Hours* ends with "This Love of Mine." (More than singing it and even introducing it, as he did in 1941 with Tommy Dorsey's orchestra, Sinatra cowrote the song with his own manager-sidekick Hank Sanicola and composer Sol Parker.) "This Love" opens with a gentle flourish from Mance's keyboard, then Scott sings "this" as quietly as possible, before laying it on much more dramatically on "lovvvvve of miiiiiinnne . . . goes onnn annnnnd onnnn . . ."—he even stretches the "and," as if to indirectly stress the on-and-on-ness of the phrase. Overall, it's neither as subtle as "Motherless Child" nor as dramatic as "Day by Day" and "Unchained Melody"; rather, it finds a copasetic point of agreement between the two for an inspired closer. Like *Wee Small Hours,* the album ends with an unanswered question, "What's to become of it, this love of mine?"

What was to become of it? Unfortunately, not very much.

First, there was the matter of the cover. Dorn's bosses at Atlantic made the decision to go with the picture of a very hip-looking African American model, with a big Afro. That's right—no Jimmy. Scott was always a distinctive entertainer to look at, and just like his sound, there was never mistaking his image for anybody else's. Yet he was no matinee idol, and Atlantic capitulated to the time-honored tradition of putting pretty models on the covers of albums by jazzmen, famously on Erroll Garner's *Most Happy Piano* and Miles Davis's *Miles Ahead.*

"I hit the ceiling! It was an insult to Jimmy. Who cared that he didn't look like Belafonte? He looked just fine, and, besides, it was his God-damned record." Said Dorn, "Their decision to go with the model made me feel very small. I was ashamed." Scott, characteristically, was gracious. "Naturally I would have preferred to see myself on the cover, but if they thought that would help sell the thing, I could only hope that they were right." (Dorn is being hard on his bosses at Atlantic; Scott's picture was, notably, not on the cover of *Falling in Love Is Wonderful* either.)

What happened next was an all-too-typical moment in the career of James Victor Scott—a combination of milestone and catastrophe, of defeat being snatched from the mouth of victory. The closest thing we have to an explanation: sometime in the 1950s, Scott had apparently signed some sort of lifetime contract with Herman Lubinsky of Savoy Records. This proved to be a major career roadblock in 1962: when Tangerine Records (Ray Charles's personal imprint at ABC-Paramount) released *Falling in Love with Love,* Lubinsky sent the company a cease-and-desist and the label stopped distributing the album. The same thing, according to Dorn, Scott, and David Ritz, happened again in 1969. Clearly, it doesn't make sense. Dorn suggests that the very threat of a lawsuit was enough to get Atlantic to pull the album; although they had invested roughly $15,000 (in Dorn's estimate), they decided it wasn't worth going to court to keep the album in print.

Even Lubinsky's son admitted that his father was a vindictive man, but one has a hard time believing that if he legitimately owned a piece of Scott's career, why didn't he do what Tommy Dorsey tried to do with Sinatra, which was to simply sit back and collect a portion of the proceeds? Why not let other record companies do the work for him and save him the trouble of actually producing records. While, yes, there's no denying we all have individuals in our lives who are spiteful on a satanically sadistic level (you're telling me?), but was Lubinsky so determined to make Scott suffer that he was willing to sabotage one of his assets for the sheer evil pleasure of bringing Jimmy down with him?

"Another Jimmy Scott masterpiece bit the dust,"

said Dorn, "and just like that, Jimmy was back in Cleveland." Not singing, either, but working as a shipping clerk at the Sheraton.

Yet *The Source* was not quite Jimmy Scott's last stand, nor Joel Dorn's, either. In 1972, Dorn decided to produce another album with his favorite male singer. He was in a much more powerful position than he had been three years earlier, with some very lucrative hits and signings (Roberta Flack, Bette Midler) under his belt. So, for no reason other than that he knew he and Scott could produce a classic album together, he summoned the singer back out of involuntary semi-retirement. As both participants told Ritz, neither "held any illusions about a breakthrough album that would ignite [his] career." They just made a good record for the sake of making a good record.

So what kind of music do people make in those circumstances, when the only goal is to do the best that they can possibly do? Not only were they not thinking about commercial considerations—said Dorn, "no one even mentioned the word 'airplay'"—they had no idea if anybody would ever hear the tracks that they were laying down.

As before, Dorn commissioned the string charts from the best orchestrator he could get, in this case the Brazilian Eumir Deodato (who had presided over some of the classic Sinatra–Antonio Carlos Jobim sessions), an expert pianist and accompanist in Ray Bryant, an all-star rhythm section in bassist Richard Davis, drummer Billy Cobham, and guitarist David Spinozza. This time, the tenor saxophone soloist is an improvement even over Fathead, one of Newman's own inspirations, longtime Basie-ite Frank Wess. Overall, Deodato's charts are somewhat lighter than Fischer's and Mardin's (and especially Marty Paich's in 1962); as on the Sinatra-Jobim sessions, they're more like stars shimmering in the background than the big string sections we hear in Beethoven and Brahms.

The fate of the tracks is somewhat bizarre: in 1993, Dorn sanctioned the release of *Lost and Found,* an odd little CD that consisted of five previously unissued tracks from 1972 followed by five tracks from the 1969 album. If Dorn only thought five of the 1972 tracks were worth hearing, he should have simply put them out as bonus tracks at the end of a complete issue of *The Source.* As it was, Jimmy Scott fans had to wait almost another ten years to get a complete CD release of *The Source.* It seems like there's very little about Jimmy Scott's career that isn't frustrating.

Lost and Found begins with "I Have Dreamed," one of the big ballads from Rodgers and Hammerstein's *The King and I.* And here, we find, is the major smoking gun, the piece of evidence that indisputably indicates that no one was actually planning to ever issue these five tracks. We've seen that there are a couple of minor lyric fudges on *The Source* (as on "Unchained Melody" and "I Wish I Knew"). But the lyric screw-up in "I Have Dreamed" is truly a whopper. He starts with "Lun Tha's" transitional passage—which is more of a singspiel intro than a true verse ("Alone and awake, I have looked at the stars / The same that smile on you . . .")—with just Bryant's piano. This intro, which is almost never heard outside the show itself, is well beyond rubato, even for him; it's slow beyond slow, as far away from anything as can be. When LJS reaches the chorus, then the bass and drums stealthily enter. "I have dreamed / that your arms are lovely." As written, the next line is "I have dreamed / what a joy you'll be," but instead he sings, somewhat Ebonically, "I have dreamed / what a joy *it be.*" Clearly, no producer would have allowed that to pass if he had any inkling at all that anybody would ever listen to this performance. (Of lesser importance: in the last line he sings "that by now I think *you* know" rather than "I think *I* know.")

Which shouldn't be held against Scott. He sings exquisitely on all five cuts. On "I Have Dreamed" he sounds like he's holding back, which is altogether appropriate for a song about restrained emotions and forbidden passion. In the verse and the first part of the chorus, Scott seems to be singing from within the context of someone who knows he's dreaming; like he has an inkling of what these emotions might feel like, but is at least an arm's length away from them. (And he has some very long arms.) We're talking slow here. How slow? Let's just say that if Jimmy were a waiter in a restaurant, you'd starve to death before you got your soup.

Yet by the end of the chorus—the track is only one chorus (and, at 4:37, it's a very long and slow chorus), he's no longer describing the dream from the outside, he sounds like he's actually experiencing it from the inside. He builds to a huge climax, going from understated to extreme in a way that's almost mind-blowing, almost as if he's going from "Motherless Child" to "Unchained Melody" within the course of a single song. And a highly unlikely one at that, a Broadway anthem, the apogee of Rodgers and Hammerstein, and a song rarely heard in pop or jazz contexts; as if to underscore its unlikeliness, pianist Ray Bryant ends with a sort of gospel blues piano flourish, something like you'd expect to hear at the end of Ray Charles doing "Georgia on My Mind."

The second track, "Stay with Me," comes from even further out of left field; you have to wonder exactly which hat it was that Dorn pulled this particular rabbit out of. This 1963 song was adapted from the main theme of the rather heavy religious drama *The Cardinal;* while the movie won numerous awards, few paid attention to the score, which was by Jerome Moross, a Hollywood composer with Broadway cred (he had composed *The Golden Apple,* generally regarded as a "cult show"). The lyrics are by Carolyn Leigh, who among many other things had a special gift for taking something as unpromising as a piece of music titled "Main Theme from *The Cardinal*" and turning it into a truly wonderful song. Prior to Scott, the only notable recording of "Stay with Me" had been by Sinatra, and it's a little-known gem that generally gets lost in the Chairman's vast treasure chest. (Bob Dylan later recorded it for his 2015 album, *Shadows in the Night.)*

Leigh's lyric is a love song couched in the rhetoric of Catholic theology; it could be sung equally well by a church choir or a crooner: "Like the lamb that in springtime wanders far from the fold, / Comes the darkness and the frost, I get lost, I grow cold"; it almost sounds like a mash-up of the Lord's Prayer and "Glad to Be Unhappy"— Rodgers and Hart meet the New Testament. Like Sinatra, Scott is one of the few singers who can live up to the expectations of both halves of that equation, and like Sinatra he is at once blessed and cursed with the power to take us down the path of righteousness at the same time he's leading us into temptation.

Scott told David Ritz that, like so many, he first discovered "The Folks Who Live on the Hill" from Peggy Lee's classic album *The Man I Love.* He taped "The Folks Who Live on the Hill" right after "Stay with Me" and, unlike any other interpretation of this classic Kern-Hammerstein song, it could be that Scott still has the Bible on his brain; again there are spiritual overtones, and he makes the house on the hill sound like one and the same "cabin in the sky" that Ethel Waters sang about in one of the greatest of all Broadway spirituals. Both Waters's cabin and Scott's "home on a hilltop high" might be seen as secular manifestations of the "mansion" referred to in John 14:2. As Jesus said, there are many rooms in His Father's house, and in Scott's slow and exacting vocal we feel as if we're taking a tour of this mythical house room by room. As always, Scott transforms the grandiose into the personal—and the other way around.

His "Folks" has all the slow stateliness of the iconic Peggy Lee interpretation but with a couple of crucial differences: he adds the verse at the beginning, which Lee didn't sing, and he changes Hammerstein's reference to "Darby and Joan" to himself and his current wife, "Ruthie and Jim," who used to be "Jack and Jill." It's already a highly personal interpretation of a great standard, and now he has made it even more so.

As the tracks progress from one song to another, Deodato's tempos and arrangements are so similar that we can't actually tell where one song ends and the next one begins, particularly as "For Once in My Life" follows "The Folks Who Live on the Hill." Once again, Scott starts with the verse, yet this time it seems particularly off-center: it's not only a verse we have absolutely never heard, but that verse is followed by a very familiar song with a completely different—and unsettling—attitude. "For Once in My Life," as sung by Stevie Wonder, Tony Bennett, and especially Frank Sinatra, is almost always an aria of male confidence and self-reassurance—in very much the same vein as "Once in a Lifetime" (the two titles, as you've no doubt noticed, are practically identical). It's an odd choice for Scott, who tends to be considerably more self-effacing than self-aggrandizing in his selection of songs. Yet he recasts "For Once in My Life" in his own image; he's the only singer I've heard who makes the song actually sound vulnerable. Directed inwardly rather than outwardly, he sings it with hesitation and even trepidation but grows considerably more assured as the six-minute track progresses.

"Dedicated to You," the fifth and last of the tracks that have thus far been issued from the 1972 sessions, is another odd fit here. All four previous songs can be described as "heavy," not necessarily pretentious, but they certainly couldn't be called "light listening" under any circumstances. "Dedicated to You" is a swing era bauble that Ella Fitzgerald put on the map, light and bouncy (and, as Fitzgerald sang it, completely memorable), which John Coltrane and Johnny Hartman transformed into something considerably more romantic, but hardly dark. (The song was an early collaboration of Sammy Cahn and Saul Chaplin, in which lyricist Hy Zaret—later to write "Unchained Melody"—also participated. Sinatra never recorded it, but there was an early Columbia Records album of Sinatra tracks entitled *Dedicated to You*.) What is consistent with the other five tracks is that Scott sings it slowly and dramatically—even so, it seems the odd man out. Possibly Dorn intended it for contrast, but unless the remaining unissued tracks are someday issued we'll never know how,

exactly, it fit into the full picture of the proposed album.

Still, we should be grateful that even five of the nine (or is it ten?) 1972 tracks finally were first heard by the world twenty-one years later. In 1975, Scott recorded his last album for Savoy, *Can't We Begin Again*, which is a worthy addition to his pitifully small catalogue—his discography is his littler than he was—but hardly a masterpiece on the order of the 1962, 1969, and 1972 sessions. Then he was out of the studio for fifteen years (he produced his own album, *Doesn't Love Mean More*, in 1990) but it wasn't until after the death of his rabbi, Doc Pomus, in 1991 that he was able to start recording regularly again. He received a genuine "hurrah" in the 1990s and 2000s—it's debatable whether this amounted to a last or a first hurrah—but still not close to what his talent deserved.

The last time I saw Jimmy Scott was in July 2011 at the Blue Note in New York. By then he was even frailer than when he first started to appear onstage in a wheelchair, which had been about five years earlier. He sang less than half the set, about four or five numbers tops, and what he did sing could hardly be described as robust. But the voice endured, the soul remained, that indomitable spirit still permeated every note that he sang. As noted, Scott outlived his champions, like Dorn, Pomus, and Ray Charles, as well his detractors, like Lubinsky. Scott himself made it to eighty-eight years, but his music, it's clear, will survive us all.

35

Bobby Short

Bobby Short

(1956)

Bobby Short (1924–2005) played a key role in the development of the Great American Songbook; no classic songs would be written expressly for him, but he had an enormous influence on the way the great songs of Cole Porter, the Gershwins, Harold Arlen, etc. would be heard. He wasn't a name-above-the-title headliner—you wouldn't see him on *The Ed Sullivan Show*, nor did he have hit singles climbing the charts with a bullet. But as yesterday's show and movie tunes became tomorrow's classics, Short did as much as anyone to ensure this music would have a home—perhaps no longer on Broadway or in dancehalls, but in tony, high-priced supper clubs and on long-playing albums. To this day, there are still pianists and singers in clubs across New York, America, and the world who want nothing more than to sound like him.

Short's early 12-inch LPs, recorded for Atlantic, are an important part of the classic album era, the period when giants like Sinatra and Fitzgerald were defining the meaning of a standard and the parameters of what would become the songbook. Where Sinatra frequently transformed the basic character of a song, Short colored more carefully within the given lines, and maintained something closer to what could be loosely construed as the composer's original intention. He was less likely to take a song written as a ballad and swing it, the way Sinatra would, or take a medium-tempo blues-styled piece like "Stormy Weather" and change it into a ballad tempo so slow it would make your skin crawl. Still, once in a while, he too could retool a standard and radically change its entire complexion, as he does on his gloriously slow and moving "Bye Bye Blackbird."

Short brought dash, style, energy, and color to the classic songbook, of a kind that it might not otherwise have had. Throughout his early albums in particular—and throughout a long career that began when he was a child performer on the Colored Vaudeville circuit—he sings the classic songs with both imagination and swing. Even the most reactionary songwriters around, your Richard Rodgers or Irving Berlin, couldn't complain that Short was taking unnecessary liberties with their words and music. Yet even so, he was interpreting their music to a remarkably personal degree. At the time when Sinatra and Fitzgerald were increasingly moving to more formal settings—theaters and concert halls—Short was rethinking the idea of the nightclub. Sinatra made the songbook respectable by singing it in concert halls, Short's answer was to sing it in high-class clubs—the very idea of which was unknown a generation or two earlier. From Prohibition on, nightclubs were mob-owned enterprises where you got bombed and picked up chippies. Bobby Short made gin joints respectable; the Café Carlyle, in particularly, represented the high end of a new breed of high-class watering holes in which wealthy playboys were not ashamed to bring their dowager mothers, in their tiaras and on their best behavior. Traditionally, one wore a false mustache to nightclubs and brought one's "secretary," but the opposite was true for the Carlyle, it was where you wanted to see and be seen.

By the 1950s, it was generally understood that jazz and the Broadway-based songbook were two distinct animals; Dizzy Gillespie had little interaction with Rodgers and Hammerstein. But Short's music brought them back together, and stressed their compatibility and interconnectedness. Short's music had an impact on a whole string of presenters and gatekeepers who supported the songbook as well as jazz: live music impresarios like George Wein, record men like George Avakian, music moguls like Ahmet and Nesuhi Ertegun, and Norman Granz, who did all of the above, were all inveterate supporters of the songbook as well as jazz. For the Erteguns (who produced the essential albums by Short and Mabel Mercer), it was more of an apparent stretch; their day job was recording and promoting rhythm and blues and later rock 'n' roll, yet they made room for Mabel and Bobby in between Ray Charles and Bobby Darin in the 1950s and Aretha Franklin and Otis Redding in the 1960s.

As a live entertainer, Short was best known for his thirty-five-year run in the Café Carlyle; if the American Songbook can be said to have had a permanent address, that was it. Yet that was only the concluding chapter—albeit the most famous one—of a long and rewarding career. At the time of his classic Atlantic albums of 1955–60, he had barely worked in New York at all, but was already a rising star thanks to long runs in Los Angeles and Paris. (He also was fiercely proud of having come from Danville, Illinois.) Atlantic Records would later make him the focal point of an anthology titled The Erteguns' New York Cabaret (1987) but, ironically, Short might have never come to New York at all if not for the Ertegun brothers. The Erteguns had first encountered Short in Los Angeles, and, largely through their support, and from the exposure generated by his Atlantic albums, the singer was able to shift his home base to Manhattan—and in fact, to become the virtual symbol of what became known

as East Side Cabaret, even though there was little in his early career to suggest that was where he would wind up, geographically or otherwise.

As a recording artist, Short's career came in two major stages: apart from an early prelude of some oddball (and generally unheard) singles, he emerges full blown with his first Atlantic album at age thirty in 1955; between that year and 1960 he would make six uniformly outstanding albums for Atlantic. These are the gems of his career; there isn't one that isn't worthy of space in your trunkful of desert island discs. Following the 1960 Bobby Short on the East Side, he would then more or less sit out the 1960s, even as the Erteguns paid more attention once again to not only R&B (that is, music for black people) but also now to rock 'n' roll (that is, music for white people) as well.

The biggest sea change in Short's artistic evolution was signaled by three major developments in 1968. One, he became ensconced at the Carlyle, when a two-week fill-in for the vacationing house pianist mushroomed into an engagement that lasted three and a half decades. Two, in May, Short did the first of two celebrated Town Hall concerts, which not only renewed his relationship with the Erteguns but launched one with impresario George Wein and also his fellow artist Mabel Mercer. And it was the combined success of both of these developments that led to a new series of albums for Atlantic, starting with a double disc of the May 1968 Town Hall concert. (The first new Short studio album, Jump for Joy, followed in 1969.)

There had been a seismic shift between the two Atlantic periods. Most people know only the Bobby Short of 1968 on, the Carlyle incarnation. In the 1970s, Short was now firmly part of the intelligentsia, part of the crowd of Upper East Side movers and shakers that centered around Elaine's and seemed always to be wearing turtle-necked sweaters and puffing away on pipes. (It was a different world, or so they tell me, before Mayor Bloomberg banned smoking.) At that point, lovers of the traditional American Songbook were on the defensive, they read George Plimpton, they went to the new Sondheim shows, and they listened to Jonathan Schwartz on WNEW (God help them!). And they rallied around Short as if his Carlyle gig was

Custer's Last Stand. Unlike Sinatra, Bennett, and Tormé, who were constantly on the road, Short had a fixed location, which made it easier to gather the wagons around him.

How different is the Bobby Short we hear on those early Atlantic albums of the late 1950s. Here, he is neither defensive nor conservative, but rather a brash young man with lots of bright ideas. Even today, the big six albums of 1955–60 have a palpable freshness to them, an audacity even, that was somehow no longer permissible later on, when the songbook became something to preserve and protect. Short doesn't sound like he's preserving anything in the early albums, but merely having fun with the songs—and reinvigorating them in the process.

One can't imagine him singing a song by Jerry Leiber and Mike Stoller in the 1970s or later, yet he does a brilliant job with "Down in Mexico" on *Speaking of Love* (1957). In an age when the lines were not yet drawn in the sand, all things were possible—Bobby Short could sing Leiber and Stoller, and Elvis Presley could sing Cole Porter. Likewise, by the 1970s, one can't imagine Short singing goofy novelties, however vintage they might have been, like "Nagasaki" and "Tiger Rag," as he does on the excellent album *The Mad Twenties* (1958). One unfortunate consequence of the music being performed in places like Town Hall was that it now had to take itself seriously, and such frivolity had to go. (After-hours was another story: once I was fortunate enough to be sitting on Bobby's piano bench when he treated a small, after-midnight crowd to what became one of my all-time favorite songs, "Princess Poo-Poo-Ly Has Plenty Papaya (She Loves to Give It Away)," which he doubtless learned from Nellie Lutcher.)

Something would be gained, but something was lost—Short's work from 1968 onward includes many classic moments and entire albums. But, on the whole, the 1955–60 albums are a lot more fun.

The 1968 Town Hall concert was so successful that it was followed, a year later, by a sequel, which, like the first, was also released as a double-LP package by Atlantic. At this point, Short became inextricably associated with Mabel Mercer—which he had never been before. Doubtless Short was proud of the connection, but it was more professional than musical. Vocally, he had little in common with the celebrated diva twenty-five years his senior—she was fundamentally a European artist, biologically of partial African descent, but stylistically more of a proper Englishwoman than anything else. Short, however, was an African American and fiercely proud of it, who had been born and raised and continued to spend most of his time in the company of other African Americans. Where Mercer was more likely to sing a waltz, Short had a right to sing the blues. Where Mercer championed the dour ditties of Alec Wilder, Short swung the funkier melodies of Ellington and Strayhorn.

Vocally, Short's chief influences were the great African American song stylists of the 1930s, primarily Ethel Waters, Bessie Smith, and Duke Ellington's most celebrated female singers, Ivie Anderson and Adelaide Hall. (No, his primary influences were not male pianist-singers, like Fats Waller or Nat King Cole.) Short's high baritone was roughly in the same sonic range as Waters's low soprano (particularly in the later years, as her voice got lower and lower). Like Waters, he liked to juxtapose the highbrow with what was then generally thought of as the lowbrow—you'll hear the rolled r's of a proper operetta tenor in the same phrase as the low moans and growls of the blues.

In a rather audacious move, he begins his self-titled album *Bobby Short* by *not* sounding like Bobby Short. The first number is "At the Moving Picture Ball," which he sings in a highly stylized, deliberately artificial way, after the fashion of those tenuous tenors of the teens and early twenties. The song, by Joseph H. Santly, is an archetypical vaudeville novelty number from 1920, a list song that's essentially a set of gags, puns, and clever rhymes connected to a running list of silent-era movie stars. It was a widely recorded hit in its day, with Billy Murray doing perhaps the best-known version; another early recording, by tenor Maurice Burkhart, takes advantage of the Edison Records technology and is actually a full four minutes long, including some verses and gags not included in any other version, even the modern ones. (If Short omitted the gag about Fatty Arbuckle for reasons of propriety, it's surprising that he retained the line "Handsome Wallace Reid / stepped out full of speed," making light of how the early cinema leading man suffered from a drug addiction that eventually killed him.)

Short sings in a voice higher than even those stratospheric 78 rpm tenors—his goal isn't to accurately reproduce another time and place, but to boldly caricature the stylistic excesses of the vaudeville era. To that end, he squeals and yelps, occasionally cracks notes, and sounds generally like a singing squirrel (or even a chipmunk)—but also growls on lines like "Mary Pickford did a toe-dance *grand . . . and . . .*" His piano playing is even more stylized; he plays in a single dynamic, never getting louder or softer, and with a deliberately mechanical rhythm. The overall idea is to sound like a player piano, thereby further evoking the ragtime era. The lyric continually references silent-picture tropes—the whole occasion is described as "some scenario" (the early name for a screenplay) which Santly rhymes with "they were merry-o!" This is one of several exclamations that he wrote directly into the song as syncopated breaks between the lines.

In 1960, Short sang "Moving Picture Ball" on Hugh Hefner's TV series *Playboy's Penthouse;* here he shows that his live performances were even more animated than the recording. During the instrumental break in the center, Short directs his gaze up in the air at some unseen activity. It gradually becomes clear that Short is miming a piano player accompanying a silent film, looking at the screen and mirroring the imaginary cinematic action.

The second song, "The Most Beautiful Girl in the World," puts the whole album on a completely different footing, both rhythmically and mood-wise. It's not exactly swinging, not like Fitzgerald or Anita O'Day, but it's certainly driving, full of rhythmic momentum. Both the voice and the piano flow together as in a river; in the verse, especially, Short indulges in little filigrees and curlicues, which stand as minor tributaries from the central melody itself. Rodgers and Hart wrote this as a straightforward waltz (for the 1935 *Jumbo*); Short imbues it with considerable vigor. There's nothing effete or sentimental about this waltz, and somehow that makes it all the more moving. After a chorus, he goes into the verse, which arrives in the

middle (a structural device we associate with Bing Crosby) and at first is in full tempo, but then, in the last few lines of the verse, slows all the way down to a virtual standstill. He stays in this snail's pace for the start of the second chorus, and then just as you think he's going to go back into tempo, he ritards again for the closing, which he delivers on a big, Broadway-style belting note. While none of this is heavy-handed, Short underscores how Richard Rodgers was able to write a robust waltz in all phases of his career.

"Bye Bye Blackbird" is Short's most notable departure from the composer's original intentions. This archetypical 1920s roarer of a tune was almost always done in gay, bouncy cut-time (2/4). Short, however, brings out the song's inner melancholia—something nobody probably realized that "Blackbird" ever had—and makes it into something bittersweet. It's now a song about endings, and at the same time is a song about beginnings, and a song about how maybe they're both the same thing. Only thirty at the time when he made this album, Short was already a veteran of roughly twenty years in show business, and he's the master of the art of taking an old-time traditional lyric and making it sound as if the words are only the tip of the iceberg of what he's feeling. He doesn't have to change the lyrics to imbue them with a deeper meaning. However, as mentioned, he does change the tempo, which instills the words with a wholly different and much more powerful message. It's said that Miles Davis was inspired to play "Blackbird" at a slow crawl tempo from hearing Bobby Short play it, and a generation of jazz listeners thus grew up thinking of "Blackbird" as a ballad rather than a peppy Jazz Age fox-trot. (Short omitted the verse—as well he should have, it's not at all necessary—and that too explains why the verse to "Blackbird" has hardly ever been heard over the last sixty years.)

The second Rodgers and Hart number, "I've Got Five Dollars" (a Depression song from the 1931 *America's Sweetheart*), takes us back to classic Bobby. Less than two minutes long, it's filled with characteristic energy, ginger, and even pep, of the kind you'd expect from a leading man (juvenile) in a 1931 Broadway musical, pledging his troth to his leading lady (ingenue) and putting his cards, not to mention his assets, on the table. Short sings it in a way that's innocent yet erotic at the same time—it's not only the slow bluesy numbers that are sexy: he can achieve the same effect with the fast and peppy (2/4) show tunes—especially with those bluesy growls in the general style of Miss Waters and Adelaide Hall. This is also the number where trumpeter Pete Candoli is most audible, especially on the intros to each of the two central refrains.

The verse, which begins with a reference to Peggy Hopkins Joyce, the real-life gold-digger (as they were then called), doesn't seem the least bit scholarly, but here it's a necessary part of the song. The "Five Dollars" verse also includes one of Short's major idiosyncratic moments: when he reaches the line "though I'm poor as a church mouse," he pronounces the word as "chitch" mouse; then, as it to make sure we know he's doing it deliberately, he pauses and repeats the words again, "chitch mouse!" And then goes on with the verse. It makes absolutely no sense—other than that it's endearingly silly. It's obviously just a piece of shtick that he came up with in his zillions of accumulated hours of playing for live audiences in supper clubs, saloons, and bars. There's no earthly reason why it should be so amusing. It just is.

There's a similar moment on the next cut, "I've Got the World on a String." Sinatra had already claimed this as a cheerful, upbeat opener for a million concerts. Short's treatment is no less euphoric, while reminding us that the song did in fact originate at the Cotton Club. The verse is also essential here. He sounds joyous but slightly restrained in rubato, then as soon as he gets to the chorus he sings, again slowly, but with unbridled rapture. The classic Short moment arrives in the bridge; when he gets to "I'd be a silly so-and-so" he says the word "silly" over and over, deliberately picking the silliest word he can to emphasize the joyful silliness of the whole thing. In later years, when I saw him in the 1980s and '90s, he was stretching it even further—as on "chitch mouse," he would stop the tempo and just repeat "silly, silly, silly" so many times that it was truly beyond silly; in fact, he was pronouncing it "sealy" by that time.

Clearly, Short needs to slow things down at this point, and there's no one better for a slow-down than Alec Wilder. "Is It Always Like This?" is one of the composer's least depressing songs. (It was recorded by Mabel Mercer, a much bigger supporter of Wilder than Short, and, surprisingly, as a pop single by Lena Horne.) It's also just two minutes long, and it supplies a brief moment of introspection—the song is meant to be sung to oneself—in what is otherwise a boisterously exuberant album.

There are thirteen songs on *Bobby Short* rather than the usual twelve, yet so many of them are under two minutes, the total playing time is still just under thirty-seven minutes. One suspects that Short was performing the next two numbers together, not exactly as a medley but without a perceptible break. These are also Short perennials, which I heard him sing many times forty years later: "Sand in My Shoes" and "Carioca." Both are classic Hollywood–Tin Pan Alley exotica, the first by Frank Loesser and Victor Schertzinger. The second (by Vincent Youmans, Gus Kahn, and Edward Eliscu) was introduced in a spectacular production number starring Fred Astaire and Ginger Rogers in their first appearance together, *Flying Down to Rio* (1933). Although both are Hollywood concoctions, the first evokes Havana and the second Brazil. ("Carioca" was most famously reinterpreted by Artie Shaw in a hard-swinging, completely non-Latin treatment.) "Sand" was introduced by Connee Boswell and Eddie "Rochester" Anderson in *Kiss the Boys Goodbye* (1941). Each of them sang a distinct and separate chorus—the idea of a white woman and a black man actually singing together was altogether *too* exotic for Hollywood to consider in 1941.

The two tracks, together, are just about five minutes. "Sand in My Shoes" opens with bongos and muted trumpet, very Havana-after-hours; you can easily imagine Sky Masterson and Sister Sarah dancing a polite rhumba to it. After the intro, Short sings one flavorful chorus, but just when we expect some kind of variation on that theme, instead he goes into "Carioca." It's not understated, there's a big intro and a gradual rhythmic shift as it goes from something like a rhumba to something like a tango. Short is still rapturously romantic on both. He very subtly slows down and speeds up throughout and also gets louder and louder without ever quite reaching belt level. This pairing is the portion of the album I find myself listening to the most often, the two tracks flowing together marvelously and giving us a good idea of how Short moved from song to song even in these early, pre-Carlyle days.

"Down with Love" is more Harold Arlen (Yip Harburg rather than Ted Koehler), and though it was written for one of the composer's earliest Broadway shows, it still sounds more like Arlen's Harlem period. This is the track where bassist Buddy Woodson and drummer Maurice Russell are given the most to do; the trio really comes to life here. It's a very up tune, especially considering that the lyric has Short frequently shouting the word "down." Most singers set it up more like a list song, but Short treats it like a traditional narrative, with a steady progression from A to B. He colors his phrasing with more growls and stop-time—abruptly cutting a note off and pausing—to give his treatment of the lyric more flavor. In no way does it sound like a laundry list.

The next number is even more of a showstopper. "Hottentot Potentate" (Arthur Schwartz–Howard Dietz) is one of Ethel Waters's big numbers from the hit 1935 revue At Home Abroad. As with "Supper Time" and "Harlem on My Mind," which Irving Berlin wrote for Waters in As Thousands Cheer, the opportunity to write for this greatest of African American divas brought out something remarkable in these Jewish American songwriters. Howard Dietz in particular loves having fun with references to the depiction of African Americans in mainstream pop culture: just as "Harlem on My Mind" is a riff on Josephine Baker, "Hottentot Potentate" goofs on Paul Robeson as the Emperor Jones in Eugene O'Neill's groundbreaking play. The idea of making fun of a dark-skinned monarch might today be considered racist or at least patronizing, but Short, like Waters, makes it clear that he's the one making the fun—not the songwriters—and that's what makes it acceptable. The text makes abundant references to contemporary black culture, as in the way Emperor Jones conquered a nation with his "trickeration," a phrase that served

as the title of a 1931 tune by Cab Calloway. (The other reference lost on most contemporary audiences is "I brought my bottle of Chanel with me / I brought along the script of Lulu Belle with me." This was a 1926 play about a black diva of rather loose morals. The character was widely believed to have been based on Florence Mills, much to the outrage of Miss Mills herself.) This is the closest Short ever came to totally copying Waters. He even reprises her exhortation to the band, "Growl it out, baby doll!" Actually, Short is the one growling, as if he's trying to out-Waters Waters.

Not to be Short-changed, "Any Place I Hang My Hat Is Home" is even louder, livelier, and bluesier; the rollicking intro, boogie-woogie-esque piano, plus wailing muted trumpet could easily pass for the start of a Big Joe Turner record. This third of four Arlen tunes on the 1955 album is also the album's most recent song. "Any Place I Hang My Hat Is Home" is from the 1946 Broadway effort St. Louis Woman, with lyrics by Johnny Mercer. Like the great divas and showmen of the 1920s, Short knows well that the blues is foremost an urban tradition, and a highly theatrical one. It might have been the country cousins with guitars and overalls that attracted all the white imitators much later on, but the heart of the blues resides in artists like Waters (Ethel, not Muddy) and Short and composers like Ellington and Arlen. Bobby Short is at least as great a blues artist as Muddy Waters or Howling Wolf—probably better. "Any Place I Hang My Hat Is Home" brilliantly conveys the notion of restless motion; Short chants exuberantly over a rocking vamp that suggests a honky-tonk train chugging its way through the Mississippi Delta, and when it comes to the stop-time breaks, it suggests the train pulling into and out of tiny Southern whistle-stop towns. Short's vibrato is a bit florid, but if you were to add a saxophone or two to the arrangement, this could be a performance by Louis Jordan and his Tympany Five.

Short had obviously picked up "Bedelia" (by Bernard Michel and Maurice Pon) during one of his protracted stays in Paris, and he sings it in French here; the only other important recording by an American was that of saxophonist James Moody, with a French string section, from 1951. He sings it slowly and carefully, enunciating the words for those of us for whom French might as well be Greek. French numbers would be a key part of Short's arsenal from the beginning, no less than the blues numbers (like "Gimme a Pigfoot" and "Down in Mexico") and the exotic numbers (in that "Sand in My Shoes" and "Carioca" would lead to "Montevideo," "Island in the West Indies," and many other representations of romance set in far-off lands and climes). "Bedelia" is a stunning performance. The vocal is loaded with style and color, and it tells a story—enhanced by a board-fade ending—even if we have no idea what it's saying.

We owe Bobby Short a debt for not letting "Fun to Be Fooled" become a footnote. He rescued this thoroughly delightful song from a 1934 revue titled *Life Begins at 8:40*, for which Ira Gershwin joined Harold Arlen and E. Y. Harburg. (Ira participated mainly as busywork while his brother George was orchestrating *Porgy and Bess*.) It's also a footnote in that Harburg would later reuse the phrase "that old devil moon" as the title of a much better known song in *Finian's Rainbow*.

For Short's purposes, this is a perfect closer in that it points to the future: this is more like Short in the Carlyle era, singing and playing in a more straightforward fashion. The closer is without the special effects we have heard in the preceding twelve tracks, there's no rushing or slowing down or radical tempo changes, no growling or exotic rhythms, no trumpet or bongos. The melody is played and sung with far less embellishment—he still pauses for dramatic effect, he still builds in excitement as he heads toward the climax, but there's no "chitch"mouse or "sealy-sealy" silliness. He ends the album on a calmer, more contemplative note. Where "Any Place I Hang My Hat Is Home" is highly extroverted, sung to other people in a party atmosphere, on "Fun to Be Fooled" he sounds like he's singing to himself, in an introverted moment of contemplation. The last line in the song is "This little dream won't end," and it's never 100 percent clear in the text exactly what "little dream" he's referring to. Ultimately, this serves to underscore the idea that he's thinking to himself rather than speaking aloud. It's a clear-cut foreshadowing of the mature Bobby of multiple decades later. It may be fun to be fooled, but you don't have to indulge in foolishness to have fun.

The later work—the records that span the period from the 1968 Town Hall concert to his final album, the 2001 *Piano*—is, for the most part, brilliant, as were the many live shows at the Carlyle and elsewhere that I was fortunate enough to attend. (There was an especially rewarding series of songbook projects, which began with a Cy Coleman songbook titled *My Personal Property*, which was recorded in 1963 but not released until some years later, as well as what might be the best Noël Coward album ever.) But these six albums from 1955 to 1960, particularly *Bobby Short*, have an exuberance and a vitality that's unlike anything else in his remarkable career.

36

Nina Simone

Nina Simone and Piano!

(1969)

Another personal note: of all the major singers of jazz and the Great American Songbook—of those who have been actively performing since, say, 1980—Nina Simone was virtually the only one I never had the chance to experience live, and she was one of the few with whom I had enjoyed no direct, personal contact. To a certain extent, this was because Simone (1933–2003) was mostly out of the country in these years, and her New York appearances were few and far between in those final decades. There was an occasion in the late 1990s in which she was booked to play the New York JVC Jazz Festival, and I was set to go—but Dr. Simone, as she was then insisting on being addressed—first postponed and then canceled the concert.

I like to think that had I been able to see her work live, I might have gotten the point a lot sooner than I actually did. Or maybe that's giving myself too much of the benefit of a doubt. I will admit it: I was extremely slow to appreciate Simone and what made her special. Essentially, she was coming from a whole other direction than the one that I was accustomed to looking in. And in the long run, those very factors—the ones that made me overlook her for too long—are the same ones that, in retrospect, make her seem even more important. As I had defined it, a jazz singer was generally someone who came up through the ranks of the jazz army. For older singers, that meant the

big bands; for the younger ones, it meant having received the stamp of approval of such modern jazz masters as Miles Davis, Art Blakey, or John Coltrane. And, to a lesser extent, jazz singers had to sing primarily the songbook of jazz standards. Those criteria covered almost everybody at least up to the 1960s: even Betty Carter and Sheila Jordan, radical as they were, had both emerged out of the jazz mainstream.

Simone's background was entirely different. Eunice Kathleen Waymon grew up in North Carolina at the exact midway point between classical music and the blues. She was a piano prodigy who studied the European classics obsessively and felt in the depths of her soul that she was a failure because she never made it as a concert pianist. Simone's music, at the beginning at least, was fundamentally a fusion of Southern American gospel and European classical piano; in bringing the two together, she created something wholly original, which closely paralleled the achievements of Ray Charles (when he brought together gospel and R&B at roughly the same time), but which was uniquely her own. The soul music that Simone gave birth to was every bit as potent as that of Brother Ray, or of the brand-new bag that Papa James Brown opened for the world, or that of the entire Motor Town foundry. Nearly every other major jazz singer of the 1960s had sung at some point with Charlie Parker, or Horace Silver, but Simone came up entirely on her own, and needed no one's imprimatur. Yet her music not only was jazz, it continually transcended the genre—it transcended every genre, in fact.

I only became a convert to Nina Simone when it became impossible not to be; when, in the 1990s and 2000s, virtually every contemporary singer I respected, most notably Cassandra Wilson, Dianne Reeves, and Barb Jungr, began citing her as a primary influence. It was clear that the major artists of the current generation valued her even more highly than anyone I considered to be part of the pantheon; today, there are far more singers out there who sound like Simone than like Ella Fitzgerald or Sarah Vaughan. Every season brings a new tribute show or album, and though Simone trumpeted her blackness from the rooftops, many of the most astute Simone tribute projects have been the work of white artists like the inspired alt-cabaret belter Lady Rizo, the soulful Broadway singer Morgan James, and the miraculously subtle British artist Barb Jungr, who are all as different from each other as they are from Simone. I counted at least a half dozen Simone tribute projects in 2012, far more than for any other legendary artist, even Judy Garland or Sinatra.

In 1966, Simone signed a new long-term contract with RCA Records. At the time, she was in a unique place, in her career or in anybody else's. She was beloved of the jazz world, and also of the lovers of the traditional American Songbook, whose treasures she continued to explore even while heading in other directions. The black pop audience loved her, even though she was more likely to do a song by Bob Dylan than by Smokey Robinson, and she still had her ears open for new show tunes that might work in her style. Musically, she would have been perfectly at home at either the Newport Jazz Festival or Woodstock.

The only thing she didn't have was a real hit single all her own. She was a true member of the advance guard, who went out ahead of the rest of the pack, blazing the trails that others would soon follow and making the discoveries from which others reaped the benefits. She wasn't shy about telling you so, either; she never let it be misunderstood that it was her version—and no one else's—of the traditional folk blues "House of the Rising Sun"

that inspired the chart hit by the Animals; and their version of "Don't Let Me Be Misunderstood" also sold a lot more than Simone's. She didn't write or introduce "I Put a Spell on You," but Creedence Clearwater Revival and the other rock bands who subsequently played the song learned it from her—not Screamin' Jay Hawkins. What seems ironic is that these pop acts appreciated her a lot earlier than the jazz world—no other jazz singer shows anything like a Simone influence until at least a generation later. (She was understandably bitter: she had helped make these songs into hits, but since she didn't own any of the copyright or publishing, there was no way she could have participated in the profits.) In 1968, she combined two songs from the musical *Hair* (which was just making the move to Broadway), "Ain't Got No" and "I Got Life," into a short medley, which, when released as a single, became a sizable hit in Europe—but even that failed to put her on the top of the American charts.

If that was the closest thing she had to a domestic hit single, albums don't seem to have mattered much to her. She's generally said to have made about forty original albums, not counting after-the-fact compilations and "greatest hits" sets. Yet very few of these albums stand out as albums. Nearly all of them are excellent representations of what she was doing at the time: the early albums for Bethlehem and Colpix include more jazz standards; the 1964–67 albums for Philips include more foreign songs, American folk songs, and contemporary show tunes; the RCA albums of 1967–74 feature more politically charged "protest" songs and more of her own brand of soul. But few of these Simone subgenres rated an album of their own.

As far as coherent album packages go, Simone made a rather offbeat Ellington songbook in 1962, and then in 1963 she killed two birds with one stone, so to speak, with *Folksy Nina*, which was a collection of folk songs recorded live at Carnegie Hall. Her first album for RCA (in 1967) was an excellent set entitled *Nina Simone Sings the Blues* although it's far from entirely the blues. Except for these few exceptions, it's hard to tell one of her albums from another—or remember which song is on which album. And yet who needs to? They're all great—you can't go wrong with virtually anything she ever did.

The 1968 *Nina Simone and Piano!* is both a unique album and an exceptionally excellent album, even by the artist's own high standards. It's the single best document extant of her piano playing and the formal training that produced it. That classical background would be a major factor in the makeup of Simone's personality. In Simone's lifetime, there were all manner of black pop stars, including many who were embraced by all audiences (well beyond the black audience), but black classical artists were another matter, and instrumentalists had an even tougher time than opera singers. Of all her experiences, that was the one that most resonated with her—the one that came closest to explaining the lifelong chip on her shoulder. Throughout her life, Simone always thought of herself as an underdog, although in the larger picture she had everything going for her, starting with prodigious talent as a pianist, singer, and occasional songwriter. She also possessed an enviable gift for finding exceptional material, which wasn't confined to any one category—she indisputably was a jazz artist, but there wasn't necessarily a jazz bias in her repertoire.

Sometimes misinformation can be useful. The *Piano* album includes a track called "Compassion (aka Compensation)," the authors of which are generally given as "Dunbar, Simone." Simone is obviously Nina, but in some sources her coauthor is given as the reggae drummer-producer Lowell "Sly" Dunbar (half of the team of Sly & Robbie). In actuality, Simone based her song on a poem by the pioneering African American poet Paul Laurence Dunbar (1872–1906, the selfsame one who told us why the caged bird sang). The album also contains a song titled "Nobody's Fault but Mine." The liner notes to the CD edition state that she learned this song from the 1967 recording by Otis Redding. However, this seems unlikely: Simone sings a completely different song with the same title; hers is a traditional African American quasi-spiritual recorded by Blind Willie Johnson in 1927.

With anyone else, the inclusion of a reggae song would have quickly raised a red flag. With Simone, such detours somehow makes perfect sense:

Simone is the only musical artist of her time who could conceivably be doing reggae, blues, spirituals, turn-of-the-century black poetry, and contemporary British pop songs all in the same breath. You wouldn't see Carmen McRae leaping among these genres in this way, although you would see plenty of singers attempting to combine the different forms and sources later on, as they followed in Simone's path.

Nina Simone and Piano! is especially valuable in this period of her life when most of what she sang was extremely confrontational. Indeed, she sounds particularly hostile on nearly everything from this period—studio recordings, concert tapes, TV appearances. She's boiling over with anger about the injustices visited upon black people by white people and about those visited on women by men, and personally pissed off about those distinctly Caucasian bands that made more money than she did from songs they learned from her. Yet in a stroke of good fortune that she never seems to have appreciated, she was in precisely the right time and the right place to express that anger in music—the Simone we first hear on records in the late 1950s is much more buttoned-down and outwardly cheerful—and very different from the embittered and embattled Simone of 1969.

Piano is an exceptional and special album: her most intimate, the one where she seems the most vulnerable, the one where she lets us see the most of her soul. It's the album where we get to see the real Nina beneath all that anger and bitterness. It was less of a commercial success than many of her other ones, but more honest. Her previous release, titled *'Nuff Said!,* was ostensibly a live album, but a number of tracks on it were recorded in the studio and then doctored up with overdubbed applause in order to sound live, whereas everything on *Piano* is almost brutally honest—and completely exposed.

Here, Simone is alone with just the piano—no other musicians, no audience to respond to even as they respond to her. Here, her deep contralto sounds warm and expressive and highly human, more sultry than hostile, compassionate and forgiving, more transcendent than transgressive, more contemplative than aggressive. One is reminded of Samuel Goldwyn's famous line "You have to take the bitter with the sour," which applies to the majority of Simone's music, yet here there's some genuine sweetness to offset all the bitter as well as the sour.

This is true from the first track, "Seems I'm Never Tired Lovin' You," onward. This is one of the most obscure numbers Simone ever sang; Dave Nathan, one of Simone's biographers and the president of her U.K. fan club, has identified this as a piece with what might be deemed personal and professional connections. Throughout the 1960s, the artist was married to her manager, Andy Stroud, and among his other clients was an act called the Swordsmen. However unlikely the name, this was a lesser-known two-man team of soul singers, not all that unusual in the age of the Righteous Brothers and Sam & Dave, and one of their few singles was "Seems I'm Never Tired Lovin' You," released on Ninandy Records, a label owned by Stroud and titled from the combination of his and his wife's name. Thanks to the connection with Simone, the Swordsmen also eventually released an album on RCA, and sang behind her on her 1969 Philharmonic Hall concert (released on the album *Black Gold*).

Simone sets the mood for the album here: it's particularly contemplative and introspective. Although the lyric is addressed to another "you," it's mainly directed inwardly. At times it seems more like a prayer—or even a mantra—than a love song. It gets particularly churchy in the bridge, wherein lines like "Should the mountains crumble to ashes / And the rain should cease to fall / And if the river stopped its flowing . . ." are probably better sung to God than to another human being.

"Nobody's Fault but Mine" illustrates the solidarity of African American music in that the song is equal parts spiritual and blues. It's laid out in regulation twelve-bar blues form, but the inherent message is solidly religious. Simone does such an outstanding job both playing and singing that it seems like an Old Testament miracle that one person is doing both at the same time. She learned the song from one of the player-singer icons who preceded her in the black music tradition, such as Sister Rosetta Tharpe and, earlier, Blind Willie Johnson. Blind Willie is particularly rough and

scabrous; he sings like he's personally already experienced the fires of hell and thus is in a good position to warn us that if we are sent to the inferno in the afterlife, it's nobody's fault but our own—after all, admonishes Blind Willie, our mothers already taught us how to pray and how to sing the Gospel, and that's everything we need to make it into Paradise. Simone's vocal is more confessional, as if she's bemoaning her own fate on a very personal level rather than trying to dictate behavioral standards for others. Her playing is a veritable textbook on piano phrases and chord voicing for spiritual accompaniment. The composition is credited to Simone herself on the album, meaning that if the Animals or Creedence Clearwater were to pick it up, nobody would collect the royalties but her.

Randy Newman introduced "I Think It's Going to Rain Today" on his first album, *Randy Newman*, in 1968. Simone had a knack for finding songs well before everyone else; she did two songs by the Bee Gees in 1968, well before anyone else had heard of them, but "Rain Today" was already well on its way to becoming one of Newman's most widely heard songs even before Simone included it on the *Piano* album. "Nobody's Fault but Mine" shows what gospel and blues have in common, but on "Rain Today" Simone's interpretation illustrates a fundamental difference between the two forms: the blues is often associated with hopelessness and futility, whereas in gospel songs the underlying hope is that things will get better, even if only in the next life; they don't always have to be as miserable as they may be right now. She includes a touch of Bach in her intro (much as she did, more famously, on her early version of "Love Me or Leave Me") and is especially moving on Newman's unusual bridge ("Lonely, lonely, tin can at my feet / Think I'll kick it down the street, that's the way to treat a friend"). In the songwriter's own recording, when he sings the lines "Help the needy and show them the way / Human kindness is overflowing," he clearly means it ironically—human kindness, he implies, is anything but overflowing. Newman implies that the rain isn't metaphorical, but a literal flood sent by the Almighty to wash our sins away—and us along with it. This time it's Simone, not Newman, who sings it in a way that's more hopeful. God still loves us and believes in us, even if we don't believe in Him the way we should. This may not be Newman's message, but it's Simone's.

In that "spirit," the next track, "Everyone's Gone to the Moon," seems like a direct continuation of "Rain Today." Here, Simone suggests that He has already passed judgment. The lyrics depict what seems to be a world suddenly bereft of people: "Streets full of people, all alone / Roads full of houses never home." The song was the one hit of Jonathan King, a British singer-songwriter who turns up on many a list of one-hit wonders. King's hit single was feather light, a wistfully, extremely youthful voice, whose naïveté was enhanced by the waltz tempo—3/4 time being a long-established signifier of old-fashioned innocence. The title suggests that morality and values have gone the same way as technology—to another planet—but Simone makes it sound like Judgment Day; whether we're raptured up to Heaven or banished to the fiery furnace is something that only He knows. Or could it be that, as Newman suggests, the Creator has already sent down another flood to purge the earth of our existence?

There follows a sequence of texts that are both more personal and even more spiritually driven. "Compensation" (which is listed on the 1999 CD as "'Compassion,' aka 'Compensation'"), is the 1905 poem by Paul Laurence Dunbar as performed by what sounds like an entire church ensemble consisting of three distinct voices and two keyboards. Not surprisingly, they're all Simone: one melody voice and two harmony voices overdubbed, with accompaniment played mostly on the piano but supplemented by organ chords in the background. Simone herself composed this setting for Dunbar's words, in which the poet suggests that God offers us the gift of song to reward our capacity for love. Lest that sound too cheerful, Dunbar further suggests that God extends to us "the boon of Death" as a respite from "having loved so vainly and sung with faltering breath."

In the 1960s, Simone basked in the company of the leading African American intelligentsia of the period, playwrights and poets, and they in hers. She was close with Lorraine Hansberry (the author of *A Raisin in the Sun,* who died at thirty-four in

1964) and Langston Hughes (who cowrote one of her signature songs, "Backlash Blues"). "Who Am I?" suggests that Simone was keeping the company of the upper echelon of New York's cultural elite even beyond the Harlem Renaissance and the civil rights movement. This is from a lesser-known work by Leonard Bernstein, his 1950 adaptation of *Peter Pan,* which, despite starring two major Hollywood icons, Boris Karloff and Jean Arthur, and running almost a year on Broadway, was completely overshadowed by the 1954 Mary Martin vehicle. For Simone to even know about it shows that she or someone in her circle was close to Bernstein and was deeply immersed in the musical theater—this song is virtually unknown, and was only heard briefly on the long-out-of-print cast album. Simone's recording contains much more of the song than the 1950 album, which makes it clear that she learned it from the sheet music. In the show, one of the Lost Boys begs Wendy for a lullaby, and she obliges with this lovely tune, which starts innocuously enough but soon becomes a contemplation on the notion of reincarnation: "Will I ever live again / As a mountain lion / Or a rooster, a hen?" Simone's treatment is anything but a lullaby: it opens with jangly discordant notes that will wake you up rather than put you to sleep, and continues with a passionate entreaty, which quickly becomes more like a diatribe—Simone was evidently a firm believer in the idea.

"Another Spring" is a highly intimate tour de force, half spoken and half sung and thoroughly acted on both sides of that equation. It's at once a poem, a monologue, and a song, with music by Angelo Badalamenti, the film soundtrack composer, famous for his long collaboration with David Lynch (notably the *Twin Peaks* theme), and a text by one John Clifford. The piece starts out rather gnarly, with Simone first describing, then portraying a very bitter old woman who talks about trying to avoid the cold of winter and watching her friends dying off even while admitting to herself that death—hers—is primarily what she has to look forward to. (It's all very Jacques Brel.) But as the piece continues for three and a half minutes, it grows increasingly more upbeat emotionally and more musical. By the end of the track, the woman is resolved that there will be another spring, and the piece is especially convincing in its optimism because it has earned the right to be so.

The most obscure song out of all fourteen cut at the sessions is "The Human Touch" by Charles Reuben, about whom we know nothing. It completes a four-song arc, all of which are virtually unique to Simone and all of which are about causes and ideas rather than the customary song subjects, e.g., love affairs, sadness, elation, and heartbreak. In "The Human Touch," the author bemoans the increasing lack of humanity he sees in day-to-day life. "Have we lost the touch that does so much?" the lyrics ask, "Have we lost the human touch?" It's a brief statement at two minutes, one thirty-two-bar chorus all the way through, more like a short poem than a lyric, and, on top of that, almost more of a haiku or even a limerick. It's over before we've had much chance to think about it, and ends with some unusual breathing patterns, almost like a machine, from Simone, over some dissonant piano notes.

Up to here, the first eight songs on the album would have been almost completely new to Simone's listeners in 1969—the closest thing to a standard would have been "I Think It's Going to Rain Today." The only jazz classic on the album is track nine, "I Get Along Without You Very Well (Except Sometimes)"; this is the sole selection most listeners would have been familiar with—the one they would have in their heads (most often sung by male singers, especially Frank Sinatra and Chet Baker). Yet, paradoxically, this is the most intimate song here, the one Simone most makes sound like her own personal experience. The words of Jane Brown Thompson seem to be coming straight out of Simone's heart, using her piano and Hoagy Carmichael's melody as a conduit. This is the track that most satisfyingly justifies the premise of the album: in the middle of a torrent of hostility, Simone finds the courage to sound exposed and vulnerable.

On most of the rest of the album, Simone sounds as if she's thinking out loud, which is a blissful thing for a performer to achieve, but here she takes it a notch deeper—it sounds more as if she's feeling out loud. She gets out of the way of the words, lets them speak for themselves, and delivers

them with as few embellishments as possible—you can practically hear the soft rains falling and dripping from the leaves. She personalizes everything with knowing little touches like "I've forgotten you just like *I said I would* . . ." and then "or *maybe* except when I hear your name . . ." and "I should never *ever* think of spring." One protracted chorus is all she needs. By delivering it internally, singing it not only from her own heart but back into her own heart, she touches all of us in the same place.

The original LP ended with "The Desperate Ones" (originally known as "Les Désespérés"; Simone likely heard it in *Jacques Brel Is Alive and Well and Living in Paris,* which opened Off-Broadway at the start of 1968. This particular song isn't on the cast album (and, more curiously, Brel's name is not on the composer credits in the Simone album), and that she chose it suggests that she must have actually seen the show, a sign that she was continuing to monitor the worlds of both musical theater and European songs. It's even more talky than "Another Spring." Simone delivers much of it in what could be described as a rather dynamic stage whisper. Even while refraining from full-on singing, Simone is very dramatic, it takes the tone of an actor who happens to be doubling as her own piano accompanist—although some of her devices for emphasizing the text, like the repeated phrase ("They cry to us for help / We think it's all in fun—we think it's all in fun—we think it's all in fun") derive more from music than spoken drama. It's an especially cryptic slice of verbiage; even while reading the libretto I'm not totally sure what's going on or what Simone is singing about, but her performance undeniably conveys a suitable atmosphere of mystery. She turns the lack of clarity into an asset. Even though we don't know who the desperate ones are, Simone makes it clear that we can't deny their ineffable sense of desperation.

It's a rather desperate, albeit moving, note to end the LP on. The 1999 compact disc edition adds four more (previously unissued) tracks from the September 16, 1968, session, starting with "Music for Lovers" by Bart Howard, the inclusion of which further testifies to still another ongoing interest of Simone's: the New York cabaret scene. For most of his life, Howard was known exclusively as Mabel

Mercer's accompanist, who also tossed out the occasional song, which would only be performed by those cabaret insiders who were friends of Mabel. Still, "Fly Me to the Moon" would be the only Bart Howard song to achieve widespread fame; "Music for Lovers" had been earlier recorded by Portia Nelson and the Hi-Los.

"Music for Lovers" further speaks to Simone's penchant for classical keyboard. She sings over her own organ here, but it's more Bach than Baptist church (though, of course, Bach wrote most of his best music for the church as well)—in fact, it sounds more like a traditional pipe organ rather than a soul-jazz Hammond B3. The previous versions are both more like American lieder, very self-consciously artsy (Nelson in particular is so quasi-operatic she almost sounds like a parody), but Simone finds the soul at the heart of Howard's song. Her vocal is rich and deep, full of nuance, almost too personal to be a religious incantation— could it be that Simone is telling us that the relationship between two people is potentially even more intimate than that between man and the Creator? This is a stunning performance, it's hard to imagine why Simone wasn't satisfied with it. Nearly ten years later she returned to the song for her album *Baltimore*, with a *concerto grandioso* arrangement—but this one has the charm.

Looking in the other direction, two of the remaining three songs are remakes of standards that Simone had cut earlier, "I'll Look Around" and "Man with a Horn." The last three songs on the CD all derive from what is generally regarded as the Great American Songbook. Lyricist Leo Robin realized the dream of a lifetime when he was assigned to write with Jerome Kern for the film *Centennial Summer*, which turned out to be one of the great composer's final projects. The movie wasn't released until 1946, well after Kern's death, and it failed to become one of his best-remembered scores. Still, "In Love in Vain" was especially beloved of black female singers: Lena Horne, Shirley Horn, Gloria Lynn, Sarah Vaughan, Carmen McRae, and Simone all recorded it (among many others). Simone's single-chorus version is short (2:29) and to the point. Her piano intro hits a lot of unexpected notes—it's like something just won't

let her be straightforwardly romantic; the course of true love never did run smooth, and neither does Simone's piano playing. Her vocal is full of operatic contours, surges, and diminuendos.

As mentioned, both of the remaining songs are remakes of numbers she'd cut earlier in the 1960s on her Colpix albums. George Cory and Douglass Cross's "I'll Look Around" was a classic recording by Billie Holiday, but otherwise, in a rough parallel to Bart Howard and "Fly Me to the Moon," the team would have been known as just a pair of insiders before 1962 when Tony Bennett recorded their "I Left My Heart in San Francisco." This treatment is stark and bereft of embellishment, Simone sounds like she's so resigned to heartbreak that she's not even looking around. At the end, she seems to have an idea for a climax—to increase the contrast, to go from a very quiet, rather mono-tonal interpretation to a big ending. Alas, she doesn't quite make it—her voice cracks. Loudly, unmistakably. Ideally, she should have done another take. Instead she put it aside. Apparently, though, she approved the 1968 track for release on the 1999 CD, bum notes and all.

"The Man with the Horn" uses a similar arrangement: quiet, quiet, *quiet,* then LOUD and dramatic at the end for contrast. But here she makes the high note. It's a lovely performance and far superior to her earlier recording. The song, with its title inspired by Dorothy Baker's famous jazz novel, is one of the major ballads of the big band era, credited to three unlikely characters: short-lived trombonist Jack Jenney, his then-wife, singer Bonnie Lake (who was also the sister of the famous film star Ann Sothern), and arranger-bandleader-songwriter Eddie DeLange. Where Simone's earlier treatment is merely sentimental, this one is full of feeling, expressed in those notes that she holds for so long that you keep expecting them to go flat, although they never quite do. Even though Simone never intended to end the album with this track, it makes for an effective closer.

When she cut her final studio album for RCA in 1973, Simone was only forty, but this was, with several significant exceptions, the end of her consistent recording career. Other jazz singers stopped recording equally early in their careers because the market was essentially finished with them, but it's especially tragic that Simone, who had more than enough popularity to keep going, took herself out of the running because of her own personal demons. As mentioned, *Nina Simone and Piano!* was not as successful as her previous release, the semi-live *'Nuff Said!* (which featured the best-selling *Hair* medley). The intrinsic worth of *Piano* was apparently invisible to record buyers in 1969, but appreciation for it has grown steadily in the nearly fifty years since then. In retrospect it seems especially valuable, not least because Simone seems to be saying goodbye to the era when she would sing of love rather than protest. The signs of the Zodiac were all correctly aligned, not least of which was a record label that was willing to let her do whatever she wanted. She would never have that opportunity again. Thank God she was prescient enough to take advantage of it.

37

Frank Sinatra

In the Wee Small Hours

(1955)

Near the end of the first act of Oscar Wilde's *An Ideal Husband,* the leading man (whose ethics, we learn, have been compromised), states the observation that "perfect people don't need love."

For most of the earlier part of his career, the young Frank Sinatra had dealt in idealized, perfect love. In his recordings with bandleader Tommy Dorsey and musical director Axel Stordahl, the young Sinatra took the idea of love and put it on a pedestal. In his twenties and thirties, he had succeeded in making the whole idea of love more concrete and believable than virtually any other vocalist of the era, and the love he sings about resides securely on a lofty plateau. In much of Sinatra's early work, love is a superhu-

man force that ennobles all those whom it touches; Sinatra's early performances of the Gershwin perennials "Embraceable You," "Someone to Watch over Me," and "I've Got a Crush on You" are stunning examples of this kind of musical and emotional perfection. In his big band and wartime-era work, even when love is other than idyllic, then it's grandly tragic, as in the semiclassical "None but the Lonely Heart." But happy or sad, it's almost always larger than life.

Still, there are foreshadowings, in the early recordings, of the deeper and more mature Sinatra, in songs like "She's Funny That Way," "It Never Entered My Mind," and "Guess I'll Hang My Tears

out to Dry." Here, we get a sense of the young singer beginning to explore all the peaks and valleys between elation and sadness.

By 1955, Sinatra's musical and personal evolution has achieved a whole new level. The singer is now fully able to chart every microscopic pinpoint of feeling—the microtones, as it were—between the notes of the emotional keyboard. Sinatra had already explored perfection, and he was now about to build the rest of his career on romantic dysfunction. Taking Wilde at his word, he shows how we are all imperfect people, therefore we all need love. From the mid-1950s on, he sings about people who seem more real, who may not be perfect but are gloriously human in their failings. Sinatra didn't have to read *Anna Karenina* to realize that there was only so much that could be done with perfection, but that each unhappy love affair was special and different in its own way. More than simply singing sad songs, Sinatra was now fashioning himself as a combination of detective and forensic psychologist probing through the ruins of busted-up love affairs: Why did this one go wrong? What happened here? His genius as an artist was both in the very big picture and in the tiniest details.

The popular and more simplistic view of Sinatra's artistic evolution was that the remarkable growth he had achieved by the mid-1950s was the direct result of his personal experiences of a few years earlier. Specifically, his emotionally super-charged ballad singing of this period and later stems from his tumultuous relationship with Ava Gardner, his second wife and, from everything that we know about Sinatra, his number-one gal-that-got-away. Some of those close to him insist that it was the Ava experience that empowered him to sing these songs more movingly. His daughter Nancy Sinatra, in talking about that grandly tragic off-again, on-again love affair, observed, "Frank Sinatra put that pain to good use." And even Nelson Riddle—the brilliant arranger-conductor whose collaboration with Sinatra was now reaching its highest point—said, "It was Ava who did that, who taught him how to sing a torch song." He added, "That's how he learned. She was the greatest love of his life, and he lost her."

However, experience can only teach you so much; merely undergoing something wouldn't necessarily endow just anyone with the ability to express feelings so movingly. In the words of Mitch Miller, who can hardly be accused of being a Sinatra sycophant, it wasn't Sinatra's experience that empowered him, or even his own inner turmoil, it was his craft. The art of singing has nothing to do with whether or not an artist himself can personally feel a given emotion, it's about what he can communicate to an audience and make them feel. And, as Miller said, "Frank had that."

In the Wee Small Hours (1955) was the first of a series of slow and sad ballad albums that the mature Sinatra would make for Capitol Records, all of them in collaboration with arranger Nelson Riddle (in addition to several with Gordon Jenkins). By 1955, Sinatra had been in the concept album business for an entire decade, having essentially invented the idea with *The Voice*. Recorded in 1945, this was an eight-song collection released in a four-disc "album" binder by Columbia Records in 1946. Well before the introduction of the long-playing record, Sinatra was already thinking in terms of a multi-song musical program in which all the numbers would be linked to each other via mood, dynamics, tempo, and texture. Record-changing phonographs allowed listeners to hear four tracks uninterrupted, making the early Sinatra 78 albums, starting with *The Voice*, no less "conceptual" than *Miles Ahead* or *Sgt. Pepper*. With the invention of microgroove technology, Columbia released *Sing and Dance with Frank Sinatra* (1950), the singer's first original long-play project. When Sinatra signed with Capitol in 1953, he recorded two more 10-inch albums, *Songs for Young Lovers* (1953) and *Swing Easy* (1954). *In the Wee Small Hours* would be his first effort in the 12-inch long-play format, although the sixteen-track set was also widely distributed, for consumers who hadn't yet upgraded to 12-inch turntables, in the 10-inch format as a two-LP set.

When constructing a concept package, the challenge for Sinatra was to achieve consistency and variety at the same time—and also to avoid repetition in the process. His plan was to gather songs from a wide range of sources, yet make them sound as if they belonged together; the risk was that they would sound so similar as to become monotonous. On *In the Wee Small Hours*, the material does indeed come from all over the map musically, although it's considerably more focused chronologically. Apart from the newly written title track, the songs date from 1929 ("What Is This Thing Called Love" and "Can't We Be Friends?") to 1942 ("I'll Be Around"), with the majority from the early and mid-1930s. As great as the popular song had been in the 1920s, in the 1930s it achieved new heights of sophistication and experimentation—partly in reaction to the Great Depression. After 1943, most of the major talents in songwriting dedicated themselves to the new book-style Broadway shows, and songs became secondary. It was the songs of the 1930s, from Broadway and Hollywood, the years when Sinatra was coming up, learning his craft, and paying the most attention, that became his sweet spot.

Four songs on *Wee Small Hours* come from jazz sources: violinist Matty Malneck and pianist Frank Signorelli's "I'll Never Be the Same," Hoagy Carmichael's "I Get Along Without You Very Well," and two songs first heard at the Cotton Club, Duke Ellington's "Mood Indigo" and Harold Arlen's "Ill Wind." The majority of the selections, however, are from Broadway musicals: Rodgers and Hart's "It Never Entered My Mind" and "Glad to Be Unhappy" came from early (meaning pre-*Oklahoma!*) book musicals, namely *Higher and Higher* and *On Your Toes;* "Can't We be Friends?" was written for the revue *The Little Show.* Two more were written for films: "Last Night When We Were Young" being written for the great opera star Lawrence Tibbett in *Metropolitan* (but ultimately not used) and "When Your Lover Has Gone" for the 1931 Depression comedy *Blonde Crazy.* Some songs came from incredibly prolific composers with long, rewarding careers—Ellington, Arlen, Carmichael; others were by writers who achieved a sort of distinction for writing only one or two classic songs: Betty Jane Thompson ("I Get Along Without You Very Well"), Paul James (Warburg) ("Can't We be Friends?"), and Einar A. Swan ("When Your Lover Has Gone").

Although the songs derive from a wide range of sources, Sinatra and Riddle utilize a specific set of tools to forge them into a unified statement. The quality of his voice and of the orchestrations is consistent from song to song—Riddle's strings are dark but not heavy.

The album is also identified by its famous cover painting, bearing the immediately iconic image of the singer with fedora hat and cigarette on a street corner in the middle of the night. It could be the cover of a Mickey Spillane paperback. As Dave Mann, the composer of the title song, described it, "It was a torch kind of a thing, with the lamp post and the slouch hat and him standing there looking disconsolate, like a loser." The cover also could have also passed for a poster for a film noir of the period, but there's little direct connection between the album and actual noir, in either a literary or a cinematic mode. Most of the music from Hollywood film noir is very European, Miklós Rósza and the like, and there's very little that sounds like Sinatra or Riddle. More importantly, noir narrative is usually a variation on a detective story: Philip Marlowe or Mike Hammer is looking up and down these mean streets to find a killer. It's an external search. Sinatra's *Wee Small Hours* and *Only the Lonely* songs find the hero gazing internally for the source of his troubles, deep into his own soul. There's mystery involved, but only in the form of self-reflection.

The songs all had certain key things in common—none could be described as cheerful or upbeat—and Sinatra now credited a new tool that would help to unify these numbers that came from such a wide array of sources into a cohesive package: a title song.

The title song for this album, "In the Wee Small Hours of the Morning," derives from Sinatra's relationship with pianist and composer Dave Mann. They had known each other since roughly 1939, when both were sidemen at the height of the big band era. Mann described the young Sinatra as lovable but arrogant, but he also said that even at that early stage Sinatra was "marvelous! There was nobody around that could sing like that. He was head and shoulders above the others."

Around 1943, when Sinatra was making his initial breakthrough, he launched a music-publishing venture in partnership with the former vaudevillian and industry veteran Ben Barton. "Benny had a music firm in the Brill Building," said Mann. "When you looked out the window you could see all of Times Square and everything. One day, I saw Frank, right after he had just had his first hit. He stood in front of that window and he looked right into the panorama of Times Square and said, 'It's mine, all mine!' He was very ambitious."

During the war, Mann played piano on several Sinatra sessions. Then, in the late 1940s, he transitioned from musician to songwriter with such hits as "No Moon at All" and "There, I've Said It Again." In 1947, Sinatra recorded one of Mann's early songs, a catchy but forgettable novelty titled "I Went Down to Virginia."

In 1954, Mann was working with the very successful lyricist Bob Hilliard (responsible for such Sinatra favorites as "The Coffee Song" and "Ebb Tide"). Unlike many songwriting teams who wrote words and music separately, Mann preferred to work directly with his librettist, crafting both melody and text simultaneously—and they often found themselves working together in the middle of the night. "It was about three AM, and Bob said, 'I got a good title—'In the Wee Small Hours of the Morning.' I started fiddling around on the piano and the song wrote itself in fifteen minutes."

The following afternoon, the songwriters were heading to their publisher, which happened to be near the New York office of Capitol Records. As they were walking down Broadway and West Fifty-fourth Street, they saw a cab pull up, and Sinatra and Riddle emerged. Upon following them into the building, Mann got their attention, and "of course, Frank was glad to see us. We told him we had a song and played it for him. He loved it instantly. He said, 'Fellas, that's my kind of song. We'll do it.'"

Sometime earlier, Sinatra had taped "Last Night When We Were Young," which suggests that he was already thinking about a new album of ballads. When he heard "In the Wee Small Hours," the pieces gradually fell into place, and he was ready to record the remaining fifteen titles in February and March 1955.

The song and the album begin with pianist Bill Miller tinkling the first few notes of Mann's melody so lightly that he almost seems to be blowing on the keyboard rather than actually touching it with his fingers. Every time I hear this famous introduction (as iconic in its own way as the cover painting) I assume that he must be playing a celeste. (The celeste makes its appearance soon enough, on track three, "Glad to Be Unhappy.") Although the album is entirely slow numbers, this is, in fact, one of the great jazz sets of Sinatra's canon—no less, for instance, than his team-ups with Count Basie. *Wee Small Hours* is hardly a swing album, yet it's jazzy as all hell. Don't confuse tempo with texture: *Wee Small* may be a slow album, but it's one of the classic collections of jazz vocals, a bluesy and intensely felt extended performance that, overall, represents the closest Sinatra came to emulating one of his original inspirations, Billie Holiday. As in Holiday's best work, the singer continually personalizes and reshapes the original melodies to increase their immediacy, to make the words sound even more as if they're occurring to him spontaneously. The jazz values of *Wee Small* are underscored by the presence of the exceptional trumpeter Harry "Sweets" Edison, and of four cuts on which the singer is accompanied only by a rhythm section—quite a unique occurrence on a Sinatra record.

Sinatra's favorite jazz-derived device, throughout much of his career and on *Wee Small* in particular, is a way of bending notes that involves a downward swoop. On the final notes of the title cut, for instance, on the words "of all," Sinatra throws in a grace note, swooping down from E-flat to G-flat, and very lightly touching on that G-flat before heading back up to B (as written). He employs a similar kind of ornamentation, though considerably more aggressively, on the second line of "What Is This Thing Called Love?" On the words, "this funny thing *called love*," Sinatra is supposed to simply go up from B to C, but instead he starts at E-flat (not just touching on it but lingering there), then very dramatically swings a full octave up to the next-higher E-flat before dropping down to the C.

The emphasized notes serve an even stronger programmatic purpose on Arlen and Harburg's semi-operatic "Last Night When We Were Young." Originally this was big baritone stuff, but Sinatra cuts it down to size, making it credibly intimate. When he stretches and bends the note on "*Ages ago* last night," he makes it sound most aged indeed. Those three syllables, "*Ages a-*go," are written to be sung as a triplet, but Sinatra makes the line work for him by placing a very heavy stress on the first note and understating the following two beats, thereby blurring the distinction between speech and song. He makes the word sound incredibly *aged* and world-weary. In the process, he drops down an octave, from G-flat to the next-lower G-flat, which projects the sense of an emotional drop, and then goes back up to B. He stretches the word "love" in much the same fashion on the line "*Love* was a star / A song unsung." Songwriter Sammy Cahn compared Sinatra's voice in this period to a cello (as opposed to his lighter, more violin-like vocal sound in the 1940s), and these extended notes here recall nothing so much as an arco cello.

One sure indicator of Sinatra's artistic intentions is the inclusion of a full three songs by the poet laureate of romantic dysfunction, Lorenz Hart: "Glad to Be Unhappy," "Dancing on the Ceiling," and "It Never Entered My Mind." (The latter is a superior remake of a number he'd recorded in 1947.) Surely, no singer has ever nailed a Hart lyric so exactly, capturing perfectly the poet's "funny valentine" vision of romance: even when love is good, it's never perfect, and, as Tolstoy tells us, often it's those very imperfections that make it even more special.

Based on recorded evidence, the songs of Rodgers and Hart were mostly introduced by period-style tenors who were still the fashion for musical comedy leading men in the 1920s and into the 1930s, even at a time when Bing Crosby was popularizing a more intimate, romantic baritone style. We tend to think of male singers in the period as dentist-drill tenors and overwrought belters, yet the way Sinatra sings Hart's lyrics, with a perfect match of music to credible emotion, is so overwhelmingly on-target that one imagines this must be the way Hart heard his own words being sung in his head.

It's quite possible that Richard Rodgers himself cringed when he heard the liberties Sinatra took with his old songs—although it's unlikely he took the time to listen—but even he couldn't deny that Sinatra makes these classic songs communicate on an extremely high level. Take "Dancing on the Ceiling" (first heard in the 1930 West End show *Ever Green*): Sinatra employs all kinds of slurs and swoops to transform the song from a rather fanciful air about an inverted terpsichoran (à la Fred Astaire in *Royal Wedding*) into a torch song, both whimsical and tragic. He descends tellingly on the line "has brought *my lover* to me" in the verse, but that's only the beginning. A few bars later he comes to the words "never *sleep* in bed," and while these were originally written to be sung on one note, Sinatra begins the phrase a whole tone higher than written, and from there launches a massive slur downward. Instead of hitting F, he goes from G to F to E, hitting all the microtonal points in between. This is an extremely erotic moment. What both he and Hart leave out is what paints the most vivid picture. On the face of it, the hero is merely telling us what he isn't doing in bed, i.e., sleeping. It's up to us to imagine what he *is* doing in it.

Sinatra's most significant alterations to the central refrain of "Dancing on the Ceiling" involve adding words. He inserts the word "all" at the start on the fourth line, making it "*all* through the night," and uses this "all" to start another slur,

in which he sings the word "through" a half step higher than written. Hart's lyrics are so perfect that they hardly require anyone to improve them, but Sinatra adds minor modifications that make them work even better for his purposes. "There's my love / Up *there* above" and "I'm so grateful to discover / *That* she's still there." As with everything Sinatra does, these extra words make the lyric seem more conversational and, ultimately, more believable. Then there's the line "I love my ceiling more / Since it is a dancing floor." The phrase "dancing floor"—as opposed to the more familiar "dance floor"—always struck me as odd; was that an actual expression, possibly from England circa 1930, or did Hart just need to fill one extra beat? Yet it seems incredibly down-to-earth when Sinatra sings it.

About the only Hart line that Sinatra can't do anything for comes in the last eight bars of "Glad to Be Unhappy," when he comes to the words "Like a *straying* baby lamb / With no mammy and no pappy." It's a rare example of Hart coming up with a phrase that would make sense if read to oneself but is very difficult for a singer to put over. For sixty years, listeners have found it tough to make out exactly what Sinatra is singing here—some hear "Like a *strange* baby lamb," others, "Like a *string of* baby lambs." Still, even when he *strays,* Sinatra couldn't pick a better word to do it on.

"Glad to Be Unhappy" begins with the end of love. While another songwriter might have expressed a downtrodden mood with grandly epic imagery, Hart refuses to act all tragic about it— no drama queen, he. He undercuts what could be a potentially melodramatic narrative with slangy euphemisms: "toothpaste grin," "sadly mumble," "mammy" and "pappy." Sinatra's brilliance is that he takes that jargon and makes a powerful statement about love and loss with it, as if the speaker is trying to downplay his own tragedy—his way of dealing with it is to trivialize it, as if it were a series of Madison Avenue slogans. Hart's strength as a lyricist—more than anyone else's (with the exception of Cole Porter)—is about the pull between happy and sad, between laughing and crying. Surely no other artist could animate both halves of this equation as purposefully as Sinatra, whose happys are mountaintops of elation and whose sads are great yawning caverns of despair.

Sinatra told stories in song, but what he does on *Wee Small Hours* is more akin to painting a picture: a series of scenes, of vignettes, random moments in a series of broken love affairs. The cover image perfectly sets the after-hours mood—virtually the whole album transpires "while the whole wide world is fast asleep." "Deep in a Dream" hardly describes a daydream, and the feeling known as "Mood Indigo" sets in, naturally, "in the evening / when the lights are low." "Deep in a Dream," "Dancing on the Ceiling," and "I See Your Face Before Me" are driven by the idea of a departed loved one invading the nocturnal unconsciousness. On "Face," that image "crowds" the hero's "every dream"; lyricist Howard Dietz uses "crowd" as a verb to imply that this subconscious intrusion is far from welcome. The speaker doesn't want to see the faces of his departed beloved, even in his sleep, yet she comes anyway, like it or not.

On "It Never Entered My Mind," even though the protagonist may "awaken with the sun," the story is less concerned with what happened the morning after than the night before—"Last Night When We Were Young." Some of these songs are so bleak that they make Sinatra's so-described "saloon songs" seem cheerful by comparison: in "One for My Baby" (on *Only the Lonely*), for instance, Sinatra is in a gin joint, spilling his troubles to a barkeep; in "It Never Entered My Mind," it seems like he can't even summon the strength to get out of bed. "I sit alone and sadly mumble," he tells us. Virtually every song on the album explicitly transpires at night, except "What Is This Thing Called Love?"—and that, perhaps ironically, is the only song originally written in a minor key.

There's nothing on the entire album that could conceivably transpire in the sunlight. "This Love of Mine" makes reference to the day but only as it exists to provide contrast for the night. "It's lonesome through the day," the lyric tells us, but what goes on after dark is so bad that it makes "lonesome" look good by comparison. What happens at night is apparently so disturbing that Sinatra (as both lyricist and singer) won't even tell us what it is—the most he can do is avoid the issue by saying,

"But oh, the night." It's a great example of communicating by not being specific—he merely lights the spark in our imaginations.

As we've seen, Sinatra recorded four of the songs with just a rhythm section, featuring guitar (George Van Eps), bass (Phil Stephens), and drums (Al Stoller), plus two keyboards: Sinatra's regular pianist, Bill Miller, plus Paul Smith on celeste. (Since the piano and celeste are rarely heard at the same time, the group could be regarded as a quartet, even though they're manned by two separate musicians.) The absence of horns and strings on these titles gives the overall album both extra variety and increased intimacy. Sinatra had been experimenting with this format and these same musicians in a radio series of the early Capitol era called *To Be Perfectly Frank* (a selection of these tracks was finally released legitimately in the 2015 package *Frank Sinatra: A Voice on Air (1935–1955)*. Between the tracks with strings and those with the rhythm section alone, Sinatra achieves a perfect balance of consistency and diversity—the songs all feel like they're of a piece, yet never redundant or repetitive.

There's one other underlying message here: love is something that can devastate you, wipe you out, reduce you to ruins, but, ultimately, it is a cyclical occurrence. It's happened before and it will happen again. "Where or When" might have made a good choice for this album, but overall it's too hopeful—not nearly melancholy enough. A similar feeling of déjà vu—but much more suitably bleak—occurs in "I'll Be Around," by Sinatra associate Alec Wilder. The circular ideal resounds in the title, which puns on "around" (meaning nearby) and "round" (as in circular) and the notion is transmitted even before Sinatra enters with the lyric. Using celeste and guitar, Nelson Riddle devised a brilliant intro, a circular pattern that like Wilder's melody is based on the cycle of fifths.

When Sinatra sings "Goodbye again" at the start of the bridge, it's a clear indication that this breakup scenario has transpired before, probably more than once. When he reprises the bridge, he pronounces the words "Goodbye *again*," and then leaves for the rest of the line, leaving Paul Smith and George Van Eps to "sing" the remaining syllables nonverbally on their instruments. Clearly, the most important word in that line is "again." Then, when Sinatra returns at the end of the bridge, he sings "now and then" very fully and musically, with a comparatively big, open sound, but then contrasts this by ritarding out of tempo with "Drop a line" and even more so with "to say you're feeling fine," in a very small, humble voice.

"What Is This Thing Called Love?" likewise uses a circular-style countermelody, played by clarinetist Mahlon Clark, as do "I See Your Face Before Me" with a much-repeated triplet articulated by the flutes (particularly behind the oboe solo) and the oriental wind chime figure on "I'll Never Be the Same." Love is a story with a beginning, middle, and end, but it's also a cycle that repeats itself *senza fine*—without conclusion. The conflict between those two ideas finds its greatest expression in the final song.

In the Wee Small Hours might be described as a set of fourteen classic show and film standards (another pop music concept pioneered by Sinatra) that begins and ends with two very different kinds of songs which are both extremely personal statements. It's not much of a stretch to assume that the title song held deep personal relevance for him: it was a roadmap of his inner turmoil, particularly of his tumult of the early 1950s. Sinatra could do other types of story as well, but when he was being directly autobiographical, the results were devastating.

If the opener was deeply personal, the closer was perhaps even more so; "This Love of Mine" is the rare song that Sinatra actually wrote, at least partially, back in 1941. The inspiration for it came, surprisingly, from Ernest Hemingway. Around 1940, there was a rumor being bruited about that Hemingway's *For Whom the Bell Tolls* was going to be made into a film (eventually released in 1943). At that time, one Sol Peskin was employed as a song plugger for a music publisher who dreamed of being a successful songwriter. After changing his last name to "Parker," he started work on a song titled "For Whom the Bell Tolls," thinking that the name would help the song get published or possibly even noticed by a Hollywood studio. "I wrote

a forty-eight-bar melody with lyrics, of which all I can remember is, 'I know it's you / For whom the bell tolls,'" Parker once told me. "I played it for Hank Sanicola and we went up to the Paramount Theatre. Within minutes, Frank was listening to me sing this song. He's rubbing his chin with his two skinny little fingers, and he immediately said, 'Let's make it more commercial.'

"We knew exactly what [Frank] meant, and it showed his intelligence with respect to music. I had written a forty-eight-bar song, whereas the average song is only thirty-two bars. So Hank and Frank condensed the music and, two days later, Hank came to me with sixteen bars of lyrics and he said, 'This is what we got so far, Solly.' I looked at the opening line, 'This love of mine . . .' I said, 'This looks like a good title. I'll wind up the song with 'this love of mine' and that'll be it.' Basically, half the music was mine and half the lyric was mine, so I assume that Frank and Hank together wrote the other half."

One of the great strengths of "This Love of Mine" is the way it compresses a long melody into a short space. The song's format is ABAB' (B prime), and the primary eight-bar section (A) sounds like it could be a song all by itself. Its melody seems to be continually changing, with very little repetition. The B section (or bridge) contrasts this by starting with a four-bar strain and then repeating it but ending on a higher note the second time around ("But oh, the *night*"). Sinatra, working as both coauthor and performer, incorporates a trombonelike portamento slide on the key word "shine," leading to the final line. The melody continually rises and falls, and it's a particularly adroit piece of work to come from three newcomers to the songwriting biz.

Although "This Love of Mine" was one of Sinatra's most successful numbers from the Tommy Dorsey period, the song remained more or less unique to him. He revived it in 1953 for *To Be Perfectly Frank* and also sang it live in a semi-spontaneous reunion with Dorsey on February 2, 1955; two weeks later, on February 17, he recorded it at the Capitol studio in Hollywood for *In the Wee Small Hours*.

Other singers recorded "In the Wee Small Hours" (both Johnny Hartman and Tony Bennett added the verse), but the song became totally identified with Sinatra. Thus the format of the album is, metaphorically, a sandwich: the meat inside consists of classic songs by Harold Arlen, Cole Porter, Rodgers and Hart, Duke Ellington, etc., but the "bread" on the outside—the beginning and ending—are two songs unique to Sinatra, one that he was introducing and the other that he had cowritten and was already closely associated with.

There's also a direct trajectory that connects the two. For all of the noir melancholia the song suggests, the eight simple lines of "In the Wee Small Hours" are actually quite restrained—you don't get hysterical or drink yourself to death, the worst that you do is "lie awake and think about the girl." Fifteen songs later, Sinatra has gradually modulated to a more emotionally intense state: on "This Love of Mine," written in the first person ("this love of *mine*") rather than the more detached second ("*you* lie awake"), the protagonist cries his heart out and then lets it break, and even takes his case to the cosmos, calling on "the sun and the moon / The stars that shine" for guidance. (Their reaction, if any, is not recorded.) It's clear that by now he's doing more than just thinking about the girl; the mood has progressed from the most intimately internal to the most cosmically extroverted and external.

Sinatra tellingly ends both the album and the last song with a question: "What's to become of it / This love of mine?" And to make things more ambiguous, he reprises part of the opening line at the very end—the part about love going on and on—and he further underscores that message with a few notes of celeste. The album is ending exactly where it began, even as love itself goes on and on. Sinatra is finishing not with a period but with a set of ellipses.

In the Wee Small Hours represents a singular achievement. Sinatra's classic albums are often categorized by tempo, with the fast "swing" albums on one side of the dividing line and the slow "ballad" albums falling on the other. This division makes

sense, but as mentioned above, *Wee Small Hours* is the one case where one of his comparatively slow-tempo projects is also inarguably a jazz album. Its influence on contemporary jazz musicians is amazingly widespread: In 1994, pianist Keith Jarrett recorded "In the Wee Small Hours" on his classic 1994 live *At the Blue Note* set, in a stunning interpretation that was clearly taking its cues from Sinatra. A dozen years after that, the contemporary jazz singer Kurt Elling took Jarrett's improvisation on the song, wrote lyrics to it, and combined that version with the original Mann-Hilliard words and music. The result, heard on his album *Night Moves*, was a brilliant contemplation of the larger meaning of the idea of confronting the void during the wee small hours of the morning.

Sinatra still had many great ballad albums ahead of him, particularly *Close to You* (1957), *Where Are You?* (1957), *Frank Sinatra Sings for Only the Lonely* (1958), and *No One Cares* (1959)—the latter three, especially, are perfect examples of song collections that are so dark, so hopeless in their outlook that, as Frank Sinatra Jr. famously said, "They should be sold by prescription only." But none of them has the amazing blend of jazz and balladry, romance and even humor, that's pervasive in *In the Wee Small Hours*.

Having shown that he could make torch songs more believable by incorporating elements of jazz, the very next step in Sinatra's musical evolution was to approach the same idea from the opposite perspective. Instead of making a ballad jazzier, he would take a swing number and make it more romantic. Or, more accurately, he would start with a number that had begun life as a straightforward love song—say, Cole Porter's "I've Got You Under My Skin"—and then he would make a swing number out of it, put it to a beat. He had the idea that a song could be both things at once, jazzy and romantic. No one had ever done anything like that before, but he and Riddle were game to try. And if he could pull it off even once, would he have the audacity to try and sustain it for an entire album?

He would call it *Songs for Swingin' Lovers!*

38

Frank Sinatra

Songs for Swingin' Lovers!

(1956)

The received wisdom regarding Frank Sinatra's comeback is that it began with the release of *From Here to Eternity*. This was, the argument goes, his first hit movie in a long time, and also launched his career as a "serious" dramatic actor. But symbolically, his portrayal of James Jones's "Maggio" more accurately represents the end of the first phase of his career. As Mitch Miller, who, to the distaste of both men, was in the middle of Sinatra's life at the time, observed, Sinatra's comeback couldn't properly begin until his old life was completely dead, and, as Miller put it, "by getting stomped to death in that movie"—referring to Maggio's famous Oscar-winning death scene—"he did like a penance, you know?"

Eternity was released in August 1953, and it might be said that he was born again four months later with the recording of "Young at Heart." It's no coincidence that Sinatra begins this new phase with a song about new beginnings and fresh starts, and likewise it's no coincidence, either, that he began what might have been his most important album, *Songs for Swingin' Lovers!*, with "You Make Me Feel So Young," a similarly themed song about rebirth and renewal.

In the Wee Small Hours, his immediately previous album, is widely viewed from an autobiographical perspective; he was obviously channeling his own inner turmoil from the period when his tumultuous relationship with Ava Gardner was

driving him to desperation and worse. There was a lot more to it, obviously, but by being able put those emotions into his art, Sinatra was able to achieve a kind of closure. I'm referring to an artistic and a spiritual closure; in reality, Gardner would always be his one great love, and they would never be completely out of each other's lives until her death in 1990. (It's probably safe to say that, in the Sinatra saga, she was the only woman he ever really carried a torch for or, as he might have put it, went out and got drunk over.)

So, in musical terms, he was saying goodbye both to her and to that whole infamous down period of his life, with *In the Wee Small Hours*. As we've seen, it ends with a song that asks a question without answering it— "What's to become of it, this love of mine?" He begins the next phase and the next album with a genuine answer, and that is to start all over again: if life or love has knocked you flat on your . . . back, well, you pick yourself up and dust yourself off. You go back to the beginning: you somehow make yourself feel so young.

Soon enough, hopefully, you'll start to feel like there are bells to be rung, and, more importantly, songs to be sung.

"You Make Me Feel So Young" has Sinatra stating the album's intentions—it's like Babe Ruth pointing to the side of the stadium where he intends to send the ball. "You Make Me Feel So Young" in particular shows how Sinatra's singing varies between poles of seriousness. At various points in the lyric, he reads each line like a Method actor, as if it were an absolute reality, at other times he just plain trashes the words and has fun with them, playing with them as if they were rhythmic place holders and melodic baubles, bouncing them, as the lyric states "like a toy balloon." Throughout the swing albums of the mid-1950s on, he frequently alternates between the two modes—sometimes even just within a few notes of each other—and especially more so in later concert performances of this song. By the 1970s, this song became an even more exaggerated anthem of playfulness. In the 1970 Royal Festival Hall concert from London, for instance, he surprises us by momentarily delving into silly voices: in the second chorus, he sings "the moment that you *shpeak*," mimicking a little boy with a lisp, and, a few lines later, he affectionately ribs his English audiences by affecting a British accent, "joshing"—instead of "running"—"about the meadows." There's a concert from the Sands in Las Vegas, 1961, where he detours into a Chico Marx–style mock-Italian accent, "You make-a me feel-a so young!" It's just plain childish—and that's precisely the point. Sinatra is getting in touch with his juvenile side.

The significance of *Songs for Swingin' Lovers!* wasn't necessarily that it was a jazz album: in fact, as we've seen, *In the Wee Small Hours* was as much a pure jazz album as anything Sinatra would ever do, and then too he had always sung up-tempo numbers more than occasionally (particularly on his weekly radio shows). Still, it was the ballads that had made him famous.

To understand why *Swingin' Lovers* was so amazingly influential in its day and sixty years later is still revered as a milestone accomplishment, we have to start with the title. "Swingin' lovers" was not just a catchy turn of phrase. Sinatra meant it literally. As a concept, it would signify a major breakthrough in the evolving art of interpreting the American Songbook. Up until this point, in Sinatra's music and pop music in general, "swingin'" and "lovers" were two separate concepts. Jazz meant up-tempo, riff numbers, which, when they had words at all, tended to celebrate nonsense—

things like "A-Tisket, A-Tasket," "Sing, Sing, Sing," or "Hit That Jive, Jack!" Many of these were direct descendants of Gershwin's archetypical rhythm song, "I Got Rhythm," which supplied a template (both harmonically and philosophically) for hundreds of so-named "rhythm songs" throughout the swing era.

There already were (in the parlance of a later generation) "jazz standards" by the 1930s. For the most part, these were traditional numbers from the early days in New Orleans ("Tiger Rag," and suchlike), but occasionally they were certain popular songs that were favored by improvising jazzmen. "I Can't Give You Anything but Love" was originally rendered in something close to ballad time (granted that nearly all pop music and jazz was in fox-trot time or faster in the Jazz Age), but it quickly became a custom to jazz it up, especially after Louis Armstrong made his famous recording of the song in 1929. A disproportionate number of the songs recorded by Armstrong had a huge jazz afterlife, but generally they were transformed from ballads to swingers with their romantic elements neutered—in a sense, a love song became a rhythm song.

With *Swingin' Lovers,* Sinatra announced that it was possible to do both. His innovation, both in his own singing and in the arrangements that he worked out with orchestrator and key collaborator Nelson Riddle, was to treat a song rhythmically—to swing it—but in such a way that the lyrics retained their romantic resonance. By combining the two, Sinatra brought the formerly separate pursuits of "swingin'" and "lovin'" to new heights together. By adding a beat to a great love song, he proved that it could be both erotic and rhythmic, that the two didn't negate but rather enhanced each other. The beat made the lyrics more passionate, and the romance made the beat more compelling—he showed that the heart is an instrument of rhythm as much as emotion. He proved that the human heart could beat in solid four swing time.

As with *Wee Small Hours,* Sinatra makes a key statement with his choice of opening and closing songs (although here he also uses the first number of Side B as the album's emotional-musical climax). Those bookends, the first track ("You Make Me Feel So Young"), the last track ("How About

You?") and the entr'acte ("I've Got You Under My Skin"), are not, unlike on *Wee Small Hours,* new songs, but they come from the same twenty-five-or-so-year span of pop songs that Sinatra culled from for the rest of the album, ranging from the 1923 "Swingin' Down the Lane" to the 1947 "Old Devil Moon." One thinks of the songs from the 1920s ("You Brought a New Kind of Love to Me," "Makin' Whoopee," and "Swingin' Down the Lane") as songs that Sinatra heard when he was a little kid in his father's saloon. Most of the remaining songs are from the 1930s, when he was starting to think of himself as a professional singer and beginning to keep track of what distinguished a great song from all the others.

More recently, a pair of contemporary Canadian songwriters, Don and Jeff Breithaupt, had the very creative notion to pose the question: What if *Songs for Swingin' Lovers!* actually did have an original title song, like *Wee Small Hours* or *Come Fly with Me*? They came up with a perfectly engaging tune that begins, "Play one of those songs for swingin' lovers. / The key to romancin' is in the dancin' . . ." and set it in the same heartbeat tempo of the classic Sinatra-Riddle albums. But even though no such title song is to be found on the actual album, *Songs for Swingin' Lovers!* holds together brilliantly. This is the project where Riddle fully perfected his trademark introductions: after a few spins, even a casual listener can tell what tune is coming next just by the intros, none of which use the actual melody of the song in question. (In 1993, a pair of modern jazzmen, trumpeter Tom Harrell and baritone saxist Per Goldschmidt, recorded a bebop tribute to Sinatra entitled *Frankly.* They commence their version of "You Make Me Feel So Young" with a bop rearrangement of Riddle's original intro.)

Whereas Sinatra would outline the general content of the arrangement to Riddle—the tempo, the structure, the general feeling—the intros were one of Riddle's key areas of creativity, an area where Sinatra rarely, if ever, told him what to do. It seems clear sixty years on that Sinatra and Riddle intended these brief but memorable compositions-in-miniature to serve not merely as introductions to individual songs but something more like connected passages that help link fifteen separate

tracks to each other and unify them into a kind of extended work. Conceptually, it's but a mere half step from the 1956 *Swingin' Lovers* to the completely continuous *Miles Ahead* a year or so later.

In 1954, Sinatra and Riddle had recorded a jazz-styled album titled *Swing Easy!,* which employed a more traditional dance band instrumentation—brass, reeds, and rhythm—sans strings. That seems to have been the original idea: in June 1955 they went into the KHJ Studio in Hollywood (the more famous Capitol Tower studio wouldn't be operational until February 1956) and laid down one track, "I Thought About You." This too just used the standard swing band format, and was significantly different from the version later issued. Clearly, Sinatra wasn't satisfied. In October, they recorded "Love Is Here to Stay," now also using the full string section, and this time it worked. They recorded fifteen more tracks for the album in January 1956 (on the 10th, 12th, and 16th).

Riddle later wrote, "In planning *Songs for Swingin' Lovers,* Frank commented on 'sustained strings' as part of the background to be used. Perhaps unconsciously, my ear recalled some of the fine arrangements Sy Oliver had done for Tommy Dorsey, using sustained strings, but also employing rhythmic fills by brass and saxes to generate excitement. The strings, by observing crescendos in the right places, add to the pace and tension of such writing without getting in the way. It was a further embroidery on this basic idea to add the bass trombone [George Roberts] plus the unmistakably insinuating fills of Harry Sweets Edison on Harmon-muted trumpet." Those sustaining strings are all over *Swingin' Lovers.* They're particularly effective throughout "How About You?" and behind the celeste part on "Pennies from Heaven." On "I've Got You Under My Skin," the strings provide a background for half of each eight-bar portion, coming in, for instance, at the midway point of each of the first two A sections.

In *Swingin' Lovers,* Riddle integrates strings into the jazz-pop ensemble more successfully than any other orchestrator, from Ellington and Strayhorn to Gil Evans, would ever do. The strings are an absolutely essential component of his sound; it wouldn't be Riddle without them. They provide the crucial cornerstone of his harmonic foundation. Gordon Jenkins claimed (probably correctly) to be the first arranger to back vocalists with pure harmonic backgrounds, leaving the melody out of the accompaniment and giving it all to the star singer. Riddle's own approach, however, was to do something even more unique with the harmony. He all but removed it from the background, except in the strings—the strings play the harmony while the arranger empowers the rest of the ensemble to focus on countermelodies, such as those heard in the introductions. The countermelodies were increasingly his focus; he was endlessly inventive in devising all manner of riffs, licks, and background patterns to set off and contrast the central tune. Instead of distracting from the foreground activity, these melodic tchotchkes help center our attention on it. (Even on a ballad, like "I See Your Face Before Me" on *Wee Small Hours*, the chart is all secondary melodies and precious little harmony.) The strings are absolutely the core element of "Anything Goes," for instance, holding it together both melodically and harmonically. This frees the horns in particular from any "serious" musical responsibility; now they're free to offer wry commentary on the lyrics. Following the colossal inspiration of Duke Ellington, Riddle has his key musicians (in particular trombonists Milt Bernhart and George Roberts, woodwinds Harry Klee and Skeets Herfurt, and trumpeter Sweets Edison) engage in what amounts to an ongoing dialogue with Sinatra. The interplay's the thing.

As we've seen, that dialogue begins with "You Make Me Feel So Young" by Mack Gordon and Josef Myrow, written for the 1946 film *Three Little Girls in Blue*; like many Sinatra signatures, it's a song that was largely ignored prior to him (the one notable pre-Sinatra recording is by ex–Benny Goodman vocalist Martha Tilton on Capitol). In addition to everything else, the opening track also illustrates Sinatra's often surprising use of dynamics. In fact, throughout both *Wee Small Hours* and *Swingin' Lovers* the dynamics are amazingly consistent, both from song to song and even between the two albums. Comparing them to each other, the surprising conclusion is that he's only slightly

louder on the swingers than he is on the ballads. In both cases, he knows enough to let the orchestra do much of the work—the snappy-peppy brass intro that begins "You Make Me Feel So Young" and the euphoric trombone melee in the center of "I've Got You Under My Skin." Unlike his disciple Tony Bennett, Sinatra rarely sings louder or softer, especially in this period—he achieves the same effect by extending a note rather than belting it—"a wonderful fling to be *flunnnnnng . . .*" Later on, by his concert period, he tended to make greater use of louds and softs (partly because he has much more control of every little circumstance in a recording studio than he could ever have in a stadium), and he tends to belt more often, but here he varies the volume only with microscopic increments.

In many ways, the second track is one of the most radical on the album. "It Happened in Monterey" (Billy Rose, Mabel Wayne, from the 1930 film *King of Jazz*) is one of the two most famous songs by Mabel Wayne, the other being "Ramona," and both are waltzes with a quasi-Latin flavor. Sinatra had done something like this with his 1953 single of "South of the Border," also a sentimental old ersatz-Mexican number, but with "Monterey" he took the idea one step further in that he de-waltzed the song from 3/4 to 4/4 swing. Even more than on "South of the Border," on "Monterey" you can tell he's doing more than just swinging a song that was never intended to be swung—there's much more of a note of regret, as if his indiscreet heart really does long for the sweetheart that he left in old Monterey. In both songs, Sinatra's reputation as a ladies' man serves him well, it's not too hard to be believe that he's left sweethearts pining for him all over the map.

"You're Getting to Be a Habit with Me" (Al Dubin, Harry Warren from the 1932 film *42nd Street*) starts with a truly distinctive introduction, and makes heavy use of celeste, played by Sinatra accompanist Bill Miller. In fact, illustrating Sinatra and Riddle's desire to swing lightly, the celeste is prominent all over the album, but especially here. Sinatra had all but introduced this diminutive keyboard to mainstream pop with Tommy Dorsey on the 1940 "I'll Never Smile Again," and it remained one of his signature sounds throughout the 1940s and early 1950s. Miller plays both keyboards at different points, soloing on it on "You're Getting to Be a Habit with Me" (where it's considerably lighter than Ruby Keeler's tap dancing to the song in *42nd Street*), "How About You," "Pennies from Heaven," and "Swingin' Down the Lane." In fact, it's only on the intro to "Love Is Here to Stay" that we get a distinct piano passage. With these two 1955 albums, Sinatra's interest in the celeste peaks, and it's never heard from again quite so extensively. (He uses it fleetingly on "Easy to Remember" on *Close to You*.) This was one of many elements of the Sinatra legacy that Mel Tormé, Nat Cole, and others were keen to pick up on, using a celeste to create a more intimate sound than a full pianoforte. "You're Getting to Be a Habit with Me" is a particularly successful example of a danceable number on a "swingin'" album that's rapturously romantic and intimate, and more than justifies the album title.

"You Brought a New Kind of Love to Me" (Irving Kahal, Pierre Norman, Sammy Fain, written for Maurice Chevalier in *The Big Pond* and also sung memorably by Bing Crosby and the Marx Brothers) was obviously a Sinatra favorite, he sang it several times on his 1940s radio shows (once memorably in a duet with Peggy Lee) and later reprised it on *Sinatra's Sinatra* (1963) in a very different Riddle arrangement. Riddle's intro sounds like a sly wink, especially with Harry "Sweets" Edison's muted trumpet making its presence known. Sinatra's phrasing on the central melodic line is exquisite, especially the way he finesses the high notes in "if the night-*IN*-gales / Could sing *LIKE* you . . ." The strings enter in the instrumental break and become a metaphoric dancing partner. Riddle, for once, uses the violins to carry the melody—and it sounds nothing short of rapturous when, at the start of the second eight, they jump an octave higher and then continue playing the tune.

"Too Marvelous for Words" (Johnny Mercer and Richard A. Whiting, from the 1937 movie musical *Ready, Willing and Able*) is all about the bass: first, it opens with George Roberts's bass trombone grunting, and then, in the instrumental break, there's something almost never heard on a pop record of the period—a string bass solo. It's

played by the virtuoso Joe Comfort, best known for his tenure with Nat King Cole's trio; like Edison, Comfort was a prominent example of an African American musician thriving in the recording studios at a time when segregation was still the law in most of the country. Riddle's framing of the solo was clearly informed by Duke Ellington ("Jack the Bear," "Koko"), and today contemporary bassists like Christian McBride use the song to pay homage to both Sinatra and Comfort. Sinatra and Riddle heighten tension and excitement at the end by delaying the resolution (in the last line), which Sinatra belts.

From the 1947 Broadway hit *Finian's Rainbow*, "Old Devil Moon" (E. Y. Harburg, Burton Lane) is the newest tune on the album, and one that Sinatra was slated to sing in a proposed animated feature film based on the show (the music was recorded but the movie never produced). The *Finian's* soundtrack recording of "Devil Moon" (from August 1954) includes a remarkable jazz interlude costarring Oscar Peterson and Red Norvo, and also features Broadway leading lady Ella Logan, but otherwise the Riddle orchestration that backs Sinatra is essentially the same as on *Swingin' Lovers*. Sinatra starts with the first section rubato, so that it sounds like a verse. There's no intro, barely a note before Sinatra starts in with the first line "*IIIII* . . . look at you and suddenly . . . ," languorously stretching the first word, and his hip phrasing is the polar opposite of most of the feet-on-the-ground two-beat we hear in Broadway shows. In "New Kind of Love," a wall of lovely strings enters in the break, here it's a devilish brass section, which dances around Edison's trumpet solo, allowing Sinatra to reenter with the appropriate words "razzle-dazzle." He comes close to cracking on the high note on "laugh *like* a loon" but makes it—in the twenty-first century, the producer would have called for another take or the engineer would have finessed it, but it makes the performance so much more vital to hear the note exactly as he sang it, with all the pure excitement that only Sinatra could create.

"Pennies from Heaven" (Arthur Johnston, Johnny Burke) was an obvious homage to Bing Crosby, a signature song that the legendary crooner introduced in the 1936 film of the same title—and one of dozens, if not hundreds, of songs that Sinatra learned from his childhood hero. This arrangement was later replaced by a more aggressive chart with Count Basie's orchestra, but the 1955 version has a surplus of charm; Riddle opens with a veritable hurricane of strings, as if to suggest an impending storm, before Sinatra enters with Johnny Burke's famous words of inspiration, celeste (taking a prominent solo), and one of his gentlest, subtlest vocals.

Speaking of subtlety, "Love Is Here to Stay" (often cited as the last song to be written by George Gershwin, with lyrics by Ira Gershwin, from *The Goldwyn Follies,* 1938) opens with a remarkably inviting passage by Bill Miller that turns out to be his fullest statement on piano (rather than celeste) on the album. (This piano intro is also a blueprint for the one that opens Riddle's iconic arrangement of "The Lady Is a Tramp" on *A Swingin' Affair!,* 1956). Miller's presence gives the whole vocal the feeling of Sinatra with a jazz trio (Miller, Comfort, and, on this track, Irv Cottler on drums) and an underpinning of strings and then brass. It's another example of Sinatra sticking to a low dynamic—never raising his voice at all—and letting the orchestra do all the work, thus conveying stability and, as the lyric suggests, steadfastness and permanence.

If Side A, track one, "You Make Me Feel So Young," establishes the album's intentions, it's the first song of Side B that signifies the album's high point, and the most beautifully realized result of those ambitions. Cole Porter wrote "I've Got You Under My Skin" as a rather torrid torch song, introduced by femme fatale Virginia Bruce in the 1936 Eleanor Powell vehicle *Born to Dance;* it was dark and dramatic, although the song always had a strong beat, a light bolero that made it a somewhat more conventionally structured sibling of "Begin the Beguine," Porter's Caribbean-inspired love song of the year before. The early vocal recordings, such as Lee Wiley's (with Victor Young's Orchestra, which Sinatra likely heard), and that of Britain's piano-vocal star "Hutch," are filled with gravitas but don't try to swing, and the dance band versions (like Hal Kemp or Shep Fields) supply a steady beat but there's nothing that would make your temperature rise. Sinatra's treatment, comparatively, is both more swinging and more romantic.

We know (from the testimony of musicians on the session, like bass trombonist George Roberts) that Nelson Riddle had been partly inspired by "23 Degrees North—82 Degrees West," an original composition by arranger-conductor Bill Russo for Stan Kenton's orchestra. Indeed he was, but there already was a vague trace of pan-Latin rhythm in the DNA of "Skin" that Riddle elaborated upon. In fact, the Sinatra-Riddle "Skin" begins almost like a 1930s dance band, with a fox-trot-y riff, although unlike most swing bands it's primarily voiced by a bass clarinet. Sinatra sings over that riff—there's no hint of Porter's melody in Riddle's arrangement—in a way that sounds like he's holding back, like enormous emotion is mounting within him but he's trying not to let it show.

Then, following the first chorus, it must have sounded, to pop music listeners in 1955, like all heck was breaking loose: the instrumental passage resembles Kenton at his most chaotic—first there's a gaggle of trombones that sound like warring rhinoceri, then trombonist Milt Bernhart plays a brief solo that does more shouting in eight bars than Sinatra does in the entire album. But, in a sense, Bernhart loses his cool so that Sinatra doesn't have to. Sinatra ends with a half chorus (sometimes called an "out chorus," in which he comes back at the bridge, "I would sacrifice anything . . .") that illustrates his approach to climaxes, especially with regard to dynamics: he reenters at the loudest point on the track and then gradually winds down for the ending—rather than going for a big, long, loud note at the end, as, say, Judy Garland (and Tony Bennett) might do.

After all that euphoria, we wake up to reality with "I Thought About You," an iconic song in which the central mystery is why lyricist Johnny Mercer and composer Jimmy Van Heusen didn't become an ongoing partnership once they had this classic under their belts. This seems to have been the first tune in the project that Sinatra and Riddle attempted; on June 30, 1955, they recorded a very different arrangement that so far has only been issued surreptitiously on an underground bootleg release *(From the Vaults, Vol. 1).* The June take features only a seventeen-piece big band—indicating that perhaps Sinatra was originally thinking of doing the *Swingin'* album without strings—and there's a trombone solo in a vaguely Tommy Dorsey manner. Apparently upon hearing the playback, Sinatra canceled the rest of the session, and six months later returned with the arrangement now decked out with a solid string background rather than brass and prominent flute (Harry Klee) instead of trombone. This quieter treatment is much more contemplative, and far better suited to conveying the act of thinking. With other singers, the song is about taking "a trip on a train," but when Sinatra sings it, the song is about thinking about someone, the state of being haunted by a lover (past or present) at the precise moment when one should be focusing on something as distracting as train travel.

"We'll Be Together Again" may be the album's most purely romantic moment (except perhaps for the deleted "Memories of You"), to the point where it's hard to believe that it was written by the titanium-tonsiled shouter Frankie Laine (and his accompanist, Carl Fischer). It's also the slowest and the longest track at four and a half minutes. The first chorus sounds like it could be a leftover from *Wee Small Hours*, but it gets brassier in the break, and the instrumental section is a moving mixture of strings and Harry Edison's trademark beeps—he makes his trumpet sound like blinking lights on a Christmas tree. In spite of Edison's always valuable contribution, the most significant instrumental presence is the lead alto saxophonist, Arthur Herfurt (known familiarly as "Skeets"), who had been working with Sinatra frequently since the Dorsey era. Herfurt plays a beautifully moving alto passage—reminiscent of both Johnny Hodges and Jimmy Dorsey—at both the beginning and the end. When Sinatra sang this on his 1958 TV series, he even spontaneously acknowledged the saxophonist by declaring "Yeah, Skeets!" at the coda. Overall, it's a perfect blend of Sweets and Skeets.

"Makin' Whoopee" (Gus Kahn, Walter Donaldson) was the title track from Eddie Cantor's most famous vehicle, both on Broadway (1928) and in Hollywood, *Whoopee!* (1930). This is more or less a Sinatra one-shot, he never sang it again, although its ironic view of love and commerce suits him superbly. Sinatra renders the lyrics with something close to Cantor's deadpan delivery, letting Gus Kahn's incriminating lyric more or less speak for itself. For the first chorus, his chief instrumental companion is clarinetist Mahlon Clark; for the second, Roberts offers more sardonic commentary on bass trombone.

That second chorus—not only here but also on "Too Marvelous for Words" and "Anything Goes"—also keys into a legitimate criticism of Sinatra. For all three of these songs, lyricists Kahn, Mercer, and Porter wrote a mess of extra choruses, enough for these numbers to be extended at great length in a supper club or on a Broadway stage. But rather than singing any of these second choruses, Sinatra just repeats the first set of lyrics. Although this repeat is jazzier than the original ("a mess of shoes, a gang of rice . . ."), I've always found that disappointing. In the second chorus of "Whoopee," he lays out entirely during the bridge, letting the orchestra take over for eight bars, before he returns with the last eight. Viewed from another perspective, this can be taken as an illustration of Sinatra clearly thinking of himself as a band singer, rather than a cabaret singer like Bobby Short or his beloved Mabel Mercer, who would beguile crowds with chorus after chorus.

Chicago-based lyricist Gus Kahn also wrote the words to "Swingin' Down the Lane" (which predates Duke Ellington's "It Don't Mean a Thing (If It Ain't Got That Swing)" by almost a decade as a pop song with "swing" in the title). The composer was one of the major dance band leaders of all time, Isham Jones, and the song is the earliest on the album (1923). Sinatra goes from a sardonic contemplation of love and marriage and the consequences of "makin' whoopee" back to an uncomplicated dance, with couples strolling "hand in hand / swingin' down the lane." Yet even here the song turns melancholy when the singer gradually reveals that he's not part of that procession of parading sweethearts (the song is a philosophical antecedent of Louis Armstrong's famous "Sweethearts on Parade"), but that he's merely "watching lovers making eyes like we used to do" rather than participating. Sinatra imbues this graceful dance with just enough of an undercurrent of regret. If Riddle's introduction sounds familiar, British listeners in particular probably know it as the riff behind Matt Monro's 1961 hit "My Kind of Girl"; arranger Johnnie Spence borrowed it from Riddle note-for-note without even changing the key.

"Anything Goes" opens with a unique intro featuring flute (Harry Klee) and harp (Katherine Julye), something that you truly would never expect to hear on an album with "Swingin'" in the title. This interpretation reminds us that for all of his verbal wit and passion, Cole Porter also liked to throw a party where people danced. The first chorus here, especially, brings out the whimsical and terpsichorean sides of Porter; on the second chorus, Sinatra himself gets heavier, louder, and more serious overall, even as the band gets brassier— Sinatra makes the second chorus sufficiently different from the first even though he sings the same set of lyrics. Quite possibly this is the track that Porter had in mind when he described Sinatra as "the only person singing today with some passion" (as quoted in William McBrien's biography, *Cole Porter*). Sinatra's vocal isn't merely a wry commentary on contemporary mores, as expressed in what's often treated as a purely frivolous bonbon of a song, but is full of passionate intensity.

After singing tongue-in-cheek about modern chaos and the breakdown of old-guard rules— e.g., how a glimpse of stocking, for instance, is no longer looked on as something shocking—Sinatra makes the most extraordinary move. In effect, he steps out of the song and addresses the audience directly, calling attention to the performance medium itself by adding an original coda. In what are possibly his own lyrics (or those of Sammy Cahn) he sings, "May I say before this record spins to a close / I want you to know . . . anything goes!" He's been playing the hero of a musical love story for over three quarters of an hour—the equivalent of a leading man in a classic show—so he now steps forward in front of the curtain for a bow.

"Anything Goes" would have been a perfect way to conclude *Lovers*, but what Sinatra and Riddle actually ended with was better still. Where "Anything Goes" provides a conclusive statement, "How

About You?"—the album's equivalent of a postscript, winds up the disc on a note of ambiguity. (Sinatra had first recorded the song, by Ralph Freed and Burton Lane, from the 1941 *Babes on Broadway*, around the time it was new, with Tommy Dorsey's orchestra.) After telling us everything he knows about love for fifteen songs, Sinatra now concedes that this is hardly the last word on the subject. Now he wants to know what *we* think, indicating that it's impossible to come to a pat conclusion where love is concerned. When it comes to love, Sinatra is admitting, Sinatra has no more of a clue than the rest of us. For all the breeziness of the album, Sinatra has decided to wind up on a low note— literally—as he dives for a deep F in the coda (a pitch that puts him in the basso range).

Sinatra recorded sixteen songs for *Swingin' Lovers* (making it just as long and ambitious as *Wee Small Hours*), but here had to drop one song for length before the set's release. So far, that sixteenth cut, Eubie Blake and Andy Razaf's "Memories of You," is most easily found on *The Capitol Years*, a three-CD anthology issued by EMI around the time of Sinatra's seventy-fifth birthday. "Memories of You" includes one of the archetypical examples of mature Sinatra phrasing, when he puts the proper emphasis on the first note of the lines (in the out-chorus) "*Your* face beams / *in* my dreams" to help drive home the lyric. He makes it increasingly bigger and louder up to this point—as if he's finding an optimistic interpretation for what is generally regarded as a sad song—but then backs off in time for the final line. This is, after all, a song about a busted love affair. It's been suggested that the performance was too slow, but it's neither as slow nor as romantic as "We'll Be Together Again." It also would have made the album forty-eight minutes long, but even with that track, it's still shorter than the full-length *Wee Small Hours*, which is a few seconds shy of fifty minutes. It's my contention that "Memories of You" fits the album perfectly, and should be restored to a future digital edition of *Swingin' Lovers*.

Wee Small Hours and *Swingin' Lovers* represent a watershed moment in American music. The very least of their achievements was establishing beyond question the artistic validity of the pop album. Prior to 1955, Sinatra had only made one album a year, or less. But from this point onward to his temporary retirement in 1971, he would now customarily release two or three LPs annually. But more than being economic or technological milestones, *Wee Small Hours* and *Swingin' Lovers* represent a zenith in terms of showing the world exactly what pop music was capable of. Never before had technique, warmth, wit, and especially emotion, from the pinnacle of elation down to the nadir of despair, been distilled into such flawless packages. What *Citizen Kane* did for American cinema and *The Great Gatsby* did for American literature, *In the Wee Small Hours* and *Songs for Swingin' Lovers!* did for American vernacular music.

It's no coincidence that traditional American pop was now, after decades of being dismissed by deep thinkers, being gradually recognized as the Great American Songbook, and achieving a level of respectability. Perhaps it took the emergence of a new species of pop music to make people appreciate the more traditional kind. Nineteen fifty-five is generally regarded as the official start of the rock 'n' roll era: this was the first year that there were more rock-oriented singles than "traditional pop" records on the singles charts. The generations were already beginning to gap, the music favored by grown-ups was getting ever more sophisticated (in both jazz and in Broadway musicals), while that offered to kids was increasingly dumbed down (note the shift, for instance, in Elvis Presley's recordings of the late 1950s from authentic blues and country music to puerile kiddie songs). There could never be a true successor to Sinatra, in the sense that Sinatra might be said to be a successor to Crosby (and, perhaps, Jolson) simply because Sinatra would do everything that it was possible to do with the traditional songbook. He would take it as far as it could go, there was nothing left for anyone else. The next big noise and sea change in American pop would therefore have to be someone like Presley, who sang a completely different kind of music and who was, in many ways, as un-Sinatra-like as possible.

Yet Sinatra's influence even extended to some singers who had started more as Elvis types rather than fraternity types: Bobby Darin most famously. And Darin was only the best known of an entire generation of singers who based much of their careers on Sinatra's "swingin' lover" concept, such as Jack Jones and Steve Lawrence, and the album also had a profound influence on veteran artists such as Buddy Greco, Vic Damone, Mel Tormé, and Tony Bennett. *Songs for Swingin' Lovers!* can be said to have inspired an entire industry of dozens if not hundreds of albums by mostly male singers doing passionate love songs with a swinging dance beat. (The album was so iconic that it was also spoofed in the titles of such subsequent albums as *Songs for Chubby Lovers* by Broadway's Stubby Kaye, and Peter Sellers's *Songs for Swingin' Sellers,* the cover of which showed the British comic hanging from a tree.)

Many years later, in one of the few interviews he ever gave, Sinatra was asked to explain the success of *Songs for Swingin' Lovers!* and his work with Nelson Riddle in general. "Nelson had a fresh approach to orchestrations, it was a kind of a sophisticated sound, and I made myself fit in with what he was doing," Sinatra modestly said. (For his part, Riddle always insisted that he had very specifically tailored his work for Sinatra to the singer's own outlines, not the other way around.) The Chairman continued, "I wish I could explain it but I can't: it just happened. It came out that way, and it was a happy marriage of an idea that he had, orchestrally, which I made my vocal effort fit. And the ultimate result was apparently accepted by everybody, because people still play [those records], and they like them. For which, of course, I'm very pleased."

39

Jo Stafford

Jo Stafford Sings American Folk Songs (1948 and 1961) and
Jo Stafford Sings Songs of Scotland (1953 and 1956)

There's more than one kind of soul. The word was first widely employed—with reference to music at least—to describe the black popular music of the 1960s, a specific sound that combined R&B and gospel. But even so, Ray Charles and Aretha Franklin didn't have a monopoly on soul. Hank Williams and Patsy Cline had long since

demonstrated that they had a kind of soul that was all their own, even as Cole Porter and Billy Strayhorn crafted songs that were no less soulful in their own way. And, Jehovah knows, there's also a distinctly Jewish kind of soul, which is clearly audible in musicians as varied as Al Jolson and the klezmer clarinet king Naftule Brandwein. There's French soul (Edith Piaf), Italian soul (Dean Martin . . . yes, Dean Martin), Gypsy-Romany soul, and Russian soul (don't ask me for an example).

Jo Stafford was one of the strongest examples of the uniquely Anglo-American brand of soul; one completely immune to the influences of Africa,

Broadway, or Eastern Europe, yet meeting every conceivable definition of what soul is.

"Wayfaring Stranger," as sung by Stafford on her album *American Folk Songs*, is almost indescribably beautiful; Stafford taps into a vast wellspring of emotion, as deep as it is understated. The song, which is listed on the album as "Poor Wayfaring Stranger," is evocative even just in the title. Most of us today would think of the term "wayfarer" as an archaic word for traveler. It's the sort of expression one finds in old sea shanties, even though it technically refers to someone traveling on foot. It also sounds like the Old World more than the New, especially the British Isles, or at least a time when Young America was more deeply connected to Mother England.

The title "Wayfaring Stranger" is both somewhat cryptic and slightly redundant in a way that seems positively poetic when Stafford sings it; anyone is a stranger when he travels to a place he's never been to before, but Stafford's wayfaring stranger is making a trip more significant than from Brooklyn to Queens or Minneapolis to St. Paul—it's more like someone paying a call on St. Paul himself, on the other side of the River Jordan. The song uses the idea of traveling in the sense of transitioning from one world to the next—in other words, dying. Stafford makes it sound monumentally significant, a tale of Heaven and Earth, but at the same time warm and personal. The line "I'm going home to see my father" momentarily makes us wonder what she means by "home" in this context, but it's not the place where she grew up; rather, it's the place where she'll travel to meet her parents—in other words, to join them in the hereafter. Stafford's treatment is at once intimate and epic; she makes the song itself into a kind of a wayfaring stranger, helping it to travel across time, from the nineteenth century to the mid-twentieth and through her performance, making it relevant to all time.

Stafford's singing is opulent, but still understated, and, it turns out, perfectly suited to the simple yet profound music and lyrics; when she sings of the Shenandoah, the river seems amazingly wide and deep; when she tells us that black is the color of her true love's hair, there can be no doubt that his hair is black as black can be; when she tells us that her true love died today and that she will die tomorrow, we have no choice but to believe it. These songs are forthright and direct, compared to a contemporary show tune like "The Gentleman Is a Dope," which encompasses multiple levels of irony, and yet Stafford is equally convincing when singing either one. Her voice is as deep and rich as the Shenandoah itself, and her credibility is greater still.

In 1947, when Stafford recorded "Wayfaring Stranger," the song was well over a hundred years old. And yet, seventy years after 1947, this historic recording also anticipates the future, pointing to the folk revival of the 1950s and '60s and the subsequent folk-rock boom, which to a degree has been with us ever since. In a bit of irony that Stafford couldn't possibly have foreseen, it seems a sure bet that most listeners in 2017 will be more familiar with "Wayfaring Stranger" than with any of the contemporary songs that Stafford sang in 1947 that may have been number-one hits.

In a very direct way, Stafford is the immediate progenitor of such later folk divas as Joan Baez and Judy Collins; there's the same directness, the same purity of expression in their singing. In the contemporaneous words of Paul Weston, who arranged and conducted the project, "In being a singer and not just a song stylist, and because of family ties reaching back to Tennessee, Miss Stafford possesses the vocal equipment and the native 'feel' for the music which is so important to a proper interpretation."

In the immediate postwar era when Stafford recorded "Wayfaring Stranger" and the six other songs that comprise *American Folk Songs*, there was considerable baggage, both political and cultural, attached to folk and country songs. One faction apparently insisted that the kind of songs on this album, which were written by largely anonymous authors over the decades and centuries, were less complex, not only musically but dramatically, than the show tunes and other popular songs that dominated musical taste in Stafford's era. Whether or not that's actually true is irrelevant: Stafford could sing "Itsy Bitsy Spider" and make it every bit as emotionally significant and musically rich as "Begin the Beguine" or "Lush Life."

In the first half of the twentieth century, folk songs had occasionally been heard in mainstream music in two ways. They were increasingly included in the repertoire of what were then known as "concert singers," who were, essentially, opera singers performing outside opera; artists like Lawrence Tibbett, Nelson Eddy, and, most famously, Paul Robeson would perform Anglo-American folk songs and Negro spirituals together with Puccini arias and Schubert lieder.

Then, at the start of the big band era, there was a vogue for swing versions of traditional songs, starting with Maxine Sullivan's "Loch Lomond." At the same time, Ella Fitzgerald's "A-Tisket, a-Tasket" launched a parallel trend of swinging traditional nursery rhymes, which were often interchangeable with folk songs. As a young harmony singer, Jo Stafford recorded several swinging folk songs at around this time: "Would'st I Could Kiss Your Hand, Oh Babe" with the Stafford Sisters and "Polly Wolly Doodle" with the Pied Pipers.

In 1947, when she recorded the first tracks for *American Folk Songs,* pop music meant Broadway, Hollywood, and big bands. By 1961, when Capitol released the very different 12-inch version of *American Folk Songs,* the music industry was drastically changing, and the singles market especially was driven by sounds that were far from new but sufficiently different, with more of a foundation in rhythm and blues and country music. Among singers who had graduated from the swing bands of a decade earlier, a few were better equipped than others to weather the change: both Peggy Lee and Dinah Washington had a unique capacity for singing the blues, with the result that they were more likely to be boosted by the changes rather than marginalized by them. Jo Stafford, too, had a gift for singing the most sophisticated show tunes as well as the most essential and basic folk songs—in her music, "Shenandoah" is no less worthy of a place at the table than "Haunted Heart."

American Folk Songs originated with Stafford's then-surprising decision to sing a traditional folk song on her radio show. At that time, pop singers sang nothing but the latest pop songs on the air—even to go back to less-than-current popular songs, the Gershwins or Rodgers and Hart (as Frank Sinatra was then doing) was relatively rare. Just to test the waters, it was on one 1947 episode of *The Chesterfield Supper Club* that Stafford and Weston experimented with "He's Gone Away," a nineteenth-century air that is variously described as having originated in either Appalachia or North Carolina, or possibly some combination of the two. A year later, Weston wrote about the results in an article for *Capitol News,* the label's house organ (distributed to employees and retailers), "the mail response was considerably more gratifying than was expected, and over a six-month period more requests were received for this song than for any popular ballad of the day. With this as a stimulus, more songs were gathered and presented, and thus the idea of the album was based on an actual expression of opinion by the listening public."

The idea of a pop singer doing such material to begin with was unprecedented, but the way Weston and Stafford presented the songs was even more so.

Weston said that he expected "loud wails will be heard from the 'purists' who believe that American folk songs should be presented with an accompaniment of only guitar, zither, or dulcimer." Instead, he explained, their idea was to present these songs "with orchestral accompaniment in a style which may, at first, seem rather unusual." Weston compared the idea of putting these songs in orchestral settings to the adaptations of Bach chorales into orchestral form conducted by Leopold Stokowski. "What the objectors failed to realize was that Bach's music was thus made palatable to a portion of the public who knew little of him."

As it turned out, 1947–48 was the perfect moment to put such a project in motion, and for reasons that were both technological and political/cultural. The long-playing album format was brand-new at the time, but cutting-edge as the technology was, the format lent itself to looking backward rather than forward. *American Folk Songs* would help establish the idea that albums of songs, like photo albums, were about collecting rather than creating, gathering what already existed rather than making something completely new. In this album, Stafford and Weston were creating something that was both old and new at the same time.

"The preparation of the material was not just the work of a week or two, for there are more than 100 versions of 'Barbara Allen' alone," wrote Weston. "Careful research was employed in an attempt to present an interesting yet authentic version of each song." In the early postwar years, most activity in the folk music world was highly politically charged, from Paul Robeson and Pete Seeger outward. In the 1940s and '50s, folk music was embraced by Marxist music lovers as an antidote to what they perceived as the commercial excesses of the capitalist music industry.

It might be said that *American Folk Songs* was born in the shadow of a political event, the passing of the Taft-Hartley Act of 1947, which, in plain language, obligated labor unions to give plenty of warning time before calling a strike. Not long after the bill was passed, the American Federation of Musicians called just such a strike against record companies (the second one of the decade). From September to December, anyone with a recording contract was under the gun to produce as much product as possible before the strike was set to start, on January 1, 1948. Stafford herself partook in a dozen or so sessions from September to December, and these included all six of the songs that would be issued in 1948 in the first edition of *American Folk Songs*. There wasn't a single session of this material. The folk songs were mixed in with the pop songs. On November 21, she cut "Black Is the Color of My True Love's Hair" along with "Once and for Always" (the big ballad from Bing Crosby's new movie, *A Connecticut Yankee in King Arthur's Court*), and on her last session of the year, December 31, "Wayfaring Stranger" and "Barbara Allen" were recorded shortly before "It Was Written in the Stars" (the big ballad from Tony Martin's new movie, *Casbah*).

Some of the tracks were issued as singles at the time, others were first heard on the album, which was issued in the 78 rpm album format in April 1948, containing six tracks on three discs. A year later, in May 1949, Stafford taped one more traditional song, "I Wonder as I Wander," which was released as a single in December of that year in time for Christmas. Then, in 1950, the album was released in the new 10-inch long-playing format, with "I Wonder as I Wander" added as a seventh track.

The 10-inch LP version starts with "Poor Wayfaring Stranger"; the very different 1961 12-inch LP, however, begins with "Shenandoah." "Wayfaring Stranger," as we have seen, lets us know that Stafford is taking us on an unexpected journey. We quickly realize that we're not about to hear the same *Lucky Strike Hit Parade*–type tunes that virtually every other pop singer of the era was doing. "Stranger" immediately takes us to a place where pop music had never gone before.

The second track, "He's Gone Away," is the song that served as the test pilot (the canary in the coal mine, as it were) for the whole project when Stafford performed it on the *Chesterfield Supper Club*; ironically, it's the major 1947 entry that's not repeated in the 1961 album. Compared to some of the other songs, it's certainly not dire—there's a lot of attention paid to the idea that though "he" may be gone, "she" (the singer) is optimistic that "he's coming back," and that her friends will com-

fort her during his absence. Lines like "Who will tie my shoe? And who will glove my hand? And who will kiss my ruby lips when he is gone?" make us wonder about the exact nature of the relationship between the two.

"I Wonder as I Wander," as mentioned, was recorded eighteen months or so after the other six tracks, in May 1949, and included on the 10-inch LP but not the 78 album. Fittingly, "I Wonder" is itself a sort of hybrid, a combination of a traditional melody and title spun into full song format by the scholar John Jacob Niles. On top of that, it's also lived two lives as both a folk song and a hymn, and one that was frequently pressed into service as a Christmas song. Stafford, in fact, recorded it for the second of three times in 1955 for Columbia on an album titled *Happy Holidays*. The second stanza does mention the way that "Mary birthed Jesus," but the more lingering image is the opening line, "I wonder as I wander out under the sky / How Jesus the Savior did come for to die." (That line is heard twice in the lyric, and three times in Stafford's arrangement.) No, it's not exactly a happy holiday song, but it's hardly morose either; it's the best kind of holiday song, not a synthetically cheerful Hallmark card with dancing snowmen and glow-in-the-dark reindeer. Stafford singing a hymn—she would make a whole album of these—is a lot like Mahalia Jackson. When either one of them sings about Jesus, you have no doubt that they're staring straight at Him, and pretty soon you can see Him too.

"Red Rosy Bush" (sometimes listed on various album covers as "Red Rosey Bush") had been recorded in concert style earlier (meaning that he treats it essentially as if it were a piece of lieder rather than a folk or a pop song) by Nelson Eddy and later by Harry Belafonte. It's a simple song that describes emotions that may not be specifically complex but are certainly highly nuanced. Like the rest of the album, it's melancholy but not somber. Stafford's voice rises and falls like a violin here, and shines brilliantly on the high notes: "I wish I was a *red rosy* bush, by the banks of the sea / And every time my true love passed, he'd take a rose off of me." This is the arrangement with the most prominent use of the harp, and like many of Weston's charts here, it sounds like a close relative to Aaron Copland in his Americana phase.

From red roses we move on to black hair. "Black Is the Color" (sometimes given as "Black Is the Color of My True Love's Hair") is a song that belongs jointly to the Old World and the New, associated with the Appalachian mountains but having its origin in Scotland. In the 1960s, various artists represented various extremes: Nina Simone and the avant-garde jazz singer Patty Waters were two of the many who came back to this song, which had become a mainstay of the American folk repertoire. It's not at all sad, but Stafford helped instill the tradition of every singer singing it close to the vest, as if she's delighted that black is the color of her true love's hair but still she's holding back, almost as if she were afraid to proclaim her good luck too loudly to the world for fear of jinxing it.

"The Nightingale" is another "American" folk song that, like much of our culture, is an import from overseas, being Celtic in origin. The song describes a flirtation between "a lady so fair" and a "soldier, a brave volunteer." The lady and the soldier talk about "going to the banks of the sea . . . to hear the nightingale sing," but when she asks him to marry her, he tells her, "Oh no, pretty lady that never can be. / I've a sweetheart in London as fair as can be." This is somewhat sanitized from most original texts, in which the soldier tells the pretty lady that he has "a wife back in London." The soldier then tells her, "Two girls in the army is too many for me" (or, in the original, "Two wives in the army is too many for me"). It's a pretty little narrative. Stafford holds our interest from beginning to end, and most people will never notice that the song doesn't have much to do with nightingales.

"Barbara Allen" is one of the most famous folk songs in the English language, probably Scottish in origin, but one that spread all over the British Isles and North America, and which has turned up in many different languages. The song remained part of the cultural bloodstream; in the wake of "Loch Lomond," Maxine Sullivan recorded it in 1940, and Doris Day did a very hard-swinging treatment in 1941 with Les Brown's Band of Renown. The song is widely heard in the pop, jazz, and country music worlds, although different versions use different sets of lyrics; Sullivan and Merle Travis sing "In Scarlet Town, where I was born, there was a fair maid dwellin'," whereas Day and Stafford begin, "'Twas in the merry month of May, when all the green buds were swellin'." This is the bleakest song in the collection, "a young man on his deathbed lay for love of Barbara Allen." In this version, the girl is sympathetic to him (in other versions she is, to put it bluntly, a bitch), but not particularly helpful—she comes in, watches him die, and then tells her mother that "my true love has died today" and now she fully expects to die tomorrow. Compared to other songs being recorded in 1947—"Too Fat Polka" or "Managua, Nicaragua" or Stafford's own blockbuster hit "Tim-tay-shun"—this is not exactly cheerful stuff—and an entirely different kind of pop music.

That finished off the original 10-inch LP. By the time it was released in 1950, Stafford and Weston were becoming a team in their personal lives as well as their professional ones, and were making a career journey from Columbia to Capitol Records, where they would remain for ten productive years. (They were married in 1952.) Over the course of that decade she recorded several additional folk songs, including a further slice of Appalachia, "Cripple Creek," as well as her second version of "I Wonder as I Wander," and she included a new version of one of the American folk songs, "He's Gone Away," in her 1959 album *Ballad of the Blues*.

But her most ambitious excursion into folk music in the 1950s was her remarkable album titled both *My Heart's in the Highlands* and *Songs of Scotland*. Like "I Wonder as I Wander," the project is a hybrid. The words are authentically Scottish; in fact, most of the texts are from the great Scottish poet Robert Burns (1759–1796)—not only the most celebrated poet and lyricist from that country, but probably the best-known Scottish writer of all time, often regarded as a veritable Scottish Shakespeare. Many of his poems had been set to music previously, but for this project, all new settings were composed by a songwriter credited on the LP jacket as "Alton Rinker." He was better known by the more informal name Al Rinker, the kid brother of the legendary jazz-pop singer Mildred Bailey and the original musical partner of Bing Crosby—and also one of the Rhythm Boys, alongside Crosby, in Paul Whiteman's orchestra.

The original liner notes to the album inform us that it was Rinker who conceived the project. "Alton Rinker, one of the country's leading composers of popular songs, first set 'My Jean' to music and became so interested that he wrote the other new songs in this collection, to form a cycle." Rinker himself is quoted: "In a few instances, it was necessary to Anglicize a number of words written in the old Scottish vernacular, in order to simplify the meaning for the general listening public."

Originally there were two sessions, one in March 1953, and the second in July of that same year; the latter date featured Mitch Miller on English horn. As with *American Folk Songs, Scotland* was produced during the height of the format wars of the early 1950s; without getting into too many arcane details, the eight original tracks were initially issued on a 10-inch LP and a double-disc EP package, both titled *My Heart's in the Highlands.* Then, in May 1956, Stafford and Weston would return to the studio to tape another four tracks, which would be included on the 12-inch edition. The cover of the 10-inch LP showed a picture-postcard-like image of a verdant Scottish countryside, with an ancient castle at the edge of a loch. The 12-inch LP was titled *Songs of Scotland* and showed the bonnie lass herself in Scottish regalia.

Both formats open with "My Heart's in the Highlands," which Burns had originally written to the melody of an earlier Scots air, "Failte na Miosg." (That tune ranks as an early example of a waltz; the Rinker setting here is in something closer to 2/4.) Burns's text illustrates the roots of a whole strain of Tin Pan Alley songs that are sentimental musings about home, from all the so-called mammy songs of the teens and twenties (even "When It's Sleepy Time Down South") up through "I Left My Heart in San Francisco" and "New York, New York." These are all vivid, potent descriptions of places that we call home, which make it plain that no matter where we might be physically, our heart is not here. No, our heart's in the Highlands, "chasing the wild-deer, and following the roe," or it's hearing the banjos ringing and the "darkies" singing or

riding the little cable cars as they climb halfway to the stars. Stafford's vocal is heartfelt in the extreme. She doesn't even faintly genuflect in the direction of sentiment.

The other major contributor to the album—who factors greatly on the opening track—is Mitch Miller. Those who think of the classical woodwind player turned pop producer as being only interested in crassly "commercial" music will doubtless be surprised to find Miller so heartily endorsing so esoteric a project as Scottish love poems. But no, that would be seriously underestimating the old reprobate. It's true that Miller's heart was generally not in the Highlands but in the lowest common denominator, but he too could appreciate the unique artistry of individuals like Burns and Stafford, and this would have been right up his alley. Miller's idea of art was often "different," and sometimes he didn't care so much if a thing was popular or even good as long as it was different. In the late 1950s, when every major singer was doing songbook albums, something like eighteenth-century Scottish poetry would have been more exciting to him simply because it *was* different. Miller, who specialized in the double reed instruments (including oboe and bassoon), is featured extensively on English horn throughout the three tracks on which he's heard.

Burns wrote "John Anderson, My Jo" as a buddy song, a homage to a best pal. The real John Anderson was a carpenter and drinking buddy of the poet. Stafford sings it as a lament to a lost love, a sweetheart, and a soul mate rather than a running mate. ("Many a happy day we had with one another.") The reminiscence is so sweet that one would assume she's singing to a long-departed lover; in reality, Anderson outlived Burns by many decades and supposedly even built his coffin. (Of course, since Burns referred to his pal John as "Jo," it could also seem as if Jo Stafford were somehow singing to herself.)

"Flow Gently, Sweet Afton" was the most popular of Burns's texts in song form—that is, on any night except New Year's. The original poem, titled just "Sweet Afton" (after a river in Ayrshire), was first set to music under the expanded title in 1837. It was rendered by Maxine Sullivan as part of the series of swinging (or, in this case, semi-swinging) traditional songs that she recorded in the wake of "Loch Lomond." It's safe to say that virtually everyone listening to Stafford's album in the mid-1950s would have been very familiar with "Sweet Afton." The straight-up text describes a young swain resting by the banks and braes of the Afton while his lady love ("my Mary") sleeps. He is rather literally speaking to the river itself, as if it were a person, telling it to keep quiet so as not to wake her. "My Mary's asleep by thy murmuring stream, / Flow gently, sweet Afton, disturb not her dream." The melody and the bittersweet quality of Stafford's voice suggest that the whole scene is a sweet memory, being played out in the protagonist's mind many years after youth and love are gone, his Mary has left him, and the relationship (at least the most romantic part of it) has ended.

The fourth track on the album is titled "Ye Banks and Braes of Bonnie Doon," although elsewhere it's known as "The Banks o' Doon" as well as "Ye Banks and Braes"; superficially it's similar to "Loch Lomond," and, like a lot of the songs on the album, it lovingly describes a place or a body of water. (No wonder Scotland continues to love Burns so much; almost everything he wrote was a love song to the Scottish countryside.) This is less of an upbeat narrative; here the tranquility of the River Doon (also in Ayrshire) is contrasted with the turbulent emotions of the woman singing: "How can ye bloom sae fresh and fair; / How can ye chant, ye little birds, And I so weary, full of care!" In a sense, it's a precursor of "Guess I'll Hang My Tears out to Dry"—here too the protagonist has to contend with "sunny weather" when rain and gloom would better suit her state of mind.

"Molly's Meek, Molly's Sweet," splits the difference between a poem, a folk song, and a nursery rhyme; it's easy to imagine little girls jumping rope—or even playing hopscotch (emphasis on Scotch)—to its singsong rhythm: "Molly's meek, Molly's sweet, Molly's modest and discreet." The poet describes a pretty young woman he sees walking down the road in her bare feet; the resulting meditation is alternately sweet and tender and kinky. He opines that such a lovely girl shouldn't have to walk around without shoes, that she should

be wearing the prettiest and fanciest shoes around ("were well laced up in silken shoes"). Mitch Miller offers a masculine point of view in his prominent English horn obbligato.

"Comin' Through the Rye" is essentially the same scenario described from the opposite point of view, a pretty girl skipping down the path while all the lads do smile on her, although this time it's described by the girl in the first person. One can't help but think of the girl from Ipanema, strolling down the beach while the *cariocas* ogle her with their tongues hanging out. The difference is that in this case the girl is talking about herself, and she first tells us that she has no one laddie of her own; therefore, telling herself that all the lads seem to dig her is her way of consoling herself. Stafford certainly sounds anything but vain. As ever, there's a slight tinge of melancholia to give gravitas to the proceedings. "Comin' Through the Rye" apparently refers to crossing a river called the Rye Water, though most of us who hear or even sing the song imagine a lassie coming through a field of grain, rather like Holden Caulfield's dream about children in a grain field in *Catcher in the Rye*.

The first two tracks on Side B bring us more Mitch Miller plus color and vegetation, red roses and green rashes (rushes), rather than geography. Side B, track one is "My Love Is Like a Red, Red Rose," a 1794 poem by Burns that, like many others, represents his reworking of material and ideas from older, more traditional sources. This is a happy text, in which the speaker pledges everlasting devotion: "Till a' the seas gang dry, my dear, And the rocks melt wi' the sun: / I will love thee still, my dear," and it isn't until the last lines that we realize that he's being so effusive with his sweetie because he's about to leave her for a protracted period. "And I will come again, my love, Tho' it were ten thousand mile." (A few years later, Jimmy Van Heusen wrote a different setting of the same Burns poem as a vehicle for Pat Boone in the film *Journey to the Center of the Earth*.) "Green Grow the Rashes, O" further connects Burns to nursery songs; I remember singing it in school in a bonnie loch somewhere in Brooklyn. Stafford again makes it bittersweet, suggesting the point of view of an old stud reminiscing about a well-spent youth:

"The sweetest hours that e'er I spent / Are spent among the lassies, oh."

The next few pieces are about tearful goodbyes to bonnie young lasses, spoken from the point of view of those swains who were compelled to leave them, and who still can recall those tender farewells many years later in vivid detail. "Annie Laurie" is the one piece on the album not credited to Burns and Rinker; it's by soldier and poet William Douglas—who supposedly actually had a relationship with a young girl named Annie Laurie—and composer Alicia Scott. In the text, our hero remembers his bonnie Annie Laurie, with the implication that he hasn't seen her again since that fateful farewell all those years ago. "Her voice is low and sweet—And she's a' the world to me; / And for bonnie Annie Laurie, I'd lay me down and die." As mentioned, the song, first written at the turn of the eighteenth century was wildly popular throughout the swing era—almost as much as "Loch Lomond." Burns's "My Jean" ties a lot of the loose ends together; he tells us how the woods and the rivers and the song of the "bony birds" remind him of his presumably long-departed "Jean." In reality, Jean Armour was the poet's wife, who bore him nine children and survived him by many years. Burns himself was hardly monogamous, but "my Jean" was the lassie he loved the best.

Like "Molly's Sweet," "The Bonnie Lad That's Far Away" is in a dance rhythm—you can just see rural British Islanders Morris-dancing to it—and the story is another tale of parted lovers. But unlike Annie Laurie and Jean, the unnamed heroine is telling us about it from the female point of view. "How can I be bright and gay," she asks us, "when the bonnie lad that I love best is over the hills and far away." The piece seems like the predecessor to a million country and western songs, especially Dolly Parton's "Down from Dover." "My father put me from his door, / My friends they have disowned me," the Burns text goes, and eventually she tells us why: "O weary winter soon will pass, And Spring will soon bring May. / And my young babe will be born, And he'll be home that's far away." This adaptation sanitizes that line to "And the bonnie lad that I love best, will be back home from far away."

"Should auld acquaintance be forgot, and never brought to mind? / Should auld acquaintance be forgot, and days of auld lang syne?" It gives one pause to hear these words on any day but December 31. Surely everybody in the English-speaking world knows these lyrics, but Stafford, more than anybody else, makes us pay attention to what they mean. Even more than any of the other tracks here, this song is a virtual synonym for both "melancholy" and "bittersweet"; Stafford treats it as the most perfect song ever written for saying goodbye and hello in the same breath.

It's hard to imagine that *Songs of Scotland* was anything other than an immensely satisfying undertaking for everyone involved: Jo Stafford, Paul Weston, Al Rinker, and even Mitch Miller. The album never became anything like a best-seller, or even a vast underground favorite like *John Coltrane and Johnny Hartman*. Surely any of Stafford's other albums—*I'll Be Seeing You (G.I. Jo)*, *Jo + Jazz*, or the two Broadway albums—sold considerably better. But *Songs of Scotland* remains a unique and completely sui generis achievement; there's simply nothing else like it in all of American music.

Stafford was still a recognized force in the commercial music world in 1961, so much so that *Billboard* deemed it newsworthy to report that her first album after leaving Columbia would be a stereo remake of *American Folk Songs* for Capitol Records. The new *Folk Songs* album was recorded in April and May 1961. *Billboard* stated that the new package would include new recordings of the original six songs and six new arrangements. (Only one song on the 1950 album, "He's Gone Away," was not redone, probably because Stafford had recently cut a new version in 1959 for her Columbia album *Ballad of the Blues*.)

The original mono album has a simplicity and a purity about it that make it perfect; the stereo remake is a much more ambitious undertaking that is totally perfect too, in its own way. I'm grateful not to have to choose. The key difference is primarily one of tempo: All seven of the original tracks are in roughly the same medium-slow tempo. Conversely, the 1961 album employs a very subtle use of rhythmic contrast; it's both slower and faster.

The seven remakes, which include "I Wonder as I Wander" (Stafford's third recording of the song), are all at least as good or better than the mono versions. Stafford's voice is perceptibly darker, deeper, and richer in 1961 than it had been in 1947. In 1947, Stafford was an excellent popular singer; by 1961, her voice is as high as a mountain and as deep as a valley, and flows as gently and strongly as the Afton or the Missouri.

The new versions are all slower than the originals. The most effective of these is "Wayfaring Stranger," which served as the opener in 1950 but is Side A, track four in 1961. The tempo is slower to the point where it's twenty seconds longer, and the overall experience is more powerful. In the original, Stafford sings the song's iconic lines with as few pauses as possible. In the remake, she takes short, subtle breaths between most of the lines, which has the effect of making the whole piece more movingly contemplative, as if she were thoughtfully pondering this journey she's undertaking, from one world to the next, up and over the River Jordan. The original is more like a conversation, the remake is more like a woman thinking out loud, and as in all such contemplation, there are pauses between one thought and the next— they don't all just come tumbling out. In all the remakes, the slower tempos give the songs more of what F. Scott Fitzgerald would call "a sort of epic grandeur."

Of the six new songs, four are up-tempo dance numbers, obviously thrown in to add some rhythmic variety. These are intermingled with the other songs in a very clearly defined pattern: "Old Joe Clark" (Side A, track three), "Single Girl" (Side A, track six), "Cripple Creek" (Side B, track three), "Sourwood Mountain" (Side A, track six), all of which feature banjo solos and prominent accompaniment by Joe Maphis. (Maphis, 1921–1986, was a prominent country and western studio player, based in Los Angeles. Although better known for his guitar solos, he was also a formidable monster of banjo.) As we can see, every third song, including the final track on each side, is one of these mood-lightening square-dance numbers.

Of the up-tempos, "Cripple Creek" is a song that Stafford had previously recorded in a rarely heard Columbia track circa 1955. "Sourwood Mountain" has her chanting "Hey ho diddle-um day!" in a clear-cut example of what Gabby Johnson, of *Blazing Saddles* fame, would describe as "authentic frontier gibberish." Other than that noteworthy distinction, the most notable of these is "A Single Girl," which is fast and tuneful but not necessarily cheerful. The lyric comes as close as a major label cared to in 1961 to skewering the institution of marriage. "Lord, I wish I was a single girl again," she sings, repeating the line for emphasis, then continuing, "When I was single I dressed in silk so fine / Now I am married, Lord, I wear rags all the time." Weston's arrangement stirs up lots of excitement, first by having Stafford slow and rubato, singing the key line of the song ("Lord, I wish I was a single girl again") before the banjo enters and kicks everything into tempo, and he throws in a key change about halfway through (before the line "When I was single, most every day was fun . . .").

There are only two new songs on the 1961 album that don't fall under the general heading of foot-stomping, toe-tapping fun, "Johnny Has Gone for a Soldier" and "Shenandoah." "Johnny Has Gone for a Soldier" joins "Barbara Allen" and "Wayfaring Stranger" as a song about death, but where the former is romantic and the latter is grandly poetic, "Johnny" finds no romance or poetry in death, just pure bloodshed. It's quite possibly the saddest of all, inspiring, as the very effective opening section states, tears that "would turn a mill." Just two years earlier, Stafford recorded *I'll Be Seeing You*, an album of love songs from World War II; "Johnny Has Gone for a Soldier" sounds more like the kind of song that would be sung during the era of Vietnam.

"Shenandoah" is the new album's opener and also its masterpiece. Up to now, the various departures from the original texts that we've noted remind us of the Hollywood Production Code (or even the Comics Code Authority). In "The Nightingale," the lyric change covers up the possibility of bigamy or some kind of extramarital shenanigans. In "The Bonnie Lad That's Far Away," the lyric change spreads a virtual layer of liquid paper over the notion of a pregnancy without the benefit of clergy. "Shenandoah" marks the one major case when a lyric change from the original makes the adaptation deeper, richer, and more moving.

This air, officially titled "O Shenandoah," dates from the early nineteenth century. The folklorists report that the song originates with the tale of a French fur trapper who fell in love with the daughter of a Native American chief. In the official lyric, the line goes "Shenandoah, I *love* your daughter," which is the way both Harry Belafonte and the famous English folksinger Richard Thompson perform it. However, Stafford sings "Shenandoah, I *am* your daughter"; the revised lyric is less specific, more general, and, overall, more effective. It opens up the narrative, transforming what was plainly concrete into what now seems like one of the eternal mysteries. A singer with a keen sense of narrative, Stafford makes me think of a pioneer woman in middle age, remembering her youth in the Shenandoah Valley, back when the Missouri River represented the very extreme end of civilization. Is she singing about her home in Shenandoah? Is she singing about a love of her childhood? As with the best of Robert Burns, it could be either—and

it doesn't really matter. Home represents so many things, from romantic love to parental love to familial love, and Stafford's interpretation captures all of them.

Her heart's not in the Highlands now, it's down in the valley. Stafford's character sings of herself as a daughter, in the metaphoric sense, of the Shenandoah Valley; but at the point at which she's singing, the frontier has been traveled further west, and much of the land from the Missouri River westward has been conquered and mapped. And Stafford herself is also a pioneer, doing what no other artists of her generation did in finding a very new way to sing these very old songs and make them available to posterity in an entirely new artistic and technological medium. (Her efforts had an influence far beyond her own time—Stafford's recording of "Barbara Allen" had a profound impact on the young Judy Collins, for one.) Stafford reminds us that even though rivers and valleys and mountaintops on God's green earth will all eventually be charted out, the imaginings of the human heart and soul are beyond measure.

40

Jo Stafford
I'll Be Seeing You (G.I. Jo)
(1959)

Whether you actually lived through World War II or not, you probably have several very distinct images in your head when you think of the music of that era. If there's any one act that signifies wartime American pop culture to subsequent generations, it's the Andrews Sisters, all jaunty and defiant, singing upbeat patriotic songs about what a lucky fellow Mr. Smith is to be an American, suggesting that the most serious thing a soldier had to worry about was that his girl back home might be sitting under the apple tree with some other dude in uniform. The Japs might have caught us off-guard at Pearl Harbor, but we'll be darned if we're about to let them sink our spirit! That was how Patty, Maxene, and LaVerne depicted the home front in 1941–42—all enthusiasm and flag-waving.

Yet those upbeat, cheerful songs were mainly heard during the early part of America's involvement in the war. Within a few years—months, even—the nation was singing a very different tune. The jingoistic energy of the early months had been dissipated by the long years of separation; instead of stressing victory over the bad guys, the prize in the eyes of songwriters in 1944 and '45 was only for lovers to be reunited, for G.I. Johnny to come marching home—in one piece. The only "victory" that mattered in most songs from the later part of the war is strictly a personal one.

No less than America's military, America's songwriters did some of their best work in this (thankfully brief) period; whereas most of the propaganda jingles from the earlier years were quickly forgotten, a disproportionate number of songs from 1943–45 would go on to become classics, and their status as standards would be confirmed during the following decade, during the early years—and the golden years—of the jazz and pop album.

These are the songs that inspired Jo Stafford to record what many regard as her finest album, *I'll Be Seeing You*, taped in 1958 and released in 1959. Most of its twelve songs were from these years—with the notable exception of the title track, and even then, while "I'll Be Seeing You" had been introduced in 1938, it also was a hit during the war, and has been closely associated with World War II ever since.

More than most of the albums discussed in this book, *I'll Be Seeing You* is a true concept album—a dozen songs that are united by mood as well as their mutual points of origin and the general content of the lyrics; songs that are connected by what the words are actually saying. Most of these numbers were written for wartime-era movie musicals, generally all-star Technicolor affairs, and many were also victims of another conflict that was raging at the time, the battle between the musicians' union and the record labels, which resulted in the

Recording Ban of 1942–44, a thirty-month strike during which union musicians were not allowed to make recordings. As a result, many songs from these years were not commercially recorded until years after the fact. In concentrating on this very specific, very rewarding period, *I'll Be Seeing You* is a laudable work of precise scholarship as well as of singing and arranging.

The orchestrations (and other aspects of the album production) were the work of Stafford's musical and personal partner, Paul Weston, and represent some of that very talented arranger's best work. It's part of Weston's brilliance that he stays generally true to the ideals of the big band era: the tempos are generally slow but still danceable, nothing is in rubato, and though strings are present, the traditional big band sections of brass, reeds, and rhythm take center stage. Like most dance band recordings, none of the tracks here uses a verse—Stafford and Weston don't need them. "No Love, No Nothin'" may be the most modern-sounding chart here—the saxophones in particular reflect the influence of Woody Herman's Second Herd—but in general the orchestrations are lush and romantic, and perfectly suited to Stafford's rich, sultry voice.

But for all of Weston's contributions, the focus is never off Stafford, who proves again and again why she's considered one of the more significant talents in American music. It's not just her sumptuously perfect voice that makes her great, but her equally perfect ear, her timing and phrasing, and, perhaps more than anything else, her remarkable taste and conviction.

At the end of the 1950s, the singers who helped pioneer the 12-inch LP were in an unusual place, career-wise and culturally. Frank Sinatra, Jo Stafford, Peggy Lee, Ella Fitzgerald, Doris Day, Margaret Whiting, Perry Como, Billy Eckstine, Dinah Shore, and Nat King Cole, to name a few, all began their careers during the swing era and the war, and by the mid-1950s were all ensconced in the LP medium. All were roughly twenty years into what would be long-running careers. At this point they were all like the double-faced Janus, looking forward and backward simultaneously. They

were focusing intently on Hollywood and Broadway, waiting for Cahn and Van Heusen or Lerner and Loewe to write them a new hit song, and at the same time they were looking back at the past, at the increasingly canonical catalogues of iconic songwriters like the late George Gershwin, Jerome Kern, and Lorenz Hart.

Some of them were also starting to look at their own catalogues: Sinatra, Cole, Eckstine, and some of the others were doing new recordings of their vintage hit songs in new technologies (hi-fi and stereo), sometimes for new labels. Sometimes there was a corporate motive, as when Eckstine re-recorded his early MGM hits for Mercury or Sinatra "covered" his own Capitol hits for Reprise Records. But equally often there was a deliberately nostalgic attitude—both Sinatra and Stafford recorded album-length tributes to their mentor (for lack of a better word) Tommy Dorsey, and Doris Day released a beautiful reflection on the 1940s, affectionately titled *Sentimental Journey*.

Jo Stafford was the least easy to define, both stylistically and technologically. She was frequently seen on TV, but she didn't dominate the medium like Perry Como or Dinah Shore; she appeared in a few films, but wasn't a movie star like Doris Day or Sinatra; she continued to land hit singles, but she wasn't primarily a singles artist like Nat Cole or Patti Page; and she didn't do live albums like Fitzgerald, Sarah Vaughan, and Mel Tormé—nor songbook albums like Fitzgerald (although she recorded enough Frank Loesser songs to fill such an album). She wasn't as thoroughly bluesy as Peggy Lee, as hard-swinging as Fitzgerald, or as overtly emotional as Billie Holiday or Sinatra. In short, Jo Stafford did a little bit—or even a lot—of everything, in every medium, and did it all extremely well. She was all of these things at the same time; she was very much of a muchness.

In 1959, Stafford recorded an album that singularly suited her: *I'll Be Seeing You*, a collection of love songs from those crucial waning years of the war. Even the LP cover conveys a narrative: Stafford, looking fabulous at forty-one in a lovely full-color photo, is ensconced in the visual iconography of the war years: she's sitting at a radio microphone (by 1960, traditional network radio was already a relic of a previous generation), positioned in front of World War II recruiting posters, holding what appears to be a publicity 8 x 10 photo of herself that she has apparently autographed for a serviceman. The entire image is framed by the red, white, and blue borders of what had been known as "V-Mail"—a special postage system designed expressly for personal communication with the GIs. It's a safe assumption that anybody who looked at the cover of *I'll Be Seeing You* automatically knew what Stafford and Columbia Records were going for: fifteen years after the war, to everyone in Stafford's demographic the depiction of her sending a V-mail letter automatically communicated the idea of wartime separation well before he or she even glanced at the track list.

Which underscores another point. Stafford, nicknamed "G.I. Jo," had been a singing sweetheart of the armed forces, her voice no less of an icon than Betty Grable's legs.

Listening to *I'll Be Seeing You* puts me in mind of an observation made to me by Stafford's occasional producer Mitch Miller. Miller astutely pointed out that a performance of a song isn't driven by whatever emotion the singer happens to be feeling, but rather by the emotion that the singer instills in the audience—and the two things aren't necessarily related to each other. Stafford has a gift that may make her unique among singers in any genre. Where Sinatra, Holiday, and Judy Garland, to name three masters, all express emotion to move listeners to feel that emotion, Stafford could communicate emotion without directly expressing it. She doesn't necessarily *sound* sad, but somehow she gets listeners to feel sad; she's rarely jumping-for-joy happy, but listening to her I feel happy whenever she wants me to feel happy.

I'll Be Seeing You opens with one of the earliest tunes in the collection, "I Don't Want to Walk Without You." In 1940, composer Jule Styne was set to work on a B-musical for Republic Pictures with lyricist Frank Loesser (loaned from Paramount)—their first collaboration. Styne already had a melody he wanted to play for Loesser, but upon hearing it, his new partner's reaction was "SHHH! Don't ever play that around here again!" Loesser

immediately decreed that this was too good a melody for a Poverty Row outfit like Republic; instead, he said, "we'll take it over to Paramount and write it there." Loesser himself later reported that Irving Berlin told him "Walk Without You" was the best song he ever heard. Some pundits have tried to deflate Styne and Loesser's achievements by stating that the melody is adapted from Felix Mendelssohn's famous "Spring Song," but this is bogus scholarship: any similarity between the first few notes of the two melodies is both coincidental and inconsequential. The song was introduced on recordings and radio just about the time of Pearl Harbor, before it was officially introduced in the 1942 Paramount Pictures musical *Sweater Girl*.

What matters is that Loesser and Styne had the enormous good fortune to have written a song of separation that was good to go just at the very moment that the United States was about to enter the war. Without even trying, they had already written a war song—and one that sounds more like the end of the war than the beginning; there would soon be many other songs about walking solo. Arranger Paul Weston begins with a pattern that suggests a dance band, although nothing on the album is in traditional fox-trot tempo—the flute behind Stafford in the second eight bars makes it sound more 1959 than 1941. Emotionally, this is one of the lighter tunes in the set. Stafford asks her absentee lover, "I don't want to walk without the sunshine / Why'd you have to turn off all that sunshine?" Here and at other points, there's an implication that the guy is gone by his own choice, which also suggests that he could come back any time he wants. In songs like "I'll Walk Alone," however, it's unstated that the separation is not anyone's choice (except possibly Hitler's). It's clear that she won't be happy until he returns, but she's not acting as if it's within his power to come back— she doesn't bother pleading with him or entreating him to return.

The second track, Johnny Burke and Jimmy Van Heusen's "It Could Happen to You," is a song out of Stafford's past: her 1944 recording was one of her first hits as a solo artist. Certainly that was a more auspicious destination for the song than the movie it was written for, *And the Angels Sing*, a rather oddly conceived remake of *Sing You Sinners* (1938), a picture that hardly warranted remaking to begin with. (Fred MacMurray, Paramount's all-purpose leading man, starred in both). Thanks partly to Stafford, "It Could Happen to You" became one of the absolute top songs of the war years and many decades after, one of the most recorded of all jazz standards in the 1950s and '60s. Of Stafford's two recordings, 1944 and 1959, neither uses the verse, but the latter, which is nearly thirty seconds longer, is much more luxuriously legato; on the original, the younger Stafford sounds serious about warning the listener of the perils of falling in love, almost as if she were warning the young GIs to proceed with caution where the opposite sex is concerned: "Loose lips sink hearts." In the later version, she sounds more as if she's resigned to being trapped in a romantic spell—contrary to her advice to us—and is actually enjoying it.

"I'll Walk Alone," written by Sammy Cahn and Jule Styne for Dinah Shore to sing in the Universal film *Follow the Boys,* is neither the first nor the last song on the album about walking alone. One simply could not have lived through World War II and not have heard both this song and this sentiment over and over. This 1944 musical comedy again included the Andrews Sisters, still dishing out the jive, this time with "Shoo-Shoo Baby," yet Shore stole the production with "I'll Walk Alone," by far the best-remembered number in the picture. Because of the American Federation of Musicians situation, the song couldn't be recorded by union musicians, although nearly all of the A-list bands played it live on the air—the song was virtually omnipresent on the radio. The only two notable recordings of it available during the war were by Louis Prima, whose label had apparently made some early settlement with the union, and by Shore herself, backed by an a cappella choir with no musicians.

Stafford had sung "I'll Walk Alone" live in 1944, but didn't get the chance to record it for fifteen years. For many reasons, hers is unquestionably the one to beat. Unlike Shore, she doesn't include the verse—she doesn't need to; she keeps everything at a bare minimum. The song isn't despondent or necessarily even torchy—a torch song would

be a lament over a man who left her for another woman. Stafford sings as if she has every hope that he'll return. The question is when, and in how many pieces. She's not crying her heart out, drinking black coffee (or worse), she's merely walking alone, stoically, without feeling sorry for herself. It comes across as incredibly real and heartfelt, and it's devastatingly sad for that very reason—in Stafford's art, the act of simply strolling solo is more poignant than hanging one's tears out to dry or impelling the willow to weep for you. "I'll Walk Alone" has a line that helped the song survive the war: "I'll walk alone. / They'll ask me why and I'll tell them I'd rather." Obviously, in 1944, nobody was asking any woman why she was walking alone. And, in fact, the song was successfully revived in the 1950s.

"I'll Remember April" is a very beautiful standard that was introduced in an Abbott & Costello movie (in *Ride 'Em Cowboy;* it was sung by Dick Foran, a traditional baritone-tenor who always looked like a stand-in for Nelson Eddy). As with "I Don't Want to Walk Without You," it became a war song by accident. Since the movie, which, unlike *Buck Privates,* is not a war comedy, was released in February 1942, it seems unlikely that it was written with the looming conflict in mind. It's an unusual choice, since it again sounds as if the "other" or the "you" in the lyric ("You loved me once in April / Your lips were warm . . .") could likely be with a new lover. It doesn't have the tone of "I'll Walk Alone" or "No Love, No Nothin'," in which there's no doubt that the two lovers have been separated by the Axis. But that doesn't matter much when one hears Stafford sing "April" by itself (apart from the rest of the album)—it's a truly beautiful, bittersweet vocal about the end of love, movingly sung in her deep, resonant, chesty contralto, a text in which the act of reminiscing about a love is in itself enough of a signifier to the listener, saying that the affair *est fini.*

"We Mustn't Say Goodbye" might have been totally forgotten if not for Stafford. It was introduced by Lanny Ross in the 1943 *Stage Door Canteen*—yet another all-star wartime musical with a quasi-revue format. Seventy years later, it must be admitted that Ross sang it very well, but at the time, his high tenor must have seemed at least two generations stylistically out-of-date—his approach is much more operetta than swing era. Two other then-young singers remembered the song from the war: Tony Bennett (who sang it on his 1959 *To My Wonderful One,* around the same time as Stafford) and Mel Tormé (on a 1990 duo set with George Shearing called *Mel & George "Do" World War II*), but no one tops Stafford. The lyrics (by Al Dubin, to a tune by storied songwriter Jimmy Monaco) are a little more stoic than usual—most songs on Stafford's album merely imply that we should all keep a stiff upper lip and face the future with a smile, but these lyrics come out and state that explicitly.

"Yesterdays" is the only song on *I'll Be Seeing You* that just doesn't belong on the album—it seems too much of a stretch to make it work in a wartime context. Nobody in wartime songs is dreaming of yesterdays, they're inevitably looking forward to the bright tomorrows ahead, a kind of nostalgia for the future as represented in the classic British song "(There'll Be Bluebirds Over) The White Cliffs of Dover." Surrounded by the rest of the album, "Yesterdays" is hopelessly dark and bleak—there's no hint of the lover coming back or things getting better. This was one of two songs deleted when the Westons reissued the album on their own label, Corinthian Records. Still, there's no denying it's one of the most moving interpretations ever of the classic Jerome Kern song (from *Roberta,* 1933). It belongs somewhere, just not here.

Composer Harry Warren and lyricist Leo Robin wrote the heartfelt "No Love, No Nothin'" for Alice Faye to sing in the 1943 Fox film *The Gang's All Here.* Counterbalanced by the circus psychedelia of "The Polka Dot Polka" and "The Lady in the Tutti-Frutti Hat," this no-frills love song is refreshingly straightforward. No frills, no love, no nothin', in fact—it's all about the deprivations that the "love-sick girl" on the home front is suffering; although the comparison is never stated directly, there's an obvious parallel with wartime rationing and shortages. It was near impossible to get sugar, rubber tires, or gasoline, among other goods, and the same thing applied to love—she's not getting any of that either ("no fun with no one"), not until her baby

comes home. Even the bone-simple rhymes (the lead-off is "home" and "roam") convey a sense of deprivation. Warren's melody is actually very rich harmonically, and is in a fetching ABAB format; Robin's lyrics on the verse utilize a triple-rhyming scheme: "froze," "suppose," "goes." Another singer might have tried to show a cheerful attitude in the face of adversity, but Stafford admirably makes it work by taking it at face value.

"I'll Be Seeing You" was another war song by default: originally written in 1938 for a flop show called *Right This Way,* it was revived for the war (much like "As Time Goes By"), although due to a somewhat morbid coincidence. The lyricist Irving Kahal died in February 1942, and according to one story bruited about by sheet music collectors, this song was played at his funeral—a suitable enough air for such a solemn occasion—because the funeral home was filled with publishers and songwriters, among them Kahal's partner, Sammy Fain. It then and there occurred to more than a few movers and shakers in the music industry that this 1938 song perfectly captured the current mood of the war. Stafford sings it slowly and movingly, almost hypnotically; I never noticed before how Kahal's lyrics use images of the most harmless, innocuous sort—"that small café, / The park across the way / The children's carousel / The chestnut trees, the wishing well"—to underscore the seriousness of the absence. It's not the big things that tell her he's gone, it's these usually meaningless little things—chestnut trees, for chrissake. After the first chorus, she starts to hum in harmony with the orchestra, almost as if her mind is drifting off into a reverie. The message is that she's thinking of her absentee lover, and the words are no longer on her mind. Her interpretation has at least a hint of optimism, but there's nothing concrete—it's obvious that she doesn't know exactly when she'll be seeing him. She may in fact be looking at the moon, but she'll be seeing him.

Whereas many of these songs had a life after the war ended, that's not what was on Irving Berlin's mind when he wrote "I Left My Heart at the Stage Door Canteen." Sammy Cahn's brilliance in "I'll Walk Alone" was to leave nearly all the details blank, to make the situation it describes universal and not totally connected to the war. Berlin's strength is to make everything completely specific, with all the precise details filled in—"I Left My Heart at the Stage Door Canteen" is a very specific song about a specific character in a very specific period of time. There were numerous cases when Berlin could be as poetic or as witty as Cole Porter or Lorenz Hart, but in many of his best songs his key asset is his ability to be as direct as possible. It was written to be sung by a young man (as part of the all-male, all-soldier cast of Berlin's 1942 revue, *This Is the Army*), so Stafford adjusts the gender pronouns as necessary: "a girl named Eileen" becomes "a handsome marine" and "a soldier boy without a heart" is now a "love-sick girl." Stafford tells the full story, such as it is: young soldier and pretty hostess meet and fall in love at the Stage Door Canteen. There are whole worlds of information communicated between the lines. Whereas most of the other songs on the album are despondent to a degree, "Stage Door Canteen" radiates pure innocence—this is a love song for two virgins. As a corollary, one can't help thinking of innocent young men being sent into battle, many without ever having experienced physical love. Paul Weston's arrangement rewrites Berlin's ending: Jo sings the closing line ending on a descending interval, then restates it, this time going up on the last note.

The last big hit movie musical of the war was *Anchors Aweigh*, which, though it had a stronger plot than *Follow the Boys, Stage Door Canteen, The Gang's All Here,* or *This Is the Army,* still retained many elements of the all-star revue format. The big ballad from *Anchors Aweigh* was "I Fall in Love Too Easily"—although if you didn't know it was from a wartime movie, you wouldn't necessarily think of it as a wartime song. In truth, how she falls in love too easily is probably the last thing a serviceman would have liked to hear his girl back home singing. Styne's melody consistently brings out the classical allusions in the arrangers who orchestrate the song, and there are Tchaikovskian touches in both Axel Stordahl's arrangement for Sinatra and in Weston's orchestration for his wife. Again, her singing is plaintive and understated—it's a minimal approach to a song about having too much.

"You'll Never Know" was inspired by a race-track bugle call, or so composer Harry Warren told Michael Feinstein. The song was an amazing, colossal hit after being introduced by Alice Faye—one of the biggest female musical stars of the war years—in the 1943 *Hello, Frisco, Hello* and subsequently winning the Academy Award. Curiously, over the last seventy years it's never been one of Warren's most performed songs of the period; one doesn't hear it nearly as often as "On the Atchison, Topeka, and the Santa Fe" or "At Last." (The latter would have been perfect for Stafford, and particularly on this album.) Whereas Warren wrote "No Love, No Nothin'" for Alice Faye as a deliberate song of wartime separation, "You'll Never Know" only became one by default—*Hello, Frisco, Hello* was a period piece, and the kind of Americana-style escapism intended to get audiences' minds off the war. Yet Mack Gordon's lyric includes lines like "You went away and my heart went with you. / I speak your name in my every prayer" that clearly spoke to wartime viewers. Stafford's treatment is surprisingly cheerful, she's not trying to sound depressed or despondent—and she sounds happy to hear a prominent tenor saxophone obbligato (probably played by Ted Nash) behind her. She liberally rewrites the melody, especially in the last eight bars, and her vocal is far more optimistic than torchy.

"I Should Care" was a major torch song of the era—but one that doesn't fit perfectly into the framework of the album; by 1959, it should have been apparent to Stafford and Weston that this was a song about a relationship that had ended. It would be a major stretch to construe it as being about two lovers separated by the war. Understandably, the Westons wanted to include it, since it was Paul Weston's single biggest hit as a composer—he wrote the melody in conjunction with fellow arranger Axel Stordahl while Sammy Cahn wrote the famous lyrics. It was a major hit of the war era, sung widely on the radio (and heard in the 1945 MGM film *Thrill of a Romance*), and it also had the good fortune to be introduced just as the AFM ban was ending, resulting in many successful recordings, none more so than Sinatra's (with co-composer Stordahl conducting).

There's no denying that the Stafford-Weston

treatment of "I Should Care" is stunning, and a perfect song for her—especially with another lovely tenor solo from Nash. And it would have been a crime had she never recorded it. Still, it's not a perfect fit for the album, especially as the closing song. It's kind of curious that Stafford and Weston buried "I'll Be Seeing You" in the middle of the album—by rights, it should have been the closer; it's a perfect note to end on, a song of farewell that carries with it an implicit note of understated optimism, and hope for a future reunion, even though that reunion may well be in the next world.

It seems as if hardly anyone noticed *I'll Be Seeing You* when it was first released in 1959. Decades later, the Westons exercised a clause in their contract with Columbia that allowed them to claim ownership of their master recordings after a certain amount of time. They started their own label, Corinthian Records, and released what looked like a budget reissue of *I'll Be Seeing You,* with a plain brown cover, two deletions, and a new title: *G.I. Jo.* They picked the right two songs to drop: "Yesterdays" and "I Should Care." Ironically, when the album was titled *I'll Be Seeing You,* it ended with "I Should Care," but *G.I. Jo* ends with "I'll Be Seeing You."

No matter what the title, the album was in itself a reunion of sorts, a reconnecting of Stafford with the songs and the era that first made her a star. World War II means a lot of different sounds to a lot of different people—from the euphoric jive of the Andrews Sisters to the stoic and sentimental songs of separation sung so brilliantly by Shore, Sinatra, Como, and others. Yet no one captured the era better than Jo Stafford did on *I'll Be Seeing You,* in which she movingly interprets the bittersweet songs of a bittersweet era with her bittersweet voice.

41

Kay Starr

I Cry by Night

(1962)

All the albums in this book represent great artists at their absolute peak, but they did their best work at different points in their careers. June Christy's *Something Cool* and Peggy Lee's *Black Coffee,* for instance, were both essentially first albums by former big band vocalists, who took full advantage of the develop-ing long-playing format to show that they were more than mere canar-ies, even more than mere jukebox acts and hitmak-ers, but capable of creat-ing fully formed artistic statements utilizing the broader canvas of the new medium. Jack Teagar-den, conversely, made his most memorable album, *Think Well of Me,* close to the end of his life. And certain other artists came through with their defini-tive statements just on the brink of a long dry spell: Jackie Paris's *The Song Is Paris, The Tony Bennett / Bill Evans Album,* and Kay Starr's *I Cry by Night.* It's as if they were aware they had reached the end of an era—and whatever they had been saving up for that moment, all of it went into these albums. *I Cry by Night* (1962) wasn't Starr's final album, but it was her last truly classic recording, as well as her all-time greatest.

Born in 1922, Starr wasn't even forty when she made this definitive, conclusive statement; she had been operating in the big time for a quarter century at that point, ever since about 1937, when, in junior high school, she had served as band singer with bandleader and jazz violin great Joe Venuti. Even

here, the signs of potent cross-cultural fertilization were apparent: Venuti was an Italian American who always claimed to have been born on the boat midway during his parents' migration, and he grew up to become one of the leading representatives of New York jazz during the Roaring Twenties. He was by far the greatest soloist of his era on the violin, an instrument that figures much more prominently in both country music and classical music than in jazz, and he worked with Starr in Tennes-see, a state that had its own jazz scene but was, obviously, much more of a hotbed of country music. The Oklahoma-born Starr herself was multi-culti even at birth: her father was a Native American, while her mother's people were of Irish descent.

The history of Ameri-can vernacular music is one of different strains of music breaking apart from each other—much like the world's continents in the Paleozoic era—and then coming back together (philosophically, at least). Kay Starr grew up literally singing to the chickens on her parents' poultry farm in a Pangaea period wherein popular songs, show music, jazz, blues, and hillbilly music were almost literally in bed together—or at the very least, in beds that may have been separate but were certainly adjacent. When she was first learning to sing, there was no one to tell her that jazz, blues, country, and pop music were supposed to be separate pursuits. By the time she was a regularly working recording artist in the 1940s, all of these musics were tabulated on separate charts in *Billboard* magazine, but she had grown up fully immersed in all of them, and was more than credible in all four.

"Bonaparte's Retreat," a number-four chart hit single for her in 1950, is a representative Starr signature song. It had been an old-time bluegrass "breakdown," going back to well before the advent of recorded sound (and was later recorded as such by fiddler W. M. Stepp), before Nashville tunesmith Pee Wee King adapted it into a contemporary country hit. Thanks to King (himself of Polish extraction), the melody made the transition from folkloric music to popular music, yet Starr completely modernized it. Her treatment uses big band brass, and the time signature is much closer to a swinging 4/4 (whereas all the previous incarnations had been in a strict hoedown 2/4). Her singing has all the harmonic and melodic ingenuity and big-band-era swing of a contemporary jazz singer, someone who has grown up with Ella Fitzgerald and Billie Holiday, as well as the texture, the twang, and the overwhelming passion of a great country singer. If Count Basie had ever made an album titled *This Time in Nashville—Basie Plays the Great Country Hits* (you can imagine the cover, with the Count in a cowboy hat instead of his customary yachting cap), this is what it would sound like. That adaptability and diversity contributed to the longevity of her career—besides Ella Fitzgerald, how many band singers who were working in 1936–37 were still active in the mid-1960s? It was a long career by the standards of almost any era; Bing Crosby had shown that the key to longevity was diversity, and those artists who kept going through the decades, like Sinatra and Cole, were able to continually reinvent themselves—even Cole was singing lots of country music by the time of his death in 1964.

Starr's recording career was almost fated to run out of steam in the mid-1960s—not because of changing times, she'd already changed with the times many times by then—but because she had already done it all; there was nothing left for her to do. She had run out of new mountains to climb. In 1962, she released *Just Plain Country,* the same year as Ray Charles's *Modern Sounds in Country*

and Western Music; both albums rendered country classics with amazing musicality and originality, but Charles, as an artist now reaching a whole new audience, had brought not just an R&B feel to C&W, but an ineffable feeling of newness.

The vocalist whom Starr has most in common with is her approximate contemporary Dinah Washington: the very timbre of her voice tells us that Starr is essentially a country singer, no matter whether she's singing Hank Williams or Puccini, just as every note out of Dinah Washington's throat is that of a blues singer, even if she's singing Rodgers and Hammerstein or Noël Coward. They both have an intense, even a searing sound, a sound that conveys a rare combination of fearlessness and vulnerability. The crucial difference between the two is that Washington inspired multiple generations of jazz and R&B singers and then soul divas. Conversely, almost no one, alas, extended Starr's legacy—no other singer would continue to mix blues, jazz, and country music into a palatable mix and then proceed to cover all the ground from Broadway to Nashville to Hollywood to the Mississippi Delta.

Starr scored the majority of her hit singles between 1948 and 1957, attaining the pinnacle of chart-topping success in 1952 with her megahit, "Wheel of Fortune." Then she consolidated her gains in a five-year span from 1958 to 1962, in which she released eight uniformly excellent albums: *Rockin' with Kay* (1958), *I Hear the Word* and *Movin'!* (both 1959), *"Losers, Weepers...,"* *Movin' on Broadway!,* and *Jazz Singer* (all 1960), *I Cry by Night* (1961), and *Just Plain Country* (1962). All but the first two were made following her return to Capitol Records, which followed a three-year relationship with RCA. These six Capitol albums can be divided handily between fast and exuberant, swinging ones (*Movin'!, Movin' on Broadway!,* and *Jazz Singer*), and three of ballads, which were no less purely jazz but certainly slower (*"Losers, Weepers...," I Cry by Night,* and *Just Plain Country*).

By the end of this run, clearly no one was paying attention: it's hard to believe that the jazz press didn't universally declare *I Cry by Night* as the best set of love songs by a jazz singer with a smoking-hot small group since Billie Holiday's Verve sessions (or even Nat King Cole's *After Midnight*). "Losers, Weepers..." was a terrific album, in which Starr sang mostly slow and sad songs of loving and losing, with a very discreet big band and string section. Released only a year later, *I Cry by Night* was an even more intimate offering, in which the Starr singer performed a flawless program of torch tunes, accompanied by a rhythm section plus one horn.

There are moments on *In the Wee Small Hours, Black Coffee,* and *After Midnight* that resemble *I Cry By Night,* and on paper it seems it could have been produced by Norman Granz (who favored the small group setting for major jazz singers), but Starr's classic album has a remarkable vibe all its own, a combination of jazz, blues, and country ideals, all united under the general umbrella of heartbreakingly sad saloon songs.

All the musicians involved were currently studio players with a long history with jazz and big bands. The rhythm section was led by Gerald Wiggins, a pianist who started his career at the top: by age twenty-one he was playing in Louis Armstrong's big band and shortly thereafter in Benny Carter's. When he settled in the Los Angeles studios, he was a favorite choice of singers while occasionally recording albums under his own name—something of a parallel career to his white counterpart Jimmy Rowles. In 1958, "Wig," as he was known, had the honor of deputizing for two of the greatest piano players of all time: the album *Welcome to the Club* (reissued as *Big Band Cole*) was a collaboration between Nat King Cole and the Count Basie Orchestra, but the pianist was neither the King nor the Count but Wiggins, who should have earned a royal title with this one job alone. The rest of Starr's rhythm section included two other gentlemen who had put in many years with Cole, bassist Joe Comfort and Lee Young; the latter was still playing occasionally with Cole in 1961, and had, in fact, been the drummer on *After Midnight.* (The sole Caucasian in the rhythm section, Al Hendrickson, had started his career with Artie Shaw.)

In Los Angeles, the first recording date took place on Thursday, November 30, 1961, and the second the next day, Friday, December 1, each session resulting in six songs, for a total of twelve on the final album. The "guest soloist" on the first date was trumpeter Mannie (sometimes spelled "Manny") Klein, who was undoubtedly also the contractor for the two sessions. Klein was one of those rare musicians whose careers spanned virtually the entire history of jazz and American pop, from early hot jazz bands like the Memphis Five in 1922, to the more elaborate dance and concert bands of the late 1920s (even the biggest of them all, Paul Whiteman's), to the swing era in the 1930s and 1940s. When he made it to Hollywood, he not only became one of the most-heard trumpet soloists in the movies (that's him bugling for Montgomery Clift in *From Here to Eternity*), but he worked at a side career as a musicians' contractor for recording dates. Klein played behind a lot of singers on a lot of records. He was less distinctive than either Bobby Hackett or Harry "Sweets" Edison, but probably even more versatile—he could play everything, from hot jazz to straight formal "reading" jobs and even to klezmer and ethnic music—which made him all the more appropriate for the equally versatile Starr.

Starr couldn't have found a better song to begin the date with than "Baby, Won't You Please Come Home," one of many tunes from the Jazz Age that evokes the blues (and is frequently sung by blues singers) without being in the strict twelve-bar format. The tune was an early success for Clarence Williams, one of the first important African American music entrepreneurs. Published in 1919 (and introduced on records by Williams and his wife, blues singer Eva Taylor, in 1922), the song was performed by a wide range of jazz and pop personalities over the decades, including Sinatra in 1957. Klein's muted opening notes could pass for Edison; Starr sings it slowly and full of feeling, slower, in fact, than most blues singers would have taken it. Wiggins's piano solo is especially spare, he almost seems to be playing just the melody in the right hand with virtually no harmony in the left. The session was off to a roaring start, although Klein's trumpet might better be described as growling rather than roaring, while Starr's singing is more like moaning the blues.

In 1931, Ruth Etting had been the first notable singer to record "Nevertheless (I'm in Love with You)" by Bert Kalmar and Harry Ruby, otherwise best known for writing most of the songs for the Marx Brothers movies. As with the same team's "Three Little Words," the song had a persistent life without ever being a major hit for any one artist. Starr had recorded it in the late 1940s on a Standard transcription, a treatment that's significantly faster and uses a full-sized big band for accompaniment. The 1961 album track is slower and more bluesy; the earlier one is more upbeat, and this one is more low-down, both musically and in attitude. The right/wrong, weak/strong duality of the lyric could get very singsongy in the wrong hands, but Starr's treatment is both playful and torchy.

"Whispering Grass" had originally been a hit for the Ink Spots in 1940, and ever since then has been one of those songs that has been thought of as part of the African American experience: Duke Ellington, Lou Rawls, Erskine Hawkins's orchestra, Dakota Staton, and the star British Grenadian singer-pianist "Hutch" (aka Leslie Hutchinson). It was an early hit for songwriter Doris Fisher, and her more famous father, the veteran songwriter Fred Fisher (of "Chicago" fame), who is credited alongside his daughter. It's a song that seems to come from a very old place, an era when people lived on the land and communed more directly with nature, as reflected in still earlier songs like "I'm Telling It to the Daisies (but It Never Gets Back to You)," and also in songs set in earlier times like "I Talk to the Trees." The speaker in "Whispering Grass" freely communicates with plants, so much so that she implores the whispering grass not to reveal her secret heart. Starr, shadowed by an open-belled Klein, sounds remarkably vulnerable—as if she's worried about the future of her love affair, and the last thing she wants is a bunch of whispering blades of grass and blabbering trees annoying her about it. At one point she declares that the grass is whispering things "that ain't so"; first the subject of their whispering is a lie, then it's a "secret," and finally she speaks of this hidden truth as an "old thing"—best left forgotten.

Starr's raw power is in full force on "Lover Man (Oh Where Can You Be?)." This is the number one song in the Billie Holiday repertoire, and even more than her other signatures like "Strange Fruit" or "God Bless the Child," was conceived with her explicitly in mind. Starr's interpretation has a very slight Nashville twang, while Wiggins's piano likewise has a hint of the "slip note" style of country keyboardist Floyd Cramer; despite the long-standing association with Holiday (the song is, rightfully, included on virtually every tribute album to Lady Day), Starr makes it her own with her distinctive sound. Klein is heard only briefly— it's almost as if he were out grabbing a smoke for most of the track.

"I'm Alone Because I Love You" is a prehistoric waltz by Ira Schuster and Joseph Young. Although popular in the very early days of jazz, it was kept alive over the decades mainly by country singers like Ray Price and Eddie Cochrane. Even when Nat King Cole recorded it in 1964, his rendition was more country and western than jazz, and there's a hearty helping of hillbilly in Starr's as well. She opens with a foreboding, uncomfortable bass vamp from Comfort, and more Cramer-ish keyboard from Wig, while Klein's Sweets-ian trumpet punctuates the proceedings. Starr sounds down and blue, but she seems to relax and open up on the bridge, with more cheerful thoughts like "yesterday's kisses" and "yesterday's sunshine"; her version, notably, is not a waltz, but a slow, steady 4/4.

"I'm Still In Love with You," not to be confused with the Hank Williams country music standard "I Can't Help It if I'm Still in Love with You" (which Starr recorded on her subsequent album, *Just Plain Country*), is a ballad by a blues artist, the singer-guitarist Aaron Thibeaux ("T-Bone") Walker. Somehow you would think that all those hard-hitting female blues singers from Dinah Washington's church would be all over this one, but no, Starr is virtually the first major artist after Walker himself to record it. (Later, there would be a treatment by Lou Rawls.) Her treatment has a hint of sixteenth-note triplets in the intro, rather subtly phrased by Hendrickson, but in general it's part of Starr's brilliance that she makes a song sound great whether it was born of Broadway or the blues, Nashville, Storyville, or Soulville. She's supremely musical here, seeming to be singing with an unmistakable smile on her face—she sings as if she's glad that she's still in love with the guy and is convinced that he's still in love with her; it's less of a torch song, or an air of unrequited love, than anything else in the set. There's a definite beat to her vocal, it's not rubato, and Starr shows us she's a master of alternating between staccato and legato, singing sometimes in short rhythmic bursts and at other times stretching out notes for emotional impact.

On the second day, she and the same rhythm section gathered at the Capitol Tower again. For all but the last of the six numbers, the guest soloist was a true jazz heavyweight. Saxophonist Ben Webster had been born and raised in Kansas City, that hotbed of jazz, and worked his way up from territorial bands in Missouri to national orchestras like those of Cab Calloway and, more spectacularly, Duke Ellington. It was in Ellington's band that Webster came to fame, and he grew increasingly recognized as one of the major tenor saxophone soloists of his time or any other. Leaving Ellington, he spent the next thirty years (until his death at sixty-four) alternating between leading his own small bands and working as a guest star in a wide range of contexts. In the early 1960s, he guest-soloed on albums by jazz singers (Joe Williams), blues singers (Jimmy Witherspoon), and, memorably, on *Sinatra and Swingin' Brass* (1962). Webster had started his career as a disciple of Coleman Hawkins, but he quickly became known as a more passionate and emotional player, which was no small feat, since the Hawk was hardly unemotional himself. Webster was also a much stronger bluesman, one of the fiercest ever to hold a horn.

Webster's presence makes all the difference on the five tracks he plays on: "I Cry by Night," "It Had to Be You," "P.S. I Love You," "More than You Know," and "My Kinda Love." The idea of a superior jazz-pop singer working with a small band was rare, although not unprecedented. But on these five tracks, the album becomes something other than *Black Coffee* or *After Midnight* and more like *Annie Ross Sings a Song with Mulligan, John Coltrane and Johnny Hartman,* and *The Tony Bennett / Bill Evans Album.* Webster is more than a supporting player like Klein (or like Edison and the soloists on *After

Midnight); he's a true partner, his presence felt just as keenly as Starr's on all five tracks; he doesn't stay in the background (nor would Starr or anyone else want him to), and yet he doesn't pull focus, either. Starr is too much of a star, to put it one way, to play second fiddle, even to a jazz legend.

The title song, "I Cry by Night," seems to have been written expressly for Starr and this album by the team of Marvin Fisher (music) and Jack Segal (lyric). This is our second encounter with the Fisher family; Marvin was the brother of Doris and the son of Marvin (composers of "Whispering Grass"). Marvin seems to have been the artiest songwriter in this illustrious family, and he thrived in the marketplace as a pop tunesmith with a knack for songs that were both popular and sophisticated. Yet "I Cry by Night" is a total surprise: until you look at the composer credit you would think that it came from the country music world, it's much more Ray Price than Bobby Short. Starr and Webster are, as always, creatures of more than one world. Starr emphasizes the downward motion of the song, both melodically and lyrically—"I may laugh by day, but I cry by night"—and for once, compared to Starr's enormous passion, Webster sounds almost detached; where she's despondent, he's almost bubbly and aloft, and the contrast makes her vocal even more moving.

"It Had to Be You" comes from the Chicago team of Isham Jones, a prolific composer who enjoyed an equally important role in American music as a key architect of the modern dance band, and Gus Kahn, who, unlike his partner, found even greater success on Broadway and then in Hollywood. Comfort and Wiggins dominate the intro, and Starr stretches it out like a true hillbilly ballad: "think-ing of you-oo . . ."; "nobody else gave me a thri-ill."

Johnny Mercer consistently named "It Had to Be You" as his favorite song, and "P.S. I Love You," written with Gordon Jenkins, was one of Mercer's own earliest successes. Hendrickson introduces Starr, who keeps it rather light and introspective; the lyric takes the form of a letter being written, and Starr sings it as if she's conversing simultaneously with both herself and the object of her affection.

Webster is relatively understated on "It Had to Be You" and "P.S. I Love You," almost as if he's saving his energy for what's about to come. He then really comes into his own on "More Than You Know" and "My Kinda Love." "More Than You Know" was introduced in one of the most notable flop shows of the 1920s—that it opened on October 17, 1929, only a week before the stock market crash, was only the start of its problems. "More Than You Know" by Vincent Youmans (music) and Edward Eliscu (lyrics) (Billy Rose is sometimes given a share of the credit), is a song that gradually grew in importance; it was barely recorded at all in its first decade, but picked up considerable momentum from the swing era; for the last fifty years it's qualified as one of the major songbook standards of all time. In fact, in recent decades it is easily the most frequently heard of all Vincent Youmans songs. Webster introduces Starr here, and his stretched-out phrasing sounds as if he's doing his best to accommodate her and fit himself to her blue country mood. He stays behind her, doggedly but discreetly, never letting her out of his sight, like a private eye shadowing a suspect. She builds to a climax at the end of the first chorus, wailing on "more than you'd ever know-ow"; at which point he plays a tag, and she repeats the phrase even more dramatically.

Composer Lewis Alter wrote a little bit of everything, from bread-and-butter pop songs ("A Melody from the Sky") to a rare collaboration with Oscar Hammerstein ("I'm One of God's Children [Who Hasn't Got Wings]"), and even a symphonic jazz classic ("Manhattan Serenade," which was successful as both a concert work and a pop song). The African American lyricist Jo Trent collaborated with everyone, black and white, Jew and Gentile. "My Kinda Love" was their major collaboration, and one that musicians favored heavily from the Jazz Age up through the early modern era. This is Webster's most extensive solo; he starts the track, and plays consistently behind Starr, so much so that you'd think she's taking a guest vocal on a Ben Webster album. She sings the words "you're happy today" bright and cheerful, with separation between the syllables, but on "you may be gone tomorrow," she blends it all together with a slurring blue note. The end of the bridge gets a

stop-time treatment, with the rhythm section laying out, but Webster surrounds her with his big, vibrato-rich tenor sound as the two head for the coda. It's indeed "one way to paradise."

Why Webster left the session with one more number to go is anyone's guess. His friend the famous New York–based bassist Milt Hinton has pointed out that Webster was often so busy that he did multiple sessions in a single day—possibly he was on his way to another date and another paycheck. In any case, the final song of the two sessions, "What Do You See in Her?" features Starr with just the four-piece rhythm section and no horn; Hendrickson is the primary accompanist here. The tune is the work of the very obscure veteran Frank Weldon and the soon to be famous relative newcomer Hal David; it was recorded, not surprisingly, by female singers such as Sarah Vaughan, Dakota Staton, Nancy Wilson, and even Helen Grayco (the underappreciated big band singer who was also Mrs. Spike Jones). It's an astute lyric that Starr gets the most out of, the wronged protagonist asking the man who left her what he sees in the other woman, but it turns out to be a self-answering question and a self-fulfilling prophecy. Like every other track on the album, it's short but poignant; if Norman Granz had produced the album, the major improvement would have been that each track would have lasted a more luxurious four or five minutes at least. (The only shortcoming of this album is that there's not enough of it.) Starr sings like a wounded woman, in the best tradition of the line from Judy Garland to Billie Holiday to Edith Piaf to Loretta Lynn. She offers a big voice and an even bigger soul, and yet consistently seems vulnerable, and, most important, human. (Barbra Streisand could have learned a lot from her.)

After *I Cry by Night*, Starr made one more album in her "classic" series, *Just Plain Country*, taped in July 1962; then there were two more for Capitol, *The Fabulous Favorites* (1963), a set of stereo remakes of her earlier hits (including "The Rock and Roll Waltz," originally recorded for RCA), and a 1966 album with the rather awkward title of *Tears & Heartaches / Old Records*. (Side A begins with "Tears & Heartaches"; Side B begins with "Old Records."

There's no debating that *Tears* is a highly listenable album, but one wishes that Starr had been given more leeway to more fully interpret these songs the way she did on *Just Plain Country* in 1962 and even more so on *I Cry by Night* in 1961.

There was life after Capitol Records: an excellent pop standards album, *When the Lights Go on Again* (1968), a superior but underappreciated big band set with Count Basie titled *How About This* (1969), the eponymous *Country* (1974), and the jazzier *Back to the Roots* (1975). Lastly, there were two final albums that amount to postscripts to an amazing career, *Kay Starr* (a truly oddball pop package, 1981) and the live album Starr fans had been waiting fifty years for, *Live at Freddy's* (recorded in 1986; I'm proud to say that I was there).

It may be that Starr's versatility worked against her in the long run. To this day, more people think of her as a pop singer than as a jazz singer or even a country singer—which isn't surprising, since millions of people have actually heard "Wheel of Fortune" and "The Rock and Roll Waltz" rather than *I Cry By Night* or *Jazz Singer*. In 2001, she recorded what will likely be her final appearance on records, a guest duet with admirer Tony Bennett on his 2001 *Playin' with My Friends: Bennett Sings the Blues*. It was an amazing run of over sixty years from her first appearance on recordings to her last.

After years of inactivity, Katherine Laverne Starks died at age ninety-four in 2016. Of her many excellent singles and albums, *I Cry by Night* in particular offers some of the best singing of the American Songbook—all the American songbooks—that's ever been done, even if there isn't a category for it.

42

Maxine Sullivan

Memories of You: A Tribute to Andy Razaf

(1956)

"My recollections of working with Maxine are many and fond. In listening to this album again, almost sixty years after it was recorded, I thought how perfect Milt Hinton's playing was, then I realized that most of that side was Wendell Marshall!

"I recall that Jerry Newman's Esoteric Studio was a small high-ceilinged room on the second floor—I don't remember what street. I must have rehearsed with Maxine, probably at Leonard's apartment on Riverside Drive. I think that any ensemble writing must have been done by Charlie Shavers, and the rest was just put together, with direction by Leonard. Maxine's voice was lighter then; I did a lot of projects with her later on, and by the time of our Shakespeare album and the subsequent one, *I Love to Be in Love* (on Tono), it had settled to a contralto. She was easy to work with and had perfect, swinging time. I was honored to be hanging out with her and that whole band."

—Dick Hyman, August 2013

Hi, this is Maxine Sullivan. I'd like to pay a tribute today to the wonderful lyrics of Andy Razaf. First, we'd like to do a song that he wrote in collaboration with the one and only Fats Waller."

Recorded in 1956, the album *Memories of You: A Tribute to Andy Razaf* arrived so early in the history of the album that its star felt it necessary to supply a spoken introduction. The logic behind that probably was that up until this time, the only occasion in which one could hear twelve songs in a single sitting were live performances, whether in person or on the radio—therefore, the spoken intro makes the album seem more like a live show.

Maxine Sullivan (1911–1987) was an essential American jazz and pop artist and a rare one whose career enjoyed no traditional middle act. Sullivan had been a major attraction following her trend-setting hit record of 1937, her ingenious swing interpretation of the traditional Scottish folk song "Loch Lomond." (Its impact was so great that even actual Scots and Brits, such as Annie Ross and Noël Coward, felt compelled to come up with their own swing versions of the iconic song.) Though her spotlight had dimmed somewhat since the war, she continued to work, both in recordings and personal appearances, up through the end of the 1950s. She then disappeared completely for an entire decade, for personal and family reasons, she said (being somewhat vague about this sabbatical in later years), and reappeared in time for what would later be described as the "jazz revival" of the 1970s. By that time, the jazz of the swing era had become a niche music, and Sullivan fit very comfortably into that niche. Within that limited audience and older demographic, she was in tremendous demand, performing (mostly at traditional-style "jazz parties") and recording (on specialist labels) as much as she wanted.

Memories of You: A Tribute to Andy Razaf arrived at the midpoint of her career, just as she was phasing out her "first act," and preparing for her ten-year intermission. In 1955 and 1956, the journalist, producer, and songwriter Leonard Feather (1914–1994) and pianist and musical director Dick Hyman put together two albums for Sullivan; and their interest in the singer suggests that Sullivan was already the province of such ultra-knowledgeable parties and sophisticated insiders, and less so of the record-buying public at large. The first of these albums was released under several different titles, but the idea was to pay homage to her late professional and personal partner, the bassist and bandleader John Kirby (1908–1952). This 1955 project was a double concept album in the sense that it not only re-created the iconic John Kirby Sextet, but nearly all the material was what was then called "traditional," either folk songs or very old jazz standards, like "St. Louis Blues" and "Rose Room."

Feather was well aware that the album format was the medium for simultaneously re-creating and preserving the music of the past, for preserving and documenting what had come before—and, in the case of those Kirby homage sessions, to re-create it. Both were produced for the short-lived Period Records, which operated at the time of the transition from 10-inch to 12-inch LPs, releasing about three dozen albums in both formats, about half of which were reissues or licenses from the French Swing label (notably a three-volume *Django Reinhardt Memorial* series). Virtually all the new material, a fairly catholic assortment of very modern jazz (Sonny Rollins, Charles Mingus), traditional jazz (Danny Barker, Jack Teagarden), blues (Big Bill Broonzy), and some especially groovy piano (Al Haig, Ralph Burns), seems to have been produced by Feather. In his memoir, Feather refers to Period Records as "another independent company that glowed brightly for a few years."

The two Sullivan projects were recorded in November 1955 (*Flow Gently, Sweet Rhythm*, which came out with trumpeter Charlie Shavers billed

over Sullivan) and August 1956 (*Memories of You: A Tribute to Andy Razaf*); over the nearly sixty years since they were taped, they've often been reissued together, especially in the CD era. Feather wrote of "the ageless Maxine Sullivan" and noted that the set was "composed entirely of songs with lyrics by Andy Razaf, to whom an album had never been devoted." This 1956 Razaf collection arrived in the middle of two marvelous songbook albums devoted to Waller, that of Louis Armstrong in 1955 and that of Dinah Washington in 1957.

Andy Razaf (1895–1973) is generally described as one of many great American songwriters whose name is less well known than his music, which is mainly because, unlike his most famous partner, Fats Waller, he did not have a notable career as a performer in his own right. Waller and Razaf, who wrote their most famous songs together (but also both worked with other collaborators), were, along with Duke Ellington, the best-remembered songwriters to come out of the Harlem experience, that almost magical interwar era when the land above Central Park was seen by the city and the world as a refreshing, tan-colored alternative to Broadway, and African American talent was creating shows that were fully the equal of anything being seen in Times Square. Most uptown entertainment was themed around nightclubs (which were often larger than the Off-Broadway theaters of today), revues, and dance orchestras, but there was considerable overlap with the so-called legitimate theater: a number of Harlem productions made it down to Times Square and the Great White Way. Still, much more frequently, white patrons came up to Harlem to sample the music, dancing, and comedy. Producers like Lew Leslie and Connie Immerman were, in effect, competing successfully with Broadway revue moguls like George White and Earl Carroll, much as composers like Ellington, Waller, and Razaf had hits and status (in the music business at least) comparable with that of Irving Berlin or Cole Porter.

By the end of World War II, this particular golden era of Harlem entertainment was over, black popular music no longer meant swing bands but rhythm and blues, and musical shows meant full-length book productions rather than revues. Razaf was sixty years old when the Sullivan album was recorded, and in a period of involuntary semi-retirement. It would have been a much more obvious idea for Feather to produce Sullivan in "A Tribute to Fats Waller," but the Razaf project came about partially because of Feather's friendship with the lyricist. They had been close for at least fifteen years by then: in 1942, Razaf and Feather had written the song "Mound Bayou" together, and when, in 1943, Feather was up for membership in ASCAP, Razaf sponsored him. Focusing the album on Razaf was a brainstorm; Sullivan's voice, dark and low and sultry—though not any deeper than when she made her first discs in 1937—and her light, swinging, highly rhythmic style perfectly suited Razaf's lyrics in all their diversity: songs of romantic happiness, songs of despair, songs about not misbehaving and keeping out of mischief.

Feather put together a band that started with two key horn players from the Kirby Sextet project, trumpeter Charlie Shavers and clarinetist Buster Bailey. The producer then filled out the group with big band veterans who had since graduated to playing full-time in the studios, starting with Hyman and also including Jerome Richardson on alto saxophone, Wendell Marshall and Milt Hinton alternating on bass, and drummer Osie Johnson. Sullivan was particularly close to Shavers and Bailey, but she would have known everybody in the band and worked with them all at some point.

"Keepin' Out of Mischief Now" is generally regarded as Waller and Razaf's sequel to their hugely successful "Ain't Misbehavin'"—even as both songs replace a "g" with an apostrophe in their titles; one of the central differences is that "Misbehavin'" is in AABA form and "Mischief" is in ABAB. "Mischief" comes from 1932, one of Razaf's peak years, in which he wrote and published over fifty songs, the majority (including this one) with Waller. "Mischief" is one of many songs the pianist composed while he was between recording contracts, and, as such he never sang it on a recording or played it with his band—but he did record a lovely solo piano treatment in 1937. It was another jazz giant, Louis Armstrong, who made the song into a jazz standard when he recorded it in 1932—much as he had done for "Ain't Misbehavin'" three

years earlier. (If all the songwriters in the world, particularly African American ones, got together and figured out how much they owed Louis Armstrong, it probably would be even more than what he owed them.)

Hyman sets the tone for Sullivan's version of "Mischief." The album begins with a quick paraphrase of the melody, played on piano but so lightly, fingers barely touching the keyboard, that it almost sounds like a celeste. Then, Sullivan delivers her spoken introduction, accompanied by a feather-light piano background by Hyman. Sullivan offers the verse ("Don't even go to a movie show . . .") ad-lib before the proceedings kick into tempo with the chorus. Rather than evoking the Kirby Sextet, here the group plays very much like Fats Waller's Rhythm, the small group that accompanied the pianist-composer-singer on the majority of his most famous recordings (and nearly everything from 1934 on). Hyman leads the charge and sets the Waller-ian tempo. After Sullivan's verse and first chorus, Hyman solos with keyboard runs that sound like he had recently listened to Waller's 1937 piano solo of "Mischief" and it was very fresh in his memory. Following Hyman, Shavers plays sixteen bars and Sullivan reenters at the second "A" ("All the world can plainly see . . .") and takes it out. In the classic Ethel Waters tradition, this second half chorus is much more playful, and ends with a particularly inspired tag wherein Sullivan repeats the final line—which is also the song title—before the coda.

The second track is "Massachusetts," with a melody by "Luckey" Roberts, from 1942. It's an absolutely terrific song, and a valid reminder that Fats was merely the biggest (in every sense of the word) of the legendary Harlem stride pianists with whom Razaf collaborated. In addition to "Mrs. Waller's little boy," he wrote songs with James P. Johnson and Eubie Blake, as well as Roberts. Charles Luckyth Roberts was a pianist frequently mentioned in the same breath as Waller, Johnson, and Willie "the Lion" Smith, and no slouch as a composer either; he had a major hit in 1942 with "Moonlight Cocktail," a 1912 composition (originally known as "Ripples of the Nile") that became a Glenn Miller favorite. During the war years, especially after

Waller's death, Roberts and Razaf worked on a number of patriotic songs, including some for the Treasury Bond effort. "Massachusetts" certainly has a jingoistic feel. In general, Razaf's lyric is in the same vein as the innumerable Southern travelogue songs that Tin Pan Alley had been turning out for decades by then; however, its geographical focus is on a prominent state above—rather than below—the Mason-Dixon. The song was a winner for Razaf and Roberts in 1942, and is best remembered for an especially vibrant Okeh disc by the nascent jazz singer Anita O'Day with Gene Krupa's orchestra.

Although some arrangements on the Sullivan-Razaf album allude to the Kirby Sextet, and others, like "Mischief," are obviously inspired by Waller's Rhythm, Sullivan's "Massachusetts" is a solid 4/4 swinger in the spirit of the great big bands. It also opens adorably, with Sullivan making a comically unsuccessful attempt to spell the word "Massachusetts." After getting a few letters in, she announces, "Come on now, let's just sing the song." There follows a verse ("Am I happy? Yes! It's my lucky day . . ."), and then Hyman prods her into tempo as she kicks into a very solid dance beat. It's an exceedingly hip performance of a highly swinging song; the songwriters use the ostensibly awkward four-syllable phrase as a rhythmic mantra, chanted variously by Sullivan, Shavers, and the ensemble. Shavers also interjects spontaneous-sounding asides throughout, like "I can hardly wait" and "I hope that train ain't late." More than any of the 1942 recordings, Sullivan and company address the whole of Razaf's lyric, and it's a prime example of the lyricist at his wittiest, "I miss Cambridge, where / They have that Harvard air"—at this point Shavers breaks in with "So very proper!" Sullivan does wonderful things with Razaf's full text, leaving little room for instrumental solos, but Shavers says more in eight bars than most trumpeters could say in eight choruses. She concludes with a cute coda, "Well, move over, Massachusetts, I'm comin' right in . . . today."

"How Can You Face Me?" comes from the Waller-Razaf peak period in 1932, but doesn't seem to have been heard until fall of 1934; why the team sat on it for two years isn't known, but the wait

worked to their advantage. In 1932, Waller was not in a position to record it, but that had changed by 1934, and he included it in one of the first sessions by his new band, the Rhythm. In the fall of 1934—the ramp-up to the swing era—"How Can You Face Me?" was widely recorded by major white bands on major labels, and the song was obviously successful.

Still, the best recording is, obviously, by Waller himself. The song fits into the continuum of "Ain't Misbehavin'" and "Keepin' Out of Mischief Now" in that it's sung from the perspective of a character who has suffered as a result of someone else's misbehaving and mischief. This is, patently, a turnabout for Waller, and he makes the most of the comic possibilities of the situation. Even Waller's opening notes resonate with jaunty defiance; as he sings, he seems to be parodying his own song, throwing in comic asides while singing Razaf's lyrics ("My angel was just *a dog known as the* devil"), and engaging in a spontaneous dialogue with trombonist Floyd O'Brien: "Ah you're a dirty dog, get out in the street . . . No, I didn't go there last night, you know I wasn't there neither! I went to the other place!"

Sullivan sings from a woman's point of view, and, let's face it, in most traditional Tin Pan Alley songs, that was usually the perspective of a victim. The verse starts out rubato (following a lovely clarinet intro by Buster Bailey), with Sullivan starting it like a torch song, or a song of self-pity ("Love 'em, leave 'em, and deceive 'em / Seems to be your game"). She admonishes the perpetrator and herself as well, but as the track continues it's clear that she has some lingering affection for the "dirty dog"—"devil" that he may be. There are solos by Bailey, Shavers, and Hyman (not doing a Fats impression here, any more than Sullivan is), and the second bridge has Sullivan stretching out the payoff, the punch line, as it were: "was—just—a—devil." She ends with a trilly little scat figure over the coda, as if to say, That dirty dog of a devil wasn't so bad after all, was he?

"S'posin'" illustrates that Razaf had fruitful collaborations with Caucasian composers as well, the two represented here both being British, namely Paul Denniker and Feather himself. Denniker was an accomplished pianist (as all of Razaf's collaborators seem to have been) born and raised in London. Remarkably, according to Barry Singer's excellent biography *Black and Blue: The Life and Lyrics of Andy Razaf*, the two began working on songs together as early as 1924; in the context of the period, this is highly unusual at a time when it was illegal in many states for black musicians and white musicians to play in the same band together. It was also rare for musicians of different skin colors to play together on recording sessions—which weren't even open to the public.

Written in 1929, "S'posin'" was their biggest hit as a team, and more than that, it was perhaps the single most successful of Razaf's songs in its day. ("Honeysuckle Rose" and "Ain't Misbehavin'" would catch up with it and surpass it only later on.) Alas, not all interracial business relationships were as ideal as that of Razaf and Denniker; "S'posin'" was a huge hit in 1929, but Razaf's publisher, the reprehensible Joe Davis (whose unscrupulousness Singer documents in great detail), contrived to swindle Razaf out of all his royalties. It could have only irked Razaf that the song became internationally famous; the great British–South African singer Al Bowlly even sang it with "the Honolulu Serenaders," an ersatz Hawaiian recording made in London.

It's easy to see why "S'posin'" was so popular in the last few months of the Roaring Twenties—before the crash and the Depression changed everything. Like a flapper, like Colleen Moore, Clara Bow, or Helen Kane, the song is cute and flirty, Razaf's well-constructed lyric sets up the character of a saucy but virginal 1920s girl rather literally dancing around the idea of telling her beau that she's in love with him, yet not coming out and actually saying it until the last line. Sullivan, who was born in 1911, grew up during the Jazz Age, and she has so much fun with the text that her pleasure becomes palpable. It's another song in the ABAB format, and Sullivan fully treats us to two different verses and two full choruses—for another singer that might be too much verbiage, but Sullivan is sweet, sincere, and lightly swinging all the way. Shavers plays a short muted solo between the two choruses, but this time it's really about Sulli-

van, the rhythm section, and how they propel each other along.

Likewise, "My Fate Is in Your Hands" was a substantial success for Waller and Razaf in 1929; like "S'posin'," it quickly transcended the Harlem showbiz milieu that created it—it was played by many mainstream dance bands, including Guy Lombardo and His Royal Canadians, with a trademark quivery vocal by brother Carmen, by British bands in London, and even by Josephine Baker in Paris. As "Fate" would have it, Waller himself never sang it on a recording, but he played a key role on an extremely lovely vocal version of the song by his friend the pioneering crooner Gene Austin; Waller also made an outstanding solo piano recording. Razaf's lyrics, which use a courtroom metaphor for a relationship ("You're my judge and jury . . . what is the verdict? / My fate is in your hands"), anticipates a later mini-movement of love songs using crime and punishment as a metaphor: "Wanted," "Guilty," "Confess," and "Prisoner of Love."

Buster Bailey intros Sullivan's verse with a lilting phrase which reminds us that, long before the Kirby Sextet, he was the star clarinetist—essentially the Benny Goodman equivalent—in Fletcher Henderson's orchestra. After the verse and chorus (AABA), Shavers and Bailey alternate eight-bar sections before Sullivan returns, even more relaxed and gently swinging for the last sixteen bars. Again, her closing tag is a winner, casual and compelling at the same time: "My fate, honey baby, is in your hands!"

"Stompin' at the Savoy" and "Christopher Columbus" were both composed by saxophonists, Edgar Sampson and Leon "Chu" Berry, and at the time were little more than pleasant chores for Razaf. However, both turned out to be highly lucrative for the lyricist. He didn't set out to write words for swing band instrumentals, he had higher aspirations for more serious and poetic lyrics ("Mound Bayou" is an example), but publishers often came to him with jobs like these. In some cases, the instrumentals were already hits and the copyright holders were convinced that they would be more valuable with lyrics even if, in some cases, those lyrics were never performed by anybody. In 1932, for instance, Waller and Razaf wrote

"Stealin' Apples," a swing band perennial, performed steadily over the next fifty years by Benny Goodman, among many others, but sung by, quite literally, no one. Yet in this case, the publishers were right: no one thought of "Stompin' at the Savoy" and "Christopher Columbus" as material for singers, but when Razaf wrote the words, that's exactly what they became.

The last tune on Side A, "Stompin' at the Savoy," is, famously, the theme song of Chick Webb and His Orchestra and of the Savoy Ballroom, on Lenox Avenue and 140th Street in Harlem, where the Webb band took on all comers. Razaf's lyrics capture the glory, grandeur, and even "sweet romance" of what it was like to dance to one of the great swing bands, and, as Singer points out, Razaf's words are not only singable but danceable; they practically whirl around the floor all by themselves. Thanks to Razaf, dozens of singers over the years have been able to perform the song, from swing era vocalists like Ella Fitzgerald, June Christy, Mel Tormé, and Sarah Vaughan (who sang it as a samba at the Savoy) to more contemporary jazz singers like Karrin Allyson and Carol Sloane. "Stompin' at the Savoy" also may be the only swing anthem introduced by Judy Garland, vocally at least; the showbiz icon's first commercial recording had the former Frances Gumm, billed here as a "12 year old swing singer" belting out "Stompin' at the Savoy."

Sullivan launches directly into "Savoy" after a very brief trumpet intro, and boom, she's off and running—there's no verse to slow things down. Still muted, Shavers then plays a full chorus solo that's so eloquent and yet simple and so armed with technique that one imagines he could make his trumpet sound muted even without a mute. Hyman plays a piano interlude and Sullivan returns at the bridge; indeed, you'll keep dancing long after the track is finished. Razaf did a brilliant job—his assignment was, after all, to write a song about dancing—and he was going beyond the call of duty when he ended the piece with a vague allusion to a romantic note: "So let me stomp away with you." Sullivan, more than Garland or Fitzgerald, really finesses that awkward last line and makes it sound amazingly intimate.

The second side opens with what amounts to a lot of business before we hear one of the most familiar melodies in all of jazz: "Honeysuckle Rose." Hyman starts with a flurry of Fats-ish flourishes, and Sullivan goes along with the gag. "Okay, Fats," she commands, "you can relax now." The tempo slows down to a gentle glissando, but instead of singing, Sullivan offers a quaint spoken intro, "This is a song about a fellow named Mr. Rose. Let's call him 'Sam Rose.'" No, this is not a hysterically funny line in and of itself, but it does have the flavor of one of Waller's famously extemporaneous semi-spoken asides. We then get the verse, which begins, "Have no use for other sweets of any kind . . ." Just by omitting the word "I," which should logically be there at the start of that sentence, Razaf makes the lyric marvelously conversational, he seems to begin with a dialogue that's already in progress, creating an instant immediacy between singer and audience. Finally, about forty-five seconds in, all the preliminaries are finished and Sullivan and the rhythm section launch into the famous melody.

She more than does justice to it, delivering the tune with a solid, steady beat, in the classic Maxine manner, lots of power without excess of volume or tempo. Hyman, fittingly—and jauntily—leads the soloists in the instrumental break, followed by Jerome Richardson on alto (whose modernistic solo suggests Charlie Parker's famous variation on "Rose," which he titled "Scrapple from the Apple"), Bailey (sounding a bit reedy), and Shavers (still muted). Sullivan reenters for a full second chorus, delivering the tune at something more like double-time, but still logically and coherently. When she gets to the second bridge and final A, she sings an entirely unfamiliar set of lyrics that seem to have been penned by Razaf specifically for this recording: "You've got what sweetness, much more than a candy store. / Oh what sweetness! You're all that I've waited for!" She ends with an imaginatively musical tag that plays with the words "honey," "suckle," and "rose" in that order.

"Memories of You" is perhaps the finest ballad of Razaf's canon, and it's the romantic high point of Sullivan's album. Richardson launches it with flute, giving the song more of a modern feel than anything else on the set, immediately taking us out of the past and more into the world of the song. Sullivan sings it passionately, but it still stays in dance tempo; there's nothing like what Frank Sinatra or Billie Holiday might do (as on her Commodore sessions) of slowing it down to crawl-time. That Sullivan manages to get so much emotion from it while still keeping the whole works eminently danceable seems remarkable. Just a little emphasis here and there, phrasing one word or syllable, makes it exceptionally powerful: "*How* I wish / *I* could forget"—not as pronounced as Sinatra's from a few months later, but marvelous just the same. Even Hyman's eight bars of piano have a blue, hesitating quality to them.

"Ain't Misbehavin'" has been recorded a zillion bajillion times, but Sullivan's treatment stands out as one of the very, very best. There's a brand-new verse, possibly never heard anywhere else, and probably again supplied by Razaf via the prodding of Feather. Actually, the passage that opens Sullivan's track is better described as a fast patter section rather than a verse: she sings about the various stations on her television set—"Channel Four, Channel Two / What a bore, where are you?"—which she then answers "I'm a lonesome Jill without a Jack / Because the TV set just won't talk back." She sings the first chorus very zingy and zippy, with much élan; no grass is growing under her feet. Then, the tempo ritards and Sullivan now gives us the familiar verse ("This is a fickle age / with flirting all the rage," followed by another full chorus (she's probably the first to sing "home and my video" instead of the familiar "radio")—and then she reprises the original patter bit as a coda: "Channel nine / Channel three / Baby mine, rescue me!"

Next comes what might be the prettiest song on the album, "Mound Bayou." "Spending a weekend out at Andy's home in New Jersey, I had noticed a sheet of lyrics lying on the small green-painted upright piano, the one on which Fats Waller had written some of his greatest songs," Leonard Feather later wrote. "Andy explained that Mound Bayou was a small town in Mississippi with an all-black population. At his suggestion, and inspired by the idea of composing on a piano Fats had visited so often, I set 'Mound Bayou' to music." With words by Razaf and music by Feather, the tune was first recorded in 1942 by a singer named Linda Keene accompanied by "Henry Levine and His Strictly from Dixie Jazz Band"—this was an ensemble that played on a highly popular radio series entitled *The Chamber Music Society of Lower Basin Street*. However, "Mound Bayou" was then suitably introduced in the first recording that everybody remembers, by the major blues-jazz singer Helen Humes with saxophonist Pete Brown's band. It's a truly lovely song, Feather's most notable success as a songwriter (other than this, most of his better efforts were R&B numbers and novelties, like "How Blue Can You Get?").

Shavers plays a relaxed, deliberately lazy-style trumpet intro that surely suggests a sleepy Southern town, one with a lazy 'Sippi steamer slowly chugging by. Sullivan sings slowly and luxuriously; she may be in a rush to get back home, but as soon as she arrives, all the hurrying is over. You can imagine how it might be draggy in the hands of a lesser singer—even if the townsfolk depicted in the lyric are decidedly stationary—but Sullivan, like Humes in 1942 and the young Ernestine Anderson (who recorded it in 1960), keeps everything mobile.

The second-to-last tune (number eleven as the crow flies), "Christopher Columbus," begins with a bass break as Sullivan starts the verseless lyric. As with "Savoy," Razaf's words transformed the piece from a hit instrumental into a song that would endure; everyone concerned was delighted when Fats Waller, who had nothing to do with writing it, played and sang it with his Rhythm in an all-time classic of jazz and jollity in 1936. There's only a brief bit of Shavers near the end, otherwise it's all Sullivan and the rhythm section, which makes perfect sense in that the charms of the piece are purely rhythmical—and more hysterical than historical. She even condenses "Mister Christopher Columbus" into *Mistopher* Columbus" at one point. Perhaps certain singers, like Fitzgerald and Washington, swung *harder* than Sullivan, but a rock-hard swing isn't always the best approach. "Christopher Columbus" shows that no one, but no one, ever swung *better* than Maxine Sullivan.

After "Christopher Columbus," the album ends with a true Razaf-Waller gem, "Blue Turning Grey over You." That Feather and Sullivan—or anyone else—knew the song at all was directly due to Louis Armstrong, who put it on the map in 1930. (All that Pops needed to make the song immortal was just one single line: "You used to be so good to me / That's when I was a novelty.") With its transcendental trumpet solo and even better vocal, "Blue Turning Grey" is a cornerstone of the Armstrong/Waller-Razaf relationship, and he recorded more songs by the two partners than he did by any other songwriters (as Satchelmouthed scholar Ricky Riccardi has thoroughly tabulated). Billie Holiday recorded a wonderful version of the song, clearly inspired by Armstrong, in 1951; and Satch's own 1955 reinterpretation, for his album *Satch Plays Fats,* is also majestic and equally marvelous.

Although Sullivan's career was closely intertwined with two major bandleaders of the swing era, Claude Thornhill and John Kirby (her first husband), she was never a big band vocalist in the traditional sense of the term. Yet she was the greatest swing band singer ever. Her reading of "Blue Turning Grey over You" is solidly jazzy as usual; she plays with the song without distorting the melody while keeping the lyrics sacrosanct. Like all those swing era singers named Helen, Sullivan can tell a whole, complex, multilayered story in a very short amount of time (this track is 2:29, and it's not even the shortest on the album) and she can get in all the emotion and drama while still remaining in dance tempo, and without compromising the tune.

"Blue Turning Grey over You" is a song about the end of a relationship, unhappy but not bitter, and Sullivan isn't the least bit whiny or morose. It turned out to be the way she concluded her career as well; she reprised the song on what turned out to be her final recording, a live concert in the Highlights in Jazz series, taped in New York in March 1987, less than a month before her death.

Many classic recordings did not have the impact on the artists' actual careers that they should have; Tony Bennett's meetings with Bill Evans would not be fully appreciated until many years later, and it wasn't until after Dinah Washington's death that everyone realized her Fats Waller songbook was her greatest work in the album format. *Memories of You: A Tribute to Andy Razaf* must be a unique and extreme example wherein the artist, having cut one of the greatest works (actually, when you count the Kirby reunion project, two of the greatest) of her career, completely disappeared. She was rapidly transitioning from a period of semi-retirement to one of total oblivion; by 1959, she disappeared entirely, only to reemerge at the very end of the flower power decade. From that point on, she about-faced from one of the most obscure to the most visible jazz singers on the scene, constantly recording and touring, right up until that final concert in New York in 1987.

Maxine Sullivan had essentially started her career in 1934 when she was asked to sing Joyce Kilmer's hoary ancient poem "Trees." She later said that she felt like she had no choice but to do it her way, which in this case meant that she had to swing it, i.e., put a jazz beat underneath it. Sullivan was one of those reluctant auteurs who simply had to do things their way, even if it didn't make sense to anybody else at the time—perhaps going into retirement right after she had made the album of a lifetime was another manifestation of that. No matter what she did, even if it meant depriving the world of her exquisite artistry for much too long, she was always herself.

43

Jack Teagarden
Think Well of Me
(1962)

Life in a tea garden has its own charm, but is not free of dangers and troubles, either.

—Hindu saying

n May 1961, Bob Brookmeyer—who, at the age of thirty-one, had already established himself as one of the top trombone players and arrangers in the highly competitive New York jazz-and-studio scene—went to see Jack Teagarden at the Village Vanguard. "Oddly enough, Jack wasn't my original hero on the trombone," Brookmeyer told me, a few days before his eightieth birthday in November 2009. When he was a student trombonist in Kansas City during the swing era, Brookmeyer's first role models were Bill Harris and Dicky Wells, the trombone stars of the Woody Herman and Count Basie bands, respectively. By the bebop era, the jazz pioneers of the Roaring Twenties—even Teagarden and his colleague Louis Armstrong—were starting to seem out of step to some younger musicians.

But not for long, Brookmeyer added. "As I grew older and my taste got more sophisticated, I started to really appreciate Teagarden. By the time I went to see him at the Vanguard, I was a big fan." The next time Brookmeyer saw Teagarden was roughly seven months later, in January 1962, on the sessions for the all-time-classic album *Think Well of Me.* "Jack was really playing well at the time, the best

that I had ever heard him, both at the Vanguard and on the sessions."

Nineteen sixty-one–sixty-two represented a unique moment in the life of Weldon Leo "Jack" Teagarden (1905–1964): the legendary jazzman was trying, and for a time, succeeding, in keeping his rather considerable demons at bay. "At that time Jack wasn't drinking—but I was," said Brookmeyer, who would eventually conquer his own addiction with the aid of Alcoholics Anonymous. Even in a field where every third guy seemed to have either a drinking or a drug problem (the difference was largely generational), Teagarden's capacity for alcohol had long since assumed mythic proportions. And Brookmeyer took note: if Jack Teagarden, of all the world-champion imbibers, somehow found the inner strength to clamber onto the wagon, it was nothing less than an inspiration and a wake-up call for Brookmeyer.

But Teagarden's sobriety was, alas, short-lived. In September 1963, eighteen months after the recording of their album together, the two trombonists ran into each other at the Monterey Jazz Festival. "He was clearly in his cups again," said

Brookmeyer. "Plus he had a woman with him who seemed . . . well, kind of seedy. He saw me, and he looked a little bit ashamed. He gave me a look like he was sorry."

Try to imagine the look that Jack Teagarden gave Bob Brookmeyer. A look that conveyed lost innocence, disillusionment, of broken hopes and shattered dreams, of role models with feet of clay, of people that you invest your trust in and who let you down, of an old lush of a trombone player sending a warning message—a cautionary tale, as it were—to his younger counterpart.

As it happened, Teagarden and Brookmeyer had already translated that look—complete with all the emotional baggage that it carried with it—into concrete musical form and lyrical form. And it went like this: "Think well of me, for I think well of you."

Think Well of Me might be said to be a combination of the work of three drunks, two of them trombonists: the singer and star instrumentalist Jack Teagarden, the arranger Bob Brookmeyer (who shared those duties with veteran orchestrator Russ Case), and the songwriter (and former bandleader and vocalist) Willard Robison.

Teagarden and Robison had known each other for forty years by 1962. At the time they first met, Teagarden was already something of a non–urban legend, who had become famous among musicians in the Southwest by playing with yet another near-mythic character, the Texas boogie-woogie piano giant Peck Kelley. Teagarden had been born in Vernon, Texas; his father played trumpet in brass bands, and Teagarden first studied the baritone horn, though he soon graduated to trombone. As a teenager, he was part of the first wave of Western jazz musicians to get hip to the new music from the New Orleans diaspora, which by 1920 was in the process of spreading to both coasts as well as the South and Midwest. As was the case with nearly all major musicians of the period (except Kelley), the call of the music eventually drew Teagarden to New York, where he soon became the talk of the jazz world—fairly unchallenged as the greatest trombonist there was—and a kick-ass blues singer besides.

Teagarden was a complex figure who didn't quite fit the profile of any other musician of the era: as an innovator, he flew very near the orbit of both Louis Armstrong and Bix Beiderbecke, and he was, in fact, very close to both of these legendary trumpeters. But he was neither a rip-roaring success by "going commercial" (as critics decried), like Armstrong, nor a self-destructive Roman candle who burned himself out at an early age, like Beiderbecke—although at times he certainly seems to have tried. Like Armstrong, Teagarden led several generations of musicians—trombonists especially—on the path into the future of jazz, and was one of the key players who helped establish the primacy of the soloist, yet he was firmly grounded in the fundamentals. He was, no less than Armstrong, one of the all-time masters of the blues, both playing and singing them.

While Teagarden doesn't fit any particular mold, getting a bead on the career of Willard Robison is even more difficult. In fact, much about him is open to question—we're not even sure exactly when or where he was born, the best we can do is to say somewhere in Missouri around 1892–94. In the early days of radio, those years when the Depression was growing ever more depressed, Robison was widely known as the leader of the then famous Deep River Orchestra, and he also recorded prolifically as both a bandleader and a vocalist in the late 1920s. By 1940, Robison was more or less a full-time songwriter, performing only occasionally, writing songs that continued to make an indelible impression on other artists—particularly those who looked for highly original, out-of-the-way songs, such as Peggy Lee and Johnny Mercer.

Speaking on the *Chamber Music Society of Lower Basin Street* show in 1940, Robison says, "I managed to get around all over the country and I listened to the songs that people sang. Most especially, I listened to the Negroes in the South, and I watched the way they live. I have tried to put a Native American philosophy in my music, the kind of music that comes from the people."

Contrary to popular mythology, not all of the great songwriters were Jewish New Yorkers: consider Cole Porter, Johnny Mercer, Harry Warren, Jimmy McHugh, Hoagy Carmichael, and the team of Johnny Burke and Jimmy Van Heusen; nor were W. C. Handy, Duke Ellington, Fats Waller, and Andy Razaf frequently seen in the synagogue. Yet it's safe to say that nearly all of these gentlemen, Hebrew and Gentile alike, were writing out of a metro-centric background. Whether it was Broadway, the Lower East Side, or Harlem, their music almost always reflected the industrialized East. Even the songs of Isham Jones and Gus Kahn, composed in Chicago, or Noël Coward, Vivian Ellis, and the stiff-upper-lip songwriters of London's West End, derive from the urban experience. (Hollywood was essentially Broadway West, a better-financed but lower-slung road-company version of the Big Apple.)

The music of Willard Robison, however, is an entirely different kettle of fish. In interwar America, Robison was the rare songwriter whose music belonged equally to Tin Pan Alley and the Mississippi Delta, whose songs could have been sung with equal authority by the Carter Family and the Andrews Sisters. Robison wrote with the unbridled backwoods passion of the great country and blues singers but the harmonic profundity of the Kerns and the Ellingtons.

"His melodies are amazingly complex and interesting," said Brookmeyer. "They never go where you think they'll go—the next note is never where you expect it to be. He does all kinds of things that I would never even try when I write a tune, but he makes it work. I think he's a terribly underrated composer."

Lyrically, Robison's songs are even more idiosyncratic. Two of Robison's greatest disciples were Johnny Mercer and Hoagy Carmichael, and even though they frequently wrote songs that depicted rural rather than urban scenes, Robison's music is much more thoroughly immersed in the Deep Southern blues. Together and separately, Mercer and Carmichael wrote of lazy rivers and moon rivers rolling along in their ambling, bucolic way across the moon country, but neither of them wrote anything as profoundly melancholy as Robison.

"Share Croppin' Blues" is an archetypical example of a song that could have been written by no one else. If Mercer or Carmichael or Harold Arlen had written it, it would never have been so defeatist and even scary. If Bill Broonzy or Louis Jordan had written it, it wouldn't have had the same kind of literary quirkiness. The hero of "Share Croppin' Blues" sings of a kind of desolation you won't find anywhere on Broadway or Tin Pan Alley, even in "protest" songs like "Brother, Can You Spare a Dime?" or "Black and Blue." Although it's laced with ironic humor, it paints a vividly bleak picture unlike anything else in American music: "They call it sharecroppin' but there's nothin' to share." He lambastes his banker for repossessing his wagon, lacerates his landlord for taking his tools, his "old lady" who left him "when the pickings got lean," his son who's incarcerated in Jefferson City ("doing ten to fifteen"), and then proceeds to curse the goat who ate his shoes. Even his dog can't cheer him up. It's almost *The Grapes of Wrath* set to music, but with more of a sense of humor.

Robison's music has much more in common with Bob Dylan or Leonard Cohen than it does with Cole Porter or Irving Berlin or any songwriter of his own generation. That's particularly true when you factor in his frequent allusions to religion and the Bible; long before "Suzanne," Robison told us that Jesus was a sailor when he walked upon the water. Can you imagine Sammy Cahn and Jule Styne writing "Move Over Jehovah"?

Robison published some of his most celebrated airs, "Old Folks," "'Round the Old Deserted Farm," and "Guess I'll Go Back Home This Summer," all around 1938 and '39. In the 1940s, his music continued to attract both the cognoscenti and, occasionally, the record-buying public. Kay Starr landed her first notable hit while with Charlie Barnet's orchestra on "Share Croppin' Blues" in 1944, and the following year Billy Eckstine brought Robison's 1930 song "A Cottage for Sale" back to the charts. At the end of 1947, Peggy Lee scored with a brand-new slice of Robisonia entitled "Don't Smoke in Bed." In the very earliest days of the pop and jazz album, there were no fewer than three entire albums of Willard Robison songs, including *Lazy Along with Willard Robison* by singer-saxophonist Tony Pastor and His Orchestra on the independent label Cosmo Records. In 1947, Johnny Mercer produced and starred on a six-song collection titled *Willard Robison's Deep Summer Music,* and in 1953 Robison himself made his only long-playing recording, an eponymous 10-inch LP on Coral arranged and conducted by Russ Case (remember that name).

Prior to 1961, Teagarden had recorded two Robison songs, both of which were characteristically quixotic, philosophical, and heavily laced with religious references. "That's What the Man Said" was performed by Louis Armstrong and the All-Stars in the 1951 MGM film *Glory Alley,* a number that included prominent solo spots for Teagarden both playing and singing, and "Old Pigeon-Toed Joad" was included by Teagarden on his 1956 Capitol album *This Is Teagarden!* Armstrong, Teagarden, and choir sing "That's What the Man Said" as if it were an upbeat message, but the outlook is actually rather bleak: "Tomorrow and tomorrow / Creeps into this veil of tears." "Pigeon-Toed Joad" is close kin to the luckless hero of "Share Croppin' Blues," with its references to the "Book of Job" and John Steinbeck. Yet even though the titular character is down—his deformed feet are only the beginning— he's not out, and Robison details Joad's ingenuity in surviving, despite all the breaks against him. As Brookmeyer suggests, Robison's songs go off in unexpected places—melodically as well as spiritually.

For most of his later career, Robison remained based in New York. At the time of *Think Well of Me* (1962), the songwriter was, as George Hoefer wrote in the original notes, "frequently seen around the Plymouth Hotel in midtown." Dan Morgenstern (who served as editor of *Down Beat* for most of the 1960s) remembers seeing Robison "and his lady friend" at the Copper Rail, usually after he had cashed his monthly royalty check from ASCAP. The songwriter clearly had seen better days; he is often described somewhat less kindly in this period as "looking like a homeless person." Said producer Creed Taylor, "He had that worn look that goes with tipping a few too many, and he was kind of fragile-looking."

In his fifties, Teagarden tried, usually in vain, to maintain his health and sanity by staying off the road. He had been a touring musician practically his whole life—with the Paul Whiteman band, his own orchestra, and then Louis Armstrong's All Stars—but his problem was he couldn't support himself by staying in any one place. Much as he loved Armstrong—and Armstrong seems to have viewed Teagarden, more than any other musician, as his musical soul mate—he couldn't keep up with the relentless pace of the All-Stars. Teagarden didn't have Armstrong's iron-man stamina, and he tended to fortify himself with alcohol, which ultimately weakened rather than strengthened him. "You spend all day traveling," said Brookmeyer, "then somehow you're supposed to be in the mood to come out and entertain people at night. You try drugs or booze to help you feel up to it, but so far no one's been able to handle that for very long. It can't be done."

Now on his own and based in Los Angeles (living with his wife, Addie, and their son, Joe), Teagarden led his own groups, usually with trumpeter Don Goldie and pianist Don Ewell. He came east regularly for the Newport Jazz Festival, and as the 1950s gave way to the 1960s, he played two important gigs in New York. In 1959 he did an extended run at the Roundtable, which was extensively recorded by Roulette Records, and as mentioned, in April 1961 he brought his sextet to the Village Vanguard, sharing a bill with pianist Junior Mance and his trio. This was one of those gigs that everybody remembers. Teagarden was sober and reaching a new plateau in his playing; he was warmly greeted by old friends, such as the pianist Charlie LaVere and his son Steve and Robison himself, and also new ones, like Brookmeyer and the producer Creed Taylor, who was then running Verve Records.

Taylor had first heard Teagarden as a high school student in Virginia in 1945. In 2009, he remembered being blown away, both by Teagarden's amazing musicianship and his remarkable coolness: "He had on his bow tie and his white tux and it was really something to see him playing and leading his own big band." Like everyone else who heard Teagarden in 1961, Taylor was extremely impressed. "Record companies in general look for whoever is au courant at the time," said Taylor. "But Jack was just out there, like a gem waiting to be dealt with, as far as I was concerned." Taylor called Teagarden and arranged a meeting. "So we got together," Taylor recalled, "and he brought his friend Willard along with him at that meeting. I was already familiar with him because I had recorded 'A Cottage for Sale' with Chris Connor a few years earlier. I loved this song and I was really impressed when I met Willard."

A few months later, in Chicago in October 1961, Teagarden and his sextet (featuring Goldie and Ewell) recorded *Mis'ry and the Blues,* the first of three albums for Verve. Even though only two of the ten songs on *Mis'ry and the Blues* were by Robison, "Don't Tell a Man About His Woman" and "Peaceful Valley," the whole album had a melancholy, Robisonian feeling to it. Taylor was increasingly taken with Robison's songs, and he especially loved the combination of blues and humor in "Don't Tell a Man About His Woman"—so much so that when the first album did well, the producer decided to build the follow-up project around the idea of the Willard Robison songbook, which would be recorded at Rudy Van Gelder's studio in Englewood Cliffs, New Jersey, in January 1962. Apart from the songbook concept, Taylor also made the rather different choice of accompanying Teagarden with a string orchestra.

It seemed like a natural idea to place Teagarden playing and singing Robison's songs, which were mostly ballads, in a string setting. Taylor chose two arrangers for the project, both brass players. Trumpeter Russ Case had played in Benny Goodman's first band in 1934, and worked with other orchestras and studio groups, including long stints with Hal Kemp and Raymond Scott. More recently, he had graduated from the dance bands for a substantial career as an arranger and conductor—mostly in pop contexts, for Perry Como and many others. Case had previously worked with both Teagarden and Robison: with the trombonist on a 1936 recording session costarring Frank Trumbauer, and with the songwriter as the musical director of his 1953 Coral album. (Brookmeyer, playing piano rather than trombone, had also once played with Case's orchestra, as a sub when Case's regular pianist was "under the influence.")

When Taylor thought of combining Brookmeyer (who played the less common valved version of the trombone) with Teagarden, he said, "I felt like that without even asking him, Bob would have bent over backwards to do an album with Jack." Even though Teagarden and Brookmeyer would not be playing together, it struck Taylor as a compelling idea to juxtapose a modern valve trombonist with a legendary slide trombonist— what he described as "Jack's super distinctive slide trombone style."

Think Well of Me was recorded at Van Gelder's in Englewood; Taylor remembers that the frequently caustic engineer was delighted to have this living legend in his studio, and that Tea, characteristically, addressed Van Gelder as "Gate." It took three consecutive days (as most orchestral albums did at the time, as per union regulations), January 17, 18, and 19, 1962. It's not certain which tunes were recorded on which dates, but it seems likely that one date included most of Brookmeyer's arrangements, another featured four of Case's, and the third was split by the two. A total of thirteen tracks were apparently recorded, twelve songs (then the norm for an album) by Robison (some with different collaborators), plus "Where Are You?" by Jimmy McHugh and Harold Adamson. The latter song was arranged by a third orchestrator, the German-born Claus Ogerman.

The final album contained ten Robison songs ("Don't Take Your Meanness Out on Me" and "Moonlight Mississippi," both arranged by Brookmeyer, were apparently recorded but not used) as well as "Where Are You?" It's not known why there's one non-Robison song in the lineup— unless it's because it's just so good, both in terms of Teagarden's singing and Ogerman's opulent chart. In any case, "Where Are You?" opens the album and serves as a kind of prelude. Under most circumstances, it's a fairly sad number, what Sinatra would call a "saloon song"—the key lines are "Where have you gone without me? / I thought you cared about me." Yet compared to some of Robison's bleak tales of desertion and love and desertion again, "Where Are You?" seems positively cheerful—at least the hero hasn't completely given up the search for his "happy ending." It's not nearly as nihilistic as "A Cottage for Sale," the second song, which is sung from the perspective of someone who has utterly abandoned all hope; there's no chance that she'll come back to the cottage.

Of the numbers arranged by Case, "Guess I'll Go Back Home This Summer" (1939) and especially "Old Folks" (1938) were two of the composer's most widely heard songs; when they were new, they were recorded by such stars as Tommy Dorsey, Tex Beneke with Glenn Miller, Bing Crosby, and Mildred Bailey, later on they were favored by such big names as Nat King Cole and George Shearing, Peggy Lee, Dexter Gordon, and even Charlie Parker.

One can immediately sense the ambiguity in the title of "Guess I'll Go Back Home"—note that it isn't "I'm Glad to Go Back Home" or even "Can't Wait to Get Back Home." The whole affair is a reluctant nostalgia trip, a tale of going home to a home that no longer feels like home. The speaker doesn't even know if his old girlfriend has gotten married since he's been gone, or to whom. Teagarden sings it like an itinerant musician who doesn't get home very often. It's bittersweet with a capital B.

"Old Folks" (lyrics credited to Dedette Lee Hill) is Robison's most richly rendered character; growing up in Missouri at the turn of the century, he would have doubtless encountered more than a few veterans of the Civil War, who told tall tales ("how he held the speech at Gettysburg for Lincoln that day") as they sat and whittled, while glossing over such minor details as whether they fought "for the blue or the gray." Once again, Teagarden sings it reflectively, as if it were autobiography, and the face of the wizened old campaigner were staring at him from the other side of a mirror.

Also arranged by Case, "Country Boy Blues" is the longest track in the album (almost 3:50). It's one of Robison's rarest songs, with only two notable recordings, Johnny Mercer's in 1947 and Teagarden's here. Like many Robison songs, it uses some of the cadences and harmonies of the blues, but there is something like a bridge, thus it's not in strict blues form. The lyric is completely through-composed, none of the words are ever repeated. Mercer's tempo was faster, so much so that even though his version is a minute shorter, he gets in more lyrics than Teagarden—but then again Teagarden finds time for an entire gorgeous chorus on trombone. It's one of Robison's funniest—but hardly happiest—songs, in his typically self-

deflating fashion: the hero is a country boy, "a sentimental farmer," who comes to the city and has his heart broken (and his pocketbook pilfered) by a slicker gal—described here as "a shoemaker's daughter who made a heel out of me," hanging "around the washtub, looking for the handle." The melody is sinewy and unpredictable, and doesn't follow the pattern of any other song. The structure is AABAABA, and the bridge sections make use of stop-time, a device that's very much in the vocabulary of the blues; Don Goldie plays a prominent muted trumpet obbligato behind Tea. No matter what's technically the form, Teagarden's solo at the end is really the blues.

The 1938 "'Round My Old Deserted Farm" (yet another Robison tune recorded by Mildred Bailey, who, like Peggy Lee, was among his biggest boosters), is about as dire as it gets: "The prayer meeting bell lends a heartache to the dell" and even "The birds flying by sing a muted lullaby." When he sings "love long ago departed / and left an old deserted farm," you start to wonder if the whole image might be metaphoric: when love leaves, the heart is like a deserted farm. Robison states the final phrase, "with tears," no less than three times for emphasis at the end. Tea ends with a trombone solo that climaxes in a cadenza that's dramatic but not melodramatic. As Brookmeyer put it, "Teagarden was inimitable, just like Billie Holiday was inimitable—you can't learn to do what they did, it just has to come to you through a process of osmosis."

The remaining numbers by Case were the title song (about which more shortly) and "I'm a Fool About My Mama"; these are the only notable recordings of either song. "Mama," the album's sole instrumental, also alludes to blues form, and harmonically is about as minor as you can get. Goldie solos briefly here, evoking the general sound of Charlie Shavers. Teagarden plays another dramatic trombone cadenza at the coda, which might be described as baroque if it weren't so immersed in the deep essence of the blues.

Brookmeyer arranged six songs, but two of his charts didn't make it to the final album (maybe someday they'll eventually surface from the vaults of Universal Music). The title of "In a Little Waterfront Cafe" suggests the possibility of quaintness and romance. Any other songwriter would have written, "In a little waterfront cafe / We fell in love and made life so gay!" However, this is Robison we're talking about. Not surprisingly, he uses the café as the setting for where she said goodbye to him as they stared at the blue Pacific moonlight and heard the seagulls cry as he kissed her tears away. Even though their bittersweet laughter sparkles like champagne, the whole affair is still hopelessly sad.

"Tain't So Honey, Tain't So" is possibly the only song in the collection that's completely affirmative. The 1928 Whiteman disc was a landmark, so much so that Teagarden (unlike on "Deserted Farm") and Brookmeyer include the verse (after a Bix-inspired intro by Don Goldie), which Tea's friend Bing Crosby sang almost thirty-five years earlier. Tea's brief solo, even more than the vocal, is upbeat and jubilant, as he tells us of another Robison character, "old Aunt Phoebe Law" (rhymes with "Arkansas") whose way of dealing with bad news, trouble, and hardship is to look the devil square in the face and tell him it ain't so. (Try it sometime.) The way Robison writes it and Teagarden sings it, you would think they were both actually from Arkansas and really did have an Aunt Phoebe Law.

Brookmeyer's charts include two of Robison's most autobiographical texts, both about the breakup of a marriage. No, they're not generic "love affairs," as they said back in the day, or "relationships," as they say today; there are enough references to let you know that these are actual marriages that are ending. Robison told the producer that "A Cottage for Sale" was his own story. Even though Larry Conley (who more normally was an arranger) was credited with the lyrics, the songwriter insisted to Taylor, " 'That wasn't just any cottage, that was my cottage!' He told me all about how it happened—a broken marriage and all that."

Interviewed by *Metronome* magazine in May 1933, Robison told a somewhat conflicting tale: it was indeed his own cottage, but he was forced to sell it because of the Depression. However, when the song caught on, and became one of the ten "leaders" (top sellers) of 1933, he was able to buy the cottage back. "Cottage," which was published in 1930, perfectly captures the overall despair of the first full year of the Great Depression—when the real estate market was gutted with cottages for sale. The text tells the tale merely by describing the empty bungalow—"our little dream castle with every dream gone"—and that's story enough; "Cottage for Sale" might be described as a site-specific torch song.

"Don't Smoke in Bed" was even more personal. Among popular singers, Peggy Lee was by far Robison's greatest postwar supporter, recording at least ten songs by him (even more than Mildred Bailey). The story Lee later told regarding "Don't Smoke in Bed" was that in 1947, Robison, who in his mid-fifties was drinking more heavily than ever, was convinced that he was dying. He had started work on a song, but all he had was a title, a general idea, and a few lines. He wanted to finish it before he crossed over the deep river to the bandstand in the sky, so he could have a new copyright (and royalties) to bequeath to his daughter. Lee, who certainly knew from alcoholics, volunteered to finish the song for him, with the help of her husband, Dave Barbour. (However, Jim Gavin, in his 2014 biography of the singer, points out that there's no actual evidence to support Lee's claim that she wrote most of the song.)

"Don't Smoke in Bed" is delivered mostly in the first person: a long-suffering wife is leaving her alcoholic (and abusive) husband. The implication is that he's a hopeless lush and she's resigning herself to the idea that he's never going to straighten out. The tone of the text is affectionate and tender, and moving in that the speaker—the departing wife—refuses to break down and get sentimental. She speaks dryly and almost without emotion, as if she ain't got no tears left. The very phrase "Don't smoke in bed" was something one said to a drunk. In those days, passing out with a lit cigarette in your mouth and setting your fleabag mattress on fire was an even greater cause of death than drinking and driving. To Lee's surprise, and, possibly, to that of the songwriter himself, he didn't die in 1947—he made it to the approximate age of seventy-three in 1968.

The song became one of Lee's big hits of the era, and thanks to her it passed on to Julie London, Nina Simone, and many more contemporary divas, including more recently Canadian country-pop star k.d. lang. Teagarden is the most notable male artist so far to sing it. "Don't Smoke" is written from a female perspective, the words principally being the text of a goodbye note that "she" left on "his" dresser, along with her wedding ring. The song is in something like AAA format—there's not even a bridge to relieve the tension; Goldie's trumpet solo is especially dramatic and forlorn here. "That sure was a sad song," says Taylor, in deliberate understatement.

Dan Morgenstern, in his notes to the 1998 CD reissue of *Think Well of Me*, suggests that the strings are occasionally superfluous: "They don't add much musical meat to the proceedings." Teagarden's onetime boss Ben Pollack made a similar, if more cryptic, comment to Leonard Feather in a *Down Beat* blindfold test (February 14, 1963). Hearing "'Round My Old Deserted Farm" prompted the drummer-bandleader to recall an occasion when Teagarden insisted on singing a love song with the Pollack band around 1930. "We had a ballad come up and Jack wanted to do it, and I said, 'Jack, this isn't for you.' He says he could sing anything. And that's the trouble with this record. I don't like to hear Jack sing this type of tune. It doesn't fit him." Despite that, Pollack adds, "The record is beautiful and [so is] Jack's trombone solo—he's the top T. I'd give this a top rating. The arrangement was very beautiful too. I'd rate it about four stars."

Regarding the strings, I do wish that Teagarden had recorded more Robison songs with a small group—songs like "Mis'ry and the Blues." I wish he had also sung "The Devil Is Afraid of Music," "Lonely Acres in the West," "We'll Have a New Home in the Morning," and at least a dozen others. The only way that *Think Well of Me* could have been improved is if it were a double LP (or a twenty-four-track CD, including the two lost songs). The arrangements, the songs, the strings, and Tea's singing and playing are all totally of a piece. Teagarden never sounds old-fashioned, even when ensconced in the cutting-edge arrangements of Brookmeyer. "Jack is and was without age," says Taylor. "He was completely classical from the moment he popped out of the womb. Recording

him, especially with Bob's charts, was like entering a time capsule—because he was my hero."

Brookmeyer's tone poem treatment of "Don't Smoke in Bed" is a brilliant case in point; the use of pizzicato strings and spaced-out percussion suggests Bartók, and perfectly complements Teagarden's majestic mastery of the blues. I get a distinct sense that Robison, Teagarden, and Brookmeyer were all on the same page; the three were uniquely sympathetic to each other at least partially because they were all alcoholics. Two of the three died practically with a bottle in their hands, but at least Brookmeyer was able to take the cure and make it last. (He died at the age of eighty-one in 2011.) Hey, one out of three is a pretty good success rate for drunks.

Teagarden's final score at Verve Records was actually three for three. Six months after *Think Well of Me*, he taped his final album for Creed Taylor, which was titled simply *Jack Teagarden!!!* For this set, Teagarden played and sang mostly well-heeled contemporary songs, such as "Moon River" and "All the Way," in the company of a stellar studio combination costarring Bobby Hackett, Bud Freeman, and Hank Jones, along with clarinet and arrangements by Bob Wilber. One of Teagarden's outstanding vocals here is "Learnin' the Blues," the title of which seems a little ludicrous in the context of Teagarden's career; at fifty-seven he knew more about the blues than practically anyone alive. Learning the blues? Teagarden was the one who taught them to everybody else.

Jack Teagarden!!! is a delight. *Think Well of Me* is a masterpiece. This is an eminently successful album that is mired in failure. Which brings us, at last, to the title song for the album, "Think Well of Me," a Robison rarity virtually unheard anywhere else. It's as bittersweet as you can get: even the title tells a story—you know without even hearing the lyric that one person is leaving another, and that the first person has behaved in such a manner that he needs to go out of his way to plead with the second person to think well of him. Like a lot of great sad songs, it's those details the lyricist leaves out—and lets the listener guess—that make the song so poignant. In this case, these are absolutely all the details you're going to get. You hear the speaker apologizing, and it doesn't matter what for. "Think Well of Me" (which quotes *Hamlet*) was apparently introduced by Teagarden on this album, and the very sound of his voice communicates as much as the actual words. He sounds for all the world like an old hound dog, looking up at you with big, sad eyes.

It's revealing to place "Think Well of Me" in the context of the last-hurrah-and-farewell songs such as Edith Piaf's "Non, je ne regrette rien," which was the thematic inspiration for all those self-aggrandizing anthems that began to flourish in the 1960s and have been omnipresent ever since (from "Once in a Lifetime" to "My Way" to the even more lugubrious "Here's to Life"). Piaf defiantly regrets nothing, but Teagarden and Robison are saying just the opposite: they regret everything. They are giving us that forlorn, guilty look Teagarden gave

Brookmeyer at Monterey in 1963, a look that says they hope we won't judge them too harshly, that they hope we'll remember the good things and try to forget the bad. Think well of me, for I think well of you.

After Monterey, Teagarden played New York one last time, the Metropole near Times Square, in the fall of 1963. (Willard Robison somehow hung on until 1968.) Teagarden died in New Orleans in January 1964, where he was given a traditional Crescent City funeral. "There was a typical street parade," said Creed, "with Jack in an open casket." A second funeral was held in Los Angeles. There were speakers and mourners, but the most touching eulogy was delivered by a choir of trombonists from Musicians Local 47. They played three numbers—two spirituals and a song: "Nobody Knows the Trouble I've Seen," "Goin' Home," and "Think Well of Me."

44

Tiny Tim

God Bless Tiny Tim

(1968)

No one knew more about old music than Tiny Tim. He studied it and he loved it. He knew all the old songs that only existed as sheet music.

—Bob Dylan

This album may well be the most controversial (some would say regrettable) choice for this book. But I loved it as a six-year-old, and unlike a lot of the things I loved at that period (the movie *Chitty Chitty Bang Bang,* for one), *God Bless Tiny Tim* still holds up. What I loved about it as a kid was that it was a brilliant introduction to the music of the 1920s and earlier; what I love about it forty years later is that it now seems like a perfect introduction to the psychedelic pop music of the late 1960s. I'm not ashamed to admit that this is an album that I would gladly bring with me to a desert island. Even more than most pop products of the *Sgt. Pepper* era, it flows beautifully from start to finish, and it even incorporates the act of turning itself over from the LP's A side to its B side. (One note: all quotes from Tiny Tim come from an interview with Ernest Clark, found on the website tinytim.org.)

Herbert Khaury (1932–1996), who was known professionally as "Tiny Tim," is generally remembered as a novelty act. He could also be cited as the most notorious example of the expression "one-hit won-der," since he only had a single single that charted, his 1968 recording of "Tiptoe Through the Tulips." "Tiptoe Through the Tulips" is, in fact, a highly representative sample of Khaury's oeuvre, and it provides a solid illustration of what might be called the entertainer's sincere perversity. As Tiny Tim, Khaury had an unusual gift for singing a song sincerely and camping it up at the same time; with "Tiptoe," it's obvious that he loves the song, and he's not intending to make fun of it—instead, he rather makes fun *with* it. He sings it straight even while stomping it to death, as if those two things were somehow not mutually exclusive.

Tiny Tim was most famous for singing in a trilly, exaggerated falsetto, the voice that he employs on "Tulips." He could sing in other ways too, but it was the falsetto that became his trademark. That was the voice, more than anything else, that made him a star in 1968–69, a brief period when both that single and his brilliant first album, *God Bless Tiny Tim,* were major hits. But people quickly tired of the sound, so much so that even by the time his next project, the equally wonderful *Tiny Tim's Second Album,* was released, his star was already waning.

With that in mind, it's hard to make the claim that Khaury was a major artist or a great singer, and it's also hard not to blame people for being immediately repulsed by the same novelty voice that attracted multitudes for a hot minute. That extreme falsetto can be difficult to take, and, even as a devoted fan of his music, I personally have a hard time spending a whole afternoon listening to his records. Still, I find the voice endearing—in reasonable doses at least—and one of the delights of *God Bless Tiny Tim* is learning that he had much more to offer than the trademark falsetto. Khaury sang in a remarkably wide vocal range, from that stratospheric soprano all the way down to a deep basso profundo (he's almost a male Carol Channing). He could sing like a baby boy, a grown woman, a hillbilly, his friend Bob Dylan, Jerry Lee Lewis, Jolson, Elvis, or a towering tenor like Bill Kenny of the Ink Spots, who had a high voice but one quite distinct from the feminine falsetto.

Tiny Tim was the first androgynous pop star, and in his gift for gender blur he anticipates dozens of glam rockers and others, from David Bowie to Prince to Boy George. Yet in retrospect, his greatest gift was for generational blur. Early in his career he was shunned for his taste in material—those goofy old novelty songs of his parents' generation—but ultimately it was those songs that put him on top, however briefly. In an age when the British invaders were evoking the bluesmen of the Mississippi Delta and Chicago, Khaury championed the old, old, almost prehistoric Tin Pan Alley of the teens and twenties, as well as more familiar fare from the 1930s and '40s. Yet he also loved classic rock 'n' roll, not to mention country and folk music. Tiny Tim also did a marvelous job with a series of newly written songs that appear on his first two albums; these were generally forced on him by his producer, Richard Perry, but he sang them brilliantly nonetheless.

In 1969, he would also make television history, with a stunt that became one of the most watched events in the history of the medium—an action that, like so much of his career, was highly personal. After that, there was no way to go but down; the craze couldn't help but be over. He would work continually for the remaining twenty-five years of his life, but after only a few short months at the top he was already a has-been, a "nostalgia act"—which is an ironic label for an artist who made us question the very concept of "nostalgia" to begin with. In those two albums, the first in particular, Tiny Tim became the only pop star in all of American music whose entire career was predicated on the clash of the generations, and who, all by himself, represented both the past and the future of pop music. In trying keep his balance with one foot on each of two tectonic plates, it's hardly surprising he couldn't maintain his footing for very long.

None of which would matter if those two albums weren't so wonderful. *God Bless Tiny Tim* is the major project from the era of *Sgt. Pepper* and the rock-concept album where past and future mingle, where the work of young songwriters (like Paul Williams) is interspersed with vaudeville songs from well before World War I. Listening to these two albums is like some goofy science fiction movie where you see a streamlined art deco locomotive flying through outer space, or a medieval knight jousting with a cowboy. And yet everything flows beautifully, the new tunes and the old-timers never detract from each other; producer Perry gave the album a logical trajectory from track to track and side to side—it progresses as meaningfully as the best Broadway original cast albums. Prior to 1970, rock 'n' roll was a series of trends succeeding one another, from rockabilly to doo-wop to teen idols to British invaders to singer-songwriters. More than any of his predecessors, Khaury showed the next generation of pop artists that they could pick and choose whatever styles they wanted to work in. In that sense, Tiny Tim was pop music's first great postmodernist.

It's a basic rule of science that every action produces an opposite reaction; every revolution leads to a counterrevolution. By 1968, the rock 'n' roll revolution was complete: the sea changes that had been occurring over the previous ten years now seemed ineradicable. For the most part, popular music was now essentially based on rhythm and blues (rather than the Broadway-associated American Songbook); with the arrival of the Beatles and Dylan, the concept of the singer-songwriter had replaced the traditional business model of songwriting and singing being two distinct professions. Now, also, there was a generation gap (which was also a very deliberate business model) firmly in place, in which very different kinds of music were marketed toward twenty-to-thirty-year-old baby boomers and their forty-to-fifty-something parents.

All these changes had washed up on our shores between the mid to late 1950s and the mid- to late 1960s, yet as soon as they were in place, there immediately began a look backward—as if in the rush to what was perceived to be the future there was a backlash and an instant nostalgia for the past that had just been buried. As early as the first rock concept albums, there were deliberate attempts to re-create the past, the most famous of which were by the Beatles and particularly Paul McCartney, who wrote several numbers that were inspired more by George Formby than Buddy Holly, most famously "Honey Pie," "When I'm 64," and "Your Mother Should Know"; the latter two were also successfully recorded by "trad" (a British variant on Dixieland) bandleader and trumpeter Kenny Ball (whose band was then wearing Beatle haircuts).

Other bands on both sides of the Atlantic followed suit. The contemporary deejay Trav S.D. refers to this style of music—1960s rock bands evoking the era of ukuleles and megaphones—as "psychedelic vaudeville." Some prime examples would be "Just like Gene Autry" by San Francisco's Moby Grape, "Magnolia Simms" and "Daddy's Song" by the Monkees, "End of the Season" by the Kinks, and Frank Zappa's "Bow Tie Daddy," the latter of which seems like a deliberate and rather mean-spirited put-down of the older generation. ("Don't try to do no thinkin' / Just go on with your drinkin'," as if the rockers of the 1960s were paragons of sobriety.) Even the original "tribal love" rock musical, Hair, featured a psychedelic vaudeville number, "Hello There," crooned by a tenor with a megaphone voice, backed up by a girl's vocal trio which emulates a skip in the record. One British group even called itself the New Vaudeville Orchestra and had a major hit with "Winchester Cathedral" in a faux–Jazz Age style.

Still, the most successful and enduring psychedelic vaudevillian was Tiny Tim. Biographies of Her-

bert Khaury, born in Washington Heights in upper Manhattan in 1932, invariably try to depict him as an outsider, a *meeskite* who sang in a strange voice and liked wacky old songs (which would immediately distinguish him, obviously, from most future rock-pop stars). Yet there was nothing so unusual about a young singer in the 1940s and 1950s going around singing what was not yet known as the Great American Songbook, even if he did prefer songs from World War I to those from World War II. He was thoroughly immersed in the older songs well before the rock 'n' roll sea change. What was unusual was that he was hanging around the folk music bars and coffeehouses playing and singing ancient Irving Berlin songs on a ukulele rather than emulating Lead Belly on a guitar, as most folkies were then doing.

Now working under the name Tiny Tim, he was already a fixture in the folk clubs when Bob Dylan arrived in New York. "He played ukulele and sang like a girl—old standard songs from the '20s," as Dylan wrote in his 2004 memoir, *Chronicles*, also recalling that they both worked at a club that paid them in all the hamburgers and French fries they could eat. In 1962 a live recording was made, supposedly at a Village club, and was released about six years later as *With Love and Kisses from Tiny Tim: Concert in Fairyland*. (The artist later described it, with justification, as the worst record he ever made.) The most significant thing about the *Fairyland* album is its very existence, which shows that someone was already interested enough in Khaury to record one of his live shows. (Other oddball early recordings by Khaury were later gathered onto a pair of collections titled *The Human Canary, 1963–70* and *Lost and Found, 1963–1974*.)

Then, around 1965, he met Richard Perry, a twenty-three-year-old Brooklyn native and aspiring producer who'd grown up on rock 'n' roll. "At the time Mr. Perry started out with me," Khaury said later on, "I have to give him credit because he did have faith in me." Perry borrowed money from his father-in-law to produce a 45 rpm single, on a makeshift label called Blue Cat, of "April Showers" backed with "Little Girl (in the Pines)"; this was the first commercial release by Tiny Tim. He continued to attract the attention of other movers and shakers of the era, including Lenny Bruce (who hired him as an opening act) and Peter Yarrow of Peter, Paul and Mary. Yarrow helped engineer a reunion between Khaury and Dylan, then working with the Band, and as a result Tiny Tim shows up on some of the famous Dylan "Basement Tapes." (He would later make a guest appearance on a Beatles Christmas record.)

Yarrow also brought Tiny Tim to the attention of Mo Ostin, president of Reprise Records, long known as Frank Sinatra's home base but also emerging as a power player in the rock era, especially since it had been absorbed into Warner Bros. Records a few years earlier. Ostin made a point of catching Tiny Tim's show at a club called the Scene in New York in 1967, and offered to sign him to Reprise, where the idea of working with Richard Perry (who had just produced the highly experimental *Safe as Milk*, the first album by Captain Beefheart and His Magic Band) presented itself. They began to plan an album together, "It was a challenge, because I've always liked to do the old songs," the singer said. "Mr. Perry said, 'We're going to have to split it. I'm going to do some parts that I want and you'll [also] do what you want.'"

The midpoint between the 1920s and the 1960s is, mathematically and culturally, the 1940s, and *God Bless Tiny Tim* opens with "Welcome to My Dream," written for Bing Crosby (to sing in *The Road to Utopia*) by his "house" songwriters, Johnny Burke and Jimmy Van Heusen, in 1944. It's a perfect opening song for an album, although no one seems to have used it as such before this. (In the movie, Crosby croons it to Dorothy Lamour, more or less as a song of seduction.) We hear what is apparently Khaury's "natural" singing voice, not up in falsetto or down in basso, delivering the lyric a cappella, with a slight reverb on his voice, which makes everything sound somewhat surreal—it's as if we already were in a dream, the very one that Tiny Tim is welcoming us into.

As the first (and only) chorus ends, the reverb increases to the point where the sound we hear is more reverb than voice, and as he hits the last word we hear a flourish of strings, wordless choir, pizzicato violin, and odd percussion; imagine an "easy

listening" album titled *Jackie Gleason Plays Bartók for Lovers*. This is the kind of instrumental music you'd hear in a dream sequence in a movie, or as if someone was being hypnotized into a flashback, where all the faces get all wavy and mushy. Then the proceedings get even more surreal and dreamlike. Where, you wonder, is he going to wind up?

We find out soon enough. The complex, semiclassical orchestral section dies and we hear a simple ukulele being strummed, with a female voice over it, which is, naturally, Tiny Tim in falsetto singing "Tiptoe Through the Tulips" (introduced by Nick Lucas in the early talking picture revue *Gold Diggers of Broadway* in 1929, written by Al Dubin and Joe Burke). Although singing in what is clearly not his natural voice, Tiny Tim is completely sincere, even when emitting a hugely exaggerated dramatic sigh at the end of the first eight bars. The accompanying band, which is more 1968 than 1929 (there's very little of what could be called syncopation), fills in gradually as the first chorus progresses, and the second chorus begins with a "soft-shoe" break that sounds as if Tiny Tim were emulating pedal taps with his tongue and mouth, accompanied by a Fender bass. "Tiptoe" would be the hit single from the album, and, briefly, rocket its singer into the loftier reaches of celebrity. Somehow, Tiny Tim had discovered a science fiction wormhole connecting the 1920s to the 1960s, a direct link between the fey, effeminate tenors of the pre–Bing Crosby era and the long-haired, unisexual hippies of the Haight-Ashbury period.

We then hear the speaking voice of Tiny Tim, in the same "Tulips" falsetto. "Hello, my dear friends! Well, here I am on record at last, and it feels so wonderful to be here with you on my first album." As if to illustrate the point, the third song starts with him singing "I'm so happy!" This turns out to be the verse to "Livin' in the Sunlight, Lovin' in the Moonlight," another early talkie tune, introduced by Maurice Chevalier in *The Big Pond* (1930), which Khaury may well have first heard on the famous record by Paul Whiteman's orchestra with an especially zesty vocal by the young Bing Crosby. He lunges into the tune: at first with just ukulele in the verse, then is joined by bass guitar and Latin percussion that instantly transport the piece from

1930 to 1968: the horn orchestrations are more like those you might hear on a dance party on *Laugh-In* (at a time when Tiny was making repeated appearances on that show), and there are piano passages that seem lifted from any number of Beatles tracks. But still, the orchestration moves from this section with a syncopated cymbal snap, and it ends with a Dixieland tag.

He introduces the next selection as "a little duet." Singing in multiple voices was one of Khaury's major shticks in live performance—he could easily be a boy-and-girl duet all by himself, and studio trickery further enabled him to do both voices at once, in harmony. "On the Old Front Porch" was one of many rather charming old-time songs about young couples spooning not quite out of the watchful eye of the parents of the girl in question. "Front Porch" was a big-selling duet record in 1913–14 by Billy Murray and Ada Jones; together, they recorded it at least twice, with slightly different lyrics, for different labels, and Miss Jones recorded it yet a third time, with the lower-voiced Henry Burr singing the male part.

The Khaury-Perry version opens with a clarinet and vibes in loose harmony, giving it an ethereal but vaguely archaic feeling; the rhythm is again subtly propelled by a Fender bass. There's little to suggest ragtime-era syncopation, and there's an electric guitar wail suggesting 1950s Nashville. The main attraction is, clearly, Tiny Tim's one-man duet; in fact, at one point he sings in yet a third voice, playing the part of the girl's father (speaking in a resonant baritone): "Will that young man go home tonight / Or have his breakfast here?" Tracks like this are why *God Bless Tiny Tim* is such a charmer, and are, in fact, much more compelling than "Tiptoe Through the Tulips." The artist is so completely disarming, and totally in love with the material. No amount of smirking can convince me that this is camp.

The first "new song" on *God Bless Tiny Tim* is "The Viper," and it doesn't completely qualify as either "new" or a "song." It's the kind of piece that's funny only the first time you hear it: it sounds like Girl Scouts trying to scare each other, huddled around a campfire, shining a flashlight under their chins for spooky effect. The spoken recitation is a

cappella, but Perry has embellished it by altering the production around Tiny's various voices for mock-horrific effect. (The funniest moment of the text is the unexpected quoting of "All Shook Up": "My head was spinning and my knees were weak / I could hardly stand on my own two feet!")

Without spoken intro, the macabre mood continues: we hear a spooky-sounding electric organ, which leads us "down below," where sits "the devil" and "his son." This turns out to be the verse for "Stay Down Here Where You Belong," an Irving Berlin song from 1914. In both world wars, Berlin wrote lots of jingoistic, patriotic airs, but this is a rare example of any Tin Pan Alley composer writing a genuinely pacifist, antiwar song, delivered with the same antic wit that Berlin brought to the best of his comedy lyrics. Even so, Berlin was somehow embarrassed by it, to the delight of Groucho Marx, who never failed to needle him about it—even to the point where Berlin offered Marx money to stop singing it (or so Groucho claimed). Groucho eventually included it in his double LP *An Evening with Groucho* and also on numerous talk shows in the 1960s. Tiny Tim's version is filled with scary effects—the most chilling of which is the singer's grisly satanic laugh—and production values that enhance the comedy but don't detract from the message, here revived in time for Vietnam. The last line is, in fact, "You'll find more hell up there than there is down here below."

"Then I'd Be Satisfied with Life" brings us the Tiny Tim–Richard Perry collaboration at its zenith. Once again, this is an old-timer unearthed by the artist, who said, "That is a great song! It was written by George M. Cohan [and is] one of the rare, rare songs in his repertoire." It was recorded for Victor in 1903 by one S. H. Dudley, and was popular enough to be parodied in an early Yiddish comedy record by Julian Rose. Cohan's song is itself a rather arch parody of the "be-happy-with-what-you-have"-type songs (typified by "The Best Things in Life Are Free"), a genre that continued to proliferate across the whole history of pop music (Bing Crosby recorded dozens), even up through the Elvis era. Most of those lyrics in this genre insist that "The moon belongs to everyone" or "You think that money means everything / but it's anybody's spring," or that we should measure our wealth in "pennies from heaven," Cohan's song employs a similar tone but substitutes extravagant symbols of copious wealth: "All I want is fifty million dollars . . . and living in a mansion made of gold."

Tiny Tim made several important updates to the sixty-year-old lyric: "'If Tuesday Weld would only be my wife' was really a line I put in. The original line in that song was 'If Hettie Green would only be my wife.' She was the richest woman in the world in 1903, and many men were dying to be her husband." Cohan sang that all he wanted was "Pierpont Morgan waiting on my table / and Sousa's band playing while I eat"; TT sings, "Rockefeller waiting on my table / and Lombardo's band playing while I eat." But it seems to have been Perry's idea to make the whole thing into a contemporary country record, with Khaury affecting a Nashville baritone throughout, accompanied by wailing guitars, including a sliding dobro, and a pianist emulating Floyd Cramer's slip-note style. Someone had the idea of gagging it up like a subtle Spike Jones: after "sealskin coats to protect me from the cold," we hear TT shiver slightly; when he refers to "Lombardo's band," we hear several saxophones wailing away in sweet band harmony; when he sings of Tuesday Weld, we hear the voice of a breathless sexpot moaning "Oh, Tiny!" (supplied by the singer Nico, of the Velvet Underground). The track actually begins with Tim singing a cappella an old vaudeville one-liner, "Never hit your grandma with a shovel / It makes a bad impression on her mind."

"I really liked 'Strawberry Tea,'" said the artist. "It was one of the songs given to Mr. Perry. I decided to take a shot and try some modern songs and take the challenge of doing more than one type of sound." "Strawberry Tea" borrows a fruit from "Strawberry Fields," while the idea of tea, whether consumed in the traditional way or smoked, was very much, you should forgive the expression, in the air. It's a surreal, psychedelic waltz, with a blurry echo around the singer's voice, like a movie character in a dream sequence.

The second side of the LP begins with something titled "The Other Side." This is the most extravagant production job on the album, and one of the truly most demented "songs," if that's the

right word, ever recorded by anyone—way beyond psychedelics and even Frank Zappa–Captain Beefheart pop surrealism territory. It starts with Tiny Tim laughing maniacally, and then briefly gasping for breath. At its most basic, it's a tale of ecological terror, depicting the world of men as engulfed and deluged by melting icecaps. The song's structure is an unusual ABC-ABC. It opens with a simple but ominous Fender bass riff, and Tiny tells us, in a sinister voice similar to that of "The Viper," "One eye is brown, the other is brown. / I am a fish, I swim around." Said fish goes on to explain that as he swims, he looks down and sees the wreckage of mankind, specifically cars trapped underwater, their windshields "wiping" in a gesture of futility. The C sections are in a perversely jubilant major key, with Tiny singing in the familiar falsetto, "The ice caps are melting, oh ho ho ho! / All the world is drowning, oh ho ho ho ho." (Why shouldn't he be jolly? To a fish, this is good news.) To further inflate the already overdone mood of this part of the song, we hear a very cheery saxophone section chugging away, oblivious to the catastrophe.

Before we get to the last section, Tiny speaks to us, and tells us in a fairly ecstatic tone: "No matter if you're out there parked in that car along the highway, or whether you're at home, sitting by the radio, or whether you're having them good meals, or whether you're by the TV set, let everyone sing about those melting ice caps! How they're coming down into the sea and let us all have a swimming time, as we sing . . ." The last lines of the song are, "The ice caps are melting, the tide is rushing in. / All the world is drowning, to wash away the sin." Thus this soggy apocalypse is not only ecological, but biblical.

The song about fish is followed by a brief interstitial bit: we hear the voice of Tiny Tim saying "The birds are coming" over and over, in a brief but endless-sounding loop, with echo, delay, and other electronic effects, including actual bird noises.

After all the weirdness involving fish and birds, we need to go back to something reliable, such as another 1913 song updated to sound like 1968. The song in question is "Ever Since You Told Me That You Loved Me (I'm a Nut)," and it represents the combined efforts of three storied songwriters with dozens of standards between them: Grant Clarke, Edgar Leslie, Jean Schwartz. The original song is a model of peppy syncopation, and Tiny Tim does the original justice, even with more electric bass, heavy drumbeats, and tambourines—the most surprising element is a Joe Venuti–style hot fiddle solo in the middle. Tiny's voice has a slight reverb effect that only makes it more endearing, and he sings with irresistible drive and energy. He's especially adorable when he reaches the end of the bridge: "I bump into people on the street—Like a fool! Like a fool! Like an OLD fool!" It's a terrific track.

And now for something completely different. After a few more bird noises, we proceed from the sheer energy of "Ever Since You Told Me That You Loved Me (I'm a Nut)" to another gonzo duet. "Daddy, Daddy, What Is Heaven Like?" opens with a child's toy keyboard, and Khaury singing in the voice of a baby boy. Whereas some of the old songs are souped up to sound new, this is a new song with more excess sentimentality than any turn-of-the-century ballad. Khaury sings the part of a little lad asking his father about heaven, needing to know, "If Mommy loved us so, why'd she go there?" He then sings back as the "Daddy," in an exaggerated Nashville baritone, something like Eddy Arnold, Ray Price, or Jim Reeves, "Maybe someday you'll go to Heaven too. / If I know your Mommy, she saved a place for you." After listening to this track for almost forty years, I still can't tell you what the original intentions were, whether those of the songwriter (Art Wayne), the producer, or the singer. Are they parodying the sentiment or indulging in it? Or possibly both? Both voices, the boy and the father, are so outrageously overdone, and in such stark contrast to each other: the baby boy voice is backed by a toy piano, the father's by wailing Nashville guitars. It's hard to believe anybody was taking anything seriously. Yet TT sings the last line completely straight, with the youngster singing, "Why is there, Daddy, a tear in your eye?" It gives one pause.

In the interview, TT avoids giving any clues as to his intentions regarding "Heaven." However, he's very clear about his feelings concerning the next track, "The Coming Home Party" (credited to

Diane Hildebrand and Jack Keller). He describes it as "the worst song! Don't get me wrong, I mean, this is a song I never would have recorded, but Mr. Perry wanted to have this on the album." I respectfully disagree: "The Coming Home Party" is genuinely entertaining; it's clearly a satire on mores and morality in suburban America in the wake of The Graduate, released in 1967. The track starts with the sounds of party chatter, over which we hear a xylophone playing a "misterioso" opening, as if a mustachioed villain were creeping up on an unsuspecting damsel in a silent melodrama. An electric organ booms away throughout, playing a harpsichord-like figure that sounds very much like 1960s pop. TT's voice is multitracked, to give it a strangely impersonal character. The opening lyrics are worth quoting in full:

I used to be the first to laugh
When Mrs. Jennings took a bath,
And left the window open for the neighbors.
But had we looked, we might have seen
That she was really very clean,
And given her the credit of her labors.

As in The Graduate, the story seems to be about a young man having an affair with an older, married lady, while her husband is off "somewhere making love to all his money." It gets kind of creepy when TT speaks in the voice of "Mrs. Jennings," and the last line is "her" saying "Nighty night, little Angel." Anybody would want to hop in the sack with Anne Bancroft as "Mrs. Robinson" (hey, hey, hey!), the original MILF of the gods, but this "Mrs. Jennings" is another story.

"Fill Your Heart," by a largely unknown twenty-seven-year-old songwriter named Paul Williams, is easily the best new song in the album, and TT's spoken introduction should be taken as completely sincere: "And now, my dear friends, I'd like to dedicate this song to all of you out there wherever you may be . . . North, south, east, or west, to everyone all over the world. This song is for you!" It opens beguilingly, with an intro of oboe, harp, and bongos, but leads quickly to the hook: "Fill your heart with love today, don't play the game of time. / Things that happened in the past, happened in your mind." This is 1960s sunshine pop at its best: the orchestration and TT's voice are winningly upbeat, and the instrumental break in the center is in march tempo, over which TT wails in falsetto, sounding like a postnuclear Bob Wills. It's one of the most genuinely optimistic songs anyone ever sang, and another true highlight of *God Bless Tiny Tim*.

From pure optimism, we go to more camp comedy: "And now, because you've all been so sweet, another duet for you!" The most popular duet of the psychedelic era was "I Got You Babe" a forgettable and devastatingly minimal single by Sonny and Cher, composed by the former, at a time when the couple enjoyed a brief vogue doing an uninspired stoner impersonation of Louis Prima and Keely Smith. The *God Bless* version is a hardly rare example where Tiny Tim's so-called parody is a much more creative and satisfying work of art than the original. It's the most minimal track on the album, with absolutely no production values, just TT singing as he would live, with just his fiercely strummed uke for accompaniment. His two duet voices were undoubtedly recorded live, not in separate tracks: taking the Sonny and Cher trifle, he sings the girl voice in his familiar trilly "Tulips" falsetto, and the male part in the voice of Bob Dylan. Tiny Tim actually anticipates the voice that Dylan himself would employ a few months later on *Nashville Skyline*. And it's very funny, especially so in the end where the boy and girl indulge in some vocal exhibitionism, trilling away together. For a moment, the two voices are heard on top of each other, as deliberately canned-sounding applause rises in the background; at least that one segment was achieved using overdubs.

How to finish? Khaury and Perry chose to end with Gordon Jenkins's "This Is All I Ask," which had by then become sort of an old-stud farewell song. Recorded definitively by Tony Bennett and then Frank Sinatra, it's the kind of thing Dean Martin or Jimmy Durante would do at the end of a TV special. The lush, tasteful orchestration is worthy of Jenkins, and TT sings it totally unaffectedly and completely straight, with genuine feeling. As a song about growing old and taking steps on the path to leaving the world behind, it's an odd choice for a new artist to do on his first album, but it's beautifully handled all around and makes an effective closer. After the song finishes, we hear a reprise of the same dream music that came in at the beginning of Side A, during "Welcome to My Dream." It sounds for all the world as if Tiny Tim is ascending bodily into Heaven, on angel's wings, as we hear him say, "Thank you, thank you everyone, goodbye . . ."

God Bless Tiny Tim was a major success, reaching number seven on *Billboard*'s pop albums chart—thus competing with the Beatles, the Rolling Stones, Jimi Hendrix, and even Reprise founder Frank Sinatra. But whereas it effectively launched the careers of two major figures in the pop music business, Richard Perry and Paul Williams (today the president of ASCAP), it represented the beginning of the end for Tiny Tim. Ten months later, Khaury, Perry, and orchestrator Artie Butler delivered the follow-up: the appropriately titled *Tiny Tim's Second Album*. This too is an excellent album. If *God Bless* rates an A, the *Second Album* is a B+. Among other successes, the sequel contains another elaborate pop treatment of a folk song with Tom Paxton's "Can't Help but Wonder Where I'm Bound." There's an update of "We Love It," a worthy 1920s song, probably learned from Annette Hanshaw, in an "Ain't We Got Fun" kind of vein. He does one "straight" country song, "Have You Seen My Little Sue," credited to Perry as songwriter, and a genuinely fiery rendition of the rockabilly classic "Great Balls of Fire." Tiny Tim also outdoes himself in the one-man-duet department with a duo medley: it starts with another Ada Jones–Billy Murray number, the 1910 "I'm Glad I'm a Boy—I'm Glad I'm a Girl," which then rather ambitiously leads into a slice of genuine operetta, "My Hero," from Oscar Straus's 1908 hit *The Chocolate Soldier*. Again, he closes the album on a sincere note with "As Time Goes By."

But *Tiny Tim's Second Album* barely sold. His third Reprise album, also released in 1969, smacked of a contractual obligation quickie. *For All My Little Friends* featured little in the way of production values, the singer working with a small ensemble and nothing like the elaborate orchestrations of

Artie Butler on the previous albums. Still, as a substantially less ambitious kiddie record, *For All My Little Friends* is not without charm—and in its own way it's even more surreal than its predecessors. TT admonishes the little friends to "Remember Your Name and Address" if they should get lost, and to "walk up to that kind policeman, the very first one you see." From there he proceeds to the conclusion, the only "grown-up" track on the album—and the only one with a full orchestra—Burt Bacharach's hit waltz "What the World Needs Now."

The week before Christmas 1969, Tiny Tim enjoyed what would turn out to be his last hurrah as a major celebrity. In front of more than twenty-one million people watching *The Tonight Show Starring Johnny Carson,* he married "Miss Vicki" (Victoria Mae Budinger)—it was the showbiz equivalent of the moon landing a few months earlier. Carson would stay on the air for another twenty-three years, but December 17, 1969, remained his highest-ever rating.

Herbert Khaury would continue working as Tiny Tim wherever he could and recording (occasionally for his own labels) sporadically until his death in 1996. That year saw the release of *Girl,* an album in which he was backed by the imaginative accordion punk band Brave Combo; this is probably the best of his post-Reprise projects.

God Bless Tiny Tim was very much a product of its time, and in this case that's a good thing. It could only have been made in 1968—the rough midpoint between the 1920s and the twenty-first century. It's proof that sometimes you can create a classic by looking backward.

45

Mel Tormé

Mel Tormé with the Marty Paich Dek-Tette (Lulu's Back in Town)
(1956)

For me, the difficulty in choosing the single best album by Mel Tormé (1925–1999) is that it's very hard to pick between the two overall strongest contenders, the 1956 *Mel Tormé with the Marty Paich Dek-Tette* and the 1960 *Mel Tormé Swings Shubert Alley,* both of which derive from Tormé's remarkably fruitful collaboration with arranger-conductor Marty Paich. The two albums are so consistent overall that they could easily be reissued on the same CD together—and yet it isn't a clear-cut case of original and sequel, the way Sinatra's *Songs for Swingin' Lovers!* and *A Swingin' Affair!* so obviously are. The singing and the orchestrations and playing on both albums are roughly equal, but the 1956 album incorporates a wider range of material—the songs come from a broader range of sources—and there's more contrast in that the 1956 album includes ballads as well as swingers, whereas in the 1960 set every song is, more or less, in a compatible tempo, and they all come from postwar Broadway shows (shows that were recent enough for Mel to have actually seen them himself). Which of the two albums is more essential? It's almost impossible to choose, but I would say that the 1956 package continues to contain more surprises for me, right up to this day.

With *Mel Tormé with the Marty Paich Dek-Tette,* Mel Tormé did something that few vocalists have

done: it would be enough for a singer to have a distinct enough vocal timbre (so many singers tend to sound like so many other singers, as do saxophonists or pianists), but in his collaborations with Paich, Tormé crafted an entire ensemble sound unique to him. Whenever you hear a Nelson Riddle–like orchestral sound, you expect to hear the voice of Sinatra; likewise, when you hear a West Coast band sound, circa the mid-1950s, in the style of Gerry Mulligan or Shorty Rogers, the voice you expect to hear in this context is inevitably that of Mel Tormé.

When I published my book *Jazz Singing* in 1989, Mel was flattered that I had so many positive things to say about him, but he was somewhat annoyed to be classified as a "cool" singer. Yet with the Marty Paich Dek-Tette album, Tormé created a whole sonic universe that was uniquely his own yet entirely bound up with the whole school of music known as cool jazz or, sometimes, West Coast jazz. The collaborations with Paich (and other accompanists working in the cool idiom, like Shorty Rogers, Johnny Mandel, and Russ Garcia) would be the sweetest of all sweet spots in Tormé's long career; after hearing his voice framed against those particular colors of brass and reeds, it's impossible to imagine why he would ever want to sing with a conventional swing band, a string orchestra, or any other kind of a group.

Yet "cool" would never be the word that I would use to describe Mel's own personality: he was passionate, he was brilliant, he was funny, he was goofy, he was smart and articulate in a very idiosyncratic kind of way (like most singers and musicians of his generation, he had never been to college); he was bright and extremely knowledgeable on a wide variety of subjects (especially music and film) without being nerdy. And yet, when he sings with Paich's ensemble, he becomes incredibly and ineffably cool—sometimes he's at his coolest when you least expect it, as on "I Love to Watch the Moonlight," an otherwise forgotten, very minor big band bouncer, which he somehow imbues with significance, without making it heavy or dark. Saying he was "cool" on the Paich albums isn't to denigrate his artistry—or to suggest that he was deliberately trying to be terminally hip—but merely to show that he and Paich made coolness into a much greater virtue than it had ever been before, or even since.

In 1954, Mel Tormé was under contract to Coral Records, a comparatively low-on-the-ladder subsidiary of Decca. Coral was like most record companies in the early LP era: chasing the hits and trying to sell singles, while occasionally allowing their jazz-oriented artists some leeway to attempt more personal projects. In about three years with Coral, Tormé had made two excellent albums, both with a pronounced jazz feel: an affectionate homage to the big band era titled *Musical Sounds Are the Best Songs* (1953) and his first of many in-person concert recordings, *Live at the Crescendo* (1955).

With his supremely lovely voice and higher-than-average musical intelligence, Tormé was an asset to a record company. Even though he only occasionally landed actual hits on the charts, he brought other attributes to the table. In fact, he'd enjoyed his most successful song as a composer rather than as a performer: his "Christmas Song" had been a major, career-changing hit for Nat King Cole. Clearly, there was some kind of an audience for Tormé's music—he already was supported by what his agent, the famous malapropster Carlos Gastel, described as "a vast minority" of fans.

As Mel told me in an interview in 1995, his contract with Coral ended at the end of 1954, and the label wanted him to re-sign. "I left Coral because of

Red Clyde, who had started Bethlehem Records," Mel recalled. "He came to me and we had dinner and a long, long talk in which he outlined his precepts and concepts for Bethlehem. He told me that he was going to sign Dizzy and Duke Ellington and Sarah Vaughan, and I felt that was the place for me. I stayed with them until my contract ran out." (Of those three artists, only Ellington would actually do an album for Bethlehem.)

Essentially, in switching from a more mainstream-oriented major subsidiary to an independent, jazz-oriented concern, Tormé was renewing his commitment to jazz, and relinquishing a certain part of his claim to pop fame. For one thing, he must have been aware that Bethlehem could hardly compete in the singles market (it was hard enough for Coral), yet the first project he would tape for Bethlehem was, to his surprise, far from a jazz album. "That surprised me," said Mel, "because Red Clyde absolutely [signed] me for the jazz aspect of my singing and the first thing he said was, 'I want to do a ballad album with you.' So *It's a Blue World* was the first Bethlehem album." *It's a Blue World* turned out to be a shimmeringly beautiful album of first-class ballads, beautifully sung with a large, romantic movie-style orchestra. Whether it was a jazz album or not seems immaterial.

One side benefit from *Blue World* was Tormé's first opportunity to work with Marty Paich. "I came to Red and I said, 'There's a guy out here who wrote some things for [drummer-bandleader] Shelly Manne and His Men, he's absolutely marvelous and I'm absolutely positive that he can write ballads as well as jazz things.' And Red said, 'Yeah, I kind of heard of him, but he's a jazz guy.' And I had to fight to get Marty to write a few of the arrangements on that album. He scored 'All This and Heaven Too,' which is one of the most beautiful arrangements that I've ever sung to. And when Marty wrote those things, I understood where he was coming from and that he was a complete arranger—not just a jazz arranger."

The next item on Tormé's list was indeed a jazz project that was right up Paich's alley. In 1949 and 1950, Mel and a lot of other music lovers had been blown away by the sound of the Miles Davis Nonet, known at the time as "the Tuba Band." "I thought, what a great sound to use behind a vocalist." Baritone saxophonist and arranger-composer Gerry Mulligan had played a key role in the Davis sessions, and he was responsible for the next step in the evolution of that idea with a series of recordings in 1953 with a group he called his Tentet. When Tormé heard those sessions, he was completely sold on the concept. "I just loved what the tuba brought to that group at the bottom of the range and the alto and lead trumpet at the top, to the point where I wanted to sing against that background. It was a wonderful mix of West Coast cool—that's all I can call it."

Tormé gratefully acknowledged Mulligan's Tentet by dubbing this new ensemble "the Marty Paich Dek-Tette," which would also provide the title for the first Tormé-Paich album, taped in January 1956.

When I spoke with both Tormé and Paich, a few years before Paich's death in 1995 and Tormé's debilitating stroke in 1996, each was keen to give credit to the other but, at the same time, retain a generous chunk for himself. At times, Mel has spoken as if he regarded Paich as what Sinatra called "a musical secretary"; in other words, that Paich took down ideas from Mel's head and made them work in real life. Paich, on the other hand, told me that the charts were "about 90 percent my ideas and 10 percent Mel's."

The truth is probably somewhere in the middle, but one thing is obvious: that there are ideas and concepts in the Paich-Tormé charts that are simply not present in Paich's accompaniments for other singers, as wonderful as those charts are. At the same time, Tormé could not have accomplished the Dek-Tette albums with any other orchestrator. Paich was also quick to point out that with most singers he had to keep their musical range and limitations in mind whenever he wrote anything, even those as versatile as Sammy Davis Jr. "But with Mel, I could write anything I wanted," he said: there was nothing he could write that Tormé couldn't sing.

Mel was always a "prefacer": if you were to ask him what time it was, he would look at his watch and say, "Let me tell you something, laddie, it's four PM." (I was never sure if he called everybody "lad-die" or if it was just me.) He would always begin to answer by telling you that he was about to tell you something. That's why the famous opening to the *Dek-Tette* album sounds like something Mel himself would have come up with. "Lulu's Back in Town" is introduced by a vamp that rises chromatically, a half step upward with every repeat; over this, Tormé sings a brief special-material lyric that sets up the idea that he's about to tell us about a very special woman: "You've heard about Margie. / You've heard about Dinah . . ." These are both earlier songs titled after feminine names that all audiences in 1956 would have been readily familiar with. In fact, Paich had actually recorded "Lulu" in 1954, as pianist on a sextet date led by valve trombonist Bob Enevoldsen, who would also play on Tormé's January 1956 session. Nothing like Tormé's vamp is heard on Paich's 1954 instrumental version.

The song itself is from 1935, and is a rare instance of a number written for a movie (by Hollywood's most storied songwriter, Harry Warren) having an association with black or jazz musicians from the moment it was introduced. It was written for Dick Powell in the 1935 *Broadway Gondolier,* and quickly taken up by all manner of jazz and black entertainers and bandleaders, most notably pianist-singer Fats Waller and trumpeter-vocalist Wingy Manone. Many songs at that time had slightly different lyrics for male and female vocalists, but owing to the racial climate of the day, lyricist Al Dubin was compelled to prepare a special set of lyrics for African American performers. In the bridge, where Dick Powell sings "You can tell all my pets / All my blondes and brunettes," Waller and the Mills Brothers sang, "You can tell all my pets / All my Harlem coquettes"—obviously it wouldn't do to suggest that a colored gentleman was consorting with blondes. "Lulu" was popular with the public and many jazz groups into the early swing era, but less so in the modern epoch.

Outfitting "Lulu" with a brand-new wardrobe, this very modern-sounding vamp, was Tormé's deliberate strategy: the old girl gained a new life and became one of Tormé's constant companions. He would tinker slightly with the arrangement over the years, but he kept the intro intact. The rest of the track is no less fresh and original: following solos by alto saxophonist Bud Shank and Bob Enevoldsen (playing valve trombone), Tormé returns to sing an artfully crafted paraphrase of the Al Dubin lyric; he changes the notes and the intervals, but sticks to the words, in a manner that, in the abstract, parallels Sarah Vaughan. Yet it's the vamp that seizes the day: like Nelson Riddle's famous intro to "You Make Me Feel So Young" at the start of *Swingin' Lovers,* this vamp instills in our ears the idea that we are about to hear something new and very special—that something different has indeed been added.

The singer's own protests aside, his voice has an indisputable coolness to it, here and throughout the album—not unemotional, like Mr. Spock, but understated. His is both a different kind of happy and a different kind of sad from Sinatra or Holiday. He couldn't ever be said to be lacking in feeling, but it's his own brand of feeling, and his own way of expressing it.

Tormé was one of the first major musicians to discover Harold Arlen and Ted Koehler's "When the Sun Comes Out," which follows "Lulu" as the second tune on the album. In 1933, Arlen and Koehler had composed one of the major songs of the era—of all time—in "Stormy Weather." Eight years later they reunited for an unofficial sequel to "Stormy Weather" titled "When the Sun Comes Out." They were no longer working together. It wasn't written for a specific assignment (a musical, a revue, a film) but because, it seems in retrospect, that the song simply had to be written. "When the Sun Comes Out" is a very literal follow-up to "Stormy Weather"—it belongs on the B side of the original 78 or 45 rpm singles.

"When the Sun Comes Out" was first recorded by, among others, Helen O'Connell with Jimmy Dorsey and Helen Forrest with Benny Goodman, both in early 1941. In 1982, Tormé reprised it in a live album, and in a spoken introduction, he reminisced about being introduced to it by Lena Horne: "Great song. Great band. Great singer." (Mel remembered hearing her do it live with Charlie Barnet's orchestra, though she didn't sing it on the band's commercial recording.) The Tormé-Paich "Sun" is slow and moody, much more about the weather being stormy than about the sun coming

out, more about darkness than light. It opens with a French horn intro, the atmosphere very similar to that on previous ballads from the Davis Nonet (like "Darn That Dream") and the Mulligan Tentet and very different from both the early swing band versions and the later big belting versions done in the wake of Barbra Streisand and Judy Garland.

He may be waiting for the sun to come out, but he also loves to watch the moonlight. Two of the very best songs he included on the *Dek-Tette* album were scarcely heard from again: "I Love to Watch the Moonlight" and "When April Comes Again." Tormé's "Moonlight" has the whimsical feeling of one of Mulligan's medium-up riff numbers, like "Bernie's Tune." And yet his own intrinsic coolness gives the song something of a hard-core edge, accentuated in the second chorus by the way he sings around brief solos (Bob Enevoldsen, valve trombone, Bob Cooper, tenor sax, probably Don Fagerquist, trumpet). The end result might be called seriously frivolous, in that it's incurably bouncy but with Tormé's own particular intensity and sense of purpose.

Tracks five and six are both the most baroque and the most basic in the album. We rev back into tempo with "Fascinating Rhythm," the Gershwin brothers classic that, as its title implies, has served as impetus for tricky rhythmic patterns ever since it was first heard in 1924. Tormé and Paich shoehorn a lot of ideas into a rather small space (a mere two and a half minutes), and there's even time for substantial solos by Enevoldsen (again) and Jack Montrose (probably) on tenor saxophone. This would become a career perennial for Tormé, one of his featured numbers on TV variety shows and other guest spots—there's a famous version from *The Judy Garland Show* in 1963, in which the horn solos were replaced by drum solos by Tormé himself. Since "Fascinating Rhythm" was from a Fred Astaire show *(Lady, Be Good),* the song can be said to anticipate the second Tormé-Paich album, *Mel Tormé Loves Fred Astaire,* recorded ten months later, in November 1956.

Only three and a half minutes long, "The Blues" is a testament to Tormé's ingenuity on many levels, starting with his ability to find worthwhile material. Along with Astaire and Gershwin, one of his favorite sources was the Duke Ellington band book; virtually every so-called jazz singer of the time or since has picked the Ducal bones clean, but "The Blues" is a number that Tormé had virtually to himself. It derives from the maestro's first full-length extended work, the 1943 *Black, Brown and Beige*; "The Blues," which started life at the end of the second full movement ("Brown"), was the only part of the work to have a vocal in the piece itself (although lyrics were later added to "Come Sunday"). Ellington, an underappreciated wordsmith, wrote his own lyrics to "The Blues," which was originally known as "Mauve." It was famously sung at its premiere at Carnegie Hall by Betty Roche.

"The Blues" is also clear evidence of Ellington's perversity, in that it isn't remotely in anything like basic blues form—in other words, "The Blues" is not the blues. "The Blues" is a piece of music that contemplates the nature of the blues without actually being the blues—it observes the blues from an objective distance. (It's a lyric that could have been written by Ralph Ellison or Albert Murray.) Ellington cast his text in what we might call a pyramid or a triangular form, in which each line grows progressively longer ("The blues. / The blues ain't / the blues ain't nothin'...") and then, at the end, gets correspondingly shorter. As heard in *Black, Brown and Beige,* the section begins with a formidable intro—which links to the "Work Song," the dramatic melody that Ellington uses to begin the whole work. Tormé's version, however, forgoes that intro, and begins with the first two words (and the title) of the text, "The Blues." He does retain the mid-section that Ellington placed in the center of "The Blues," an instrumental interlude that was substantial enough to gain its own title and be performed independently, as "Carnegie Blues." Whereas tenor saxophonist Ben Webster (later Al Sears) took the main solo in the Ellington performance, here the "Carnegie Blues" interlude is given to Bud Shank on alto.

Rodgers and Hart dominate side two of the *Dek-Tette* album, with three of the six songs: "The Lady Is a Tramp," "I Like to Recognize the Tune," and "Sing for Your Supper." The mid-1950s were the time when Sinatra and Fitzgerald were leading the charge to the discovery of the Great American

Songbook; "Tramp" would be a signature song for both of those artists, yet Tormé beat them both to it (they would each get to it later that same year). Mel's version is in a class by itself: he opens with a fast and exciting scatted intro, underscored by trumpet (probably Don Fagerquist), very much like one of the more up-tempo instrumentals by Shorty Rogers and His Giants. Yet as modern as the background is, the purpose of the whole thing is to support the lyrics and the voice of the singer; it's not a purely instrumental exercise. "Tramp" (with solos by Fagerquist, Shank, and Cooper) is a letter-perfect example of how such modern jazz devices, not least the killer-fast bebop tempo, can be used to underscore the words—the relentless pace makes the woman in question somehow seem both trampier and more ladylike.

Tormé wrote a new partial chorus of original lyrics, heard after the instrumental break ("When she goes dining, dressed in her jeans / Loves pork and beans / She gets stares, but who cares?") and made an even more personal modification to the text when he added the line "Can't make Lombardo / digs Basie and Hamp" in the coda. He elongates the final line "That's . . . that's why . . . that's why the lady . . ." and stretches it out (almost in a parallel to the form of "The Blues"), as the band plays a Latin polyrhythmic background, similar to what Shorty Rogers would use in one of his Afro-Cuban numbers, like "Tale of an African Lobster."

In the "Basie and Hamp" line, Tormé personalizes the song by making it, in those lines, a song about music. The other two Rodgers and Hart songs here are even more meaningful to him since they're already about music: "Sing for Your Supper" (from *The Boys from Syracuse*) is a song about singing, and "I Like to Recognize the Tune" (from *Too Many Girls*) is a song about listening—two things that Tormé did very well.

"Recognize the Tune" boasts one of Paich's most sonorous arrangements—it's almost as if he's going out of his way to insure that the tune is supremely recognizable. Again, Tormé makes very personal and specific lyric alterations: the original referred to "a guy named Krupa" who "plays the drums like thunder," but Tormé passes along the honors along to his personal fave, "a guy named

Buddy" (as in Rich). He gets extremely playful in the coda, passing through different styles of music and tempos, and yet the tune is never buried.

"Sing for Your Supper," unlike the other two Lorenz Hart lyrics, does not open with the verse but with a vocal scale—as if warming up to sing the lyricist's instruction to sing for one's supper. Tormé clearly relishes the line "songbirds are not dumb"—he should know—and he stretches out the phrase "si-nn-g and you'll be fed"—making a veritable song out of the word "sing" all by itself.

If Rodgers and Hart, and the sophisticated songs they wrote for Broadway, were yet another influence (following Ellington, Gershwin, and Astaire), so too was Artie Shaw. Tormé had worked with the mercurial clarinetist-bandleader on an early album of Cole Porter tunes in 1946—the idea of singing Porter with Shaw was pure manna from heaven to Mel (what he would call "very much of a muchness")—this being the combination of one of his absolute favorite composers and his personal hero of a maestro. On the 1956 album, Tormé included two Vincent Youmans songs that he clearly learned from Shaw, "Keepin' Myself for You" and "Carioca." Shaw had cut the first in 1940 with his Gramercy Five, and "Carioca" (another Astaire number, from *Flying Down to Rio*) was a Shaw classic immortalized by the original "Begin the Beguine" band of 1939.

Shaw's "Carioca" opened with nightmarish growling and then flew into a superfast 4/4; it's an archetypical example of what was known, back in the swing era, as a "flag-waver." The term "carioca" itself is Portuguese, it commonly refers to inhabitants of the city that Astaire and Rogers flew down to ("ca-RIO-ca"). Shaw, however, jettisoned any hint of Latin rhythm, and thus the Tormé-Paich version is all the more exciting because they re-Latinize the "Carioca." Tormé had done an embryonic treatment of the song in 1950 with the Red Norvo Trio, which sounds rather like a blueprint for the Paich version—the 1950 includes Tormé's own lyrical tag ("my love for you can not die . . .") and his declamatory exhortation of "the Carioca" with a large exclamation point at the end. That exclamation is delivered even more loudly at the conclusion of the 1956 track, and the horns may be small in number compared to a full-scale big band, but they are mighty, and they help Tormé deliver that final shot with a resounding wallop.

"Keepin' Myself for You," with lyrics by Sidney Clare, had been written for the 1930 film version of Youmans's 1927 Broadway success *Hit the Deck*. This and "When April Comes Again" are the two finest straight-up ballads on the album. Mel is remarkably tender, and the intricacies of the arrangement are all in support of the singer, the song, and the story—they help keep the whole performance more honest and expressive, they keep the emotion in the foreground rather than drawing attention to their own technical ingenuity. Here's more proof that with Mel, both his own vocal technique and the considerable musical ingenuity of Paich and the ensemble are all there in the service of the lyric, the narrative, and the overall feeling.

"When April Comes Again" is possibly even more touching; Mel's singing is even more heartfelt. A comparatively obscure song by arranger Paul Weston, "When April Comes Again" has a fine lyric by the even more obscure Doris Schaefer. It was recorded by Jo Stafford (the future Mrs. Weston) in 1950 and then later, in the wake of Tormé, by George Shearing, and virtually no one else. As with "I Love to Watch the Moonlight," the mere fact of his coming up with a beautiful, underperformed song like "When April Comes Again" testifies to his musical acumen—and he sings it very beautifully indeed. As with "Carioca," he adds an original tag of his own devising ("It may not come for long / I will always love you"). The composer himself told me in 1995, "Mel recorded a song of mine, 'When April Comes Again,' and it's just a most wonderful record of it—it's just great. He takes a song and he probably puts more of a proper feeling into a song than anybody singing."

When Tormé recorded "The Lady Is a Tramp," he had no idea that he was setting the stage for what would become a comparison (or even a competition) between himself, Sinatra, and Fitzgerald. Just the opposite holds true for "Lullaby of Birdland": Mel was directly inspired by Ella's classic 1955 recording of that then-new lyric and deliberately wanted to see what he could come up with in response. Was he trying to outdo her? Not necessarily. He knew he couldn't beat Ella at her own game—he wasn't trying to out-Ella her, but he could out-Mel her. "Lullaby of Birdland" is generally cited as the masterpiece of the first *Dek-Tette* album (it's neck and neck, at least, with "Lulu"), and it's an imposing piece of work. Tormé and Paich have reimagined the human voice itself as a very different kind of musical instrument while, at the same time, using the solo timbres of various horn players as if they were human voices. It's a rare instance of an orchestrator and a singer creating a perfect level playing field upon which the two can interact.

"Lullaby of Birdland" starts with bassist Red Mitchell, then Mel's singing voice. Drummer Mel Lewis joins in on the bridge (at the words "weepy old willow"), and the piano only enters with the rest of the ensemble at the start of the second chorus, and it's here that Tormé starts scatting. Yet the scatting itself is beside the point: the main attraction, starting here in the second chorus and continuing for the third and fourth, is the interaction of the human voice and the metal "voices" of the horn soloists. He joins in inspired exchanges with trumpets and saxes; he refers occasionally to quoted phrases from songs, particularly in the third chorus, where he interacts with the trumpets—one trumpeter starts the chorus, and Tormé comes back with "Love Me or Leave Me," the 1928 pop song that provided George Shearing with the harmonic foundation of "Birdland." Then, after the next trumpet phrase, Mel answers with Gerry Mulligan's "Ontet," and he responds to the next one with "Chloe"; the fourth chorus has him doing the same with Bobby Enevoldsen, although in the first two exchanges Tormé answers by throwing the trombonist's own phrases back to him rather than quoting a song, then he kicks back a little bit of "Blue Moon" and, next, "Blacksmith Blues." There's a marvelously mellifluous exchange with the combined saxophone section, and Tormé caps the exchange with "Moon over Miami." The final chorus, in which he returns to the words, also ends in what could be called a pyramid structure, since it ends as it began, with the lyrics over the bass.

· · ·

When I first met Mel, in the early 1980s, I told him how the original *Dek-Tette* album was my favorite. Mel said something like, "Let me tell you one thing, laddie . . . I called the company that owns those masters, and I told them I would redo that album, sing those old charts with a new band, for nothing. Honest to God!" (That was another expression he was fond of.) He was so unhappy with the sound of his own thirty-year-old voice of 1956 that he actually volunteered to work for bupkis. Clearly, this was an extreme measure.

That corporation didn't take Mel up on his offer, and instead reissued the 1956 album. Fortunately, the music was unscathed, but the title and the cover were both seriously botched. The original title, *Mel Tormé with the Marty Paich Dek-tette,* was apparently perceived to be a bit generic, so they renamed the album after its most identifiable song. Their strategy with the cover was completely inapposite: the original album jacket was brilliant, a caricature of Mel's face laid out in vintage automobiles. The cover they replaced it with was, in fact, boring beyond generic: mostly black, with a red and white stripe. The title on that reissue was *The Tormé Touch;* since then, the album has been re-re-issued many times all over the world as *Lulu's Back in Town*.

Like Frank Sinatra and Nelson Riddle, or Miles Davis and Gil Evans, the combination of Tormé and Paich proved to be one of the major, highly productive collaborations of the great early years of the jazz and pop album. Before 1956 was finished, they continued with *Mel Tormé Sings Fred Astaire* (1956), then there was a live show taped at the Crescendo in 1957 (which yielded enough material for two LPs, *Live at the Crescendo* and *Songs for Any Taste*). Between 1957 and 1959 there were four studio albums: *California Suite* (1957), *Prelude to a Kiss* (1957), *Tormé* (1958), and *Back in Town* (1959). Then the original Tormé-Paich series reached its climax with *Mel Tormé Swings Shubert Alley* in 1960; this was the project that came closest to knocking the original 1956 *Dek-Tette* album off its pedestal as his greatest—and it was a fitting conclusion to the series. It was a collaboration that was bookended by classics.

Nearly thirty years later, there was a worthy postscript. In 1988, the singer and the arranger-conductor reunited for a studio set *(Reunion)* and a live package *(In Concert Tokyo)*. The Tokyo package fulfills at least some of Mel's wishes to remake the 1956 charts, and there are new and excellent vocals of "When the Sun Comes Out" and "Carioca," which is slightly less cool but possibly even more animated than the original. The 1988 studio album contains an additional song from the 1956 *Dek-Tette* album, "The Blues." Mel's voice is somewhat heavier (the key has been lowered), but still remarkably fluid, and the tempo is slightly slower (the 1988 version is also a minute longer). Again, he's somewhat cooler on the original and more dramatic on the remake, but all three are exceptional vocals that he could have been proud of.

Mel told me in 1995, "Marty was very finicky and he could actually be—I hate to say this—devastatingly dictatorial. There were times when he really got all the musicians mad at him because he was . . ." Here he hesitated. "I can't say arrogant, that's not the word. He was a dogged perfectionist. He'd still be working on it and it drove the guys nuts, but eventually, we got what we wanted. And it was superb." Mel himself wasn't always beloved by everyone; he could be acerbic, say the wrong thing in the wrong way, and step on toes. He also could throw his enormous musical knowledge and technical skill around, sort of like the musical equivalent of a bully. He was also resentful of certain singers who were obviously less talented but more popular—it's hard to blame him for that.

Tormé and Paich, who were both born in 1925, both stopped making music at the age of seventy: the arranger died of colon cancer in August 1995; Tormé suffered a massive stroke a year after that and never sang again. It's a shame that they couldn't do one final project together in the early 1990s: it would have been one last chance to try and improve on perfection.

46

Sarah Vaughan

Sarah Vaughan

(1954)

She was known as "the Divine One," not only in a nod toward another Sarah (Bernhardt), but because her voice was so overwhelmingly beautiful that many assumed it couldn't possibly have emanated from a mere mortal. And yet while the voice was amazingly opulent, it was never so large that it overshadowed the emotional content or the inner essence of the song she was singing.

Sarah Vaughan's music was indeed rapturous and angelic, but on the one occasion when I had the opportunity to meet her, I was much more impressed with the humanity of the woman than with the so-called divinity. This was at the Blue Note in New York, about 1985; she had spent her entire career on the road, and a week in one city was a comparative luxury, even if it meant a minimum of twelve shows in six days. Even for a headliner, life on tour was a continual backbreaker, and backstage, Sarah seemed very old at sixty. The main thing I remember was that she was visibly exhausted, gasping for breath and—not to put too fine a point on it—literally dripping with sweat. She put so much effort into every show that she seemed barely able to talk during her brief break between the first and second sets. All of a sudden, any thoughts of Vaughan being a supernatural entity quickly evaporated (faster than the perspiration, in fact). Sarah Vaughan put her heart and soul, not to mention her blood, sweat,

and tears—and her humanity—into every note she sang.

Much of Sarah Vaughan's jazz work, like her 1955 big band album, *In the Land of Hi-Fi*, is up-tempo and what might be called "up-volume"—in other words, loud and swinging. Yet the 1954 album originally titled *Sarah Vaughan* is precisely the opposite: it's intimate, subtle, and restrained. Even the album title, just the artist's name, is understated, although it's become known to history as *Sarah Vaughan with Clifford Brown*.

When Vaughan signed with Mercury Records in 1954, she was not yet thirty, but this was already her third long-term relationship with an important label. Previously, she had been "pacted to" (as *Variety* would have said) Musicraft Records (a minor concern that never achieved its goal of becoming a major player) from 1945 to 1947, then Columbia Records (as always, the biggest) from 1949 to 1953, and then Mercury. Based in Chicago, Mercury was one of the first general-interest record companies to have a jazz imprint. Its jazz division was a variation of sorts of the parent company's name, EmArcy Records, and Vaughan's first four albums for the corporation were all released on this subsidiary: *Images, Sarah Vaughan, In the Land of Hi-Fi*, and *Sassy*.

Images, a 1954 10-incher that was expanded into a 12-incher retitled *Swingin' Easy*, was essentially what Vaughan was doing in clubs, with her working trio of pianist John Malachi, bassist Joe Benjamin, and drummer Roy Haynes. Then, *Sarah Vaughan* and *In the Land of Hi-Fi* were both arranged by the brilliant Ernie Wilkins, who had not yet done the single chart that would put him in the hall of fame: the Count Basie–Joe Williams classic "Every Day I Have the Blues."

Wilkins, a tenor saxophonist whose birth year has been given as both 1919 and 1922, hailed from St. Louis, Missouri. He played in territory bands (the Jeter-Pillars Orchestra) and army military bands (including one led by Willie Smith), and then in Earl Hines's orchestra in the late 1940s, but by 1951 was back in St. Louis. In that year, his longtime friend, the trumpeter Clark Terry helped him land a spot in Count Basie's band, and, as Terry put it, he lied to Basie when he said that Wilkins played alto (rather than tenor). The specific saxophone turned out to be unimportant, since Wilkins proved his greatest value to Basie by writing orchestrations for the band, first instrumentals, and then some of the key blues charts for Joe Williams that became some of the Basie band's most successful numbers of the entire "New Testament."

In the mid-1950s, Sarah Vaughan toured on several occasions with a Birdland all-stars package that included the Basie orchestra, which gave her the chance to hear Wilkins's orchestrations; from there, she decided to appoint Wilkins to serve as musical director on two very different, both highly jazzy albums, beginning with *Sarah Vaughan,* taped in December 1954. "You know," concluded Terry, "I shudder sometimes when I think about how all of this happened as a result of that big lie that I told Basie when I called up Ernie Wilkins, who was working in a little place over in East St. Louis, Missouri, for 75 cents a night!"

Wilkins's contributions to the *Sarah Vaughan* album were obviously major, but quite possibly the overall sound and approach used on the album were determined by producer Bob Shad. Coincidentally, a further key player was yet another member of the Basie reed section, tenor saxophonist Paul Quinichette. Quinichette had been hired by Basie for his tonal resemblance to the great-

est of the band's graduates, the legendary Lester Young. Where Young was known as "the President" or "Pres," Quinichette was frequently billed as "the Vice Pres," which was also the title of his first album as a leader, done for EmArcy in 1951–52. In November 1954, Quinichette was at the helm of two sessions that resulted in an LP titled *Moods.* The other half of the front line on *Moods* was a flute—played by Sam Most on the first date and Herbie Mann on the second. On the first date, the moods in question were laid-back and relaxed; on the second they were highly tropical and Latin, thanks to a three-piece Pan-American percussion section of congas, bongos, and timbales. The results could be called "Jazz *Tropicalia,*" and as such, the sound of Quinichette's Presidential tenor in such a setting very directly anticipated what Stan Getz would sound like playing Brazilian style a decade later.

Three weeks after the *Moods* sessions, Shad reconvened the two "horns," Quinichette and Mann, along with pianist Jimmy Jones, who had played on the second *Moods* session but who was also, for many years, Sarah Vaughan's regular musical director. Even without Latin percussion, the tropical mood of Quinichette's *Moods* hangs in the air on *Sarah Vaughan:* "April in Paris," for instance, sounds more like July in Havana.

For the *Sarah Vaughan* recording sessions, Quinichette and Mann joined Vaughan's working trio, which then consisted of Jones, bassist Joe Benjamin, and the singer's longtime drummer, Roy Haynes. Lastly, there was one other musician whom Shad thought to add, the young trumpeter Clifford Brown. In 1954, Brown was rapidly being recognized as the most imposing new musician on the jazz scene; the quintet he co-led with veteran drummer Max Roach was one of the great groups of its time (and a major attraction for EmArcy Records), and "Brownie," who was widely beloved by his fellow musicians, had a remarkable future before him. (Alas, it would be over a year and a half later, when Brown's life ended tragically in an automobile accident.)

In addition to recording the Roach-Brown Quintet, Shad also taped the trumpeter on *Clifford Brown with Strings,* one of the first and best albums in that format, a lovely set arranged and conducted by another Basie-ite, arranger Neal Hefti. Shad also cast Brown as featured soloist with Mercury's three major female jazz singers: Dinah Washington, Helen Merrill (he played behind Merrill on an album taped several days after the Vaughan sessions, under the baton of another current Basie arranger, Quincy Jones), and Vaughan. Brown was a natural at playing romantic numbers with strings as well as obbligatos behind girl singers: at the time of these sessions, he was only twenty-three and twenty-four, but his sensitivity as a ballad specialist—especially as a firebrand young player with power to spare—was remarkably developed for a musician of any age. Throughout *Sarah Vaughan,* Brown plays very softly, blending in easily with the tenor sax and flute; whether he's blowing openly or into a mute, his trumpet work is always strong and supportive, always helping the song and the singer rather than merely calling attention to itself. His presence on *Sarah Vaughan* is yet one more factor that ensured this album's iconic status.

The album opens with "Lullaby of Birdland," which actually was the second tune recorded on the first of two sessions, on December 16 and 18, 1954. This was six months after Ella Fitzgerald introduced the lyric version of the song, which for over two years had served as an instrumental theme at Birdland itself; in fact, there are several extant Sarah Vaughan airchecks from 1953 that begin with her trio playing the still wordless "Lullaby." Although there was considerable competition in the early years—"Lullaby" was also recorded by Chris Connor and Mel Tormé—more recently Vaughan's has been the most frequently heard. Dianne Reeves expanded on the Vaughan-Wilkins arrangement in her 2000 tribute to Vaughan, *The Calling.* Likewise, the version played before showtime in the current incarnation of Birdland, on West Fortyfourth Street in Manhattan, is Vaughan's.

It begins with an ingenious and memorable vocal-instrumental intro, presumably composed by Wilkins, which Vaughan hums in harmony with the reeds (and which is reprised in many later recordings by other singers, who perhaps assume

that it's part of George Shearing's written melody). There are solos for all three members of the rhythm section, Jones, Benjamin, and a break by Haynes, before Vaughan birdlands into scat exchanges with the horns, Mann, Brown, and Quinichette, trading fours back and forth for a whole thirty-two-bar chorus. She returns to the lyrics for the bridge, and, after the final A section, reprises, or rather, rescats, the opening intro melody, this time as a coda.

Vaughan's version of "Lullaby" survives in two takes, a master and an alternate; the latter has been included as a bonus track on CD reissues. Both are slower and mellower than Fitzgerald's recording, and also less of a production: Vaughan is backed by a small, intimate group whereas Fitzgerald employs a large orchestra, an organ, and a choir. But the major difference is that Vaughan's version has the feel of being a cut on an album, whereas Fitzgerald's has the feel of a single; Vaughan's track sounds like the start of something, whereas Fitzgerald's is a whole show unto itself.

Vaughan's "Birdland" is also a whole minute longer than Fitzgerald's, but "April in Paris," the second track of *Sarah Vaughan,* is longer still—six and a half minutes. *Sarah Vaughan* is one of the first projects to utilize not only the longer playing time made possible with the LP, but the more relaxed general feeling that came with not having to get up and change a record every few minutes. As good as Vaughan had sounded on her earlier recordings, "April in Paris" is something entirely new. After a brief piano intro, she sings Vernon Duke's melody and Yip Harburg's lyric in a way that's at once languid and urgent, as if she has all the time in the world but has something important to say nonetheless. After the singer's opening chorus, Jones takes a piano solo that fairly shimmers in the manner of Erroll Garner, and there are gloriously relaxed eight-bar statements from Quinichette and Brown—at this tempo, eight bars seems like plenty of time. When Vaughan returns to sing a full second chorus, Brown and Mann shadow her like Philip Marlowe. This second chorus is even more playful and musical than the first—as if the extra time has empowered Sarah Vaughan to fully become Sarah Vaughan.

"He's My Guy" is a classic big-band-era love song (by one of the era's prime songwriting teams, Don Raye and Gene de Paul), introduced simultaneously in 1942 by Helen Forrest with Harry James and Jo Stafford with Tommy Dorsey. The words are vaguely optimistic, but the song has a downish melody that makes it more torchy than tender. This time, Wilkins's whimsical intro and Vaughan's medium-tempo vocal (as well as solos by Quinichette, Brown, Jones, and Mann) make it more playful and less moody than, say, Peggy Lee's *profundo* interpretation on *The Man I Love*. Vaughan's second full chorus is more upbeat still—she really rings out with the last few lines.

Up next is the album's major slow torch song. "Jim" was credited to the head of the musicians' union, James Caesar Petrillo, and most successfully introduced by Helen O'Connell with Jimmy Dorsey's orchestra in summer 1941 (shortly before Billie Holiday with Teddy Wilson), fully a year before Petrillo would launch the disastrous ban on recording by the American Federation of Musicians. Like the "guy" in "He's My Guy," "Jim" (apparently Petrillo named this song after himself?) is both careless and callous. Jim doesn't bring her pretty flowers; Jim doesn't try to cheer her lonely hours. She takes this tale more seriously and more somberly than "He's My Guy," and at nearly six minutes it's the second-longest track on the album. Vaughan stretches it out with a sense of humor but also longing—this is the track on which Vaughan and Quinichette come closest to sounding like Billie Holiday and Lester Young. Quinichette has the main obbligato behind Vaughan, sounding like a supportive friend, but then Brown enters with a hard-edged tone, as if he's playing the role of the bounder Jim himself. Vaughan reenters with a playful half chorus, in which she says the word "sometime" three times, which has the effect of a traumatized woman trying to put a brave face on a heavy heart. Even though there's a scat intro and coda, the meaning of the words comes through: you can tell that there have been many "Jims" in Vaughan's life, and that these words are coming straight from the heart of a woman who has lived and suffered.

Vaughan is once again postulating on romantic possibilities on "You're Not the Kind"; the music is by arranger Will Hudson, the words are credited to Irving Mills, which indicates only that Mills published it; we essentially have no idea who actually wrote the lyric. (From everything we know about him, it surely was not Mills himself.) Vaughan had recorded the song with Tadd Dameron's orchestra eight years earlier, and it had been introduced by Hudson's own band in 1936. The song was mostly performed by major singing musicians with colorful names: Red Allen, Wingy Manone, Fats Waller (and even female instrumentalist-singers Frances Faye and Valaida Snow). The only canonical diva to sing it was Vaughan—as a result, it's a *primo* choice for anyone looking to do a Sarah tribute project. More important, the lyrics—whoever wrote them—are tailor-made for Vaughan's coquettish attitude: "You're not the kind of a boy for a girl like me," she begins, "I'm just a song and a dance, you're a symphony." More than Fitzgerald or Washington, Vaughan can be simultaneously coy and ironic, and can say one thing while letting you know she means something else entirely. Both of Vaughan's recordings, 1946 and 1954, are outstanding, yet this latter one has greater maturity, not to mention expert solos by Mann and, especially, Clifford Brown.

After three songs disavowing love, we come to one of the all-time-great love songs, the Gershwins' "Embraceable You." But even in a romantic mood, Vaughan is too creative to sing it completely straight, she plays with the relationship of the time and the notes even on the first utterance of the word "embraceable." "Embraceable You" features Vaughan with just the rhythm section; the horns sit this one out. Yet even though it deploys two thirds of the trio that accompanied Vaughan on *Images / Swingin' Easy* seven months earlier, the feeling couldn't be more different: the December standards are much more laid-back and relaxed, and thus more sensual. The Gershwins set the song in an ABAB format, so that more than most it seems to have a first half and a second half, and Vaughan's phrasing, in the second half especially, is so luxuriously romantic it almost sounds sinful, as if she's wearing a silk nightie and erotically teasing some "naughty baby" while both are ensconced in satin sheets. Even when she toys with the tune, it's not just a meaningless exhibition of vocal chops, but a chance to display the coy playfulness of a lover—she seems to be teasing both the tune and the naughty baby himself.

The next two songs, "I'm Glad There Is You" and "September Song," are more about maturity and consistency than youthful capriciousness. "I'm Glad There Is You" is the most successful number attributed to Jimmy Dorsey as a composer, co-credited to pianist and arranger Paul Mertz, an old friend from the Roaring Twenties. This is the most pronounced example of a verse being used on the album. Vaughan delivers it slowly and deliberately—and doesn't arrive at the central refrain until well after a whole minute in. She does an expert job of sustaining the narrative, occasionally altering a note here or a rhythmic placement there, but keeping the story going nonetheless.

"September Song"—one of the few other-than-ridiculous moments in that 1938 political cartoon of a musical, *Knickerbocker Holiday*—is an odd choice for a thirty-year-old jazz singer, but the music (Kurt Weill) and words (Maxwell Anderson) are sublime. Quinichette and Mann are lovely together, weaving around each other in the intro, before Vaughan enters on a more somber note. She sings it more soberly than most of the other songs here, as if to show how well she appreciates the severity of reaching the September of one's years—even while she's still in April. Appropriately, her vocal is unhurried—the very nature of the piece is better suited to a full-length album than to a single.

Vaughan possesses all the richness and grandeur necessary to take full advantage of everything: the extra-special quality of all nine songs, and this one in particular; the outstanding backings laid out for her by Wilkins and the three outstanding soloists playing in support of her; and the technological format that allows her to easily stretch out a song to four, five, or six minutes. All these components seem especially suitable to

a classic song about romantic steadfastness and the inevitable passage of time. Still, even here, the thirty-year-old Sassy allows herself a flourish of her trademark sassiness when she comes back (following a muted solo by Brown) for the out-chorus, starting on the word "and" ("and these few precious days")—she elongates it well beyond what we expect—and then compounds things by adding a Billy Eckstine–inspired original coda and tag at the very end: "Not January, February, June or July . . ." (She would return to "September Song" two years later, this time with a full orchestra and strings, on *Great Songs from Hit Shows*, 1956—an interpretation that's considerably less sassy.)

The album begins and ends with its two strongest rompers, "Lullaby of Birdland" and "It's Crazy." The latter was one of Nat King Cole's key swing hits from the period of his transition from trio to orchestra. This 1952 number is frequently credited to Dorothy Fields and Richard Rodgers; in fact, it's the work of songwriter Al Fields and Timmie Rogers, who was best known as an entertainer and comedian. It's a short, simple rhythmic bauble, with hardly any of the significance of "September Song"—or of "Lullaby of Birdland" for that matter. Vaughan's two short choruses are pure joy, and frame solos by the whole company, starting with Brown (a beautiful, open-bell statement that fully shows why his death at twenty-five was such a loss), then Jones, Mann, and Quinichette, that are more like a curtain call. "It's Crazy," which was also the last tune to be recorded on the last date, ends with Vaughan conclusively climaxing the album. "Crazy, crazy, crazy," she rips out, sounding as if she's hammering a door shut, and the three horns get together on a crazy-sounding boppish note.

Sarah Vaughan, the album, is very well named; it's her first album on which she sounds completely like the mature Sarah Vaughan: relaxed yet urgent, with a deep, luxurious voice. It's the forerunner of everything she would go on to do in the future, jazz, pop, or even *Sarah Slightly Classical*. Because she would make so many excellent albums over the next thirty-five years, *Sarah Vaughan* (or *Sarah Vaughan with Clifford Brown*) is rarely singled out as a classic, but make no mistake, the mature, "complete" period of the great diva begins here. The album mainly gets attention due to the presence of Clifford Brown. (Coincidentally, four years earlier Vaughan had done two sessions on which the twenty-four-year-old Miles Davis served as a sideman. It was with Vaughan that both these iconic trumpeters, Brown and Davis, did their finest work with a vocalist.)

Great as her future albums were, *Sarah Vaughan* remains a singular achievement. Its ten tracks flow very easily, and the Diva is always inspired by—and never overwhelmed by—the formidable soloists in her accompaniment. It's telling that Vaughan was such a great artist that a masterpiece like this one barely even stands out.

47
Sarah Vaughan
"Live" in Japan
(1973)

Only in the 1960s and '70s did the likes of Sarah Vaughan, Ella Fitzgerald, Anita O'Day, Carmen McRae, and Mel Tormé become labeled "jazz singers." It wasn't their music that had changed; it was that the public perception of such artists was gradually shifting. In the 1940s and '50s, when they first emerged, they were simply "singers"—no one called Sarah Vaughan a jazz singer when she first sang with Earl Hines's orchestra: she was a performer who was competing for attention with Ella Fitzgerald and Billie Holiday on one level and with Patti Page and Jo Stafford on another.

But by the 1960s, when the phrase "pop singer" became attached to Neil Diamond or Dusty Springfield, it was clear that some other expression had to be applied to Sarah and Ella. "Jazz singer," at least, was a convenient enough phrase to apply, and there was little ambiguity as to what it meant. Singers like Tony Bennett and Rosemary Clooney had a harder time of it, category-wise: eventually, NARAS (the Grammy people) got around to labeling them "traditional pop singers," but at best this was an awkward and ungainly label.

Traditional pop and jazz singers alike were finding themselves increasingly marginalized, yet what seems ironic forty years later is that the audience for singers like Sarah Vaughan was still *huge* in 1973—it's just that the market for the Jackson Five was *huge-er.* Along with everyone else who was

likely to sing "The Nearness of You," be they jazz or pop, she was being pushed out of the mainstream and into the niche markets—yet those niches were, at the time, absolutely tremendous. It was a time when Vaughan and Fitzgerald could pack concert halls all over the world and Sinatra could easily do an entire week at Madison Square Garden. Fortunately, some of the more important standards singers found their way onto boutique labels, and, again, the jazz singers had the advantage, like Fitzgerald on Pablo, Tormé on Concord, and Vaughan on Mainstream.

Mainstream Records was founded in 1964 by Bob Shad, a veteran producer who, a decade earlier, had worked with Vaughan (and Dinah Washington and many others) on Mercury and EmArcy; among other things, Shad had produced her classic 1954 album *Sarah Vaughan* (with Clifford Brown). Vaughan signed with Mainstream in 1971, by which time it was fairly impossible, or so it seems in retrospect, for any label to release any kind of an album involving the great standard songs. Vaughan's overall output for Mainstream might best be described as admirably schizophrenic. Although she was importuned to cover a lot of cheesy contemporary songs, at least half her output for the label (or roughly every other album) is worth listening to. Given the circumstances, this was a commendable trade-off.

In the middle of all this, Shad recorded at least one of Vaughan's live concerts, a show in Tokyo in

September 1973, featuring her working trio, with pianist Carl Schroeder, bassist John Giannelli, and drummer Jimmy Cobb. (The drummer will always be best known to jazz history for his participation in the seminal Miles Davis album *Kind of Blue*, though I have to confess that I've listened to *"Live" in Japan* many more times.) It turned out to be a masterstroke: it was a truly magical performance, a fact that the producer immediately recognized by issuing the results as a double LP set. After Shad died in 1985, his daughter, Tamara Shad, sold the catalogue to Sony Music, and in 1993, three years after Vaughan's death, Sony reissued *"Live" in Japan* in an expanded, and therefore improved double CD edition that included twenty-seven full tracks and nearly two hours of music altogether.

"Live" in Japan is an amazing snapshot of a great artist in a unique period. Earlier, Vaughan was loosely classified as pop, and later she was regarded as a major concert artist, but in 1973 nobody seems to have had any expectations of her whatsoever, and yet here she was probably the greatest that she had ever been or ever would be.

Sarah Vaughan begins the concert with a "chaser," that is to say, a fast, snappy quick opener that usually utilizes a very well-known standard done very up-tempo—in this case it's the Gershwins' "A Foggy Day." It's a kind of a throwaway, but it serves its purpose in the pacing of the evening. Then, the second tune, "Poor Butterfly," offers the first indication that something special is about to happen. Generally regarded as an American vernacular answer to the opera *Madama Butterfly,* this 1916 song, cowritten by Raymond Hubbell (one of the founders of ASCAP) and introduced in Broadway's *The Big Show,* was a major hit—in *This Side of Paradise,* F. Scott Fitzgerald describes it as "the song of that last year" (meaning the final year before the U.S. entered World War I). Like "Limehouse Blues," another mock-Asian tune from a revue, "Poor Butterfly" found favor with jazzmen as a jam session perennial in the swing era. "Butterfly" became one of Vaughan's signature ballads (Carmen McRae included it in her tribute album, *Sarah—Dedicated to You* after she first included it in her 1956 album *Great Songs from Hit Shows*—and it's the only

number from the Tokyo concert that contains any reference to Japanese culture, even if it's filtered through Italian opera and American pop.

Vaughan always launched "Butterfly" with the verse, sung slowly and deliberately—it's a unique example of her taking a song that had started as a serious ballad, then was jazzed up for several generations, and then was restored to full stateliness by one of the major jazz singers of that or any other time. The number begins with Schroeder tinkling some minor chords in ersatz oriental fashion before Vaughan enters, telling of the Japanese lass named "Butterfly" who was seduced and abandoned by a "fine young American." Although the singer left us many live versions, this is the longest, two whole minutes longer than the 1956 studio track, and the finest—Vaughan seems intent on showing sympathy for what appears to be the whole wide world of unfortunate women.

If "Poor Butterfly" is a show tune with operatic aspirations, "The Lamp Is Low" is just the opposite, a classical melody (Maurice Ravel's 1899 piano piece, *Pavane pour une infante défunte*) transformed into a pop song and, from there, into a jazz standard. Vaughan does it as another two-minute chaser, getting in and out of it very quickly, with John Giannelli's Fender bass being the most prominent instrument behind her. (I'm not certain if the bassist is actually playing electric or if this is some sort of sonic trick originating with the digital remastering of the compact disc edition.)

The next tune is another big ballad, Thelonious Monk's "'Round Midnight"; Vaughan was part of the Harlem jazz scene at the time that Monk composed this classic—although, oddly, she didn't get around to recording it until 1963. She left us any number of live versions, though I wouldn't think anybody identifies the song with her—unlike "Poor Butterfly" or "Misty." As the concert progresses, each of the ballads would seem to be getting bigger and deeper, a progression that's especially notable between "Poor Butterfly," "'Round Midnight," and "Willow Weep for Me," though the latter gets somewhat derailed.

"Willow Weep for Me" seems like kind of a bonus track: Vaughan makes a great show of announcing that she hasn't sung it in a while and doesn't remember the words, and, as she warned us, she doesn't. She improvises a spontaneous lyric—mainly about how she can't remember the actual lyric—and throws in some goofy scat syllables, almost as if she's parodying the idea of a scat solo. "Willow" was clearly a jinx for the Divine One: in 1957, while doing a live recording for Shad and EmArcy at Mister Kelly's in Chicago, she had loused up the song, and in 1957 she even had a lyric sheet in front of her. Unlike when Ella Fitzgerald forgot the lyric to "Mack the Knife" in Berlin 1960, and made magic out of that situation, nothing special happens here. One of Vaughan's oldest friends and staunchest supporters, Leonard Feather, in his notes to the 1993 CD edition of the Japan concert, opined, "My own feeling is that she should have skipped it." It's hard to disagree.

Another chaser follows, "There Will Never Be Another You," with further electric bass runs by Giannelli. "Misty" is a Vaughan classic, ever since she first cut it in 1958 on the album *Vaughan and Violins;* there are many of us who associate the Erroll Garner and Johnny Burke standard with her more than with Johnny Mathis, who had the hit single. This "Misty" is a serviceable rendition, but hardly one of Vaughan's all-time best.

Things get more and more interesting with the next number, "Wave." Like a lot of singers, Vaughan was drawn to Brazilian rhythms in the early and mid-1960s; she was among the first to do a bossa-centric album, the 1964 *¡Viva! Vaughan* (never mind that the word "viva" is Spanish, not Portuguese). "Wave," originally known as "Vou Te Contar" in Portuguese, was composed by Antonio Carlos Jobim and introduced by him in 1967; apparently the composer himself wrote the English lyric, which was first recorded by him and Frank Sinatra in 1969. Like so many of the major Jobim songs, "Wave" was frightfully overperformed for the next twenty years or so: with a dwindling number of good new-ish songs at their disposal, veteran singers tended to all do the same numbers (by Jobim, Cy Coleman, Michel Legrand, and a few others) over and over. It seems as if everyone sang "Wave" at one point: Sinatra, Fitzgerald, Tormé, O'Day. Vaughan's earliest version is this 1973 concert: she sings it slowly and sensually, more like a ballad than a bossa; in fact, there's nary a trace of a Brazilian beat here. More than a rhythmic showcase, the piece is a feature for Vaughan's astonishing vocal range. Jobim's melody is famously an obstacle course for singers, taking them down as low as they can go, and it's suitable fodder for Vaughan's chops. As Gunther Schuller, who played and conducted for Vaughan on several occasions, pointed out, she essentially had four ranges: soprano, alto, tenor, and baritone. "Wave" has her going as far down as she can possibly go, and you can tell she relishes the workout—for Vaughan, the use of technique always carried with it an emotional imperative. She never failed to connect the absolute lowest, highest, longest, fastest notes to a dramatic purpose—it was never merely empty technique or pure showing off; but there was an immense thrill just in the way she would hit the notes.

"Like Someone in Love," which starts a cappella, is in medium tempo, not a pure chaser—Vaughan stretches out the notes, playfully and caressingly—in fact, exactly like someone in love. She interjects a few scat phrases as she lunges into the second chorus, which, in the classic tradition solidified by Ethel Waters, is at once both more playful and more intense than the first—especially when she slows down to a low note and a gospelly melisma at the coda.

The stakes get higher with "My Funny Valentine." By 1973, this was notoriously the most overdone number in the American Songbook—the joke was, "How many singers does it take to sing 'My Funny Valentine'?" and the answer usually came back, "All of 'em!" But Vaughan had only recorded the song once before, back in 1954, and there's no understanding why it would be such a concert tour de force twenty years later. She sings it with just piano—Giannelli and Cobb presumably grab a smoke—and it becomes another six-minute workout for the Vaughan choppers, climaxed by a breathtaking low note at the end. That she invests so much of herself so movingly in a song that was already so widely done is startling—this is one of the all-time greatest of the thousands of documented performances of Rodgers and Hart's valentine. (And soon enough in the same concert, she does the same with the equally overexposed "Over the Rainbow" and "Summertime.")

"All of Me" includes an excellent scat chorus—the real thing, not screwing around this time—and although this is far from a mere chaser, it's clear that the defining moments of this concert are the ballads. Just why "(Where Do I Begin) Love Story" should be such a major moment is also completely inexplicable. The song was from a ridiculously over-the-top, banal romantic disaster of a movie based on an over-the-top, banal romantic disaster of a novel; to view it today is to puzzle over the tastes of cinemagoers in 1970. The theme song, by French composer Francis Lai, was at least better than the movie—which isn't saying much—and had Tony Bennett and Andy Williams competing with it on the same label (Columbia). For Vaughan—who sang it on this sole occasion—it's hardly a throwaway, but one of the most moving things she ever sang; it's one of many examples in this show of Vaughan readying herself for her late-career concert blockbuster "Send in the Clowns." Just as Vaughan sings, "He fills my heart with very special things / With angels songs, with wild imaginings / He fills my soul with so much love," she seems to want to fill every note with as much meaning as possible—even the rests and the spaces between notes resonate with deep feeling.

"I would like to sing a tune that I recorded when I was about two years old, and that makes me now about twenty-nine," Vaughan announces at the start of another classic song that no one would associate with her. For the record, she first committed "Over the Rainbow" to vinyl in 1955—at age thirty-one. As with "Valentine," she takes "Rainbow" with just Schroeder's piano, in such a way that's so intensely personal—and taking lots of liberties with the notes and intervals—that you forget anyone ever sang the song before her. Her treatment of the bridge in the second chorus is particularly amazing, with a remarkable trajectory of low to high notes. When we get to the ending, she repeats, "Why, why, oh why, can't I," over and over, and over, but she's not just milking the applause, she's asking a legitimate question—she really wants to know, why can't she? She truly seems to be pondering aloud why her personal life was so

much less rewarding than her career, why her marriages all ended in divorce, why she was ultimately alone. "Over the Rainbow," as sung by Judy Garland and virtually everyone else, is ultimately an optimistic song, a tale of hope, but Vaughan makes it into something much darker, something more like a torch song. Why oh why?

Before the last note ends, Giannelli and Cobb start in with the funky vamp intro to "I Could Write a Book"—as if they're trying to lift Sarah out of heading into a depression. Although it's only two and a half minutes, Vaughan is more relaxed with this than with the previous chasers. She really seems to be enjoying swinging this Rodgers and Hart love song; it's more open and expansive than what came before—although by now the electrified buzzing of Giannelli's Fender bass is starting to become annoying.

"Book" ends with Vaughan repeating a brief scat phrase over Giannelli's vamp. There's a brief bit of instrumental bow music, as if we've reached the intermission: in the 1993 two-CD edition, the second disc starts here. There should have been an additional edit—it's fully ninety seconds before the next song, "The Nearness of You," starts, which must have frustrated many a deejay. After the bow music, we hear Vaughan responding to a request to play the piano herself. At first she seems hesitant and even apologetic, but then she turns it around and seems eager to play: "Who knows, I might become the world's greatest piano player!" Looking at Schroeder, she then giggles, "You're fired!"

"Nearness of You" may well have been Vaughan's most significant signature song of all; surprisingly, she had only sung it on records once before, in 1949 for Columbia, and again shortly after for the Snader Telescriptions company (canned performances filmed for showing on early television). She introduces the song with a crystalline touch—there can be no doubt that she knew how to play the piano. (Famously, she had served as deputy pianist for Earl Hines's orchestra thirty years earlier.) The verse includes the line "when you and your magic pass by," and to hear Vaughan sing over her own piano playing, we do indeed feel we're in the presence of magic. Likewise, Ned Washington's wonderful lyric also tells us that her heart is "in a dither" when her "dear" one is far away, but when he's near, "Oh, my." No one's ever sung Washington's text better: the words "oh my" imply a feeling that goes beyond all words, and the way she swoops down on those two notes of Hoagy Carmichael's sumptuous melody emphasizes the point spectacularly. Likewise, the refrain lyric is almost an anti-list: here are the things I don't need to love you—not the "pale moon," nor "your sweet conversation," and not the "soft lights" either. Appropriately, for a "not" song, Vaughan is, by Vaughan standards, restrained: in five and a half minutes she does the verse and one chorus, and builds to a beautiful high-note climax—holding back nothing. Maybe this was Vaughan's greatest strength: there were other singers who sang words better than she ever cared to, but no one could compete with her at conveying that sense of the epic and the eternal that lay beyond the reach of any kind of verbal vocabulary. "Nearness" is easily the high point of the concert, all the more special because she only plays piano for this one number (in fact, this one five-and-a-half-minute "Nearness of You" is Vaughan's single greatest moment as an instrumentalist and is a contender for her greatest moment ever as a vocalist as well).

"I'll Remember April" starts with Schroeder suggesting a Scottish drone on his piano, but when Vaughan flies into the melody, there's a vaguely Latin element going on. It's got the chaser mentality, but Vaughan is clearly having fun with it—she certainly relishes the Basie-esque coda, with all the repeats and the trademarked three-note tag. She's still having fun with "Watch What Happens," a medium-slow romper—far from a ballad—particularly when she stretches out on "maybe just afraaaiiiddd . . ." the second time around. The song is one of Michel Legrand's early classics, before he started working with Alan and Marilyn Bergman, and while Vaughan sang it many times in concert, she never sang it in a studio, and this is certainly her best reading of it. "I Cried for You" is solidly in chaser mode: usually the term "chaser" refers to a brief number at the end of a set, often an encore (following bow music), to indicate to the audience that the show was over, but here Vaughan and her trio are chasing after each other: first Schroeder

plays some percussive notes on the piano, Cobb answers him, then Vaughan jumps in and chases the lot of them—or is it the other way around? In any case, it doesn't sound like anybody's crying for anybody.

"Summertime" brings us back to the realm of the angels—again she concentrates her energy in the slow ballads. A lot of singers made a specialty of the Porgy and Bess opener: it was also one of Fitzgerald's very best ballads, and Vaughan had featured it regularly since 1949. Where "Wave" had shown off her low notes, "Summertime" is sung mostly in her upper-soprano register. As composed by George Gershwin and DuBose Heyward, "Summertime" is already a show tune, a folk song, and a lullaby; in Vaughan's performance it becomes all that and more: she sings it like a combination of Schubert's "Ave Maria," "Addio del passato" from La traviata, and Mahalia Jackson doing "Take My Hand, Precious Lord."

She follows "Summertime" with a fast, nameless, and somewhat generic blues, over which she introduces the trio. Just when we think she's satisfied to let this be an instrumental feature, after the solo by Schroeder she enters with a series of scat choruses of her own. Giannelli and Cobb both solo, and at last the bass sounds somewhat more like an acoustic instrument here. She returns to scat out the coda, and at seven and a half minutes it's hardly a waste of time.

In 1962, Vaughan recorded Snowbound, a lovely, underappreciated album of romantic ballads with string section arranged by Don Costa. The most successful track was "I Remember You," which she continued to sing for decades to come, using a vestige of the Costa arrangement, though (as here) with only a trio, but starting with Johnny Mercer and Victor Schertzinger's verse. This live version is even deeper than the 1962 album's: a decade older, Vaughan sounds like she's mentally replaying the cherished moments of relationships long past. When she stretches words and plays with them, it's as if she's going over the scenes in her head, and the final note loops around from high to low and back up again in a way that defies the limits of memory.

"There Is No Greater Love" is one of many ballads by the Chicago-based bandleader Isham Jones that became a jazz standard, and it's a unique item in the Sarah Vaughan canon. Amazingly, she never quite gets around to the lyric. It begins with Cobb's intro and then a voice-and-drums duo, with Vaughan not exactly scatting but singing the melody wordlessly; when the bass enters and the thing kicks into a firmly set swinging tempo, it's almost anticlimactic. Still, she continues on her nonverbal path, quickly departing from the melody in a true improvised scat solo. One keeps waiting for the lyrics (by Marty Syme), but when they never show up, somehow they're not missed.

Paul Williams's "Rainy Days and Mondays" is, like "Love Story," a pop song of the day (a number two hit for the Carpenters) transformed into one of the minor miracles of the Divine One. She had done the song in a Peter Matz arrangement on the 1972 *Feelin' Good* album, but Japan is the real deal. When Vaughan is given a good song, whether it's classic or contemporary, and allowed to do with it what she wishes, the results are indeed worthy of the ages. In fact, a lot of the material on *A Time in My Life, Feelin' Good,* and even the dreadful *Send in the Clowns* album could have been potentially classic Sarah, if only the label had let her interpret the songs in her own way with her own trio. "Rainy Days and Mondays" is completely moving, from start to finish. As with her colleague Ella Fitzgerald, it's been alleged that Vaughan didn't pay attention to the words or know how to interpret a lyric: this track is one of many that prove otherwise. The way she repeats "funny, funny," going up and down the scale on increasingly high notes, is amazingly engaging—and not only funny, but "funny, funny."

Surely the way that she follows "Rainy Days" with "On a Clear Day" shows that she's paying close attention to titles and lyrics. It's just a quickie, up and exuberant, and a "clear" and deliberate follow-up to the rainy day song. (In the album notes, Leonard Feather makes the curious comment that the tune was "used from time immemorial by singers who have opened their sets with it." The song was written for the Broadway musical of the same name in 1965, so it was barely eight years old in 1973.) Vaughan says everything she wants to say with it in two choruses coming in at under two minutes.

There follows a delightful artifact: as we near the end of the evening, Vaughan is up for suggestions as to what to sing next—"Mercy! What do you want to hear?" We can't quite make out what the crowd is yelling, but Vaughan repeats the requests that come in: "Thanks for the Memory," "Lonely Serenade," "Lullaby of Birdland," "Alone Again, Naturally," "Body and Soul." Then somebody cries out "Bye Bye Blackbird" and she likes the idea—"Let's do that." She tells the crowd, "This is being recorded. We're making a record, and it'll be out . . ." She then apparently turns to Bobby Shad, watching in the wings, and asks him, "How long, Bobby?" The answer comes back, "Very shortly." She laughs, and after pointing out that she's never recorded it, she says, "But we'll do it." She picks a key with Schroeder and they get into it; after Schroeder puts down a few notes, she pushes him to take it faster, and as she starts singing, the crowd begins clapping on the first and the third beat in the measure. The second chorus is even looser and more swinging, and the third (at 2:40 or so) even more so, and for the fourth she's just chanting the words "bye bye, blackbird" over and over. She gradually abandons both the words and the melody, and in her last few choruses (surrounding a piano solo) has come up with a completely new tune all her own. She attempts to stop several times, but the crowd apparently keeps egging her on to continue, and she starts spontaneously making up silly lyrics: "Pretty pretty blackbird, see you later, blackbird, see you next time blackbird, glad to be in Tokyo so I can sing 'blackbird' for you."

The applause fades up and down, suggesting that there's been an edit. She comes back with "Tonight" from *West Side Story,* which she does quickly and easily, not at all like the anthemic treatment that the Bernstein-Sondheim classic usually receives. But then, she lets us go with one last ballad, the semi-slow—and not at all churchy— "Tenderly." It's a somewhat rhythmic waltz, and Vaughan gets the lyrics out beautifully. It's hardly reverential, or even sentimental, but it's as tender as it needs to be just the same. It ends with Vaughan thanking the audience and introducing the trio a last time. "So until the next time, until the next time, we want to say so long and God bless all of you all. Bye bye." The trio continues to play "Tenderly" as Vaughan exits.

"Live" in Japan is an amazing concert from a unique and fascinating period in the great diva's development, a wonderful document in which she turns familiar standards into quick and swinging throwaways but makes jazz masterpieces out of "Love Story" and "Rainy Days and Mondays." It's in those two songs, as in "Rainbow," "Summertime," "Funny Valentine," and "Wave," that Vaughan exemplifies what one friend, the artist and illustrator Robert Richards, said about her: "I think that she only really was a complete person when she was singing. She also told me on a few occasions that when she was onstage, nothing existed but beauty, there was no pain, there was no worry, there was no sorrow, there was just the joy of music, and that's what she was about."

There were relatively few live recordings from the final two decades in her almost fifty-year career: a mysterious, short live session from Los Angeles with Jimmy Rowles in 1974, and *Gershwin Live!* with the L.A. Philharmonic from 1982 were the only ones released in her lifetime. Luckily, others have come out over the last twenty years, including several shows from the 1970s (on the download service Wolfgang's Vault) and *In the City of Lights*, a Parisian set from 1985. One can only hope that more will find their way to our ears.

The Tokyo concert also had a fascinating echo in an inspiring two-person play-cabaret item titled *"The Devine* [sic] *One": Sassy Swings Tokyo*, written by playwright Laurence Maslon, starring the gifted young singer-actress Marinda Anderson as Vaughan. The dramatic premise is Vaughan giving an interview to a Japanese journalist before going on to do the famous concert. Repeatedly through the dialogue, she claims to be at a loss for words, even as the real Vaughan usually was during interviews, and whenever she can't quite articulate what she wants to express, she apologizes by saying, "I don't know, I just sing, that's all." Finally, at the end of the playlet, the interviewer tells her, "You don't have to say that you 'just sing.' You sing. And that's enough."

48

Dinah Washington

Dinah Washington Sings Fats Waller

(1957)

inah Washington (1924–1963) was one of the major singers in the American idiom—with her searingly intense sound, she sang blues, jazz, standards, and a great deal more—but although she worked well into the album era, she never moved into the album category: virtually all of her significant recordings were singles rather than LPs. It was more of a genre thing than a generational thing: Sarah Vaughan was born the same year as Washington, and she made album after great album. But few if any of the first generation of rhythm and blues artists even seemed interested in making the transition—not Louis Jordan or Charles Brown, for instance. Likewise the early rock 'n' rollers, like Fats Domino, Little Richard, and even Elvis, were essentially singles specialists.

The first major figure in R&B to establish himself in the long-play format was Ray Charles, who led the charge with a fruitful series of thematic concept albums that culminated in the 1962 blockbuster *Modern Sounds in Country and Western Music*. There were all kinds of great soul albums after Ray Charles, but very few before; in fact, the two most important figures in the pre-Ray world of R&B were Louis Jordan and Dinah Washington, and they were more often the inspiration for other concept albums (B.B. King saluting Louis Jordan, Aretha Franklin singing the Dinah Washington songbook) than they themselves ever made.

Washington only made one original album that qualifies as an undisputed classic, *Dinah Washington Sings Fats Waller* (1957). The follow-up, *Dinah Sings Bessie Smith* (1958), was, if not a disaster, certainly a disappointment. A case might be made for the 1963 *Back to the Blues,* but it has little of the polish, the cachet, and the reputation of Washington's tribute to Waller. Washington and Waller were highly kindred spirits, both of whom died at the ridiculously young age of thirty-nine—party animals who more or less expired due to their own foolishness. (Smith also died young, at forty-three, but from circumstances outside of her control—though it was also difficult to keep Bessie away from a party, or to get her to do anything in moderation.)

The idea for the Washington-Waller songbook album was probably that of Mercury Records' Bobby Shad, who was keen to have Washington expand into the "mainstream" jazz categories and follow, to a degree, the career path of Vaughan and Ella Fitzgerald. Yet although she was foremostly a singles artist, hers was a catalogue of remarkable diversity. It's hard to find something she couldn't or didn't sing: from the simplest blues in C to Café Society stuff like Noël Coward's "Mad About the Boy." She sang blues and novelties written for her, but she also covered hits by other artists in all genres—R&B, mainstream pop, movie and show tunes, even country and western songs.

Most recording artists of the 1950s followed a rather different business model. The singers who worked with Mitch Miller, like Rosemary Clooney and Frankie Laine, might do ten dog songs in a row and then land one blockbuster hit that paid for everything and a lot more. Washington, on the other hand, had few blockbusters, not until "What a Diff'rence a Day Makes" comparatively late in her career, but virtually no dog songs or novelties. As a result, her overall discography is highly listenable; it's what Tony Bennett would describe as a "hit catalogue." When, roughly twenty-five years after her death, Polygram Records began issuing the complete Washington output in a huge series of LPs and then CDs, it was amazing how consistently excellent the bulk of her music actually was. Most of the material in that enormous series of discs, in fact, sounds even better now than it did when it was new.

Thus, to summarize: Washington had few big hit singles and virtually no notable albums, but she did have one great individual track after another, and a cumulative catalogue of enormous value to Mercury Records. In twenty-first-century jargon, this would be called a "long-tail" approach to selling product. (Something tells me that Dinah would have responded to that term by singing a blues in C titled "He's My Long-Tail Papa.")

Washington was doing so well, selling so many records primarily to the African American market (whose tastes far exceeded the borders of R&B or "race" music), that there seems to have been little motivation for her to more fully explore the album concept. One experiment that Shad tried was the 1954 album *Dinah Jams*, which was an interesting attempt to foist a Jazz at the Philharmonic–type format upon her. Each track had one or two choruses of vocals by Washington, followed by roughly ten minutes of horn solos; even Ella Fitzgerald, who toured with JATP, never recorded in a format that so completely emphasized the instrumental players at the expense of the vocalist. (Indeed, it's hard to think of another vocal album where the singer is so marginalized.)

By 1957, the songbook format was proving itself a bonanza: Fitzgerald had defined the concept with her 1950 George Gershwin album and then demonstrated its massive commercial viability with her *Cole Porter Songbook* of 1956, and within a year Sarah Vaughan, Chris Connor, and Carmen McRae, among many others, were all doing songbook albums. Louis Armstrong had also done two songbook projects, *Louis Armstrong Plays W. C. Handy* in 1954 and *Satch Plays Fats* in 1955.

Orchestrator and saxophonist Ernie Wilkins had played on Washington's recording dates occasionally since 1949; by 1957, he had already helped both Joe Williams (and with him, Count Basie) and Sarah Vaughan do some of the best work of their careers. Bob Shad was clearly in his corner, and Wilkins was a perfect choice for the Washington-Waller mash-up, even down to the minuscule point that his name made the album a three-"W" project.

The initial sessions for the Washington-Waller-Wilkins album occurred in New York on Tuesday, October 1, 1957, followed by Wednesday the 2nd and Friday the 4th, and seven weeks later a final date on November 20. "There seemed to be easy camaraderie as Dinah and the band went over the arrangements," as Washington's biographer, Nadine Cohodas, reported. "Though everyone was casual, the men all in open-necked sport shirts and pants, Dinah was dressed up. On the first day, she wore a gray tweed dress with a matching cape and accented it with a darker gray turban on her head." Starting with Wilkins himself, the studio orchestra was somewhat Basie-centric—at least half the men playing were past or current Basie-ites, most notably guitarist Freddie Green, the rock of the Basie rhythm section for virtually all of its existence. Even the central pianist, Patti Bown, fell into that category: she never worked with the Count himself—he had no need of a pianist—but she later deputized for Basie in Quincy Jones's big band.

Washington, however, brought along her own accompanist, one Jack Wilson, whom she had found in Atlantic City less than a month earlier (it's not known if this is the same Jack Wilson who became a prominent keyboardist on the West Coast in the 1960s). This was his first recording session, and as Wilson told Cohodas, "When I walked in the record date, I was so knocked off my feet by all these cats ... a lot of them were my heroes." Wilson specifically recalled that the ranks were divided between those who smoked pot and those who didn't; those who did lit up in the men's room, and those who didn't hesitated to use the same john for fear of getting a secondhand buzz.

Said Wilson, "We were worried about reading that music," explaining that Wilkins's charts were swinging but not simple. The first drummer who had been called in, in fact, couldn't cut it. When it became obvious that he wasn't up to the job, the band took another break, while another drummer was located—the exceptional Charli Persip, eventually famous for his work with Dizzy Gillespie. Perhaps the delay in switching drummers explains why the first session yielded a mere two usable masters, about half what it should have. But then, curiously, the second and third sessions also produced only two issued songs each. "The musical standards were just the highest," trombonist Julian Priester told Cohodas; "Dinah was impeccable."

A possible source of delay was Eddie Chamblee, a B-level R&B tenor saxophonist who had recently become the fifth Mr. Washington. He's a competent player, but hardly up to the level of the other saxophonists on the date: Jerome Richardson (flute, alto), Sahib Shihab (alto), Frank Wess (tenor, flute), Benny Golson (tenor), and Charles Davis (baritone). Obviously, the reasons she married him and then wove him into the fabric of her career were not entirely artistic. For two tracks on this album, Chamblee sings in harmony with his wife, and these rather modest duets are the lesser songs on the album. It's not that he's bad, it's just that his presence is entirely unnecessary. Unlike Brook Benton in his own celebrated duets with Washington, Chamblee doesn't add anything.

The first tune on the first day, "Honeysuckle Rose," is a case in point, and reminds us of Hank Williams's duets with his unmusical wife. He sings the bridge solo in a Nat King Cole–like voice, and when Washington returns after the first chorus to sing the bridge again ("Don't buy sugar . . ."), he eggs her on ("No, baby!"). Still, when Washington sings solo, one can at least hear how great the Wilkins orchestration actually is.

Washington and Wilkins had actually begun the project with the two most important songs. "Honeysuckle Rose" and "Ain't Misbehavin'" were easily

the two biggest copyrights in the Waller catalogue. Both were from 1929, with lyrics by Waller's most important collaborator, Andy Razaf, and both were written for revues produced by Harlem showman Connie Immerman. "Honeysuckle" had its roots in an earlier song written by Razaf; about 1924, the lyricist was writing material for the Club Alabam, which featured a chorus line billed as the "Honeysuckle Rosebuds." He wrote a song for the occasion titled "Honeysuckle Rose," but it was never published or recorded or even remembered by anybody except Razaf. Five years later, as Barry Singer noted in his excellent biography of the lyricist, when he and Waller needed a new song for Connie's Inn, he decided to reuse this old title.

"Ain't Misbehavin'" is absolutely essential to the overall oeuvres of both Waller and Washington. The songwriter positively reveled in his image as an irrepressible bad boy. In one of his few recorded interviews, a Q&A session from 1941, we hear Eddie "Rochester" Anderson (introduced by no less than Edward R. Murrow) somewhat uncomfortably reading off a list of questions that he obviously didn't write. When the semi-scripted conversation turns to Wallers's theme song, the pianist states with obvious joy, "Our theme song being 'Ain't Misbehavin'—that was written while I was lodging, or rather incarcerated, in the alimony jail." When Rochester sighs in response, Waller adds, "And I wasn't misbehavin', see? You dig? You catch on? Well, all right then!" The message was obvious: Waller spent so much time partying and whooping it up that it took a prison spell to keep him out of circulation, and the idea of him actually behaving himself, even under these extreme circumstances, was so novel that he felt compelled to write a song about it. In reverse psychology, the song actually calls attention to his lifestyle of continually misbehaving; for him to be behaving himself, even for just this once, is clearly a monumental occasion, and therefore worth singing about.

The song was also significant for Washington; it was one of the few that she recorded more than once in her short career, the first time as a single for Mercury ten years earlier. The 1947 version is much more mellow: Washington employs her signature dynamics while backed by a clone of the King Cole

Trio, with piano, bass, and guitar. She certainly sounds restrained, as if she were holding back and trying not to misbehave, although there's a smoky after-hours feeling to it as well, as if she were at the end of a long and eventful evening and the misbehavior is already over with.

The 1957 Wilkins arrangement is completely different. She starts the first eight bars with just Frank Wess's flute behind her before the horns enter in their Basie-like glory. Compared to the earlier trio chart, Wilkins's treatment is brassy but highly subtle at the same time. In 1947, it sounded as if the band were trying to restrain her, like the gentle drummer-less trio was tactfully warning her about the dangers of misbehaving. In the 1957 version, the band is louder and more dynamic, and Washington seems to be the one telling everyone else not to misbehave.

Both "I've Got a Feeling I'm Falling" and "Keepin' Out of Mischief Now" deal with the same subject matter. Both stress the crucial facts that staying home, behaving oneself, and generally avoiding trouble are crucial components of romantic commitment. In the first (lyrics credited to Harry Link and Billy Rose, who probably came up with the title), an individual who was formerly flying high is now doing just the opposite. The track begins with a tenor solo (presumably by Chamblee) before Washington enters; Chamblee's playing is, at least, better than his singing. She starts a minute or so in, and only sings one chorus—but it's totally perfect, capturing every nuance of Waller's flying and falling protagonist. "Mischief" starts with the verse, accompanied by piano only; Dinah gets very breathy on the last part of said verse, and when she sings "don't even go to a movie now" she seems to predict the entire career of Nancy Wilson with just a single note. And yet even though there's a promise to toe the line and reform herself, there's also a threat implied, as if she's saying, "Don't even try to get me into any mischief, jerk!"

The three first dates, as mentioned, produced only two releaseable tunes each, and both the first two days ended with an unsuccessful attempt at Waller's "Everybody Loves My Baby (But My Baby Don't Love Nobody but Me)." Finally, on the third date, they started with "Everybody Loves My Baby"

and at last got a usable take. The song originated with two Waller colleagues, both named Williams (though not related): Spencer, who wrote it, and Clarence, who published it. The song didn't need Waller to make it a jazz classic—it was introduced by the brilliant Alberta Hunter on a session produced by Clarence Williams with Louis Armstrong on cornet; by the time Waller recorded it in 1940, he was jamming on an old favorite. Yet Waller, with his blissful piano solo and exuberant vocal, immediately claimed the song as his own, to the point where it fully belonged on a Waller songbook album. Alas, Washington, who has again saddled herself with Chamblee as her duet partner, deprived herself of a proper shot at wresting the song away from Waller.

The mood changes sharply with "(What Did I Do to Be So) Black and Blue." The piece is sometimes described as the first Broadway protest song; it was introduced by Edith Wilson in the Connie Immerman revue *Hot Chocolates,* and, like Irving Berlin's "Suppertime" a few years later, which is often cited as the second Broadway protest song, was also recorded definitively by Ethel Waters. It sounds more like a semi-blues out of the Waters-Washington continuum, the singer bemoaning that men won't pay attention to her. This is as close as the defiant Washington could come to self-pity. Razaf's text has been softened somewhat to make it less racially charged: instead of "I'm white inside" (in the first line of the bridge), Washington sings "I'm sad inside"; a few lines later, instead of "'Cause I can't hide what is on my face" she sings "'Cause I can't hide all the sorrow in my face." She also omits the line "My only sin is in my skin." (Five years later, Lou Rawls not only reinstated all those potentially controversial lines in a decidedly post-Washington rendition, he even titled his album *Black and Blue.*) Despite the lyric changes, Washington's angst is palpable. "Black and Blue" (which Waller himself never recorded) is one of the masterpieces of the album and of Washington's career.

When more or less the same band gathered again in New York to do the remaining six tunes, they began with "Christopher Columbus," which is a jolly bit of swinger's merrymaking at the expense of the celebrated explorer; early recordings of the number are subtitled "A Rhythm Cocktail." The melody would be the most famous to be written by saxophonist Leon "Chu" Berry, at that time the tenor sax soloist in Fletcher Henderson's orchestra. Curiously, the tune was widely heard, recorded, and broadcast before Henderson got to it—it had even been waxed by Benny Goodman in an arrangement by Henderson and his brother Horace a full week before Henderson himself recorded it. Then it became Henderson's property for a while; he used it as his theme song (it's heard as a program opener on one of the few surviving broadcasts by the Henderson band). It was so widely popular that supposedly a bandit who was about to rob the bandleader decided to spare him when he realized his intended victim was "the guy what plays 'Christopher Columbus.'" Over the very long haul, the song became an all-American cultural institution when arranger Jimmy Mundy worked it into an all-time mega-masterpiece of the swing era, Benny Goodman's "Sing, Sing, Sing," and though all previous recordings were in major, including Goodman's own, when Berry's melody became the second strain of the Goodman-Mundy arrangement, it was now heard in an unmistakable minor key.

Waller recorded the Berry-Razaf tune about two weeks after Henderson, in April 1936. His was by the far the best of the vocal versions. He starts with the melody in octaves, as the opener of a killer stride piano introduction, and then proceeds to romp through the lyrics in a way that must have delighted Andy Razaf. The song was silly enough already, but Waller injects more drollery into it than even Razaf might have anticipated. Fats is in especially fine form on the bridge, which like a lot of swing era songs composed by jazz musicians is based on the bridge of "I Got Rhythm." The lyrics here are:

Since the world is round
We'll be safe and sound
Until our goal is found
We'll just keep rhythm bound.

Waller, however, adds an "o" at the end of every line, and it makes the difference between mere

silliness and comic genius. Said bridge is, overall, rather minimal, which leaves Fats with a lot of room to mess around in. He comes up with one of his best asides. After the line "Since the crew was makin' merry—" he interrupts his own vocal to interject a spoken aside: "and Mary got up and went home!"

Washington can't compete with Waller in the playing field of pure antic silliness—as when Fats goes into a falsetto voice allegedly mimicking Signor Colombo himself—but she has a high comic style of her own. On the second time around (following a particularly guttural Chamblee tenor solo), when she gets to Waller's then iconic aside, she delivers her own commentary on it: "Soon the crew was makin' merry—and Mary got mad!"

Otherwise, to her credit, Washington doesn't seem to care how silly Razaf's text is, it's all about how she can deliver the words and music to a ferocious swinging dance beat. No one swung harder than Washington, not even Fitzgerald or Anita O'Day, and she takes this lyrical trifle and turns into a veritable demonstration of how the human voice can swing. Singing all around the countermelodies, Washington is on the beat in a way that makes it hard to imagine that all the horn players didn't just stand up and start dancing around the studio. Without sacrificing any of Waller's antics, she restores Chu Berry's "rhythmic cocktail" into a swing masterpiece.

The November 20 date then continued with two non-Waller compositions, "'Tain't Nobody's Business if I Do" and "Someone's Rocking My Dreamboat." The first song, sometimes spelled "'Tain't Nobody's Biz-Ness if I Do," is another product of the Clarence Williams publishing empire, co-credited to Porter Grainger, who served as Bessie Smith's pianist for a while (and later wrote the classic blues song "Nobody Knows You When You're Down and Out"), Williams himself, and one Robert Prince.

Although "refined" into its familiar eight-bar form (rough as it is, thematically) by Williams and company, "'Tain't Nobody's Business if I Do" has its origins in an old folk tune that actually predates the blues. According to Yuval Taylor in his book *Faking It*, there were many variations on the

"Nobody's Business" idea in early African American music; apart from the Williams-Grainger-Price song, popularized by Bessie Smith and Fats Waller, there's a parallel song associated with the early folk-blues singer and guitarist Mississippi John Hurt (who, Taylor tells us, didn't consider himself a blues singer and never billed himself as "Mississippi"). Hurt's version was faster and bouncier—Smith's is slow and languorous—and was titled "Nobody's Dirty Business." Nearly every artist who turned to the tune after the 1920s used the Bessie Smith–Clarence Williams model, except, notably, Ella Fitzgerald and Louis Jordan, who duetted on a version inspired by John Hurt's recording.

Waller had a long history with the song in its Williams-Smith incarnation: in 1922, at the age of eighteen, he played on one of its very first recordings, accompanying classic blues singer Sara Martin on a Williams-produced session. He also recorded a piano roll of "Business" in 1923, and, finally, in 1940, made the famous recording with His Rhythm, which is the one that doubtlessly served as a model for Washington and Wilkins.

Waller's 1940 treatment is joyous and strident, but Washington takes her cue from the slow, sensual readings of Bessie and Billie Holiday (who recorded it as part of an unfinished Bessie tribute project of her own). Her track opens stealthily with flutes (Wess and Jerome Richardson) before Washington sings it very earthily and erotically, with a prominent tenor obbligato by Chamblee; there may have been better saxophonists in the band, but none of them were better equipped to help Mrs. Chamblee get into such a sexy mood. Ever foisting him on her fans, she even refers to him directly: where the original line is "If my man and I fuss and fight," she inserts his name, "If Eddie and I fuss and fight." Wilkins brings on the high brass for fills between her lines, and even though at 3:29 it's probably the longest track on the album, she makes it seem short and sweet.

At a mere 2:03, "Someone's Rocking My Dreamboat" is way too short; one wishes it were at least twice as long. Why she recorded it at all is a mystery. Not only did Waller not write it, he never recorded it, and is not known ever to have sung it. (However, according to Laurie Wright in his thorough bio-

discography, *"Fats" in Fact,* it was sung in a concert by Waller's band in Winnipeg in 1942, though by one of the female entertainers in the company, not Waller himself.) It's by the René brothers, Leon and Otis, who were, in a sense, West Coast equivalents of Clarence Williams as songwriters, publishers, and record entrepreneurs. Apart from its inclusion on Washington's album, the song is more closely associated with Bugs Bunny (who sang it in numerous cartoon shorts) than Waller, but it's an excellent song and Washington sings it brilliantly, so it would seem churlish to complain.

"Someone's Rocking My Dreamboat" is a very lovely gift horse that one doesn't wish to look too closely in the mouth, but the next tune they tackled on that date is a disaster—lyrically speaking. Waller wrote so many excellent songs, more than could fit on a dozen albums, one wonders why the producers felt compelled to have Washington sing his instrumental "Jitterbug Waltz." Waller had written it at least as far back as 1939, and mentioned it in an article published under his own byline that year. "I wrote a little tune in Chicago once . . . my idea was to convey the picture of a jitterbug waltzing; thereby indicating a change in his techniques as of today compared with the past." He recorded it in summer 1942, eighteen months before his death, making it one of his last great melodies. During the swing era, waltzes were exceedingly rare in jazz, and the idea of writing a jazz tune in 3/4 was in itself a novelty. "Jitterbug Waltz" became more widely heard in the 1960s, when jazz waltzes came into vogue.

In Washington's recording, the two individuals who adapted Waller's instrumental into a song were Charlie Grean, a studio arranger whose chief jazz cred came from having orchestrated the string section for Nat King Cole's hit record of "The Christmas Song," and lyricist Maxine Manners, whose chief claim to fame was, well, nothing; the ASCAP index lists twenty-five songs by her, none of which I've heard of, and some of which have fairly astonishing titles, like something called "Schmatas and Chatchkas." (I'm guessing that Miss Manners wasn't exactly Spanish.) In any case, the lyric is dreadful, not even worth quoting. Further, Wilkins seems to have made the orchestration deliberately jarring and discordant, and the band sounds as if they have no idea how to play in 3/4. Washington, for her part, sings as if she's trying to get the whole thing over with as quickly as possible. At 1:50, it's the shortest tune on the album, but why it was there to begin with I'll never know. Twenty years later, composer and director Richard Maltby wrote a new set of lyrics for "Jitterbug Waltz" for the Broadway revue *Ain't Misbehavin'*, and while those words are somewhat better, nothing changes the fundamental truth that not every piece of music ever written should have words.

While "Jitterbug Waltz" is the album's major train wreck, order is restored with "Ain't Cha Glad," which is one of its unalloyed triumphs. Written in 1933, the song is classic Fats Waller and Andy Razaf—one of their all-time best, with a catchy tune and a wonderful use of contemporary slang for title and lyrics. As titles go, it's a clear-cut follow-up to "Ain't Misbehavin'" (in fact, the melodies of the bridges to the two songs are remarkably similar) and possibly also "Ain't Cha Got Music," by Waller's mentor James P. Johnson. The song (sometimes spelled "Ain'tcha Glad?") was widely popular in 1933–34, when it was played by Isham Jones, Benny Goodman, Horace Henderson, Hal Kemp, and other prominent bandleaders. The major figure who didn't record it was Waller himself, who was not making any recordings in those years; according to his own testimony, he was staying one step ahead of the alimony police and avoiding big cities (that had recording facilities). Sadly, when he began recording regularly again with the Rhythm series in 1934, he never got around to "Ain't Cha Glad."

Dinah is brilliantly dynamic, subtle, and specific, yet full of power and raw emotion. It seems to have been Wilkins who brought the song to her attention; he recorded it for a session of his own at Savoy Records in September 1957, but that performance has never been released. The Washington chart is brassy and sparkly and yet constantly reveals a superior musical intelligence; he makes particularly effective use of a stop-time break (what a classical conductor might describe as a fermata) at the end of the bridge—right after "Every

street we meet is Lover's Lane." Ain't you glad that Washington sang this song? Heck yes!

We can also be glad that she and Wilkins included "Squeeze Me," the last tune recorded at the November session. Washington is playful and coquettish, as befits a song that was inspired by a dirty old folk tune (a quasi-blues) titled "The Boy in the Boat." The meaning of the title of that song has become somewhat obscured by the mists of time, but for now we'll just say that it seems to refer to a very specific sector of the female anatomy. "Squeeze Me" is one of the composer's earliest; in 1939, he referred to it as "my first professional song" and dated it to 1919. It had become a widely known jazz standard well before Waller made his famous Rhythm record of it in 1939. His vocal is knowing and slyly flirtatious (as when he sings, "Don't let your fat daddy cry"), but even the Mighty Fats can't compete with Washington at her most kittenish, as when she substitutes "sweet mama" for "fat daddy." Where Waller is merely irascible, Washington is never less than irresistible.

With "Squeeze Me," Washington and Wilkins completed six usable titles in one date, thus finishing the album. The total tally was the customary twelve tracks, six from the three dates in the first week of October 1957, the other six from the single session of November 20. As we've seen, of the twelve, "Jitterbug Waltz" was a pure disaster, and two others, "Honeysuckle Rose" and "Everybody Loves My Baby," were severely compromised by the star's insistence on including her husband as duet partner. And yet even in those two lesser tracks, Washington's vivacity and sincerity are unmistakable.

Clearly, producer Bob Shad had conceived of Washington's two tribute/songbook albums at the same time—*Dinah Sings Bessie Smith* was released immediately after the Waller album, and Washington had begun recording it well before the Waller set was released. For whatever unfortunate reason, the personalities of Dinah and Bessie don't sync up nearly as well as those of Dinah and Fats; it's almost as if Dinah and Bessie are somehow rivals twenty years after the latter's death. Washington and Waller are similar enough but also different enough, but Dinah and Bessie don't have any of the spiritual rapport that's so abundant on the earlier album. More crucially, the *Bessie* album suffers from the lack of Ernie Wilkins: all sessions are credited to "Eddie Chamblee and His Orchestra," and the quasi-Dixieland settings suit neither spouse particularly well.

Had Washington made it to middle age, or even elder-stateswoman-hood, she would have undoubtedly gotten around to making some excellent albums. As it stands, the only other actual album that can be considered a contender is one of her final projects, the 1962 *Back to the Blues*—which, in fact, contains superior remakes of two Bessie standards from the 1957–58 album, "Me and My Gin" and "You've Been a Good Old Wagon." But while *Back to the Blues* is fairly magical, *Dinah Washington Sings Fats Waller* is supreme.

49

Margaret Whiting

Margaret Whiting Sings the Jerome Kern Song Book

(1960)

No one quite had a career to parallel to Margaret Whiting's. The typical pattern for a singer of Whiting's generation was to land a string of hit singles in one's twenties and thirties, then to make a series of more artistically profound albums in their forties and fifties, and, by the time they were in their sixties to become elder stateswomen. With Whiting, it was as if that pesky middle phase— the entire second act— was somehow just missing. Late in life she was revered, by younger singers especially, as something even more than a grand diva of the American Songbook: she was a highly accessible, super-friendly, incredibly down-to-earth living legend. I've often witnessed the look on a young singer's face when she realized that Princess Margaret was in the house—it was indeed like a royal audience—but Maggie's presence was never intimidating. She made it her business to know every singer in the jazz and cabaret rooms in New York even into the twenty-first century, and she encouraged all of them.

Yet one can't help wonder: How much did these singers, young enough to be her granddaughters, actually know about the music of Margaret Whiting? She was a major role model and inspiration to dozens if not hundreds, but compared to other notable figures from the swing and early postwar era like Jo Stafford or Peggy Lee, young singers and, indeed, listeners in the last few decades of Whiting's life had relatively few opportunities to actually experience her own recorded work. The young singers who tried to impress her at Danny's Skylight Room on West Forty-sixth Street undoubtedly had heard "My Ideal" or "Moonlight in Vermont," but, unlike the situation with Stafford or Lee, there was remarkably little Maggie easily available in the post-78 era—she left us relatively few original albums, and there weren't even that many "greatest hits" collections of her earlier work. She made two songbook albums that were among the very best that the genre had to offer, *Margaret Whiting Sings Rodgers and Hart* (1947) and *Margaret Whiting Sings the Jerome Kern Songbook* (1960), yet they were scarcely heard from after their original release. Whiting's greatness, alas, was something that younger singers were compelled to accept on good faith. It was unfortunate that, unlike Rosemary Clooney or Doris Day, Whiting didn't live long enough to see any kind of comprehensive collection of her recorded work, but she was too busy sustaining her own career—as well as helping all her spiritual progeny—to pay much attention.

On the many occasions when I interviewed Maggie, she was always keenest to talk about her breakthrough period, her salad days—the war years and the early postwar period. She was proudest of having worked with Johnny Mercer, and would eagerly tell anyone and everyone how much he contributed to her career. She was less excited to mention that, in 1948, Mercer officially stepped down from his position as general overseer of Capitol's pop singles. As the 1940s became the 1950s, Whiting continued to land hits, but many of these were coming from a surprising place. In a series of duets with hillbilly singer Jimmy Wakely, she became one of the very first "mainstream" singers to infiltrate the country and western market—well before Tony Bennett sang "Cold, Cold Heart" and other Hank Williams classics. (It was like pulling teeth to get Whiting to even acknowledge that these records even existed; later, in the 1960s, she enjoyed a brief return to the charts as a country artist, but as her daughter, Debbi, confirms, Whiting thought little of her entire Nashville career.)

She remained true to Johnny Mercer for decades after their professional association ended. In her 1987 memoir, *It Might As Well Be Spring,* she admits that her career foundered after she was separated from Mercer and especially after she left Capitol. "I guess I never found the right genius to have as a manager or agent. My mother was always saying, 'You've got to find the right person. You've got to have another Johnny Mercer to pick the right songs. You need somebody creative.' Maybe she was right, but I didn't want to listen to her."

A rough survey of Whiting's work in the long-playing era is remarkably brief. Capitol did release a few singles collections in the early 1950s, while she was still under contract there, and her last chart single on the label was "The Money Tree" in 1956. Her career was briefly on the upswing at this point, thanks to another medium entirely: from 1955 to 1957 she was featured in a TV series titled *Those Whiting Girls,* a sitcom (with occasional musical numbers) produced by Desilu, in which she costarred with her mother and her younger sister (both named Barbara); it lasted two years and twenty-six episodes, which was respectable but hardly spectacular. In 1957, she left Capitol after almost seventeen years when Randy Wood of Dot Records approached her with a deal. According to her friend Roy Bishop, there was also a possibility of a songbook record devoted to the work of her famous composer father, Richard Whiting, that was to accompany a Hollywood biopic being pro-

duced by Dot's parent company, Paramount Pictures. Neither the movie nor the album was ever produced; instead, Dot released albums like *Margaret Whiting's Great Hits* and *Ten Top Hits.*

The most notable product of the Dot relationship with Whiting—which transpired at roughly the same time as the TV series—was the 1957 album *Goin' Places.* As Whiting recalled, the label wanted her to make an out-and-out jazz album, roughly in the "swingin' lovers" style that Sinatra had only recently perfected, and which other "legacy" artists, like Peggy Lee and Ella Fitzgerald, were already trying. Whiting most definitely did not want to compete with Sinatra and company, and thus hedged her bets by bringing in six of her favorite arrangers to work on the charts. Whiting was competent at singing up-tempos, but hardly a natural swinger like Lee or Fitzgerald, and the album took her even further out of her comfort zone by compelling her to sing the blues on "I'm Gonna Move to the Outskirts of Town." (She lamented that it was nearly impossible for her to get the right inflections on that early R&B classic, but Whiting actually had done a very credible albeit highly theatrical version of the classic "St. Louis Blues" as a Capitol single about a decade earlier.)

Goin' Places is in fact, an excellent album, but it's not a distinctive one—the use of four different musical directors prevents the package from having a unified sound. Whiting sounds as if she's trying to keep up with her peers, but there's little goin' on in *Goin' Places* that captures her doing what she does best. When she reports in her memoir that she didn't feel 100 percent comfortable with the basic idea of the album, it's hard to disagree with her. It's a more than pleasant listen, if hardly earth-shattering, and, alas, her only real album to speak of in this period.

Conversely, the 1960 double album, *Sings the Jerome Kern Song Book,* is incredibly rich in purpose as well as in actual content. It's not only Whiting's best work ever, but one of the greatest songbook albums, on par with Fitzgerald's or anybody else's. Whiting sings the great songs of Jerome Kern so brilliantly at least partly because she was truly to the manor born. Other singers grew up immersed in the American Songbook, if they were lucky, but

Whiting grew up inside of it. As the daughter of the songwriter Richard A. Whiting—and the virtual niece of at least two others (her "uncles" Johnny and Jerry, Mercer and Kern), Whiting treats the songwriters and their works as if they were members of her own family, whom she regards with both affection and familiarity—and complete and utter trust. More than most of her peers, she knew from the inside out what makes a great song great, and how best to sing it—she knew how to bring out those very qualities that made these songs so special to being with.

Her voice is sunny and optimistic, yet different from, say, Doris Day's or Dinah Shore's, who could also be so described. She's focused on the sunshine, but at the same time it's a voice and a style that doesn't deny the existence of the darkness. She's upbeat and cheerful, but able to be melancholy or blue when the occasion demands. Like Day at her best, she sings in a million shades of optimism—just as the Eskimo language has dozens of words for various consistencies of snow and ice, she sings in all manner of gradations. In her wartime era work, the breakthrough hits on Capitol, Whiting sounds merely young and bright-eyed, exactly what you would want to hear if you were a GI overseas (or his gal). Rather than being disillusioned fifteen years later, she sounds like she's fully earned the license to be happy—she's got a right to sing the good news.

The *Kern Song Book* happened because she was approached by Norman Granz in about 1959—apparently shortly before he sold his label, Verve Records, to MGM. "He came up to me and the first words out of his mouth were, 'I have two favorite singers, Ella Fitzgerald and Margaret Whiting.' Why wouldn't I have liked him?" Granz signed her to a contract, which seems to have been for five albums, and then proceeded to "go back on the road managing Ella." This report seems consistent with most of his pop-vocal-oriented projects—Mel Tormé and Anita O'Day tell similar stories. Most of the singers he signed were given carte blanche to do whatever they wanted, with no interference, or even assistance. In effect, the musical directors, especially Billy May and Russell Garcia, served as de facto producers, not only writing the orchestra-

tions but helping the singers pick songs and plan the album—certainly Whiting gave plenty of credit to Garcia, her arranger-conductor, for the success of the Kern project.

Granz gave Whiting a free hand to choose any orchestrator in Hollywood, and Garcia was the one she elected to work with. Garcia, who died at age ninety-five in 2011 (the same year as Whiting, who was nine years younger), was a major musical director, both for the movies and the pop music industry, whose work was consistently excellent. If he's less well known than the three superstar arranger-conductors celebrated for their work with Sinatra (Nelson Riddle, Billy May, Gordon Jenkins), it's because his individual style was less idiosyncratically stylized, less pronounced, less easy to automatically identify in a blindfold test. Garcia also recorded less on his own (although some of his own albums, especially *Wigville* and his excellent all-trombone album, *Four Horns and a Lush Life,* are highly regarded). Still, Garcia, who later converted to the Bahá'í faith and spent several decades on a religious pilgrimage, was easily one of the best vocal orchestrators of this particular golden age.

The earliest song in Whiting's *Kern Song Book* is "Look for the Silver Lining" from the 1920 *Sally,* with a lyric by Buddy DeSylva, who would collaborate fruitfully with both Kern, already a veteran, and the young George Gershwin and others, before entering into a fulfilling partnership with two other songwriters, Lew Brown and Ray Henderson. Right away it's clear that Whiting, then about thirty-five, had matured considerably from her earlier jukebox days. In the Capitol 78 era, this would have been a brisk show tune—two-beat and upbeat—yet her reading here is considerably deeper. For more than chronological reasons, this track sets the tone for the project: she encourages us to look for the silver lining, but not in a way that's phony (she doesn't want to hear from any cheerful Pollyanna) but in a way that's completely genuine, that makes the sunshine more believable by acknowledging the dark clouds—the melancholy moods are always nearby, but she chooses not to give in to them.

Continuing forward chronologically, the next show addressed is the 1925 *Sunny,* from which

Whiting sings "D'Ye Love Me?" with a text credited to both Oscar Hammerstein, Kern's most celebrated lyricist, and Otto Harbach. As heard in the show (Binnie Hale sings it in an early London cast recording), the melody has a *schottische* quality, which is underscored by the ethnic angle suggested in the punctuation and spelling of the title, and the lyric has a bright teasing quality. Whiting and Garcia slow it down, making it more tender than tantalizing, and remarkably sincere. The original is innocent and even naive, whereas Whiting's interpretation is knowing but not at all jaded or disillusioned.

Show Boat, from 1927, with book and lyrics by Hammerstein, is easily Kern's best-known work, his sole show to be regularly revived. A very contemporary guitar solo (Barney Kessel?) opens "Why Do I Love You?," which Whiting sings briskly, essentially with just guitar and a drummer playing brushes. The bass enters behind her on the bridge, and a flute comes in after the first chorus. We expect the full orchestra on the second chorus, but instead it's just the rhythm trio—and we don't need any more than that. Where many show tunes are often "jazzed up" by musicians and singers after the fact, *Show Boat*'s "Can't Help Lovin' Dat Man" is a song that Kern and Hammerstein originally wrote in what they deliberately cast as an African American folkloric style, and it's usually performed with syncopation and something like blues feeling. Whiting sings it completely straight, like an archetypical Broadway love song, without swinging it (although her rhythmic control is absolutely perfect) or growling out any blue notes.

Whiting must have felt about "Bill" the same way Ella Fitzgerald felt about "Over the Rainbow" in her Harold Arlen songbook, that it was another singer's signature and she didn't want to touch it. Surely Whiting was familiar with Helen Morgan's definitive, unflinchingly autobiographical performance. With its full verse and chorus, "Bill" is the second-longest song on the Kern package, which suggests how Whiting could have made her version different merely by eliminating the song's longish verse. But no, she tackles the whole enchilada—this is a Kern songbook, after all—and makes it unique by bringing her own experience to it. This

isn't "Julie LaVerne's" story, or Morgan's, it's now Maggie's—for four minutes at least. It's not as dramatic or heartbreaking as Morgan's—how could it be?—but it's completely honest and subtly moving in its own way.

Having fallen in love—professionally speaking—with the wonderful Helen Morgan during *Show Boat*, Kern and Hammerstein then proceeded to write their next show specifically for her. This was *Sweet Adeline* (1929), for which the team composed two of their most powerful love songs, "Why Was I Born?" and "Don't Ever Leave Me." The two complement each other beautifully: "Why Was I Born?" is heavy and moving, singularly focused in a way that a Helen Morgan torch song has to be. The text drops hints throughout and finally answers its own question in the last line: "Why was I born? To love you." Whiting lightens it in a way that makes it more believable for her. "Don't Ever Leave Me" has a playful melody that contrasts with the potentially down nature of the text, which Kern and Hammerstein likely meant to keep comparatively light—the message is not "If you ever leave me I'll kill myself," but the kind of coyly cooing phrase lovers whisper to each other in baby talk. Whiting's reading, done with just the rhythm section (piano only for the seldom heard verse), is just cozy enough.

The Cat and the Fiddle (1931) brings us back to the lyrics of Otto Harbach (1873–1963). Kern seems to have employed him to supply the libretti whenever Hammerstein was unavailable, and some of Otto's best songs are frequently mistaken for those of the Almighty Oscar—songs like "Smoke Gets in Your Eyes" and "Yesterdays," both from *Roberta* (1933). To the extent that Harbach had an identity of his own, it was that those shows he worked on with Kern (as well as Sigmund Romberg and Rudolf Friml) tend to represent Broadway at its closest to European operetta. Even the title "Poor Pierrot" sounds *mittel*-European, with its titular reference to a key character from the commedia dell'arte. (Noël Coward, another transitional composer who represented the shift from Old Europe to New Broadway, wrote a famous song, "Parisian Pierrot," featuring the pantomime icon.) "Poor Pierrot" has a complex lyric that Whiting renders beautifully, and a text strewn with archaic cultural references suddenly becomes a timeless tale about a boy, a girl, and a love unrequited. "She Didn't Say Yes" is erotic in an exquisitely innocent way; Garcia's small-band (octet? sextet?) arrangement plays with the time: there are stop-time-like breaks for Whiting to deliver the suggestive punch lines, and at different points the background suggests a chiming clock. Throughout, Garcia's writing suggests the *Birth of the Cool* style of his 1955 *Wigville* album.

In *Music in the Air* (1932), Kern and Hammerstein returned to old Europe with a backstage comedy set in the world of operetta, with drama queen divas, histrionic tenors, and apple-faced conductors. (Whiting had already performed one excellent song from the same score, "I've Told Every Little Star," in an adorable interpretation for Capitol.) "The Song Is You" is unquestionably one of the team's greatest songs, and an absolutely perfect embodiment of everything that's great about music and song; they're old and new at the same time, looking to the future and grounded in the past. It's not surprising that Kern is the one composer equally favored by opera singers and beboppers alike. In "The Song Is You" Whiting helps the two collaborators (Hammerstein, alas, died in the year that Whiting recorded and released the Kern album) realize their concept of a text that wraps up the notions of both music and love into a single coherent bundle. Perhaps even more than Sinatra's signature performances (from throughout the 1940s), Whiting's treatment is simultaneously soaring and down-to-earth.

After *Show Boat*, *Roberta* (1933) was probably Kern's overall most successful show, the one that yielded the most hits and standards, and which was filmed three times. (In 1935, 1952, and 1969, the latter a television production in which Bob Hope reprised his role as the original 1933 Broadway lead.) Whiting sings five songs from the score here, including "I Won't Dance." The hardcore musical-theater nerds among us may be tempted to point out that "I Won't Dance" actually originated in a 1934 British show, *Three Sisters*, and was only later worked into the 1935 film of *Roberta;* that's technically correct, but it's the Dorothy Fields rewrite of the lyrics that makes this a classic song, not, in this case, the original by Hammerstein.

The 1933 Broadway *Roberta* marked Kern's definitive collaboration with Harbach, while the 1935 RKO production marked the start of a fruitful collaboration with Fields. Overall, *Roberta* is Harbach's moment of glory, he's at his most soulfully dramatic with "Smoke Gets in Your Eyes" and "Yesterdays," but at his flirtiest and sauciest with "Let's Begin," a text that could have been written by Fields, while "The Touch of Your Hand" is a rapturously tender love song that puts Harbach in a class by himself. The melody of the latter is virtually through-composed, especially in Garcia's orchestration, and thus more like a true aria than a song in song form. "The Touch of Your Hand" was recorded by relatively few pop or jazz singers, the operatically inclined Sarah Vaughan being an exception—but it's a superb song, unfairly neglected in the modern era. It's only when one thinks about it that one realizes that "The Touch of Your Hand" is no less grandly "European" than "Smoke Gets in Your Eyes" and "Yesterdays," but it's part of Whiting's brilliance that she can cut all three down to size and transmute the grandiose into the sublimely personal. "Smoke Gets in Your Eyes" is perhaps Harbach's greatest lyric. The orchestration is heavier than usual here, evoking Gordon Jenkins (though perhaps not quite that dour) and Whiting's singing is amazingly direct, sad but not morose, more realistic than in a heightened state of melodrama.

Whiting begins "I Won't Dance" by repeating the three notes of the title over and over, like the vocal equivalent of a drum break, for her intro. She proceeds from there to the verse, and when she reaches the chorus, the tuba becomes prominent in the accompanying ensemble, which again underscores Garcia's affection for the 1949 Miles Davis *Birth of the Cool* band. Whiting is at once hot and cool—in many ways the *Kern Song Book* is an even better jazz album than *Goin' Places*. Garcia's arrangement of "Let's Begin" is also highly bebop-pish, with a full alto solo that sounds like Bud Shank or Art Pepper. Harbach's text is full of lines like "love or gin/wife or sin" that were highly risqué in 1933, and brings us the same vibe—from Kern, Harbach, Garcia, and Whiting—as "She Didn't Say Yes." It's playful, sensual, at once erotic and innocent, knowing and naive.

The remaining songs on the album were written expressly for Hollywood musicals, with the major exception of the two from *Very Warm for May* (1939), Kern's last Broadway show. Overall, his best original film score was the 1936 *Swing Time*, with lyrics by Dorothy Fields—the apex of their collaboration. "A Fine Romance" is again both rhythmic and comic, with Whiting adroitly delivering Fields's witty punch lines in and around the drumbeats, and more modernistic writing from Garcia. At this point, you might expect "The Way You Look Tonight" to be another bright bouncer; instead it's one of the best ballads in the package. Her singing is slow, but not too slow, and rich with meaning; it's one of those Sinatra-grade performances where not one note, not even one inflection, is out of place. Surely it's one of the best-ever recordings of this romantic anthem, which, thanks to the 1991 movie *Father of the Bride*, is now absolutely de rigueur at weddings—from here to eternity, or so it seems.

The 1938 *Joy of Living* was the composer's fourth movie with Irene Dunne (after *Roberta*, *Show Boat*, and *High, Wide, and Handsome*), but unlike the Kern classics in those two iconic properties, "You Couldn't Be Cuter" is that great rarity: a Kern-Fields masterpiece that was extremely popular at the time but which has scarcely been heard since 1938. When it was new, there were recordings by at least a dozen major bands, two of which are worth mentioning: Ray Noble's orchestra with singer Tony Martin and, from London, Lew Stone's band with singer Al Bowlly. In a quick two minutes, Garcia and Whiting make this delightful song even more whimsical; in the instrumental break, Garcia contrasts a flute and a tuba in what seems like an emulation of some kind of clockwork windup mechanical dancer. After Whiting, Ella Fitzgerald included the song in her own *Jerome Kern Song Book* (1963)—doubtlessly, she and Granz discovered the song from Whiting. (It also turns up in subsequent Kern songbook albums by Sandy Stewart and Rebecca Kilgore, both of whom probably learned it from Ella.)

Whenever anybody wants to pull out a factoid regarding a flop show that produced a classic song, *Very Warm for May* (1939) and the unforgettable

"All the Things You Are" are usually the examples they use. The book must have been the culprit, but while Kern can't be blamed for the show's failure, part of the responsibility must go to Hammerstein, since he wrote the libretto as well as the classic lyrics. Whiting's reading of "All in Fun" (also from *Very Warm*) is pure narrative, she takes a very specific story and makes it remarkably universal. On "All the Things You Are" she does precisely the opposite, taking a big, sweeping opus of a story and making it highly specific and personal.

The last three film numbers in Whiting's *Kern Song Book* find the great composer writing beautiful, soaring melodies for such musical icons as Fred Astaire (*You Were Never Lovelier*, 1942), Gene Kelly (*Cover Girl*, 1944), Rita Hayworth (who costarred in both of the above-mentioned films), and Abbott and Costello (*One Night in the Tropics*, 1940). "Remind Me" was actually introduced by Hollywood tenor Allan Jones (father of Jack) in the latter vehicle, which also introduced Bud Abbott and Lou Costello to movie audiences. It's another stunningly lovely Kern-Fields ballad with prominent piano (Lou Levy), with guitar and flute on hand to help Whiting transport us to what amounts to another night in the tropics.

You Were Never Lovelier (1942) was Kern's last encounter with Astaire, a relationship that not only included two classic Fred and Ginger vehicles, *Roberta* and *Swing Time*, but went back to the 1922 Broadway musical *The Bunch and Judy*. No less important, it was Kern's only meeting with Hollywood's young rising lyric giant Johnny Mercer, and the two songs they wrote together are among their finest. "I'm Old Fashioned" has a baroque intro by Garcia—talk about old-fashioned and "quaint"!—that some will find obnoxious, others ingenious. Whiting's singing is anything but old-fashioned, she makes the song sound strongly contemporary. "Dearly Beloved" finds Mercer in a similarly old-fashioned frame of mind; this could be a major wedding song had not "The Way You Look Tonight" knocked all the others out of the running.

Cover Girl (1944) marked the only collaboration between Kern and his friend Ira Gershwin, though they surely would have written more together had the composer not died the following year at the comparatively young age of sixty. "Long Ago (and Far Away)" must have seemed like a surprise at the time—why was Kern writing such a sweeping, soaring, long-note-y melody for Gene Kelly, a dancer who was not nearly as endowed in the tonsils department as he was in the terpsichorean one? Kern's wisdom paid off: the song not only provided the most memorable moment in the movie, as wonderfully sung and danced by Kelly and Hayworth, but resonated as a highly poignant song of separation during the late World War II era and became a number one hit. That's the spirit in which Whiting sings it, she is almost certainly thinking of her dear departed father and uncle Jerry, and those days that she spent with them, which, even in her mid-thirties in 1960, already seemed so long ago and far away.

Margaret Whiting Sings the Jerome Kern Song Book was easily the finest work of the singer's career, as well as the greatest of the many Kern songbooks that have been recorded. I'm very glad I got to listen to it while Whiting was alive—even though it was on a pair of scratchy old LPs (much worn)—and told her repeatedly how much I loved it. It was a huge source of satisfaction to her in 2002, when she was pushing eighty, that the matchless *Kern Song Book* was reissued as a single CD, with all twenty-four tracks intact. How could you not love it? Margaret Whiting and Russ Garcia show us why it's impossible to imagine a world where the songs of Jerome Kern are not beloved by everyone.

50

Lee Wiley

Night in Manhattan

(1950)

How many singers are you going to go out of your way to hear?

—Mitch Miller

Lee Wiley. Mitch Miller. If one were to try to imagine a more incongruous combination of vocalist and producer, it probably couldn't be done. Wiley (1908–1975) spent most of her career as a cult favorite, known only to hardcore aficionados. Even though she was beloved by those in the know, it didn't amount to much. Compared to such colleagues as Connee Boswell and Mildred Bailey (not to mention Ella Fitzgerald or Sarah Vaughan), Wiley's career was minimal and her overall output minuscule. The career of Mitch Miller (1911–2010) was just the opposite: the classical-instrumentalist-turned-pop-impresario did more than anyone else to steer Columbia Records—and the entire music industry along with it—in the direction of the mega-

hit. Miller was the primary force behind the development of the genre sometimes known as "producer pop," which would be the dominant mode of the music industry for many decades, and which is still very much with us today. Miller was responsible for one blockbuster chart-topper of a hit single after another, and helped convert the music business from the equivalent of a mom-and-

pop store to a Walmart. Hits were simply what he did. Big hits. Lots of them.

Yet up until the day he died Mitch was proudest of his work with Lee Wiley. He was responsible, more or less, for setting the careers of such huge names as Rosemary Clooney and Tony Bennett in motion, and helped such established headliners as Jo Stafford and Doris Day land some of the most successful records of their long careers. But somehow Lee Wiley meant more to him than anything else he'd ever done. As he once said to me, "If you look at the record, I'm the guy who found Rosemary Clooney, Johnny Mathis, Tony Bennett, Vic Damone— these are all people that I discovered," exaggerating slightly but not by much. "Forty, fifty years later, they're all at the height of their career, wherever they go they sell out, and there's only one reason: they sang great songs, and varied types of songs, and they had quality, excellence." He then added, "And that's what I heard in Lee Wiley."

Mitch then told me something that nearly everyone who'd ever looked at his career might disagree with: "And I used to operate on a supposedly noncommercial theory that excellence will sell. Some things that didn't sell well [at the time are] good enough so that people still like them now." He laughed as he said that.

Lee Wiley represented the most extreme example of Miller putting Columbia Records' money where his own taste was. Did her records sell? "To be honest, I didn't care if they did or not. You must remember there was a guy in charge, Goddard Lieberson. He was the first to record Stravinsky, he produced [some of] the first albums of Broadway shows—the first complete albums of plays. His point was that the record company should take some of the money they earned on other things and spend it on things of quality. Not far-out things, not exotic things, things of quality that would have a long life. And that was the climate when I was put in charge of the pop division. It was important to record Lee because she was so good! How many singers are you going to go out of your way to hear?"

He went on, "Why do you suppose it was that all the Condon guys, especially Eddie himself, all liked her so much? 'Cause she was a great musician! She knew how to phrase. To me, Lee was in the same class with . . ." At this point, Mitch fumbled for a name. "Oh God, carnation in her ear? Billie Holiday. Yeah, Billie Holiday, unique! You hear four bars and you know who it is."

He was right about that; the voice is at the center of the issues regarding Wiley. In her first recordings, in her early to mid-twenties, she already sounds deep and throaty; she comes much closer to the ideal of what was then called a "torch singer" than, say, Ruth Etting, whose voice was comparatively higher and more nasal. Wiley's voice is almost always described in terms of flammable metaphors: as she got older, the voice sounded less torchy and by the 1950 *Night in Manhattan* sessions, it sounds positively smoky. She also had what could be called a burnished sound, an ashen sound. You get the idea.

It's certainly a distinctive sound, but is it an appealing sound? Mel Tormé liked to talk about the first time he heard the voice of Billie Holiday and famously compared her sound to spinach: "It may not taste good, but it's so good for you." Holiday's voice wasn't sweet or pretty like Ella Fitzgerald's,

but there's something about it that grabs you from the first note, even when it rubs you the wrong way, as it occasionally does. Wiley doesn't have that; her voice doesn't make you stop dead in your tracks, like Holiday's, make you fall in love, like Peggy Lee's or Jo Stafford's, or cast a magic spell, like Nat King Cole's.

It's also significant that Wiley only had limited experience with big bands: being out on the road with a dance band, playing mostly ballrooms for set after set, night after night, town after town, gave singers a very different background from Wiley's. Band vocalists, even very subtle ones like Peggy Lee, learned how to grab an audience's attention very quickly. Wiley never did that, never had that. She made an audience come to her rather than going to them.

Nearly all the great singers had a quality that combined identity with autobiography: when Billie Holiday sings, she has only to open her mouth and we know her whole life story. She utters a few syllables and we know who she is and where she comes from, even though the words she's singing are not usually her own. The larger point is that her very voice conveys some sort of a narrative. Wiley doesn't have that, either; I've been listening to her for thirty years and she's still a mystery to me. (By contrast, I feel that Mildred Bailey, Ella Fitzgerald, and Helen Forrest are all my best friends.) In fact, there was a TV movie (or, to be completely accurate, a 60-minute episode of *Bob Hope Presents the Chrysler Theatre*) about her life in 1963, starring Piper Laurie as the singer and directed by a young Sydney Pollack. It seems hardly a coincidence that the title was *Something About Lee Wiley*.)

But what Wiley does have is miraculous musicianship, phrasing, and incredible skills as an interpreter. It's not surprising, therefore, that she would never be a major record seller, or a pop star. Her career wasn't a lifelong love affair between herself and the general public, but rather her support would come from insiders: musicians, devotees, the jazz press, industry heavyweights like Milt Gabler, John Hammond . . . and Mitch Miller.

Miller was a jazz fan, or so he liked to say. He would have heard Wiley with various Eddie Condon combinations in the late 1930s and '40s. She turns up on Milt Gabler's Commodore Records, which was what today would be called a boutique label, aiming its product at hard-core jazz fans rather than trying to compete with RCA or the other big boys for chart hits. Wiley also recorded a series of early songbook albums (probably the first ever) for other boutique labels that catered to Broadway and cabaret buffs, among them Schirmer Records, for whom she did an eight-song Harold Arlen album in 1942. Mitch specifically remembered the "Sherman" records, as he called them, and they led to his decision to do new songbook albums with Wiley a decade later.

Toward the end of 1950, Miller formed a professional relationship with the pianist Joe Bushkin. Bushkin's entire career trajectory was somewhat special: he started playing with small groups on Fifty-second Street and became an immediate favorite of the Condon gang, both for his playing and his upbeat, party-hearty personality. Bushkin worked extensively with big bands (Bunny Berigan, Benny Goodman, and, most notably, Tommy Dorsey) and also made a lasting impression on such notables as Bing Crosby, Frank Sinatra, and Buddy Rich. In addition to being an energetic and highly entertaining, swinging piano player, Bushkin was a musician of well-above-average looks, charisma, and supreme self-confidence. He and Wiley were never involved romantically (not, at least, that Joey would ever admit to me), but he was a lifelong fan and supporter. The same way that Crosby and Sinatra constantly did whatever they could to boost Bushkin, Bushkin himself boosted Wiley at every opportunity. (Not all musicians were so enamored of Wiley; the irascible trumpeter Ruby Braff cursed a blue streak when I mentioned her name.)

Wiley's association with Miller and Columbia would mark the start of a new phase in her career. In the 1930s, there had been a concerted attempt to promote her as a pop star; she sang with mainstream dance orchestras and on mainstream radio programs, and for a brief while she was on the cover of radio-fan magazines. Her run of marquee-name stardom was sabotaged by illness, or so she said, and by the start of the war she had moved laterally to the margins of the mainstream by sing-

ing regularly with the Condonites. Eddie Condon wasn't a superstar like the major swing bandleaders, but he was the best known of all traditional-style jazzmen, and he could pack Town Hall on a weekly basis for many years—concerts at which Wiley was a regular. Her most visible moment in the immediate postwar era arrived in 1947, when in the same season she recorded a duet with Bing Crosby for Decca and not long after she cut a solo session of her own for Majestic Records, a start-up operation where another old friend, John Hammond, was producing.

When Miller recorded Wiley with Joe Bushkin and His Swinging Strings, one figure who hovered over the proceedings was the composer Victor Young. He had been a key influence in terms of the use of strings in modern popular music, having brilliantly incorporated strings into dance band orchestrations in the 1920s and 1930s, and then helped change the sound of film music in the 1940s and '50s. Along the way, he wrote a considerable number of popular songs, many that became standards. Young was also Wiley's lover—there doesn't seem to be a better word for their relationship.

Fully half the eight songs on *Night in Manhattan* were composed by Young, one with a partial credit to Wiley herself; they form the core of the album. The singer's single greatest accomplishment may be her transcendent interpretation of Young's classic song "Street of Dreams," which boasts an especially poetic lyric by Sam Lewis (otherwise best known for "When You're Smiling" and "For All We Know"). This is a perfect case of every detail of the scenario working out exactly as anticipated: Wiley's smoky voice is the catalyst and star player, carrying the basic narrative forward, with Bobby Hackett's trumpet obbligato in a very prominent supporting role, the velvety strings enhancing the whole works, providing the mise-en-scène and the overall atmosphere. In the background, Bushkin's insistent piano functions as a kind of very active director, making sure the action keeps moving at a steady pace, without a letup.

"Street of Dreams" is also where Miller's comparison of Wiley to Billie Holiday sounds the most apropos. It's on a strictly musical level, in the timbre of their voices. There's a comparable depth and emotional profundity. Like Holiday's, Wiley's music isn't necessarily dependent upon emotional highs and lows, but rather on a clearly stated wish to portray the world as it really is, not exaggerated for dramatic purposes. Wiley's singing is equally driven by the two muses of narrative and swing. Where the two singers differ is mainly in extra-musical circumstances, although with artists on this level of honesty, it's not totally possible or even desirable to keep one's personal life out of the music. We know that Wiley was hardly as self-destructive as Holiday but, rather, a woman in control of her own destiny, both musical and marital. The "Street of Dreams" narrative, with its colorful verse describing "brothers as blue" lining up to purchase dreams at midnight, is Wiley at her most evocative and Lady Day–like. Other than Wiley's, the most famous version of the song is by Tommy Dorsey and Frank Sinatra. This 1942 disc features a big string section, but overall it's a much lighter affair—without the verse, it's much easier to interpret the lyric as wistful, metaphoric, and romantic. Still, Tony Bennett, who also recorded the song with the verse, told me that he had no doubt that the song was all about drug addicts scoring and then shooting up in the depths of the night, making the lyric literal rather than metaphoric. Wiley's interpretation is both at the same time.

The remaining three Young songs all have words by Ned Washington, a brilliant lyricist who, despite having written many classic songs with Young (as well as "The Nearness of You" with Hoagy Carmichael), never seems to advance to the front of the line whenever anybody is trying to pick a subject for a cabaret show or a songbook album. "I Don't Stand a Ghost of a Chance with You" is perhaps Young's most widely sung standard, a song introduced by Bing Crosby (who is given a composer co-credit), and is still frequently heard today.

Wiley's voice, as always, makes us think of cigarettes and wineglasses. You might think it would be more haunted and otherworldly, given the content of this song, but her voice is resiliently solid here and not at all ghostly. Which makes sense, as Washington was referring to "a ghost of a chance," meaning a very slim chance, a remote possibility, as opposed to something that's already dead or running around in a white sheet and hollering "boo!" There's little sign of hope in Wiley's voice; instead she sings it with an air of resignation as she asks, "What's the good of scheming?"

"Anytime, Any Day, Anywhere" starts with a lively trumpet intro by Hackett, and then an especially jubilant vocal by Wiley. She's one of the rare vocal artists of any generation whose ability to express a mood was not constrained by tempo. The metronomic count on this number isn't particularly fast, yet Wiley sounds happy and even rapturous. This is the song where the lyric is co-credited to Wiley (and Washington) and it had an odd career after being introduced here, mainly because there are so many other songs with similar titles (like Sinatra's very different "Anytime, Anywhere") that it's tricky to keep track of which song is which.

If "Ghost of a Chance" is possibly Victor Young's most famous song, "A Woman's Intuition" is among his most obscure, and certainly the least known on *Night in Manhattan*. To me, it's always suggested those songs in the repertory of another Lee who was close to Young, namely Peggy Lee. (The lyric suggests those inherently masochistic songs that Miss Lee was writing in those years when she was married to a hopeless alcoholic, such as "What More Can a Woman Do?") Was it written expressly for Wiley? Quite possibly. Following this rendering, it was only sung by artists who learned it from this album. Although she sings it well and Hackett is perfect as usual, the song's obscurity is deserved; it's not surprising that it never became any kind of a jazz or pop standard.

Among the non-Young songs, "Manhattan" and "Sugar" are stunning examples of the Wiley-Hackett-Bushkin-strings format at its apogee of perfection. The arrangements anticipate a lot of movie underscoring from the 1950s, in Hollywood romances like *The Eddy Duchin Story*. You know the setup: Boy and girl are listening to a singer in a small intimate club. At first we just hear voice and piano, but then as the couple get more involved with each other, the strings stealthily enter—we almost subconsciously leave the physical world of the setting itself and enter the emotional world of the characters. (Obviously, the place is too small for twenty customers, let alone a section of two dozen violinists on its stage.) Maybe we'll then take off on a love montage with the couple strolling past romantic vistas (like the fountain in Central Park) as we hear the strings continuing to play the theme underneath. "Manhattan," which is one of the signature New York songs of all time, is especially prime fodder for opulent movie romance underscoring.

"Sugar" had come from an interesting place racially. It had been composed by the pioneering African American songwriter Maceo Pinkard but was made into a jazz standard (and a cornet masterpiece) by Bix Beiderbecke, after which it became a kind of theme song of the Condon gang and other white jazzmen of the 1920s—and was precisely a perfect song for Lee Wiley. Of the singer's immediate contemporaries—her friend Mildred Bailey, the very successful Connee Boswell, Frances Langford, Helen Ward, and the other early swing era "canaries"—no one is as rapturously romantic as Wiley. They all have their strong points, but no one else makes you quite feel like slow dancing close with your best girl. You have to wait for a later generation, for the likes of Dinah Shore or even Peggy Lee, before anyone even comes close.

Night in Manhattan, it must be admitted, contains one unmitigated disaster—and, to compound the infraction, it's the only song on the album actually composed by Joe Bushkin. I've played this album a million times and every time I do, I have to either skip this track or suppress the desire to hurl the disc out the window and under the feet of passersby. Bushkin composed his most famous song, "Oh Look at Me Now," when he was playing in Tommy Dorsey's rhythm section during a time when the Dorsey band was part of a songwriting contest on the radio. Bushkin wrote the tune and his friend, another Condon associate named John DeVries, came up with the lyric. It was a contest winner and an immediate hit. You know where this is going: There's this guy, see, who claims to have never "cared about love"; in fact, he tells us that he even "laughed at those blue diamond rings." That was then. Now, see, he confesses that ever since he met that certain dame, he has become obsessed with such romantic folderol; now, see, he describes

himself as a "new man, better than Casanova at his best." The original "Oh Look at Me Now" is an undisputed classic of the big band era, and, more than that, truly a memorable song. God knows why Bushkin and DeVries wanted to mess with it. With a few simple minor pronoun alterations, the lyric would have worked equally well for a female artist as for a male, but for some reason known only to DeVries, he felt compelled to come up with an all-new lyric for Wiley in 1950.

The result was a catastrophe, easily one of the most misogynistic texts ever produced in the golden age of American songwriting. In DeVries's view, women have no need whatsoever for love and romance—or even sexual gratification; the only thing that interests them is cold, hard cash. One can only surmise that in the years between 1941 and 1950, DeVries had been through some kind of bitter divorce in which his departing spouse took him to the cleaners and frisked him of every last cent (including the royalties for this song). That's the only explanation I can think of for such an unflattering depiction of female intentions. Essentially, he's lashing the entire gender of womanhood to the mast.

But one also has to wonder what Wiley was thinking of, if anything. A major musical theater diva like Eartha Kitt or Carol Channing could have sung the thing with irony and humor. But not Wiley. She's utterly sincere, her tongue is nowhere near her cheek. A few contemporary female singers out there, like Daryl Sherman and Barbara Fasano, have sung this lyric, but I do my best to argue them out of it. Perhaps the one useful thing about the lyric is that it establishes Wiley's musical persona as fully opposite to Holiday's perpetually wounded, perennial victim. She's completely in charge and totally empowered. (From what we know about Wiley's personal life, she didn't conform to either extreme of the stereotype: she was neither destroyed by love, like Holiday, nor financially enriched by it, like the woman depicted by DeVries.)

"I've Got a Crush on You" is a veritable Pandora's box of intertwined relations between Wiley, Miller, Hackett, Bushkin, plus two additional giants of twentieth-century music, Frank Sinatra and Fats Waller—not to mention the songwriters George and Ira Gershwin. Wiley first recorded "Crush" in 1939 as part of her first album, the Gershwin songbook produced by Liberty Music Shop. The backing band then was a Condon affair, with a rather special surprise guest on piano—the legendary Waller, who was then a much bigger star and celebrity than Wiley or anyone else in the room, but was there strictly to express his admiration for her. According to some accounts, Bushkin was also on hand as a precaution, to spell Waller in the likely event he became too inebriated to finish the session. However it's undeniably Waller playing on "Crush"; the Waller stride flourish intro is unmistakable.

As already mentioned, Liberty Music Shop was a boutique enterprise aimed at specialists and connoisseurs; few members of the lay public ever heard Wiley's 1939 LMS album, but it was appreciated by virtually the entire music industry. Among them was Ira Gershwin, who gave Wiley full credit for reconceiving "Crush" as a slow, sensual number. The song originally had the dubious distinction of being part of two Gershwin productions that never quite got off the ground, *Treasure Girl* (1928) and *Strike Up the Band* (1930). The brothers Gershwin had originally planned it as a snappy, peppy 1920s-style fox-trot. The older Gershwin was at first flabbergasted by what he perceived as Wiley's radical reinterpretation, but he quickly admitted that the song worked better that way, and went to the trouble of acknowledging the singer in his book-length collection, *Lyrics on Several Occasions.*

Another individual better known than Wiley who knew that 1939 album well was Frank Sinatra. I asked Mitch if Sinatra ever listened to Wiley, and he responded with a loud, dismissive laugh, as if I had just asked the stupidest question in the world. "Are you kidding?" he bellowed. "Frank listened to everything and learned from everyone!" In 1947, Sinatra recorded his own version, with trumpeter Bobby Hackett, a string quartet, a rhythm section, and a few woodwinds, one of whom was Miller. "I was on that date," Miller proudly told me. Where the 1939 Wiley disc begins with a Fatsian flourish, Sinatra starts with Hackett playing a trumpet intro

that would come to be iconic. In terms of tempo, structure, and overall dynamics, Sinatra had obviously studied the Wiley disc and was determined to improve on it, which he did. Then, three years after Sinatra, Wiley and Miller built on what Sinatra had achieved. The 1950 Wiley-Hackett version adheres to the format of the 1947 Sinatra-Hackett disc even more closely than Sinatra followed the outline of the 1939 Wiley version. Her 1950 "Crush" is definitive, quite possibly the most essential interpretation of that oft-recorded Gershwin masterpiece. Like Sinatra, she strikes the perfect note. This isn't "So in Love" or "Night and Day," a song of undying devotion and even obsession, it's a much breezier kind of attraction. It's about a "crush," one serious enough for the crush-ee to consider constructing a "cunning cottage" (much like the "little home" in the Gershwins' "The Man I Love"), but basically a much lighter affair, the kind that makes those involved "coo" and "care" even as they address each other as "Sweetie Pie." Lee Wiley's 1950 "I've Got a Crush on You" deserves to be on every Gershwin anthology collection ever.

Following the *Night in Manhattan* sessions, Miller produced two more 10-inch LPs with Wiley. These would be songbooks representing Irving Berlin and Vincent Youmans, two composers not covered in her 1939–42 songbook series. Rather than backing the singer with either a jazz band or a string section (let alone both), on each of these Columbia songbooks the accompaniment is provided by the twin pianos of Stan Freeman and Cy Walter, a then famous keyboard team who were also, at the time, better known than Wiley—they had a show of their own on New York radio titled *Piano Playhouse.* Neither of these two other albums is as splendid as *Night in Manhattan,* but there's little in Wiley's career—or anyone else's—that is. (Her second-best album is the 1956 *West of the Moon* with Ralph Burns and His Orchestra.)

Along with the reputations of Wiley and Miller, the acclaim for *Night in Manhattan* mushroomed, but unlike the history of many of the albums in this book, it eventually tapered off. Columbia eventually made a 12-incher out of *Night in Manhattan* by adding four random tracks from the Berlin and Youmans albums, and in that format it was steadily appreciated by cognoscenti. By the end of the LP era, *Manhattan* was, like a lot of vintage albums owned by the corporation, distributed by Columbia Special Products. At one point in the early 1980s—shortly before the coming of the compact disc—a sales rep from CSP informed me that *Manhattan* had, over a period of slightly more than thirty years of being in print more or less continually, reached the million-unit mark.

Wiley died in 1975, concluding a forty-year career of intermittent success. It may be that her influence extended for twenty years or so after her death; it was in the 1970s and '80s that you were most likely to see a singer in a New York cabaret do a tribute show to Wiley or sing "A Woman's Intuition," a song they could have only learned from her. That period now seems long gone; Wiley is barely known at all among younger singers today—way

less than Billie Holiday, which isn't surprising, but I've heard many more aspiring vocalists learning songs and arrangements from the Boswell Sisters than from Lee Wiley. All of which has nothing to do with the quality of her best work. Even if her influence isn't what it was all those decades ago, that takes nothing away from *Night in Manhattan,* which is one of the best albums ever made in the spheres of vocal jazz and the classic songbook. There's no recording that so vividly captures the late-night, smoke-filled-room mood more effectively, in which even the relatively cheerful songs like "Manhattan" and "Sugar" have an air of resignation about them. Slow or fast, famous or obscure, melancholy or optimistic, it ultimately doesn't matter: they're all waiting for you at midnight in that Manhattan saloon somewhere on the street of dreams, where love laughs at a king and broken hearts can be made like new.

Cassandra Wilson

Belly of the Sun

(2002)

n August 2001, a few weeks before 9/11, Cassandra Wilson and her band went to work in an abandoned train station—or rather, the structure that had formerly been the station stop for Clarksdale, Mississippi—in the heart of the Mississippi Delta. They set up recording equipment, and over ten days they recorded fifteen tracks for an album that was released a few months later. *Belly of the Sun,* as it was titled, is a unique example of what might be called a "location recording." The term has generally been used to refer to live albums, in the sense of an album taped in front of an audience at Carnegie Hall or Birdland, but it's also a term used in relation to the concept of "field recordings," of the kind associated with anthropological and ethnomusical projects.

Wilson's idea was something altogether different. She wanted to record a blues-centric album in the very heart of the country that produced the blues, but not necessarily like Alan Lomax or the Library of Congress taping field hollers being hollered out in the middle of an actual cotton field. Wilson wanted the spirit of the blues to be all around them, quite literally, in the very air that they were breathing. Even though she and the musicians and the technical crew were all indoors—hopefully enjoying the benefit of air-conditioning—the general idea was that the spirit of the blues would seep in through the transoms.

"No one goes to the Mississippi Delta in the middle of August!" As Wilson pointed out in an interview done around the time of the release, "Most of the people who live there stay indoors. I thought it'd be a great time to test our resolve and experience the hottest point in the calendar year. It's also a good time to go because there aren't a lot of people traveling there. Nothing happens in August except maybe preparation for the harvest." Wilson's preferred engineer, Danny Kopelson, she added, "is great at adapting spaces, and he had to do a lot of tweaking to get that space in order. But it was well worth it because it had such an incredible ambience. I really enjoy going into spaces like that and changing them."

Wilson had been born (in 1955) in nearby Jackson, Mississippi. In the album notes, the singer's friend and manager Michael Simanga, talks about hearing her in a "little juke joint" in Laurel, some time in the mid-1970s. "Even then in that small, dark, crowded, smoke-filled place, smelling of fried chicken, catfish, and alcohol . . . it was clear that Cassandra was a special artist." This album was her bid at returning to her roots: although she was clearly a product of the land where the blues (supposedly) were born, most of us heard her for the first time in the late 1980s when she was part of a decidedly postmodern group of musicians based in Brooklyn.

Thus listeners (myself included) were surprised when she started including some very traditional blues in her albums, especially the two Robert Johnson tunes ("Come on in My Kitchen" and "Hell Hound on My Trail") heard on the 1993 *Blue Light 'til Dawn.*

From a certain perspective, Wilson's involvement with the very "far-out" musicians of Brooklyn's cutting edge of the 1980s (like Steve Coleman, whose music is steeped in highly idiosyncratic scientific theory, something like Anthony Braxton's or even Sun Ra's) and the most basic, fundamental blues makes perfect sense: part of the intention of Ornette Coleman and the early free-jazz players was not to make the music more complicated but more simple, not more intellectual but more accessible. In this regard, one of Wilson's key mentors was the trumpeter and vocalist Olu Dara (a native of Natchez, Mississippi), well known in jazz circles for his involvement with postmodern gurus like David Murray and Henry Threadgill, but whose own music is the most fundamental and joyful Delta-style blues; Dara's own singing is rather like avant-garde yodeling. Dara performs on several key albums with Cassandra Wilson, including the 1987 *Days Aweigh* as well as *Belly of the Sun,* and his spirit hovers over her entire output.

An equally surprising aspect of *Belly* and, indeed, Wilson's overall career, is her approach to repertory. On most of her earlier albums, she wrote nearly all of her material herself; when she graduated, as it were, to songs written by others, it was not, as we expected at the time, to familiar jazz standards by Irving Berlin or Duke Ellington, but to a surprising number of popular songs from the 1960s onward. Since she also includes material from the traditional American Songbook, the body of work that most jazz singers draw on, Ms. Wilson's sets can be very eclectic indeed. The set list started with the idea of a blues album, but it evolved to the point where it contained a wide variety of music, all of it with a certain bluesiness to it, as Stephen Colbert might say.

The accompaniment also uses the vocabulary of the blues, but not the loud, dissonant, antisocial blasting of the electrified Chicago blues, which is the aspect of the blues that 1960s rock 'n' rollers were keen to pick up on. As on most of Wilson's recordings, her key collaborator here is Marvin Sewell, a gifted guitarist who has amazing technique as well as a unique capacity for utter simplicity; he's one of the few guitarists playing today (possibly of all time) with an idiosyncratic sound, or certainly one of the few whose playing can be readily identified in the same way that the leading saxophonists and trumpeters all sound different from each other. Most of the tracks use acoustic guitar as opposed to electric guitar—Ms. Wilson's original composition "Just Another Parade" employs a bouzouki, the Greek equivalent of the guitar. Most also use hand drums as opposed to trap drum kits with cymbals and drumsticks—Robert Johnson's "Hot Tamales" utilizes what is identified as a "plastic tub."

Asked when she came up with the idea for the album, Wilson responded, "It occurred to me this past summer [2001], and it was really a selfish reason. I wanted to go home for the summer and wanted my friends to join me. I thought it'd be a great idea for all of us to get together in the Delta and make the next record. It's the first time I've been able to really do something like that on location, sort of the way you would do a movie. The Delta is the Holy Land for this music, American popular music. I looked at this as a pilgrimage. It was a galvanizing experience." The idea of "going home" was merely the first step in the evolution of the album; ultimately, she would travel all over the map, and be anything but confined to one particular comfort zone.

Like the material, Wilson's voice seems to split the difference between jazz and blues. In fact, about the only thing that seems straightforward about her sound is that it could only belong to an African American female; you can't imagine it coming from anyone other than a black woman from Mississippi. On some songs, like "Only a Dream in Rio," the voice is light and ethereal as a vocal will-o'-the-wisp, mimicking the qualities of the sky and the sun. On other songs, like "Wichita Lineman," she drops to a considerably lower register, almost like a female Louis Armstrong, singing in a voice that makes us think of the earth. The two most basic realities of life in the Mississippi Delta are the hot, baking sun above and the dark, oozing mud below, and the sound of Cassandra Wilson is thoroughly saturated with both. They're in every note she sings.

Belly of the Sun opens with what, for many, would be the best-known song, "The Weight," a classic rock number by the Band, which is heard on their 1968 debut album, *Music from Big Pink,* and which they performed, famously, at Woodstock. Both the album and the song are iconic: *Big Pink* contains at least three songs I know well, though I've barely ever listened to the Band, and the song itself, according to those who compile numerical lists of such things, is surely one of the most familiar tunes of the last fifty years. Even though I'd heard it many times, I never quite knew what the lyrics were all about or even what the title was—I always thought it was titled "Take a Load of Fanny."

The song is especially noteworthy in that nearly everyone knows its "hook"—which is "Take a load off, Annie"—and since the words "the weight" never actually appear in the lyrics, that phrase, "Take a load off, Annie," is the closest reference to anything weighty. This is the line that everybody sings along with, especially in bars, even if they don't know the rest of the lyrics or, indeed, have any idea what the song is about. It's to Wilson's credit that she makes this crucial line sound less like a barroom chant and more like an actual lyric, a part of a coherent narrative. The piece is rendered slowly and evocatively, with bongo drums—more as if Nazareth were in the Caribbean rather than Pennsylvania (or even Mississippi), and the end result is that we actually listen to the lyrics more than we do in any other performance of the song, particularly those by the Band. When the Band perform it, it's kind of a group chant; when Wilson sings it, it becomes a genuine song. When she gets to the passage:

> I picked up my bag, I went lookin' for a place
> to hide,
> When I saw Carmen and the devil walkin'
> side by side.

> I said, "Hey, Carmen, come on let's go
> downtown."
> She said, "I gotta go, but my friend can stick
> around."

I still don't know what's going on, but it's clear, at least, that *something* is happening.

Wilson's first original is "Justice," about which she said, "I wrote 'Justice' about the time of the presidential election. I was so frustrated and so disappointed in the outcome. I really felt for those people whose vote did not count. It just seemed so sad to me that in the year 2000 there were still black people who were having difficulty voting. That's why that song was written. That was the inspiration." Wilson's vocal is soft and sensual, so much so that one actually has to read the lyrics printed on a page before one fully realizes the political implications of her text:

> Give me a box of reparation
> I'll take that box of reparation
> No, not the little one,
> I want the big one that matches my scars.

She brings the track to a series of escalating climaxes—you could call them "sub-climaxes"—by building to the phrase, "I think I'll have some of that!" In fact, just as "The Weight" could be called "Take a Load Off, Annie," "Justice" might be better titled, "I Think I'll Have Some of That!"

"Darkness on the Delta," more properly titled "(When It's) Darkness on the Delta," is the closest thing to a songbook standard on *Belly of the Sun,* and, to me at least, it's unchallenged as the highlight of the album. The three-way collaboration of Jerry Livingston, Al J. Neiburg, and Marty Symes wrote at least three jazz standards: "Under a Blanket of Blue," "It's the Talk of the Town," and "(When It's) Darkness on the Delta." Wilson performs "Darkness" as the most open and spare number on the album, yet undisputedly the warmest. Done only with voice and piano, played by a Mississippi musician named Boogaloo Ames, "Darkness on the Delta" is both subtle and deeply moving.

It came about, as she explained, "When I was

in Mississippi, I was searching for older musicians that I could work with, older musicians that I could learn from. And I heard a lot about Boogaloo while I was there. One thing led to another, and I called and asked him if he might like to play on the recording. I was especially fascinated with him because he symbolized a missing link, so to speak, between jazz and blues. He was equally facile in both, and you hear it in what he's playing. In Mississippi, there is sometimes a gray area where jazz and blues meet. I thought he was perfect for 'Darkness on the Delta.' That was the tune he suggested from his repertoire, a song I'd never heard before."

If Boogaloo Ames had been, say, eighty-five in 2001, then he would have been a teenager in 1932, when "Darkness on the Delta" was introduced. The song held obvious significance for both him and Wilson, as Delta musicians, and especially for its time. A year earlier, Louis Armstrong premiered "When It's Sleepytime Down South," and, by the point when he was broadcasting regularly, he already knew that "Sleepytime" was destined to be his theme song. "Darkness on the Delta" could be described as a rather obvious sequel to "Sleepytime Down South," and later there would be "It's Slumbertime Along the Swanee" as well as "Twilight Time in Tennessee." But there was a tradition of songs that went back earlier, including the 1930 waltz "Lazy Louisiana Moon" and "Carolina Moon. Using Tin Pan Alley as a guide, one would think that all anyone ever did south of the Mason-Dixon line was go to sleep.

As already stated, Wilson and Ames do it starkly but cheerfully, Ames beginning with major chords that suggest the sun coming up rather than going down. As usual, Wilson is restrained, but for her the overall mood is very optimistic indeed, as she sings,

Fields of cotton all around me,
*Voices ringing sweet and low.**
Lord, I'm lucky that you found me
Where the muddy Mississippi waters flow.

* The original line, in 1932, was "Darkies singing sweet and low."

She's especially convincing at the end of the bridge, wherein the three-man songwriting team made their number especially "Southern" by alluding to a key line from a well-known spiritual: "Laughter on the levee / No one's heart is heavy, / All God's children got someone to love," which comes from "Going to Shout All Over God's Heaven." Although the white songwriters were trying to depict black people in the South, as Wilson sings it "Darkness" isn't about race or geography, but about warmth, family, and community, about feeling safe when the sun goes down, putting one in mind of Jack Kerouac's famous line about "the coming of complete night that blesses the earth." The performance of Wilson and Ames is indeed a blessing, but one, alas, that the pianist did not live to enjoy; Boogaloo died sometime between summer 2001 and spring 2002, when *Belly of the Sun* was released.

Wilson recorded one other track with Ames, the unreleased "Rock Me Baby," the archetypical blues by B. B. King. It seems fitting that Ames was her collaborator on both the album's most standard-y standard and its bluesiest blues. We hear the voice of Ames, laughing and expressing his joy nonverbally, and we also hear Wilson clapping her hands and snapping her fingers as she addresses him directly, "Rock me, Boogaloo!" I can't imagine why she elected to leave it off the final album, unless she thought that it was inappropriate to include something so intimate and personal right after Ames's death.

Ames was probably already gone when Wilson chose to follow "Darkness on the Delta" with Antonio Carlos Jobim's "Waters of March." (The original Portuguese title of the song was "Águas de Março," but Jobim actually did write the much heard English lyrics himself.) Even without that knowledge in mind, it's a perfect sequence: "Darkness on the Delta" is about going to sleep, possibly even the final sleep, whereas "Waters of March" is about the ever-renewing cycle of existence, life going on despite the deaths of those near to us: "A life, the sun, / A knife, a death, / The end of the run." Both songs illustrate the flowing and renewing of life using the ever-flowing river as a metaphor.

It was partly due to Wilson that "Waters of March" became conspicuously overdone over the next decade. Although introduced by Jobim himself, playing and singing, in 1972, the gospel of the song was widely spread in American clubs by the singer Susannah McCorkle, who sang it consistently up to her death in spring 2001. The song was omnipresent, on albums and especially live, throughout the first decade of the twenty-first century, much as "Lush Life" had been in the 1980s and '90s—both were "art" songs that jazz and cabaret singers somehow just could not leave alone. (In the second decade, "Ballad of the Sad Young Men" seems to be the artier-than-usual song that I keep hearing.)

"Waters" has been performed by many singers whom I adore, like Rosemary Clooney and John Pizzarelli (together), Mark Murphy, and Paula West, yet the only recording I've gone near in the last ten years is Wilson's. She's virtually the only artist to do anything creative with it, namely to downplay the Brazilian rhythm. In fact, the remarkable Brazilian percussionist Cyro Baptista was, at this time, part of Wilson's touring ensemble—but part of his talent is that he doesn't overplay; rather, he supplies just enough of a South American feel without making the whole thing a samba. Only Wilson would have thought to use such simple but effective devices as, at the halfway point, ritarding dramatically and having the whole ensemble drop out before she comes back with the line "It's the promise of spring." How better to depict death and rebirth than having the whole song essentially die, then come back to life, a musical resuscitation?

While "Waters of March" is one of the most complex pop songs ever written, the beauty of "You Gotta Move" is that it's such a simple, almost primitive melody, a blues with lyrics that give it spiritual relevance (which seem to have directly inspired Bob Dylan's "Gotta Serve Somebody"), in such a way that it's infinitely interpretable. The piece is credited to "Mississippi" Fred McDowell, a traditional Mississippi blues-singer-songwriter-guitarist, and is probably best known through Sam Cooke's more openly erotic treatment on his 1963 album Night Beat and then later by the Rolling Stones.

Wilson's treatment sticks closer to McDowell (and the Stones) than to Cooke, with Sewell's guitar sounding very, very Delta—although it should be noted that he's just playing fills and obbligatos rather than chords behind the singer—and the musicians are mostly chanting behind her at key moments, instead of playing. "You Gotta Move," which features her longtime drummer Jeffrey Haynes playing "plastic tub," is one of two tracks that weren't cut in the ex–train station, which apparently was booked that day for a wedding. Thus, the resourceful Kopelson set up his digital recording hardware in a boxcar. I seriously doubt there was any ventilation, and one can certainly feel the heat and the perspiration from all concerned on both tunes cut there, "You Gotta Move" and "Hot Tamales," which also suggests the balmy atmosphere.

Perhaps the railway station and the boxcar were a metaphor for travel: the next stop on the trip is back to Brazil for James Taylor's "Only a Dream in Rio." Like the singer-songwriter, Wilson takes the title rather literally. Yet this isn't a literal story or a distinct narrative but a series of images that add up to a vivid picture; it's a dream in Rio, not an episode that actually transpired there. ("It's all right, you can stay asleep," the lyric goes. "You can close your eyes.") At moments the images grow somewhat less tranquil—"On the run from the soldier's gun / Shouting out loud from the angry crowd." The song was first heard on Taylor's 1985 That's Why I'm Here, but unlike "The Weight," "Wichita Lineman," or "Shelter from the Storm," "Only a Dream in Rio" can't be described as a well-known contemporary classic, just a song that Wilson happened to like. She's probably the only major artist to sing it after Taylor himself. Wilson's backing is all guitars, gentle percussion, and other voices—how better to support a "samba floating in the summer breeze"? Her arrangement is much more danceable than Taylor's. The composer also collaborated with one Jim Maraniss to produce a Portuguese translation of the lyrics, of which Wilson sings a small portion.

Wilson is a talented songwriter, but it's hard to imagine why she would choose to bookend one of her originals with "Only a Dream in Rio" and

"Wichita Lineman." Her "Just Another Parade" is a fine song, and even has the benefit of India.Arie, the R&B star and admitted Cassandra-ite, joining her on vocals, along with Rhonda Richmond, a singer-pianist-violinist-songwriter who makes a contribution to this album in almost all of those categories. But you barely notice the song lodged between James Taylor and Jimmy Webb—even the title seems to put itself down in the company of all these classic songs: it's just another parade. Yet it's a solid piece of songwriting, and one that I'm inclined to pay more attention to when I hear it separated from the rest of the album on the radio or on random play.

Next, Wilson takes us to Kansas; Toto, I don't think we're in Oz anymore. She may have been the first notable female artist to sing "Wichita Lineman" (more recently it has been performed by two additional Cassandra-ites, Barb Jungr and Paula West). Introduced by Glen Campbell in 1968, this is one of the most uniquely male love songs ever written, one of the few to address the subject of romantic love and deprivation of same from a specifically masculine perspective. Wilson sings it with appropriate pronoun adjustment: "My man's a lineman for the county / and he drives the main road . . ." In a way, she makes it even more empathetic, because it's not her own abject loneliness that she's singing about, but that of her man. As he proceeds down the wires of that impossibly flat Kansas landscape, gazing at one telephone pole after another, she feels his pain. Webb's text was specific as to gender but not to genre: it was embraced early by country and pop artists alike, while Ray Charles made a brilliant soul treatment and Freddie Hubbard played it as jazz instrumental.

Wilson's arrangement has a lightly Latin underpinning—for one thing, she removed that telegraph signal/Morse code rhythmic pattern on the original; her undulating strings and bongos are both evocative and erotic. The way she sings it, it's now a love song, also one of the rare ballads about long-term commitment (in that respect, it's a precursor of many 1970s love songs like those by Alan and Marilyn Bergman). Where most songs are about falling in love, this one is about sustaining a relationship over the long haul. Fortunately, this

Wichita lineman is able to keep these metaphorical wires buzzing as well; they can well stand the strain. Wilson has a unique vocal trick of dipping into a basso profundo to emphasize a phrase here and there, diving for a low note rather than shooting for a high one; it sometimes makes her sound like a distaff Satchmo—"Mama Dip," if you will—but it's a marvelous technique for refocusing and sustaining our attention.

Bob Dylan wrote many songs that continue to be widely sung by other artists (particularly in the 1960s, when singers were, in general, more inclined to do songs composed by individuals other than themselves), yet somehow "Shelter from the Storm" is not one of them, even though, as Wilson sings it, it's one of his very best. Dylan introduced the song on his 1975 *Blood on the Tracks*, a treatment that recalls the early, folkish side of Dylan, stressing harmonica and acoustic guitar; however, a year later, he delivered a very different, extremely hard-rocking version on his live album *Hard Rain*. (Here the drummer kicks like he's got ants in his shoes and Dylan snarls like a punk rocker.) The lyrics use biblical references that somewhat anticipate the songwriter's slightly later Christian period and which clearly spoke to Wilson; "void without form" is from Genesis, while "they gambled for my clothes" references the Jesus of Saint Matthew. (27:35, to be specific).

Wilson's "Shelter from the Storm" is much more maternal and nurturing than Dylan's own rather severe readings. Her arrangement stresses acoustic guitar, and even though there's a Fender bass, it's played in a way that's more soothing than harsh. She also has adjusted the lyrics into the third person: "Now there's a wall between us" becomes "Now there's a wall between them," and "I'm livin' in a foreign country now" is "He's livin' in a foreign country now," etc. At the start of the track, she rushes certain lines ("Everything up to that point had been left unresolved") in a way that recalls the nervous energy of the songwriter himself. But gradually she gets more and more relaxed, increasingly stressing a fermata at the end of every third line, pausing dramatically before the fourth, payoff line: "Come in," she said, "I'll give you shelter from the storm." By the last few lines, her treatment is much more sheltering and much less stormy than Dylan's.

We're now entering the home stretch, with three originals (the last one by Rhoda Richmond) in a row. "Drunk as Cooter Brown" stands out because of its catchy melody, emphasized by steel drums and a pan-Caribbean beat. I have to wonder if the title might have been a familiar phrase, in Mississippi at least, that Wilson turned into a song, as Arthur Herzog had done with "God Bless the Child."

There's a natty guitar solo by Sewell at one point, and Wilson gets so caught up in it that she starts snapping her fingers loudly—as polished as the track is, it still has a live, spontaneous feeling. I still couldn't tell you what "Drunk as Cooter Brown" is actually about, or even who he is—however, in his defense, I will say that anyone with a name like "Cooter Brown" could hardly be expected to be sober.

"Little Lion" was originally intended to follow "Cooter Brown" and is one of two tracks that were recorded and not issued on the finished CD. It's a true product of the Afro-Caribbean diaspora, with African-style guitars and West Indian percussion. The tune is apparently another Wilson original, although it may have a folk source. The lyrics are distinctly maternal, in an anthropomorphically animalistic sort of a way, as in "I love to see you smile, little lion." This and "Rock Me, Baby" were included on an early advance edition of the album, but have not been heard from since.

On the finished album, "Cooter Brown" leads directly to "Show Me a Love." This is the first of two consecutive tracks that showcase two local singer-musicians who contributed their instrumental abilities as well as songs to the project. "Show Me a Love," co-credited to Wilson and guitarist Jesse Robinson, is much simpler and more direct than most of the songs written solely by Wilson; unlike "Cooter Brown," it's not the least bit gnomic: you're not left scratching your head and wondering what's going on. Despite lines like "Show me a love that's pure enigma / And a Kodak picture...," the over-all meaning is crystal clear: she wants someone

to show her a love. There's a brief scat sequence here, but the piece is mainly propelled by three percussionists all going to town together: Xavyon Jamison, Cyro Baptista, and Jeffrey Haynes. Wilson's tune is pure hook; it would have made a great Motown single circa 1970.

Rhonda Richmond's "Road So Clear" changes the texture, adding, at long last, Olu Dara's trumpet to the mix of guitars and drums. The Harmon mute sound inevitably puts everyone in mind of Miles Davis, but Dara is his own man—he sounds more like Bunk Johnson than Miles. One is immediately struck by how Wilson takes Richmond's basic description of walking down a country road and makes it sound so completely erotic: "I need to feel some rich black...soil...that's moist...between my...toes." The road itself is fairly distinct, although one can't be sure exactly where it's leading her or us. It's evident, however, through the descriptions of the local landscape and the spirit guides that seem to be escorting the superstitious traveler, that the song does indeed belong on an album that's a musical portrait of the American South.

"Road So Clear" seems like the conclusion of the CD journey, but the thirteenth track, listed as "Hot Tamales" (also taped in the boxcar), is a worthy encore. Credited to Robert Johnson, this number was originally recorded by the legendary bluesman as "They're Red Hot." Although it was also sung by Eric Clapton in his tribute to the legendary Mississippi musician, it's more of a hokum song than a traditional country blues, a fast-moving shuffle with jokey lyrics ("I got a man who's long and tall / He sleeps in the kitchen with his feet in the hall"). This is probably the most fun and frivolous of Johnson's songs, which generally tend to be about death, life, the devil, and death again (and even "Dead Shrimp Blues"). Here, Johnson is in step with many other prewar bluesmen who actually had a sense of humor; this is the kind of thing he would have played for people to dance to. Wilson's vocal, accompanied by Sewell and Haynes (again on "plastic tub," which makes me wonder if he was in the musicians' union or the laundrymens'), is fast and snappy like a chaser—just a hundred seconds and we're outta here.

Some of Wilson's earlier albums are fairly flaw-less, especially *Blue Light 'til Dawn* (1993), *New Moon Daughter* (1995), and *Traveling Miles* (1999), as are some of her more recent releases, like *Glamoured* (2003) and *Loverly* (2008), the latter also recorded in a "location" situation. But *Belly of the Sun,* which was released in early 2002, is the most perfect, the album where everything—the mate-rial, the concept, the band, the arrangements, and the singer herself in her various voices—all come together seamlessly. It's the Wilson album I would most want to take with me to a desert island, heaven forbid—or, even worse, an abandoned train station in Mississippi.

Discography

1.

Louis Armstrong, *Louis Armstrong Meets Oscar Peterson* (1957)
LP: Verve Records MG V-8322
CD: Verve Records MG V-8322

2.

Fred Astaire, *The Astaire Story* (1952)
4-LP boxed set: Mercury MGC 1001/4
2-CD set: Verve Records 835 649-2

3.

Chet Baker, *Let's Get Lost: The Best of Chet Baker Sings* (1954–56)
LP (contains six tracks; not a direct equivalent of the 1989 CD): Pacific Jazz Records PJLP-11
CD: Capitol Records 0777 7 92932 2 3

4.

Tony Bennett and Bill Evans, *The Tony Bennett / Bill Evans Album* (1975)
LP: Fantasy F-9489

Tony Bennett and Bill Evans, *Together Again* (1977)
LP: Improv 7117

CD (includes both LPs, and additional material, on a 2009 2-CD set, *The Complete Tony Bennett / Bill Evans Recordings*): Fantasy FAN-31281

5.

Ray Charles, *Modern Sounds in Country and Western Music* (1962)
LP: ABC-Paramount ABC-410
CD: Rhino Entertainment Company R2 70099

6.

June Christy, *Something Cool* (1955)
LP (original mono recording): Capitol Records T-516
LP (stereo remake): Capitol Records ST-516
CD (contains all tracks from the mono and stereo LPs, 2001): Capitol Jazz 7243 5 34069 2 9

7.

Rosemary Clooney, *Blue Rose* (1956)
LP: Columbia CL-872
CD: Columbia CK 65506

8.

Nat King Cole, *After Midnight* (1957)
LP: Capitol Records W-782
CD (*After Midnight: The Complete Session*): Capitol Jazz 7243 5 20087 2 8

9.

Nat King Cole, *St. Louis Blues* (1958)
LP: Capitol Records SW993
CD: Capitol Records CDP 7243 8 32162 2 2

10.

Bing Crosby, *Bing with a Beat* (1957)
LP: RCA Victor LPM-1473
CD: Bluebird 82876-60142-2

11.

Bing Crosby and Louis Armstrong, *Bing & Satchmo* (1960)
LP: MGM Records E3882P
CD: EMI (DRG Records) 91515

12.

Doris Day, *Day by Day* (1956)
LP: Columbia CL 942

Doris Day, *Day by Night* (1957)
LP: Columbia CL 1053
CD (Europe and Australia; includes both LPs, 1994): Columbia 475749 2

13.

Doris Day and Robert Goulet, *Annie Get Your Gun* (1962)
LP: Columbia Masterworks OS 2360
CD: DRG Records 19112

14.

Blossom Dearie, *My Gentleman Friend* (1959)
LP: Verve Records MG V-2125
CD: Verve Records 314 519 905-2

15.

Matt Dennis, *Matt Dennis Plays and Sings Matt
  Dennis* (1954)
LP: Trend TL-1500
CD (Britain; included in a 2-CD set with three other
  albums, entitled *Welcome Matt*): Jasmine Records
  JASCD 697

Bobby Troup, *Bobby Troup Sings Johnny Mercer* (1955)
LP: Bethlehem Records BCP19
CD (Japan): Bethlehem Records CDSOL 6081

16.

Billy Eckstine, *Billy's Best!* (1958)
LP: Mercury MG-20333
CD: Verve Records 526 440-2

17.

Ella Fitzgerald, *Lullabies of Birdland* (1955)
LP: Decca DL 8149
CD (Japan): Decca MVCJ-19220
CD (included in a 2-CD set with *Sweet and Hot*, also
  from Decca): Universal International Music B.V.
  Verve Records 0600753359068

18.

Ella Fitzgerald and Louis Armstrong, *Ella & Louis*
  (1956)
LP: Verve Records MG V-4003
CD: Verve Records 825 373-2

19.

Ella Fitzgerald, *Mack the Knife: Ella in Berlin* (1960)
LP: Verve Records MG VS-64041
CD: Verve Records 825 670-2

20.

Judy Garland, *Judy at Carnegie Hall* (1961)
LP: Capitol Records WBO 1569
CD: Capitol Records CDP 7 46470 2

21.

Johnny Hartman, *John Coltrane and Johnny Hartman*
  (1963)
LP: Impulse! A-40
CD: MCA Impulse! GRD-157

22.

Dick Haymes, *Rain or Shine* (1956)
LP: Capitol Records T 713
CD (Britain, included in a 2-CD set entitled *Dick
  Haymes: The Complete Capitol Collection*): EMI
  0946 3 71389 2 2

23.

Billie Holiday, *Lady in Satin* (1958)
Mono LP: Columbia CL 1157
Stereo LP: Columbia CS 8048
CD (as this book goes to press, Sony is issuing *Lady
  in Satin: The Centennial Edition*, a 3-CD set that
  includes all the additional session material on the
  French 2-CD set *Masters of Jazz: Billie Holiday*):
  Columbia 88875076132

24.

Lena Horne, *Lena Horne at the Waldorf Astoria* (1957)
LP: RCA Victor LOC-1028
CD (included in a 2002 2-CD set with *Lena at the
  Sands*, recorded in Las Vegas in 1960): Collectables
  COL-CD-2841.

25.

Barb Jungr, *Every Grain of Sand: Barb Jungr Sings Bob
  Dylan* (2002)
CD: Linn Records AKD 187

26.

Dave Lambert, Jon Hendricks, and Annie Ross, *Sing
  a Song of Basie* (1957)
LP: ABC-Paramount ABC-223
CD: Verve Records 314 543 827-2

Annie Ross, *Sings a Song with Mulligan!* (1957)
LP: World Pacific WP-1253
CD: DRG Records 91511

27.
Eydie Gormé and Steve Lawrence, *Eydie and Steve Sing the Golden Hits* (1960)
LP: ABC-Paramount ABCS-311
CD: MCA Records MCAD 22016

28.
Peggy Lee, *Black Coffee* (1953 and 1956)
10-inch LP: Decca Dl 5482
12-inch LP: Decca Dl 8358
CD: Verve Records B0003093-02

29.
Peggy Lee, *The Man I Love* (1957)
LP: Capitol Records T-864
CD: DRG Records DRG-CD-94783

30.
Marilyn Maye, *Meet Marvelous Marilyn Maye* (1965)
LP: RCA Victor LSP-3397
CD (included in a 2001 2-CD set with *The Lamp Is Low*, 1966): Collectables 2807

31.
Carmen McRae, *As Time Goes By: Live at the Dug* (1973)
LP: Catalyst Records CAT-7904
CD (Japan): JVC VICJ-61037

32.
Anita O'Day, *Anita O'Day Sings the Winners* (1958)
Mono LP: Verve MG V-8283
Stereo LP: Verve v6-8485
CD: Verve 837 939-2

33.
Della Reese, *Della Della Cha Cha Cha* (1961)
LP: RCA Victor LSP 2280
CD (Germany): BMG Music 886828

34.
Jimmy Scott, *The Source* (1969)
LP: Atlantic SD 8242
CD: Label M 495722

Jimmy Scott, *Lost and Found* (1972)
LP (released as *The Source* in 1970, containing some of the material on the 1972 CD): Atlantic SD 8242
CD: Rhino Records R2 71059

35.
Bobby Short, *Bobby Short* (1955)
LP: Atlantic 1230
CD: Collectors' Choice Music CCM 02372

36.
Nina Simone, *Nina Simone and Piano!* (1969)
LP: RCA Victor SF 8074
CD: RCA 07863681002

37.
Frank Sinatra, *In the Wee Small Hours* (1955)
LP: Capitol Records W-581
CD: Capitol Records CDP 7 96826 2

38.
Frank Sinatra, *Songs for Swingin' Lovers!* (1956)
LP: Capitol Records W-653
CD: Capitol Records CDP 546570

39.
Jo Stafford, *Jo Stafford Sings American Folk Songs* (1948 and 1961)
10-inch Mono LP, 1948: Capitol Records CC-75
12-inch Stereo LP, 1961: Capitol Records ST-1653
CD: Corinthian Records 110

Jo Stafford, *Jo Stafford Sings Songs of Scotland* (1953 and 1956)
10-inch LP (entitled *My Heart's in the Highlands*): Columbia C-6274
12-inch LP: Columbia CL 1043
CD: Corinthian Records 122

40.
Jo Stafford, *I'll Be Seeing You (G.I. Jo)* (1959)
LP: Columbia CS 8080
CD: Corinthian Records 105

41.
Kay Starr, *I Cry by Night* (1962)
LP: Capitol Records T 1681
CD (Britain; included in a 2-CD set with *Losers, Weepers*, 1960): EMI Capitol Records 7243 8 56058 2 6

42.
Maxine Sullivan, *Memories of You: A Tribute to Andy Razaf* (1956)
LP: Period SPL 1207
CD: DCC Compact Classics LPZ-2038

43.
Jack Teagarden, *Think Well of Me* (1962)
LP: Verve Records V6 8465
CD: Verve Records 314 557 101-2

44.
Tiny Tim, *God Bless Tiny Tim* (1968)
LP: Reprise Records RS 6292
CD: Rhino Records 8122-79904-9

45.
Mel Tormé, *Mel Tormé with the Marty Paich Dek-Tette (Lulu's Back in Town)* (1956)
LP: Bethlehem Records BCP 52
CD: Bethlehem Archives (Avenue Jazz) R2 75732

46.
Sarah Vaughan, *Sarah Vaughan* (1954)
LP: EmArcy MG-36004
CD: EmArcy 841 641-2

47.
Sarah Vaughan, *"Live" in Japan* (1973)
LP: Mainstream Records ULS-119-120
CD: Mainstream Records (Legacy) J2K 57123

48.
Dinah Washington, *Dinah Washington Sings Fats Waller* (1957)
LP: EmArcy MG-36119
CD: EmArcy 818 930-2

49.
Margaret Whiting, *Margaret Whiting Sings the Jerome Kern Song Book* (1960)
LP: Verve Records MGVS 6142-2
CD: Verve Records 314 559 553-2

50.
Lee Wiley, *Night in Manhattan* (1950)
10-inch LP: Columbia CL 6169
12-inch LP: Columbia CL 656
CD: Columbia Special Products 75010

51.
Cassandra Wilson, *Belly of the Sun* (2002)
CD: Blue Note 7243 5 35072 2 0
LP (a limited-edition 2-LP vinyl pressing): Pure Pleasure Records PPAN BST35072

Photographic Credits

The following foundations, museums, archives, and collectors generously provided either electronic scans or the actual covers for the following album covers reproduced in this book.